Planning Enforce

Second edition

Planning Enforcement

Second Edition

Richard Harwood QC

Thirty Nine Essex Street Chambers

Bloomsbury Professional

Bloomsbury Professional Limited,
Maxwelton House,
41-43 Boltro Road,
Haywards Heath,
West Sussex RH16 1BJ

© Bloomsbury Professional Limited 2013

Bloomsbury Professional is an imprint of Bloomsbury Publishing plc

ISBN: 978 178043 178 9

Typeset by Phoenix Photosetting, Chatham, Kent
Printed in the United Kingdom by Hobbs the Printers Ltd, Totton, Hampshire

To my parents

Preface

The first edition of this book was written in 1996, less than four years after the coming into force of the Planning and Compensation Act 1991 reforms. The 1991 Act had given effect to the recommendations of Robert Carnwath QC in his report *Enforcing Planning Control*. Recognising the inevitable complexities of the topic, the report attempted to minimise the technicalities, which had bedevilled planning enforcement.

Returning to the book some 17 years later it is remarkable that few words of the 1991 legislation have been changed. What has though happened is that the regime has been added to, not least by the introduction of temporary stop notices and planning enforcement orders. The secondary legislation has been comprehensively replaced and procedural guidance was reissued in 1997 but is now looking very dated. Case law has continued to develop.

In this second edition I have sought to reflect the changes which have taken place in law, policy and practice. Whilst the technicalities of the various notices can prove troublesome, the greatest difficulties in practice are on questions such as whether something is a breach of planning control and the application of time limits. The only two planning enforcement cases which have gone to the highest court in the land in the last 20 years have been on time limits: *Sage* and *Welwyn Hatfield*. I have significantly expanded and separated out the discussion of these issues.

Enforcement is the field where any clash between the public interest and the interests of landowners or occupiers is at its sharpest. The Human Rights Act 1998 and duties to consider effects on groups and individuals in the Equality Act 2010 and the Children Act 2004 have added a dimension to planning enforcement. I have attempted to set out how these bear on the decision to take action.

The impact of European environmental law has been more muted in enforcement than in other areas of planning law. However the understandable thought that environmental impact assessment was not likely to be a real issue in enforcement because no one would build a large factory without planning permission, was blown away by the *Ardagh Glass* saga where someone did just that.

As well as new powers, there are new statutory regimes to enforce in the context of development consent orders and the community infrastructure levy. The enforcement powers under these provisions are considered.

Another change in the last 20 years has been the separation of English and Welsh secondary legislation and policy. That trend began under John Major's Government in the 1990s but has accelerated since the creation of the National Assembly for Wales. In planning enforcement the difference has been more one of form rather than substance but I have endeavoured to deal with the legislation and guidance at either end of the Severn Tunnel.

I have been able to pick up the enforcement changes consequent on the abolition of conservation area consent in England and the introduction of listed building lawful works certificates in the Enterprise and Regulatory Reform Act 2013. At the time of writing these changes are not in force and the relevant secondary legislation has yet to be made.

The result is that this book conforms to the basic rule of second editions, which is that they must be much longer than their first editions. I can only hope that on this occasion it is seen as a good thing.

Thanks are due to clients, colleagues, opponents, inspectors and judges, with, for, against and in front of whom I have debated enforcement issues. Many will find their cases discussed in a dispassionate and neutral manner in these pages. Thanks are also due to colleagues in chambers who have road-tested various chapters of the book without noticeably adverse effects.

The greatest thanks of all must go to Gráinne and Cathan, James and Sophie. The price of book writing by practising lawyers is borne by their families as, train journeys aside, tapping away is squeezed into late nights and weekends. They can be pleased that it is finished, although the children will find that it contains fewer evil magicians, fearsome beasts and youthful heroes than they hoped for.

Richard Harwood QC
Thirty Nine Essex Street
London
June 2013

Contents

Contents

Contents

Contents

Contents

Table of Statutes

Table of Statutory Instruments

Table of European Legislation

Table of Cases

A

B

C

H

N

O

P

Q

R

S

Y

Z

Chapter 1

Introduction

PURPOSES OF ENFORCEMENT POWERS

1.01   The nationwide system of planning control introduced in the Town and Country Planning Act 1947 is based on the view that the use of land is a matter of public interest. Most obviously activities on land have a visual impact. But they can also affect neighbours by noise, fumes and disturbance. There are wider effects: for example most development generates traffic on roads, and an out-of-town shopping centre could affect the quality of retailing in the town centre. Wildlife habitats or archaeological remains may be threatened. There is also a need to provide the business premises, housing, shops, schools, and transport infrastructure that a modern society requires. Food must be grown, minerals worked and waste recycled or disposed of.

1.02   Much of this requires proper consideration in planning applications to public bodies. The need for this consideration carries with it the expectation that the procedures are gone through and that landowners and occupiers do not simply go ahead without necessary permission. It is also essential that when permissions are obtained, they are adhered to.

1.03   Planning enforcement is concerned with keeping to these procedures. It seeks to prevent development from occurring without a necessary planning permission and to ensure that the requirements of a planning permission are met. A useful description of the responsibilities of councils in enforcing planning controls was given by Purchas LJ in *Runnymede Borough Council v Ball*:[1]

> 'the duties of the Council under the planning legislation was not merely to enforce penalties for past offences but was also to do all within their power to ensure through properly observed planning control the natural amenities of their area.'

Planning enforcement is though a matter for the discretion of the planning authorities. There is no general duty to enforce, and it might only be in very limited circumstances that enforcement is required under European law or as the only rational, and so lawful, response to a particular situation. As the planning system as a whole is concerned with the public interest, so enforcement powers are to be exercised in the public interest. There is no point in enforcing against development which is and which will remain, innocuous.

THE STRUCTURE OF PLANNING CONTROL

1.04   Planning control is in the hands of three tiers of government:

---

[1]   [1986] JPL 288.

- district or unitary councils;

- county councils; and

- the Secretary of State for Communities and Local Government (for English matters)[2] and the Welsh Assembly Government (these powers being exercised by the 'Welsh Ministers').[3]

1.05　At the local level, most planning matters are dealt with by district councils. County councils deal with minerals and waste planning ('county matters') as well as their own projects. Planning enforcement powers are generally exercisable by district councils, except for county matters.[4] Unitary authorities have the responsibilities of district and county councils. There is a mix of different local authority structures across England. In Greater London and the former metropolitan counties (Greater Manchester, Merseyside, South Yorkshire, and Tyne and Wear, West Midlands – the Birmingham conurbation – and West Yorkshire) there are unitary authorities. The rest of England is a mixed bag of counties with a two-tier (county/district) system throughout: counties with a two-tier system but some unitary authorities (usually major cities) and counties which are administered by one or more unitary authorities. Welsh local government consists of unitary authorities, styled as counties or smaller county boroughs.

1.06　All councils with planning responsibilities are referred to as local planning authorities ('LPAs').[5] The powers of local planning authorities are sometimes exercised by other bodies. In national parks, national park authorities are the planning authority for all purposes.[6]

1.07　Urban development corporations are normally made, by order under the Act, the local planning authority for their area. The Secretary of State and Welsh Ministers are also empowered to make enterprise zone authorities, housing action trusts and (in England) the Homes and Communities Agency the local planning authority for particular areas.[7] The Mayor of London may make a mayoral development corporation the local planning authority for an area.[8] How planning powers are exercised within these bodies' areas will vary. Enforcement and smaller planning applications might be left to the existing councils.

---

[2] The name of the department responsible for planning has changed frequently in recent years. Prior to 1972 the Ministry of Housing and Local Government dealt with these matters. It then became the responsibility of the large Department of the Environment. In 1997 the Department for the Environment, Transport and the Regions was created under John Prescott (prompting the quip by Norman Fowler MP 'Deputy Prime Minister, Secretary of State for the Environment, Transport and the Regions, the only minister with a job title bigger than his vocabulary'). In 2001 this became the Department for Transport, Local Government and the Regions. This department was abolished in 2002 and the planning powers were exercised by the Office of the Deputy Prime Minister, with the Minister, John Prescott, exercising his powers as First Secretary of State. In 2006 the powers were transferred to a new Department of Communities and Local Government, whose remit is quite similar to the old Ministry of Housing and Local Government.

[3] Where powers are in substance the same in England and Wales, the Secretary of State and the Welsh Ministers will often be referred to as 'the Minister'.

[4] Town and Country Planning Act 1990, Sch 1, paras 3, 11.

[5] Town and Country Planning Act 1990, s 1.

[6] Environment Act 1995, s 67.

[7] Town and Country Planning Act 1990, ss 6–8A.

[8] Town and Country Planning Act 1990, s 7A. The Mayor may become the local planning authority for particular strategic planning applications but does not have enforcement powers except in respect of planning obligations entered into in relation to planning applications for which he has become the local planning authority: Town and Country Planning Act 1990, s 2E(5).

1.08   The powers of the Secretary of State and Welsh Ministers need not be exercised by the minister personally; civil servants can act in his name without express delegation.[9]

MAIN SOURCES OF LAW AND POLICY

1.09   Planning legislation is principally contained in the Town and Country Planning Act 1990 ('the Act'), the Planning (Listed Buildings and Conservation Areas) Act 1990 ('the Listed Buildings Act'), the Planning (Hazardous Substances) Act 1990 ('the Hazardous Substances Act') and the Planning (Consequential Provisions) Act 1990. This comprised the first consolidation of planning legislation since the Town and Country Planning Act 1971. References in this book to 'the Act' are to the Town and Country Planning Act 1990 as amended. Sections and Schedules referred to are those of the Act, unless otherwise specified.

1.10   The principal enforcement provisions are contained in Part VII of the Act, ss 171A–196C. This legislation has been amended several times since 1990. The principal changes have been in:

- the Planning and Compensation Act 1991 ('the 1991 Act') – amongst other matters, this implemented the report by Robert Carnwath QC on planning enforcement;

- the Planning and Compulsory Purchase Act 2004, which introduced temporary stop notices;

- the Planning Act 2008, introducing the new regime for major infrastructure and the Community Infrastructure Levy; and

- the Localism Act 2011, which for enforcement dealt with exceptions to time periods and mechanisms for dealing with advertisements.

1.11   The Enterprise and Regulatory Reform Act 2013 proposes various changes to historic environment legislation, in particular bringing the demolition of buildings in conservation areas within planning control. The Growth and Infrastructure Act 2013 brings forward various changes to planning, although not particularly important for enforcement.

1.12   The Secretary of State, Welsh Ministers, planning inspectors and local planning authorities are expected to take into account government guidance. To use the language of the courts: it is a material consideration in the exercise of the decision-maker's discretion. Guidance also expresses the Government's view as to the law. Frequently this is a useful and concise guide to the legislation, but it must be approached with caution. Only the courts can determine what the law is and it is not unknown for the guidance to be wrong. Government guidance in England is contained in the National Planning Policy Framework, Planning Policy Statement 10 on waste, national planning statements on major infrastructure and circulars. More informal government advice is given by practice guides and letters from the Chief Planner.

---

[9]   *Carltona Ltd v Commissioners of Works* [1943] 2 All ER 560.

1.13   In planning, circulars principally provide advice on procedural matters. They are identified by their number in the year of publication by the relevant department and by that year (eg 10/97 is the 10th circular of 1997 for that particular department). When a circular was published jointly by the Department of Environment and Welsh Office prior to devolution then the circulars had different numbers. In this book, joint circulars are usually referred to by their English Departmental number, with Welsh Office numbers being footnoted.

1.14   Enforcement is mentioned briefly in the National Planning Policy Framework and detailed guidance on the working of the regime is given in Department of the Environment circular 10/97 *Enforcing Planning Control: Legislative Provisions and Procedural Requirements.* At the same time as the circular, the Government published *Enforcing Planning Control: Good Practice Guidance for Local Planning Authorities.* The circular and the practice guidance are both dated and whilst the circular remains useful it should be considered with care. The practice guidance is likely to be cancelled.[10] Various circulars have been published on particular elements of the process, usually when legislation has changed.[11]

1.15   In Wales, non-statutory planning policy is contained in Planning Policy Wales (5th Edn, 2012) and Technical Advice Notes (TANs) along with some circulars published by the Welsh Office prior to devolution. TAN9 *Enforcement of Planning Control* provides guidance on when enforcement powers should be used. Detailed procedural guidance is contained in Welsh Office Circular 24/97, which is materially the same as the DoE Circular, and has the same name.

Planning enforcement powers

1.16   Planning enforcement is principally concerned with local planning authorities taking action against physical works or activities on land which do not have the required planning permission or which have been carried on in breach of a condition attached to a planning permission. These are known as breaches of planning control.

There are five powers which authorities can use against such breaches:

(i)   Issue an enforcement notice requiring the breach of cease and remedying any harm caused. Enforcement notices can be appealed to the Secretary of State or Welsh Ministers and do not come into force until any appeals have been determined.

(ii)   Serve a breach of condition notice . As the name suggests, this may only be used against breaches of conditions on planning permissions, rather than things done without planning permission. There is no right of appeal against such a notice.

(iii) Serve a stop notice. An enforcement notice will take at least 28 days to take effect, so a stop notice may be served with or after it to prohibit unlawful activity until the enforcement notice has to be complied with.

---

[10] Cancellation without replacement was recommended by Lord Taylor in *External Review of Government Planning Policy Practice Guidance* (December 2012).

[11] For example, Circular 02/02: Enforcement appeals procedures, Circular 02/05 Temporary Stop Notices, Procedural Guidance: Enforcement appeals and determination of appeal procedure (PINS 02/2009).

(iv) Serve a temporary stop notice. Temporary stop notices work like stop notices but can be served before any enforcement notice. They have effect for up to 28 days.

(v) Apply to the court for an injunction. The High Court or the County Court can grant an injunction restraining breaches of planning control. This is the only power available before a breach takes place.

Failure to comply with any of the notices is a criminal offence. Where an enforcement notice has been breached, the local planning authority may carry out the works in the notice.

1.17   There are a number of other powers which whilst not directed to unlawful development may be used against it or related problems. In the Town and Country Planning Act 1990 these are the making of discontinuance or revocation orders and issuing section 215 notices to clean up land. Special regimes of control, authorisation and enforcement apply to trees, advertisements, listed buildings, demolition in conservation areas, scheduled monuments, the keeping of hazardous substances and nationally significant infrastructure projects. These give rise to immediate criminal liability and powers to seek injunctions and in most cases to serve notices.

Principles of public law

1.18   The Secretary of State and LPAs are subject to the principles of public law which control all government bodies. These seek to ensure that decisions are taken lawfully, whilst leaving their merits to the public bodies concerned. A decision taken unlawfully is ultra vires. These principles are applied by the High Court in judicial review proceedings and in various statutory rights of challenge under the Planning Acts. There are three main grounds of challenge.

Error going to jurisdiction

1.19   This ground, which is also known as illegality, comes into two categories:

(a) *Error of law*
    If the decision-maker makes an error of law in coming to his or her decision then it will be *ultra vires*.

(b) *Error of fact*
    The court can determine whether a fact essential to the decision-maker's ability to exercise his or her power is correct. For example, the court can determine whether the site is within the LPA's area.

Unreasonableness

1.20   This ground, also called irrationality, is concerned with defects in the way the decision was thought through. Unreasonableness in its broad sense includes: acting for an improper purpose; failing to take account of material considerations; taking account of immaterial considerations; opposing the policy of Parliament; and making a finding of fact on no evidence. Unreasonableness in its narrow sense means making a decision that no reasonable person could have come to. This is known as *'Wednesbury* unreasonableness',[12] or sometimes as perversity.

Natural justice

1.21   This ground, which is also known as procedural impropriety, is concerned with errors in the way the decision was made and comprises three categories:

(a) *Failure to comply with procedural requirements*
    These requirements may be set out in statute or in rules or regulations, for example, how notice is given of a hearing.

(b) *Failure to give a fair hearing*
    Even if any procedural requirements have been met, the decision-maker may have failed to give a party a fair opportunity to state his case and challenge any opposing case.

(c) *The appearance of bias*
    This is a real danger, from his or her interests or behaviour, that the decision-maker is biased against a party.[13]

The court's powers

1.22   In judicial review if a decision is ultra vires then the High Court has a discretion whether to quash it. If quashed, the decision is considered to be void ab initio, to have had no legal effect from the date of its making. In judicial review proceedings the court can make the following orders:

- a quashing order (formerly certiorari) – to quash a decision;

- prohibition – to prevent the public body from making a decision or doing an act;

- a mandatory order (formerly mandamus) – instructing the public body to make a decision or do an act;

- injunction – instructing the public body to do or not do an act;

- declaration – setting out the law in a particular situation or stating the validity of a decision; and

- damages – if there is a private right of action, for example, in tort or contract.

Where the power to apply or appeal to the Court to challenge a decision is contained in legislation then the Court's powers are set out in statute. So on an appeal to the High Court against an enforcement notice appeal decision[14] the Court is empowered to remit the appeal decision back to the minister for redetermination.

---

[12] From Lord Greene MR's judgment in *Associated Provincial Picture Houses Ltd v Wednesbury Corporation* [1948] 1 KB 223, 229.
[13] Because of local authorities' many responsibilities and interests, this rule is applied with less rigour to decisions by LPAs (*R (Lewis) v Redcar and Cleveland Borough Council* [2008] EWCA Civ 746, [2009] 1 WLR 83).
[14] Town and Country Planning Act 1990, s 289.

Nullity, validity and the circumstances in which challenges can be brought

1.23   The ability to challenge an unlawful decision can be contentious, particularly where the challenge arises at a relatively late stage. In the enforcement context this includes questioning the validity of notices when they are being enforced or the planning conditions which underlie the enforcement action. It may be helpful to set out the circumstances in which an authority's decisions can or have to be challenged and the principles underlying these:

- *Government must act in accordance with the law.*

- *Unless excluded by legislation, a person with sufficient interest in the matter is able to challenge the lawfulness of a government decision.*

- *As a general rule, a decision will be treated as valid unless and until it is set aside by a court of competent jurisdiction. Once it is set aside it will be treated as never having had legal effect.*[15]

- *If legislation provides a mechanism to challenge the decision in the Administrative Court of the High Court then it should be used (a statutory application or appeal), otherwise a challenge may be brought by judicial review. The relevant procedural requirements have to be followed, not least in the timing of the proceedings, subject to the Court's ability to disapply the requirement.*

- *In judicial review the court has a discretion whether to set aside the unlawful decision, although it will normally do so.*

- *The ability to challenge a decision except by applying to the Administrative Court is limited.*

- *A decision or document is a nullity if it is so defective on its face that it is not the type of decision that its maker would have wished it to be.* For example, an enforcement notice issued against a claimed breach of planning control would be a nullity if, correctly interpreted, it failed to identify the land, set out the steps which had to be taken or the activity required to cease, or say by when this had to be done. A document is a nullity if on its face it fails to include an element (or contains conflicting material) which means that it cannot be given effect. In those circumstances it must be ignored.

- *A person may defend themselves in any civil or criminal proceedings by establishing that the public law decision which is the basis of the allegation against them is unlawful, unless statute provides that the point cannot be raised.* In *Boddington v British Transport Police*[16] the House of Lords affirmed the principle that a defendant in criminal proceedings can rely on the unlawfulness of a public law decision which has not been quashed by the Administrative Court as a defence in criminal proceedings. The unlawfulness of an act can be raised as a defence in civil proceedings.[17] For example the validity of a breach of condition notice can be challenged in defence to a prosecution.[18] However, because of the legislative regime, the validity of a planning enforcement notice cannot be challenged in criminal proceedings except in limited circumstances.[19]

---

[15]   *Hoffmann-la Roche v Secretary of State for Trade and Industry* [1975] AC 295 at 365 per Lord Diplock.
[16]   [1999] 2 AC 143.
[17]   *Wandsworth London Borough Council v Winder* [1985] AC 461.
[18]   *Dilieto v Ealing London Borough Council* [2000] QB 381.
[19]   Town and Country Planning Act 1990, s 285; *R v Wicks* [1998] AC 92.

- *The bringing of a challenge by an ordinary claim is likely to be an abuse of process if there is no private law cause of action alleged and it may be appropriate to transfer to public law proceedings if a private law claim relies on public law illegality.* In *Trim v North Dorset District Council*[20] it was held to be an abuse of process to seek a declaration in ordinary proceedings that a breach of condition notice had been served out of time. On occasions local authorities have threatened to carry out works on a site pursuant to a notice and landowners have sought injunctions in private law proceedings to prevent the works on the basis that the decision is unlawful in public law terms and so the works would be trespass. The courts have often been prepared to entertain such claims, albeit with dicta that the claim should have been brought, and an injunction sought, in judicial review.

- *Landowners have been able to contend before local planning authorities, Ministers and Inspectors that conditions on earlier planning permissions are unlawful.* This again is a collateral challenge reflecting the principle that a person should not be subject to an unlawful decision. In *Tarmac Heavy Building Materials UK Ltd v Secretary of State for the Environment, Transport and the Regions* the High Court ruled in an enforcement notice appeal that a condition imposed 47 years earlier was invalid.[21]

- It is questionable whether a public authority or third party should be able to raise the unlawfulness of a decision in proceedings other than by way of judicial review or statutory application to the High Court. The scenario would be that a public authority grants a consent and then brings proceedings against the person acting in reliance upon it, saying that the consent was unlawful. The doctrine of ultra vires provides that if a decision is quashed then it had no effect – so if development takes place under a planning permission which is subsequently quashed then that development was without planning permission and can be enforced against. However the Administrative Court only acts if person with standing brings proceedings in time (or with an extension of time) and it exercises a discretion to quash. Any other court or body dealing with an allegedly unlawful decision does not have these procedural controls nor any discretion as to how it deals with illegality. If a public authority wishes to enforce on the basis that its decision was unlawful then it might be thought that an Administrative Court challenge would have to be brought first, unless the decision was a nullity on its face. In *White v South Derbyshire District Council*[22] the Divisional Court quashed convictions for operating a caravan site without a site licence which had been obtained on the basis that there had been no power to grant the site licence nine years previously. The authority should have arranged for judicial review proceedings to be brought if it wished to challenge the licence. However in *Fenland District Council v Reuben Rose (Properties) Limited*[23] a local planning authority had granted listed building consent without notifying the Secretary of State prior to doing so as was required by legislation. Four years later the council raised the validity of the consent and then took almost a year to assert that it was invalid. The developer said that the consent had been implemented and more

---

[20] [2010] EWCA Civ 1446, [2011] 1 WLR 1901.
[21] (2000) 79 P & CR 260. See also *Earthline Ltd v Secretary of State for the Environment, Transport and the Regions* [2002] EWCA Civ 1599, [2003] 1 P & CR 24. In that case a local planning authority had imposed an unlawful time limit on a review of an old mining permission and on a subsequent application to vary the condition the Inspector on appeal failed to recognise the error.
[22] [2012] EWHC 3495 (Admin).
[23] [2000] PLCR 376.

works would be carried out under it. The Council then applied to the County Court for an injunction and a declaration that the consent was void. The Court of Appeal held that an injunction could be granted on the basis that there was no valid consent and so a criminal offence would be committed. The decision seems to bypass the protections of judicial review. Any challenger to the decision five years after its grant would have to deal with the immense delay in bringing proceedings and establish why the decision should be quashed. That would have been a difficult task. Those issues were bypassed by finding that the County Court could treat the consent as invalid. The Council could have arranged for judicial review of its own decision, perhaps by a councillor, and for an interim injunction to be sought to hold the line in the meantime.

ESTOPPEL/RES JUDICATA

1.24   Estoppel is the concept that a previous decision or representation prevents a party from subsequently contending for a different position. It is a private law concept and its application to public law regulatory matters is limited to formal judicial or planning appeal decisions. As explained below, the courts have rejected the application of estoppel by representation to public law processes.

Res judicata/issue estoppel

1.25   Estoppel *per rem judicata* prevents the reopening of matters which have been determined by a competent body. It was two elements, cause of action estoppel in respect of the claim, and issue estoppel, which covers individual conditions establishing a claim. It applies to court proceedings and findings by Inspectors (or by the Secretary of State on appeal) which are essential to their decision. The House of Lords in *Thrasyvoulou v Secretary of State for the Environment* held that *res judicata* is applicable to determinations in public law, in that case a planning enforcement appeal as Lord Bridge of Harwich said:[24]

> 'The doctrine of *res judicata* rests on the twin principles which cannot be better expressed than in terms of the two Latin maxims "interest reipublicae ut sit finis litium" and "nemo debet bis vexari pro una et eadem causa."[25] These principles are of such fundamental importance that they cannot be confined in their application to litigation in the private law field. They certainly have their place in criminal law. In principle they must apply equally to adjudications in the field of public law. In relation to adjudications subject to a comprehensive self-contained statutory code, the presumption, in my opinion, must be that where the statute has created a specific jurisdiction for the determination of any issue which establishes the existence of a legal right, the principle of *res judicata* applies to give finality to that determination unless an intention to exclude that principle can properly be inferred as a matter of construction of the relevant statutory provisions.'

1.26   In enforcement an estoppel can arise on one of the 'legal' grounds of appeal. Consequently an inspector's finding that there was no breach of planning control or that the time for enforcement action had expired cannot be re-opened by the

---

24   *Thrasyvoulou* at 289.
25   Loosely translated as 'it is in the public interest that there be an end to litigation' and 'no one shall be tried or punished twice in regards to the same event'.

issue of a fresh enforcement notice.[26] However, a decision that planning permission should not be granted cannot give rise to estoppel *per rem judicata* as it is a matter of discretion and planning judgment, allowing different bodies to lawfully come to different views.

1.27 A decision of the High Court as to the planning status of law will bind the parties in later proceedings. In *Payne v Caerphilly County Borough Council*[27] the President of the Lands Tribunal, George Bartlett QC, held that a permanent injunction under s 187B of the Town and Country Planning Act 1990 gave rise to the doctrine of *res judicata* in respect of the determination of the lawfulness of activities for the purposes of stop notice compensation under s 186. The issue was left slightly open in *R (Mid-Suffolk District Council) v Secretary of State for Communities and Local Government*[28] where an Inspector on a lawful development certificate appeal wrongly dismissed as irrelevant a High Court ruling on the meaning of a planning permission in injunction proceedings.

1.28 In estoppel by representation, a party is prevented from going back on a statement because another person has relied on it to his detriment. This was often said to arise when a local planning authority made an informal statement as to whether a particular development or use of land was lawful and it was argued that the authority could not resile from that view in later enforcement action. A narrow view of estoppel by representation as it applied to public bodies exercising their statutory functions was taken by the Court of Appeal in *Western Fish Products Ltd v Penwith District Council*.[29]

1.29 However in *R (Reprotech (Pebsham) Ltd) v East Sussex County Council*[30] it was argued that local planning authority was bound by its planning officer's opinion that the generation of electricity at a waste transfer station was not a material change of use. The House of Lords disagreed and rejected the application of estoppel by representation to public authorities. Lord Hoffmann said:[31]

> 'I think that it is unhelpful to introduce private law concepts of estoppel into planning law. … It seems to me that in this area, public law has already absorbed whatever is useful from the moral values which underlie the private law concept of estoppel and the time has come for it to stand upon its own two feet'

A representation by a public authority may have an effect in public law. It may give rise to a legitimate expectation, or it may be unreasonable or unfair to resile from it. Broadly speaking a public authority would be expected to follow the procedure it has promised although it is much less likely to be bound as to its outcome. It might also be an abuse of process to prosecute a person who relied on the local planning authority having said that what was going to be done was lawful.[32]

---

[26] See also *Forrester v Secretary of State for the Environment* (1997) 74 P & CR 434 (previous Inspector's finding as to the planning unit gave rise to issue estoppel).

[27] [2009] RVR 66, LCA/109/2006, LCA/158/2006 (Lands Tribunal, 6 January 2009).

[28] [2009] EWHC 3649 (Admin) at paras 27–29.

[29] (1978) 38 P & CR 7.

[30] [2002] UKHL 8, [2003] 1 WLR 348.

[31] *Reprotech*, at paras 33–35.

[32] *Postermobile plc v London Borough of Brent* [1998] Crim LR 435, where the local authority had said that temporary advertising hoardings (up for less than a month) did not need consent.

Chapter 2

Breach of Planning Control

2.01   The key concept in planning enforcement under Part VII of the Town and Country Planning Act 1990 is 'breach of planning control'. This is the prerequisite to taking enforcement proceedings. Breach of planning control is defined by s 171A(1) of the Town and Country Planning Act 1990 as constituting:

> '(a) carrying out development without the required planning permission; or
>
> (b) failing to comply with any condition or limitation subject to which planning permission has been granted.'

This chapter considers what is development, the need for planning permission for development and the concept of breach of condition and limitation.

DEVELOPMENT WITHOUT PLANNING PERMISSION – SUBSECTION (A)

The meaning of development

2.02   The first element is the carrying out of development without the required planning permission. 'Development' is defined by s 55(1) of the Town and Country Planning Act 1990:

> 'Subject to the following provisions of this section, in this Act, except where the context otherwise requires, "development," means the carrying out of building, engineering, mining or other operations in, on, over or under land, or the making of any material change in the use of any buildings or other land'.

This definition divides into two categories: operational development – 'building, engineering, mining or other operations'; and the making of a material change of use. Lord Denning MR observed in *Parkes v Secretary of State for the Environment*:[1]

> 'in the first half "operations" comprises activities which result in some physical alteration to the land, which has some degree of permanence to the land itself: whereas in the second half "use" comprises activities which are done in, alongside or on the land but do not interfere with the actual physical characteristics of the land.'

Land means any corporeal hereditament[2] and this includes water (tidal or otherwise) in a river.[3]

---

[1]   [1978] 1 WLR 1308 at 1311.
[2]   Town and Country Planning Act 1990, s 336.
[3]   *Thames Heliport v London Borough of Tower Hamlets* [1997] JPL 448.

11

2.03   *Breach of Planning Control*

2.03   Several general principles apply to interpreting the meaning of development:

(a) Planning is concerned with works which physically alter the land or change its use.

(b) Planning is concerned with protecting the public interest and development will, therefore, tend to be interpreted in a way which includes activities and works which should be regulated in the public interest.

(c) The Town and Country Planning Act and the secondary legislation made under it provide a 'comprehensive code of planning control'. The courts must give effect to the intention of Parliament as evinced by that comprehensive statutory code.[4]

(d) To give effect to European law, 'development' should be construed as far as possible as including all projects which fall within the Environmental Impact Assessment Directive unless they are subject to other English legislation requiring EIA.[5]

Operational development

2.04   Operational development involves making a physical change to land. It must though fall within one of the four categories of operational development.

Building operations

2.05   By s 55(1A), 'building operations' includes:

'(a)   demolition of buildings;

(b)   rebuilding;

(c)   structural alterations of or additions to buildings; and

(d)   other operations normally undertaken by a person carrying on business as a builder.'

Consequently building operations is defined in an inclusive fashion in subsection (1A).

2.06   Whether building operations have been carried out can often be answered by asking whether they have resulted in a building. Building must be considered in its wide definition in the Town and Country Planning Act 1990 as including any structure or erection or part of a building.[6] Whether an object is a building is often judged by reference to three factors: size; the nature and degree of attachment; and the degree of permanence. Permanence was concerned with 'a sufficient length of time to be of significance in the planning context'[7] and this may be something erected on a seasonal basis.

---

4   *Pioneer Aggregates (UK) Ltd v Secretary of State for the Environment* [1985] AC 132 at 140 to 141 per Lord Scarman.
5   *R (SAVE Britain's Heritage) v Secretary of State for Communities and Local Government* [2011] EWCA Civ 334, [2011] LGR 493; *R (Save Woolley Valley Action Group Ltd) v Bath and North East Somerset Council* [2012] EWHC 2161 (Admin), [2013] Env LR 8 at paras 112 to 114.
6   Town and Country Planning Act 1990, s 336(1).
7   *Skerritts of Nottingham v Secretary of State for the Environment, Transport and the Regions* [2000] JPL 1025 at 1034 per Schiemann LJ.

2.07   Examples of structures which the courts have said could be buildings include a seven-bay marquee erected in the grounds of a hotel for eight months in a year,[8] a tower crane resting on a steel track[9] and polytunnels over large areas of farmland for nine months a year.[10] The setting up of umbrellas and side panels to create a marquee type structure in the rear garden of a shisha lounge was also a building operation.[11] 'Poultry units' each housing up to 1,000 birds and said to be moved periodically around their paddocks could also be buildings (or the product of building operations).[12] An object may be a building in planning law without being incorporated into the land, as part of the realty.[13]

2.08   Some building operations do not result in buildings. For example, laying a tarmac drive is normally undertaken by a builder. Similarly the categories include structural alterations to buildings. Painting the exterior of a building has permitted development rights[14] so legislators must have assumed that painting could be development, even though it would not be a structural alteration.

Engineering operations

2.09   It is perhaps too simplistic to suggest that engineering operations are operations carried out by engineers. Operations in planning are concerned with effects on land, so engineering operations tend to fall within the civil engineering disciplines. Those operations include the construction of roads, earthworks, lakes and ponds, so tend to be physical works to land which do not result in buildings, structures or erections. Many of these operations will not be carried out by engineers at all.

Mining operations

2.10   Mining operations include:[15]

'(a)   the removal of material of any description—

(i)   from a mineral-working deposit;

(ii)   from a deposit of pulverised fuel ash or other furnace ash or clinker; or

(iii) from a deposit of iron, steel or other metallic slags; and

(b)   the extraction of minerals from a disused railway embankment'.

Mineral working deposit and minerals are further defined:[16]

'"mineral-working deposit" means any deposit of material remaining after minerals have been extracted from land or otherwise deriving from the carrying out of operations for the winning and working of minerals in, on or under land;

---

[8]   *Skerritts of Nottingham*, above.

[9]   *Barvis Ltd v Secretary of State for the Environment* (1971) 22 P & CR 710.

[10]   *Hall Hunter Partnership v First Secretary of State* [2006] EWHC 3482, [2007] 2 P & CR 5.

[11]   *Islam v Secretary of State for Communities and Local Government* [2012] EWHC 1314 (Admin), [2012] JPL 1378.

[12]   *R (Save Woolley Valley Action Group Ltd) v Bath and North East Somerset Council* [2012] EWHC 2161 (Admin), [2013] Env LR 8.

[13]   *R v Swansea City Council, ex p Elitestone* (1993) 66 P & CR 422.

[14]   Town and Country Planning (General Permitted Development) Order 1995, Sch 2, Pt 2, Class C.

[15]   Town and Country Planning Act 1990, s 55(4).

[16]   Town and Country Planning Act 1990, s 336(1).

"minerals" includes all substances of a kind ordinarily worked for removal by underground or surface working, except that it does not include peat cut for purposes other than sale.'

Minerals therefore include sand, gravel, stone and coal but also oil and gas.

2.11   The extraction of further minerals from an existing quarry or the digging of the ground to gain access to it is a mining operation. Even where mining has taken place on land, it is still a mining operation to carry out further extraction on that land, such as by digging deeper. Lord Denning MR said in *Thomas David (Porthcawl) Ltd v Penybont Rural District Council*:[17]

'Every shovelful is a mining operation.'

Other operations

2.12   Such is the breadth of building, engineering or mining operations that the final category of 'other operations' has rarely been relied upon. This residual category is not limited to operations of the same class as building, engineering or mining operations.[18] *Beronstone*[19] concerned the erection of hundreds of wooden stakes to mark out plots of land and accessways, which amounted to other operations.[20] In *Save Woolley Valley* the construction or installation of the poultry units could have been other operations if it were not within building operations.

Exclusions from operational development

2.13   Section 55(2) sets out various operations or uses of land which do not involve development. With respect to operational development these are:

'(a) the carrying out for the maintenance, improvement or other alteration of any building of works which—

(i)   affect only the interior of the building, or

(ii)   do not materially affect the external appearance of the building,

and are not works for making good war damage or works begun after 5th December 1968 for the alteration of a building by providing additional space in it underground;'

This exception is of considerable practical importance as it excludes from control a very large number of building operations, although its meaning and application have been open to some debate. In *Sage v Secretary of State for the Environment, Transport and the Regions*[21] the House of Lords held that the sub-paragraph only applied to an existing building. This was described in *Sage* as a 'fully detailed

---

[17]   [1972] 1 WLR 1526 at 1531.

[18]   *Coleshill and District Investment Co Ltd v Minister of Housing and Local Government* [1969] 1 WLR 746 and *Beronstone Ltd v First Secretary of State* [2006] EWHC 2391 (Admin), *R (Save Woolley Valley Action Group Ltd) v Bath and North East Somerset Council* [2012] EWHC 2161 (Admin), [2013] Env LR 8 at para 74 (the latter decision disagreeing with *Tewkesbury Borough Council v Keeley* [2004] EWHC 2954 (QB), [2005] JPL. 831 at para 37, which appears to decide to the contrary.

[19]   *Beronstone v First Secretary of State* [2006] EWHC 2391 (Admin).

[20]   Small plots had been sold on the dubious potential of development in the green belt and stakes were used to mark the plots to avoid restrictions on permitted development rights for fences.

[21]   [2003] UKHL 22, [2003] 2 All ER 689.

structure of a certain character'.[22] Consequently it would not be possible to partly construct a building and then use sub-paragraph (a) to alter the internal layout from the approved plans, although that could be done as soon as the building was complete.

2.14   There has been some debate as to whether internal works are development if they are part of a project which includes external alterations which are development. The issue has arisen in unusual circumstances, as if planning permission is granted for the external works it rarely matters whether it is actually required for the internal works. However the view was taken in *R (Prudential Assurance Limited) v Sunderland City Council*[23] that planning permission was required for the insertion of internal walls in a retail unit as part of a sub-division, which involved material alterations to the exterior of the building.

2.15   Under the second proviso to the exception, materially affecting the external appearance of a building involves an impact capable of having some effect in planning terms. Whether an alteration is material does depend upon the building, its character, the change and the available viewpoints. For example an alteration which is only visible from an aircraft would not be material.[24] In *Royal Borough of Kensington and Chelsea v CG Hotels,*[25] 11 floodlights had been fixed to the walls of a hotel or placed on balconies, but as these were unnoticeable and virtually invisible from the street during the day an inspector held that they were not development because of the paragraph (a) exception. This was upheld by the Divisional Court, who considered that the effect of floodlighting at night did not alter the external appearance of the building.

2.16   The exception for internal works allowed the installation of mezzanine floors in retail warehouses (unless restrained by planning condition) which could significantly increase sales floorspace and so retail and traffic impact. Section 55 was consequently amended by the Planning and Compulsory Purchase Act 2004 to allow specified floorspace additions to be removed from the exception from development.[26] Consequently, in England, operations which have the effect of increasing the gross floor space of a building by more than 200 square metres are capable of being operational development if the building is used for the retail sale of goods other than hot food.[27] Sub-paragraph (b) provides as follows:

> '(b) the carrying out on land within the boundaries of a road by a highway authority of any works required for the maintenance or improvement of the road but, in the case of any such works which are not exclusively for the maintenance of the road, not including any works which may have significant adverse effects on the environment;'

---

[22]   *Sage* at paras 18, 23 per Lord Hobhouse of Woodborough.

[23]   [2010] EWHC 1771 (Admin), [2011] JPL 322.

[24]   *Burroughs Day v Bristol City Council* [1996] 1 PLR 78.

[25]   (1981) 41 P & CR 40.

[26]   Inserting Town and Country Planning Act 1990, s 55(2A).

[27]   Town and Country Planning (Development Management Procedure) (England) Order 2010. No order has been made in Wales.

Sub-paragraph (b) provides a general exception for maintenance or improvement works carried out by the highways authority[28] within the existing boundaries of a road. Permitted development rights apply to works which may have significant adverse effects, maintenance or improvement works adjoining[the road and street furniture.[29]

> '(c) the carrying out by a local authority or statutory undertakers of any works for the purpose of inspecting, repairing or renewing any sewers, mains, pipes, cables or other apparatus, including the breaking open of any street or other land for that purpose;'.

This exception relates to existing apparatus. There are extensive permitted development rights for new apparatus.

Demolition

2.17   Section (g) provides that:

> '(g) the demolition of any description of building specified in a direction given by the Secretary of State to local planning authorities generally or to a particular local planning authority'.

Demolition is dealt with in planning in this way:[30]

(a) Considering s 55(1) on its own, demolition will tend to fall within the categories of operational development. The demolition of buildings is a building operation under subsection (1A), and the demolition of other works (such as a road or bund) may be an engineering operation or other operation.

(b) The demolition of the whole of a building with a cubic content (measured externally) which does not exceed 50m³, or the demolition in whole or part of any gate, fence, wall or other means of enclosure, is excluded from the definition of development by the Town and Country Planning (Demolition – Description of Buildings) Direction 1995.[31]

(c) Where demolition is development, it will need planning permission, even if scheduled monument, listed building or conservation area consent[32] is also required.

---

[28] The Highways Agency (as the Secretary of State for Transport) is the highways authority for motorways and trunk roads, Transport for London (as part of the Greater London Authority) is the highways authority for certain important roads in Great London, whilst the county or unitary council is the highways authority for the remainder.

[29] Town and Country Planning (General Permitted Development) Order 1995, Sch 2, Pts 12 and 13.

[30] This issue is discussed in more detail in Richard Harwood, *Historic Environment Law* (Institute of Art and Law, 2012) at pp 160–170.

[31] The Demolition Direction had excluded from the definition of development demolition which was authorised by scheduled monument, listed building or conservation area consent or the demolition of any building which was not a dwellinghouse or adjoining a dwellinghouse. The effect was that most commercial, infrastructure and public buildings could be demolished without being subject to planning control. The Court of Appeal in *R (SAVE Britain's Heritage) v Secretary of State for Communities and Local Government* [2011] EWCA Civ 334, [2011] JPL 1016 held that these exclusions were contrary to the Environmental Impact Assessment Directive as those projects could avoid a need for EIA. Those parts of the Demolition Direction were declared unlawful, bringing almost all demolition within the need for planning permission.

[32] The Enterprise and Regulatory Reform Act 2013 proposes to abolish conservation area consent in England, replacing it with strengthened enforcement provisions for demolition in conservation areas: see Chapter 16.

(d) Planning permission may be granted on application to the local planning authority or by permitted development rights. The permitted development rights may be withdrawn by an Article 4 Direction or may need to be subject to a determination that Environmental Impact Assessment is not required.

(e) Unless planning permission, scheduled monument, listed building or conservation area consent has already been granted for the demolition, or demolition is required by a planning obligation, the local planning authority must be asked whether prior approval of the method of demolition and any proposed restoration of the site is required.

Fish farming

2.18   One inclusion within operational development is fish farming (including shellfish) in non-tidal waters. 'The placing or assembly of any tank in any part of any inland waters for the purpose of fish farming' is treated as engineering operations if it would not otherwise be development.[33] In this context 'tank' includes any cage and any other structure for use in fish farming.

MATERIAL CHANGE OF USE OF LAND

2.19   Material change of use requires a 'material change in the definable character of the use of the land'.[34] The character of a use is broad and does not allow the planning authorities to exercise detailed control over the use of land in the way that conditions on a planning permission may do. Usually a material change of use will involve a change in the description of the use, for example from office to residential, or shop to café. In some cases the character of the use may change because the purpose of the activity may affect its extent. For example, a home occupier using his garage for repairing his cars would usually be within the residential use, but if he repairs other people's cars, particularly for payment, then this is likely to be a material change of use.[35] It is possible that a mere intensification of a use of land can be a material change of use – doing more of the same thing – but such cases will be very rare. Usually the new use is capable of being described differently by the activity or its purpose. It is possible that a material change of use resulting from changes in intensity can affect the overall character of the use, even though the descriptions of the uses do not change.[36] However, it is important to remember that any intensification must change the character of the use.[37] In assessing whether there has been a change of character in the use, the impact of the use on other premises is relevant, but cannot be considered in isolation from what is happening on the land.[38]

---

[33]   Town and Country Planning Act 1990, s 55(4A).
[34]   *Hertfordshire County Council v Secretary of State for Communities and Local Government* [2012] EWHC 277 (Admin), [2012] JPL 836 at para 46 per Ouseley J, approved by the Court of Appeal [2012] EWCA Civ 1473 at para 11 per Pill LJ.
[35]   See the comments of Sullivan J in *R v Thanet District Council ex p Tapp* (2001) 81 P & CR 37 at para 54.
[36]   See *Fidler v First Secretary of State* [2004] EWCA Civ 1295, [2005] 1 P & CR 12 at para 29 per Carnwath LJ doubting the relevance to the post-1991 legislation of Donaldson LJ's comment in *Kensington and Chelsea RBC v Secretary of State and Mia Carla Ltd* [1981] JPL 50 that: 'If the planners were incapable of formulating what was use after intensification and what was use before intensification then there had been no material change of use'.
[37]   *Lilo Blum v Secretary of State for the Environment* [1987] JPL 278 at 280 per Simon Brown J.
[38]   *Hertfordshire County Council v Secretary of State for Communities and Local Government* [2012] EWCA Civ 1473 at para 26 per Pill LJ.

Primary and ancillary uses

2.20   A use of land includes uses which are ordinarily incidental or ancillary to the primary use. This is a judge-made concept[39] designed to cater for the common situation that different and smaller uses will be part a main use (for example, a shop may have an office for its management;[40] a sports centre might have a store for equipment). There must be a relationship between the potential ancillary use and the main use:[41] otherwise there would be two separate uses or a mixed use.

2.21   'Ordinarily' excludes particularly unusual uses, but is wider than 'commonly'. In *Harrods Limited v Secretary of State for the Environment*[42] the courts held that whilst a car park was an incidental part of the retail use of a department store, a helicopter landing pad on the roof for the Harrods chairman was not. Sullivan J focused his judgment on the ordinarily incidental issue. In the Court of Appeal, Schiemann LJ agreed in broad terms with the High Court analysis, but said the proper approach was to consider whether, ignoring the Use Classes Order, what is involved amounts to a material change of use.[43] Examples of activities found not to be ancillary to the main use are: the keeping and slaughtering of chickens for sale (some 300 per week) was not incidental to the shop use of the premises;[44] providing coin-operated booths for viewing films in a shop;[45] and holding major festivals at a residential theological college.[46]

The planning unit

2.22   In considering whether a material change of use has taken place, the local planning authority should identify the appropriate planning unit. This is the most appropriate physical area against which to determine whether a material change has taken place. The planning unit is a judge-made concept – it is not in the legislation – but which enables the identification of the relevant land in s 55.

2.23   Three broad categories for determining the planning unit were identified by Bridge J in *Burdle v Secretary of State for the Environment*:[47]

> 'First, whenever it is possible to recognise a single main purpose of the occupier's use of his land to which secondary activities are incidental or ancillary, the whole unit of occupation should be considered. That proposition emerges clearly from *G Percy Trentham Ltd v Gloucestershire County Council [1966] 1 WLR 506*, where Diplock LJ said, at p 513:
>
>> "What is the unit which the local authority are entitled to look at and deal with in an enforcement notice for the purpose of determining whether or not there has been a 'material change in the use of any buildings or other land'? As I suggested in the

---

[39]   First appearing in *Percy Trentham Ltd v Gloucestershire County Council* [1966] 1 WLR 506 at 512 per Lord Denning MR and 514 per Diplock LJ.
[40]   An example used in *Brazil Concrete Ltd v Amersham RDC* (1967) 18 P & CR 396 at 399 per Lord Denning MR.
[41]   *Main v Secretary of State for the Environment* (1999) 77 P & CR 300.
[42]   [2001] EWHC Admin 600, [2002] JPL 437.
[43]   Court of Appeal at paras 20, 21.
[44]   *Hussain v Secretary of State for the Environment* (1971) 23 P & CR 330.
[45]   *Lydcare Ltd v Secretary of State for the Environment* (1984) 49 P & CR 186.
[46]   *International Society for Krishna Consciousness v Secretary of State* [1992] JPL 962.
[47]   [1972] 1 WLR 1207.

course of the argument, I think for that purpose what the local authority are entitled to look at is the whole of the area which was used for a particular purpose, including any part of that area whose use was incidental to or ancillary to the achievement of that purpose."

However, secondly, it may equally be apt to consider the entire unit of occupation even though the occupier carries on a variety of activities and it is not possible to say that one is incidental or ancillary to another. This is well settled in the case of a composite use where the component activities fluctuate in their intensity from time to time, but the different activities are not confined within separate and physically distinct areas of land.

Thirdly, however, it may frequently occur that within a single unit of occupation two or more physically separate and distinct areas are occupied for substantially different and unrelated purposes. In such a case each area used for a different main purpose (together with its incidental and ancillary activities) ought to be considered as a separate planning unit.'

Applying the categories is not always simple.

The carrying on of a use

2.24   A use may be carried on even if at that moment there is no activity on site. For example, a building and land would still be in a factory use if the factory was closed for the weekend or for a summer holiday.[48] Similarly an area of pavement was used for seating ancillary to a restaurant even though the tables and chairs were put away at night and during cold weather.[49]

2.25   A lawful use will survive a lengthy period of inactivity on the land. Abandonment is possible in relation to prior use[50] though not in relation to rights acquired under a planning permission still capable of being implemented according to its terms.[51] There is some debate as to whether a use instituted under a planning permission can be abandoned by lack of use.[52] Conversely, if a use is not lawful then it will need to be actively carried out for the limitation period to become lawful. This is considered further in Chapter 3 below.

2.26   Identifying in legal terms the start of a use is not straightforward. It could not be later than the actual commencement of a use (for example, when the shop started trading). However, the physical conversion of a building might give rise to a change of use before the use by the occupiers commences, for example, carrying out works to convert a building to residential use. The point in the process that the change takes place has not been firmly resolved by the courts: Donaldson LJ suggested in *Impey v Secretary of State for the Environment*[53] that the test may be whether the premises are usable for the new use.

---

[48]   *Thurrock Borough Council v Secretary of State for the Environment* [2002] EWCA Civ 226, [2002] JPL 1278, at para 28 per Schiemann LJ.

[49]   *Westminster City Council v Secretary of State for Communities and Local Government* [2013] EWHC 23 (Admin) at paras 57–61.

[50]   *Hartley v Minister of Housing and Local Government* [1970] 1 QB 413; Secretary of State for the Environment, Transport and the Regions v Hughes (2000) 80 P & CR 397.

[51]   *Pioneer Aggregates (UK) Ltd v Secretary of State for the Environment* [1985] AC 132 143.

[52]   See *Stockton on Tees Borough Council v Secretary of State for Communities and Local Government* [2010] EWHC 1766 (Admin), [2011] JPL 183.

[53]   (1980) 47 P & CR 157.

2.27 *Breach of Planning Control*

Exceptions to material changes of use

2.27   By s 55(2) various matters are not material changes of use:

'(d) the use of any buildings or other land within the curtilage of a dwellinghouse for any
      purpose incidental to the enjoyment of the dwellinghouse as such;'.

Such uses include gardens, swimming pools for the use of occupants, the keeping
of family pets, car parking and storage. The use must be incidental to the enjoyment
of the dwellinghouse as such, rather than the particular interests of the owner. It
is legitimate to consider what people normally do in dwellinghouses, and so the
keeping of 40 dogs or having a replica Spitfire aircraft in the back garden were not
incidental.[54]

'(e) the use of any land for the purposes of agriculture or forestry (including afforestation)
      and the use for any of those purposes of any building occupied together with land so
      used;'.

Agriculture has a special, and relaxed, status in planning law. A material change of
use from any use to agriculture or forestry is not development and agricultural and
forestry operational development has substantial permitted development rights. The
definition of 'agriculture':[55]

'includes horticulture, fruit growing, seed growing, dairy farming, the breeding and
keeping of livestock (including any creature kept for the production of food, wool, skins
or fur, or for the purpose of its use in the farming of land), the use of land as grazing
land, meadow land, osier land, market gardens and nursery grounds, and the use of land
for woodlands where that use is ancillary to the farming of land for other agricultural
purposes, and "agricultural" shall be construed accordingly.'

2.28   The sale of produce grown on a site is part of the agricultural use, but the
sale of products grown elsewhere is not.[56] The stationing of a caravan for mixing
cattle food and for the farmer to shelter in during the day (but not to live) was also an
agricultural use.[57] In *Millington v Secretary of State for the Environment, Transport
and the Regions*[58] the growing of grapes for winemaking and the making of wine at
the farm from those grapes was an agricultural use, the latter being ancillary to the
farming activities. The keeping of horses is not agricultural unless they are used in
farming,[59] as at least in the United Kingdom they are not kept for the production of
food or skins.

2.29   There may be exceptions to agricultural uses, for example, in *Winchester
City Council v Secretary of State for Communities and Local Government*[60] the
production of pathogen free eggs was an industrial rather than an agricultural
process.

---

[54] *Wallington v Secretary of State for Wales* [1991] JPL 942 and *London Borough of Croydon v Gladden*
      (1994) 68 P & CR 300 respectively.
[55] Town and Country Planning Act 1990, s 336(1).
[56] *Williams v Minister of Housing and Local Government* (1967) 18 P & CR 514.
[57] *Wealden District Council v Secretary of State for the Environment* [1988] JPL 268, CA.
[58] [2000] JPL 297. The case contains a useful examination of the agricultural use authorities.
[59] *Belmont Farm Limited v Minister of Housing and Local Government* (1962) 13 P & CR 417.
[60] [2007] EWHC 2303 (Admin), [2008] JPL 315.

2.30

'(f) in the case of buildings or other land which are used for a purpose of any class specified in an order made by the Secretary of State under this section, the use of the buildings or other land or, subject to the provisions of the order, of any part of the buildings or the other land, for any other purpose of the same class.'

2.31   The use classes are set out in the Town and Country Planning (Use Classes) Order 1987. Where a building or other land is within one use class a change of use to another use within the same use class is not development.[61] In *R v Bolsover District Council ex p Ashfield District Council,*[62] it was left open whether a use needed to have commenced by activity (in that case by shops starting to trade) before the Use Classes Order could be relied upon.

2.32   The use classes are not comprehensive. There will be uses of land or buildings which fall outside the wording of all of the classes. Certain uses are excluded by the Order even if they would otherwise be within a class: theatre, amusement arcade or centre, or a funfair, launderette, sale of fuel for motor vehicles, sale or display for sale of motor vehicles, taxi business or business for the hire of motor vehicles, scrapyard, or a yard for the storage or distribution of minerals or the breaking of motor vehicles, a registrable alkali works, a hostel, waste disposal installation using incineration or chemical treatment, the landfill of hazardous waste, a retail warehouse club, a night club or a casino.[63]

2.33   The concept of primary and ancillary uses remains, so land will be within a use class because of its primary use and may still have ordinarily incidental uses.[64] A mixed use comprising one or more use classes, or a use class and a sui generis use does not have the benefit of the use classes order.[65] For example, if a sandwich shop was in mixed A1/A3 use, the use classes order could not be relied up to change to an A1 or A3 use.

2.34   The Use Classes Order applies to part of a building as well as the whole, so sub-division of a building is not a material change of use.[66] Since internal works would not be operational development, the only element giving rise to the need for planning permission may be external alterations.

Changes of use which are material

2.35   Section 55(3) provides that the following are material changes of use (whether they would be otherwise):

'(a) the use as two or more separate dwellinghouses of any building previously used as a single dwellinghouse involves a material change in the use of the building and of each part of it which is so used;'.

---

[61] Town and Country Planning (Use Classes) Order 1987, Art 3(1).
[62] (1995) 70 P & CR 507.
[63] Town and Country Planning (Use Classes) Order 1987, Art 3(6).
[64] Town and Country Planning (Use Classes) Order 1987, Art 3(3).
[65] *Fidler v First Secretary of* State [2004] EWCA Civ 1295, [2005] JPL 510 per Carnwath LJ at para 28, endorsing *Belmont Farm v First Secretary of State* [2003] EWHC 1895 (Admin), [2004] JPL 593.
[66] Except for the sub-division of a dwelling where the operation of the Use Classes Order is excluded by Art 4.

2.36 *Breach of Planning Control*

The conversion of a dwellinghouse into flats is, therefore, development (and also does not benefit from the Use Classes Order), as would be the subdivision of an existing flat within a building. A change of use to another form of residential use, such as a house in multiple occupation or lodgings, is not covered by this subsection although such changes will often be material in any event. Changing from two or more dwellinghouses into a single dwellinghouse is not within the subsection. Whether such a change is material has to be considered on its own facts.[67]

"(b) the deposit of refuse or waste materials on land involves a material change in its use, notwithstanding that the land is comprised in a site already used for that purpose, if—

(i) the superficial area of the deposit is extended, or

(ii) the height of the deposit is extended and exceeds the level of the land adjoining the site.'

The deposit of waste on a temporary or permanent basis tends to be seen as a use of land. To provide a degree of planning control over long-established sites, the area and height of waste deposits is restricted.

2.36   Additionally, by s 55(5):

'the use for the display of advertisements of any external part of a building which is not normally used for that purpose shall be treated for the purposes of this section as involving a material change in the use of that part of the building.'

This enables the planning enforcement powers to be used against unlawful advertisements in addition to advertising controls. If the advertisements are displayed in accordance with the relevant Advertisements Regulations then they have deemed planning permission.[68]

Short-term lettings in London

2.37   A local variation to the meaning of development is provided by s 25 of the Greater London Council (General Powers) Act 1973 which makes the use of residential premises in Greater London for short-term lets a material change of use. The section provides:

'(1) For the purposes of [section 55(1) of the Town and Country Planning Act 1990], the use as temporary sleeping accommodation of any residential premises in Greater London involves a material change of use of the premises and of each part thereof which is so used.

(2) In this section —

(a) "use as temporary sleeping accommodation" means use of sleeping accommodation which is occupied by the same person for less than 90

---

[67] In *Richmond upon Thames London Borough Council v Secretary of State for the Environment, Transport and the Regions* [2001] JPL 84 an Inspector's decision that the conversion of a house back from seven flats to a single dwelling was not development was quashed as the Inspector did not consider that small flats may fulfil a planning purpose.

[68] Town and Country Planning Act 1990, s 222. The regulations are the Town and Country Planning (Control of Advertisements) (England) Regulations 2007 and, in Wales, the Town and Country Planning (Control of Advertisements) Regulations 1992.

consecutive nights and which is provided (with or without other services) for a consideration arising either —

(i) by way of trade for money or money's worth; or

(ii) by reason of the employment of the occupant; whether or not the relationship of landlord and tenant is thereby created;

(b) "residential premises" means a building, or any part of a building, which was previously used, or designed or constructed for use, as one or more permanent residences.'

Even if a change from temporary sleeping accommodation to longer-term residential accommodation is not a material change of use, a reversion to temporary sleeping accommodation would be a material change of use.[69]

The need for planning permission

2.38 Section 57(1) of the Town and Country Planning Act 1990 provides:

'Subject to the following provisions of this section, planning permission is required for the carrying out of any development of land.'

This subsection demonstrates that the concept of development is central to the planning system. Essentially, if development is carried out then it requires planning permission. Conversely, if what is done is not development then it does not need planning permission.

2.39 Planning permission can be granted either following an application made to the local planning authority or under permitted development rights. The Town and Country Planning (General Permitted Development) Order 1995[70] ('the GPDO') grants planning permission for specified classes of development subject to various conditions and in certain cases the approval of details. These permitted development rights can be restricted by 'Article 4 directions' made by the local planning authority under the GPDO. Planning permission may also be granted either for particular projects or specific classes of development by local development orders, neighbourhood planning orders, community right to build orders or simplified planning zones. Where consent is granted by the Secretary of State or Welsh Ministers under particular enactments they may also grant a deemed planning permission under s 90 of the Town and Country Planning Act 1990.

2.40 The development authorised by a planning permission can normally only be carried out once. For example, when planning permission was granted for a garage and, following the construction of the garage, part of it was demolished with a view to rebuilding to enable an order to be made diverting a public footpath, the permission did not authorise the rebuilding of the garage: *Hall v Secretary of State for the Environment, Transport and the Regions*.[71] Most obviously this applies where the relevant part of the development has been completed: a building is constructed

---

[69] *Fairstate Ltd v First Secretary of State* [2005] EWCA Civ 283, [2005] JPL 1333, affirming [2005] JPL 369. In *Fairstate*, the occupation of temporary sleeping accommodation for 155 days by one person meant that the next short period of occupation was a material change of use.

[70] SI 1995/418.

[71] [1998] JPL 1055.

and is subsequently demolished in whole or part and rebuilt. In *Hall,* Nigel MacLeod QC said:

> 'it does seem to me that it is right that when a discrete and substantial part of a planning permission is completed in accordance with that permission, then that part of the permission has been completed and achieved, and is spent in so far as that aspect of the permission is concerned. To knock the garage down and rebuild it is not in my judgment authorised by this planning permission.'

A different situation may arise if part-way through construction part of the works have to be taken down and rebuilt, for example because they turn out to be unstable or are damaged by fire. In those circumstances the authorised building will not have been constructed until the works, including the repeated works, have been concluded.

2.41   Similarly in *Cynon Valley Borough Council v Secretary of State for Wales*[72] planning permission had been granted to make a material change of use to a fish and chip shop (an A3 use class[73]). The use of the shop had reverted to A1 retail use (an antiques shop) under permitted development rights. It then changed to a Chinese takeaway (again, an A3 use). Both changes were material changes of use and the local planning authority enforced against the change to a takeaway). The Court of Appeal held that original planning permission was spent when the change of use to a fish and chip shop took place could not be used to authorise a subsequent change back to an A3 use.[74]

2.42   There is however no reason in principle why a planning permission should not expressly authorise repeated development. This might be a seasonal use of land or a building erected and dismantled on a seasonal basis (such as a large marquee, tennis dome or agricultural polytunnels) but the consent ought to be explicit.

Exceptions to the need for planning permission

2.43   There are several exceptions to the requirement for planning permission which are concerned with an alternative means of approval and returning to earlier uses following temporary or unlawful activity:

- If development consent is required as part of a nationally significant infrastructure project then no planning permission is required: s 57(1A).[75]

- Where planning permission has been 'granted for a limited period, planning permission is not required for the resumption, at the end of that period, of its use for the purpose for which it was normally used before the permission was granted': s 57(2). A permission for a limited period will most obviously include a permission for a defined period of time. In *Westminster City Council v Davenport,*[76] the Court of Appeal held that s 57(2) applied to a permission

---

[72]   (1987) 53 P & CR 68.
[73]   In England, hot food takeaways including fish and chip shops and Chinese takeaways are now in the A5 use class: Town and Country Planning (Use Classes) Order 1987.
[74]   *Cynon Valley* at 76. The reversion to an A3 use was lawful for another reason, based on what is now s 57(3) of the Town and Country Planning Act 1990, as discussed below.
[75]   The requirement for development consent rather than planning permission is in the Planning Act 2008, s 33(1).
[76]   [2011] EWCA Civ 458, [2011] JPL 1325.

for diplomatic uses, which was personal to the Commissioner of particular governments. The temporary permission must be implemented for this provision to be relied upon.[77] 'Normal use' does not include any use begun in breach of planning control[78] so it is not possible to revert to the previous use of the land if that was started without planning permission, even if it had become lawful by the passage of time before the temporary permission was granted. The provision can be relied upon even if the temporary use had ceased to be carried on before or after the permission required cessation, and does not have to be carried out immediately the period expires.[79]

• If a development order, local development order or neighbourhood development order grants planning permission subject to limitations, planning permission is not required for the use of the land for its normal use: s 57(3).[80] The Town and Country Planning (General Permitted Development) Order 1995 grants permissions 'subject to any relevant exception, limitation or condition specified in Schedule 2' of that Order.[81] In *Cynon Valley Borough Council v Secretary of State for Wales*,[82] it was held that the permitted development rights to change uses imported the limitations in the Use Classes Order. Since Class A1 of the Use Classes Order provided for use as a shop except for certain purposes, the planning permission was subject to limitations. It was therefore possible to revert to the previous use of the shop, namely class A3 hot food. The text of the Use Classes Order has subsequently changed and the particular limitation in the *Cynon Valley* case no longer arises.

• Section 57(4) applies to the resumption of uses following an enforcement notice:

'Where an enforcement notice has been issued in respect of any development of land, planning permission is not required for its use for the purpose which (in accordance with the provisions of this Part of this Act) it could lawfully have been used if that development had not been carried out.'

2.44   Where an enforcement notice has been issued s 57(4) therefore permits a reversion to the previous use if that was a lawful use. There is no right to revert to the previous lawful use if no enforcement notice has been issued. One consequence is that if two successive unlawful material changes of use take place (neither becoming lawful by passage of time) and an enforcement notice is issued against the second material change of use, then there is no right to revert to the original lawful use.[83] This applies even if the original and final uses are the same.[84] A lawful use for the purposes of s 57(4) includes uses which have become lawful by passage of time.[85] Land which

---

[77] *Smith v Secretary of State for the Environment* (1984) 47 P & CR 194 at 204–205 per Woolf J.
[78] Town and Country Planning Act 1990, s 57(5). This includes any breach of planning control under the Town and Country Planning Act since the 1947 Act: Town and Country Planning Act 1990, s 57(6).
[79] *Smith v Secretary of State for the Environment* (1984) 47 P & CR 194 at 205.
[80] Community right to build orders are 'a particular type of neighbourhood development order' (Town and Country Planning Act 1990, s 61Q) so are also subject to section 57(3).
[81] Town and Country Planning (General Permitted Development) Order 1995 ('the GPDO'), Art 3(2).
[82] (1987) 53 P & CR 68.
[83] *Young v Secretary of State for Environment* [1983] 2 AC 662.
[84] *Fairstate Ltd v First Secretary of State* [2004] EWHC 1807 (Admin), [2005] JPL 369 at paras 27, 28 per Sullivan J.
[85] *Hillingdon London Borough Council v Secretary of State for Communities and Local Government* [2008] EWHC 198 (Admin), [2008] JPL 1486. This is the effect of the passage of time conferring lawfulness rather than merely immunity as a result of the new s 191 introduced by the Planning and Compensation Act 1991. *LTSS Print and Supply Services Ltd v Hackney London Borough Council* [1976] QB 663 on the previous legislation is no longer good law.

was in a particular use on 1 July 1948 was able to continue in that use, subject to compliance with the previous systems of planning control.[86] The resumption of various uses which had been carried on before 1 July was permitted if begun before 6 December 1968.[87]

SUBSECTION (B)

2.45   The second breach of planning control is failing to comply with a condition or limitation. Conditions can be attached to a grant of planning permission.[88] These can require the development to be carried out in a certain way (eg materials in an extension matching the existing building) or make it subject to other acts being done first ('negative conditions'). Some permitted development rights are subject to conditions in the GPDO.

2.46   'Limitation' includes limitations specified in the General Permitted Development Order.[89] There is considerable uncertainty as to whether 'limitation' includes the ambit of the permission granted. One view is that a limitation must be in the form of a condition.[90] The High Court in *I'm Your Man v Secretary of State for the Environment*[91] held that limitations were only those identified in the GPDO. In that case planning permission had been granted for a use for what the description of development said was a temporary period of seven years. No condition was imposed requiring the cessation of the use at the end of that period. When the use duly continued Robin Purchas QC held that it was not a breach of planning control. It was common ground that in the particular circumstances the change from a temporary use to a permanent use was not a material change of use. In the absence of a time limiting condition, nothing prevented the change to a permanent use. *I'm Your Man* does not mean that the description of development does not matter – on the contrary it is important in determining what the planning permission authorises and so part of the basis for deciding whether subsequent changes are development.

2.47   Whether there has been a failure to comply with a condition depends upon the planning permission having been implemented and the interpretation of the permission. Development is only carried out in breach of a condition or limitation in a permission if the permission is implemented: see *Newbury District Council v Secretary of State for the Environment*[92] where a condition requiring the removal

---

[86]   The Town and Country Planning Act 1932 had allowed local authorities to introduce schemes over land, meaning that authorisation would be required. However the Town and Country Planning (Interim Development) Act 1943 provided that all land was deemed to be subject to a scheme and permitted applications for permission under interim development orders: ss 1, 2. By s 77(1) of the Town and Country Planning Act 1947, planning permission was deemed to be granted for development authorised by an interim development permission which had been approved after 21 July 1943.

[87]   Town and Country Planning Act 1990, s 57(7) and Sch 4. Given the 10-year time limit, these provisions are now redundant.

[88]   Town and Country Planning Act 1990, ss 70, 72.

[89]   Town and Country Planning (General Permitted Development) Order 1995, Art 3(2). The power to impose limitations in a development order is in the Town and Country Planning Act 1990, s 60(1). These are the only limitations identified in Circular 10/97: see Sch 2, para 2.7.

[90]   *Peacock Homes Ltd v Secretary of State for the Environment* (1984) 48 P & CR 20.

[91]   (1999) 77 P & CR 251. There is extensive consideration of the history of limitations in planning legislation in that judgment.

[92]   [1981] AC 578. See also *Sheppard v Secretary of State for the Environment* [1975] JPL 352.

of buildings by a particular date did not apply when the planning permission was unnecessary.

Implementation of a planning permission and the consequences for enforcement

2.48   The implementation of a planning permission is taken to require the carrying out of development comprised in the planning permission, although this can be at a very limited level. Examples of material operations which can constitute the beginning of development are in s 56(4) of the Town and Country Planning Act 1990:[93]

'(a) any work of construction in the course of the erection of a building;

(aa) any work of demolition of a building;

(b) the digging of a trench which is to contain the foundations, or part of the foundations, of a building;

(c) the laying of any underground main or pipe to the foundations, or part of the foundations, of a building or to any such trench as is mentioned in paragraph (b);

(d) any operation in the course of laying out or constructing a road or part of a road;

(e) any change in the use of any land which constitutes material development'

A retrospective planning permission will take immediate effect.

2.49   As a general principle the implementation must also comply with any conditions in the planning permission. This principle was explained for planning permissions by the Court of Appeal in *FG Whitley & Sons v Secretary of State for Wales*.[94] Woolf LJ held:

'It is only necessary to ask the single question: are the operations … permitted by the planning permission read together with its conditions. If the operations concerned contravene the conditions, they cannot be properly described as commencing the development authorised by the permission.'

The question of compliance with conditions and implementation tends to arise if negative conditions prohibit the commencement of development before something has happened (such as an approval of details) or require something to happen before development commences.[95] In limited circumstances, non-compliance with a pre-commencement condition does not prevent the implementation of the permission. This is most easily explained where it would be irrational in public law terms to enforce against the particular breach,[96] although there may be some other cases where the effect of a breach of condition might not invalidate the implementation.[97] If a

---

[93]   That they are examples was identified by Sullivan J in *Field v First Secretary of State* [2004] EWHC 147 (Admin), [2004] JPL 1286.

[94]   (1992) 64 P & CR 296.

[95]   Negative conditions are often referred to as Grampian conditions following the House of Lords decision in *Grampian Regional Council v Secretary of State for Scotland* 1984 SC (HL) 58.

[96]   See *R (Hammerton) v London Underground Limited* [2002] EWHC 2307 (Admin), [2003] JPL 984.

[97]   The ambit of any wider approach than irrationality of enforcement is open to debate: see *R (Hart Aggregates Ltd) v Hartlepool Borough Council* [2005] EWHC 840 (Admin), [2005] JPL 1602 and *Greyfort Properties Ltd v Secretary of State for Communities and Local Government* [2011] EWCA Civ 908, [2012] JPL 39.

2.50 *Breach of Planning Control*

failure to comply with a condition means that the permission is not implemented, then the breach of planning control is the carrying out of development without planning permission, rather than a breach of condition.

2.50 Departure from the approved plans might mean that a planning permission is not implemented at all or affect the lawfulness of part or all of the works. The case law has not been consistent, or often fully reasoned as to where distinctions are drawn. An initial departure from the plans has been held to still be works commencing development under a planning permission when considered as a whole.[98]

2.51 In *Handoll v Warner Goodman & Streat*[99] permission was given for a dwelling and garage subject to a condition that it should only be occupied by persons engaged in agriculture ('an agricultural occupancy condition'). The dwelling was built some 90ft west of the approved location. The Court of Appeal held that it was materially different to the planning permission granted and so that permission was not implemented. Overruling *Kerrier District Council v Secretary of State for the Environment*,[100] they held that the condition did not therefore apply. Similarly a development which exceeds the size thresholds in the General Permitted Development Order would be unlawful in its entirety – not simply in the excess – if there is a difference in substance. Lord Denning MR said in *Garland v Minister of Housing and Local Government:*[101]

> 'Suppose that a man is given permission to build a bungalow, and, instead, he builds a two-storey house. He has built the house without any permission at all. Suppose next that a man is given permission to make an extension which is two storeys high, and, instead, he makes an extension of three storeys. Again, he has built the extension without any permission at all. This is the very thing which has happened in this very case. On the figures which have been given in the inspector's report, Mr. Garland, under the General Development Order, was given permission to make an extension of 11,711 cubic feet, and, instead, he has made an extension of 14,491 cubic feet. This seems to me to be, as in the other examples, so substantial an excess that the whole was without any permission at all. If there were only a trifling excess, it would be different. There might then be only an excess over a limitation. But, when there is a difference in substance, then the whole is done without any permission at all.'

2.52 *Sage v Secretary of State for the Environment, Transport and the Regions* concerned time limits on a building constructed without planning permission. Whilst considering a holistic approach to what are operations, Lord Hobhouse commented:[102]

> 'if a building operation is not carried out, both externally and internally, fully in accordance with the permission, the *whole* operation is unlawful'.

2.53 In *Welwyn Hatfield* Mr Beesley had planning permission for a hay barn but whilst externally it looked like the approved barn it was internally constructed as a dwellinghouse. This was therefore constructed without planning permission.[103]

---

98   *Spackman v Wiltshire County Council* (1977) 33 P & CR 430; *Commercial Land Limited v Secretary of State for Transport, Local Government and the Regions* [2002] EWHC 1264 (Admin), [2003] JPL 358; *Aerlink Leisure Ltd v First Secretary of State* [2004] EWHC 3198 (Admin), [2005] 2 P & CR 15.
99   (1994) 70 P & CR 627 (CA).
100 (1980) 41 P & CR 284.
101 (1969) 20 P & CR 93 at 101–102.
102 [2003] UKHL 22, [2003] 1 WLR 983 at para 23.
103 *Welwyn Hatfield Borough Council v Secretary of State for Communities and Local Government* [2010] 2 P & CR 10 at para 25 per Richards LJ (CA); [2011] 2 AC 304 at paras 11–13 per Lord Mance.

2.54   Except where a planning permission includes the retrospective authorisation of development which has been carried out, a time limit condition for the commencement of development is deemed to be included if it is not express on the permission.[104] After that period the permission is considered to have lapsed, and any subsequent development should be viewed as development without planning permission rather than development in breach of the condition.

Conditions remaining in force

2.55   A planning condition must remain in force for a contravention of it to be a breach of planning control. A condition may cease to have effect in the following circumstances:

(a) Most obviously, where a planning permission is granted for the same development but with a different condition under s 73 of the Town and Country Planning Act 1990 and that permission is implemented, or a retrospective permission is granted under section 73A.

(b) Where another planning permission supercedes the earlier permission or the relevant part of it. Whether it does depends upon the scope of the later permission and the relationship between the two consents.[105]

(c) Where new development extinguishes the original permission.[106]

(d) When the time period under a temporary planning permission expires, it may be that conditions governing the use also expire.[107]

Interpretation of planning permissions

2.56   The classic summary of the principles applicable to the interpretation of planning permissions was given by Keene J in *R v Ashford Borough Council ex p Shepway District Council*:

> '1. The general rule is that in construing a planning permission which is clear, unambiguous and valid on its face, regard may only be had to the planning permission itself, including the conditions (if any) on it and the express reasons for those conditions: see *Slough Borough Council v Secretary of State for the Environment* [1995] J.P.L. 1128, and *Miller-Mead v Minister of Housing and Local Government* [1963] 2 Q.B. 196.
>
> 2. This rule excludes reference to the planning application as well as to other extrinsic evidence, unless the planning permission incorporates the application by reference. In that situation the application is treated as having become part of the permission. The reason for normally not having regard to the application is that the public should be able to rely on a document which is plain on its face without having to consider whether there is any discrepancy between the permission and the application: see *Slough Borough Council v Secretary of State (ante); Wilson v West Sussex County Council* [1963] 2 Q.B. 764; and *Slough Estates Limited v Slough Borough Council* [1971] A.C. 958.

---

[104] Town and Country Planning Act 1990, ss 91, 92.

[105] See *Stevenage Borough Council v Secretary of State for Communities and Local Government* [2010] EWHC 1289 (Admin).

[106] See the discussion in *Welwyn Hatfield Borough Council v Secretary of State for Communities and Local Government)* [2011] 2 AC 304 at para 23 per Lord Mance.

[107] *Avon Estates Ltd v Welsh Ministers* [2011] EWCA Civ 553, [2012] PTSR 958.

3. For incorporation of the application in the permission to be achieved, more is required than a mere reference to the application on the face of the permission. While there is no magic formula, some words sufficient to inform a reasonable reader that the application forms part of the permission are needed, such as "… in accordance with the plans and application …" or "… on the terms of the application …", and in either case those words appearing in the operative part of the permission dealing with the development and the terms in which permission is granted. These words need to govern the description of the development permitted: See *Wilson* (ante); *Slough Borough Council v Secretary of State for the Environment* (ante).

4. If there is an ambiguity in the wording of the permission, it is permissible to look at extrinsic material, including the application, to resolve that ambiguity: see *Staffordshire Moorlands District Council v Cartwright* [1992] J.P.L. 138 at 139; *Slough Estates Limited v Slough Borough Council* (ante); *Creighton Estates Limited v London County Council* (1958) *The Times*, 20th March 1958.

5. If a planning permission is challenged on the ground of absence of authority or mistake, it is permissible to look at extrinsic evidence to resolve that issue: *see Slough Borough Council v Secretary of State* (ante); *Co-operative Retail Services v Taff-Ely Borough Council* (1979) 39 P. & C.R. 223 affirmed (1981) 42 P.& C.R. 1.'[108]

2.57   This statement applies to outline planning permissions and is subject to important qualifications. A planning application must include all the drawings and details necessary to describe the development to be authorised. In *Barnett v Secretary of State for Communities and Local Government*,[109] Sullivan J pointed out that the cases cited in *Ashford* and *Ashford* itself concerned outline planning permissions:

'If it is plain on the face of a permission that it is a full permission for the construction, erection or alteration of the building, the public will know that, in addition to the plan which identifies the site, there will be plans and drawings which will describe the building works which will have been permitted precisely because the permission is not, on its face, an outline planning permission. In such a case those plans and drawings describing the building works were as much a part of the description of what has been permitted as the permission notice itself. It is not a question of resolving an 'ambiguity'. On its face, a grant of full planning permission for building operations is incomplete without the approved plans and drawings showing the detail of what has been permitted. In the absence of any indication to the contrary, those plans and drawings will be the plans listed in the application for permission. If the local planning authority does not wish to approve the plans submitted with the application and wishes to approve amended plans, then it can include a statement to that effect in the decision notice. Absent any such statement, the reasonable inference, against the statutory background provided by Section 62 of the Act and the 1988 Regulations, is that a grant of full planning permission approves the application drawings.'

These observations were followed by the Court of Appeal in that case, in particular by Keene LJ.[110] Consequently application drawings are approved in full planning permissions, whether or not this is stated expressly.

2.58   From 2006, outline planning applications were required to state the approximate location of buildings, routes and open spaces, and the upper and lower dimensions for buildings, along with the location of access points to the development

---

[108]   Paragraph 5 is about the lawfulness of planning permissions, rather than their interpretation.
[109]   [2008] EWHC 1601 (Admin), [2009] JPL 243.
[110]   *Barnett v Secretary of State for Communities and Local Government* [2009] EWCA Civ 476, [2009] JPL 1597 at paras 17–22.

even when layout, scale and access were reserved. Those requirements have now been removed in England (other than for access) but remain in Wales.[111] If those provisions applied to the planning application at the relevant time then those parameters would be approved.[112]

Interpretation of conditions

2.59   The documents considered in interpreting a planning condition are the same as for the planning permission as a whole. Principles for interpreting conditions were set out by Elias LJ in *Hulme v Secretary of State for Communities and Local Government*:[113]

'(a) The conditions must be construed in the context of the decision letter as a whole.

(b) The conditions should be interpreted benevolently and not narrowly or strictly: see *Carter Commercial Development Limited v Secretary of State for the Environment* [2002] EWHC 1200 (Admin) para 49, per Sullivan J, as he was.

(c) A condition will be void for uncertainty only 'if it can be given no meaning or no sensible or ascertainable meaning, and not merely because it is ambiguous or leads to absurd results' per Lord Denning in *Fawcett Properties v Buckingham County Council* [1961] AC 636, 678. This seems to me to be an application of the benevolent construction principle.

(d) There is no room for an implied condition[114] (although for reasons I discuss more fully below, the scope of this principle needs careful analysis). This principle was enunciated by Widgery LJ, as he then was, in *Trustees of Walton on Thames Charities v Walton and Weighbridge District Council* [1970] 21 P&CR 411 at 420, in the following terms:

"I have never heard of an implied condition in a planning permission and I believe no such creature exists. Planning permission [...] is not simply a matter of contract between the parties. There is no place, in my judgment, within the law relating to planning permission for an implied condition. Conditions should be express, they should be clear, they should be in the document containing the permission."

14 Accordingly, whilst there must be a limit to the extent to which conditions should be rewritten to save them from invalidity, if they can be given a sensible and reasonable interpretation when read in context, they should be.'

---

[111] Town and Country Planning (Development Management Procedure) (England) Order 2010, Art 4 (from 31 January 2013); Town and Country Planning (Development Management Procedure) (Wales) Order 2012, Art 3.

[112] Discussed in *R (Wrenn) v Wiltshire Council* [2011] EWHC 2198 (Admin).

[113] [2011] EWCA Civ 638 at paras 13, 14. On the absence of implied conditions, see also *Sevenoaks District Council v First Secretary of State* [2004] EWHC 771 (Admin).

[114] There are minor errors in Elias LJ's citation of *Walton*. These are corrected in this text.

Chapter 3

Time Limits on Enforcement

TIME LIMITS

3.01 Enforcement action must be taken within a certain time of the breach of planning control occurring. There are two principal time periods in s 171B of the Town and Country Planning Act 1990: four years and ten years. In limited circumstances it may be possible to take action outside those periods. The purpose of the time limits was explained by Schiemann LJ in *Secretary of State for the Environment v Holding and Thurrock Borough Council*:[1]

'The rationale of the immunity is that throughout the relevant period of unlawful use the LPA, although having the opportunity to take enforcement action has failed to take any action consequently and is it would be unfair and/or could be regarded as unnecessary to permit enforcement.

… [the authority's] position is much the same as that of a landowner who lets the world regularly walk along a path over his hand. There comes a time when he has lost his right to object.'

THE FOUR-YEAR RULE

3.02 Enforcement action in respect of operational development undertaken without planning permission or the change of use of any building to use as a single dwelling house can only be taken within four years.[2]

Operational development

3.03 Section 171B(1) of the Town and Country Planning Act 1990 provides:

'Where there has been a breach of planning control consisting in the carrying out without planning permission of building, engineering, mining or other operations in, on, over or under land, no enforcement action may be taken after the end of the period of four years beginning with the date on which the operations were substantially completed'

The actions enforced against are, therefore, those in the operational development limb of s 55(1). The time limit applies to operations carried on without planning permission. Operational development carried out in breach of a planning condition is subject to the ten-year period in s 171B(3).

---

[1] [2002] EWCA Civ 226, [2002] JPL 1278 at paras 15, 25.
[2] Town and Country Planning Act 1990, s 171B(1), (2). The Enterprise and Regulatory Reform Act 2013 proposes that there be no time limit for planning enforcement action against the unlawful demolition of a building in a conservation area: see Chapter 16.

3.04   Time runs for operational development from the date when the operations were substantially completed.[3] In *Sage* there had been constructed what the House of Lords described as an 'unfinished dwelling house' which was unfit for habitation:[4] the floor at ground level consisted of rubble; there were no service fittings or staircase; and the interior walls were unfinished, without lining or plaster. None of the windows were glazed (although there was some dispute whether they had ever been glazed). The High Court and Court of Appeal had allowed Mr Sage's appeal on the basis that the internal works had not required planning permission because of the exception to development in s 55(2)(a) of the 1990 Act and so the building was substantially completed. However the Lords held that the internal works exception only applied to buildings once they were completed.

3.05   In *Fidler v Secretary of State for Communities and Local Government,*[5] a house had been constructed without planning permission behind a screen of hay bales. The landowner claimed that the operations were substantially completed when the house was built and occupied. The Inspector and the High Court disagreed, considering that substantial completion took place when the hay bales were removed some four years later.

3.06   If the operations are still within the time limit, then all the works, including those carried out more than four years ago, can be enforced against. In *Robert Reginald Howes v Secretary of State for the Environment,*[6] a vehicular access to a garden had been created by removing the hedge and tipping hardcore onto the grass. Hodgson J held that if the substantial completion, by laying hardcore, took place within the four-year limit, then the whole operation, including the opening of the fence, could be enforced against.

3.07   Mining operations are treated differently to building or engineering operations. Each shovelful or bulldozer cut is a separate operation.[7] This has the consequence that any enforcement action can only deal with the last four years' activities (unless there is a breach of condition), but also means that carrying mining operations in the future on a site cannot be lawful because of previous working. An operator has no right to dig deeper because land has already been worked.[8]

Change of use to a single dwelling house

3.08   Section 171B(2) provides:

> 'Where there has been a breach of planning control consisting in the change of use of any building to use as a single dwelling house, no enforcement action may be taken after the end of the period of four years beginning with the date of the breach.'

---

3   Town and Country Planning Act 1990, s 171B(1).
4   Per Lord Hobhouse at para 16.
5   [2010] EWHC 143 (Admin), [2010] JPL 915.
6   [1984] JPL 439.
7   *Thomas David (Porthcawl) Ltd v Penybont RDC* [1972] 1 WLR 1526.
8   Prior to 1948, mining had been seen as a use of land as mining operations were not separately identified in the definition of development in the Town and Country Planning Act 1932. They were included in the operational development categories in the Town and Country Planning Act 1947.

3.09 *Time Limits on Enforcement*

The single dwelling house time limit of four years is more generous to developers than the usual material change of use time limit of ten years. This is to protect long-term residential occupation.

3.09   The relevant breach is a 'change of use' rather than a 'material change of use'. Consequently a change of use to residential occupation in breach of a condition is subject to the four-year rule. In *Arun District Council v First Secretary of State*[9] planning permission had been granted for an extension of a house subject to conditions that it should only be occupied by a named dependent relative of the householder and then when she vacated the extension it was to be used at all times for purposes incidental to the house as a single dwelling house and not be occupied or disposed of as separate residential accommodation. The extension was not in fact used by the relative but as part of the house until it began to be let to students, who occupied it independently as separate living accommodation. Eight years after that separate use began, the Council issued an enforcement notice. The Court of Appeal held that the four-year period applied to that breach.[10] Subsection (2) is concerned with a 'change of use' not merely a 'material change of use' and omits the reference to 'without planning permission' which is in subsection (1). Consequently the change of use to a dwelling house took place eight years before the enforcement action and so was lawful. In reaching this conclusion the Court of Appeal followed dicta of Keene J in *King's Lynn and West Norfolk Borough Council v Secretary of State for the Environment.*[11]

3.10   Circular 10/97 considers that a breach of an occupancy condition attached to a dwelling house is governed by the ten-year rule.[12] Unless the contrary intention appears in the legislation, building includes 'any part of a building'.[13] The conversion of a building into flats is governed by the four-year rule: see the conjoined appeals of *Doncaster Borough Council and Van Dyck v Secretary of State for the Environment.*[14] Similarly if a potentially self-contained part of a house is occupied separately in breach of a condition limiting it to ancillary accommodation (such as a granny annex or staff flat), then that is a change of use of a building (being *part* of the building) and subject to the four-year rule.

3.11   Subsection (2) relates solely to the change of use of a building and so the building must have been in a non-dwelling house use prior to the change. Consequently if a building is constructed as a dwelling house and put to that use there is no change of use of a building to use as a dwelling house. The four-year time period in subsection (2) does not apply and the use of the building is subject to the ten-year period in subsection (3): see *Welwyn Hatfield Borough Council.*[15]

---

[9]   [2006] EWCA Civ 1172, [2007] 1 WLR 523.
[10]   *Arun* in particular per Auld LJ at paras 22 to 27, Sedley LJ at para 35 and a very useful discussion of the history of four-year time limits by Carnwath LJ at paras 37 to 51.
[11]   *King's Lynn and West Norfolk Borough Council v Secretary of State for the Environment* [1995] JPL 730.
[12]   Circular 10/97, Annex 2, para 2.4.
[13]   Town and Country Planning Act 1990, s 336(1).
[14]   (1992) 66 P & CR 61. This followed contradictory decisions at first instance in *Doncaster* (1991) 63 P & CR 61, *Van Dyck* [1992] 2 PLR 5 and *Worthing Borough Council v Secretary of State for the Environment* (1992) 63 P & CR 446.
[15]   *Welwyn Hatfield Borough Council v Secretary of State for Communities and Local Government* [2011] UKSC 15, [2011] 2 AC 304 at paras 14, 17.

3.12   A change which does not create separate dwelling houses, such as a conversion into a house in multiple occupation, is subject to the ten year rule rather than the four year rule.

THE TEN-YEAR RULE

3.13   Section 171B(3) provides:

> 'In the case of any other breach of planning control, no enforcement action may be taken after the end of the period of ten years beginning with the date of the breach.'

These categories are material changes of use and failing to comply with conditions or limitations, other than conversion to a single dwelling house.

3.14   Where the change of use occurred and then continued without alteration, it is straightforward to determine if the time limit bites. However, change of use, such as from storage to a scrapyard, may be gradual and vary over time. Here the question is whether the present use is materially different from that of ten years previously. If it is, that material change can be enforced against. Sullivan J has rationalised the ten-year period as:[16]

> 'felt to be fair to both parties, since it would give the local planning authority sufficient time to identify any significant planning problem arising as a result of the breach of planning control, whilst at the same time it would not place an undue evidential burden upon the landowner, who could rest assured that after 10 years he would be free of the threat of enforcement action.'

3.15   All breaches of conditions or limitations, except a condition preventing the change of use of any building to use as a single dwelling house, are subject to the ten-year rule. Section 171B, introduced by the 1991 Act, therefore altered the previous position in respect of operational development. Formerly a condition or limitation which related to operational development was governed by the four-year rule.[17] A condition prohibiting the occupation of a building before access works are carried out does relate to the carrying out of operations.[18]

3.16   Until 27 July 1992, unauthorised changes of use had to have begun by the end of 1963 to have the benefit of a time limit.[19] A rolling ten-year period was introduced following the recommendations of the Carnwath Report. This led local planning authorities to rush out hundreds of enforcement notices against unauthorised uses which had begun between 1963 and 1982 in the spring of 1992. However, if the breach had become immune from enforcement by reason of the earlier four-year rule by 27 July 1992 (when the section was brought fully into effect), then no further enforcement action could be taken.[20]

---

[16]   *North Devon District Council v First Secretary of State* [2004] EWHC 578 (Admin), [2004] JPL 1396 at para 21.

[17]   Town and Country Planning Act 1990, s 172(4)(b) as originally enacted: see *Harvey v Secretary of State for Wales* [1991] 2 PLR 1, CA and *Peacock Homes Ltd v Secretary of State for the Environment* (1984) 48 P & CR 20, CA.

[18]   *King's Lynn and West Norfolk Borough Council v Secretary of State for the Environment* [1995] JPL 730.

[19]   Town and Country Planning Act 1990, ss 172, 191 before substitution by the 1991 Act; SI 1991/2905, Art 5(b).

[20]   Planning and Compensation Act 1991, s 4(2); Planning Compensation Act 1991 (Commencement No 5 and Transitional Provisions) Order 1991 (SI 1991/2905).

Breaches of occupancy conditions

3.17   A breach of a condition which prohibits a change of use of a building to a dwelling is subject to the four-year rule: see *Arun District Council v First Secretary of State.*[21] A condition which restricts who may occupy a dwelling house is subject to the ten-year rule, as a breach would not be a change of use to a dwelling house. These conditions most often restrict occupation to those employed in agriculture or another rural activity where the building has been allowed as an exception to the restrictions on residential development in the countryside.

Continuity of breaches

3.18   The time period is based on the particular breach of planning control which is being enforced against. For operational development, time runs from substantial completion and is discussed above. A material change of use will start and a condition may first be breached on a particular day. In applying the time limits the question is whether it is the same breach as any which took place four or ten years early or whether a fresh breach has taken place.

Material change of use

BREACH OF CONDITION

3.19   In *Nicholson v Secretary of State for the Environment,*[22] Robin Purchas QC suggested a three-stage test to judge whether enforcement action could be taken against a breach of condition:

(1) identify the failure to comply;

(2) look to see when as a matter of fact and degree that failure began; and

(3) decide whether a period of ten years (or four years, as appropriate) has since expired.

3.20   The starting point for applying the time limit is to identify what the breach of condition is. Some conditions can be breached to different degrees. For example, in *St Anselm Development Co Ltd v First Secretary of State,*[23] a residential and office building was constructed with 19 car parking spaces in the basement. A condition required the whole of the parking to be retained for the vehicles of the users and occupiers of the building. In practice the parking spaces were let out to unconnected persons most of the time. Fourteen of the spaces had been let out in breach of the condition continuously for more than ten years, but the other five spaces had been let out over a shorter period. Sullivan J held that whilst the condition applied to the whole car park, and the first breach of the condition arose more than ten years ago, the use of each space was a particular breach of the condition and so the more recent breaches could be enforced against. The judge said:

---

[21]   [2006] EWCA Civ 1172, [2007] 1 WLR 523 and discussed above.
[22]   [1998] JPL 553 at 560.
[23]   [2003] EWHC 1592 (Admin), [2004] JPL 33.

'The question is not: could *an* enforcement notice alleging *a* failure to comply with this condition have been issued 10 years ago, but could *this* enforcement notice alleging *this* failure to comply with the condition and requiring this failure to be remedied by taking *these* steps, have been issued 10 years ago?'[24] [original emphases]

3.21   Time runs on a breach of condition as long as it is the same breach of condition. Often it is said that a breach as to have continued or been continuous for the period, but neither term is in the statute. Legislation simply refers to a period beginning with the date of the breach. Whether a breach has continued or been continuous may be a helpful way of applying the test in most cases, but it is not the test itself. Some breaches continue at every moment after the period for compliance (for example, a condition requiring noise attenuation to be installed prior to the occupation of a building would be breached from the time that occupation began until the installation of the measures). Other breaches have been considered to have taken place even if they have not been carried on at every moment. For example, breach of a condition restricting the occupation of holiday bungalows to a period between March and November each year was lawful because it had been carried on for more than 10 years. A fresh breach did not start each November and end in March of the following year.[25] Similarly a condition prohibiting the operation of a factory on Sundays or a restaurant being open beyond midnight could be breached for more than 10 years even though the breach would only be carried on at particular times or days.[26]

3.22   Where there are gaps in the occasions that the breach was being carried on, a judgment needs to be made as to whether it is still the same breach. In *Trim v North Dorset District Council,*[27] Carnwath LJ suggested it was arguable that an occupancy condition was breached on each day that the unlawful occupation occurred, so the ten-year period would start again each day and there would be no time limit. In the absence of argument he expressed no view.

Breaches involving operational development and a change of use

3.23   It may be that a breach of planning control consists of both operational development and a change of use. Where the time periods are the same length (in the case of a change of use of a building to a dwelling house) and expire at the same time then there is in practice no problem. Complications arise when the breach is potentially both operational development subject to the four-year period and a material change of use subject to the ten-year period. Two distinct questions arise:

(a) what time period or periods apply; and

(b) whether operational development can be removed as part of enforcement action against the material change of use?

3.24   In *Welwyn Hatfield Borough Council v Secretary of State for Communities and Local Government,* the Secretary of State argued that when an unlawfully constructed building had become lawful under s 171B(1) the use of the building

24   *St Anselm* at para 27.
25   *North Devon District Council v First Secretary of State* [2004] EWHC 578 (Admin), [2004] JPL 1396.
26   See *North Devon* at paras 24, 25 per Sullivan J.
27   [2010] EWCA Civ 1446, [2011] 1 WLR 1901, at para 14, 15.

was also lawful. The Court of Appeal declined to express a view on that point.[28] The Supreme Court proceeded on the basis that a four-year period could apply the operational development of constructing a building but use would still be governed by the ten-year period. However Lord Mance suggested, going to the discretion to enforce, that:[29]

> 'there is a potential answer to this apparent anomaly, one which would apply as much to a dwelling house as to any other building. It is that, once a planning authority has allowed the four-year period for enforcement against the building to pass, principles of fairness and good governance could, in appropriate circumstances, preclude it from subsequently taking enforcement steps to render the building useless.'

Lord Brown agreed with Lord Mance, saying:

> 'Parliament appears to have contemplated that a dwelling house built by way of unpermitted operational development would be enforced against, if at all, within the requisite four-year period provided for by section 171B(1) – failing which the authority probably would not seek ordinarily to enforce against its continued use as a house.'[30]

3.25   An enforcement notice against a material change of use can require the land or buildings to be restored to their condition prior to the change of use, even if that requires the removal of operational development which would have been lawful by the passage of time.[31] This may be confined to ancillary operational development[32] and be related to the scale of the operational development. For example, in *Newbury District Council v Secretary of State for the Environment and Mallaburn,* the four-year period was applied to a tennis court constructed on land which was also the subject of an unlawful change of use to residential garden.[33] In *Welwyn Hatfield* Richards LJ doubted that the *Murfitt* approach could be applied to require the removal of the dwelling under a ten-year rule.[34]

3.26   There are a range of potential circumstances, from modest operational development in support of a material change of use to a situation where a substantial building or structure has been erected and the material change of use flows from that. The potential outcomes are that the operational development is subject to the same time limit as the change of use, that separate time limits apply or possibly that the operational development time limit applies either formally or because it would be unlawful to enforce against the use if the building had become lawful.

Time limits not running in the event of fraud

3.27   The time limits had been applied in practice without any regard as to why no enforcement action had been taken within the necessary period. In some cases landowners had lied about what had taken place and then changed their explanation when enforcement action was taken or a lawful development certificate sought. The

---

[28]   [2010] 2 P & CR 10 at para 26 per Richards LJ.
[29]   [2011] 2 AC 304 at para 17 and see also para 30.
[30]   [2011] 2 AC 304 at para 68.
[31]   *Murfitt v Secretary of State for the Environment* (1980) 40 P & CR 254.
[32]   See Waller LJ in *Murfitt*.
[33]   [1995] JPL 329. Subsequently discussed in *Ball v Secretary of State for the Environment, Transport and the Regions* [2000] PLCR 299.
[34]   [2010] 2 P & CR 10 at para 32.

issue came to attention in two high profile cases which began in the late 2000s. In the first case, a Mr Fidler, living in the greenbelt in Surrey, had engaged in a series of planning enforcement battles before he constructed an entire house in a space enclosed by hay bales and covered with a tarpaulin. Four years after occupying the house, he removed the hay bales and claimed the house had become lawful. In *Welwyn Hatfield Borough Council v Secretary of State for Communities and Local Government*, Mr and Mrs Beesley had obtained planning permission for an agricultural barn as a cover for their actual intentions. They then constructed a building which externally looked like the barn for which they had been granted planning permission, but which was from the outset internally constructed and fitted out as a dwelling house. Again they sought to rely on the four-year rule.

3.28   Both cases were contested initially on interpretation and application of the four-year rules in s 171B(1) and (2). Whilst allowing the Beesleys' appeal, Mummery LJ expressed his puzzlement that there had been no argument that 'Mr Beesley's reprehensible conduct in obtaining planning permission by deception' prevented reliance on the time limits.[35] This inspired the local authority to argue in the Supreme Court that the time limits did not apply in the case of fraud. The Supreme Court allowed the authority's appeal. Since the application of the decision is often debated in practice, it is useful to consider it in some detail.

3.29   The reprehensible conduct was summarised by Lord Mance JSC as:[36]

'First, Mr Beesley intended to deceive the council from the outset, that is (at least) when he made each of his successive planning applications in March 2000 and January 2001; in each application he described the proposed building as a hay barn, said that the application involved no change of use of land, and, in relation to sewage disposal, answered not applicable. Secondly, when building his house, he deliberately refrained from giving the notice under the building regulations, applicable to a house but not an agricultural barn, so committing an offence triable summarily and punishable by a fine. Thirdly, he did not register for council tax or on the electoral register at the building. Fourthly, he gave the council as his address his office, whereas all other correspondence was to and from the house. Fifthly, he lived a low-key existence, the house being at the end of a lane or track apparently accessible from the road only by a locked gate.

32. The aim of this conduct was, firstly, to obtain a planning permission which would not have been granted had the application been for a dwelling house, secondly, to conceal the fact that what was being built was and was to be a dwelling house and, thirdly to live in the house without being detected or therefore having enforcement steps taken for the four-year periods.'

3.30   However he found that:

'The real gravamen of the council's case is to be found in the deception involved in the obtaining of false planning permissions which Mr Beesley never intended to implement, but which were designed to and did mislead the council into thinking that the building was a genuine hay barn and so into taking no enforcement step for over four years. This was deception in the planning process and directly intended to undermine its regular operation.'[37]

---

[35]   *Welwyn Hatfield Council v Secretary of State for Communities and Local Government* [2010] EWCA Civ 26, [2010] JPL 1095 at paras 43 to 47.
[36]   *Welwyn Hatfield Borough Council v Secretary of State for Communities and Local Government* [2011] UKSC 15, [2011] 2 AC 304 at paras 31, 32.
[37]   At para 43.

The other aspects in paragraph 31 (building regulations, council tax, electoral register, address and being low-key) were ancillary and Lord Mance was not prepared to assume for the present case that they would, without more, disentitle reliance on the time limits.[38] Lord Mance held, and the rest of the Court concurred, that Mr Beesley could not rely on the time limits on public policy grounds where his conduct 'consisted of positive deception in matters integral to the planning process (applying for and obtaining planning permission) and was directly intended to and did undermine the regular operation of that process'.[39] He considered that there was no need for a criminal offence to have been committed.[40] Lord Rodger agreed, as Mr Beesley 'deliberately set out to conceal the true nature of the development during the whole four-year period, with the aim that the council would be prevented (as happened) from taking enforcement action within the four-year period'. Lord Brown emphasised that:

> 'it would be impossible to superimpose upon the statutory scheme any sort of broad principle to the effect that no one guilty of wrongdoing can be allowed to benefit from the limitation provisions of the 1990 Act.'[41]

He considered the principle would only apply in 'highly exceptional circumstances' and, for example, would not have included the letting of a granny flat to students in *Arun District Council v Secretary of State for Communities and Local Government* (as discussed under s 171B(2) above).[42]

3.31   Permission to appeal to the Court of Appeal had been granted to Mr Fidler before the Supreme Court decision in *Welwyn Hatfield*. The Secretary of State then successfully applied to set aside that permission. Sullivan LJ said:[43]

> '12. ... In the present case the deception was not the making of a false planning application, but the deliberate hiding of building operations behind a shield of straw bales the top of which was covered by a tarpaulin. On the appellant's own evidence, the bales were deliberately erected to conceal the construction of the dwelling; this was not a case of someone merely refraining from drawing attention to themselves by, for example, not applying for building regulations approval; here, there was positive conduct, and the avowed intention of that positive conduct was to deceive the local planning authority so that it would not realise building operations had been carried out until after the four-year period had expired.
>
> 13. It seems to me that upon the facts found by the Inspector, this is a paradigm case of deception which disentitles an appellant from relying upon the four-year rule; it simply does not lie in this appellant's mouth to say that this local planning authority should have spotted the building which he had so carefully concealed at some earlier stage, were he to do so it would indeed frustrate the underlying statutory purpose. It is therefore of no consequence whatsoever whether the bales were or were not part of the building operations; the short point is that this was a deliberate deception which plainly falls within the principles set out in the Welwyn Hatfield case, the consequence of which is that this appeal has no prospect whatsoever of succeeding.'

---

[38]   At para 44.
[39]   At para 56.
[40]   At para 53.
[41]   At para 73.
[42]   *Welwyn Hatfield* at paras 75 to 79, 84.
[43]   *Fidler v Secretary of State for Communities and Local Government* [2011] EWCA Civ 1159 at para 12, 13. Longmore LJ added at para 15: 'A deliberate deception by conduct can be just as serious as deliberate deception by a written misrepresentation'.

PLANNING ENFORCEMENT ORDERS

3.32   Concern about landowners benefitting from planning breaches which they had concealed or lied about was shared in government. The *Fidler* and *Welwyn Hatfield* cases had received a great deal of press attention, including in their early stages when it looked as if the landowners might get away with it. Prior to the Supreme Court decision in *Welwyn Hatfield*, the government had devised its own solution to the problems thrown up by those cases. The Localism Act 2011 introduced new ss 171BA–171BC into the Town and Country Planning Act 1990 to allow local authorities to apply to the magistrates' court for a planning enforcement order to allow enforcement action to be taken which would otherwise be out of time where concealment of the breach has taken place. A planning enforcement order allows a local planning authority to take enforcement action. It does not itself order the landowner to do, or refrain from doing, anything.

3.33   The relevant local planning authority may apply to a magistrates' court for a planning enforcement order.[44] Such an order allows the authority to take enforcement action in respect of the apparent breach and any of the matters constituting the apparent breach in a one-year period beginning 22 days after the decision to make the order or the day on which any appeal to the High Court by case stated is finally resolved ('the enforcement year').[45] Enforcement action can be taken within the 'enforcement year' whether or not the time limits in s 171B have expired.[46]

3.34   A planning enforcement order may only be made if:[47]

'(a)   the court is satisfied, on the balance of probabilities, that the apparent breach, or any of the matters constituting the apparent breach, has (to any extent) been deliberately concealed by any person or persons, and

(b)   the court considers it just to make the order having regard to all the circumstances.'

The language of subsection (a) was tightened up during the Bill's passage. At one point it would be met if the court was satisfied 'that the actions of a person or persons have resulted in, or contributed to, full or partial concealment of the apparent breach or any of the matters constituting the apparent breach'.[48]

3.35   There must now be deliberate concealment. Concealment involves some active step and intention must be established. However questions do remain. It would appear that concealment will occur if a false answer is given (such as a denial that works have been carried out or claiming that the use of the property is agricultural when it is now residential). A failure to respond to a statutory request for information might be concealment, although the question becomes more debatable where the request is informal. An issue may be whether a failure to register a building or its occupiers is concealment (such as non-domestic rates, council tax or electoral registration). There might also be the question of who the concealment is from. A long leaseholder might not tell its landlord about works or changes in use. There might also be mixed cases, where the local authority is told about the use or development

---

44   Town and Country Planning Act 1990, s 171BA(1).
45   Town and Country Planning Act 1990, s 171BA(3), (4).
46   Town and Country Planning Act 1990, s 171BA(5).
47   Town and Country Planning Act 1990, s 171BC(1).
48   Localism Bill 2011, cl 109, as introduced in the House of Lords.

for particular purposes (such as Council Tax) but not for others (most obviously, planning control). Of course, the *Welwyn Hatfield* approach to fraud is highly fact sensitive and its application at the margins is not straightforward, but the planning enforcement order approach does not provide a clearer solution. The ultimate test of the provision is not whether it catches the flagrant breaches (there would have been deliberate concealment in *Welwyn Hatfield* and *Fidler*), but whether it avoids catching people whose conduct has not been so morally reprehensible as to justify belated enforcement action.

3.36 What is just in all the circumstances is not defined, but relevant circumstances could include whether the concealment was by the landowners or occupiers and whether they still have the site, or whether an innocent purchaser might become the subject of enforcement action.

3.37 The local planning authority may only apply for a planning enforcement order:[49]

> 'within the 6 months beginning with the date on which evidence of the apparent breach of planning control sufficient in the opinion of the local planning authority to justify the application came to the authority's knowledge'.

There may be debate as to when the authority had sufficient evidence of the breach to justify the application. It is evidence of the breach which matters, not evidence that the conventional time limits might have expired. In some cases an authority will suddenly become aware of an issue. In others it may be an accumulation of material, or it might that the authority had information suggesting a breach long before it appreciated that there might be a breach. A certificate signed on behalf of the authority, 'stating the date on which evidence sufficient in the authority's opinion to justify the application came to the authority's knowledge, is conclusive evidence of that fact'.[50] That assertion is not as robust as it appears on the face of the Act. The certificate is amenable to challenge in the magistrates' court proceedings on judicial review grounds, as an abuse of process or, if there is fraud, additionally the certificate must comply in substance and form with the statutory requirements.[51]

3.38 When making the application, the authority are required to serve a copy of the application on the owner and occupier of the land and any other person having an interest in the land which they consider may be affected by enforcement action against the apparent breach.[52] The persons entitled to appear 'include' the local planning authority who applied, any person served with the application and 'any other person having an interest in the land that is an interest which, in the opinion of the court, would be materially affected by the taking of enforcement action in respect of the apparent breach'.[53] That the list of persons entitled to appear is inclusive rather than comprehensive could be significant. There are other categories of person who might wish to appear, such as those accused of deliberate concealment or previous owners who disposed of the property on the basis of representations about its planning status.

---

[49] Town and Country Planning Act 1990, s 171BB(1).

[50] Town and Country Planning Act 1990, s 171BB(2).

[51] *Burwell v Director of Public Prosecutions* [2009] EWHC 1069 (Admin). There is a degree of judgment involved in assessing what evidence justifies making the application: see *RSPCA v Johnson* [2009] EWHC 2702 (Admin).

[52] Town and Country Planning Act 1990, s 171BB(4).

[53] Town and Country Planning Act 1990, s 171BB(5).

3.39   A planning enforcement order will identify the apparent breach of planning control to which it relates and state the date on which the court's decision to make the order was given.[54] The date of the decision will be when the court pronounces its decision rather than when the order is drawn up. The local planning authority's register of enforcement and stop notices will include details of every planning enforcement order. On the register will be the address or identification by plan of the land, the name of the authority which applied for the order and the court which made it. The date of the court's decision, the beginning and end of the enforcement year and any postponement of the date by an appeal will be included, along with the apparent breach of planning control and details of where in the register any enforcement notice or breach of condition notice issued in relation to that breach can be found.[55]

3.40   The planning enforcement order provisions came into force in England and Wales on 6 April 2012.[56] If the time limits under s 171B for enforcing against a breach of planning control expired before 6 April 2012 then the planning enforcement order provisions cannot be used to enable enforcement action to take place.[57]

3.41   It is questionable whether any concealment which planning enforcement orders are intended to control would not be caught by the anti-fraud approach of *Welwyn Hatfield Borough Council v Secretary of State for Communities and Local Government* in any event. At the time of the Localism Bill's passing and subsequently it has been commented that the provisions are unnecessary and to the extent that they go wider than *Welwyn Hatfield*, are undesirable.[58]

EXTENSIONS OF THE TIME LIMITS

3.42   Section 171B(4) provides two extensions to the time limits.

Breach of condition notices following enforcement notices

3.43   If an enforcement notice is in effect, a breach of condition notice can be served in respect of the same breach of planning control at any time as s 171B(1) to (3) does not prevent:[59]

> 'the service of a breach of condition notice in respect of any breach of planning control if an enforcement notice in respect of the breach is in effect.'

An enforcement notice is 'in effect' when the time for compliance with it has started to run, either at the end of the initial period set out in the notice or following the final

---

54   Town and Country Planning Act 1990, s 171BC(2).
55   Town and Country Planning (Development Management Procedure) (England) Order 2010, Art 38(1). No similar provisions have yet been made for Wales.
56   Localism Act 2011 (Commencement No 4 and Transitional, Transitory and Saving Provisions) Order 2012, Art 8.
57   Localism Act 2011 (Commencement No 4 and Transitional, Transitory and Saving Provisions) Order 2012, Art 13(3).
58   For example, the case comment [2011] JPL 1183 at 1208–1209 and Emma Hatfield, 'Concealed Development: did we really need section 124?' [2013] JPL 19.
59   Town and Country Planning Act 1990, s 171B(4)(a).

determination or withdrawal of an appeal.[60] The enforcement notice must have been issued within the time limit to take effect.

Second bite

3.44 Enforcement action may be taken for a breach of planning control if the local planning authority had taken or purported to take enforcement action in respect of that breach in the previous four years.[61] This is even if the conventional time limit has expired by the time of the later notice. This allows a second attempt if the previous notice was dismissed on appeal, withdrawn or found to be a nullity.

3.45 In *William Boyer (Transport) Ltd v Secretary of State for the Environment,*[62] enforcement notices alleging a material change of use to car breaking since 1963 were issued on 24 July 1992. They were then withdrawn and new enforcement notices issued in August 1992. The Court of Appeal, upholding Jeremy Sullivan QC, sitting as a Deputy High Court Judge, held that the original enforcement notices must have been issued within the time for enforcing under the new time limits for it to be possible to issue further notices under s 171B(4)(b). The second bite provisions cannot be used to create a new time limit for development which was lawful at the time of the original notices.

3.46 It is not yet determined whether a local planning authority can have a third bite of the cherry by issuing a second enforcement notice on this basis and issuing a further enforcement notice within four years of the issue of the second notice relying on the same provision. The wording appears to allow it (and the first instance judge in *William Boyer* accepted this as the case), but as a matter of principle it is objectionable.

3.47 The second bite provisions apply where the authority has taken or purported to take enforcement action. 'Purported' is important in the working of the provision as a second notice may be served because the first notice had a fatal legal defect. That error may well have been in the description of the site or the breach of planning control. The provision is intended to allow local authorities to remedy such errors by a subsequent notice and that may result in a second notice which identifies different land or characterises the breach in a different way. However it must not be used to challenge a different breach. Perhaps the best approach is to consider what in substance the authority were trying to enforce against in the first notice and then ask whether the second notice is directed towards the same issue.

3.48 In *Jarmain v Secretary of State for the Environment, Transport and the Regions*[63] a council originally issued an enforcement notice for breach of a condition in failing to remove a mobile home at the expiry of a planning permission. The owner had replaced that caravan with another caravan, altered to be a permanent structure. A second enforcement notice against operational development could use the second bite provisions. The notices were challenging the same matter on the ground. In

---

[60] Town and Country Planning Act, ss 173(9), 175(4).
[61] Town and Country Planning Act 1990, s 171B(4)(b).
[62] *The Times* 7 February 1996, CA; (1994) 69 P & CR 630, Jeremy Sullivan QC, sitting as a Deputy High Court Judge.
[63] [2000] JPL 1063.

Fidler v First Secretary of State,[64] the local planning authority had issued enforcement notices against particular uses on particular land within a larger planning unit. Those notices were vague and a subsequent notice which dealt with those and other uses could not use the second bite provisions. A second bite notice was upheld in *Romer v First Secretary of State*[65] where the appellant had owned two adjacent properties and constructed a building in mixed residential and workshop use at the rear of one of the plots. The planning authority's original enforcement notice had been against the wrong plot. Judge Gilbart QC held that the second notice was dealing with the same development and indeed, the same owner.

TIME LIMITS FOR OTHER ENFORCEMENT PROCEEDINGS

3.49   The s 171B time limits only apply to enforcement action, the issuing of enforcement notices or the serving of breach of condition notices. Action for the breach of one of those notices, for example criminal prosecution, is not subject to the s 171B time limits. But a prosecution for a summary only offence must be brought within six months of the date on which the offence is alleged. A stop notice may not prohibit activity which was carried on more than four years before the notice was served.[66] No time limits apply to unlawful works to listed buildings or the unlawful demolition of a building in a conservation area.

PLANNING INJUNCTIONS

3.50   No express time limit is provided for seeking injunctions under the planning legislation however it would make little sense if use or development or a breach of a condition which was lawful under s 191 of the Town and Country Planning Act 1990 could be the subject of a s 187B injunction.

3.51   Lawfulness arises under s 191 when the time limit for enforcement action has expired and the activity does not contravene an enforcement notice or breach of condition notice which is in force. The realistic interpretation is that a planning injunction cannot be sought against a breach of planning control has become lawful.

---

[64]   [2003] EWHC 2003 (Admin), [2004] JPL 630.
[65]   [2006] EWHC 3480 (Admin), [2007] JPL 1354.
[66]   Town and Country Planning Act 1990, s 183(5).

Chapter 4

The Decision to Enforce and the Developer's Response

4.01   This chapter considers how planning authorities should decide whether to take enforcement proceedings and also how developers should respond to the possibility that action may be taken.

ENFORCEMENT PROCEEDINGS AS AN EXERCISE OF DISCRETION

4.02   There is no statutory duty on local planning authorities to take action against a breach of planning control in any particular circumstances. Authorities do have a general responsibility for planning in their area, which includes enforcing planning control as well as setting policy and dealing with applications before them. If authorities fail to enforce at all then the planning system would fall into disrepute. However, there is no expectation that every breach of planning control must be regularised by the grant of planning permission or terminated. Essentially, authorities are expected to consider the extent of harm which does or might result from the breach. That will need to be balanced, to varying degrees, against the impact of taking enforcement proceedings.

EXPEDIENT

4.03   It is common in the planning enforcement provisions for local planning authorities to have to consider it 'expedient' to take action: enforcement notices; stop notices; temporary stop notices; and injunctions ('necessary or expedient'). For breach of condition notices the local planning authority is given a simple discretion 'may', but that makes little practical difference.

4.04   In deciding whether to issue an enforcement notice, the authority is required to have 'regard to the provisions of the development plan'.[1] The duty to have regard to the development plan means that the statutory presumption in favour of the development plan in s 38(6) of the Planning and Compulsory Purchase Act 2004 applies:

> 'If regard is to be had to the development plan for the purpose of any determination to be made under the planning Acts the determination must be made in accordance with the plan unless material considerations indicate otherwise.'

The primary consideration is therefore the acceptability of the unlawful development in planning terms.

---

[1]   Town and Country Planning Act 1990, s 172(1)(b).

4.05   Some guidance on expediency is given for England in the National Planning Policy Framework, para 207; Circular 10/97 Annex 2, para 2.3; and in Circular 03/09 on costs at Part B paras B32 to B42. Welsh guidance is contained in TAN9, the Welsh version of Circular 10/97 and the Welsh Costs Circular. This is considered below.

PERSONAL CIRCUMSTANCES

4.06   Planning considerations are normally concerned with the character of the use of the land and not the particular personal circumstances of a particular occupier.[2] Personal circumstances may, however, be relevant in certain circumstances. Such circumstances may be relevant in two respects: they may affect whether the development is acceptable in planning terms;[3] and, even if the development is unacceptable, whether enforcement proceedings should be taken and the nature and extent of those proceedings. A need to consider may arise as a matter of general planning considerations and by reason of various statutory duties.

4.07   The importance of considering the personal circumstances of occupants was emphasised in *R v Kerrier District Council, ex p Uzell*.[4] In that case the District Council, as local planning authority, had issued an enforcement notice requiring the removal of caravans occupied by travellers from land owned by Cornwall County Council. When the local planning authority resolved to prosecute or seek an injunction against the County Council if it did not evict the travellers, several occupants of the site challenged the decision by judicial review. Latham J held that considerations of common humanity, particularly the need for shelter, were material in decisions to take enforcement action and in pursuing enforcement matters.

Human Rights Act 1998

4.08   The European Convention on Human Rights has a greater prominence in enforcement than in other areas of planning as it affects existing buildings and uses, and many enforcement cases have involved gypsies or travellers. Section 6(1) of the Human Rights Act 1998 imposes the general duty:

> 'It is unlawful for a public authority to act in a way which is incompatible with a Convention right.'

Convention rights which more usually arise in enforcement cases are Article 8 'Right to respect for private and family life', Article 14 'Prohibition of discrimination' and Article 1 of the First Protocol 'Protection of property'. The procedural right to a fair trial under Article 6 applies, but in planning cases has added little to the common law, apart from a requirement to deal with cases within a reasonable time.[5] Occasionally other rights are raised in planning enforcement,

---

[2]   *East Barnet Urban District Council v British Transport Commission* [1962] 2 QB 484 per Lord Parker CJ.
[3]   *Westminster City Council v Great Portland Estates plc* [1985] 1 AC 661, per Lord Scarman at 670.
[4]   (1996) 71 P & CR 566, [1996] JPL 837.
[5]   See *Vergos v Greece* (2005) 41 EHRR 41.

such as Article 9 'Freedom of thought, conscience and religion'[6] and Article 10 'Freedom of expression'.[7]

Right to respect for private and family life

4.09

ARTICLE 8

'1. Everyone has the right to respect for his private and family life, his home and his correspondence.

2. There shall be no interference by a public authority with the exercise of this right except such as is in accordance with the law and is necessary in a democratic society in the interests of national security, public safety or the economic well-being of the country, for the prevention of disorder or crime, for the protection of health or morals, or for the protection of the rights and freedoms of others.'

Prohibition of discrimination

4.10

ARTICLE 14

'The enjoyment of the rights and freedoms set forth in this Convention shall be secured without discrimination on any ground such as sex, race, colour, language, religion, political or other opinion, national or social origin, association with a national minority, property, birth or other status.'

Protection of property

4.11

PROTOCOL, ARTICLE 1

'Every natural or legal person is entitled to the peaceful enjoyment of his possessions. No one shall be deprived of his possessions except in the public interest and subject to the conditions provided for by law and by the general principles of international law.

The preceding provisions shall not, however, in any way impair the right of a State to enforce such laws as it deems necessary to control the use of property in accordance with the general interest or to secure the payment of taxes or other contributions or penalties.'

4.12 The substantive rights (Articles 8, 13, Protocol 1 Article 1) which arise in planning cases are all qualified rights, in that a balance has to be struck between the right and the public interest. The Convention has been interpreted to give states a wide discretion in regulating planning matters.[8] Article 14 prevents discrimination in

---

[6] See *Iskcon v United Kingdom* (1994) 18 EHRR CD133 where a complaint against enforcement action which limited the number and size of religious festivals at a residential college was held to be inadmissible.

[7] For freedom of expression and advertising control, see *Butler v Derby City Council* [2005] EWHC 2835 (Admin), [2006] 1 WLR 1346.

[8] See *Sporrong and Lönroth v Sweden* (A/52):(1983) 5 EHRR 35 and *Hatton v United Kingdom* (36022/97) (2003) 37 EHRR 28.

respect of the rights enjoyed under the Convention, rather than creating a freestanding right against discrimination.

4.13   A preliminary question is whether the rights are engaged in the particular case and in respect of which persons. A person whose land is enforced against will have their Protocol 1 Article 1 rights 'engaged'. Similarly someone who is being forced out of their home (including a residential caravan) will have Article 8 rights engaged. The impact of development on neighbours may be so substantial as to engage their Article 8 or Protocol 1 Article 1 rights, usually where there is severe environmental pollution.[9]

4.14   The general approach to considering qualified rights was identified by Dyson LJ in *Samaroo v Secretary of State for the Home Department*:[10]

> 'At the first stage, the question is: can the objective of the measure be achieved by means which are less interfering of an individual's rights? ...

> The question at [the second] stage of the consideration is: does the measure have an excessive or disproportionate effect on the interests of affected persons?'

This approach is relevant to considering the effect of enforcement on the human rights of the person being enforced against[11] but is less use when a balance is being struck between the human rights of persons living close to a site and the ability of the landowner to develop.[12]

4.15   The relationship between planning and Article 8 rights was considered by the European Court of Human Rights in *Chapman v United Kingdom,* when it recognised the vulnerability of gypsies and the need for respect for their way of life but continued:[13]

> '102. Where a dwelling has been established without the planning permission which is needed under the national law, there is a conflict of interest between the right of the individual under Article 8 of the Convention to respect for his or her home and the right of others in the community to environmental protection. When considering whether a requirement that the individual leave his or her home is proportionate to the legitimate aim pursued, it is highly relevant whether or not the home was established unlawfully. If the home was lawfully established, this factor would self-evidently be something which would weigh against the legitimacy of requiring the individual to move. Conversely, if the establishment of a home in a particular place was unlawful, the position of the individual

---

[9]   *Lopez Ostra v Spain* (1994) 20 EHRR 277 and *Guerra v Italy* (1998) 26 EHRR 357, considered in *Lough v First Secretary of State*.
[10]   [2001] EWCA Civ 1139, [2001] UKHRR 1150 at paras 19, 20.
[11]   *R (O'Brien) v Basildon District Council* [2006] EWHC 1346, [2007] 1 P & CR 16 at 142 per Ouseley J:

> 'The value, to my mind, of the decision in Samaroo is that it points out that whether a decision is proportionate and lawful may involve both the proportionality of the end and the proportionality of the means deployed to achieve that end. Whatever the logical sequence of consideration of the stages in Samaroo , the decision was not intended to impose a sequential straitjacket on the stages of decision making in all cases, especially outside the deportation context'.

Cf *McCarthy v Secretary of State for Communities and Local Government* [2006] EWHC 3287 (Admin).
[12]   *Lough v First Secretary of State* [2004] EWCA Civ 905, [2004] 1 WLR 2557 at para 50 per Pill LJ and para 55 per Keene LJ.
[13]   (2001) 33 EHRR 18.

objecting to an order to move is less strong. The Court will be slow to grant protection to those who, in conscious defiance of the prohibitions of the law, establish a home on an environmentally protected site. For the Court to do otherwise would be to encourage illegal action to the detriment of the protection of the environmental rights of other people in the community.

103. A further relevant consideration, to be taken into account in the first place by the national authorities, is that if no alternative accommodation is available, the interference is more serious than where such accommodation is available. The more suitable the alternative accommodation is, the less serious is the interference constituted by moving the applicant from his or her existing accommodation.'

Children Act 2004

4.16 County, district and unitary councils in England are required by section 11 of the Children Act 2004 to make arrangements for ensuring that:[14]

'their functions are discharged having regard to the need to safeguard and promote the welfare of children'.

This duty is relevant where planning enforcement would result in displacing children, such as requiring the removal of residential caravans from land. A decision needs to meet s 11 to be accordance with the law for the purposes of Article 8(2), and the best interests or wellbeing of the child needed to be not just a consideration but a primary consideration. A primary consideration was not the same as the primary consideration.[15] As with other duties, what matters is substance rather than form. For example in the Dale Farm litigation, Ouseley J considered that whilst there had not been explicit consideration of the duty, the crucial factors for children in the case were health and education and that those had been treated as primary considerations.

Equality Act 2010

4.17 The Public Sector Equality Duty is introduced by s 149 of the Equality Act 2010. It replaces and widens previous duties with respect to race relations[16] to extend to various 'protected characteristics': age; disability; gender reassignment; pregnancy and maternity; race; religion or belief; sex; and sexual orientation. It provides that:

'(1) A public authority must, in the exercise of its functions, have due regard to the need to—

(a) eliminate discrimination, harassment, victimisation and any other conduct that is prohibited by or under this Act;

(b) advance equality of opportunity between persons who share a relevant protected characteristic and persons who do not share it;

---

[14] Children Act 2004, s 11(2)(a).
[15] *ZH (Tanzania) v Secretary of State for the Home Department* [2011] UKSC 4. This immigration case is cited in one of the Dale Farm cases, *R (Sheridan) v Basildon District Council* [2011] EWHC 2938 (Admin) at para 98 per Ouseley J. Dale Farm was a large traveller site cleared by Basildon Council using direct action powers under s 178 of the Town and Country Planning Act 1990 in October 2011. The high profile site prompted a series of High Court cases.
[16] Under the Race Relations Act 1976, s 71, discussed in the planning injunction case of *South Cambridgeshire District Council v Gammell* [2008] EWCA Civ 1159.

(c) foster good relations between persons who share a relevant protected characteristic and persons who do not share it.

(2) A person who is not a public authority but who exercises public functions must, in the exercise of those functions, have due regard to the matters mentioned in subsection (1).

(3) Having due regard to the need to advance equality of opportunity between persons who share a relevant protected characteristic and persons who do not share it involves having due regard, in particular, to the need to—

(a) remove or minimise disadvantages suffered by persons who share a relevant protected characteristic that are connected to that characteristic;

(b) take steps to meet the needs of persons who share a relevant protected characteristic that are different from the needs of persons who do not share it;

(c) encourage persons who share a relevant protected characteristic to participate in public life or in any other activity in which participation by such persons is disproportionately low.

(4) The steps involved in meeting the needs of disabled persons that are different from the needs of persons who are not disabled include, in particular, steps to take account of disabled persons' disabilities.

(5) Having due regard to the need to foster good relations between persons who share a relevant protected characteristic and persons who do not share it involves having due regard, in particular, to the need to—

(a) tackle prejudice, and

(b) promote understanding.

(6) Compliance with the duties in this section may involve treating some persons more favourably than others; but that is not to be taken as permitting conduct that would otherwise be prohibited by or under this Act.

(7) The relevant protected characteristics are—

age;
disability;
gender reassignment;
pregnancy and maternity;
race;
religion or belief;
sex;
sexual orientation.

(8) A reference to conduct that is prohibited by or under this Act includes a reference to—

(a) a breach of an equality clause or rule;

(b) a breach of a non-discrimination rule.'

4.18   Section 149 comprises nine needs, as Judge Vosper QC identified in *R (RB) v Devon County Council*:[17]

'It is possible to identify nine needs from section 149. They are:

(1) the need to eliminate discrimination;

---

[17] [2012] EWHC 3597 at para 20.

(2)   the need to advance equality of opportunity between persons who share a relevant protected characteristic and persons who do not;

(3)   the need to remove or minimise disadvantages suffered by persons who share a relevant protected characteristic that are connected to that characteristic;

(4)   the need to take steps to meet needs of persons who share a relevant protected characteristic that are different from the needs from persons who do not share it;

(5)   in particular the need to take steps to take account of disabled person's disabilities;

(6)   the need to encourage persons who share any relevant protected characteristic to participate in public life or in any other activity in which participation by such persons is disproportionately low;

(7)   the need to foster good relations between persons who share a relevant protected characteristic and persons who do not;

(8)   the need to tackle prejudice, and

(9)   the need to promote understanding.'

4.19   There is a need to comply with the duty in substance, not in form – a failure to mention it is not in itself determinative – conversely it needs to be apparent how the duty has been addressed The duty must be performed with vigour and an open mind. General awareness of the duty does not amount to the necessary due regard, being a 'substantial rigorous and open-minded approach'. If a risk of adverse impact is identified, consideration should be given to measures to avoid that impact before fixing on a particular solution.[18] There needs to be a basis for equalities issues to arise. A late assertion in a challenge is not likely to be persuasive[19]

OTHER POTENTIALLY RELEVANT AND IRRELEVANT MATTERS

4.20   The fact that the development has taken place is essential to the ability to enforce, but may also be relevant to whether retrospective planning permission should be granted. In deciding whether to grant retrospective planning permission a local planning authority is entitled to ask whether it would consider it expedient to take enforcement action to require the removal of the development. Schiemann LJ said in *R v Leominster District Council ex p Pothecary*:[20]

'I therefore reject the submission that a planning authority is never entitled to consider the likelihood of enforcement action at the time when the application for retrospective planning permission for a building erected without planning permission is before them. It is not rare that buildings are put up without the appropriate planning permission. Sometimes there is no planning objection at all. Sometimes there is an insuperable objection. There are many situations between the two ends of what is a continuum. There are situations where the authority would not have given permission for the development if asked for permission for precisely that which has been built, but the development is not so objectionable that it is reasonable to require it be pulled down. To require this would be a disproportionate sanction for the breach of the law concerned. That is why Parliament has imposed the requirement of expediency. What weight the authority gives to the existence of the building is a matter for the authority.'

---

[18]   *R (JM & NT) v Isle of Wight Council* [2011] EWHC 2911 (Admin) at para 95 to 105.
[19]   See *Ilyas v Aylesbury Vale District Council* [2011] EWCA Civ 1377 at para 26.
[20]   (1998) 76 P & CR 346.

Walker LJ also said:

'I agree that the planning authority was not merely entitled, but in practice bound, to take account of the existence of the large metal and wood lambing shed which had been constructed without planning permission having been granted. It was a relevant fact that had to be taken into account. The weight to be attached to the fait accompli was another matter.

The policy of the law must be to discourage any belief that persons who carry out development without planning permission are likely to obtain an advantage by breaking the law. Nevertheless, circumstances vary: the range of possible cases extends from a flagrant and deliberate breach of planning control to an inadvertent breach in some minor respect, for instance an error of a few metres in siting a building.'

Of course, the effect of a few metres difference in siting will depend on the location and proximity of neighbours.

4.21   In *R v Caradon District Council ex p Knott*,[21] Sullivan J held that it was not lawful to issue an enforcement notice 'for the sole purpose of reducing the compensation payable to that landowner if his land was going to be acquired by the local planning authority, for example, under a compulsory purchase order'. The emphasis on sole purpose is important. If the development is unacceptable in planning terms then a collateral benefit of reducing compensation is permissible.

NATIONAL PLANNING POLICY FRAMEWORK

4.22   The National Planning Policy Framework says 'the purpose of the planning system is to contribute to the achievement of sustainable development'.[22] This has three dimensions: economic, social and environmental. In considering the merits of any unauthorised development the policies of the NPPF will be relevant. Its only guidance on enforcement is at para 207:

'Effective enforcement is important as a means of maintaining public confidence in the planning system. Enforcement action is discretionary, and local planning authorities should act proportionately in responding to suspected breaches of planning control. Local planning authorities should consider publishing a local enforcement plan to manage enforcement proactively, in a way that is appropriate to their area. This should set out how they will monitor the implementation of planning permissions, investigate alleged cases of unauthorised development and take action where it is appropriate to do so.'

Other English guidance

4.23   Some other extant planning guidance in England bears on the desirability of enforcement action:

* The practical outcome of the enforcement notice: for example, what is the fallback position or could a notice lead to reconstruction under permitted development rights, possibly in a less acceptable way? (Circular 10/97 Annex 2, para 2.3.)

---

[21] (2000) 80 P & CR 154 at 171.
[22] NPPF, para 6.

- Judicial authority, government guidance and appeal decisions should be considered (Circular 03/09 Part B para B33). The previous costs circular had referred to 'well-reported' appeal decisions but the Government now seems to expect authorities to be aware of any decision. That said, appeal decisions are rarely useful in another appeal unless they are directly on point.

- 'Authorities should be able to show, on appeal, that they had reasonable grounds for concluding that the breach of control would unacceptably affect public amenity or the existing use of land and buildings meriting protection in the public interest; and it was expedient to issue the enforcement notice in the particular case' (Circular 03/09, Part B, para B34).

- It is generally unreasonable (in the normal sense) to issue an enforcement notice solely to remedy the absence of a valid planning permission if there is no significant planning objection to the breach of control (Circular 03/09 Part B para B40).

The former Planning Policy Guidance Note 18

4.24   PPG18 has been revoked and so is no longer government policy. A number of its comments on expediency are worth having in mind:

- Whether the breach 'would unacceptably affect public amenity or the existing use of land and buildings meriting protection in the public interest' (PPG 18, para 5(3)).

- Whether the breach is trivial or purely technical (PPG 18, para 5(4))

- If the local planning authority consider that the development would be permissible if conditions are attached but the developer refuses to make a planning application (PPG 18, paras 8,9)

- Unauthorised minerals development should be stopped as soon as it is detected (PPG 18 para 20)

CONSIDERATIONS ON EXPEDIENCY

4.25

- development plan or draft plan policies on the merits of the development or on enforcement;

- whether the development accords with development plan or draft plan policies;

- the council's enforcement policies;

- previous local planning authority and appeal decisions on the site and on similar sites;

- the local planning authority's prospects of success on appeal and the risk of costs being awarded against it in an appeal;

- the possibility that failure to take enforcement action that is plainly necessary will amount to maladministration in the view of the Local Commissioner for Administration; and

- the personal circumstances (insofar as they are known) of the occupants, particular if the notice will require persons living on the subject land to move.

THE PRINCIPLES OF TAN9 IN WALES

4.26   Technical Advice Note 9 *Enforcement of Planning Control* sets out the general approach to breach of planning control that local planning authorities in Wales should take. It is important for authorities to show that they have followed its advice in deciding on enforcement proceedings. There were many similarities with the advice in Planning Policy Guidance Note 18 (PPG18) *Enforcing Planning Control.* Since the current English guidance is now short, the TAN9 may be of some use in England.

4.27   The TAN sets out a number of general principles:

(i) 'The town and country planning system regulates the development and use of land in the **public interest**' (para 4).

(ii) 'Although it is not a criminal offence to carry out development without first obtaining any necessary planning permission, such action is to be discouraged. The fact that enforcement action is discretionary and should be used as a last resort and only when it is expedient, should not be taken as condoning the wilful breach of planning controls.' (para 5).

(iii) 'In considering enforcement action, the decisive issue for the local planning authority should be whether the breach of planning control would unacceptable affect public amenity or the existing use of land and buildings meriting protection in the public interest.' (para 6).

(iv) 'Enforcement action should be commensurate with the breach of planning control to which it relates; it is usually inappropriate to take formal enforcement action against a trivial or technical breach of control which causes no harm to public amenity. The intention should be to remedy the effects of the breach of planning control, not to punish the person(s) carrying out the breach. Nor should enforcement action be taken simply to regularise development for which permission had not been sought, but which is otherwise unacceptable.' (para 6).

(v) That 'unauthorised development [was] carried out in good faith because the developer believed that planning permission was not needed ... is not relevant in determining whether or not to take enforcement action, the cost to the developer of responding to enforcement action may represent a substantial financial burden and this should be taken into account by the local planning authority when deciding how to handle a particular case. It should not, however, prevent action being taken when it is clearly necessary to do so.' (para 7).

(vi) 'The initial aim should be to explode, in discussion with the owner or occupier of the land, what steps, if any, could be taken to reduce any adverse effects on public amenity to an acceptable level. However, local planning authorities should bear in mind the statutory time limits for taking enforcement action and that prompt initiation of enforcement action may be necessary to prevent an unacceptable breach of planning control from becoming well established and more difficult to remedy.' (para 8)

4.28 *The Decision to Enforce and the Developer's Response*

4.28   TAN9 characterises the circumstances where enforcement action may have to be taken into the following categories:

(a) *Where acceptable, but unauthorised, development has been carried out*
The TAN advises that if an unconditional planning permission is likely to be granted, the developer should be advised to submit a planning application even though it would be generally regarded as unreasonable to enforce solely to remedy the absence of a valid planning permission.[23] The guidance says it should be pointed out that the absence of a planning permission may affect disposal of the land.[24]

(b) *Where unauthorised development can be made acceptable by the imposition of conditions*
The local planning authority should invite the owner or occupier to submit a planning application. If that is not done then the authority can take enforcement action, explaining what harm has been caused and how the conditional grant of planning permission can remedy it.[25]

(c) *Where the unauthorised development would be acceptable on alternative sites*
The local planning authority should set a reasonable time limit for relocation. The local authority's economic development bodies are encouraged to suggest alternative sites. If an agreed timetable for relocation is ignored it will usually be expedient to enforce. Particular regard should be had to the effect of enforcement on small businesses or the self-employed.[26]

(d) *Where the unauthorised development is unacceptable and relocation is not feasible*
The owner or occupier should be informed that the development will not be allowed to continue at its present level (or at all). If the development provides valued local employment, the authority should try to agree a timetable to end the breach. If no agreement is reached, enforcement action is usually justified.[27]

(e) *Where the unauthorised development is unacceptable and immediate remedial action is required*

'Where a local planning authority considers that an unauthorised development is causing unacceptable harm to public amenity, and there is little likelihood of the matter being resolved through negotiations or voluntarily, they should take vigorous enforcement action to remedy the breach urgently, or prevent further serious harm to public amenity.'[28]

4.29   When considering enforcement action against private householders who appear to have relied on permitted development rights but exceeded a specific limitation, local planning authorities should have regard to what could have been done under those rights. Action should not be taken to remedy development only slightly exceeding the householder's permitted development rights.[29]

---

[23]   TAN9, paras 9 and 11.
[24]   TAN9, para 10. Of course, in those circumstances a landowner might simply record the works done and wait for the time limit to expire.
[25]   TAN9, paras 12 to 14. This might arise where the new building or material change of use, or the demolition of a building is to be accepted not conditions are required to avoid or remedy harm to amenity or require the restoration of the site.
[26]   TAN9, paras 15 to 19.
[27]   TAN9, paras 20–21.
[28]   TAN9, para 23.
[29]   TAN9, para 24.

4.30   The TAN draws attention to the potentially irremediable nature of mineral working, the speed at which damage can be caused and the lack of restoration and aftercare provisions. Effective liaison to avoid breaches and speedy enforcement action may be required.[30]

4.31   Welsh Office Circular 23/93 *Award of costs incurred in planning and other (including compulsory purchase Order) Proceedings* advises that costs may be awarded against local planning authorities for unreasonable decisions to issue enforcement notices. Annex 3, para 24 warns:

> 'It will generally be regarded as unreasonable for a planning authority to issue an enforcement notice solely to remedy the absence of a valid planning permission, if it is concluded, on an enforcement appeal … that there is no significant planning objection to the breach of control alleged in the enforcement notice. … Authorities should be able to show, on appeal, that they had reasonable grounds for concluding that the breach of control would unacceptably affect public amenity, or the existing use of land and buildings meriting protection in the public interest; and it was expedient to issue the enforcement notice in the particular case.'

Enforcement Concordat and Regulatory Compliance Code

4.32   As part of a general approach to regulatory enforcement, central government has promoted various initiatives to encourage effective but proportionate actions by central and local government. These were primarily aimed at regulation of business, but in the planning context will include all landowners and users.

4.33   The Enforcement Concordat was published in 1998. It set out Principles of Good Enforcement, which in policy were standards (of performance by regulators), openness, helpfulness, complaints about service, proportionality and consistency.[31] The Concordat has been widely adopted by local government.

4.34   In March 2005 the Government published a report by Philip Hampton entitled *Reducing Administrative Burdens: Effective Inspection and Enforcement.* In response, the Legislative and Regulatory Reform Act 2006 set principles for the exercise of regulatory functions:[32]

> '(a) regulatory activities should be carried out in a way which is transparent, accountable, proportionate and consistent;
>
> (b)   regulatory activities should be targeted only at cases in which action is needed.'

Ministers were able to publish a statutory code of practice to be considered when setting general policies, principles and standards with respect of exercising regulatory functions or giving guidance.[33] A code was published in 2007 as the Regulators' Compliance Code, with specific obligations on allowing economic progress, comprehensive risk assessment, giving advice and guidance, inspections to be for a reason, not requiring unnecessary information or duplication of information requirements, use of proportionate sanctions, and regulators' accountability.

---

[30]   TAN9 paras 25–26.
[31]   The text of the Concordat is in *Enforcement Concordat: Good Practice Guide for England and Wales* (DTI).
[32]   Legislative and Regulatory Reform Act 2006, s 21(2).
[33]   Legislative and Regulatory Reform Act 2006, s 22.

4.35 The principles and the code apply to various national bodies with planning interests (the Environment Agency, English Heritage). Whilst they apply to local authorities in respect of numerous functions, these do not include town and country planning.[34]

The landowner's response to the potential for enforcement action

4.36 When faced with the potential for enforcement action to be taken, landowners and occupiers have four broad options:

(i) *Do nothing and wait for the time limit to expire*
A great number of breaches of planning control are neither regularised by obtaining a retrospective consent nor subjected to enforcement proceedings. They might simply not be noticed by nor reported to the local planning authority, or they may involve development which is seen as harmless or beneficial in planning terms. Any harm might be so small that the local planning authority would not take action. An approach of masterly inactivity may be the best one to adopt. It can be cheaper, and even less stressful, than trying to regularise a position which would not have been challenged. Several points do need to be borne in mind:

(a) if consent was not required or there was no breach of a condition, then a record should be kept at the time (for example, photographs of measurements showing a tree was below the size requirements for notice to be given of it being cut down in a conservation area);

(b) if reliance is going to be placed on the breach becoming lawful by passage of time then a record must be kept of when the works were substantially completed, the use begun or the matters relating to the condition incurred. The greater the risk of enforcement action being taken, the more detailed should be the evidence collected;

(c) it is important not to prevent time limits from running by fraudulent conduct or allow a planning enforcement order to be made due to deliberate concealment;

(d) no time limits apply to listed building or conservation area control breaches;

(e) an apparent breach of planning control may have to be addressed when the property is sold, let or mortgaged. Insurance can be purchased against enforcement proceedings, and where there has been no intimation of action and the works do not appear harmful then this can be readily and inexpensively obtained. Where action appears to be a real possibility, then insurance is unlikely to be available.

(ii) *Seek to dissuade the local planning authority from taking action*
The landowner may seek to persuade the authority that there was no breach or that no action should be taken about any breach. This will usually need some correspondence although a meeting on site is also likely to be required. Depending upon the particular issues there may be a need to provide information, submit arguments or even produce a legal opinion. It is important to ensure that false information is not provided nor is information concealed which affects the

---

[34] Legislative and Regulatory Reform (Regulatory Functions) Order 2007.

running of the time limits. That said, it is a legitimate tactic to keep discussions going until a time limit expires.

On some occasions it may be useful to seek a lawful development certificate ('LDC').[35] If granted, that will state the position. An application also provides a formal mechanism for debating the lawfulness of what has been done before enforcement action has been taken. That said, lawful actions do not need a certificate to validate them. A landowner or developer who considers the position to be clear might decide not to spend their money on an LDC application

(iii) *Seek to regularise the position by applying for consent*
   If consent appears to be needed or there has been a breach of condition, the developer may wish to make a retrospective application for approval. If granted, that will resolve the issues (subject to any pre-existing criminal liability). If refused, it may appear more attractive to fight an appeal on a retrospective application rather being forced into trying to demonstrate the planning merits in an enforcement appeal.

(iv) *Comply with planning control*
   This is affected by the extent of any benefit from the breach, the chances and expense of seeking to retain that benefit, the costs and losses of compliance and whether any compromise position can be reached.

---

[35]   See Chapter 22.

Chapter 5

Obtaining Information

5.01   The first that the local planning authority may know of a suspected breach of planning control is a complaint by a member of the public or a councillor. The information may be sketchy or incomplete. The local planning authority will want the following information:

(a) whether a breach of planning control is taking, or has taken, place;

(b) whether any time limits apply;

(c) who is involved in the land: and

(d) sufficient evidence to support enforcement proceedings.

Landowners, occupiers and developers will want to halt enforcement proceedings as soon as possible. An explanation may do that. For reasons of commercial secrecy or privacy, or to avoid giving the local planning authority ammunition, they might want to say as little as possible. If the local planning authority's information gathering can be lawfully frustrated this could delay, if not prevent, enforcement proceedings. Developers will also want to obtain evidence to show that the activities are authorised or that action is time-barred.

5.02   The local planning authority has a number of statutory powers to obtain information. These are now considered.

PLANNING CONTRAVENTION NOTICES

5.03   Planning contravention notices were introduced by the Planning and Compensation Act 1991 and are the local planning authority's most potent method of finding out information. They seek information about breaches of planning control. Guidance on their use is provided in Circular 10/97, Annex 1. Around 5,000 planning contravention notices are served each year.[1]

Issue

5.04   A planning contravention notice may be served 'where it appears to the local planning authority that there may have been a breach of planning control' (s 171C(1)). That a breach is anticipated is insufficient. The service of a planning contravention notice was successfully challenged in *R v Teignbridge District Council, ex p Teignmouth Quay Company Ltd*.[2]

---

[1]   In the period 2002 to 2012 district planning authorities served between 4,103 and 5,366 PCNs a year, with an additional 100–200 PCNs served on county matters: CLG Enforcement Statistics 2011/2012.
[2]   [1995] JPL 828. The decision is referenced at Circular 10/97, Annex 1, para 1.4.

5.05   Teignmouth Quay were carrying out works at their docks pursuant to permitted development rights. Judge J considered that planning contravention notices were an intrusive procedure which could not be deployed unless it appeared to the local planning authority, acting reasonably, that a breach of planning control might have taken place. Refusal by a landowner to co-operate with council inquiries was not sufficient. The appearance of the breach must be to the local planning authority, not to third parties, such as local residents. Nothing suggested a breach of planning control and the issue of the planning contravention notice was quashed.

5.06   The planning contravention notice may be served on the owner, occupier or any person with an interest in the land or any person carrying out operations on the land or using it for any purpose.[3] A planning contravention notice does not have to be served before taking enforcement proceedings.[4]

Contents

5.07   The notice can require information as to:

'(a)   any operations being carried out on the land, any use of the land and any other activities being carried out on the land; and

(b)   any matter relating to the conditions or limitations subject to which any planning permission in respect of the land has been granted.'[5]

Planning contravention notices often ask detailed questions, tailored to each notice. Section 171C(3) provides examples of matters that can be covered, including the persons interested in the land, details of uses and operations and information going to the applicability of any planning permission.

5.08   The planning contravention notice may give the recipient notice of a time and place where the recipient can make representations or offer to apply for planning permission or undertake remedial works.[6] This provision is intended for use where the local planning authority considers that enforcement action could be avoided by discussions or a planning application.[7] It need not be used if the planning contravention notice is simply to obtain information for use in an enforcement notice, and it does not prevent informal discussions. The planning contravention notice must also set out the consequences of non-compliance, in particular that enforcement action may follow, and the effect on stop notice compensation. A model notice is contained in the Appendix to Annex 1, Circular 10/97.

Failure to comply

5.09   Compliance with the planning contravention notice must be by a response in writing,[8] which includes email. If the failure to provide the information required, or co-operation requested, by a planning contravention notice (or notices under s 330

---

[3]   Town and Country Planning Act 1990, s 171C(1).
[4]   Town and Country Planning Act 1990, s 171C(7); also Circular 10/97, Annex 1, para 1.3.
[5]   Town and Country Planning Act 1990, s 171C(2).
[6]   Town and Country Planning Act 1990, s 171C(4).
[7]   Circular 10/97, Annex 1, para 1.10.
[8]   Town and Country Planning Act 1990, s 171C(6).

of the Act or s 16 of the Local Government (Miscellaneous Provisions) Act 1976: see below) results in loss or damage because of the issue of a stop notice, compensation is not recoverable.[9] Failure to comply with a planning contravention notice more than 21 days after service is a summary offence with a level 3 (£1,000) fine.[10] It is a defence to show a reasonable excuse for non-compliance.[11] Knowingly or recklessly making a false or misleading statement in purported compliance with a planning contravention notice is a summary offence, with a level 5 (£5,000) fine.[12]

THE POWER TO ACQUIRE INFORMATION: SECTION 330 NOTICES

5.10   Section 330 of the 1990 Act provides the local planning authority and the Secretary of State with the power to require information as to interests in land and the use of the premises.

Issue of a section 330 notice

5.11   The notice must be in writing and must require a response in writing. The notice is normally a standard form, with blank spaces for the addressee to answer the requests. The notice must be:

> 'for the purpose of enabling the Secretary of State or a local authority to make an order or issue or serve any notice or other document which, by any of the provisions of this Act, he or they are authorised or required to make, issue or serve'.[13]

This would include: obtaining information to decide whether to take enforcement action; determining who to serve with an enforcement notice; or identifying persons for the purpose of prosecutions or injunctions under the Act. The power is applied to the Listed Buildings Act and the Hazardous Substances Act.[14] A notice issued for the purposes of other Acts or where there is an intention to take no further action on the matter (save for a prosecution for not returning the notice) is ultra vires. The notice may be served on the occupier of the premises and any person who directly or indirectly receives rent in respect of the premises.[15] As a matter of practice, notices are usually served on those persons believed to be involved in the land and also addressed to 'The Occupier' and 'The Owner'.

Contents

5.12   The notice can request the following information:

(a) the interest of the person served;

(b) the name and address of any other person known as having an interest;

(c) the purpose for which the premises are used;

---

[9]   Town and Country Planning Act 1990, s 186(5)(b). See Chapter 12 below.
[10] Town and Country Planning Act 1990, s 171D(1), (4).
[11] Town and Country Planning Act 1990, s 171D(3).
[12] Town and Country Planning Act 1990, s 171D(6).
[13] Town and Country Planning Act 1990, s 330(1).
[14] Listed Buildings Act, s 89; Hazardous Substances Act, s 37.
[15] Town and Country Planning Act 1990, s 330(1).

(d)   when that use began;

(e)   the name and address of any other person known as having used those premises for that purpose;

(f)   when activities being carried out on the premises began.

By including 'activities' (which can be the subject of a stop notice), the section 330 notice can seek information about operational development in progress, in addition to the use of the land.

5.13   The notice will require the information to be given within 21 days of service or any later, specified period.[16]

Failure to comply

5.14   Failure to comply with a notice (which includes answering only some requests) is a summary offence with a level 3 (£1,000) fine. It is a defence to show a reasonable excuse for not complying.[17] This would include being away until after the period expired. False information is more damaging to local planning authority enforcement than a failure to provide information. Consequently, knowingly making a misstatement in respect of information requested is an either-way offence, subject to a maximum fine in the magistrates' court (£5,000) and two years' jail and/or an unlimited fine in the Crown Court.[18]

THE GENERAL POWER TO OBTAIN INFORMATION OF PERSONS INTERESTED IN LAND

5.15   A more general power to obtain information as to persons' interests in land is provided by section 16 of the Local Government (Miscellaneous Provisions) Act 1976. This can be used for any of the local authority's statutory powers. It is, however, rarely used in planning matters since more specific powers are available. The notice may be served on the occupier, any person with an interest in the land and any person authorised to manage the land. It must specify the statutory function the local authority is concerned with. The person served has 14 days (or any longer specified period) to give his or her interest and those of other people who could be served.[19] Failing to comply (there is no reasonable excuse defence) or knowingly or recklessly making a false statement is a summary offence with a level 5 (£5,000) fine.[20]

RIGHTS OF ENTRY

5.16   Site visits are essential in planning control. Sometimes a sufficient view can be obtained from the public highway, but private land will often need to be entered. The local planning authority may authorise any person, normally a planning officer, in writing but without a warrant, to enter any land for certain enforcement purposes

---

[16]   Town and Country Planning Act 1990, s 330(3).
[17]   Town and Country Planning Act 1990, s 330(4).
[18]   Town and Country Planning Act 1990, s 330(5).
[19]   Town and Country Planning Act 1990, s 16(1).
[20]   Town and Country Planning Act 1990, s 16(2).

under section 196A. The power is to ascertain whether there is or has been a breach of planning control, whether any Part VII powers should be exercised and if so how, and to ascertain whether any requirements under that Part have been complied with. The authorised person may enter the subject land or any other land, for example to view the site. These rights of entry do not allow works to be carried out by the local planning authority to determine whether action should be taken. The powers may only be exercised at a reasonable time, and if there are reasonable grounds for their use. Guidance is on the use of rights of entry is provided in Circular 10/97, Annex 6.

5.17   A dwelling house may only be entered if 24 hours' notice has been given to the occupier.[21]

Entry under warrant

5.18   Force may only be used to enter the land if a warrant is issued by a justice of the peace or district judge under section 196B. A sworn information must satisfy the court that there are reasonable grounds for entering for section 196A purposes and:

'(a) admission to the land has been refused, or a refusal is reasonably apprehended; or

(b)   the case is one of urgency.'[22]

A refusal is deemed 'if no reply is received to a request for entry in a reasonable period'.[23] The warrant permits one entry, within a month of the issue of the warrant. It must be at a reasonable hour, unless the case is urgent.[24] The Secretary of State has equivalent entry powers to the local planning authority under sections 196A and196B for the purpose of deciding whether an enforcement notice should be issued, exercised after consultation with the local planning authority.[25]

Failure to comply

5.19   It is a summary offence to wilfully obstruct any person exercising a right of entry under these sections, punishable by a level 3 (£1,000) fine.[26] Conversely, it is an offence for a person exercising such a right of entry to disclose any manufacturing process or trade secret he discovers, except in the course of his duties in connection with the entry.[27] This is punishable by a maximum fine in the magistrates' court or two years' jail and a fine in the Crown Court.[28]

OTHER POWERS OF ENTRY

5.20   Parallel powers are provided in respect of tree controls in ss 214B, 214C and 214D. There is a power to take samples from trees and soil samples.[29] A general

---

[21]   Town and Country Planning Act 1990, s 196A(4).
[22]   Town and Country Planning Act 1990, s 196B(1).
[23]   Town and Country Planning Act 1990, s 196B(2).
[24]   Town and Country Planning Act 1990, s 196B(3).
[25]   Town and Country Planning Act 1990, s 196A(2), (3).
[26]   Town and Country Planning Act 1990, s 196C(2).
[27]   Town and Country Planning Act 1990, s 196C(5), (6).
[28]   Town and Country Planning Act 1990, s 196C(7).
[29]   Town and Country Planning Act 1990, s 214D(1).

right of entry for powers other than the enforcement powers in Pt VII is provided in s 324 of the Act. This includes the powers in respect of land adversely affecting the amenity of the neighbourhood and advertising.[30] The other Planning Acts have equivalent provisions to ss 196A–C in the Listed Buildings Act at ss 88, 88A and 88B and the Hazardous Substances Act at ss 36, 36A and 36B.

COURT ORDERS TO OBTAIN INFORMATION

5.21   A defendant in civil proceedings may be ordered to disclose, on affidavit, the identity of other wrongdoers and other matters. Such an order could be obtained alongside interim relief, such as an interlocutory injunction.[31] For example, an interim injunction may be sought against a housing developer for breach of a negative condition requiring landscaping to be carried out before houses are occupied. The local planning authority could seek an order that the housing developer swear an affidavit disclosing the identities of the purchasers of the houses, as they will be in breach of planning control if they go into occupation.

SURVEILLANCE

5.22   The ability of local planning authorities to carry out covert surveillance or investigations is limited by the Regulation of Investigatory Powers Act 2000. Local authorities are not able to conduct intrusive surveillance, that is, covert surveillance in residential premises or private vehicles.[32] They are only able to carry out directed surveillance (which is covert surveillance[33] likely to result in the obtaining of private information about a person other than in residential premises or private vehicles) to prevent or detect criminal offences punishable by a maximum term of at least six months' imprisonment.[34] In practical terms these powers would not be used for planning matters as the only offences which carry such sentences are unlawful demolition of listed buildings or in conservation areas. If it was believed that such demolition was taking place or about to take place, a local planning authority would use powers of entry rather than attempt covert surveillance. Covert human intelligence sources may be used to prevent or detect crime[35] but only with the approval of the magistrates' court.[36]

OTHER SOURCES OF INFORMATION

Council records

5.23   The planning files and register entries for the subject site and neighbouring site should be checked. Other licence records, for example for caravan sites or goods

---

[30] Town and Country Planning Act 1990, s 324(1)(c).
[31] *Loose v Williamson* [1978] 1 WLR 639.
[32] Defined in Regulation of Investigatory Powers Act 2000, s 26.
[33] Surveillance is covert if 'it is carried out in a manner that is calculated to ensure that persons who are subject to the surveillance are unaware that it is or may be taking place': Regulation of Investigatory Powers Act 2000, s 26(9).
[34] Regulation of Investigatory Powers (Directed Surveillance and Covert Human Intelligence Sources) Order 2010, art 7A.
[35] Regulation of Investigatory Powers Act 2000, s 29.
[36] Regulation of Investigatory Powers Act 2000, s 32A.

vehicle operations, may be relevant. They will show previous decisions on the site and may indicate the history of uses on the site. Some councils keep photographs of potential advertising hoarding sites in the event that hoardings are subsequently erected and the period of use needs to be determined.

Aerial photographs

5.24   Aerial photographs may reveal the physical extent of buildings and works. Care needs to be taken with the quality and date of freely available internet images (sometimes, but usually inaccurately, described as satellite photographs). Much higher quality images are available and there are also experts in analysing such images.

Land ownership

5.25   Title to registered land can be ascertained by a search of the Land Registry.[37] Two points should be born in mind: the date of a transfer is the date of entry on the register, which may be several months after the conveyance; and the addresses given for owners and other persons are not updated. Office copies of the register are admissible in evidence in legal proceedings.[38]

Companies

5.26   Details of companies, including their accounts and the names and addresses of directors, are available online from Companies House. A number of agencies provide services searching these records.

Site Visit

5.27   Enforcement action will rarely be possible without a site visit. Officers will be particularly concerned to ascertain the exact nature of the breach and who is carrying it out. Photographs should be taken and, if an unauthorised business is alleged, flyers, take-away menus and business cards should be requested as appropriate.

Interviews

5.28   Persons, including those involved in the activity investigated, can be questioned. Where the questioning is of a suspect by a person charged with the investigation of crime, the Police and Criminal Evidence Act 1984 (PACE) applies.[39] Whether a person is charged with investigating crime is a matter of fact: one test is whether a prosecution might result from the investigation.[40] In the planning context, questioning by council officers is likely to fall under PACE if it is of a person who may have committed an offence and it is about facts which may be elements in the offence. For example, asking a landowner whether an enforcement notice which has taken effect has been complied with would come under PACE. If PACE applies, then

---

[37]   Under s 129 of the Land Registration Act 1925.
[38]   Land Registration Act 1925, s 113.
[39]   Police and Criminal Evidence Act 1984, s 67(9).
[40]   *R v Bayliss* (1994) 98 Cr App R 235.

the interview should be in accordance with Code C made under PACE. This sets out rules on, inter alia, the conduct of interviews with suspects. The suspect should be cautioned before interview. The caution shall be in the following terms:

> 'You do not have to say anything. But it may harm your defence if you do not mention when questioned something which you later rely on in court. Anything you say may be given in evidence.'[41]

HOW DEVELOPERS CAN OBTAIN INFORMATION

5.29   Developers and landowners may seek information on the history of the subject site to show that there was not a breach of planning control (eg the acts did not amount to a material change of use) or that a breach is now time-barred. Additionally developers should look for information about procedural errors by the local planning authority, any evidence justifying judicial review of the decision, and evidence that the local planning authority or its officers considered that there was no breach of planning control or that any breach was not serious. The developer's best source of information is the local authority. Local authorities keep extensive records, much of which the public is entitled to see. There is very little that the public is prevented by law from seeing. Reports and entries concerning nearby properties may shed light on the history of the subject property.

The planning register

5.30   The local planning authority must keep, available to the public, a planning register containing copies of all planning applications and decisions upon them.[42] The register also includes information on applications for certificates of lawfulness of existing or proposed use or development.

The enforcement register

5.31   Similarly, an enforcement register is kept by local planning authorities. It is available for inspection by the public at reasonable hours.[43] This contains information on planning enforcement orders, enforcement notices, stop notices and breach of condition notices served in the local planning authority's area.[44] It includes dates of issue and service and a summary of the breach of planning control alleged.[45]

Council minutes and officers' reports

5.32   The minutes and agenda of committee meetings and council meetings, together with officers' reports and background papers, should be available to the

---

[41]   Code C: Code of Practice for the Detention, Treatment and Questioning of Persons by Police Officers, para 10.4

[42]   Town and Country Planning Act 1990, s 69; Town and Country Planning (Development Management Procedure) (England) Order 2010 ('the DMPO'), art 37; Town and Country Planning (Development Management Procedure) (Wales) Order 2012 ('the 2012 DMPO'), art 29.

[43]   Town and Country Planning Act 1990, s 188(3).

[44]   Town and Country Planning Act 1990, s 188(1).

[45]   2010 DMPO, art 38; 2012 DMPO, art 29.

public for six years from the date of the meeting.[46] The limitation upon this right is that minutes and reports relating to proceedings during which the meeting was not open to the public are not available. This limitation applies when 'exempt information' is discussed, the public interest in withholding disclosure of the information outweighs that in favour of disclosure and the councillors present resolve to exclude the public.[47] Exempt information includes counsel's opinion, actions relating to criminal offences, and decisions to issue notices or make orders or directions if that might enable a person affected by the decision to defeat its purpose.[48]

Freedom of Information Act/Environmental Information Regulations

5.33   Wide rights of access to information are provided by the Environmental Information Regulations 2004 and the Freedom of Information Act 2000.

The Environmental Information Regulations 2004 implement European Council Directive 2003/4/EC and applies to environmental information which is defined as:[49]

'any information in written, visual, aural, electronic or any other material form on–

(a)   the state of the elements of the environment, such as air and atmosphere, water, soil, land, landscape and natural sites including wetlands, coastal and marine areas, biological diversity and its components, including genetically modified organisms, and the interaction among these elements;

(b)   factors, such as substances, energy, noise, radiation or waste, including radioactive waste, emissions, discharges and other releases into the environment, affecting or likely to affect the elements of the environment referred to in (a);

(c)   measures (including administrative measures), such as policies, legislation, plans, programmes, environmental agreements, and activities affecting or likely to affect the elements and factors referred to in (a) and (b) as well as measures or activities designed to protect those elements;

(d)   reports on the implementation of environmental legislation;

(e)   cost-benefit and other economic analyses and assumptions used within the framework of the measures and activities referred to in (c); and

(f)   the state of human health and safety, including the contamination of the food chain, where relevant, conditions of human life, cultural sites and built structures inasmuch as they are or may be affected by the state of the elements of the environment referred to in (a) or, through those elements, by any of the matters referred to in (b) and (c);'.

Public authorities have a duty to make this information available within 20 working days of a request.[50] Limited exceptions are provided including where disclosure would adversely affect the course of justice, information provided voluntarily to the public body, internal communications, the protection of the environment and

---

[46]   Papers relating to the full Council meeting and regulatory committees, including development control are accessible under the Local Government Act 1972, ss 100C,100D; those relating to executive decisions by the Council's Cabinet or Executive and members and officers under those arrangements can be accessed, on similar terms under the Local Authorities (Executive Arrangements) (Meetings and Access to Information) (England) Regulations 2012.

[47]   Local Government Act 1972, s 100A(4).

[48]   Local Government Act 1972, Sch 12A.

[49]   Environmental Information Regulations 2004, reg 2

[50]   Environmental Information Regulations 2004, reg 5.

personal data.[51] These exceptions are subject to the public interest in maintaining the exception outweighing the public interest in disclosing the information and data protection principles.

5.34   The Freedom of Information Act 2000 applies to public bodies including local authorities, government agencies and central government. Authorities will have publication schemes setting out what information is published. Additionally, any person may request information, without giving a reason for the request, and the request must receive a substantive response within 20 working days.[52] The grounds for withholding information are limited. A public authority can decline to provide information if the cost of complying with the request exceeds the 'appropriate limit' which is £600.[53] Vexatious or repeated requests can also be declined.[54]

5.35   Part II of the Freedom of Information Act 2000 contains a variety of exemptions from the duty to provide information. The exemptions which are most likely to be relevant to planning enforcement situations are:

- information held for the purposes of criminal investigations;[55]

- information for potential civil proceedings by the authority which comes from confidential sources;[56]

- other information whose disclosure would, or would be likely to, prejudice criminal justice or the purpose of ascertaining whether any person has complied with the law;[57]

- information whose disclosure is likely to prejudice the free and frank provision of advice or exchange of views or otherwise the effective conduct of public affairs;[58]

- personal information under the Data Protection Act 1998;[59]

- information subject whose disclosure would give rise to an actionable breach of confidence;[60] and

- information subject to legal professional privilege.[61]

In most cases, including these examples, the information can only be withheld if 'the public interest in maintaining the exemption outweighs the public interest in disclosing the information'.[62] Finally the Freedom of Information Act regime does not apply to information subject to the Environmental Information Regulations[63] but it is prudent to make any request under both provisions. If a request is refused,

---

[51] Environmental Information Regulations 2004, regs 12, 13.
[52] Freedom of Information Act 2000, s 10.
[53] Freedom of Information Act 2000, s 12; Freedom of Information and Data Protection (Appropriate Limit and Fees) Regulations 2004, reg 3.
[54] Freedom of Information Act 2000, s 14.
[55] Freedom of Information Act 2000, s 30(1).
[56] Freedom of Information Act 2000, s 30(2).
[57] Freedom of Information Act 2000, s 31.
[58] Freedom of Information Act 2000, s 36.
[59] Freedom of Information Act 2000, s 40.
[60] Freedom of Information Act 2000, s 41.
[61] Freedom of Information Act 2000, s 42.
[62] Freedom of Information Act 2000, s 2(2).
[63] Freedom of Information Act 2000, s 39.

in whole or part, the public body's internal review procedures should be followed before a complaint is made to the Information Commissioner's Office.

5.36 Requests for information are more effective, and more likely to be answered, if they are precise about what information is required. A request should identify the particular land and may want to address the type of information, whom it concerns and a range of dates.

5.37 The Data Protection Act 1998 gives individuals a right of access to personal data about them.[64] The exceptions to this right are very limited and so it may result in the production of more material.

Inspector's decision letters and reports

5.38 Decision letters and reports by government inspectors appointed on planning matters can help in putting together the history of a site. This is even if the decision was about neighbouring land, as inspectors often describe the local area. Decisions from 2006 are on the Planning Casework Service part of the Planning Portal website.

The developer's records

5.39 Correspondence with the local authority should be checked. Where time limits may apply financial or business records may show when works were carried out or operations began. Solicitor's or surveyor's papers on obtaining the property may be helpful. Where a dwelling house is concerned, family photographs may show, for example, when a wall was built.

Neighbours and former occupants

5.40 Neighbours, former occupants and users of the site may be able to say when the use began. Usually they will not have records, but if the witness can remember, for example, getting her car resprayed at the site just after getting engaged, that can date the use.

OBTAINING INFORMATION ON APPEAL

5.41 Inspectors holding public inquiries have a power to require any person to attend to give evidence or produce documents under s 250(2) of the Local Government Act 1972:

> 'For the purpose of any such local inquiry, the person appointed to hold the inquiry may by summons require any person to attend, at a time and place stated in the summons, to give evidence or to produce any documents in his custody or under his control which relate to any matter in question at the inquiry, and may take evidence on oath, and for that purpose administer oaths:

---

[64] Data Protection Act 1998, s 7.

Provided that—

(a) no person shall be required, in obedience to such summons, to attend to give evidence or to produce any such documents, unless the necessary expenses of this attendance are paid or tendered to him; and

(b) nothing in this section shall empower the person holding the inquiry to require the production of the title, or of any instrument relating to the title, of any land not being the property of a local authority.'

This power is applied to inquiries under the Town and Country Planning Act by s 320 of that Act, and inquiries held under the hazardous substances[65] and listed buildings regimes.[66] Any such application should be made at the inquiry or a pre-inquiry meeting, although it is prudent to give advanced written notice if possible. Whilst such applications are rarely, if ever, granted, they tend to focus the other side's mind on the material and the Inspector may suggest that material is produced.

---

[65]   Planning (Hazardous Substances) Act 1990, Sch 1, para 6.
[66]   Planning (Listed Buildings and Conservation Areas) Act 1990, s 89(1).

Chapter 6

Enforcement Notices

6.01   The principal method used by local planning authorities against breaches of planning control is the enforcement notice.[1] It can apply to breaches of conditions or limitations as well as unauthorised development. An enforcement notice will specify the breach of planning control alleged and the steps required to remedy the breach. It will give a certain time to do those steps. Failure to comply within that time gives rise to criminal offences. An appeal against a notice can be made to the Secretary of State, and then to the High Court.

THE ISSUE OF AN ENFORCEMENT NOTICE

6.02   A local planning authority has a power to issue an enforcement notice when it appears to them that the two criteria in s 172(1) are met:

(a) there has been a breach of planning control; and

(b) it is expedient to issue the notice, having regard to the provisions of the development plan and any other material considerations

Actual rather than apprehended breach of planning control

6.03   First, there must appear to the local planning authority 'that there has been a breach of planning control'.[2] Therefore an enforcement notice cannot be issued against an anticipated breach of planning control, even if that breach occurs before a copy of the notice is served. The need for an actual breach is illustrated by *R v Rochester upon Medway City Council, ex p Hobday*.[3] Land was being used as a market. Permitted development rights allowed temporary market use for up to 14 days per calendar year. The local planning authority authorised the issue of an enforcement notice on the 15th market day, when the use had commenced but before 14 days' use had occurred. This decision was void. Enforcement action could not be authorised unless it appeared to the local planning authority that a breach of planning control had occurred. This was even though the council were in error in considering that there was no breach until the 15th day. If the market use was permanent, then the 14 days' rights did not apply.[4]

6.04   As would be expected, the local planning authority must be acting reasonably in concluding that a breach of planning control has occurred: see *R v Teignbridge*

---

[1]   Since 2002 the number of enforcement notices issued in England has ranged between 4,471 and 5,909 per year: CLG Enforcement Statistics 2011/2012.
[2]   Town and Country Planning Act 1990, s 172(1)(a).
[3]   [1989] 2 PLR 38.
[4]   *Tidswell v Secretary of State for the Environment* (1976) 34 P & CR 152.

District Council, ex p Teignmouth Quay Company Ltd.[5] Conversely in *R v Sevenoaks District Council, ex p Palley,*[6] a decision not to take enforcement action was quashed because the local planning authority proceeded on a materially false basis: they relied on an earlier ultra vires determination that the subject land was agricultural land.

6.05   Since enforcement action can be taken where there 'has been a breach of planning control' it would appear possible to serve an enforcement notice to remedy injury to amenity where the breach of control has ended (for example, if an unlawful building has been removed but the site needs restoration).

Discretion to issue

6.06   If there appears to be a breach of planning control and if the issuance of an enforcement notice is expedient, the local planning authority then has a discretion to issue the notice.[7] This discretion must be exercised having regard to all material considerations, although these factors are essentially accounted for within expediency.

DRAFTING THE NOTICE

6.07   The requirements of a valid enforcement notice are set out in the Act, the Town and Country Planning (Enforcement Notices and Appeals) (England) Regulations 2002[8] ('the Enforcement Notices and Appeals Regulations') or the Town and Country Planning (Enforcement Notices and Appeals) (Wales) Regulations 2003 ('the Welsh Enforcement Notice and Appeals Regulations').[9] It must state:

(i)   the breach of planning control which appears;[10]

(ii)   the paragraph of s 171A(1) breached;[11]

(iii)   the steps required to be taken, or the activities required to cease;[12]

(iv)   the date upon which the notice shall take effect;[13]

(v)   the period or periods for compliance within which steps are to be taken or activities ceased;[14]

(vi)   the reasons why the local planning authority consider it expedient to issue the notice;[15]

---

[5]   [1995] JPL 828.
[6]   [1995] JPL 915.
[7]   Town and Country Planning Act, s 172(1).
[8]   SI 2002/2682.
[9]   SI 2003/394.
[10]   Town and Country Planning Act, s 173(1)(a). This must be sufficient for any person served to know what is alleged: s 173(2).
[11]   Town and Country Planning Act, s 173(1)(b).
[12]   Town and Country Planning Act, s 173(3).
[13]   Town and Country Planning Act, s 173(8).
[14]   Town and Country Planning Act, s 173(9). A notice which fails to specify both the date when it is to become effective and the date by which it has to be complied with is invalid: *Mead v Chelmsford Rural District Council* [1953] 1 QB 32.
[15]   Enforcement Notices and Appeals Regulations, reg 4(a); Enforcement Notice and Appeals (Wales) Regulations, reg 3(a).

(vii)   all policies and proposals in the development plan which are relevant to the decision to issue the enforcement notice; and[16]

(viii)   the precise boundaries of the land to which the notice relates, whether by reference to a plan or otherwise.[17]

6.08   Additionally each copy of an enforcement notice shall be accompanied by an explanatory note, which shall include the following:

'(a)   a copy of sections 171A, 171B and 172 to 177 of the Planning Act, or a summary of those sections including the following information—

(i)   that there is a right of appeal to the Secretary of State against the enforcement notice;

(ii)   that an appeal must be made by giving written notice of the appeal to the Secretary of State before the date specified in the enforcement notice as the date on which it is to take effect or by sending such notice to him in a properly addressed, pre-paid letter posted to him at such time that, in the ordinary course of post, it would be delivered to him before that date, or (where electronic communications are used to send such notice to the Secretary of State) by sending the notice to him at such time that, in the ordinary course of transmission, it would be delivered to him before that date;

(iii)   the grounds on which an appeal may be brought under section 174 of the Planning Act;

(iv)   the fee payable under regulation 10 of the Town and Country Planning (Fees for Applications and Deemed Applications) Regulations 1989 for the deemed application for planning permission for the development alleged to be in breach of planning control in the enforcement notice;

(b)   notification that an appellant must submit to the Secretary of State, either when giving notice of appeal or within 14 days from the date on which the Secretary of State sends him a notice so requiring him, a statement in writing specifying the grounds on which he is appealing against the enforcement notice and stating briefly the facts on which he proposes to rely in support of each of those grounds.

(c)   a list of the names and addresses of the persons on whom a copy of the enforcement notice has been served.'[18]

Model enforcement notices are provided in the Appendices to Circular 10/97 Annex 2. The explanatory note can be an annex to the notice (models for this note are also in 10/97) accompanied by the DoE booklet 'Enforcement Appeals – A Guide to Procedure'.

6.09   If the notice is against operational development on a small area of the site they should make clear in the notice that the alleged breach of planning control is confined to that area.[19]

---

[16]   Enforcement Notices and Appeals Regulations, reg 4(b); Enforcement Notice and Appeals (Wales) Regulations, reg 3(b).

[17]   Enforcement Notices and Appeals Regulations, reg 4(c); Enforcement Notice and Appeals (Wales) Regulations, reg 3(c).

[18]   Enforcement Notices and Appeals Regulations, reg 5; in Wales the words 'National Assembly' are substituted for 'Secretary of State' Enforcement Notice and Appeals (Wales) Regulations, reg 4.

[19]   A point made in the previous Circular 31/92 Appendix 1, para 10.

STEPS REQUIRED

6.10   The enforcement notice specifies steps required to be taken, or activities required to cease, or, wholly or partly, to remedy the breach or any injury to amenity arising from it.[20] An enforcement notice can require steps which are both concerned with remedying the breach of planning control and remedying harm to amenity, whether they are the same or different steps in a notice.[21] This may be partial restoration of the status quo coupled with other work designed to remedy the injury to amenity caused by the breach, or the removal of the contravention and restoration of site. Remedying the breach includes making any development comply with a planning permission (including terms and limitations), discontinuing use of the land or restoring the land to its pre-breach condition.[22]

6.11   Possible requirements in an enforcement notice include:

(a) the alteration or removal of buildings or works;[23]

(b) carrying out building or other operations;[24]

(c) limiting activity on the land;[25]

(d) contouring refuse or waste deposits; and[26]

(e) constructing a replacement building where demolition has occurred in breach of planning control.[27]

6.12   Planning permission is deemed to be given for a replacement building constructed in accordance with an enforcement notice.[28] The enforcement notice may cover more than one breach of planning control.[29] The enforcement notice must identify the particular breach and enforce solely against that. For example, where a condition can be breached in several different ways or on different areas on the site, the particular breach must be identified. In *St Anselm Development Co Ltd v First Secretary of State,*[30] enforcement notices against a non-resident user of a car park identified the particular parking spaces which were being enforced against.

6.13   The steps should be precise and should not provide for later approval of details – for example of a restoration scheme. Later approval of details can be required if planning permission is granted, but there is no appeal mechanism for dealing with such approvals in steps as part of an enforcement notice.[31] The notice

---

[20] Town and Country Planning Act, s 173(3),(4). An enforcement notice must take some action against a breach of planning control identified in it: *Tandridge District Council v Verrechia* [2000] QB 318.

[21] *Wyatt Brothers (Oxford) Ltd v Secretary of State for the Environment, Transport and the Regions* [2001] EWCA Civ 1560, [2002] PLCR 18 per Kennedy LJ at para 22. The Court disapproved advice in Circular 10/97, Annex 2, paras 2.30, 2.31 that the notice or steps had to be for one purpose or the other.

[22] Town and Country Planning Act, s 173(4).

[23] Town and Country Planning Act, s 173(5)(a).

[24] Town and Country Planning Act, s 173(5)(b).

[25] Town and Country Planning Act, s 173(5)(c).

[26] Town and Country Planning Act, s 173(5)(d).

[27] Town and Country Planning Act, s 173(6), (7).

[28] Town and Country Planning Act, s 173(12).

[29] *Valentina of London Ltd v Secretary of State for the Environment* [1992] JPL 1151.

[30] [2003] EWHC 1592 (Admin), [2004] JPL 33.

[31] *Kaur v Secretary of State for the Environment* (1991) 61 P & CR 249.

should not restrict existing rights, such as existing use rights, those lawful by the passage of time, permitted development rights and ancillary uses (*Mansi v Elstree Rural District Council*).[32] The *Mansi* doctrine operates:

(a) as a matter of drafting, in that notices should not be worded to prohibit lawful development; and

(b) as a matter of interpretation, so that a notice should be interpreted as far as possible to avoid such a conflict.

6.14 *Mansi* itself is an example of the first category. A plant nursery had an ancillary use of the sale of plants grown on the site and some imported plants. That changed to a fully retail use on part of the site. The local authority's enforcement notice required the discontinuance of the sales. The Divisional Court considered that the enforcement notice should be varied to allow the limited retail sales and any non-material intensification of that user.

6.15 In *Duguid v Secretary of State for the Environment, Transport and the Regions*,[33] the Court of Appeal held that an enforcement notice which prohibited markets and car parking on land did not need to specifically safeguard the permitted development rights to use the land for markets on up to 14 days a year. There was no need to specifically preserve the rights in the notice. Whilst in *Mansi* there was an established use and there was a benefit in defining what it was, permitted development rights are set out in the development order and are readily identified.[34] However the *Mansi* doctrine does not allow any existing lawful use of the land to be raised in a later defence to proceedings under an enforcement notice, even if it is backed by a lawful development certificate. If not raised as a ground of appeal, the right might be lost. Keene LJ said in *Challinor v Staffordshire County Council*:[35]

> 'what this line of cases indicates is that an enforcement notice will be interpreted so as not to interfere with permitted development rights under the General Development Permitted Order or with rights to use land for a purpose ancillary to a principal use which is itself not being enforced against. The authorities go no further than that and certainly do not establish any general right to assert existing use rights at a time when the enforcement notice has come into effect after an unsuccessful appeal or in the absence of an appeal. Such rights must be asserted at the time of appeal against the enforcement notice. If the landowner sleeps on those rights, he will lose them.'

The cases on *Mansi,* therefore, point to care in drafting enforcement notices and caution in appealing to be certain that lawful activities are not prohibited.

6.16 An enforcement notice against an unauthorised change of use can require the removal of operational development protected by the four year limit,[36] allowed under permitted development rights or works, such as an internal staircase,[37] which are not development if they are integral to the change of use. A common example is that an unlawful residential use of agricultural land (such as by caravans or occasionally houses) is often accompanied by the erection of fences or walls. Whilst

---

[32] (1964) 16 P & CR 153.
[33] (2001) 82 P & CR 6.
[34] *Duguid* at para 28 per Ward LJ, following *R v Harfield* [1993] 2 PLR 23.
[35] [2007] EWCA Civ 864, [2008] JPL 392 at para 52.
[36] *Murfitt v Secretary of State for the Environment* (1980) 40 P & CR 254.
[37] *Somak Travel Ltd v Secretary of State for the Environment* (1987) 55 P & CR 250.

those means of enclosure may have permitted development rights,[38] an enforcement notice against the use can require their removal.[39] This point was overlooked when Basildon District Council sought to remove large numbers of travellers from Dale Farm. The enforcement notices required the cessation of the residential use and the removal of tipped material from most plots but did not require the removal of the fences and walls which had been erected around the 54 caravan plots. Consequently the Council was not able to permanently remove the enclosures when taking direct action to enforce the notices.[40] The result was that on the completion of the works most plots contained large craters where material had been removed, enclosed by fences and walls.

UNDER ENFORCEMENT

6.17   An enforcement notice may identify a breach of planning control but not take all the steps necessary to end the contravention. If that notice is then complied with, any remaining development responsible for that breach of planning control is deemed to have planning permission. This is the effect of s 173(11) which provides:

'Where–

(a) an enforcement notice in respect of any breach of planning control could have required any buildings or works to be removed or any activity to cease, but does not do so; and

(b) all the requirements of the notice have been complied with,

then, so far as the notice did not so require, planning permission shall be treated as having been granted by virtue of section 73A in respect of development consisting of the construction of the buildings or works or, as the case may be, the carrying out of the activities.'

The under-enforcement permission is tied to the breach of planning control alleged in the notice.[41] Permission is not given in respect of other breaches of planning control on the site. The provision does not oblige:

'a local planning authority to scour a planning unit for potential breaches of planning control (whether or not it has sufficient evidence to prove those breaches) for fear that planning permission for any such breaches might otherwise be deemed to be granted'.[42]

6.18   Similarly, if the notice is solely directed at remedying injury to amenity from the breach, then the breach of planning control will have planning permission insofar as it continues. For example, if a building is unlawfully demolished and a resulting enforcement notice imposes restoration requirements then planning permission would be granted for the demolition once the restoration is complete. Of more practical use, a notice imposing controls on an unlawful restaurant (such as requiring an extractor fan and limiting hours) would grant permission for the restaurant.

---

[38]   Under the Town and Country Planning (General Permitted Development) Order 1995, Sch 2, Pt 2.
[39]   *Cash v Secretary of State for Communities and Local Government* [2012] EWHC 2908 (Admin), para 28–32.
[40]   *Egan v Basildon District Council* [2011] EWHC 2416 (QB), [2012] PTSR 1117.
[41]   For there to be underenforcement, the notice must have been capable of specifying remedial measures but have not done so in that respect. It would appear that underenforcement would in practice apply where partial remedial measures are proposed as an enforcement notice which requires no steps in respect of an identified breach is unlawful: see *Tandridge District Council v Verrechia* [2000] QB 318.
[42]   *Maldon District Council v Hammond* [2004] EWCA Civ 1073 at para 42 per Brooke LJ.

TAKING EFFECT

6.19   An enforcement notice 'takes effect' on a date specified in the notice. As the notice must be served not more than 28 days after it is issued and not less than 28 days before it takes effect,[43] the notice must take effect at the earliest 28 days after issue. Periods of 42 or 56 days are common to allow for delays in service. Appeals to the Secretary of State must be made so as to arrive before the notice takes effect.[44] Once the notice takes effect, there is then a specified period for compliance.[45] The period for compliance must run from the date that the enforcement notice takes effect and cannot start before that date.[46] For example, in *Koumis v Secretary of State for Communities and Local Government* it was not open to the local planning authority to vary an enforcement notice to provide for a six-month compliance period from a date which was before the High Court appeal against the notice had been finally determined.[47]

6.20   The local planning authority should consider this period carefully: it is a ground of appeal to the Secretary of State that the compliance period is unreasonable. PPG18 advised that if the enforcement notice will compel a small business or self-employed person to relocate their trading activities, the period should minimise disruption to the business and, if possible, avoid any permanent loss of employment.[48]

6.21   Different periods for compliance can be provided for different steps or activities.[49] For example, use of land for heavy goods vehicle parking could be required to cease in eight weeks and the operational development associated with it, eg hardcore which has been laid, to be removed in 12 weeks.

SUSPENSION OF TAKING EFFECT

6.22   When an enforcement notice appeal is brought, the enforcement notice shall be 'of no effect pending the final determination or the withdrawal of the appeal'.[50] Final determination is the date of the Secretary of State's decision letter if there is no further appeal to the High Court. If the decision is appealed to the High Court under s 289, then there is no final determination until that process has ended.[51] This includes the determination of any appeals in the Court of Appeal or Supreme Court or the dismissal of applications for permission to appeal to those bodies. If the Secretary of State's decision is quashed on a s 289 appeal, then the enforcement notice cannot take effect until his re-determination of the appeal and the resolution of any consequent High Court proceedings. An enforcement notice can, therefore, be delayed from taking effect for a considerable period. The Act was therefore amended by the 1991 reforms to allow the court to order that the enforcement notice have effect during a

---

[43]   Town and Country Planning Act, s 172(3).
[44]   Town and Country Planning Act, s 174(3).
[45]   Town and Country Planning Act, s 173(9).
[46]   *R (Lynes) v West Berkshire District Council* [2002] EWHC 1828 (Admin), [2003] JPL 1137 at para 30, 31 per Harrison J.
[47]   *Koumis* [2012] EWHC 2686 (Admin), [2013] JPL 215 at paras 26, 29 per Walker J.
[48]   PPG 18, para 16
[49]   Town and Country Planning Act, s 173(9).
[50]   Town and Country Planning Act, s 175(4).
[51]   *R v Kuxhaus* [1988] QB 631.

s 289 appeal to it.[52] The extent to which it has effect will be specified by the court, and the court may set down terms, including requiring the local planning authority to give an undertaking as to damages.

WHO TO SERVE

6.23   Copies of the enforcement notice must be served on the owner and occupier of the subject land and any other person whom the local planning authority considers has an interest in the land which is materially affected by the notice.[53] 'Owner' is defined by s 336(1) of the Town and Country Planning Act 1990 as:

> 'a person, other than a mortgagee not in possession, who, whether in his own right or as trustee for any other person, is entitled to receive the rack rent of the land, or, where the land is not let at a rack rent, would be so entitled if it were so let.'

The 'rack rent' is the full market rent of the property.[54] So a freeholder would be entitled to the rack rent if the property is let out at a market rent or is not let out at all. If the property is let out at a sub-market rent then the person who leases at a sub-market rent is the owner. This covers leaseholders with notional or modest ground rents and those paying substantial rents which were less than the the the market value when they were entered into.[55] The effect of the definition in the enforcement context is to put greater responsibilities on persons who 'own' the property, even if only for a limited period, than on those who would conventionally be seen as renting. Different parts of a building may have different owners. For example, in a block of flats the freeholder will be the owner of the structure of the building and the common parts, but flats let on long leaseholds will be owned by their lessees.

6.24   There are inconsistent authorities on the relationship between ownership under s 336 and proprietorship of registered land. In *East Lindsey District Council v Thompson,*[56] the Divisional Court held that the owner was the proprietor and where land had been conveyed the purchaser only became the owner when he was entered as the proprietor by the Land Registry. Unfortunately the judgment makes no reference to the decision of Potts J in *R v Surrey County Council ex p Bridge Court Holdings*[57] that a person who had acquired the site but was not the registered proprietor was the owner. The decision in *East Lindsey* is to be preferred.

6.25   'Occupier' may include licensees, trespassers and squatters.[58] The status of occupier depends upon the facts and circumstances of each case. The factors include the degree of control exercised by the person and the duration of enjoyment of the premises.[59] If a mortgagee or chargee is disclosed by a Land Register entry for the property, they should be served as the value of their security might be affected. The local planning authority may serve other persons outside these categories.[60] They

---

[52]   Town and Country Planning Act, s 289(4A).
[53]   Town and Country Planning Act, s 172(2).
[54]   *Compton Group Ltd v Estates Gazette Ltd* (1978) 36 P & CR 148.
[55]   *London Corporation v Cusack-Smith* [1955] AC 337.
[56]   [2001] EWHC Admin 81, (2001) 82 P & CR 33.
[57]   *R v Surrey County Council, ex p Bridge Court Holdings Ltd* [2000] PLCR 344.
[58]   *Scarborough Borough Council v Adams* [1983] JPL 673.
[59]   *Stevens v Bromley London Borough Council* [1972] Ch 400.
[60]   *Scarborough Borough Council v Adams* [1983] JPL 673.

should serve any person whom they may wish to prosecute for failing to comply with the notice. Those persons will not then have the defence of not being aware of the existence of the notice.[61] Local planning authorities are asked to provide three copies of an enforcement notice when serving, along with three copies of the appeal form, so that one form can be sent to the Secretary of State with any appeal.[62]

MANNER OF SERVICE

6.26   The service or giving of notices under the Act must be done in certain specified ways. If service is defective, the act may be of no legal effect or it might form a ground of appeal. Modes of service are contained in s 329 of the Town and Country Planning Act 1990 and s 233 of the Local Government Act 1972.

6.27   Four methods are provided for anyone to give or serve a notice or other document under the 1990 Act (s 329(1)):

'(a)   by delivering it to the person on whom it is to be served or to whom it is to be given; or

(b)   by leaving it at the usual or last known place of abode of that person, or, in a case where an address for service has been given by that person, at that address; or

(c)   by sending it in a prepaid registered letter, or by the recorded delivery service, addressed to that person at his usual or last known place of abode, or, in a case where an address for service has been given by that person, at that address; or

(d)   in the case of an incorporated company or body, by delivering it to the secretary or clerk of the company or body at their registered or principal office, or sending it in a prepaid registered letter, or by the recorded delivery service, addressed to the secretary or clerk of the company or body at that office.'

6.28   If the name of a person interested in the land cannot be ascertained after reasonable inquiry, then the document can be sent to 'the owner' or 'the occupier' by methods (a), (b) or (c) above.[63] Alternatively it can be marked 'Important – This Communication affects your Property' and:

(a)   sent to the premises by prepaid registered letter or recorded delivery and not returned; or

(b)   delivered to a person on those premises or affixed conspicuously to some object on those premises.[64]

The same methods can be used for occupiers, whether their names are known or not. If unknown, the document should be addressed to 'the occupier'.

---

[61]   Town and Country Planning Act 1990, s 179(7).

[62]   Circular 10/97 Annex 2 paras 2.24, 2.25.

[63]   Town and Country Planning Act 1990, s 329(2)(a).

[64]   Town and Country Planning Act 1990, s 329(2)(b); Town and Country Planning General Regulations 1992, reg 13. The requirement to deliver to a person on those premises in s 329(2)(b)(ii) was not complied with in respect of the occupiers of mobile homes when copies of an enforcement notice had been given to the owner of the land with a list of persons to be served attached to the back: *Cash v Secretary of State for Communities and Local Government* [2012] EWHC 2908 (Admin) at para 16–25.

6.29   If land appears unoccupied then service can be effected by fixing the document, addressed to 'the owners and any occupiers', to an object on the land. If a person interested in that land has given an address for service, then they must be served in the usual manner.[65] The local planning authority is empowered to serve documents by the methods in s 233 of the Local Government Act 1972.[66] In addition to the Planning Act methods, this allows service by post to the proper address; the last known address or the registered or principal office.[67] Where time of service of an enforcement notice was not vital to a prosecution for non-compliance, it did not matter whether the notice served in accordance with the Town and Country Planning Act provisions had actually been received.[68] If time of service is vital, then the presumption of delivery by post can be rebutted.[69]

THE ENFORCEMENT REGISTER

6.30   Various details of enforcement notices must be entered on the enforcement and stop notice register kept by the local planning authority.[70] The register will contain the address of the site, the name of the issuing authority, the dates of issue, service and taking effect of the notice, details of any postponement of taking effect by reason of an appeal, the date of the final determination of any appeal with a summary of the breach of planning control alleged and the requirements of the notice.[71] It must also include with the enforcement notice entry the date of service and (if appropriate) withdrawal of a stop notice referring to that notice and a summary or statement of the activity prohibited by the notice. Importantly the register must also record the date on which the authority are satisfied that the steps required by the enforcement notice have been taken. The local planning authority must make entries as soon as practicable, at the latest within 14 days.[72]

VARIATION AND WITHDRAWAL

6.31   An enforcement notice might turn out to be defective or not to properly cover or remedy the breach. The breach might have been remedied and the notice become redundant because of the lapse of time. The steps required may be excessive, or an agreement be reached with the developer to meet the concerns in a different way. In those circumstances, the local planning authority may wish to withdraw or vary the notice.

---

[65]   Town and Country Planning Act 1990, s 329(3).
[66]   Town and Country Planning Act 1990, s 329(4).
[67]   Local Government Act 1972, s 233(2), (4).
[68]   Interpretation Act 1978, s 7; *Moody v Godstone Rural District Council* [1966] 1 WLR 1085 (which applied this rule to enforcement notices).
[69]   Interpretation Act 1978, s 7; *R v London County Quarter Sessions Appeal Committee ex p Rossi* [1956] 1 QB 682; *Gidden v Chief Constable of Humberside* [2009] EWHC 2924 (Admin), [2010] RTR 9. Service is deemed to take place when the letter would arrive in the ordinary course of the post.
[70]   Town and Country Planning Act 1990, s 188(1).
[71]   Town and Country Planning (Development Management Procedure) (England) Order 2010, art 38(2); Town and Country Planning (Development Management Procedure) (Wales) Order 2012, art 30(1).
[72]   2010 DMPO, art 38(8); 2012 DMPO, art 30(5). A failure to include an enforcement notice on the register may give rise to a defence (s 179(7) of the Town and Country Planning Act 1990) if the defendant had not been served with a copy of the notice and was unaware of it. Authorities should ensure that the register is updated in a timely manner, rather than filling in omissions after proceedings start and, as one planning officer was caught doing, claiming that the entries had been made at the earlier dates.

6.32   A local planning authority can withdraw an enforcement notice, or waive or relax any of its requirements.[73] The variation power includes extending the period for compliance, but does not allow additional requirements to be made or requirements strengthened. An unlawful variation will not have effect and so will not affect the lawfulness of a valid enforcement notice.[74] Notice must be given to those who were served with the notice or would have to have been served if the notice was re-issued.[75] So if ownership changed after service, the old and new owners would be notified. The withdrawal or variation can be made before or after the notice has taken effect. This allows a settlement to be reached before or during an appeal, without the approval of the Secretary of State. The appeal can then be withdrawn. An award of costs against either party is still possible if they acted unreasonably.[76] The withdrawal of an enforcement notice does not prevent the issuance of a further notice.[77] The extended time limit in s 171B(4)(b) is applicable to allow another notice to be issued within four years of the issue of the original notice even if the time limits would have otherwise expired.

6.33   The variation of an enforcement notice should not, in principle, prevent a further notice being issued. If the effect of the variation is to under-enforce, by not requiring all the steps necessary to remedy the breach, then planning permission would be granted for the under-enforced element once the notice is complied with. A fresh enforcement notice could not then be issued against that development. More generally, it will be harder to show that the subsequent issuance is expedient and that the steps required are necessary.

THE EFFECT OF A SUBSEQUENT PLANNING PERMISSION

6.34   An enforcement notice ceases to have effect to the extent that it is inconsistent with a planning permission for existing development which is granted after the enforcement notice has been served. Enforcement notices are concerned with breaches of planning control. Where that breach has been validated by a subsequent planning permission there is no reason for that enforcement notice to stand. The Act provides:[78]

> 'Where, after the service of—
>
> (a)   a copy of an enforcement notice [...]
>
> planning permission is granted for any development carried out before the grant of that permission, the notice shall cease to have effect so far as inconsistent with that permission.'

6.35   The notice, or the relevant part of it, ceases to have effect on the grant[79] of the permission without any further act. It is simply a matter of comparing the notice with what is granted planning permission. It does not matter whether the permission

---

[73]   Town and Country Planning Act 1990, s 173A(1).

[74]   *Koumis v Secretary of State for Communities and Local Government* [2012] EWHC 2686 (Admin); [2013] JPL 215 (where in the course of High Court appeal the local planning authority varied the notice to set the time for compliance as 'six calendar months after 4 May 2012', meaning the period started before the notice took effect).

[75]   Town and Country Planning Act 1990, s 173A(3).

[76]   Circular 03/09, especially Pt B, paras B43, B55.

[77]   Town and Country Planning Act 1990, s 173A(4).

[78]   Town and Country Planning Act 1990, s 180(1).

[79]   *Havering LBC v Secretary of State for the Environment* (1983) 45 P & CR 258; [1983] JPL 240.

is implemented (although it will normally be retrospective, at least in part anyway), the terms of any conditions attaching to it (unless the notice is against a breach of condition), or whether the permission is temporary.[80] No express recognition by the local planning authority of this effect of the permission, or variation of the enforcement notice, is required. It is important when action is taken under an enforcement notice to consider whether any subsequent permissions have affected it.[81] The subsequent permission need not cover precisely the matters covered by the enforcement notice to remove its effect entirely. But to do so it should cover the same operational development or use and the same area of land. The conditions attached to the subsequent planning permission need not be complied with for the enforcement notice to cease to have effect.[82] A failure to so comply may give rise to a separate breach of planning control. An enforcement notice might cease to have effect in part.[83]

6.36   There is a lacuna in the Act. Where a planning permission is granted between the issuance and the service of an enforcement notice, the notice does not lose its effect. The proper course, in these unlikely circumstances, is to appeal the notice if the local planning authority does not withdraw it. The appeal would almost certainly succeed to the extent that the enforcement notice is inconsistent with the permission. Although it ceases to have effect, the notice remains in being and can still be appealed against. If the local planning authority fails to withdraw the enforcement notice it may have costs awarded against it in the appeal for acting unreasonably.[84] Whilst the effects of an enforcement notice will be removed by a subsequent permission, a person served with a notice should not fail to appeal because a planning application is pending and it is believed likely to succeed.

6.37   The enforcement notice only ceases to have effect from the date of the planning permission. Criminal liability for an earlier failure to comply with the notice is not affected.[85] However, the local planning authority would have to consider whether it was in the public interest to prosecute for development which was now acceptable in planning terms. Any sentence is likely to be low.[86]

EFFECT ON SUBSEQUENT DEVELOPMENT

6.38   The enforcement notice is not discharged by compliance with its requirements.[87] It runs with the land and the use of the land enforced against must be discontinued permanently unless planning permission is obtained or is no longer required.[88] The enforcement notice will apply to the reinstating or restoration of buildings or works which have been required to be removed or altered.[89] These

---

[80]   A temporary permission means that the enforcement notice ceases to have effect permanently. A breach following the expiry of the temporary permission would have to be addressed by a fresh notice: *Cresswell v Pearson* (1998) 75 P & CR 404.

[81]   For an example of insufficient care being taken, see *R (Rapose) v Wandsworth London Borough Council* [2010] EWHC 3126 (Admin); [2011] JPL 600.

[82]   *London Borough of Havering v Secretary of State for the Environment* [1983] JPL 240.

[83]   *R v Chichester Justices, ex p Chichester DC* (1990) 60 P & CR 342.

[84]   *R v Secretary of State for the Environment ex p Three Rivers District Council* [1983] JPL 730.

[85]   Town and Country Planning Act 1990, s 180(3).

[86]   *R v Newland* (1987) 54 P & CR 222.

[87]   Town and Country Planning Act 1990, s 181(1).

[88]   Town and Country Planning Act 1990, s 181(2).

[89]   Town and Country Planning Act 1990, s 181(3).

provisions are designed to ensure that a developer cannot comply with the enforcement notice and then restore his development, leaving the local planning authority to start the enforcement process again. Whether the new use or operational development is covered by the enforcement notice must be carefully considered.

ENFORCEMENT ON CROWN LAND

6.39   The Crown is not bound by a statute unless it is mentioned either expressly or by necessary implication. In *Lord Advocate v Dumbarton District Council.*[90] the Ministry of Defence proceeded to cone off one mile of a carriageway a public road for the storage of portable workmen's cabins and building materials whilst improving the perimeter fence of the Faslane submarine base. The House of Lords held that the Crown was not bound by the Town and Country Planning (Scotland) Act 1972 and so the enforcement and stop notices served by the local authority had no application. The same position remained in England and Wales until changes made by the Planning and Compulsory Purchase Act 2004 were brought into force in 2006. The immunity of the Crown from planning control did not extend to other persons on Crown land who were not acting on its behalf. Prior to 2006, 'special enforcement notices' could be issued in respect of such breaches if consent was given by the Crown.

6.40   Crown land means land in which there is a Crown interest or a Duchy interest. A Crown interest is:[91]

(a)   an interest belonging to Her Majesty in right of the Crown or in right of Her private estates;

(b)   an interest belonging to a government department or held in trust for Her Majesty for the purposes of a government department; or

(c)   such other interest as the Secretary of State specifies by order[92]

A Duchy interest means an interest belonging to Her Majesty in right of the Duchy of Lancaster or belonging to the Duchy of Cornwall. This includes military bases, many government offices, roads owned by the Highways Agency (eg motorways), but not land owned by local government.

6.41   The Planning and Compulsory Purchase Act 2004 amended the Crown land provisions of the 1990 Act. Subject to exceptions, the Town and Country Planning Act 1990 bound the Crown.[93] Local planning authorities are able to serve notices and make orders in relation to Crown land,[94] but they need the consent of the appropriate authority for any other step for the purpose of enforcement in relation to Crown land (ie in connection with enforcement) including to enter land, bring proceedings or make applications.[95] The appropriate authority is the part of the Crown or government responsible for managing that particular Crown land.[96] The Crown cannot be guilty

---

[90]   [1990] 2 AC 580.
[91]   Town and Country Planning Act 1990, s 293(1).
[92]   This has been used to extend Crown interest to the Houses of Parliament: Planning (Application to the Houses of Parliament) Order 2006.
[93]   Town and Country Planning Act 1990, s 292A.
[94]   Town and Country Planning Act 1990, s 296A(2), (6).
[95]   Town and Country Planning Act 1990, s 296A(2), (6).
[96]   The relevant authorities are listed in Town and Country Planning Act 1990, s 293.

of an offence under the Town and Country Planning Act 1990.[97] Special provisions apply to breaches of planning control by the Crown in the Second World War but the likelihood of these arising is little more than theoretical.[98]

ENFORCEMENT NOTICES ISSUE

6.42   The Secretary of State may issue enforcement notices with the same effect as an enforcement notice issued by a local planning authority (s 182(1)):

> 'If it appears to the Secretary of State to be expedient that an enforcement notice should be issued in respect of any land, he may issue such a notice.'

Unlike local planning authority notices, the expediency test is not expressly based on the development plan and other material considerations. Additionally, the appearance of a breach of planning control is not expressly required.[99] In practice the test for issuing is the same. An enforcement notice could not rationally be issued without considering whether there was a breach of planning control and whether planning permission would be granted for the development. The Secretary of State must consult with the relevant local planning authority before issuing the notice.[100] An enforcement notice issued by the Secretary of State shall have the same effect as a notice issued by the local planning authority.[101] The enforcement provisions are, with limited exceptions, the same. Additionally the right of appeal to the Secretary of State remains.

'OLD' ENFORCEMENT NOTICES

6.43   Enforcement notices issued under repealed provisions, such as the Town and Country Planning Act 1971, continue to have effect and breaches can be prosecuted under the current legislation.[102]

---

[97]   Town and Country Planning Act 1990, s 296A(1).
[98]   Town and Country Planning Act 1990, s 302.
[99]   Cf Town and Country Planning Act 1990, s 172(1).
[100] Town and Country Planning Act 1990, s 182(2).
[101] Town and Country Planning Act 1990, s 182(3).
[102] Planning (Consequential Provisions) Act 1990, s 2; *Reigate and Banstead Borough Council v Drift Bridge Garage Limited* [1994] JPL B133 (unreported).

Chapter 7

Appeal against an Enforcement Notice

THE RIGHT TO APPEAL

7.01   There is a right of appeal to the Secretary of State or Welsh Ministers against an enforcement notice. An appeal is on specified grounds, which allow the Minister to determine the merits of the notice and grant planning permission for the breach of planning control if that is considered appropriate. The appeal is decided by the minister, or an inspector appointed by him, following either an inquiry, an 'informal' hearing or the consideration of written representations. There is an ability to appeal this decision in the High Court on the basis of an error of law.

7.02   Some 3,000 to 3,500 enforcement notice appeals are made each year in England. Of the appeals determined, notices are upheld in around 42 per cent of cases, varied in 31 per cent to 35 per cent of the time and quashed in 25 per cent of cases.[1] Variations will cover a range of situations from tidying up of the notice (which does not benefit the appellant), to longer compliance periods and cases where significant benefits are achieved by the appellant.

Who may appeal

7.03   A person with an interest in the subject land or a 'relevant occupier' are entitled to appeal, even if they have not been served with an enforcement notice (s 174(1)). A relevant occupier is a person occupying the land under a licence when the enforcement notice is issued and when the appeal is brought.[2] The licence may be oral or in writing. This provision extends tenants' rights of appeal to licensees. Even though occupiers must be served they only have a right of appeal if they have an interest in land or are a relevant occupier. Trespassers do not have a right to appeal.[3]

7.04   A person who was mistakenly served does not have a right of appeal, as the mere fact of service does not attach legal liabilities to them. However, if the notice is not complied with, local planning authorities usually consider bringing criminal proceedings against those served in the event of non-compliance with the notice. So a person wrongly served should aim to resolve the issue with the local planning authority. In the absence of agreement, the option would be to appeal to seek a ruling that no appeal can be brought because the person should not have been served or to bring judicial review proceedings of the decision to serve a copy of the notice on that person (rather than strictly a challenge to the validity of the notice itself).

---

[1]   Planning Inspectorate Statistical Report: England 2011/12.
[2]   Town and Country Planning Act 1990, s 174(6).
[3]   *R v Secretary of State for the Environment, ex p Davis* [1989] 3 PLR 73.

The time for appeal

7.05   The appeal must be made in writing to the Secretary of State or Welsh Ministers *before* the date on which the notice is to take effect.[4] If the notice of appeal is sent in a properly addressed and pre-paid letter such that in the ordinary course of post it should be delivered in time or by electronic communications within that period then if it then arrives late, it is allowed.[5] The address for appeals in England is: The Planning Inspectorate (PINS AA 4), PO Box 326, Bristol BS99 7XF. The appeal can be faxed to the Inspectorate's office in Bristol on 0117 987 8782 or 0117 987 8679. The address for appeals in Wales is: The Planning Inspectorate, Crown Buildings, Cathays Park, Cardiff CF10 3NQ and can be faxed on 029 2082 5150. Appeals may also be submitted via the Planning Portal website.[6] The appeal form is filled in online and copies of documents can be attached electronically. The Minister has no discretion to accept a late appeal.

Grounds of appeal

7.06   Appeals can be brought on any number of the seven grounds in s 174(2). They are commonly referred to by the letters of their sub-paragraphs:

> '(a) that, in respect of any breach of planning control which may be constituted by the matters stated in the notice, planning permission ought to be granted or, as the case may be, the condition or limitation concerned ought to be discharged;'

This is effectively an application for planning permission and is judged on the same grounds as a conventional application. It will be decided in accordance with the development plan unless other material considerations indicate otherwise.[7]

> '(b) that those matters have not occurred;'

Ground (b) relates to the factual allegation made in the notice. This will encompass what is physically said to have happened and how it is described. For example, if the allegation is that mineral extraction has taken place, an appellant might want to contend that the digging was not mineral extraction but was the construction of a lake.

> '(c) that those matters (if they occurred) do not constitute a breach of planning control;'

This ground includes claims that the matters do not constitute operational development or a material change of use (including having the benefit of the Use Classes Order), did not need planning permission under s 57, that they are authorised by an planning permission granted on application or under the General Permitted Development Order 1995, or a deemed planning permission.

> '(d) that, at the date when the notice was issued, no enforcement action could be taken in respect of any breach of planning control which may be constituted by those matters;'

---

[4]   Town and Country Planning Act 1990, s 174(3)(a).
[5]   Town and Country Planning Act 1990, s 174(3)(b), (c).
[6]   www.planningportal.gov.uk
[7]   Town and Country Planning Act 1990, s 177(2); Planning and Compulsory Purchase Act 2004, s 38(6).

This ground is that the time limits in s 171B apply to prevent enforcement action and the local planning authority do not have the benefit of a planning enforcement order under which they can issue a late enforcement notice.[8] However, it must be read as 'no enforcement notice can be issued' because a breach of condition notice can be served anytime if an enforcement notice is in effect for that breach.[9] A further enforcement notice may only be served if the breach is within the original time limit or less than four years after an earlier enforcement notice was issued.

'(e) that copies of the enforcement notice were not served as required by section 172;'

Copies of the notice have to be served on owners and occupiers and on any other person having an interest in the land which the authority believes will be materially affected by the notice.[10]

If a person required to be served was not served, the Secretary of State must quash the notice unless neither the appellant nor the person required to be served has been substantially prejudiced by the failure to serve.[11] Where there is no substantial prejudice the Secretary of State has a discretion whether to quash. A good test of substantial prejudice is whether the case against the enforcement notice at appeal or in other possible proceedings could have been materially strengthened if that person had been served and so known of the notice.

Ground (e) tends to be of limited utility as an appellant must know of the notice, whether or not it has been correctly served. A failure to serve another person can be corrected by the planning authority, if necessary by the issue of a fresh notice.

'(f) that the steps required by the notice to be taken, or the activities required by the notice to cease, exceed what is necessary to remedy any breach of planning control which may be constituted by those matters or, as the case may be, to remedy any injury to amenity which has been caused by any such breach;'

The ground of appeal may be that the requirements restrict activities which are lawful, or alternatively that the breach or injury to amenity can be remedied by other means. It is necessary to identify whether the particular requirement in the notice is to remedy a breach of control or injury to amenity. In *Wyatt Bros (Oxford) Ltd v Secretary of State for the Environment, Transport and the Regions*[12] the Court of Appeal held that where the steps required by the enforcement notice were all for the purpose of remedying the breach of planning control, it was not possible to appeal on the ground that the steps or activities exceeded what was necessary to remedy an injury to amenity. The merits of not requiring the reversal of the breach of planning control should be tested on a ground (a) appeal.

'(g) that any period specified in the notice in accordance with section 173(9) falls short of what should reasonably be allowed.'

---

[8]   Time limits and planning enforcement orders are discussed in Chapter 3 above.
[9]   Town and Country Planning Act 1990, s 171B(4)(a).
[10] Town and Country Planning Act 1990, s 172(2).
[11] Town and Country Planning Act 1990, s 176(5).
[12] [2001] EWCA Civ 1560, [2002] PLCR 18 at paras 26–28 per Kennedy LJ. The reasoning was followed in *Mata v Secretary of State for Communities and Local Government* [2012] EWHC 3473 (Admin).

The period specified will not necessarily be the minimum in which it is possible to cease the activity or take the steps required. Often time will be given to make alternative arrangements, for example to find another site or for an orderly wind-down of the offending business. Conversely there may be cases where the harm caused is so great that an immediate cessation is required.

7.07 Even if no ground (a) appeal is brought, the 1991 provisions deemed that an application for planning permission was made in any enforcement notice appeal for the matters stated in the enforcement notice as constituting a breach of planning control. This would include the discharge of a condition or limitation. The result was that there could simultaneously be a ground (a) appeal and a deemed planning application, or a deemed planning application when the appellant had chosen not to make a ground (a) appeal. Amendments introduced by the Localism Act 2011 mean that in England a deemed application only arises if a ground (a) appeal is raised in the notice of appeal or subsequent statement.[13] Even if the ground (a) appeal is in respect of part of the alleged breach, the deemed application would still arise for the entirety of the matters in the enforcement notice. In Wales a deemed planning application still arises on all enforcement notice appeals. In practice, for Welsh cases an appeal under ground (a) should be brought if permission is sought as this allows the issues to be more clearly identified.

7.08 There is no discernable, let alone good, reason why there should be a deemed application at all. The grant of planning permission can be raised expressly on a ground (a) appeal and does not need to arise twice.

7.09 A concern has been that enforcement notice appeals have sought planning permission when a planning application has failed or conversely that a planning application has been made whilst an enforcement notice has been issued. This can lead to additional effort or delay to a justified enforcement notice. Amendments introduced by the Localism Act 2011 limit the circumstances (in England) in which planning applications and enforcement appeals on ground (a) can run simultaneously:

- A ground (a) appeal cannot be made if the enforcement notice was issued after the making of a related application for planning permission but 'before the end of the period applicable under section 78(2) in the case of that application'. A planning permission is 'related to an enforcement notice if granting planning permission for the development would involve granting planning permission in respect of the matters specified in the enforcement notice as constituting a breach of planning control'.[14] The section 78(2) period is the time to decide the application before a right of appeal for non-determination arises (s 174(2A));

- A local planning authority *may* decline to determine a planning application if approving the application would involve granting planning permission for the whole or part of any matters specified in a pre-existing enforcement notice as a breach of planning control (s 70C(1)). A 'pre-existing enforcement notice' is an enforcement notice issued before the application was received by the local planning authority.[15]

---

[13] Town and Country Planning Act 1990, s 177(1C), (5). This change only has effect for notices issued on or after 6 April 2012: Localism Act 2011 (Commencement No 4 and Transitional, Transitory and Saving Provisions) Order 2012, Art 13(2).
[14] Town and Country Planning Act 1990, s 174(2B).
[15] Town and Country Planning Act 1990, s 70C(2).

7.10 *Appeal against an Enforcement Notice*

7.10   Periods for the determination of planning applications are set out in the Town and Country Planning (Development Management Procedure) (England) Order 2010:

- 16 weeks from the receipt of the application for development accompanied by an Environmental Statement;

- 13 weeks for defined major development; and

- eight weeks for any other development.[16]

Under s 78(2) the applicant and the local planning authority may agree in writing to extend the time limits. The restriction on a ground (a) appeal would appear to be applied even if the application is determined before the end of the period and an enforcement notice issued within the period. It may be debatable whether the prohibition on making a ground (a) appeal applies if the enforcement notice is issued in any agreed extension period. The consequence is that a ground (a) can be pursued if the enforcement notice is issued after the end of the non-determination period, including if the planning application has been unsuccessfully appealed.

7.11   For the purposes of declining to consider a planning application, the pre-existing enforcement notice would appear to have to still be in existence, without having been withdrawn or quashed. Section 70C(1) refers to 'the land to which a pre-existing enforcement notice relates', suggesting that the notice must still be in existence. The authority is given a discretion not to determine the application, so it must act reasonably and with regard to relevant considerations. Good reasons not to decline to consider the application would include a change in circumstances, the unlawful development could be acceptable if planning permission were granted subject to conditions, or the planning application related only to a part of the enforcement notice subject matter which might be acceptable. If the authority does decline to consider the application then the applicant has no right of appeal to the Secretary of State but instead can only challenge the decision by judicial review.

7.12   A fee is charged for a ground (a) appeal or deemed planning application. This fee does not have to be submitted with the appeal but will be asked for by the Secretary of State or Welsh Ministers during the appeal process. If the fee is not paid within the time period requested then the ground (a) appeal and the deemed application shall lapse.[17] The fee is charged for each appellant raising ground (a), so in circumstances where there could be multiple appellants it is common for only one appellant to pursue a ground (a) appeal. This election may be made when the fee is demanded: so several appellants could all identify ground (a) in their notices of appeal but then one would choose to submit the fee.

Nullity

7.13   If the enforcement is so defective as to be a nullity and so of no legal effect (such as failing to include a date for compliance: see Chapter 1), then it cannot be appealed against.[18] If on an appeal the Minister considers the notice to be a nullity

---

[16]   Town and Country Planning (Development Management Procedure) (England) Order 2010, Art 29.

[17]   Town and Country Planning Act 1990, s 177(5A).

[18]   *Rhymney Valley District Council v Secretary of State for Wales* [1985] JPL 27. The possibility that a notice may be a nullity is recognised in the fees regulations which provide for the return of any fee paid in that eventuality.

then he will state that opinion and take no further steps on the appeal. If a potential appellant considers that the enforcement notice is a nullity then the prudent course is to appeal and raise nullity in the appeal. The nullity challenge should be raised in a letter enclosed with the appeal. If that argument fails, the appellant can then rely on the grounds of appeal. However, there is authority that a challenge to the lawfulness of a notice (or the decision to issue a notice) which falls short of a nullity cannot be raised on appeal to the Minister and has to be taken by judicial review.[19] This may be unlawful consideration of expediency or improper purpose.

HOW TO APPEAL

Who determines appeals?

7.14   Appeals are determined by the Secretary of State or Welsh Ministers (in practice a minister or official) or by an inspector. An appeal determined by an inspector is called a transferred appeal, transferred under Sch 6 of the Act. All enforcement notice appeals are transferred except appeals by statutory undertakers in respect of their operational land or land they hold or propose to hold for their undertaking (section 266 land).[20] However, the Minister may direct that a particular appeal is determined by him or her.[21] This is known as a recovered appeal and tends to occur only in the most important cases. Where an appeal is to be determined by the Minister, an Inspector will be appointed. The Inspector will conduct any hearing or inquiry and report in writing to the Minister. The appeal will then be determined by the Minister or an official.

How appeals are determined

7.15   An Enforcement Notice appeal is dealt with in one of three ways:

(a) by public local inquiry;

(b) by informal hearing;

(c) by written representations.

7.16   A public local inquiry ('inquiry') is held by an inspector appointed by the Secretary of State or Welsh Ministers at a location near the subject land. This will usually be the local planning authority's offices, but may be at a village hall or, for long-running inquiries, hotels or dedicated conference facilities. The appellant and the local planning authority will give evidence orally (though some may be taken as read) and make submissions. Other persons, such as local residents or other public authorities, ('third parties') may also present their cases with witnesses and submissions. The public and press may attend. An informal hearing takes place between the appellant, the local planning authority and any other persons in front of a Planning Inspector. This may be adjourned to continue discussion at the site.

---

[19]   *R v Wicks* [1998] AC 92 (strictly obiter as this concerned challenge in criminal proceedings), *Britannia Assets (UK) Ltd v Secretary of State for Communities and Local Government* [2011] EWHC 1908 (Admin).

[20]   Town and Country Planning (Determination of Appeals by Appointed Persons) (Prescribed Classes) Regulations 1997, reg 4.

[21]   Town and Country Planning Act 1990, Sch 6, para 1(2).

7.17 *Appeal against an Enforcement Notice*

Determination by written representations is done on the basis of written submissions by the appellant, local planning authority and third parties. These will be considered by an Inspector. In all cases, the site will be visited by the Inspector. This may be unaccompanied, in a written representations case if the site can be seen adequately from the highway. If the Inspector needs to enter private property, or a party wants to point out something particular and this is agreed, the site visit will be accompanied. Site visits on hearings and inquiries are accompanied. A representative of the appellant (or the appellant themselves) and a representative of the local planning authority will attend. An accompanied site visit is not a further opportunity to argue the case (this is distinct from adjournment of a hearing to the site, where further discussion is expected). Legal representatives do not usually attend site visits but should always get a report from their party's representative on what had happened.

Choosing an inquiry, informal hearing or written representations

7.17 In Wales the appellant and the local planning authority are each entitled to appear before a person appointed by the Welsh Ministers, that is, at an inquiry or hearing.[22] If both agree, the appeal can be dealt with by way of written representations. The right to an oral hearing was withdrawn in England in amendments made by the Planning Act 2008. Section 175(3A) of the 1990 Act removes the right to a hearing. By s 319A of the 1990 Act, the Secretary of State shall decide whether a local inquiry, hearing or written representations are the most appropriate. This decision is made within seven working days from the receipt of a valid appeal[23] and is in practice made by the Planning Inspectorate. Criteria for determining the mode of appeal have to be published[24] and for enforcement appeals are contained in *Procedural Guidance: Enforcement appeals and determination of appeal procedure* PINS 02/2009.

7.18 The Secretary of State considers that if there is dispute about relevant facts, particularly under grounds (c) (whether a breach of planning control) and (d) (time limits), an inquiry is generally essential.[25] A hearing may also be inappropriate if many members of the public are likely to be present, if the appeal raises complicated matters of policy, if there are likely to be substantial legal issues raised, or if there is a likelihood that formal cross-examination will be needed to test the opposing cases. An informal hearing may be more appropriate than an inquiry for disputes about the planning merits or the period for compliance. A dispute on evidential facts or most legal grounds in s 174(2) will make an informal hearing inappropriate.[26] The mode of determination can be changed, for example, following further representations by the parties to the Planning Inspectorate or if the Inspector decides that the appeal cannot properly be dealt with by that method. An example of the latter situation would be if it becomes apparent at a hearing that cross-examination of witnesses is required.

7.19 In recent years, 60–73 per cent of enforcement notice appeals have been determined by written representations, 12–14 per cent by hearing and 15–26 per cent by inquiry.[27]

---

[22] Town and Country Planning Act 1990, s 175(3).
[23] Town and Country Planning (Determination of Appeal Procedure) (Prescribed Period) (England) Regulations 2009, reg 2.
[24] Town and Country Planning Act 1990, s 319A(6).
[25] Circular 10/97 Annex 2, para 2.37.
[26] Circular 10/97 Annex 2, para 2.37.
[27] Planning Inspectorate Statistical Report: England 2011/12. The figures are taken for the last three years.

The notice of appeal

7.20   There is no prescribed form for the notice, but standard forms are provided by the Planning Inspectorate. Different forms are used in England and Wales. In Wales, appeals can be made in English or Welsh. An explanatory booklet, 'Making your appeal: How to complete your enforcement appeal form', provides assistance on completing the form. A copy can be obtained from the local planning authority or via the Planning Portal website.[28] It is not obligatory to use the appeal form – the statutory requirement is that the appeal is in writing – but it is normal practice to do so. A separate form is used for each enforcement notice and each appellant. A copy of the relevant enforcement notice should be sent with each appeal form.

Statement of appeal

7.21   An appellant is required to produce:[29]

'a statement in writing—

(i)   specifying the grounds on which he is appealing against the notice; and

(ii) setting out briefly the facts on which he proposes to rely in support of each of those grounds'.

If the statement is not included with the appeal, then it shall be delivered to the Secretary of State 'not later than 14 days from the date on which the Secretary of State sends him a notice requiring him to do so'. The appeal may be dismissed if the information is not provided in this time.[30] The details required by the standard appeal form will provide the information required by this provision. The existence of the further time also shows that a failure to provide this information with the notice of appeal does not render the appeal invalid. In *Howard v Secretary of State for the Environment*,[31] an enforcement notice appeal was validly made by a letter that said that it was a formal notice of appeal and did not identify any grounds or facts relied upon. A similarly pragmatic approach was taken by the Court of Appeal in *R (McKay) v First Secretary of State*,[32] that a notice of appeal was valid where the appellant had erroneously referred to an enforcement notice that had been withdrawn and the Planning Inspectorate was aware that he had intended to refer to a new enforcement notice.

Filling in the form

7.22   The Planning Inspectorate have produced guides to completing the enforcement notice appeal form, which is available on the Planning Portal website for England and Wales.

Section A: appellant's details
Fill in the appellant's name, address and other details as required.

---

[28]   www.planningportal.gov.uk
[29]   Town and Country Planning (Enforcement Notices and Appeals) (England) Regulations 2002, reg 6. Sub-paragraph (i) of the requirement is also in s 174(4) of the Town and Country Planning Act 1990.
[30]   Town and Country Planning Act 1990, s 176(3)(a).
[31]   [1975] QB 235, CA.
[32]   [2005] EWCA Civ 774, [2005] 1 P & CR 19.

Section B: agent details
Fill in the details of any agent or professional representative who is running the appeal. The agent will be responsible for communicating with the Inspectorate and other parties.

Section C: details of the appeal
The enforcement notice should be identified with the date of issue, issuing local planning authority and the date it takes effect. If several enforcement notices were issued on the same day on the same land, the appellant should try to describe the particular notice, either by any reference given to it (eg notice A) or by the description of the land or breach. The grounds on which the appeal is brought (under s 174(2)) should be marked in this section.

Section D: appeal site
The full address and National Grid Reference (from an Ordnance Survey map) of the subject land should be provided. Questions are asked about any health and safety issues which might arise on a site visit (such as need for boots, hard hats, any particular dangers, use of ladders, any need to view from a height[33] and wheelchair accessibility). The appellant's interest in the land or status as a relevant occupier should be stated.

Section E: grounds and facts
The grounds of appeal being pursued should be marked and brief submissions set out. The Planning Inspectorate say that the development should be discussed with the local planning authority before the appeal is submitted to identify the key areas of contention for the appeal.[34] However the reasons for issuing the notice should make clear what it contentious. Any draft planning obligation which is available should be sent with the appeal form. The Inspectorate encourage the submission of evidence with the appeal form. It may be sensible to do this in appeals likely to be dealt with by written representations or a hearing, as the ability of third parties in particular to comment on later representations is limited.

Section F: choice of procedure
The appellant should indicate whether the written representations, hearing or inquiry procedure is preferred. Since there is no right to be heard in England, the appellant should explain, by reference to the published criteria, why the preferred procedure should be adopted. An estimate for the length of any inquiry should be given. Hearings ought not to last more than one day in any event. The appellant should also say whether the whole site can be seen clearly from the road or other public land. The question is whether the Inspector can see everything he or she ought to see without going onto private land (and in particular whether the Inspector will need to go inside buildings). If not, the Inspector will need to be accompanied by representatives of the appellant and the local planning authority whilst entering the appellant's land (and possibly that of third parties).

Section G: the fee
This section of the form needs amendment in England as the entire fee is payable to the local planning authority.

---

[33]   One appeal was compromised where the Inspector had a fear of heights so did not view the site from all the points which were required.
[34]   *Making your appeal – How to complete your enforcement appeal form – England*, p 6.

Section H: other appeals
The reference numbers of any related appeals which have not yet been decided should be included. This is to see if the cases can be determined together, although this will often not be possible if appeals are submitted at different times.

Section I: signature and date
The form should be signed. This can be done by the appellant or his agent named on the form. It should also be dated, which may assist if issues arise as to when the form should have been received.

Environmental impact assessment
The local planning authority may have to consider whether environmental impact assessment would be required for any planning permission granted on an enforcement notice appeal prior to the issue of the notice. See Chapter 10.

Fees

7.23   A fee is payable for the Secretary of State or Welsh Ministers to consider a ground (a) appeal or deemed planning permission application. The appellant will be notified of the amount due by the Planning Inspectorate. In England the fees are set out in the Town and Country Planning (Fees for Applications, Deemed Applications, Requests and Site Visits) (England) Regulations 2012 ('the 2012 Fees Regulations')[35] and in Wales they are contained in the Town and Country Planning (Fees for Applications and Deemed Applications) Regulations 1989 ('the 1989 Fees Regulations').[36] Both sets of regulations set out fees for planning applications which are based on the size of the development and the type of use. Regulation 10 in each set deals with the fees for deemed applications in enforcement appeals which double the fees due on a planning application for the development as stated in the enforcement notice.[37] The principal difference between the two jurisdictions is that the whole sum is payable to the local planning authority in England for appeals against enforcement notices which had been issued from 22 November 2012.[38] Wales continues the practice of splitting the doubled fee: half payable to the Inspectorate and half to the local planning authority.[39]

7.24   Where the fee varies according to the site area, the Secretary of State or Welsh Ministers will calculate the fee according to the actual area occupied by the allegedly unlawful development. However, no fee is payable for a deemed application if a planning application for the development subject to the enforcement notice:

(a)   was made and not determined by the local planning authority before the notice was issued; or

(b)   was refused by the planning authority and an appeal made to the Secretary of State before the notice took effect but the appeal had not been determined before the notice was issued.[40]

---

[35]   SI 2012/2920.
[36]   SI 1989/193.
[37]   2012 Fees Regulations, Sch 1, para 1(4); in different terms, see 1989 Fees Regulations, Sch 1, para 9.
[38]   2012 Fees Regulations, reg 10(3), (5).
[39]   1989 Fees Regulations, reg 10(3).
[40]   2012 Fees Regulations, reg 10(7); 1989 Fees Regulations, reg 10(5).

7.25 *Appeal against an Enforcement Notice*

The fee is payable by each person who has appealed.[41] So, seven appellants would each have to pay a fee. Persons served with an enforcement notice should, if possible, agree for only one person to appeal on ground (a) and the deemed application, with the financial and other backing of the remaining persons served.

7.25 A separate fee is payable for each enforcement notice. Where one notice alleges a number of different activities, the fee payable is the highest amount calculated. If the fee is not paid during the period specified by the Secretary of State, the planning permission ground of appeal lapses.[42] The Secretary of State cannot accept fees paid after the specified period, although he may extend the period before it expires. The fee is repaid if the Secretary of State:[43]

(a) declines jurisdiction on the appeal on the grounds that the enforcement notice does not comply with s 172;

(b) dismisses the appeal on the basis that the appellant has failed to give the information required by s 174(4);[44]

(c) allows the appeal because the local planning authority failed to provide the information or submissions required by s 175(1)(a), (b), (d) and the relevant Enforcement Notices and Appeals Regulations; or

(d) decides that the enforcement notice is a nullity.[45]

If the local planning authority withdraws the enforcement notice before it takes effect, the fee is repayable.[46] In all these circumstances the Secretary of State has not been able to determine the merits of the appeal.

7.26 The fee is also refunded if the appeal is withdrawn at least 21 days before the inquiry date or, for written representations, the site visit date.[47] If the Secretary of State allows the appeal:

(a) on any of grounds (b) to (e) (that there was no actionable breach of planning control or the enforcement notice was not properly served); or

(b) because the notice is invalid, or it contains an informality, defect or error which cannot be corrected by the Secretary of State under s 176(1),

the fee is refundable.[48]

7.27 A partial refund is obtained if the notice is varied (otherwise than by planning permission in the appeal) and the fee due for the matters in the varied notice is less than that paid.[49] Guidance on the Fees Regulations is provided in England in

---

[41] 2012 Fees Regulations, reg 10(4); 1989 Fees Regulations, reg 10(3)(a).
[42] Town and Country Planning Act 1990, s 177(5A).
[43] 2012 Fees Regulations, reg 10(8); 1989 Fees Regulations, reg 10(8).
[44] Provision of grounds of appeal and brief facts.
[45] 2012 Fees Regulations, reg 10(12); 1989 Fees Regulations, reg 10(11).
[46] 2012 Fees Regulations, reg 10(12); 1989 Fees Regulations, reg 10(11).
[47] 2012 Fees Regulations, reg 10(9); 1989 Fees Regulations, reg 10(9).
[48] 2012 Fees Regulations, reg 10(13); 1989 Fees Regulations, reg 10(13). Unless the Minister issues a lawful development certificate or, in Wales, the appeal concerns the use of land as a caravan site.
[49] 2012 Fees Regulations, reg 10(14); 1989 Fees Regulations, reg 10(14).

Circular 04/08 *Planning-related fees*[50] and in Wales by Welsh Office Circular 73/92 *The Town and Country Planning (Fees for Applications and Deemed Applications) (Amendment) (No 2) Regulations 1992.*

THE MINISTER'S ACTIONS ON RECEIVING THE APPEAL

7.28   On receiving the appeal, the Minister will check that it is validly made (in practice this is done by the Planning Inspectorate). If the Minister refuses to accept an appeal, this decision can be challenged by judicial review.The Secretary of State or Welsh Ministers will send the appeal form to the local planning authority. Formally, the Minister's duty to notify the authority arises when the regulation 6 statement is received.[51] The authority is told that an appeal has been made and is sent the appeal along with the regulation 6 statement of the grounds. In practice that is the appeal form. Foreshadowing the approach to security matters, the Minister is not obliged to:[52]

> 'disclose information as to national security or the measures taken or to be taken to ensure the security of any premises or property where, in the Secretary of State's opinion, public disclosure of that information would be contrary to the national interest.'

The local planning authority is then required to provide a certified copy of the enforcement notice and the names and addresses of those served to the Secretary of State. It must comply within 14 days of notification of the appeal.[53] If the local planning authority fails to comply, the Secretary of State or Welsh Ministers may quash the enforcement notice.[54] This is very rarely done and the Minister will give the authority seven days' notice of the intention to quash, giving it time to provide the information or explain itself.[55]

PREPARING FOR AN INQUIRY, HEARING OR WRITTEN REPRESENTATIONS

7.29   Procedural requirements for inquiries are contained in the national Enforcement Notices and Appeals Regulations and the relevant procedural rules and regulations. These provisions are:

(a) for appeals determined by written representations, the Town and Country Planning (Enforcement) (Written Representations Procedure) (England) Regulations 2002 ('the Written Representations Regulations') and the Town and Country Planning (Enforcement) (Written Representations Procedure) (Wales) Regulations 2003 ('the Welsh Written Representations Regulations');

---

[50]   This circular has not been revoked or replaced notwithstanding publication of the 2012 Fees Regulations.

[51]   Enforcement Notice and Appeals Regulations, reg 7(1); Welsh Enforcement Notice and Appeals Regulations, reg 6(1).

[52]   Enforcement Notice and Appeals Regulations, reg 7(2); Welsh Enforcement Notice and Appeals Regulations, reg 6(2).

[53]   Town and Country Planning Act 1990, s 175(1)(d); Enforcement Notices and Appeals Regulations, reg 8; Welsh Enforcement Notice and Appeals Regulations, reg 7.

[54]   Town and Country Planning Act 1990, s 176(3)(b).

[55]   Circular 10/97 Annex 4, para 2.25.

(b)   for hearings, the Town and Country Planning (Enforcement) (Hearings Procedure) (England) Rules 2002 ('the Hearings Rules'); the Town and Country Planning (Enforcement) (Hearings Procedure) (Wales) Rules 2003 ('the Welsh Hearings Rules');

(c)   for appeals determined by an inspector following an inquiry, the Town and Country Planning (Enforcement) (Determination by Inspectors) (Inquiries Procedure) (England) Rules 2002 ('the Inspectors Inquiries Rules') and the Town and Country Planning (Enforcement) (Inquiries Procedure) (Determination by Inspectors) (Wales) Rules 2003 ('the Welsh Inspectors Inquiries Rules'); and

(d)   for appeals retained by or recovered by the Minister and determined following an inquiry, the Town and Country Planning (Enforcement) (Inquiries Procedure) (England) Rules 2002 ('the Inquiries Rules'); the Town and Country Planning (Enforcement) (Inquiries Procedure) (Wales) Rules 2003 ('the Welsh Inquiries Rules').

Where the rule or regulation number is the same in England and Wales, the footnotes refer to the legislation collectively, for example the English and Welsh Inquiries Rules.

PRELIMINARY STAGES OF AN APPEAL

7.30   The initial stages of an enforcement notice appeal have similar elements whichever mode of determination is adopted, so these can be considered together. Documents may be sent electronically or in hard copy, and multiple copies are therefore only required for paper copies.

The starting date

7.31   Shortly after an appeal is received, the Secretary of State or Welsh Ministers will set a 'starting date', which is the date from which various obligations to produce submissions run. Whilst the regulations refer to the 'starting date', the point is in practice known as the 'start date'. The starting date is the later of:[56]

(a)   the date that the Secretary of State gives notice under reg 10 of the Enforcement Notices and Appeals Regulations that he has all the documents necessary to entertain the appeal; or

(b)   the date that notice is given that the appeal would be dealt with by a hearing or inquiry.[57]

Notice of the starting date, the reference number of the appeal, the Minister's address for communications about the appeal and the grounds of appeal is to be given by the Minister as soon as practicable after receipt of the written notice of appeal.[58]

---

[56]   Enforcement Notices and Appeals Regulations, reg 9(3). The Welsh provisions are similar: Welsh Enforcement Notices and Appeals Regulations, reg 8(3).

[57]   This is formal notice under r 4 of the Hearings Rules, r 4 of the Inspectors Inquiries Rules or r 4 of the Inquiries Rules.

[58]   English and Welsh Written Representations Regulations, reg 4; English and Welsh Hearings Rules, r 4(1), English and Welsh Inquiries Rules, r 4(1); English and Welsh Inspectors Inquiries Rules, r 4(1).

Notice to interested parties

7.32   Within two weeks of the starting date, the local planning authority shall give written notice of the appeal to:[59]

(a) any person who has been served with a copy of the enforcement notice;

(b) any 'occupier of property in the locality in which the land to which the enforcement notice relates is situated'. The reference to the locality includes land outside the enforcement notice site and so provides for neighbour notification; and

(c) any other person who in the authority's opinion is affected by the breach of planning control.

7.33   The notice shall contain:

(a) the name of the appellant and the address of the land to which the appeal relates;

(b) the starting date;

(c) the reference number allocated to the appeal;

(d) a description of the alleged breach of control;

(e) a statement specifying the reasons why it was expedient to issue the notice, the relevant development plan policies and proposals and the precise boundaries of the land;

(f) the ground, or grounds on which the appeal is made;

(g) a statement that representations may be submitted to the Secretary of State (or Welsh Ministers, as approapriate) within six weeks of the starting date and the address to which such representations should be sent;

(h) a statement that those representations will be sent to the appellant and the local planning authority; and

(i) a statement that any such representations will be considered by the Secretary of State/Welsh Ministers when determining the appeal unless that person withdraws them within six weeks of the starting date.

The local planning authority's questionnaire

7.34   The Secretary of State and Welsh Ministers have prepared standard questionnaires for local planning authorities to provide information in enforcement appeals. These are usually accessed and submitted online via the Planning Portal. The questionnaire will ask about the mode of determination of the appeal, whether the appeal fee has been paid, the nature of the notice, any previous applications or appeals, any circumstances which might require consultation with particular persons, environmental impact assessment screening, any relevant local planning policies and any other relevant information, which can include the reports and decisions authorising the enforcement notice. The questionnaire should be sent to the Minister

---

[59]   English and Welsh Written Representations Regulations, reg 5; English and Welsh Hearings Rules, r 4(2); English and Welsh Inquiries Rules, r 4(2); English and Welsh Inspectors Inquiries Rules, r 4(2).

within two weeks of the starting date along with a copy of all the documents referred to in it.[60] This is to be copied to the appellant.

SIX-WEEK STATEMENTS

7.35   Six weeks after the starting date is a critical point in all forms of appeal as it is the main deadline for written submissions. Whilst the timescale is common to all procedures, the purpose, and so the content, of the submissions will vary depending upon the mode of determination. The Enforcement Notice and Appeals Regulations require local planning authorities in all enforcement appeals to provide a written statement within six weeks from the starting point.[61] This statement will indicate the submissions they propose to put forward on the appeal and contain a summary of the authority's response to each of the grounds of appeal raised and say whether they would be prepared to grant planning permission and any conditions that ought to be imposed. If the local planning authority fails to serve a statement or statement of case as required by the Rules and Regulations, the Secretary of State may quash the enforcement notice.[62] If the enforcement notice was issued by the Secretary of State or Welsh Ministers then they must produce a similar statement.[63]

7.36   For *written representations*, the appellant is able to make further representations (supplementing those in the appeal documentation) by the six-week point, but is not required to do so.[64] As appeals have to be dealt with fairly, appellants should try to ensure that new material is with the notice of appeal rather than the six-week statement.

7.37   The local planning authority has to produce its six-week statement under the Enforcement Notice and Appeals Regulations but may also make further written representations under reg 7(4) of the English and Welsh Written Representations Regulations. Those further representations have to include the same matters as the Enforcement Notice and Appeals Regulations statement. The duplication is entirely pointless. An even stranger part of the regulations is that if the authority just want to rely on their Enforcement Notice and Appeals Regulations statement and their questionnaire response, they have to say so with the questionnaire, even though none of the other statements would be due for a further four weeks at least.[65] In reality an authority should simply put in a six-week statement which can refer to both regulations.

7.38   The six week statements from the main parties have to be dated and 'submitted to the Secretary of State on the date they bear',[66] presumably to stop parties submitting late and blaming the post for the delayed arrival of the representations.

---

[60]   English and Welsh Written Representations Regulations, reg 6; English and Welsh Hearings Rules, r 4(2); English and Welsh Inquiries Rules, r 4(2); English and Welsh Inspectors Inquiries Rules, r 4(2).

[61]   Enforcement Notice and Appeals Regulations, reg 9; Welsh Enforcement Notice and Appeals Regulations, reg 8.

[62]   Town and Country Planning Act 1990, s 176(3)(b).

[63]   The requirements are modified by the Enforcement Notice and Appeals Regulations, reg 11 and the Welsh Enforcement Notice and Appeals Regulations, reg 10.

[64]   Written Representations Regulations, reg 7(1), (3); Welsh Written Representations Regulations, reg 7(1), (3).

[65]   This drafting should be simplified when the enforcement regulations are next revised.

[66]   Written Representations Regulations, reg 7(5) and repeated in the other English and Welsh provisions.

7.39   For *hearings*, the appellant and the local planning authority are required to send two copies of their hearing statement to the Planning Inspectorate in this period.[67] A hearing statement:[68]

> 'means, and is comprised of, a written statement which contains full particulars of the case which a person proposes to put forward at a hearing, and copies of any documents which that person intends to refer to or put in evidence'.

There is no further procedure for proofs or statements of evidence to be submitted so the hearing statement and the documents with it have to include all the evidence which the party intends to submit, whether this would be statements from individuals or reference to documents. There is no formal calling of witnesses at a hearing so there is no organised mechanism for bringing further evidence forward at that point. New facts will no doubt emerge at a hearing, but this is likely to be in response to questions or points raised. The hearing statement therefore needs to be comprehensive in the light of the other material already submitted in the appeal. Any other person notified by the local planning authority of the appeal under r 4(2)(b) of the Hearings Rules is required to send three copies of their written comments in the same period.[69]

7.40   If *an inquiry* is held, the local planning authority and appellant must serve two copies of a statement of case on the Secretary of State and copies on any other person served with the enforcement notice.[70] The statement is to be served within six weeks of the starting date unless the Minister has instructed a pre-inquiry meeting to be held, in which case the statement is required within four weeks of the conclusion of that meeting. In the inquiry context the statement of case:[71]

> 'means, and is comprised of, a written statement which contains full particulars of the case which a person proposes to put forward at an inquiry, and a list of documents which that person intends to refer to or put in evidence'.

An inquiry statement of case sets out, in relatively summary form, the arguments that will be advanced. It would not itself contain evidence – that is left to the documents referred to or later proofs of evidence. It is therefore similar to a pleading in legal proceedings (although there is no requirement for the document to be verified by a statement of truth). The Planning Inspectorate advise:[72]

> 'It should set out both the planning and legal arguments that a party intends to put forward at an inquiry, and describe, but not contain, the evidence. It should also cite any statutory provisions and case law that parties intend to call in support of its arguments.'

The statement should briefly say what the case will be rather than simply the topics which will be covered. For example, 'the site is at the end of a single track road, which is well-used by walkers and horse riders' is more useful than 'the location of the site will be described in evidence'.

---

[67] English and Welsh Hearings Rules, r 5(1).
[68] English and Welsh Hearings Rules, r 2(1).
[69] English and Welsh Hearings Rules , r 5(3).
[70] Inquiries Procedure Rules. r 8(1), (3); Inspectors Inquiries Rules, r 6(1), (3) and the same paragraphs of the equivalent Welsh Rules.
[71] Rule 2(1) of the English and Welsh versions of the Inquiries Rules and Inspectors Inquiries Rules.
[72] *Procedural Guidance: Planning appeals and called-in planning applications* PINS 01/2009, para 6.7.2.

THIRD PARTY REPRESENTATIONS

7.41 For present purposes third parties are anyone who wishes to participate in the appeal process other than the appellant and the local planning authority. They may include neighbouring local authorities, statutory bodies, commercial rivals, neighbours and local groups. They can make their own representations in an appeal in these ways:

(a) written representations – written submissions within six weeks of the start date;

(b) hearings – written submissions within six weeks, oral submissions at the hearing or handing written representations to the Inspector at the hearing;

(c) inquiries – written submissions within six weeks, becoming a rule 6 party and being entitled to take a full role at the hearing, making oral submissions as allowed by the Inspector or handing written representations to the Inspector at the hearing.

7.42 Additionally, third parties may be called by other parties to give evidence, for example evidence of what happened on a site or the calling of a statutory consultee by a local authority in support of its case. The major parties may also submit written evidence from third parties as part of their cases. Local planning authorities would be expected to hand in late representations, which they had received in hearings or inquiries.

7.43 A third party who intends to play a very active role in the inquiry, including cross-examining witnesses, ought to seek what is informally referred to as rule 6 status. This requires them to serve a statement of case (for planning appeals this is under rule 6 of the inquiries rules, hence the name) and produce proofs of evidence to the same timescale as the main parties. They are then entitled to appear and more importantly are seen as having a more formal role in the proceedings. A person can only become a rule 6 party with the Minister's agreement, so merely volunteering a statement of case will not be enough. In some cases the Minister will impose rule 6 status on a party, usually if they appear to be preparing a substantial case which the parties and Inspectorate need to know about in advance. Consequently the Minister may require any other person who has informed him of an intention to appear at the inquiry to serve a statement of case within four weeks on him and any person specified by the Minister.[73] The Minister or an inspector may require that third party to provide further information and copy it to the persons served with the statement of case.[74] Third parties who serve statements of case on the local planning authority must provide copies of the relevant parts of documents in their list of documents, unless they are already available for inspection with other statements of case.[75]

Comments on third party representations

7.44 The Planning Inspectorate will copy third party representations which they receive to the appellant and local planning authority. In written representations cases

---

[73] English and Welsh Inquiries Rules, r 8(6); English and Welsh Inspectors Inquiries Rules, r 6(6). If provided in hard copy, three copies should be sent to the Planning Inspectorate to allow copies to be sent to the appellant and local planning authority.

[74] English and Welsh Inquiries Rules, r 8(8), (10); English and Welsh Inspectors Inquiries Rules, r 6(8), (10).

[75] English and Welsh Inquiries Rules, r 8(11); English and Welsh Inspectors Inquiries Rules, r 6(11).

the appellant and the authority may comment on those representations in a timescale offered by the Inspectorate, which shall be not less than two weeks.[76] In hearings the appellant and local planning authority may respond to any representations made in the six-week period by third parties as part of any response at the nine-week stage.[77]

NINE-WEEK STATEMENTS

7.45 Within nine weeks of the starting date the appellant and the planning authority are able to send comments on each other's six-week statement. In hearing cases they may also comment on third-party representations and in inquiries, on any other party's statement of case.[78] Comments may only be submitted by the appellant and planning authority at the nine-week point. Whilst in hearings and inquiry cases other parties do have a later opportunity to comment, the Written Representations Regulations do not give third parties any further role in the appeal. This can produce unfairness if new material is produced at the six-week point.[79] In those circumstances the Inspectorate should ensure that all interested persons are allowed to make further comments.

LATER RULE 6 PARTY COMMENTS

7.46 A third party who has become a rule 6 party may comment on another party's statement of case up to four weeks before the inquiry date.[80]

INSPECTION OF DOCUMENTS

7.47 The local planning authority must allow any person to inspect and, where practicable, copy:

(a) any statement of case, written comments, further information or other document served on them under reg 8; and

(b) the planning authority's completed questionnaire, statement of case and the documents in the list of documents with the statement or otherwise served by them under r 8.[81]

This requirement can be met by giving notice of where on a website the documents may be accessed.[82]

---

[76] English and Welsh Written Representations Regulations, reg 8(2). Regulation 8(3) empowers the minister to disregard comments made by the local planning authority on third party representations where the authority have failed to notify third parties of their right to comment. This is a wholly unjustified sanction which misses the point that a failure of notification should be corrected.

[77] English and Welsh Hearings Rules, r 5(4).

[78] English and Welsh Inquiries Rules, r 8(14); English and Welsh Inspectors Inquiries Rules, r 6(14).

[79] Two cases where planning appeal decisions have been quashed because of such unfairness are *Phillips v First Secretary of State* [2003] EWHC 2415 (Admin), [2004] JPL 613, when details of the alternative site search area for a mobile phone antenna were provided by a telecommunications operator at the six-week stage, and *Ashley v Secretary of State for Communities and Local Government* [2012] EWCA Civ 559, [2012] JPL 1235, where the developer submitted a noise report at that point.

[80] Inspectors Inquiries Rules, r 6(15).

[81] Welsh Inquiries Rules, r 8(13)

[82] English and Welsh Hearings Rules, r 5(6A); English and Welsh Inquiries Rules, r 8(13A); English and Welsh Inspectors Inquiries Rules, r 6(13A).

7.48   The local planning authority and the appellant may require the other to copy any document, or the relevant part of any document, in the list of documents in the statement of case to them.[83]

FURTHER INFORMATION IN INQUIRY CASES

7.49   The Minister may require any person who has served a statement of case to provide further information about the matters in the statement.[84] This is primarily a mechanism for seeking clarification about a party's case and the request will often be initiated by another party. A party who does not understand what case the opposition are going to advance should first try to clarify it in correspondence and if that fails, might ask the Minister to make a request.

Pre-inquiry meetings

7.50   A pre-inquiry meeting is a procedural meeting intended to enable the Inspector to explain how the inquiry will run, obtain information from the parties to assist with programming and to allow the parties to raise procedural issues. Pre-inquiry meetings are only held for long inquiries. Where the appeal is to be determined by the Secretary of State, he shall hold a pre-inquiry meeting if the inquiry is expected to last for four days or more (unless the meeting is considered unnecessary) and for any shorter inquiry where a meeting is considered necessary.[85] In Wales the equivalent time estimate is eight days.[86] In Inspector-determined appeals, the Inspector is subject to the similar duties to consider calling a pre-inquiry meeting.[87] In both England and Wales the relevant estimate for the duration of the inquiry is four days where Inspectors are considering whether to hold a pre-inquiry meeting. In a recovered jurisdiction case, if the Minister has not called a pre-inquiry meeting, the Inspector may do so.[88]

7.51   If the Minister calls a pre-inquiry meeting, the appellant and local planning authority must produce an outline statement within eight weeks of the starting date.[89] The Minister may also require any other person who intends to take part in the appeal to produce an outline statement within four weeks of any request.[90] In ministerial cases, the Minister will notify the appellant and local planning authority of the pre-inquiry meeting and the authority will then advertise it.[91] Where an Inspector calls a pre-inquiry meeting, the Planning Inspectorate will give notice to the appellant, the local planning authority, any person entitled to appear and any other person whose attendance appears desirable.[92]

7.52   Pre-inquiry meetings should resolve the order in which evidence is to be heard, which parties make opening statements and the detail of document numbering

---

[83]   English and Welsh Inquiries Rules, r 8(5); English and Welsh Inspectors Inquiries Rules, r 6(5).
[84]   English and Welsh Inquiries Rules, r 8(8); English and Welsh Inspectors Inquiries Rules, r 6(8).
[85]   Inquiries Rules, r 6(1). As formulated, the rules mean that a pre-inquiry meeting is held if the Minister thinks it is necessary, but subject to a presumption for longer inquiries.
[86]   Welsh Inquiries Rules, r 6(1).
[87]   Inspectors Inquiries Rules, r 7(2); Welsh Inspectors Inquiries Rules, r 7(2).
[88]   English and Welsh Inquiries Rules, r 9(1).
[89]   English and Welsh Inquiries Rules, r 6(2)(c).
[90]   English and Welsh Inquiries Rules, r 6(4), (5).
[91]   English and Welsh Inquiries Rules, r 6(2)(a), (b).
[92]   English and Welsh Inquiries Rules, r 9(2); English and Welsh Inspectors Inquiries Rules, r 7(3).

and arrangements for their circulation. Venue arrangements should be clarified where possible (finding the venue being the responsibility of the local planning authority). The main parties should be able to indicate the number of witnesses they will have and the topics they will cover. For programming purposes, the Inspector may ask how long the parties will take to call their witnesses-in-chief. However the critical programming matter is how long cross-examination will take, and that is difficult to judge until the evidence has been seen. It is also an opportunity for the parties to raise any procedural points. These tend to be requests for clarification of statements of case or attempts to obtain documents.

Statement of matters

7.53   If the appeal is being determined by the Minister, then he must send a statement of the matters about which he particularly wishes to be informed in considering the appeal either with notice of any pre-inquiry meeting he calls or within 12 weeks of the starting date.[93] An Inspector may produce a statement of matters in a delegated inquiry case.[94]

Timetable

7.54   If an inquiry is expected to last for four days or more, the Inspector is required to prepare a timetable for the proceedings. A timetable can be prepared for shorter inquiries and the timetable may be changed at any time. This timetable may alter the dates for sending proofs and statements of evidence.[95] The timetable for the hearing does not set absolute deadlines for particular stages, but the Inspector would wish to try to keep to the schedule. It may be particularly useful for parties who do not intend to attend throughout the hearing, so they know when they will be involved.

Persons entitled to appear at the inquiry or hearing

7.55   In England, the following persons are entitled to appear as of right at the inquiry:[96]

(a) the appellant;

(b) the local planning authority;[97]

(c) the following, if the site is in their area:

    (i)   a county or a district council;

    (ii) an enterprise zone authority;

    (iii) the Broads Authority;

    (iv) a housing action trust;

---

[93] English and Welsh Inquiries Rules, rr 6(2)(a) and 8(12).
[94] English and Welsh Inspectors Inquiries Rules, r 7(1).
[95] English and Welsh Inquiries Rules, r 10; English and Welsh Inspectors Inquiries Rules, r 8.
[96] Inquiries Rules, r 13(1); Inspectors Inquires Rules, r 11(1).
[97] The local planning authority might be a national park authority or an urban development corporation.

(d) if in an area previously designated as a new town, the Homes and Communities Agency;

(e) any person on whom a copy of the enforcement notice has been served; and

(f) any other person who has served a statement of case or outline statement having been required to do so by the Secretary of State in accordance with the rules.

In hearing cases, those entitled to appear are a simplified list of public authorities (albeit for no obvious reason) and of course there are no other parties required to produce statements of case in hearings. Those entitled to appear at hearings are therefore the appellant, the local planning authority, anyone served with a copy of the enforcement notice and anyone having an interest in the land subject to the notice.[98]

7.56   The Welsh inquiry provisions are the same except for the geographical differences that county and country borough councils are entitled to appear, and there is no reference to the Broads Authority as it is in Norfolk.[99] The Welsh legislation still refers to the Commission for the New Towns as having a right to appear for areas previously designated as a new town, but it has been abolished and its functions transferred to the Welsh Ministers. It should be noted that a person served with a copy of the enforcement notice is entitled to appear even if they are not entitled to appeal. The right to appear is given to certain locally-based public authorities concerned with land use. Government departments and agencies, such as the Department for the Environment, Food and Rural Affairs or the Environment Agency, are not entitled to appear as of right. It would, however, be remarkable for such bodies not to be allowed to play a full role, subject to preparing outline statements, statement of case and proofs as required under the rules. Parish and town councils and neighbourhood fora are not entitled to appear but ought normally to be allowed to do so. If they wish to do more than read out a statement they might wish to seek rule 6 status.

7.57   The Inspector may permit any other person, including government departments, to appear at the inquiry or hearing 'and such permission shall not be unreasonably withheld'.[100] In practice, inspectors will permit anyone with something to say that appears relevant to speak. The inspector will normally ask at the start of the inquiry who wishes to speak. If other persons indicate during the inquiry that they wish to speak they will normally be heard, but all third parties must speak before the appellant's closing submissions.

7.58   There might be a distinction between the planning permission application in ground (a) and the factual/legal inquiries of grounds (b) to (d). On the latter grounds, it has been suggested that third parties would not have standing as objectors, but they can appear as witnesses of fact as to the issues on them.[101] That view is outdated. Third parties will often be concerned to ensure that the planning status of land is correctly identified. That is recognised in standing to bring High Court proceedings and in the Aarhus Convention on Access to Environmental Justice. There is no reason why they should not be able to play a full role in appeals on the legal grounds, cross-examining and making submissions.

---

[98] English and Welsh Hearings Rules, r 9(1).
[99] Welsh Inquiries Rules, rule 13(1); Welsh Inspectors Inquiries Rules, r 11(1).
[100] English and Welsh Inquiries Rules, r 13(2); English and Welsh Inquiries Rules, r 11(2).
[101] *Thrasyvoulou v Secretary of State for the Environment* [1990] 2 AC 273.

7.59   A person appearing at the inquiry may call witnesses or put in documents and letters, so allowing other people's views or information to be put forward.

Representatives of government departments at the inquiry

7.60   The appellant may require a representative of a Minister of the Crown or government department to attend the inquiry and give evidence if:[102]

(a) the Minister or department has expressed a view on the appeal in writing to the local planning authority; and

(b) the local planning authority refer to that view in their statement of case.

7.61   For example, the Highways Agency may have expressed concern about the effects of the development on a trunk road. The attendance must be requested in writing to the Secretary of State determining the appeal at least four weeks before the date of the inquiry.[103] The Secretary of State will then provide a representative or pass the request to the Minister or department concerned who will provide the representative.[104] Similar provisions apply in Wales where the request is made to the Welsh Ministers and a representative of the Welsh Ministers or the UK Minister or government department would be required to attend.[105] The representative shall give the reasons for the expressed view and is subject to cross-examination in the usual way.[106] This provision is rarely invoked. If a government department has supported the authority's decision on an important issue then it is likely to appear with its own advocate and witnesses or provide one or more witnesses for the local planning authority.

Date of the inquiry

7.62   In a ministerial case, the inquiry will be held not later than 22 weeks after the starting date or eight weeks after the conclusion of the pre-inquiry meeting, unless the Minister considers that that would be impractical, in which case it will be held at the earliest practical date.[107] In practice the appellant and local planning authority are offered a date, with each party being entitled to one refusal. If the appeal is being determined by an Inspector, the inquiry should be held within 20 weeks of the starting date, or the earliest practical date if later.[108] Hearings should be held within 12 weeks of the starting date unless that is impracticable.[109] The Minister can vary the date, time or place of the hearing or inquiry.[110] A decision on the date of an inquiry is amenable to judicial review, but such an application would be exceptional.[111] There would need to be some very strong basis for considering it would be unfair to proceed on the proposed date.

---

[102]   Inquiries Rules, r 15(1); Inspectors Procedure Rules, r 13(1).
[103]   Inquiries Rules, r 15(1); Inspectors Inquiries Rules, r 13(1).
[104]   Inquiries Rules, r 15(2); Inspectors Inquiries Rules, r 13(2).
[105]   Welsh Inquiries Rules, r 15; Welsh Inspectors Inquiries Rules, r 13.
[106]   English and Welsh Inquiries Rules, r 15(3); English and Welsh Inspectors Inquiries Rules, r 13(3).
[107]   English and Welsh Inquiries Rules, r 11(1), (2).
[108]   English and Welsh Inspectors Inquiries Rules, r 9(1).
[109]   English and Welsh Hearings Rules, r 6(1).
[110]   English and Welsh Inquiries Rules, r 11(4), (5); English and Welsh Inspectors Inquiries Rules, r 9(4); English and Welsh Hearings Rules, r 6(3).
[111]   *R v Secretary of State for the Environment ex p Leeds City Council* [1995] JPL B61.

7.63 *Appeal against an Enforcement Notice*

Notification of the inquiry or hearing date

7.63   Notice of the making of the appeal and the arrangements for any pre-inquiry meetings have been discussed earlier in this chapter. Parties and the public at large also need to know when and where the hearing or inquiry will take place. Unless a lesser period of notice has been agreed with the appellant and the local planning authority, the Planning Inspectorate shall give not less than four weeks' written notice of the date, time and place of the inquiry or hearing to every person entitled to appear.[112] Similar notice, unless otherwise agreed, must be given if the date of the inquiry is varied.[113] The Inspectorate and the parties entitled to take part in the appeal may agree to notice being given via a website.[114] If the time or place of the inquiry is varied, the Minister must give reasonable notice.[115]

7.64   The Minister may require the local planning authority to do any of the following in inquiry cases:[116]

'(a) not less than 2 weeks before the date fixed for the inquiry, to publish a notice of the inquiry in one or more newspapers circulating in the locality in which the land is situated;

(b) to send a notice of the inquiry on such persons or classes of persons as he may specify, within such period as he may specify;

(c) to post a notice of the inquiry in a conspicuous place near to the land, within such period as he may specify.'

7.65   Where the subject land is under the appellant's control, the Minister may require him to fix a notice of the inquiry 'firmly' to the land or an object on or near the land. The notice must be readily visible to, and legible by, the public. The appellant must not remove it, or cause or permit it to be removed, for such period before the inquiry as the Secretary of State may specify.[117] Any notices of the inquiry shall contain:[118]

'(a) a clear statement of the date, time and place of the inquiry and of the powers enabling the [Minister or inspector] to determine the appeal in question;

(b) a written description of the land sufficient to identify approximately its location;

(c) a brief description of the subject matter of the appeal;

(d) details of where and when copies of the local planning authority's completed questionnaire and any document sent by and copied to the authority pursuant to [the rules] may be inspected.'

Similar rules apply to giving notice of hearings, but the Minister has no power to require the display of site notices.[119]

---

[112] English and Welsh Inquiries Rules, r 11(3); English and Welsh Inspectors Inquiries Rules, r 9(2); English and Welsh Hearings Rules, r 6(2).

[113] English and Welsh Inquiries Rules, r 11(4); English and Welsh Hearings Rules, r 6(3).

[114] English and Welsh Inquiries Rules, r 11(3A); English and Welsh Inspectors Inquiries Rules, r 9(3A); English and Welsh Hearings Rules, r 6(2A).

[115] English and Welsh Inquiries Rules, r 11(5); English and Welsh Inspectors Inquiries Rules, r 9(3); English and Welsh Hearings Rules, r 6(4).

[116] English and Welsh Inquiries Rules, r 11(6); English and Welsh Inspectors Inquiries Rules, r 9(5).

[117] English and Welsh Inquiries Rules, r 11(7); English and Welsh Inspectors Inquiries Rules, r 9(6).

[118] English and Welsh Inquiries Rules, r 11(8); English and Welsh Inspectors Inquiries Rules, r 9(7).

[119] English and Welsh Hearings Rules, r 6(5), (6).

7.66   It is a matter for ministerial discretion as to whether the authority and appellant have to give notice. Consequently these parties should be alert for any direction being given and ensure that it is complied with. At the start of the hearing or inquiry the Inspector will usually ask the local planning authority's advocate or representative if the notice requirements have been complied with. The authority should have a copy of any direction and certification of notices and advertisements. If it appears that notice has not been given correctly and there may be people who would have wished to take part or simply attend but who are not present or are unable to play a proper role because of the error, then it is likely that the hearing will be adjourned. If such a notification error is not corrected, then the appeal decision is likely to be quashed if substantial prejudice arises.[120] However, a failure to provide additional notice, even if it was intended to do so, will probably not justify the quashing of the decision.[121] Where there has been a representation that notice will be given (whether by the Planning Inspectorate or the local planning authority) then failure to give such notice is a breach of a legitimate expectation.[122]

7.67   The Planning Inspectorate will notify those entitled to appear of the name of the inspector and any assessor and the matters on which the assessor is to advise the inspector.[123] If a replacement inspector is appointed, the Planning Inspectorate will, if practicable, notify this before the inquiry begins. The inspector will in any event announce his or her name at the start of the inquiry. It is of some use to know what the Inspector's professional background is (such as planner, architect, solicitor) and the Inspector's previous decisions can be examined.

Advocates and witnesses

7.68   The roles of advocates and witnesses are distinctly different. The responsibility of a witness is to give relevant evidence. That evidence should be truthful. Witness evidence is of two types: evidence of fact and expert evidence. Evidence of fact is evidence of what happened or what the position is or, sometimes, what a party intends to do. Expert evidence is the professional view of an expert on a matter within their professional expertise. For example, a highways consultant in an appeal might give evidence of the acceptability of an access to a site. The consultant's evidence should be the consultant's own opinion, rather than running whatever argument is best for his client. Hopefully, if the client is listening to his experts, conflict does not arise. In planning appeals, views on the merits of the scheme are likely to be presented by individuals without professional expertise. Those views can be given as evidence and in inquiries can be tested in cross-examination. They will often be right. An intelligent layperson is quite capable of exposing flaws in expert evidence and it is a mistake, made sometimes but too often, to assume that local residents cannot contribute on technical matters.

7.69   The role of the advocate is quite different from that of a witness. An advocate's task is to put his client's case as effectively as it can be put. An advocate is not giving evidence or expressing their own opinion, even on matters within

---

[120]   *R v London Borough of Lambeth Council ex p Sharp* (1988) 55 P & CR 232, CA.

[121]   *R v Secretary of State for the Environment ex p Kent* [1988] 3 PLR 17.

[122]   *R(Majed) v London Borough of Camden* [2009] EWCA Civ 1029, [2010] JPL 621; *R (Vieira) v London Borough of Camden* [2012] EWHC 287 (Admin).

[123]   English and Welsh Inquiries Rules, r 5; English and Welsh Inspectors Inquiries Rules, r 5; English and Welsh Hearings Rules, r 7.

their expertise, such as the law. The advocate's conduct of the case is constrained by professional rules. An advocate may not say something that they know to be untrue or to mislead the tribunal, they must not put an argument which is so poor as to be unarguable and should ensure that the tribunal is aware of any case which contradicts their submissions. Whilst promoting their client's interests, advocates should contribute to the effective management of the case. Questioning of witnesses can be robust, but advocates should not raise irrelevant matters or subject a witness to ridicule or abuse. They should avoid criticising third parties who are not before the tribunal where possible and should only criticise a witness if they have taken the opportunity to put that criticism to the witness.

THE INQUIRY

Assessors

7.70   An assessor may be appointed to assist an inquiry inspector on particular matters.[124] The assessor will normally be a member of the Planning Inspectorate and will have expertise in a particular aspect of the case. Because of the narrow range of issues in enforcement notice appeals, the appointment of assessors is rare. In the inquiry the assessor will sit and retire with the Inspector. An assessor may ask questions. Conventionally, in a case decided by ministers, the assessor will produce their own report, which will be appended to the Inspector's report and taken into account by the Inspector in preparing their own report. The formal recommendation to the Minister will be from the Inspector. In practice the Inspector and assessor will have been working together closely in the inquiry process.

Proofs and statements of evidence

7.71   A proof of evidence is a statement from a witness setting out his evidence. A proof must be submitted in advance where a party who is entitled to appear (so including the appellant, local planning authority or rule 6 party) intends to give evidence by reading from a statement. Historically, the obligation only arose when the witness was dealing with a ground (a) appeal or deemed planning permission (reflecting the position on planning appeals) but advance knowledge of the detail of factual evidence or planning judgment on the other grounds is also important. In Wales the parties are required to prepare statements of evidence but these are exactly the same as proofs of evidence. In the rest of this chapter, proofs of evidence will include statements of evidence.

7.72   A proof will frequently be 'taken as read' at the inquiry with the summary only read out along with any supplementary questions in examination in chief. Planning inquiries have not moved as far as the civil courts in simply asking a witness to confirm their written statement with very limited room for further questions-in-chief. In part this reflects the absence of a formal mechanism for written response to the other side's proof and the need for the public to be able to follow the proceedings, but also a more relaxed approach by Inspectors so they can see how witnesses explain their evidence.

---

[124]   For notification of the appointment of an assessor, see English and Welsh Inquiries Rules, rule 12, English and Welsh Inspectors Inquiries Rules, rule 10.

7.73   The proof should concisely but comprehensively set out the witness's evidence. It should be clearly structured. If a planning witness is dealing with all the issues on the appeal then the headings may be along these lines:

Introduction: Witness's Qualifications

Site Location and Description

Planning History

Relevant Planning Policies

The Issues:

(i)   **The Ground (e) Appeal**

(ii)   **The Ground (b) Appeal**

(iii)   **The Ground (c) Appeal**

(iv)   **The Ground (d) Appeal**

(v)   **The Ground (a) Appeal**

(vi)   **The Ground (f) appeal**

(vii)   **The Ground (g) Appeal**

Conclusions

The structure of the issues reflects the logical sequence of the grounds of appeal – procedural failure, whether there is a breach which can still be enforced against, whether planning permission should be granted for it, whether the steps are excessive and whether more time should be allowed.   The pages and paragraphs should be numbered. Appendices should be provided in a separate, paginated bundle, preferably in A4 size, although some plans and photographs may be best seen in A3. Guidance on the contents of proofs in inquiries is given in *Procedural Guidance: Planning appeals and called-in planning applications* PINS 01/2009, section 6.8.

7.74   The Inspectorate's aim is for a proof to be no longer than 3,000 words,[125] although that aspiration is often not achieved. A summary should be produced if the proof is more than 1,500 words long. It should itself be less than 1,500 words and should summarise the evidence in the proof. It must not contain new material or merely state the topics that are covered by the proof.

7.75   Expert evidence (including the views of local authority officers on the merits of schemes) should include an endorsement that the evidence is the professional opinion of the witness. Some professional bodies use a set format; alternatively, the Planning Inspectorate recommends:[126]

> 'The evidence which I have prepared and provide for this appeal reference APP/xxx (in this proof of evidence, written statement or report) is true and has been prepared and is given in accordance with the guidance of my professional institution and I confirm that the opinions expressed are my true and professional opinions.'

---

[125]   *Procedural Guidance: Planning appeals and called-in planning applications* PINS 01/2009, para 6.8.3.
[126]   PINS 01/2009, para 1.13.2.

Whilst not required by Inspectorate guidance, it is appropriate for proofs or statements on factual matters in enforcement appeals to contain a statement of truth that the maker of the statement believes the facts stated in the document are true.

7.76 If a person entitled to be heard at the inquiry proposes to call a witness giving evidence by reading a proof (or in Wales, a statement), three copies of the proof and any summary should be sent to the Planning Inspectorate at least four weeks before the inquiry, or as specified in any timetable arranged by the inspector.[127] Copies would then be circulated by the Planning Inspectorate, if the parties had not already supplied copies to each other. Producing evidence at the inquiry for the first time tends to lead to delay as it is read and possible adjournment whilst matters are investigated. There is no provision in the rules for supplementary proofs dealing with matters raised in other parties' proofs. It might be agreed at a pre-inquiry meeting that these can be produced, but usually the opportunity to respond to the other side's evidence is in examination-in-chief. Supplementary proofs can be useful if the response is so technical or detailed that it is useful to have it available in writing. These should be sent to the other parties and the inspector as soon as possible. Third parties (other than those entitled to be heard) are not obliged to serve proofs. As a matter of practice they should if the evidence is detailed or amounts to expert evidence. They are entitled to copy proofs received by the local planning authority under the Rules.

Statement of common ground in inquiries

7.77 The appellant and local planning authority are required to provide an agreed statement of common ground not less than four weeks before the inquiry.[128] The statement will usually try to set out a description of the site, the planning history, identify the relevant policies, the matters not in dispute between the main parties and those which are in dispute. A model format is on the Planning Portal website. Whilst the statement is required to be produced by the same time as the proofs of evidence, it is more useful if it can be worked up by the parties before the proofs are written. That way, the parties can avoid including descriptive material in their proofs and the statement of common ground. The statement of common ground is not required to be agreed with third parties, although there may be occasions when this would be useful. For example, it may be possible to agree a statement of common ground on highways matters between the appellant, local planning authority and the highway authority.

THE INQUIRY PROCEEDINGS

7.78 Procedure at the inquiry is essentially a matter for the inspector. The normal form is set out here. The inspector will introduce themselves and explain the procedure to be followed. The inspector will ask who wishes to appear. The advocates present will state who they are, in the case of counsel who instructs them and their professional client's address, the name and address of the party they represent and the

---

[127] English and Welsh Inquiries Rules, r 16(1), (3); English and Welsh Inspectors Inquiries Rules, r 15(1), (3).
[128] English and Welsh Inquiries Rules, r 17; English and Welsh Inspectors Inquiries Rules, r 16.

witnesses they propose to call.[129] Any person appearing on their own behalf will give their name and address. Journalists present are asked to give the name and address of their organisation so that a copy of the decision letter can be sent to them.

7.79   The Inspector will set out what he considers to be the main issues to be considered and any matters on which he requires further explanation.[130] This statement is important in practice as an indication of what the Inspector has understood about the case from pre-reading. However it does not prevent parties from raising any relevant issues.[131] Unless the Inspector invites discussion of what are the main issues at that point, the parties can set our their views of the main issues in opening.

7.80   The appellant will open with an opening speech setting out his case. The Inspectorate preference is for short, 5–10 minute openings, except in major inquiries. Practice varies as to whether the local planning authority and any rule 6 parties also make opening statements. If the inquiry is likely to last for several days (or longer) or there are reasonable numbers of members of the public present, then it is useful for those parties to deliver short openings.[132] Where a one-day inquiry only involves the appellant and local authority, a local authority or other opening may be unnecessary. There is no obligation to provide written skeleton arguments for opening or closing speeches, except for closing submissions in inquiries lasting four or more days. However, it may be useful to the inspector and the parties and save time note taking. The High Court has encouraged the use of skeleton arguments in inquiries where there are points of law that may go to the courts on appeal.[133]

7.81   The appellant will then call his witnesses. The usual rule in enforcement inquiries is that the appellant goes first, but on appeals against the refusal or non-determination of planning applications, the local planning authority is expected to call its evidence first to focus discussion on the reasons for refusal. Where an inquiry deals with both an enforcement appeal and a planning appeal, the rules point in different directions. It may be that the best approach is for the appellant to start if legal grounds of appeal are raised and the local authority to start if a ground (a) appeal is the main issue.

7.82   Evidence-in-chief is subject to the normal rule against leading questions. The restrictions on admissibility of evidence in criminal or civil proceedings do not apply. The inspector will give appropriate weight to the evidence: if it is hearsay, then less reliance is likely to be placed upon it. Repetitious or irrelevant evidence or questioning may be ruled out by the Inspector.

7.83   On the usual basis that the inspector and the other parties have had sufficient opportunity to read the proof, the summary only will be read out.[134] The main proof will then be taken as read and considered as part of the witness's evidence. Questions may be asked in chief to highlight areas in the main proof or to address matters in the other side's evidence or new developments.

---

[129]   The advocate can simply say that the addresses will be in the papers. A note can be handed up with these details to save the Inspector's writing.

[130]   Inquiries Rules, r 18(2); Inspectors Inquiries Rules, r 17(2).

[131]   Inquiries Rules, r 18(3); Inspectors Inquiries Rules, r 17(3).

[132]   Public and press attendance usually declines after the first morning.

[133]   *P G Vallance Ltd v Secretary of State for the Environment* [1993] 1 PLR 74, 78.

[134]   English and Welsh Inquiries Rules, r 16(5); English and Welsh Inspectors Inquiries Rules, r 15(5) require only the summary to read out unless the Inspector permits or requires otherwise.

7.84 Witnesses at planning inquiries are normally not examined on oath. However, if factual disputes are likely to arise, as is common on enforcement appeal grounds (b) to (e), witnesses on those issues will be sworn or affirmed by the Inspector under s 250 of the Local Government Act 1972. The appellant's witness will then be open to cross-examination by the local planning authority. This cross-examination may include questions on any relevant matters on which the witness can be expected to give factual or expert evidence. This will include parts of the proof that were not read out. The Inspector may then permit cross-examination by other parties opposing the appeal. The appellant, local planning authority and any person served with a copy of the enforcement notice are entitled to cross-examine (implicitly witnesses they disagree with), other public authorities entitled to appear and rule 6 parties are not given the statutory right to do so.[135] Other cross-examination is said to be at the Inspector's discretion. However, that discretion has to be exercised fairly.[136] It is inconceivable that a rule 6 party or other person entitled to appear would not be able to cross-examine witnesses whose evidence they were challenging. The Inspector may refuse to permit the giving of evidence, cross-examination or submissions that he considers to be irrelevant or repetitious.[137] That allows proper control over the proceedings, but the Inspector must be careful to act fairly and not to exclude relevant matters. Any such error could leave the decision vulnerable to challenge. The witness can then be re-examined by the appellant's advocate. Re-examination can only cover matters raised in cross-examination and should not be leading.

7.85 The inspector may then question the witness. If the Inspector raises new points, the appellant's advocate (and sometimes the authority's advocate), with the Inspector's permission, may ask further questions on those points. This further questioning is relatively rare. The Inspector's role is more inquisitorial than that of a judge in adversarial court proceedings. However the Inspector's interventions must be fair and not show a risk of bias. Inspectors can raise questions with witnesses whilst they are being examined by advocates, but that is best confined to ensuring that questions are answered and that the answers are clear. An Inspector should not take over the examination of a witness or disrupt an advocate's questions more than is necessary.

7.86 The appellant will then call his remaining witnesses, following the same procedure. Organised supporters of the appellant, such as other persons served, may give evidence at this point. They may be cross-examined by the local planning authority and, at the Inspector's discretion, other opponents of the appeal. The authority's witnesses may be cross-examined by the appellant and questioned by the Inspector.

7.87 After the local planning authority's evidence is concluded, third parties can give evidence or make statements. Those opposing the appeal are open to cross-examination by the appellant and those supporting to cross-examination by the local planning authority. Cross-examination of a third party by another third party will rarely be permitted.

---

[135] English and Welsh Inquiries Rules, r 18(5); English and Welsh Inspectors Inquiries Rules, r 17(5).

[136] *Nicholson v Secretary of State for Energy* 76 LGR 693, [1978] 1 EGLR 111.

[137] English and Welsh Inquiries Rules, r 18(6), English and Welsh Inspectors Inquiries Rules, r 17(6). If oral evidence is prevented under this provision then the person restrained may submit evidence or submissions in writing by the close of the inquiry.

7.88   Conditions to be imposed in the event of planning permission being granted will usually be discussed after the evidence has been heard. The local planning authority will propose any conditions it wants (without prejudice to its opposition to the grant of planning permission). These will be discussed in a more informal session,[138] along with any proposals by the appellant and third parties. Even if conditions are agreed between the parties, the Inspector is likely to still have questions about them. If there are major factual or judgment issues about potential conditions then these should be addressed in the witnesses' evidence. Any planning obligation will also be discussed in that session, usually beginning with an explanation of its terms by the appellant's advocate or solicitor.

7.89   Closing submissions will then be made. Third parties will speak first, followed by the local planning authority and the appellant is entitled to the final word unless otherwise agreed.[139] Inspectors will often request a written text of the closing to be handed up when it is delivered.[140] Where the Inspector is reporting to the Secretary of State a full written text is essential as this will provide the basis of the Inspector's summary of the party's case in the report and will also be available to the Minister.[141] Even where a written text is produced, the closing will still be delivered orally, allowing the Inspector to make notes of further submissions. After the closing speeches, applications for costs can be made. The inspector will then close the inquiry, unless otherwise agreed, further material or submissions may not be made after this point. An accompanied site visit will usually take place at this point, although it may have occurred at an earlier break in the proceedings. Whilst inquiries are normally very orderly, an Inspector can require any person behaving in a disruptive manner to leave and refuse to permit them to return or allow them to return only on conditions.

HEARINGS

7.90   Until 2002 in England (and 2003 in Wales) there was no statutory procedure for hearings. Some preliminary matters were dealt with by the Enforcement Notices and Appeals Regulations. Hearings rules were introduced in those reforms.

7.91   The accommodation for the hearing should be informal, with the Inspector and the parties sitting round a table. Small committee rooms have been recommended. At the start, the Inspector will explain that the hearing will take the form of a discussion, which she will lead. She will review the case as he sees it and outline the main issues and matters that require clarification. This does not prevent parties from raising other issues.[142] The appellant or his agent will start the discussion. Questions may be asked informally during the proceedings, provided they are relevant and the discussion is orderly. Interested third parties may be present and may join in the discussion.

---

[138]   Advocates and witnesses tend to make comments in these sessions without the formality of giving evidence.

[139]   English and Welsh Inquiries Rules, r 18(4); English and Welsh Inspectors Inquiries Rules, r 17(4).

[140]   It is essential to have copies for the other advocates and desirable to have sufficient copies for those attending the session, including members of the public. If the inquiry is programmed to last for four days or more than a written copy of the closing is required by the English and Welsh Inquiries Rules, r 18(14) and the English and Welsh Inspectors Inquiries Rules, r 17(14).

[141]   It will usually be helpful to the Inspector's writing of the report to the Minister to provide by email a Word file of the closing as well as a hard copy.

[142]   English and Welsh Hearings Rules, r 11(4), (5).

The discussion is intended to be 'inspector-led' and inquisitorial, but the rules of natural justice must be observed.[143] If it becomes apparent that cross-examination is required, then the Inspector will need to decide, having consulted the main parties, whether to close the hearing and hold an inquiry (on a different occasion) instead. It is still possible to cross-examine, with the Inspector's permission, in a hearing.[144] The rules refer to evidence being called[145] but in practice there is not the formal calling of evidence. Where a party has an advocate and one or more expert or factual witnesses then there can be a rough distinction between evidence and submissions. Where a party's main representation also provides their sole or main evidence (such as a planning consultant or planning officer), the role of advocate and witness is essentially merged.

7.92   A party is entitled to be represented by any other person,[146] and so can attend with a solicitor or counsel. However, for many years the Planning Inspectorate thought it odd for lawyers to appear at hearings. That view has softened, particularly because the Inspectorate have been pushing cases down to hearings which would previously have been dealt with by inquiries. Parties consequently often consider they need to have professional advocates as well as witnesses. An advocate/witness combination can be effective in hearings, especially where there are legal or merits based submissions to make or several witnesses to marshall. In the hearing it is useful to distinguish between points best made by submission or by an expert explaining their professional view. The Planning Inspectorate has asked that the other side is told in advance if a party intends to be represented at the hearing by a lawyer. Third parties may take part, at the Inspector's discretion, although if many other people want to take an active part then it may be more suitable to hold an inquiry. The appellant will have the last word. The hearing may be adjourned for discussion to continue on site or if the appellant or the local planning authority wish, an accompanied site inspection will be carried out following the close of the hearing.

SITE VISITS AND THE ADJOURNMENT OF HEARINGS TO THE SITE

7.93   Almost all enforcement appeals require a site visit before they can be sensibly decided.[147] There are no statutory procedures for site visits in written representations appeals, but the normal practice is to carry out an accompanied or unaccompanied site visit. An accompanied site visit will be attended by the appellant (or a representative) and a local planning authority officer. In the company of both persons, the Inspector will go onto the appeal site and look at the site from the surrounding area. The Inspector may also look at the appeal site from third parties' properties if previously asked to do so. On an unaccompanied site visit the Inspector will turn up, without notice, and view the site and its surroundings from the highway and any other publicly accessible points. The Inspector would not go on private land (including the appeal site). Prior to a hearing or inquiry the Inspector will usually try to view the site from the highway or other land on which the public have a right of access. Such a visit will be informal and unaccompanied. The Inspector will normally inform the parties at the hearing if such an informal visit has taken place and if there was anything particular to note.

---

[143]   *Rydon Homes v Secretary of State for the Environment* (1995) 70 P & CR 657.
[144]   English and Welsh Hearings Rules, r 11(2), (3).
[145]   English and Welsh Hearings Rules, r 11(6).
[146]   English and Welsh Hearings Rules, r 9(3).
[147]   Exceptions would be cases that turn solely on points of law.

7.94   A hearing may be adjourned to the site for the discussion to be concluded. Alternatively the Inspector may close the hearing and may then hold a site visit at his initiative and shall conduct a site visit if requested by the appellant or local planning authority.[148] During an inquiry or after its close the Inspector may carry out an accompanied site visit and has to do so if requested by the appellant or local planning authority.[149]

7.95   If the Inspector needs to enter private property, or a party wants to point out something particular and he agrees, the site visit will be accompanied. A representative of the appellant (or the appellant himself) and a representative of the local planning authority will attend as may any other person served with a copy of the enforcement notice. An accompanied site inspection is not a further opportunity to argue the case, so the parties' role is confining to pointing out matters and ensuring fair play. Where an Inspector and the local planning authority attended for an accompanied site visit but the appellant's representative was not present, it was unfair for the Inspector to proceed accompanied by the planning officer.[150]

7.96   'Adjourning the hearing to the appeal site' or inspecting the land under the hearing or inquiries rules requires the Inspector to go onto the appeal site. Simply viewing the appeal site from the road is insufficient,[151] although that might be excused if there has been the willing consent of the parties.

7.97   It is important that the Inspector sees sufficient to decide the case with regard to all relevant matters. In *Chichester District Council v First Secretary of State,*[152] the local planning authority contended that a building which had been unlawfully constructed on a farm was a new dwelling. The Inspector granted planning permission for the building, conditioned to use as an agricultural workshop and feedstore. Having carried out an unaccompanied site visit in the written representations appeal, the Inspector failed to look inside the property even though the authority had asked for this to be done.

THE DECISION

Ministerial decision-making

7.98   Where the appeal is being decided by the Minister, the Inspector will write a report setting out procedural matters, summarising the notices, identifying policy and summarising the parties' submissions.[153] The critical part of the report is the Inspector's assessment of the appeal and recommendation to the Minister. If an assessor has been appointed, any assessor's report will be appended to the Inspector's report and the Inspector will state his conclusions on it. The Inspector will not take into account any representations received after the close of the inquiry unless he has specifically requested them to address particular points. The Minister has a discretion

---

[148]   English and Welsh Hearings Rules, r 12(2).
[149]   English and Welsh Inquiries Rules, r 19(2); English and Welsh Inspectors Inquiries Rules, r 18(2).
[150]   *R (Tait) v Secretary of State for Communities and Local Government* [2012] EWHC 643 (Admin).
[151]   *Payne v Secretary of State for Communities and Local Government* [2010] EWHC 3528 (Admin), [2011] JPL 767.
[152]   [2006] EWHC 1876 (Admin), [2007] JPL 389.
[153]   English and Welsh Inquiries Rules, r 20(1). The summaries will usually be edited versions of the parties' closings, so a cogent, written closing is essential.

whether to take into account any later material[154] but that must be exercised fairly and ensuring that the Minister has regard to all material matters. In practice, the parties should say everything they need to say to the Inspector and only make representations to the Minister on later developments.

7.99   An Inspector's report is the Inspector's own work and view. Sometimes Inspectors will ask other Inspectors to read the draft report to check for clarity and obvious errors but the Planning Inspectorate has no control over the report. The report will be sent with all the inquiry documents to the Department of Communities and Local Government or the Welsh Assembly Government. It will then be considered by civil servants or WAG officials. They will then prepare a briefing for the Minister or senior official deciding the appeal which will be sent with the report and any critical documents. The determining Minister or official will then decide the case. A decision letter will be prepared. If the Minister differs from the Inspector on a material matter of fact or takes into account any new evidence or new fact (other than changing government policy) and consequently is disposed to disagree with the Inspector's recommendation, then notice must be given to the persons who were entitled to appear at the inquiry and did so.[155] They must be told of the disagreement and the reasons for it, and given an opportunity to make written representations on the point within a three-week period. If the notice is because of new evidence or a new matter of fact, these parties may ask for the inquiry to be reopened to address those matters.[156] The decision will be transmitted by a decision letter accompanied by the Inspector's report.

Inspector's decision-making

7.100   The Inspector will write up the decision, having considered any assessor's report. If the Inspector proposes to take into account any new evidence or new matter of fact then notice must be given to the parties who were entitled to and did appear, allowing them three weeks to make written representations or request a re-opening of the inquiry or hearing.[157]

The decision

7.101   Whether the appeal is decided following an inquiry or hearing, Ministerial or Inspectorial decisions must be accompanied by written reasons.[158] There is no statutory duty to give reasons in written representations cases although conventionally reasons are given. In practice the reasons are contained in the same document as the formal decision. The Ministerial decision letter will contain the Minister's reasons. The letter will explicitly adopt the Inspector's reasons or set out where the Minister disagrees with the Inspector and why. An Inspector's decision will set out the entirety of the reasoning although it will be much shorter than a report. A decision is aimed primarily at the parties, who know what has happened at the inquiry or hearing and

---

[154]   English and Welsh Inquiries Rules, r 20(4).
[155]   English and Welsh Inquiries Rules, r 20(5), (6). Similar rules apply in the very rare event of a hearing being determined by a Minister: English and Welsh Hearings Rules, r 13.
[156]   English and Welsh Inquiries Rules, r 20(7) to (9).
[157]   English and Welsh Inspectors Inquiries Rules, r 19(3), (4); English and Welsh Hearings Rules, r 14(3) to (5)
[158]   English and Welsh Inquiries Rules, r 21; English and Welsh Inspectors Inquiries Rules, r 20, English and Welsh Hearings Rules, rr 15(2), 16(2).

what is in the appeal papers, whereas a report has to explain the case to ministers and civil servants.

7.102 The adequacy of reasons in planning decisions and other contexts has generated a mass of case law. Since a reasons challenge is inherently fact-sensitive it is unproductive to search the cases for too many detailed rules. What may be an acceptable omission in one case might not be acceptable in another. The most useful, and most often quoted, summary of the Court's approach to reasons was given by Lord Brown of Eaton-under-Heywood in *South Buckinghamshire District Council v Porter (No 2):*[159]

> 'The reasons for a decision must be intelligible and they must be adequate. They must enable the reader to understand why the matter was decided as it was and what conclusions were reached on the "principal important controversial issues", disclosing how any issue of law or fact was resolved. Reasons can be briefly stated, the degree of particularity required depending entirely on the nature of the issues falling for decision. The reasoning must not give rise to a substantial doubt as to whether the decision-maker erred in law, for example by misunderstanding some relevant policy or some other important matter or by failing to reach a rational decision on relevant grounds. But such adverse inference will not readily be drawn. The reasons need refer only to the main issues in the dispute, not to every material consideration. They should enable disappointed developers to assess their prospects of obtaining some alternative development permission, or, as the case may be, their unsuccessful opponents to understand how the policy or approach underlying the grant of permission may impact upon future such applications. Decision letters must be read in a straightforward manner, recognising that they are addressed to parties well aware of the issues involved and the arguments advanced. A reasons challenge will only succeed if the party aggrieved can satisfy the court that he has genuinely been substantially prejudiced by the failure to provide an adequately reasoned decision.'

7.103 The decision with its reasons must be sent[160] to the appellant, the local authority, those who were entitled to and did take part in the inquiry or hearing, along with anyone who did take part in the inquiry or hearing and had asked to be sent a copy of the decision.[161]

7.104 The Minister, or the Inspector, can do the following in determining the appeal:[162]

(a) He can correct any defect, error or misdescription in the enforcement notice, or vary the terms of the enforcement notice, if he is satisfied that the correction or variation will not cause injustice to the appellant or the local planning authority.

This power includes deleting part of the site as outside the planning unit or narrowing the description of the activity. However, it does not allow a correction that goes to 'the substance of the matter' (*Miller-Mead v Minister of Housing and Local Government*).[163] The power cannot correct a notice that is a nullity.

---

[159] [2004] UKHL 33, [2004] 1 WLR 1953 at para 36.
[160] Traditionally this has been by post, but may be by email or by informing participants that the documents have been put on a website and how to access them.
[161] English and Welsh Inquiries Rules, r 21; English and Welsh Inspectors Inquiries Rules, r 20; English and Welsh Hearings Rules, rr 15, 16.
[162] Town and Country Planning Act 1990, s 176(1).
[163] [1963] 2 QB 196.

(b) Where the Secretary of State determines to allow the appeal, he may quash the notice.[164]

(c) He may grant planning permission in respect of the matters stated in the enforcement notice as constituting a breach of planning control (in respect of all or part of the matters or land).[165]

(d) He may discharge any condition or limitation subject to which planning permission was granted.[166]

(e) He may determine whether, on the date on which the appeal was made, any existing use of land, operations or failure to comply with conditions or limitations was lawful, and issue a certificate of lawfulness of existing use or development (CLEUD) under s 191.[167]

COSTS

7.105 Normally each party to an enforcement notice appeal bears its own costs.[168] Costs are only awarded against a party if it has acted unreasonably and this has caused another party to incur wasted costs; in contrast to civil litigation, costs do not follow the event. A number of different provisions apply the power to award costs. By s 250(5) of the Local Government Act 1972, the Secretary of State may order the payment of parties' costs at inquiries. This is applied to enforcement notice appeals by s 320 of the 1990 Act. The power is also applied to hearings by s 322 and to written representation appeals by s 175(7). Where an inquiry or hearing is arranged but cancelled, s 250(5) is applied by s 322A. These powers can also be exercised by Inspectors. The current English advice is contained in DoE Circular 03/2009, *Costs awards in appeals and other planning proceedings*.[169] Welsh advice remains that in Welsh Office Circular 23/93 which is the same as the previous English Circular 08/93.

7.106 An award of costs will normally be made if:[170]

'• a party has made a timely application for an award of costs

• the party against whom the award is sought has acted unreasonably and

• the unreasonable behaviour has caused the party applying for costs to incur unnecessary or wasted expense in the appeal process – either the whole of the expense because it should not have been necessary for the matter to be determined by the Secretary of State or appointed Inspector, or part of the expense because of the manner in which a party has behaved in the process.'

'Unreasonable' has its normal meaning, rather than its special meaning in judicial review.[171] A costs award can cover the whole of a party's costs ('a full award') or

---

[164] Town and Country Planning Act 1990, s 176(2).
[165] Town and Country Planning Act 1990, s 177(1)(a).
[166] Town and Country Planning Act 1990, s 177(1)(b).
[167] Town and Country Planning Act 1990, s 177(1)(c). See Chapter 23.
[168] Circular 03/2009, para A7.
[169] A short addendum to the circular was published in December 2012.
[170] Circular 03/2009, para A12; WO Circular 23/93, Annex 1, para 1.
[171] *Manchester City Council v Secretary of State for the Environment* [1988] JPL 774; *R (Hann) v Secretary of State for the Environment, Transport and the Regions* [2001] EWHC Admin 930. Circular 03/3009, para A22.

a part of those costs ('a partial award'). A partial award might cover the costs of a particular issue or ground or a particular stage or period of time in the proceedings. Various types of unreasonable behaviour are set out in the Circular and these can be divided into procedural failures or substantive matters going to the merits of a party's case in whole or in part. These are all examples and parties should focus on the broad questions of whether the conduct was unreasonable and whether it caused wasted expense.

Substantive unreasonable behaviour by the local planning authority

7.107   If the local planning authority fails to take into account relevant judicial authority, government policy and well-publicised appeal decisions in issuing an enforcement notice, they may be liable in costs. They should be able to produce evidence substantiating each reason.[172] If an enforcement notice is withdrawn because it was not expedient to issue it or it had an incurable defect, then costs may be awarded. If the notice is quashed because of an incurable defect, costs are likely to be awarded if clearly established principles of law are misunderstood.[173] It is generally unreasonable to issue an enforcement notice solely to remedy the absence of a valid planning permission if an appeal concludes that there is no significant planning objection to the breach of control alleged.[174] The LPA must show reasonable grounds for concluding that the breach would unacceptably affect public amenity or that the existing use of land merited protection in the public interest.[175] Refusal by the LPA to discuss the possibility of granting planning permission for the development alleged in the enforcement notice or to provide reasonably requested information when a more helpful approach would have enabled the appeal to be avoided may lead to costs.[176]

7.108   There should be reasonable grounds for concluding that there was a beach of planning control.[177] Costs may follow a failure to undertake reasonable investigations to establish whether there has been a breach of planning control, for example by making enquiries, examining records or using investigatory powers.[178] But failure to serve a planning contravention notice does not in itself justify an award of costs.[179]

Unreasonable behaviour by the appellant

7.109   It may be unreasonable to appeal if the appeal or ground of appeal had no reasonable prospect of succeeding on the available evidence.[180] Ground (a) appeals may be unreasonable if:

(a)   there has been a recent planning appeal dismissed on the same or substantially the same site and the same or a very similar development proposal;[181]

---

[172]   See generally Circular 03/2009, para B15 to B29, B32.
[173]   Circular 03/2009, paras B35, B55; WO Circular 23/93, Annex 3, para 22.
[174]   Circular 03/2009, para B40; WO Circular 23/93, Annex 3, para 24.
[175]   Circular 03/2009, para B34.
[176]   WO Circular 23/93, Annex 3, para 27.
[177]   WO Circular 23/93, Annex 3, para 23.
[178]   Circular 03/2009, para B12; WO Circular 23/93, Annex 3, para 28.
[179]   Circular 03/2009, para B39; WO Circular 23/93, Annex 3, para 23.
[180]   Circular 03/2009, para B13.
[181]   Circular 03/2009, paras B13, B31; WO Circular 23/93, Annex 3, para 1.

(b) when it must have been obvious from the development plan, the Government's planning policy guidance or from judicial authority that the appeal has no reasonable prospect of success.[182]

If appeals on other grounds have no reasonable prospect of success, then costs may be awarded.

Unreasonable behaviour in procedural matters by the appellant and the local planning authority

7.110 Various acts by either party could be unreasonable, for example:

(a) failure to comply with the rules or regulations applicable to the appeal;

(b) failing to provide an adequate statement of case;[183]

(c) unreasonably late submission of a statement of case, or amendment to a statement of case, or proof of evidence or summary, causing the inquiry or hearing to be adjourned or unnecessarily prolonged;[184]

(d) introducing a new issue forcing the adjournment of the inquiry or prolonging the appeal;[185]

(e) causing a party to call an professional witness to attend unnecessarily;[186]

(f) failure to co-operate in settling agreed facts, or supplying relevant information, so that the proceedings are adjourned or prolonged unnecessarily;[187]

(g) uncooperative behaviour (the English guidance refers to resistance to or lack of co-operation, the Welsh circular describes 'deliberately uncooperative behaviour');[188] or

(h) failure to complete a timely statement of common ground or unreasonably failing to agree factual matters.[189]

If following negotiations or other material change in circumstances, an enforcement notice is withdrawn or varied or an appeal withdrawn, then costs will not be awarded unless there was a protracted delay in withdrawing the notice or appeal.[190]

Cancellation of inquiry or hearing

7.111 Where the late cancellation of an inquiry or hearing (that is after the formal notification by the Planning Inspectorate of the arrangements) occurs because of unreasonable behaviour by a party, then costs may be awarded under s 322A. An

---

[182] Circular 03/2009, para B13; WO Circular 23/93, Annex 3, para 3, 5.
[183] WO Circular 23/93, Annex 2, para 3(1).
[184] Circular 03/2009, para B4; WO Circular 23/93, Annex 2, para 3(4).
[185] Circular 03/2009, para B4; WO Circular 23/93, Annex 2, para 3, 4.
[186] WO Circular 23/93, Annex 2, para 3(5).
[187] WO Circular 23/93, para 4(3) Annex 2.
[188] Circular 03/2009, para B4; WO Circular 23/93, para 3, Annex 2.
[189] Circular 03/2009, para B4.
[190] WO Circular 23/93, Annex 3, para 25.

appellant who withdraws any appeal without any material change in the planning authority's case or the circumstances is likely to have acted unreasonably.[191]

Third parties

7.112   Awards of costs either in favour or against third parties are made only in exceptional circumstances.[192] Generally third parties will not receive costs because the appeal or the refusal is unreasonable. Costs may be awarded to (or against) third parties for unreasonable behaviour in procedural matters.[193] Persons entitled to appear (including rule 6 parties) are expected to comply with the procedural rules and so are more likely to have costs awarded for or against them.[194] Where unreasonable conduct causes the cancellation of an inquiry or hearing, third parties may be awarded costs if they have forewarned the appellant and local planning authority of their intention to appear.[195] Third parties should check with the planning authority whether discussions might lead to the inquiry not proceeding.[196]

THE COSTS APPLICATION

7.113   The application for costs should normally be made at the inquiry or hearing before the close of the proceedings.[197] The applications are dealt with after closing submissions. Historically, any written submissions in support of a costs application were only produced as the oral application was made. Parties often made explicit or implicit threats during the course of an appeal, such as using a proof of evidence to describe the other side's position as 'unreasonable'. The 2009 Costs Circular envisages a more up-front, and less tactical, approach. It advises that written applications should be submitted to the Inspector and copied to the other side prior to the hearing when a clear basis for an application is seen and a party intends to apply for costs. The written submissions can be updated orally in the light of events at the inquiry or hearing.[198] If a costs application is made in the absence of the party against whom the order is sought, then it will be dealt with on written representations.[199]

7.114   The costs decision will be in a separate letter to the decision letter on the appeal. If the appeal is determined by the Secretary of State, the Inspector will report on the costs application and usually make a recommendation.[200] If the inquiry or hearing is cancelled, applications for costs should be made to the Costs and Decisions Team in the Planning Inspectorate, no later than four weeks after having received confirmation of the cancellation. The Secretary of State prefers applications to be made immediately.[201] Costs may be awarded where appeals are dealt with by written representations. In such cases the application should be made with the statement of case, or at the latest the nine-week statement, unless the grounds for making the

---

[191]   WO Circular 23/93, Annex 2, para 9.
[192]   Circular 03/2009, para D5.
[193]   WO Circular 23/93, Annex 4, para 2.
[194]   Circular 03/2009, para D6.
[195]   Circular 03/2009, para D13; WO Circular 23/93, Annex 4, para 4.
[196]   Circular 03/2009, para D15; WO Circular 23/93, Annex 4, para 5.
[197]   WO Circular 23/93, Annex 5, para 1.
[198]   Circular 03/2009, paras A31–33.
[199]   Circular 03/2009, para A35.
[200]   Circular 03/2009, para A34.
[201]   Circular 03/2009, paras A46, A47; WO Circular 23/93, Annex 5, para 2.

application arise later.[202] Late applications for costs can be made in any case provided that good reason can be shown.[203]

7.115 A costs award will identify the appeal for which costs are awarded and in the event of a partial award, the particular element of the appeal which are covered (usually by reference to ground, issue, time or stage of the process). The Inspectorate will not determine the quantum of costs and are not interested in any costs estimates, beyond needing to be satisfied that some wasted costs arose from the unreasonable behaviour. The quantum of costs will be determined by a costs judge of the Senior Courts Costs Office ('the SCCO') if not agreed between the parties. The costs award must be registered with the SCCO before a detailed assessment can be carried out by a costs judge. For major costs claims the receiving party (ie the one which got the costs award) may need to instruct costs draftsmen and, if there is a difficult issue or hearing, costs counsel.

CORRECTION OF ERRORS IN DECISIONS

7.116 A decision once issued is final, subject to challenge in the Courts. It confers rights, ends processes or imposes liabilities on parties. It is not implicit that even obvious errors can be corrected by administrative means. The Planning and Compulsory Purchase Act 2004 introduced a statutory slip rule for planning appeals, including enforcement notice appeals.[204] Where a decision contains a 'correctable error' the Minister or the Inspector have a power to issue a fresh decision.[205] A correctable error is an error:[206]

'(a) which is contained in any part of the decision document which records the decision, but

(b) which is not part of any reasons given for the decision.'

This power can only be exercised if a request to make a correction has been received or the Minister or Inspector have informed the applicant or appellant that they are considering making a correction within the High Court challenge period.[207] In Wales, corrections require the consent of the appellant and any other person who owns the land.[208] A correction would be made by issuing a correction notice[209] which will be the decision as corrected with an introductory paragraph saying that it is a correction notice. A correction notice would become the determination of the appeal. Time for bringing High Court proceedings, or the taking effect of an enforcement notice would run from that date.[210] Any High Court proceedings brought against the original decision would become academic (save for costs issues) and any proceedings should be brought again against the correction notice.

---

[202] Circular 03/2009, paras A37, A38.

[203] Circular 03/2009, para A48.

[204] Planning and Compulsory Purchase Act 2004, s 59(4). Listed building, conservation area enforcement notice and hazardous substances contravention notice appeal decisions may also be corrected under the slip rule.

[205] Planning and Compulsory Purchase Act 2004, s 56.

[206] Planning and Compulsory Purchase Act 2004, s 59(5).

[207] Planning and Compulsory Purchase Act 2004, s 56(4). This does not include any potential extension of time for appealing.

[208] Planning and Compulsory Purchase Act 2004, s 56(3)(c), (6).

[209] Planning and Compulsory Purchase Act 2004, s 57(1).

[210] Planning and Compulsory Purchase Act 2004, s 58.

NATIONAL SECURITY CASES

7.117   The general principle is that the planning process operates in public. In public inquiries, it has long been the case that oral and documentary evidence has to be heard by and available to the public, subject to limited exceptions for national security or measures to ensure the security of any premises or property in the national interest (although fairness ensured that the parties could still be present).[211] In conjunction with the extension of planning control over Crown land, the Planning and Compulsory Purchase Act 2004 introduced a system of special advocates in certain planning cases.[212]

7.118   If the Secretary of State is proposing to direct that the persons able to see particular evidence in an appeal is restricted for national security or property protection purposes, then the Attorney General or Counsel General to the Welsh Assembly Government may appoint a special advocate to represent the interests of persons excluded from the proceedings.[213]

7.119   The enforcement rules and regulations are amended to provide that the Minister is not required to disclose information which could harm national security or disclose measures to protect property where a national security direction has been made. Evidence and statements of case would be split between open and closed evidence, the closed evidence only being available to the Inspector and security-vetted participants, essentially government representatives and special advocates. There would then be open and closed inspector's reports and decisions.

---

[211] Town and Country Planning Act 1990, s 321.
[212] For a discussion of this change see Stephen Tromans, Martin Edwards, Richard Harwood and Justine Thornton *Planning and Compulsory Purchase Act 2004: A guide to the new law* (The Law Society, 2005), Chapter 7.
[213] Town and Country Planning Act 1990, ss 321(5), 322A, 322B.

Chapter 8

Challenges to Enforcement Notices

8.01   Enforcement notices can be challenged by statutory appeal to the High Court and to a limited degree in judicial review and other civil and criminal proceedings. Challenges are tightly controlled, as enforcement notices are intended to be a certain and relatively quick means of enforcement. Competing with this is the need to keep public authorities under proper control and to protect the rights of the individual and the public at large.

CHALLENGING THE SECRETARY OF STATE'S DECISION ON AN ENFORCEMENT NOTICE APPEAL IN THE HIGH COURT

8.02   Three different mechanisms apply, in different situations, to challenges to appeal decisions by the Secretary of State, Welsh Ministers or an inspector:

(a) appeal to the High Court under s 289;

(b) application to the High Court under s 288 to quash a grant of planning permission in the enforcement notice appeal; and

(c) judicial review.

These challenges must be considered against the background that Parliament and the courts want to minimise delays and the opportunity for unmeritorious delaying tactics in enforcement proceedings.

Appeal to the High Court under s 289

8.03   This challenge is against any decision of the Secretary of State in proceedings on an appeal against an enforcement notice.[1] This includes decisions on costs applications,[2] but not the Secretary of State declining jurisdiction to consider the appeal, which is challengeable by judicial review.[3] The decision of an inspector is considered to be the decision of the Secretary of State and an action would be brought against the Secretary of State or Welsh Ministers, as appropriate. An appeal may be brought by 'the appellant or the local planning authority or any other person having an interest in the land to which the notice relates'.[4] Any other challenger would have to bring judicial review proceedings. The challenge is normally by the appellant if the notice is upheld, and by the local planning authority if it is not. An appeal is in principle concerned with a challenge to the substantive decision rather than the reasoning. So as a general rule it is not possible to appeal against a decision

---

[1]   Town and Country Planning Act 1990, s 289(1).
[2]   *Botton v Secretary of State for the Environment* [1992] 1 PLR 1.
[3]   *Lenlyn v Secretary of State for the Environment* (1983) 50 P & CR 129.
[4]   Town and Country Planning Act 1990, s 289(1).

where the formal decision is favourable but part of the reasons or other findings are objected to.[5] There may be exceptions, particularly if the objectionable part of the decision has consequences for other decisions.[6] The availability of this remedy satisfies the requirements of the European Convention of Human Rights that there be an 'independent and impartial tribunal'[7] in the enforcement notice process.[8]

8.04   Section 289(1) allows rules of the court to provide for a person to:

(a)   appeal on a point of law; or

(b)   require the Secretary of State to state and sign a case for the opinion of the High Court.

The Civil Procedure Rules do not provide for a case stated under this section and so this option is not available.[9] The only challenge provided for is an appeal on a point of law.[10] A section 289 appeal would be against the decision on the enforcement notice appeal.

Grounds of challenge

8.05   The appeal is confined to points of law only, meaning public law grounds. As it is an appeal against 'a decision in proceedings on an appeal' there is authority that the point must have arisen in the appeal, otherwise there is no decision to challenge in the High Court appeal.[11] The court is not empowered to set the decision aside or vary it. If the decision is erroneous in law the court can remit the matter to the Secretary of State or Welsh Ministers with the opinion of the court for re-hearing and determination.[12] The court cannot examine questions of fact, except where a factual error amounts to a public law error. Indeed, it has been said that the court should not receive evidence put before the inspector unless it is argued that the inspector has not properly summarised, or has disregarded, some material evidence.[13]

Standing

8.06   The High Court appeal may be brought by 'the appellant or the local planning authority or any other person with an interest in the land to which the notice relates'.[14]

---

[5]   *Young v Secretary of State for the Environment* (1990) 60 P & CR 560 (but note the minority view of Woolf LJ). The use of judicial review to challenge the reasoning in a favourable decision is confined to exceptional circumstances: *R (Redditch Borough Council) v First Secretary of State* [2003] EWHC 650 (Admin), [2004] JPL 21.

[6]   One example would be if an enforcement notice appeal is allowed on ground (a) (granting planning permission) and dismissed on the legal grounds (grounds (b) to (d)) and the appellant wished to succeed on a legal ground so compensation could be obtained for losses caused by a stop notice.

[7]   Article 6.1.

[8]   *Bryan v United Kingdom* (1996) 21 EHRR 342.

[9]   Practice Direction 52E on appeals by way of case stated says that procedures for statements of case by ministers may be in the enactment or rules of procedure: para 3.1. However no rules of procedure provide for a case stated against an enforcement notice appeal decision. This continues the longstanding position under the planning legislation: see *Hoser v Minister of Housing and Local Government* [1963] Ch 428.

[10]   CPR 52.20(1).

[11]   *Beach v Secretary of State for the Environment, Transport and the Regions* [2001] EWHC Admin 381, [2002] JPL 185 at para 37 to 44 per Ouseley J.

[12]   Practice Direction 52D, para 26.1(15).

[13]   *Clarke v Secretary of State for the Environment* (1993) 65 P &CR 85, 90.

[14]   Town and Country Planning Act 1990, s 289(1).

8.07   *Challenges to Enforcement Notices*

Relevant occupiers who did not exercise their right to appeal, persons who were served but without a right of appeal to the Secretary of State, other public authorities entitled to appear at the inquiry and third parties are not entitled to proceed under s 289. Such persons may be able to challenge the decision by judicial review.[15]

Bringing proceedings

8.07   The appeal must be brought by an Appellant's Notice under Pt 52 of the Civil Procedure Rules, with further procedures set out in Practice Direction 52D – statutory appeals and appeals subject to special provision, section II and section III, para 26.1. The Practice Direction says that the application must be in writing, with the reasons why permission should be granted and include any necessary application for an extension of time.[16] It must be accompanied by:[17]

'(a) a copy of the decision being appealed;

(b) a draft appellant's notice;

(c) a witness statement or affidavit verifying any facts relied on; and

(d) a witness statement or affidavit giving the name and address of, and the place and date of service on, each person who has been served with the application. If any person who ought to be served has not been served, the witness statement or affidavit must state that fact and the reason why the person was not served.'

Since an appellant's notice includes space for requesting permission to appeal, as well as the grounds of appeal, it is common practice for the application for permission to appeal to be in the draft appellant's notice rather than in a separate application document (such as a conventional application notice form or another document). Whilst the Practice Direction appears to be anticipating some separate document, it is logistically easier to put all matters on the draft appellant's notice and no problems appear to have arisen with the court.

8.08   The Secretary of State or Welsh Ministers, as appropriate, will be named as the first respondent. The appellant or the local planning authority, if they are not appealing, will be the second respondent. It is unusual to join other persons interested in the land in the proceedings, although the application, draft appellant's notice and witness statement must be served upon them.[18]

Obtaining permission to appeal

Permission from the High Court must be obtained[19]

8.09   Permission from the High Court must be obtained for an appeal to be brought.[20] The application for permission must be brought 'within 28 days after notice of the decision is given to the applicant'.[21] The prudent view is to take notice

---

[15]   See below.

[16]   Practice Direction 52D, para 26.1(2).

[17]   Practice Direction 52D, para 26.1(4).

[18]   Practice Direction 52D, para 26.1(3), (12).

[19]   Town and Country Planning Act 1990, s 289(6).

[20]   Town and Country Planning Act 1990, s 289(6).

[21]   Practice Direction 52C, para 26.1(1).

as being given on the date the notice is sent (taken as the date on the decision letter): *Ringroad Investments and Courtburn v Secretary of State for the Environment.*[22] This was a majority decision of the Divisional Court on the former requirement of the Rules of the Supreme Court Order 55, r 4(4) that the period 'shall be calculated from the date on which notice of the decision was given to the appellant'. The majority considered itself bound, with reluctance, by the Divisional Court's decision in an industrial tribunal appeal, *Minister of Labour v Genner Iron & Steel Co (Wollescote) Limited.*[23] However the *Genner* decision was described by the Court of Appeal in *Griffiths v Secretary of State for the Environment* as *obiter* and the Court disagreed with *Ringroad* considering that given means received.[24] *Griffiths* however concerned an application from a planning appeal (what is now under s 288) and so the point was itself obiter. In *Smith v Secretary of State for the Environment,*[25] the Court of Appeal considered it to be correct that time ran from the date on which the notice of the decision was received. The *Griffiths* and *Smith* approach was followed by the High Court in *Ynys Mon Borough Council v Secretary of State for Wales*[26] and *R v East Sussex County Council ex p ARC Ltd.*[27] There is therefore ample basis for saying that time from receipt of the decision rather than it being sent out. That said, in the absence of *Ringroad* being explicitly overruled, it is cautious to work from the earlier date. There may be uncertainty or dispute as to when a decision was received. Since the Planning Inspectorate will often email decisions to appellants, the question of a difference between the sending and receipt of a decision would not apply in many cases.

8.10   The proceedings must be brought 'within 28 days after' notice was given. This date does not include the date on which notice was given, as it refers to a number of days after the dates of the decision.[28] So if notice was given on a Tuesday then the last date for filing is the Tuesday four weeks later. This time may be extended with the leave of the court.[29] The application, the draft appellant's notice, the decision and witness statement (or affidavit) verifying any facts relied upon must be filed in the Administrative Court in the 28-day period along with a witness statement or affidavit:[30]

> 'giving the name and address of, and the place and date of service on, each person who has been served with the application. If any person who ought to be served has not been served, the witness statement or affidavit must state that fact and the reason why the person was not served.'

The form of the application, as distinct from the draft appellant's notice, is unclear. Since the appellant's notice includes room for applying for permission to appeal, the Administrative Court's practice is to accept an appellant's notice without a separate application form. The application is required to set out the reasons why permission

---

[22] (1980) 40 P &CR 99.
[23] [1967] 1 WLR 1386.
[24] [1983] 2 AC 51 per Templeman LJ at 56.
[25] [1987] *The Times*, 6 July.
[26] [1992] 3 PLR 1.
[27] [2000] Env LR D8.
[28] Following the reasoning in *Pritam Kaur v s Russell & Sons Ltd* [1973] QB 336. Without giving any analysis, this was also the view of the Court of Appeal in *Smith v Secretary of State for the Environment* [1987] *The Times*, 6 July.
[29] CPR 3.1(2).
[30] Practice Direction 52D, para 26.1(4). It is easier and conventional to use witness statements rather than affidavits as these do not have to be sworn before an independent solicitor.

should be granted.[31] A skeleton argument should be filed with the appellants or within 14 days.[32] However, until permission to appeal is granted, the appellant's notice in an enforcement notice case is in draft, so the requirement would seem not to apply. However, the judge considering the permission application will need to be fully informed of the issues and so a sensible course is to either file a skeleton and grounds within the original application or to include the grounds in that application and send a skeleton in within 14 days.

8.11   The permission application is heard by a single judge sitting in open court. Unfortunately there is no procedure for a judge to consider the permission application on the papers (as happens in judicial review). The consequence is that permission hearings may last a matter of seconds if the judge has decided on reading the papers that the case is arguable and no respondent attends to resist permission. Respondents may appear at the hearing to challenge the application for permission.[33] If they wish to produce evidence at this hearing, it must be filed with the Administrative Court and served on the applicant as soon as practicable and in any event, at least two days before the hearing.[34] The court may allow the applicant for permission to use a further witness statement or affidavit.[35]

8.12   If permission is granted, the appellant's notice must be served and filed in the court within seven days.[36] The appellant's notice must be served on the Secretary of State, the local planning authority or appellant (whoever is not appealing), any other person having an interest in the land.[37] A certificate of service then needs to be filed.[38] On granting permission, the court may impose terms as to costs and giving security,[39] and may give directions.[40] The High Court, or at a later stage the Court of Appeal, may order that the enforcement notice shall have effect in whole or to a specified extent, pending the final determination of those proceedings and any re-hearing and determination by the Secretary of State.[41] This effect may be on such terms including an undertaking as to damages by the local planning authority. Permission may be refused if the case is not arguable.[42] There may be other circumstances in which it can be refused. It was suggested by Henry J, in *P G Vallance Ltd v Secretary of State for the Environment*[43] that leave could be refused if it was plain that no substantial wrong or miscarriage of justice had been occasioned by any misdirection in relation to the law. If permission to appeal to the High Court is refused by the High Court the challenge ends. The Court of Appeal cannot consider

---

[31]   Practice Direction 52D, para 26.1(2).
[32]   Practice Direction 52A, para 5.9.
[33]   Practice Direction 52D, para 26.1(7): 'Any person served with the application is entitled to appear and be heard'.
[34]   Practice Direction 52D, para 26.1(8).
[35]   Practice Direction 52D, para 26.1(9).
[36]   Practice Direction 52D, para 26.1(11)(c).
[37]   Practice Direction 52D, para 26.1(12).
[38]   Practice Direction 52B, para 6.1.
[39]   Practice Direction 52D, para 26(11)(a), although this is rare, perhaps because appellants are usually local authorities or landowners.
[40]   Practice Direction 52D, para 26(11)(b).
[41]   Town and Country Planning Act 1990, s 289(4A).
[42]   *Kensington & Chelsea Royal London Borough Council v Secretary of State for the Environment* [1992] 2 PLR 116, [1993] JPL 139.
[43]   [1993] 1 PLR 74, [1994] JPL 50.

an appeal against that refusal.[44] There is also an interim power in the court to require the Minister to provide further information,[45] although that will rarely be needed.

The substantive hearing

8.13 Following service of the appellant's notice, the appellant (in the High Court) is required to serve an appeal bundle within 35 days of filing the appellant's notice.[46] This will contain the originally filed material, the permission decision and any further material produced by the parties. A skeleton should be filed with or within 14 days of the appellant's notice, if it has not already been submitted.

8.14 CPR52 and the relevant practice directions leave the status of evidence from the respondents unclear. It may be sensible for the parties to seek to agree directions to be made as to evidence and skeletons if permission is granted. Unless it orders otherwise, the High Court will not receive oral evidence or evidence which was not in front of the Inspector or Minister prior to the decision.[47] The respondents may wish to add in other documents from the appeal and that is straightforward. If an issue arises as to what happened in the conduct of the appeal (such as events on the site visit) it would be usual for all parties to be able to put in evidence. The rules on respondents' skeletons are unclear, although such skeletons are essential in enforcement notice appeals. The parties should seek to agree a timescale for skeletons.

8.15 The court's power is to remit the enforcement notice appeal back to the Minister for redetermination in accordance with the judgment of the court.[48] The enforcement notice remains in being, but its taking of effect is suspended until the appeal is redetermined (unless the suspension is lifted by the court). The court is able to give directions as to the service of stop notices and breach of condition notices, or the institution of proceedings relating to those notices, prior to the final determination of the appeal.[49]

8.16 On remission of an enforcement notice appeal the Minister is required to remedy the error identified and that does not necessarily require the appeal to be considered entirely afresh: *R (Perrett) v Secretary of State for Communities and Local Government*.[50] For example, if the decision is remitted because of a legal error on the ground (a) appeal (as to whether planning permission should be granted), the Minister is not obliged to reconsider whether there a breach of planning control which can be enforced against (grounds (b) to (d)). Whether the steps required are excessive and extensions of time might arise regardless of the grounds of the remission. An error as to whether planning permission should be granted might affect the balance of the planning considerations so the planning merits would have to be reopened in their entirety, subject perhaps to the parties agreeing that the issues can be narrowed.

---

[44] *Wendy Fair Markets Limited v Secretary of State for the Environment* [1996] JPL 649. This has been re-affirmed by the Court of Appeal in *Walsall Metropolitan Borough Council v Secretary of State for Communities and Local Government* [2013] EWCA Civ 370. There is a residual discretion in the Court of Appeal to allow an appeal to proceed if there was misconduct or unfairness in the High Court process: *Walsall* at para 15 per Sullivan LJ.
[45] Practice Direction 52D, para 26(15).
[46] Practice Direction 52B, para 6.3.
[47] CPR 52.11(2).
[48] Practice Direction 52D, para 26(14).
[49] Practice Direction 52D, para 26(16).
[50] [2009] EWCA Civ 1365, [2010] LGR 336.

Consequently if the Minister offers to submit to judgment it is necessary to consider what issues would be capable of being reopened in the remitted appeal. The result may be that the High Court proceedings have to continue to resolve the basis of the remission.[51]

Costs

8.17   The general rule is that 'the unsuccessful party will be ordered to pay the costs of the successful party'.[52] Consequently, the winner of the final hearing will usually recover its costs. Costs do though remain in the discretion of the court. A party who has been ultimately successful but failed on a significant number of its arguments might not recover its full costs. However, the losing party will not normally be expected to pay more than one set of costs, for example to the Secretary of State and the respondent developer, unless this is justified by the case.[53]

8.18   There is a little more debate about the costs of permission hearings. There are four possible situations:

(1) permission to appeal is granted and the appeal is ultimately successful;

(2) permission to appeal is refused;

(3) permission to appeal is granted but the appeal ultimately fails; and

(4) permission to appeal is granted on a limited number of the grounds advanced.

The position of an ultimately successful appellant is straightforward: the appellant will recover its costs of the permission hearing on the same basis as the costs of the overall proceedings.

8.19   In 1994 the Court of Appeal held in *R v Secretary of State for Wales ex p Rozhon*[54] that, as respondents are entitled to attend the permission hearing, they should receive their costs if permission is refused. However, that decision pre-dates the changes introduced by Civil Procedure Rules, in particular the Practice Directions to the appeal rules. Practice Direction 52B, para 8.1 provides:

> '**Attendance at permission hearings:** Where a respondent to an appeal or cross-appeal attends the hearing of an application for permission to appeal, costs will not be awarded to the respondent unless–
>
> (a) the court has ordered or requested attendance by the respondent;
>
> (b) the court has ordered that the appeal be listed at the same time as the determination of other applications;
>
> (c) the court has ordered that the hearing of the appeal will follow the hearing of the application if permission is granted; or
>
> (d) the court considers it just, in all the circumstances, to award costs to the respondent.'

---

[51] As happened, for example, in *Elvington Park Ltd v Secretary of State for Communities and Local Government* [2011] EWHC 3041 (Admin), [2012] JPL 556.

[52] Civil Procedure Rules, Part 44.2(2)(a).

[53] See *Bolton Metropolitan Borough Council v Secretary of State for the Environment (Practice Note)* [1995] 1 WLR 1176 (on s 288 applications).

[54] [1994] JPL 801.

Respondents are still entitled to appear at the permission hearing[55] but (unless a direction is made) their attendance is neither ordered nor requested. It is also notable by analogy that whilst defendants are entitled to attend judicial review permission hearings, they will not normally receive their costs: Practice Direction 54A, para 8.6. The issue has not been fully considered in the courts.[56]

Appealing to the Court of Appeal

8.20   If permission to appeal to the High Court has been granted, then its decision on the substantive appeal may be appealed to the Court of Appeal. Section 289(6) provides that any appeal to the Court of Appeal may only be brought with the leave of the High Court or Court of Appeal, but this has been restricted further by the Civil Procedure Rules. As the High Court proceedings are an appeal rather than an application, any appeal to the Court of Appeal is treated as a second appeal. Consequently permission to appeal can only be granted by the Court of Appeal.[57] The usual rule for the grant of permission to appeal is in CPR 52.3(6):

> 'Permission to appeal may be given only where—
>
> (a)   the court considers that the appeal would have a real prospect of success; or
>
> (b)   there is some other compelling reason why the appeal should be heard.'

However, for enforcement notice appeals to the Court of Appeal, the second appeals rule in section 55 of the Access to Justice Act 1999 also applies:[58]

> 'no appeal may be made to the Court of Appeal from that decision unless the Court of Appeal considers that—
>
> (a)   the appeal would raise an important point of principle or practice, or
>
> (b)   there is some other compelling reason for the Court of Appeal to hear it.'

Application to the High Court under s 288 to quash a grant of planning permission

8.21   The grant of planning permission in an enforcement notice appeal is treated in the same way as the grant of permission under a s 77 call-in or s 78 planning appeal. A grant of planning permission or the discharge of a condition or limitation on an enforcement notice appeal can be challenged by an application to the High Court under s 288.[59] Refusal of planning permission in an enforcement appeal is not covered by these provisions. A distinction is drawn between the need for speed in enforcement proceedings and treating the local planning authority and third parties

---

[55]   Practice Direction 52D, para 26.1(7).

[56]   *Rozhon* was noted as the approach to enforcement notices by the Court of Appeal when it considered judicial review permission hearing costs in *R (Mount Cook) v Westminster City Council* [2003] EWCA Civ 1346, [2004] 2 P &CR 22 at para 70. There was limited consideration following a substantive appeal hearing in *Williams v Secretary of State for Communities and Local Government* [2009] EWHC 475 (Admin) but the court refrained from expressing a view on the principle as the issue had not been fully argued and the costs involved in a skeleton from the Secretary of State for the permission hearing (without attendance) were extremely small.

[57]   CPR 52.13(1).

[58]   This requirement is repeated in CPR 52.13(2).

[59]   Town and Country Planning Act 1990, ss 284(3), 288(4).

as if the Secretary of State had granted permission in a planning appeal. There will also need to be an appeal under s 289 to the decision to allow the enforcement notice appeal.[60] The s 288 proceedings are able to quash the planning permission, but the s 289 proceedings are required to remit the enforcement notice appeal decision back to the minister. Separate proceedings therefore have to be filed, but it is conventional to have identical grounds and a common bundle of evidence. The proceedings would be dealt with together, except that there will have to be a permission to appeal hearing in the s 289 proceedings. There is no good reason why two sets of proceedings should have to be brought against a single decision. It merely increases costs and encourages procedural error.

Grounds of challenge

8.22   The s 288 challenge is on the grounds:[61]

'(i)   that the action is not within the powers of this Act, or

(ii)   that any of the relevant requirements have not been complied with in relation to that action.'

The relevant requirements are those under the Act and the Tribunals and Inquiries Act 1992 and of orders, regulations and rules made under those Acts.[62]

8.23   The High Court may quash the grant of planning permission if it is satisfied that it:[63]

'is not within the powers of this Act, or that the interests of the applicant [to the Court] have been substantially prejudiced by a failure to comply with any of the relevant requirements in relation to it.'

The tests are essentially those in judicial review. These include errors of law going to jurisdiction, unreasonableness in acting without evidence, taking into account irrelevant considerations or failing to take into account relevant considerations, or failure to comply with the statutory procedures or the principles of natural justice (see *Seddon Properties Ltd v Secretary of State for the Environment*[64] and *Ashbridge Investments Ltd v Minister of Housing and Local Government*).[65]

Standing

8.24   The challenge may be brought by a 'person aggrieved'.[66] The local planning authority is entitled to apply under this section. A person is aggrieved in the ordinary sense of the word for a s 288 application.[67] Third party pressure groups have been

---

[60]   *R (Wandsworth London Borough Council) v Secretary of State for Transport, Local Government and the Regions* [2003] EWHC 622 (Admin), [2004] P &CR 32.

[61]   Town and Country Planning Act 1990, s 288(1).

[62]   Town and Country Planning Act 1990, s 288(9).

[63]   Town and Country Planning Act 1990, s 288(5).

[64]   (1981) 42 P &CR 26.

[65]   [1965] 1 WLR 1320.

[66]   Town and Country Planning Act 1990, s 288(1).

[67]   *Times Investment Ltd v Secretary of State for the Environment* (1991) 61 P & CR 98.

allowed to challenge planning permissions.[68] Broadly speaking, a claimant must show that they took part in the appeal proceedings, were not told about the appeal and would have taken part if they had known, or are directly affected by the proposal.[69] For example, in *Bannister v Secretary of State for the Environment*,[70] a neighbouring landowner was allowed to apply under s 288 against a planning permission granted in an enforcement appeal.

Bringing proceedings

8.25   The procedure is set out in Pt 8 of the Civil Procedure Rules and its practice direction, particularly para 22. The Pt 8 claim form[71] will identify the decision to be challenged and set out the grounds of challenge. Conventionally, the Secretary of State or Welsh Ministers will be the first defendant. The appellant and the local planning authority will be added as defendants if they are not a claimant. No leave is required to bring an application, unlike a s 289 appeal. The application must be brought within six weeks from the date of the decision,[72] so if a decision is dated on a Tuesday then the claim must be made on or before the Tuesday six weeks later.[73] Subject potentially to human rights or European law issues, this time limit cannot be extended.[74] The proceedings should be served within the six-week period but the court may extend time for service.[75] A defendant must file an acknowledgment of service within 14 days of receiving the claim form if it wishes to take part in the hearing.[76]

8.26   Evidence is to be filed and served by the claimant within 14 days of serving the claim form and by the defendants 21 days after service of the claimant's evidence.[77] Evidence is by witness statement,[78] although witnesses are occasionally called where events at the hearing or inquiry are disputed. The High Court may suspend the challenged planning permission by interim order until the final determination of proceedings,[79] although this is rarely if ever done. The case is heard by a single judge, either a High Court or Deputy High Court Judge.

Costs of High Court appeals and applications

8.27   As in other court proceedings the costs of the action will follow the event. Where there is multiple representation in a s 288 application the losing party will not

---

[68]   Eg *Save Britain's Heritage v Secretary of State for the Environment* [1991] 2 All ER 10.

[69]   See *Walton v Scottish Ministers* [2012] UKSC 44, [2013] JPL 323; *Ashton v Secretary of State for Communities and Local Government* [2010] EWCA Civ 600, [2010] JPL 1645 and the Aarhus Convention on Access to Environmental Justice, art 9.

[70]   [1995] JPL B13.

[71]   Form N208.

[72]   Town and Country Planning Act 1990, s 288(3).

[73]   There is authority that the claim form needs to be with the court office rather than delivered to the court building after the office has closed: *Barker v Hambleton District Council* [2011] EWHC 1707 (Admin).

[74]   See the similar development plan challenge provisions considered in *Barker v Hambleton District Council* [2012] EWCA Civ 610, [2013] 1 P &CR 1, but cf *Pomiechowski v Poland* [2012] UKSC 20, [2012] 1 WLR 1604 on short time limits and human rights.

[75]   For the principles on extending time see *Corus UK Limited v Erewash Borough Council* [2006] EWCA Civ 1175, [2007] 1 P & CR 22.

[76]   Civil Procedure Rules, r 8(3). If there has been a failure to acknowledge service then the permission of the court is required to take part in the hearing: r 8(4).

[77]   Practice Direction 8A, para 22.8–10.

[78]   Practice Direction 8A, para 22.7.

[79]   Town and Country Planning Act 1990, s 288(5).

normally be required to pay more than one set of costs unless the recovery of further costs is justified by the circumstances of the particular case. Following conflicting case law, the House of Lords in *Bolton Metropolitan District Council v Secretary of State for the Environment (Practice Note)*[80] set out tests for these cases.

Appealing to the Court of Appeal on s 288

8.28   An appeal may be brought from the High Court to the Court of Appeal. Permission may be sought from the High Court or the Court of Appeal and the usual tests that appeal would have a real prospect of success or there is some other compelling reason why the appeal should be heard are applied.[81] Section 288 applications are not subject to the provisions on second appeals, which apply to s 289.

SECTIONS 288 AND 289 COMPARED

	Section 288	Section 289
Subject of challenge	To grant of planning permission on enforcement appeal, or decision on an appeal or call-in on a planning application	To determination of enforcement notice appeal
Time allowed for challenge	42 days	28 days
Leave to challenge required	No	Yes
Leave to appeal to Court of Appeal required	Yes	Yes

Validity of enforcement notices

8.29   The general intention is that enforcement notices should only be challenged by appeal to the Secretary of State and by a limited appeal from that decision under s 289 except in rare circumstances. It is helpful, therefore, to consider the general prohibition on challenge before addressing other means of questioning the validity of an enforcement notice. Section 285(1) provides:

> 'The validity of an enforcement notice shall not, except by way of an appeal under Part VII, be questioned in any proceedings whatsoever on any of the grounds on which such an appeal can be brought.'

If the challenge is on any of the grounds in s 174(2), then it can only be brought by appeal under that section. For example, an argument that the use had become lawful by passage of time before the issuance of the enforcement notice cannot be raised as a defence in criminal proceedings.[82] The section does not directly prevent the notice's validity being raised on other grounds. However, in *R v Wicks* the House of Lords considered that the enforcement notice regime, including s 285(1), meant that in criminal proceedings '"enforcement notice" means a notice issued by the planning

---

[80]   [1995] 1 WLR 1176.
[81]   Civil Procedure Rules, Pt 52.3(6).
[82]   *Vale of White Horse v Treble-Parker* [1997] JPL 660.

authority which is formally valid and has not been quashed'.[83] In this context, formally valid meant valid on its face. Other public law grounds (outside the s 174 grounds of appeal) could be raised in judicial review.[84] *Wicks* was followed by the Divisional Court in *Palacegate Properties Ltd v Camden London Borough Council*[85] in holding that it could not be argued in criminal proceedings that there had been no authority to issue the enforcement notice.

8.30   Section 285 applies to prevent judicial review proceedings being brought to quash an enforcement notice even if those same proceedings seek the quashing of related stop notices.[86] Section 285 is of no effect to prevent a challenge to a decision to issue enforcement notice if the notice is not issued, even if the grounds could arise on appeal.[87] The validity of an enforcement notice cannot be challenged on the grounds that:

(a)   if it was issued by the district planning authority, they failed to comply with a requirement to consult the county planning authority; or

(b)   if it was issued by the county planning authority, that it did not relate to a county matter.[88]

Judicial review

8.31   Decisions of public bodies are generally subject to judicial review. The main exceptions are if a statutory right of appeal is expressed to be exclusive or the court considers that an alternative remedy is effective and convenient.[89] Provided that the High Court challenge is not on any of the grounds on which the enforcement notice could have been appealed or is to the Secretary of State's decision on an appeal, judicial review can be brought. Because of the bars in s 285, such judicial review challenges would normally be on public law grounds related to expediency. It is appropriate to challenge the lawfulness of the decision that it was expedient to issue an enforcement notice by judicial review.[90]

8.32   An alternative ground of judicial review challenge is that the notice is a nullity: it fails to comply with the legal requirements of an enforcement notice and is therefore of no effect. For example, it may not provide reasons for its issuance or the date on which it takes effect. The steps specified may be so vague as to be unenforceable and the notice thereby a nullity.[91] Judicial review could be brought to rule that enforcement notices which did not specify a period for compliance were nullities,[92] Or the point raised on appeal to the Minister.

---

[83]   *R v Wicks* [1998] AC 92 at 119C per Lord Hoffmann.
[84]   *Wicks* at 122E per Lord Hoffmann.
[85]   (2001) 82 P &CR 17.
[86]   *R (JRP Holdings Limited) v Spelthorne Borough Council* [2007] EWCA Civ 1122, [2008] JPL 696 (permission decision).
[87]   *R v Basildon District Council ex p Martin Grant Homes Limited* (1987) 53 P &CR 397.
[88]   Town and Country Planning Act 1990, s 286(2).
[89]   *R v Chief Constable of the Merseyside Police ex p Calveley* [1986] QB 424.
[90]   For example, in *R (Gazelle Properties Ltd) v Bath and North East Somerset Council* [2010] EWHC 3127 (Admin), [2011] JPL 702 where amongst other points it was irrational not to negotiate; *Britannia Assets (UK) Ltd v Secretary of State for Communities and Local Government* [2011] EWHC 1908 (Admin).
[91]   *Metallic Protectives Ltd v Secretary of State for the Environment* [1976] JPL 166.
[92]   *R (Lynes) v West Berkshire Council* [2002] EWHC 1828, [2003] JPL 1137.

8.33   The failure of a local planning authority to bring enforcement action can be challenged by third parties in judicial review. Since the decision to take enforcement action is discretionary, proceedings tend to concern one or more of the following types of issues:

(a) error of law in considering that the activities were not a breach of planning control: for example, errors in concluding that poultry units were not development (*R (SWVAG) v Bath and North East Somerset Council*[93]) or that the development was permitted development (*R v Sevenoaks District Council ex p Palley*[94]);

(b) failure to consider taking enforcement action: in *R v Stroud District Council ex p Goodenough*[95] the Divisional Court agreed with a local action group's challenge that a local planning authority should consider taking action to prevent the demolition of listed buildings;

(c) unlawful exercise of the discretion not to take enforcement action: since the discretionary power is in broad terms, an error is difficult to establish; and

(d) taking action to address a breach of European Union law: in *Ardagh Glass*[96] the High Court directed a council to issue an enforcement notice.

Judicial review is the appropriate mechanism for challenging a refusal of the Secretary of State to hear an enforcement notice appeal.[97] It is also the only way in which someone who is not an appellant, local planning authority or person interested in the land can challenge an enforcement notice appeal decision.[98] This does raise potential conflicts with the s 285(1) prohibition on challenging enforcement notices on appeal grounds other than under the Town and Country Planning Act 1990 and the approach in *R v Wicks* to treat other public law grounds as within the prohibition on collateral challenge. However public law dislikes persons being prevented from challenging decisions which they have an interest in and some enforcement notice appeals will be subject to the rights of access to the justice in the Environmental Impact Assessment Directive, Art 11, the Human Rights Act 1988 and the Aarhus Convention on Access to Justice, Art 9.

The costs of re-determining an appeal

8.34   The effect of a successful challenge under ss 288 or 289 is that the appeal returns to the Minister for re-determination whether by quashing or remission. In either event there will be a need to re-determine the appeal unless the appeal or enforcement notice are withdrawn. The costs to the parties of that re-determination are not part of the costs of the High Court proceedings and so not recoverable under a court order. Where the re-determination arises because of an error by an Inspector, the Planning Inspectorate or a Minister then the reasonable costs of re-determination will be paid as ex gratia compensation by the Inspectorate. This scheme operated for many years before being scrapped (without announcement) in April 2011. It was resurrected in 2012 following two judicial reviews, which the Secretary of State

---

[93] [2012] EWHC 2161 (Admin), [2013] Env LR 8.
[94] [1995] JPL 915.
[95] (1980) 43 P &CR 59.
[96] *R (Ardagh Glass Ltd) v Chester City Council* [2009] EWHC 745 (Admin), [2009] Env LR 34.
[97] *Lenlyn v Secretary of State for the Environment* (1985) 50 P &CR 129.
[98] For example, *R (Samuel Smith Old Brewery (Tadcaster)) v Secretary of State for Communities and Local Government* [2009] EWHC 3238 (Admin).

conceded, and severe criticism by the Parliamentary Ombudsman.[99] Compensation arrangements are set out in the Planning Inspectorate's Good Practice Advice Note 15 *Feedback, complaints and challenges.*[100]

Challenges to costs decisions in enforcement and planning appeals

8.35   The Secretary of State, Welsh Ministers or a Planning Inspector may order a party to pay all or part of the costs incurred by another party in a planning or enforcement appeal.[101] Those costs decisions may be challenged on public law grounds in the High Court. The procedure to be adopted depends on the nature of the appeal before the Inspector or Minister. A costs decision in an enforcement notice appeal may be challenged by way of appeal under s 289 as it arises 'in proceedings on an appeal against an enforcement notice'.[102] If a challenge is being brought to the enforcement notice appeal decision then the costs challenge can be brought in the same proceedings. A costs decision in an appeal (or call-in) on a planning application falls outside s 288 as those proceedings concern a 'decision on an appeal' which has been held to mean the substantive decision only.[103] Therefore it can only be challenged by judicial review. Where planning permission is granted on a deemed planning application or ground (a) enforcement appeal then any costs decision would still be in proceedings on the enforcement notice appeal. It would be challengeable in that case by an appeal under s 289. Where an appeal deals with both a planning application and an enforcement notice then costs decisions in respect of each appeal may have to be dealt with by different High Court proceedings.

8.36   In practice, where multiple challenges are brought against decisions in the same substantive appeal the court would normally wish to deal with the cases together. The parties should inform the court of the related cases in correspondence and seek an order that the cases are heard together at the earliest opportunity. However a permission to apply for judicial review application would usually be considered on the papers (whereas a s 289 permission application has to go to a hearing). It would be prudent to ensure the judge is aware on a costs judicial review of any related substantive appeal.

8.37   The merits of challenging a costs decision are affected by the wider context of the case. For example, a costs award may have been made against the local authority on the basis that it was unreasonable to issue the enforcement notice, which was quashed on appeal. If the local authority appeal the decision on the enforcement notice successfully, then the costs decision will almost certainly also be unlawful. The flaw in the Inspector's substantive decision is likely to have infected the costs decision and the costs grounds can include reliance on the substantive challenge.[104] If a claimant's substantive appeal to the Secretary of State had failed as did its application for costs, it might be that the costs decision ought to be remitted if the substantive section 289 succeeds. In that latter case a claimant will need to show why

---

[99]   *R(Koumis) v Secretary of State for Communities and Local Government* ; *R (Payne) v Secretary of State for Communities and Local Government* . The Parliamentary Ombudsman published *A false economy?* in October 2012.

[100] On the Planning Portal website: www.planningportal.gov.uk

[101] See Chapter 7.

[102] See *Botton v Secretary of State for the Environment* [1992] 1 PLR 1 at 15 per Roch J.

[103] *North Kesteven District Council v Secretary of State for the Environment* [1989] JPL 445.

[104] For one of many examples, see *Mid-Suffolk District Council v Secretary of State for Communities and Local Government* [2009] EWHC 3649 (Admin).

re-determination of the substantive appeal might affect the costs decision or identify separate legal errors in the costs decision. Consequently if the substantive appeal decision is being challenged in the High Court it will often be sensible and relatively straightforward to challenge the costs decision as well.

8.38   Different issues arise if the sole challenge is to the costs decision to award or not to award costs. Since costs decisions are an exercise of discretion and based primarily on the Inspector's view of what was reasonable conduct, the court will give a fair degree of latitude to the decision maker if the substantive appeal decision was lawful. Additionally the courts have on occasion expressed concern at challenges being brought where the costs of the High Court proceedings will equal or exceed the likely quantum of the costs award. Sullivan J said in *R v Secretary of State for the Environment ex p Ealing London Borough Council*:[105]

> 'The decision whether or not to make an award of costs is pre-eminently a discretionary matter, and the Inspector who actually heard the evidence is in the best position to judge, not merely whether or not the evidence is well-founded in terms of the planning merits of the matter, but also whether or not a party has or has not acted unreasonably. Only very rarely will it be proper for this court to intervene and strike down such an exercise of discretion. Where one has the position that the costs of investigating the exercise of discretion are likely to be equal to if not more than the costs the subject of the award, parties should think long and hard before deciding to seek leave to move for judicial review.'

NULLITY ISSUES ON AN APPEAL TO THE SECRETARY OF STATE

8.39   If an enforcement notice is so defective as to be a nullity, then the Secretary of State will make this finding on an enforcement notice appeal. This may be decided as a preliminary point or during the determination of the appeal. The Secretary of State will not take further steps on the appeal on the basis that the notice is of no legal effect. He will not, for example, grant planning permission on a ground (a) appeal.[106] If the notice is merely invalid then the Secretary of State cannot quash the notice, only the High Court is able to. Any determination on nullity by the Secretary of State may be challenged by judicial review.[107]

COLLATERAL CHALLENGE

8.40   Challenging the enforcement notice in other proceedings is constrained by the statutory bar in s 285(1) and by general principles of public law.

CIVIL PROCEEDINGS

8.41   In principle, direct challenges to public law decisions should be brought by judicial review (or any statutory appeal) rather than by ordinary civil proceedings. This is because the public interest in good administration requires the use of the quick and safeguarded judicial review procedure: *O'Reilly v Mackman*.[108] In civil proceedings

---

[105]   22 April 1999 (unreported).
[106]   *Dennard and Dennard v Secretary of State for the Environment* [1996] JPL B26.
[107]   *Rhymney Valley District Council v Secretary of State for Wales* [1985] JPL 27.
[108]   [1983] 2 AC 237.

which are not directly concerned with validity, the validity of a public law decision may be raised 'collaterally' by way of a defence to the proceedings: *Wandsworth London Borough Council v Winder*.[109] However, with respect to enforcement notices, the statutory bar on challenging on enforcement notice appeal grounds applies by reason of s 285(1). The extent to which other public law grounds may be raised is debatable. In the planning injunction case of *Broadland District Council v Trott*[110] the Court of Appeal considered, obiter, that a notice which is formally valid on its face and has not been quashed has to be complied with, following the criminal decision of *R v Wicks*. The reasonableness of a decision to institute injunctive proceedings should be challenged by separate judicial review proceedings rather than raised as a defence.[111]

CRIMINAL PROCEEDINGS

8.42   The most important difference in criminal proceedings is that s 285(2) provides that the bar on questioning the validity of an enforcement notice in s 285(1) does not apply in a criminal prosecution for failing to comply with the notice against any person who:

'(a)   has held an interest in the land since before the enforcement notice was issued under that Part [of the Act];

(b)   did not have a copy of the enforcement notice served on him under that Part; and

(c)   satisfies the court–

(i)   that he did not know and could not reasonably have been expected to know that the enforcement notice had been issued; and

(ii)   that his interests have been substantially prejudiced by the failure to serve him with a copy of it.'

This subsection does not itself create a defence or mean that the notice is invalid in those proceedings because the subsection is satisfied. However, it does have that effect. An enforcement notice can be challenged on appeal because copies have not been served (ground (e)). The Secretary of State is obliged to quash the notice if the failure to serve has caused substantial prejudice to the appellant or the person not served (s 176(5)). So establishing that s 285(2) applies also establishes that the notice should have been quashed.

8.43   Interest in land in (a) applies to owners and those with a proprietary interest, such as lessees. Licensees and trespassers cannot rely on s 285(2). The interest must be held when the notice is issued and on the date of the alleged offence.

8.44   The date at which knowledge is tested in (c)(i) is not clear. The probable position is that it is when the substantial prejudice could not have been cured. If no person appealed the notice, this would be the last day for appealing (when the notice took effect). If an appeal was brought, it would be when the person charged was unable to play an effective part in any inquiry. This could include insufficient time to obtain evidence.

---

[109]   [1985] AC461.
[110]   [2011] EWCA Civ 301 at para 40 per Sullivan LJ.
[111]   *Waverley Borough Council v Hilden* [1988] 1 WLR 246. A stay of the injunction proceedings should be sought.

8.45   Other public law grounds cannot be raised to challenge an enforcement notice in criminal proceedings unless the notice is a nullity. Lord Hoffmann held in *Wicks* 'that 'enforcement notice' in s 179(1) means a notice issued by a planning authority which on its face complies with the requirements of the Act and has not been quashed on appeal or by judicial review'.[112]

---

[112]   [1998] AC 92 at 122F.

Chapter 9

Enforcing Enforcement Notices: Prosecution and Direct Action

9.01   If, after the period for compliance with the enforcement notice has expired, the notice has not been complied with in whole or part, further steps will need to be taken. Failure to comply imposes criminal liability. Additionally the local planning authority or the Secretary of State can carry out works on the land required by the notice. As with other situations involving breaches of planning control, injunctions are available. These are considered in Chapter 14 below.

OFFENCES

9.02   Two separate offences for breach of enforcement notices are created: one committed by owners, the other committed by persons having control of or an interest in the land. The owner offence creates strict liability if the enforcement notice has not been complied with. The control offence applies to causing or permitting activities contrary to the notice.

Owner

9.03   The owner offence is created by s 179(2) of the Town and Country Planning Act 1990 which makes it an offence for the owner of the land to be in breach of the notice. The owner is in breach of the notice in the circumstances set out in s 179(1):

> 'Where, at any time after the end of the period for compliance with an enforcement notice, any step required by the notice to be taken has not been taken or any activity required by the notice to cease is being carried on, the person who is then the owner of the land is in breach of the notice.'

Elements of the owner offence

9.04   The prosecution must prove:

(a) the defendant was the owner at the relevant time;[1]

(b) the terms of the enforcement notice;

(c) the date on which it should have been complied with (this must be alleged in the information);[2] and

(d) the failure to comply on the date alleged.

---

[1]   *R v Ruttle ex p Marshall* (1989) 57 P & CR 299.
[2]   *Maltedge Ltd v Wokingham District Council* (1992) 64 P & CR 487.

143

The owner of registered land is the proprietor registered at the Land Registry. If property is sold then it remains in the transferor's ownership until the new proprietor is registered, even if this is some time after the conveyance and transfer of possession.[3] So, ownership should be proved by producing the office copy of the Land Registry entry for the property. Where land is unregistered, completed Planning Contravention Notices or s 330 notices can also provide evidence. There is a presumption of continuing ownership where there is evidence of ownership at a particular date.[4]

9.05   If the notice was complied with and then buildings or works were reinstated or restored in breach of the enforcement notice, the owner is not liable under s 179 for failing to remove or alter this development. This is the effect of s 181(5)(b):

> 'no person shall be liable under section 179(2) for failure to take any steps required to be taken by an enforcement notice by way of removal or alteration of what has been so reinstated or restored.'

However the person who reinstates or restores the buildings will have committed a summary offence under s 181(5)(a).[5] It is not necessary to prove that the local planning authority decision to issue the notice was valid and within its powers, for example that authority had been properly delegated.[6]

Control or interest

9.06   The control or interest offence is under s 179(5). The offence is committed by 'a person who, at any time after the end of the period for compliance with the notice, contravenes subsection (4).' Section 179(4) provides:

> 'A person who has control of or an interest in the land to which an enforcement notice relates (other than the owner) must not carry on any activity which is required by the notice to cease or cause or permit such an activity to be carried on.'

Elements of the control offence

9.07   The control offence is solely concerned with the carrying on of an activity. It does not cover a failure to take required steps to remedy a breach of planning control. Only the owner is criminally liable for a failure to reverse unlawful operational development. The prosecution must prove:

(a)   the defendant had control of or an interest in the land at the relevant time;

(b)   the terms of the enforcement notice;

(c)   the date on which it should have been complied with (as said above, this must be alleged in the information);[7]

---

[3]   *East Lindsey District Council v Thompson* [2001] EWHC Admin 81, (2001) 82 P & CR 33 but see to the contrary, *R v Surrey County Council ex p Bridge Court Holdings Ltd* [2000] PLCR 344. *East Lindsey* is the better view.
[4]   *Whitfield v Gowling* (1974) 28 P & CR 386.
[5]   See para 9.36 below.
[6]   *R v Wicks* (1995) 93 LGR 377.
[7]   *Maltedge Ltd v Wokingham District Council* (1992) 64 P & CR 487.

(d) the activity required by the notice to cease was being carried on the date alleged; and

(e) the defendant caused or permitted the activity to be carried on.

'Permitting' includes giving express permission but also failing to take reasonable steps to prevent it. A failure to take unreasonable steps does not constitute permitting.[8] Whether steps are reasonable is a matter for the tribunal of fact (the magistrates or the jury). However, it is unreasonable to require a defendant physically to remove persons contravening the enforcement notice. Depending on the circumstances, it may be reasonable for the defendant to take legal proceedings against the contraveners.[9] The defendant must have the power to forbid the contravener from carrying on the activity.

CHARGING OFFENCES

9.08   Local planning authorities should have regard to the Code for Crown Prosecutors in bringing prosecutions.[10] This is based upon the principles endorsed by the Attorney General for all those who prosecute on behalf of the public. There are two main criteria that must be satisfied:

(a) Evidential sufficiency – that there is sufficient, admissible and reliable evidence that a criminal offence has been committed by an identifiable person. The test is usually whether there is a reasonable prospect of a conviction.

(b) Public interest – once there is sufficient evidence, the prosecutor must consider whether it is in the public interest to prosecute. In a planning context the factors include harm caused in planning terms and whether the offence is continuing when the prosecution is brought.

During the course of a prosecution, the local planning authority should continue to review the appropriateness of continuing the prosecution. New evidence may affect the prospects of conviction or the balance of the public interest may change, for example because of compliance.

9.09   As either way offences, which can be tried in the magistrates' court or the Crown Court, there is no time limit on the period for bringing a prosecution. However, an excessive delay, particularly where it causes prejudice to the defendant, may amount to an abuse of process. The offences are single rather than continuing, but may be charged by reference to a particular day or a longer period of time.[11] It is common to charge for a day on which an inspection by the local planning authority took place. If a longer period is charged, this will usually be between the dates of two inspections. Alternatively, Lord Roskill in *Chiltern District Council v Hodgetts*[12] suggested that a failure to cease an activity should be charged from the date compliance was first required and the date when the information was laid or the notice was complied with, whichever was the earlier.

---

[8]   *Test Valley Investments Ltd v Tanner* (1964) 15 P & CR 279.
[9]   *Ragsdale v Creswick* [1984] JPL 883.
[10] Issued with respect to the Crown Prosecution Service under s 10 of the Prosecution of Offences Act 1985.
[11] Town and Country Planning Act 1990, s 179(6).
[12] [1983] 1 All ER 1057.

9.10   Further offences can be charged in respect of a later period of time. It is provided that 'a person may be convicted of a second or subsequent offence under the subsection in question by reference to any period of time following the preceding conviction for such an offence'.[13] It has been held at first instance that an offence can be committed after an earlier acquittal: the enforcement notice remains in being. The prosecution should be heard even if a planning application has recently been submitted, unless there is a prospect that the application will be determined shortly.[14] Even then, since the application does not affect the commission of the offence, the arguments for delay are slim. However, adjournment of sentence pending determination of the planning application is more common.

ASSURANCES OF NON-PROSECUTION

9.11   A local planning authority may give a person a binding, but revocable, assurance that they will not be prosecuted for breach of an enforcement notice, or breach of specified elements of the enforcement notice. This power is contained in s 172A, inserted by the Localism Act 2011, and binds all prosecutors.[15] Section 172A(1) provides:

'When, or at any time after, an enforcement notice is served on a person, the local planning authority may give the person a letter—

(a)   explaining that, once the enforcement notice had been issued, the authority was required to serve the notice on the person,

(b)   giving the person one of the following assurances—

(i)   that, in the circumstances as they appear to the authority, the person is not at risk of being prosecuted under section 179 in connection with the enforcement notice, or

(ii)   that, in the circumstances as they appear to the authority, the person is not at risk of being prosecuted under section 179 in connection with the matters relating to the enforcement notice that are specified in the letter,

(c)   explaining, where the person is given the assurance under paragraph (b)(ii), the respects in which the person is at risk of being prosecuted under section 179 in connection with the enforcement notice, and

(d)   stating that, if the authority subsequently wishes to withdraw the assurance in full or part, the authority will first give the person a letter specifying a future time for the withdrawal that will allow the person a reasonable opportunity to take any steps necessary to avoid any risk of prosecution that is to cease to be covered by the assurance.'

9.12   Two issues arise on the formality and technical compliance of the assurance. A person who relies upon an assurance should not be at risk of prosecution because of a technical or formal error in the document prepared by the authority. This can be addressed by a reasonable construction of the provisions and care as to what errors render an assurance unlawful. For example, whilst s 172A(1) refers to a letter, it could be sent electronically and need not be written in letter form. A failure of the letter to state that the notice had to be served or that it could be withdrawn ought not to remove the recipient's protection before it is withdrawn.

---

[13]   Town and Country Planning Act 1990, s 179(6).
[14]   *R v Beaconsfield Magistrates ex p South Buckinghamshire District Council* (1993) 157 JP 1073.
[15]   Town and Country Planning Act 1990, s 172A(5).

9.13   There is an important drafting error in subsection (1)(a).[16] The letter has to explain to the recipient that the authority was required to serve the notice on the person, but there will be cases where a person is at risk of prosecution having become involved in the land after the enforcement notice was issued. That person would not have been served with a copy of the enforcement notice. It may be sensible for a purchaser of land to have time to remedy its predecessors' breaches without being at risk of prosecution. Indeed, it is unlikely that someone would buy land if they thought they would put themselves at risk of prosecution under a previously served notice. An assurance in those circumstances would not fall within all the terms of s 172A(1), although that ought not to matter or such a prosecution might be an abuse of process.

9.14   An assurance under s 172A can be withdrawn in full or in part at any time in writing. Such a withdrawal will be from a specified time, which 'will give the person a reasonable opportunity to take any steps necessary to avoid any risk of prosecution that is to cease to be covered by the assurance'.[17] A prosecution may only be brought for breaches following the specified time.[18]

DEFENCES

9.15   A number of defences are set out in s 179. The ability of the defendant to challenge the validity of an enforcement notice in criminal proceedings is also considered in Chapter 8 above.

The owner offence

9.16   It is a defence for a person charged under s 179(2) 'to show that he did everything he could be expected to do to secure compliance with the notice'.[19] In *R v Beard*[20] the Court of Appeal held:

> 'Before a defence can arise under that sub-section the owner must show that compliance with the notice is not within his own unaided powers otherwise no question of his having to secure compliance with the notice can arise. Thus, if there are other persons in occupation of the land, it is enough if he has done everything he could reasonably be expected to do to secure that they comply with the notice. If compliance would require, for example, some engineering work and the owner is not himself able to do that work and does not have the resources to employ another to do it, he will have a defence if he can show that he did everything he could reasonably be expected to do to secure compliance with the notice. These examples suffice to illustrate the application of sub-section (3). We accept as does counsel for the prosecution that the phrase 'everything he could be expected to do' must implicitly be read as 'reasonably expected'. It applies an objective criterion of reasonableness having regard to all the relevant circumstances, in particular any disability to which the owner of the land is subject.'

9.17   The defence is concerned with the defendant's inability to comply, rather than excusing any unwillingness to comply or indicating that it is undesirable to

---

[16]   A more minor error is that an authority will serve a copy of an enforcement notice rather than the notice itself.

[17]   Town and Country Planning Act 1990, s 172A(2), (3).

[18]   Town and Country Planning Act 1990, s 172A(4).

[19]   Town and Country Planning Act 1990, s 179(3).

[20]   [1997] 1 PLR 64 at p 70.

comply. In some cases a defendant might be entitled to do nothing if there was nothing he could reasonably be expected to do.[21] However, the defence not established by demonstrating that the reason for non-compliance with an enforcement notice is that no alternative site has become available where the activity in question could be continued.[22] Similarly it is not open to a defendant to seek to rely on the defence on the basis that compliance with the notice would breach his rights under the European Convention on Human Rights as these matters are considered earlier in the enforcement process.[23] Additionally the defence cannot operate as a disguised challenge to the validity of the enforcement notice, which is prohibited by s 285(1).[24] The question of whether or not a defendant has done all that he can 'reasonably be expected' to do is a matter for the tribunal of fact whether the magistrates or the jury.[25] In *Wood* a conviction was quashed where the Crown Court judge had ruled that the defence was not available before hearing any evidence, although there may be circumstances where this is appropriate.[26] In terms of the ability of a landowner to secure compliance when there are other persons on the land it should be noted that the owner can obtain an order from the magistrates' court requiring the occupier to permit him to take the steps required in the enforcement notice.[27] The defendant's personal and financial circumstances are also relevant, although the courts should be rigorous in the proof expected of an impecunious defendant.[28]

Defence of lack of knowledge

9.18   There is no mental element required for the enforcement notice offences and lack of knowledge of the existence or effect of an enforcement notice is not in itself a defence.[29] A limited lack of knowledge defence is provided by s 179(7):

> 'Where—
>
> (a)   a person charged with an offence under this section has not been served with a copy of the enforcement notice; and
>
> (b)   the notice is not contained in the appropriate register kept under section 188,
>
> it shall be a defence for him to show that he was not aware of the existence of the notice.'

The defence therefore applies to both s 179 offences. The person need not have been entitled to be served with a copy of the enforcement notice, he may have come onto the scene later. The appropriate register is the Enforcement Register. The register entry should be adequate to show what steps are required, or which activity must cease. It is probably not necessary for all the requirements of s 188 and the Development Management Procedure Order[30] in respect of the register to have been complied with.

---

[21]   *R v Beard* [1997] I PLR 64.
[22]   *Wycombe District Council v Wells* [2005] EWHC 1012 (Admin), [2005] JPL 1640.
[23]   *R v Clarke* [2002] EWCA Crim 753, [2002] JPL 1372 at paras 18, 19.
[24]   See *R v Clarke* [2002] EWCA Crim 753, [2002] JPL 1372 at para 14.
[25]   *Kent County Council v Brockman* [1996] 1 PLR 1.
[26]   *R v Wood* [2001] EWCA Crim 1395 at para 11; cf. *R v Clarke* [2002] EWCA Crim 753, [2002] JPL 1372.
[27]   Public Health Act 1936, s 289.
[28]   *Kent County Council v Brockman* [1994] Crim LR 296; [1996] 1 PLR 1.
[29]   *R v Collett* [1994] 1 WLR 475.
[30]   Town and Country Planning (Development Management Procedure) (England) Order 2010, art 38; Town and Country Planning (Development Management Procedure) (Wales) Order 2012, art 30.

9.19   The defendant's knowledge is of the existence of the notice. This is different to knowing its precise terms, but knowledge in broad terms of the land affected and the substance of the prohibitions or steps required may be necessary for a person to be aware of the existence of a notice. Knowledge is tested on the date on which the offence is alleged to have been committed.

LIABILITY OF DIRECTORS

9.20   If a corporate body is guilty of an offence under the Town and Country Planning Act 1990, then its managers would also be guilty of that offence if it was 'committed with the consent or connivance of, or to be attributable to any neglect on their part. Section 331(1) provides:

> 'Where an offence under this Act which has been committed by a body corporate is proved to have been committed with the consent or connivance of, or to be attributable to any neglect on the part of—
>
> (a)   a director, manager, secretary or other similar officer of the body corporate, or
>
> (b)   any person who was purporting to act in any such capacity,
>
> he as well as the body corporate shall be guilty of that offence and be liable to be proceeded against accordingly.'

This provision is also applied to offences under the Planning (Listed Buildings and Conservation Areas) Act 1990[31] and the Planning (Hazardous Substances) Act 1990.[32]

9.21   Where consent is alleged a defendant has to be proved to know the material facts which constitute the offence by the body corporate and to have agreed to its conduct of the business on the basis of those facts although this may be established by inference as well as by proof of an express agreement. In a health and safety case Lord Hope of Craighead observed:[33]

> 'it will be a relatively short step for the inference to be drawn that there was connivance or neglect on his part if the circumstances under which the risk arose were under the direction or control of the officer. The more remote his area of responsibility is from those circumstances, the harder it will be to draw that inference.'

PROCEDURAL RULES

9.22   Criminal procedure is now largely set out in the Criminal Procedure Rules 2012. The Criminal Procedure Rules, first produced in 2005, replace in a structured fashion, a mass of procedural rules for the magistrates' courts and Crown Courts.

The most important provisions in planning cases are:

- Part 1: the overriding objective

- Part 7: starting a prosecution in the magistrates' court

---

[31]   By Planning (Listed Buildings and Conservation Areas) Act 1990, s 89(1).
[32]   Planning (Hazardous Substances) Act 1990, s 37.
[33]   *R v Chargot Ltd* [2008] UKHL 73, [2009] 1 WLR 1 at para 34.

- Part 9: allocation and sending for trial

- Part 10: committal for trial

- Part 14: the indictment

- Part 21: initial details of the prosecution case

- Part 22: disclosure

- Part 27: witness statements

- Part 37: trial and sentence in the magistrates' court

- Part 39: trial on indictment

Additionally appeals from the magistrates' court to the Crown Court, or from either court to the High Court by case stated are dealt with by Parts 63 and 64 respectively.

The information or written charge

9.23   An information or written charge to begin a prosecution must contain:[34]

'(a) a statement of the offence that—

(i)   describes the offence in ordinary language, and

(ii) identifies any legislation that creates it; and

(b) such particulars of the conduct constituting the commission of the offence as to make clear what the prosecutor alleges against the defendant.'

As mentioned earlier, the period for compliance with the enforcement notice must be alleged in the information (and later, any indictment).[35]

Mode of trial

9.24   As an either way offence, the prosecution can be tried in the magistrates court' or the Crown Court. Unless a fine over £20,000 is anticipated, the local planning authority will normally wish summary trial, for the following reasons:

(i)   it is usually quicker and cheaper;

(ii) an acquittal can be appealed. Since prosecutions do fail on technical points, this can be important;

(iii) detailed factual or legal disputes are difficult to explain to a jury.

The choice for the defence is more finely balanced. One factor is whether a jury or bench of magistrates are more likely to have sympathy with the defendant in the particular circumstances. The particular defence to be run may work better in different tribunals.

---

[34]   Criminal Procedure Rules, r 7.3(1).
[35]   *Maltedge Ltd v Wokingham District Council* (1992) 64 P & CR 487.

Form of an indictment

9.25   Each count on an indictment sets out a statement of offence and particulars, for example:

Indictment

IN THE CROWN COURT AT NORTH LONDON

THE QUEEN v JOHN SMITH

charged as follows

Statement of Offence

Breach of an enforcement notice, contrary to section 179(2) of the Town and Country Planning Act 1990

Particulars

John Smith, between 10 January 2013 and 1 April 2013, failed to take a step required by an enforcement notice issued by the London Borough of Middlesex under the Town and Country Planning Act 1990 and dated 2 October 2011, namely to demolish the rear extension to the house at 1, Green Road, London N1 4DH when that notice had to be complied with by 9 January 2013, in breach of the enforcement notice.

Duties of disclosure

9.26   Disclosure refers to providing the defence with copies of, or access to, any material which might reasonably be considered capable of undermining the case for the prosecution against the accused, or of assisting the case for the accused, and which has not previously been disclosed.[36] The prosecution should make all unused material available, subject to public interest exceptions, to the defence if it has some bearing on the offences charged and the surrounding circumstances of the case.[37] The same rules apply to summary trial.[38] In the Crown Court the defendant must give a defence statement and the defendant may give a defence statement in the magistrates' court.[39] Following service of a defence statement, the defendant may apply for an order that the prosecution disclose material,[40] having ordinarily asked the prosecution for the material. In practice, it is for the defence to request disclosure. Officer's reports, notes of inspections, internal memoranda and letters of complaint can be sought. The whole of the planning files relating to the property (or even neighbouring properties) could be relevant. This can undermine the prosecution case, such as what was found at an inspection, or support a defence, for example by bringing evidence that the use may have become lawful by passage of time and so prejudice has occurred within s 285(2).

---

[36] *Attorney General's Guideline on Disclosure of Information*, para 8.
[37] *Attorney General's Guideline on Disclosure of Information to the Defence in Cases to be tried on Indictment*, para 2.
[38] *R v Bromley Justices ex p Smith* [1995] 1 WLR 944.
[39] Criminal Procedure and Investigations Act 1996, ss 5, 6.
[40] See Criminal Procedure Rules, r 22.5 for the process.

9.27   In enforcement notice cases the width of disclosure is narrowed by the limited scope for challenging the validity of the notices.[41] If the point to which the material relates cannot be raised in those criminal proceedings, disclosure cannot be required. The defence is under no general duty of disclosure. However, expert evidence to be used by the defence, including the professional opinion of a planning consultant, should be disclosed to the prosecution as soon as practicable after committal to the Crown Court.[42] There is an exception for expert evidence going only to sentencing which need not be disclosed.[43]

SENTENCES

9.28   On summary conviction the maximum sentence is a fine of up to £20,000. On conviction on indictment, the fine is unlimited.[44] By s 179(9) determining a fine the court shall particularly 'have regard to any financial benefit which has accrued or appears likely to accrue to [the defendant] in consequence of the offence'. The clearest example is where the defendant carried on a business in breach of the enforcement notice. A lack of financial benefit must also be taken into account as a factor militating against a large sentence.[45] However, there was no obligation to order a fine in the full amount of that benefit, or even a large proportion of it.[46]

9.29   The harm caused in planning terms is an important factor in sentencing. The sentence would be lower if planning permission for the development is granted after the breach of the enforcement notice. Where a planning application or appeal in respect of the development covered by the enforcement notice is in progress it may be sensible to adjourn sentence until the outcome is known.[47] Factors identified as relevant to sentencing in the Health and Safety case of *R v F Howe and Sons (Engineers) Ltd,*[48] may be relevant to planning offences, with appropriate adjustments. Aggravating factors include financial profit from the breach, deliberate breaches and a failure to heed warnings. Mitigating factors include prompt admission of responsibility and a timely plea of guilty, steps to remedy deficiencies after they are drawn to the defendant's attention, and a good record. Other relevant factors will include the extent of the breach or breaches, for example whether it was an isolated incident or continued over a period and, importantly, the defendant's resources and the effect of the fine on its business.

9.30   Prosecuting authorities in regulatory offences are encouraged to prepare a schedule setting out the facts of the case and relevant aggravating factors (and it is suggested, mitigating factors): *R v Friskies Petcare (UK) Ltd.*[49] If there is a guilty plea the defendants should set out in writing the mitigating features that the court should take into account. These documents are known as Friskie schedules.[50]

---

[41]   See Town and Country Planning Act 1990, s 285 and *R v Wicks* [1998] AC 92.
[42]   Crown Court (Advance Notice of Expert Evidence) Rules 1987 (SI 1987/716).
[43]   Rule 3(1).
[44]   Town and Country Planning Act 1990, s 179(8).
[45]   *R (Manorgale Ltd) v Thames Magistrates Court* [2013] EWHC 535 (Admin).
[46]   *R v Rance* [2012] EWCA Crim 2023, [2013] Crim LR 74.
[47]   *R v Newland* (1987) 54 P & CR 222.
[48]   [1999] 2 All ER 249.
[49]   [2000] 2 Cr App R(S) 401.
[50]   If guilt is contested, it would be better for the magistrates' court not to see the schedule before conviction to avoid prejudicing the court with irrelevant material.

It should then be apparent whether there are issues between the parties which need to be resolved in a Newton hearing prior to sentence. Compensation orders may be made, for example for the benefit of neighbours, but the loss must be capable of being quantified.[51]

Checklist for prosecutors in sentencing

9.31   A number of matters should be shown in evidence in respect of sentence, if applicable. These matters would be irrelevant and potentially prejudicial with respect to determining guilt or innocence so should not be put into the trial:[52]

(a) *Seriousness of the breach of planning control*
The effect the breach has had on amenity or other interests of planning importance. A planning officer can give evidence of this. Alternatively it can be shown by committee reports or by any appeal decision.

(b) *Wilful disregard of the enforcement notice*
If the defendant knew of the notice and failed to comply with it despite warnings from the local planning authority, his offence will be treated more seriously. Warning letters, the defendant's replies and his involvement in any appeal can be put in evidence.

(c) *Profit from the breach*
The local planning authority will rarely know the income derived from the breach, but they can show where commercial advantage has been gained from a breach.

(d) *Whether the breach is continuing on the date of conviction*
If the defendant has failed to comply after the date for which he is prosecuted, and even after the prosecution has been brought, this should be shown.

PROCEEDS OF CRIME ACT 2002

9.32   The Proceeds of Crime Act 2002 ('POCA') provides for confiscation orders made by the Crown Court for the recovery of money made or property received from criminal activity. Confiscation orders are made where a defendant is convicted in the Crown Court or committed to the Crown Court for sentence and the prosecution asks for an order or the court believes it is appropriate to do so.[53] The order may be in respect of the particular criminal conduct in the conviction or for a criminal lifestyle in respect of which the defendant has benefited.[54] A criminal lifestyle arises when an offence 'constitutes conduct forming part of a course of criminal activity' (that is, being convicted in those proceedings of three or more offences from which he has benefited or having convictions on at least two previous separate occasions offences from which he has benefited in the six years before the current proceedings were begun) or the offence was committed over a period of at least six months and he has benefited from it.[55] If a person has a criminal lifestyle, then all income in the previous six years is assumed to be from crime unless proven otherwise.

---

[51]   *R v Briscoe* (1994) 15 Cr App R (S) 699.
[52]   *R v Sandhu* [1997] JPL 853, [1997] Crim LR 288.
[53]   Proceeds of Crime Act 2002, s 6.
[54]   Proceeds of Crime Act 2002, s 6(4).
[55]   Proceeds of Crime Act 2002, s 75.

9.33   The confiscation order will require the defendant to pay the 'recoverable amount' which is the defendant's benefit from the conduct, reduced to the 'available amount' if the defendant has insufficient resources.[56] The benefit is recoverable whether or not it has been retained and is the value of the property or advantage obtained by the defendant, not his net profit after deduction of expenses or any amounts payable to co-conspirators.[57] Breaches of enforcement notices can lead to substantial benefit from criminal conduct, and may be within the criminal lifestyle definition. This will often be the case when the enforcement notice prohibits the carrying on of a use which generates an income. In *R v del Basso*[58] land was being used to provide a park and ride facility for passengers using Stansted Airport in breach of an enforcement notice. The recoverable amount was assessed as the total income received, before payment of staff costs, rent and tax and was over £1.8 million.

9.34   In a number of cases substantial confiscation orders have been made against landlords who rented out unlawfully converted flats in breach of planning enforcement notices: for example, orders of £186,000 and £112,500 have been made[59] There are though occasions when it is simpler for any profit to be reflected in a fine,[60] not least because of the immense complexity of the confiscation process. The benefit must be arising from the criminal conduct, so a confiscation order could not be made where a landlord of residential property was not licenced under the Housing Act 2004 but he still had a right to rent.[61]

9.35   The proceeds of crime cases do sound a warning to those operating businesses in breach of enforcement notices. As the Crown Court judge, HH Judge Michael Baker QC, said in *del Basso*:[62]

> 'I conclude with a final observation about the mentality of the [appellants] and other similar law breakers. I have received the strong impression that neither the [appellants] nor ... their accountant appreciated fully the risk that the companies and individuals involved in the park and ride operation faced from confiscation proceedings. They have treated the illegality of the operation as a routine business risk with financial implications in the form of potential fines or, at worst, injunctive proceedings. This may reflect a more general public impression among those confronted by enforcement notices with the decision whether to comply with the law or to flout it. The law, however, is plain. Those who choose to run operations in disregard of planning enforcement requirements are at risk of having the gross receipts of their illegal businesses confiscated. This may greatly exceed their personal profits. In this respect they are in the same position as thieves, fraudsters and drug dealers.'

SUBSEQUENT DEVELOPMENT IN BREACH OF AN ENFORCEMENT NOTICE

9.36   Reinstating or restoring buildings or works which have been removed or altered under an enforcement notice is a summary offence (181(5)):

---

[56]   Proceeds of Crime Act 2002, s 7.
[57]   *R v May* [2008] UKHL 28, [2009] 1 Cr App R (S) 31 at para 48.
[58]   [2010] EWCA Crim 1119, [2011] 1 Cr App R (S) 41.
[59]   Reported by the Local Government Lawyer, 30 March 2010 and 23 November 2011.
[60]   The confiscation proceedings failed in *R v Rance* [2012] EWCA Crim 2023, [2013] Crim LR 74.
[61]   *R v Sumal & Sons (Properties) Ltd* [2012] EWCA Crim 1840, [2012] HLR 46.
[62]   Quoted and endorsed by the Court of Appeal at para 46 of their judgment.

'Where without planning permission a person carries out any development on land by way of reinstating or restoring buildings or works which have been removed or altered in compliance with an enforcement notice—

(a) he shall be guilty of an offence, and shall be liable on summary conviction to a fine not exceeding level 5 on the standard scale'.

The offence is created because the enforcement notice will not, in terms, have banned the restoration or reinstatement of the operational development enforced against.The statutory defences in s 179(3), (7) and the exception to the restrictions on collateral challenge in s 285(2) do not apply to this offence. The maximum sentence is currently £5,000.

ENFORCEMENT NOTICES ISSUED BY THE SECRETARY OF STATE

9.37   A prosecution for failure to comply with an enforcement notice issued by the Secretary of State can be brought by any person, including the Secretary of State and the relevant local planning authority, under s 179.

THIRD PARTIES

9.38   Prosecutions are usually brought by the local planning authority. However, any person may bring a prosecution for failure to comply with an enforcement notice. Other public authorities, neighbours, commercial rivals and pressure groups can all bring prosecutions, although this is rare, if not unprecedented. Given the limited scope of collateral challenge in criminal proceedings,[63] evidence of how and why the enforcement notice was issued is unlikely to be relevant. This makes third party prosecutions easier.The Director of Public Prosecutions has the power to take over prosecutions began by other persons, including public authorities.[64] This may happen, and the prosecution be dropped, if a private prosecution is considered to be against the public interest.

DIRECT ACTION – CARRYING OUT WORKS IN DEFAULT OF COMPLIANCE

9.39   The local planning authority is empowered to enter land to take the steps required by an enforcement notice and recover the cost from the landowner. Section 178(1) provides:

'Where any steps required by an enforcement notice to be taken are not taken within the period for compliance with the notice, the local planning authority may—

(a) enter the land and take the steps; and

(b) recover from the person who is then the owner of the land any expenses reasonably incurred by them in doing so.'

---

[63] Town and Country Planning Act 1990, s 285 and *R v Wicks* [1998] AC 92. See Chapter 8.
[64] Prosecution of Offences Act 1985, s 6(2).

The power includes steps required in the notice (such as the removal of caravans) that incidentally cease an activity on the land.[65] The ability to carry out works not set out in an enforcement notice was considered by the High Court in *Egan v Basildon District Council*[66] where Edwards-Stuart J held that the local authority could take any step incidental to the discharge of the s 178 function[67] meaning that 'the council may do anything reasonably necessary to achieve compliance with the steps required by the enforcement notice provided that such action is not something that could itself have been the subject of an enforcement notice'.[68] In that case, which concerned the removal of travellers from Dale Farm he found:

(a) Where a notice required the removal of hardstanding it would also allow the removal of a building erected on that surface after the issue of the enforcement notice.[69]

(b) Where a building had been unlawfully constructed prior to the issue of an enforcement notice but was not mentioned in the notice, it could not be permanently removed by direct action.[70]

(c) The council could can temporarily remove structures such as gates, walls and fences to gain access to land to carry out direct action works, but it had to put these back once the works have been completed.[71]

9.40   If the intention is to remove or alter buildings or works which have been restored or reinstated after earlier compliance with the enforcement notice, the local planning authority must give 28 days notice to the owner and occupier.[72] In other circumstances there is no statutory requirement to give notice before works are carried out, but that is usually done. Direct action is normally the culmination of a long enforcement process and notice of the date of the works gives the landowner a final opportunity to comply. A confrontation may be more likely to be avoided if it is known when works will be carried out, rather than having contractors suddenly turn up at 6am.

9.41   A challenge to the exercise of the power can be brought by judicial review.[73] This could be on the grounds that the decision to enter the land was unreasonable. In *R (O'Brien) v Basildon Borough Council*, Ouseley J held whilst quashing various decisions of the Council to take direct action:[74]

> '184 It is in my view necessary for a local planning authority in deciding whether to use s 178 to consider and weigh various factors: the degree of harm done to the interests protected by planning control; the need for a swift or urgent remedy; the need to uphold

---

[65]   Such as the removal of caravans in *Midlothian District Council v Stevenson* [1985] SLT 424, [1986] JPL 913 [review decision].
[66]   [2011] EWHC 2416 (QB), [2012] PTSR 1117.
[67]   At para 27.
[68]   At para 41.
[69]   At paras 26, 28.
[70]   At paras 36–38.
[71]   At paras 36, 37. At Dale Farm the enforcement notices had not required the removal of walls, fences and gates. The consequence of *Egan* was that the council dug out hardstanding in numerous plots and had to leave the walls in place, creating a heavily cratered site.
[72]   Town and Country Planning Act 1990, s 181(4).
[73]   *R v Greenwich London Borough Council ex p Patel* [1985] JPL 851.
[74]   [2006] EWHC 1346 (Admin), [2007] 1 P & CR 16 at paras 184, 185. See also the judge's comments at paras 145 to 150 and 152 to 156.

and enforce planning control embodied in an effective enforcement notice and the criminal law; the personal circumstances and impact on the individuals of removal.

185 Part of that will involve the question of whether they have somewhere else to go or whether inevitably they will have to camp on the roadside, or in some other unauthorised Green Belt location of indeterminate harm. But it is also relevant, and the more plainly so where the conclusion is that the occupants have nowhere lawful or suitable to go, to consider the prospects of success which they might have on a planning application or on appeal, and the time scale over which that might be resolved.'

9.42   The decision to take direct action must have regard to the relevant circumstances at the time, including human rights, the Children Act and the prospects of obtaining planning permission on the current or another site.[75] There is no requirement to pursue other enforcement mechanisms, such as prosecutions or injunctions, before resorting to direct action, even if human rights are engaged.[76] The adequacy of a local planning authority's consideration of direct action was endorsed by the Court of Appeal in *R (McCarthy) v Basildon District Council,*[77] although by the time the proceedings had concluded, so much time had passed that the issue had to be reconsidered.[78]

SECURING ENTRY

9.43   It is an offence to wilfully obstruct a person acting in the exercise of these entry powers. The offence is summary-only and is punishable by a level 3 fine (£1,000).[79] An order can be obtained from the civil courts requiring an owner or occupier to allow the local planning authority to gain access under this section. Such an order can also obtained under s 222 of the Local Government Act 1972.[80] An order allowing the local planning authority to obtain access to carry out works may be possible under the s 187B injunction power.[81]

RECOVERING EXPENSES

9.44   The local planning authority can recover expenses reasonably incurred in taking the steps from the owner.[82] These include such sums as appear to the local planning authority to be reasonable in respect of their establishment charges.[83]

This liability functions primarily as a civil debt, but certain special powers are given to facilitate recovery:

(a) The local planning authority can sell any materials removed when taking the steps required unless their owner claims and takes them away within three days

---

[75]   See generally, *Sheridan v Basildon District Council* [2011] EWHC 2938 (Admin).

[76]   *R (O'Brien) v Basildon Borough Council* [2006] EWHC 1346 (Admin), [2007] 1 P & CR 16.

[77]   [2009] EWCA Civ 13; [2009] JPL 1074.

[78]   See *R (Sheridan) v Basildon District Council* [2011] EWHC 2938 (Admin) which declined to quash the later decision to take direct action.

[79]   Town and Country Planning Act 1990, s 178(6).

[80]   *Wandsworth London Borough Council v Asghar* [1989] EGCS 95.

[81]   For discussion of s 222 of the Local Government Act 1972 and planning injunctions, see Chapter 14.

[82]   Town and Country Planning Act 1990, s 178(1).

[83]   Local Government Act 1974, s 36.

of their removal from the property.[84] The balance of the proceeds, after deducting the expenses, is paid to the owner.[85]

(b)   The expenses become a charge on the property, binding on successive owners, from the date of completion by the local planning authority of the steps required under the notice.[86]

If the person pursued as the owner is receiving rent as agent or trustee for another person, then his liability is limited to the total amount of rent in his hands on and after the service of a demand for payment by the local planning authority. The balance of the expenses are recoverable from the person the agent or trustee is acting for.[87]

DIRECT ACTION AND ENFORCEMENT NOTICES ISSUED BY THE SECRETARY OF STATE

9.45   The Secretary of State is empowered to carry out works under s 178 in respect of enforcement notices he has issued, on the same basis as local planning authorities on notices they have issued.[88] 'In relation to an enforcement notice issued by the Secretary of State', s 178 is to be read as if any reference to local planning authority was to be substituted by a reference to the Secretary of State.[89] This allows the Secretary of State to take direct action but appears to remove the ability for local planning authorities to use s 178 for enforcement notices issued by the Secretary of State as the reference to the authority is substituted, not added to. There is no obvious reason why a local planning authority should not be able to take direct action to enforce a notice issued by the Minister, and this text merits amendment.

---

[84]   Public Health Act 1936, s 276(1) as applied by Town and Country Planning Act 1990, s 178(3)(a) and the Town and Country Planning General Regulations 1992 (SI 1992/1492), reg 14(1).

[85]   Public Health Act 1936, s 276(2).

[86]   Town and Country Planning Act 1990, s 178(5), Town and Country Planning General Regulations 1992 (SI 1992/1492), reg 14(2).

[87]   Public Health Act 1936, s 294 as applied by Town and Country Planning Act 1990, s 178(3)(c) and the Town and Country Planning General Regulations 1992 (SI 1992/1492), reg 14(1).

[88]   Town and Country Planning Act 1990, s 182(4).

[89]   Town and Country Planning Act 1990, s 182(4).

Chapter 10

Environmental Impact Assessment

10.01 Environmental impact assessment ('EIA') has become an integral part of the planning process for large-scale development projects.[1] It usually arises when a planning permission or other form of consent is sought. Enforcement cases will often be sufficiently small scale that EIA is not an issue. Environment Impact Assessment has been raised as relevant to enforcement in five respects:

(1) EIA of the grant of planning permission on an enforcement notice appeal;

(2) EIA of revocation, modification and discontinuance orders;

(3) whether enforcement proceedings must be taken because an unlawful project would otherwise avoid EIA;

(4) EIA and lawful development certificates; and

(5) EIA of steps required or direct action in enforcement matters.

ENVIRONMENTAL IMPACT ASSESSMENT IN OUTLINE

10.02 EIA was introduced by European Directive 85/337/EEC and subsequently amended by Directives 97/11/EC, 2003/35/EC and 2009/31/EC. In 2011 the Directive was replaced by the Consolidated Environmental Impact Assessment Directive 2011/92/EU. The critical obligation is contained in Art 2(1):

'Member States shall adopt all measures necessary to ensure that, before consent is given, projects likely to have significant effects on the environment by virtue, *inter alia*, of their nature, size or location are made subject to a requirement for development consent and an assessment with regard to their effects. These projects are defined in Article 4.'

Article 4 identifies two categories of projects. Projects listed in Annex I of the Directive will automatically require Environmental Impact Assessment, such as an oil refinery, a motorway or a large power station (described in the UK as Schedule 1 development). Where projects fall within Annex II, Member States are required to determine through a case-by-case examination or the setting of thresholds or criteria whether EIA is required. Annex II covers a wide range of projects from intensive agriculture, to mineral extraction, urban development, the food industry and flood defence works (included in the UK regulations as Schedule 2). The essential question is whether these projects are likely to have significant effects on the environment.

10.03 In the UK, environmental impact assessment has either been integrated into existing consent regimes or new regimes have been devised and in either case

---

[1] The standard work on English EIA law is Stephen Tromans QC, *Environmental Impact Assessment: Law and Practice* 2nd Edn (Bloomsbury Professional Publishing, 2012).

separate regulations have been produced. In England the regulations applying to the planning process are the Town and Country Planning (Environmental Impact Assessment) Regulations 2011 ('the EIA Regulations 2011'). Planning matters in Wales (and those applications made in England prior to 24 August 2011) are subject to the Town and Country Planning (Environmental Impact Assessment) (England and Wales) Regulations 1999 ('the EIA Regulations 1999').[2] Consents under other regimes such as highways, pipelines, harbours and electricity projects are governed by other EIA regulations. Where it takes place, EIA is usually part of the process of granting planning permission or another domestic law consent rather than a separate consent. Environmental impact assessment processes involve the following stages:

(a)   deciding whether EIA is required using selection criteria (screening);

(b)   if EIA is required, considering what impacts should be subject to assessment (scoping);

(c)   the preparation of an Environmental Statement by the developer – the statement will explain the scheme, the environmental baseline which is capable of being affected by the scheme, the likely significant effects of the scheme, the mitigation proposed in respect of those effects and the alternatives considered by the developer. As part of the statement, there will be a non-technical summary produced;

(d)   consultation of public bodies and the public on the Environmental Statement and any further information produced by the developer;

(e)   consideration of the Environmental Statement, the developer's further information and the responses to the consultation by the decision-maker; and

(f)   the production of a reasoned decision on the application.

EIA OF THE GRANT OF PLANNING PERMISSION ON AN ENFORCEMENT NOTICE APPEAL

10.04   It is possible that development requiring environmental impact assessment takes place without planning permission. This is perhaps most likely with minerals and waste development or caravans but in *R (Ardagh Glass) v Chester City Council*[3] an entire glass factory was built without planning permission. Planning permission may be granted in an enforcement notice appeal or on a retrospective planning application. In *Ardagh* the Court of Appeal rejected the argument that because of the need to enforce the EIA Directive and, to avoid a developer obtaining an advantage by developing before securing consent, planning permission could not be granted for EIA development after it had taken place. This would be contrary to common sense and disproportionate.[4] However the Court of Appeal recognised that granting permission for EIA development after it had been carried out should be the exception. It referred to the decision of the European Court of Justice in *Commission v Ireland* (C-215/06).[5] Sullivan LJ then held, citing the judgment of HH Judge Mole QC in the High Court in *Ardagh*:

---

[2]   SI 1999/293. Planning applications made before 14 March 1999 were subject to the Town and Country Planning (Assessment of Environmental Effects) Regulations 1988 (SI 1988/1199).

[3]   [2010] EWCA Civ 172, [2010] Env LR 32.

[4]   *Ardagh* at para 15 and 16 per Sullivan LJ.

[5]   [2008] ECR I-4911.

'27 In [102] of the judgment the judge said that retrospective planning permission could lawfully be granted for EIA development provided the decision taker, whether the local planning authority or the Secretary of State, made it plain,

"that a developer would gain no advantage by pre-emptive development and that such development will be permitted only in exceptional circumstances."

28 In [103] the judge referred to the approach to be adopted by the Secretary of State on an appeal against an enforcement notice, but his observations are equally applicable to a local planning authority considering an application under s 73A:

"The [decision-taker] can and in my view should also consider, in order to uphold the Directive, whether granting permission would give the developer an advantage he ought to be denied, whether the public can be given an equal opportunity to form and advance their views and whether the circumstances can be said to be exceptional. There will be no encouragement to the pre-emptive developer where the [decision-taker] ensures that he gains no improper advantage and he knows he will be required to remove his development unless [he] can demonstrate that exceptional circumstances justify its retention."

31 ... In the present case, by way of contrast, there is a discretion to grant retrospective planning permission conferred by s 73A and s 177, but there is no requirement that planning permission shall be granted. It is therefore perfectly possible for the decision taker to ensure that the discretion is exercised so as to conform with the ECJ's judgment. To that end, I would endorse those passages which I have set out in [102] and [103] of the judge's judgment. They accord with the ECJ's judgment in the Ireland case and, if the decision taker exercises his discretion in accordance with that guidance, there will, in my judgement, be no breach of community law.'

10.05   A planning permission granted in an enforcement notice appeal would be a development consent, as it entitles the developer to proceed with the project. Consequently, it was appreciated that the EIA regime should apply if planning permission was to be granted in an enforcement appeal. This would involve deciding whether EIA was needed for planning permission for the particular development which was subject of the enforcement notice and, if so, the carrying out of an EIA before the grant of planning permission. This issue was identified after the first EIA regulations had been made in 1988. Consequently, the Town and Country Planning (Environmental Assessment and Unauthorised Development) Regulations 1995 were made and applied to enforcement notices issued on or after 2 October 1995.[6] Those regulations were replaced by reg 25 of the EIA Regulations 1999. Those provisions remain in force in Wales. In England, EIA is now applied to enforcement notices by Pt 9 of the EIA Regulations 2011 (regs 30 to 41). There is little substantive difference between the two sets of regulations so they can be considered together. The Secretary of State, the Welsh Ministers and their inspectors are prohibited from granting planning permission on an enforcement notice appeal where EIA is required unless an EIA has been carried out and taken into account in the decision.[7] An appeal may be allowed on other grounds, such as there being no breach of planning control or that the time for enforcing had expired.

---

[6]   Guidance on these regulations was given in Department of the Environment Circular 13/95 (Welsh Office Circular 39/95).

[7]   EIA Regulations 2011, reg 31; EIA Regulations 1999, reg 25(1). The decision must state that the environmental information has been taken into account.

The decision whether EIA is required in an enforcement appeal

10.06   It is initially for the local planning authority which issues the enforcement notice to decide whether EIA is required. If it appears to the authority that the breach of planning control in the enforcement notice is Schedule 1 or Schedule 2 development then it must adopt a screening opinion prior to issuing the notice.[8] Schedule 1 development is the same as that listed in Annex I of the EIA Directive. Schedule 2 development is the Annex II list of projects (with minor clarifications in the UK regulations) where any part is to be carried out in a defined sensitive area or the relevant threshold or criterion in Sch 2 of the UK regulations is met or exceeded.[9] A screening opinion is a written statement of the opinion of the local planning authority whether EIA is required. All Schedule 1 development requires EIA. Schedule 2 development only requires EIA if it is likely to have a significant effect on the environment by reason of its nature, size or location.[10] If the conclusion is that EIA is required then the local planning authority must serve with the copies of the enforcement notice a notice which includes the screening opinion, the reasons for it and a statement that copies of an environmental statement have to be submitted with any appeal.[11] This notice is referred to in England as a regulation 32 notice and in Wales as a regulation 25 notice. The requirement that the notice says that an environmental statement has to be submitted with the appeal is misleading as an appeal can be considered on all grounds except seeking a grant of planning permission without an environmental statement and even in that case, an environmental statement can be sent in after the appeal has been submitted.

10.07   A person served with a regulation 32 or regulation 25 notice requiring EIA may ask the Secretary of State or Welsh Ministers to make a screening direction giving their view whether EIA is required.[12] A screening direction prevails over a screening opinion. The 2011 provisions say that the direction must be requested within three weeks of receipt of the regulation 32 notice, but any person (including third parties) may ask for a screening direction so the local authority's opinion can be overruled at any point.[13] If an appeal is submitted for Schedule 1 or Schedule 2 development without a screening opinion or direction having been made the Secretary of State or Welsh Ministers shall make a screening direction.[14]

---

[8]   EIA Regulations 2011, reg 32(1); EIA Regulations 1999, reg 25(2).
[9]   EIA Regulations 2011, reg 2(1); EIA Regulations 1999, reg 2(1). Sensitive areas are Sites of Special Scientific Interest, National Parks, World Heritage Sites, scheduled monuments, areas of outstanding natural beauty, Special Areas of Conservation, Special Protection Areas and in England, the Broads. The Secretary of State and the Welsh Ministers can require EIA of projects which are in the Annex II categories but are outside sensitive areas and fail to meet the thresholds or criteria: EIA Regulations 2011, reg 4(9); EIA Regulations 1999, reg 4(8).
[10]   Development requiring EIA is called 'EIA development': EIA Regulations 2011, reg 2(1); EIA Regulations 1999, reg 2(1).
[11]   EIA Regulations 2011, reg 32(2); EIA Regulations 1999, reg 25(3). Two copies of the environmental statement are required in England and four copies in Wales. Copies of the notices are to be sent by the local planning authority to the Secretary of State, the bodies consulted on EIAs and, in England, any persons likely to be affected by or having an interest in the notice.
[12]   EIA Regulations 2011, reg 33; EIA Regulations 1999, reg 25(6).
[13]   EIA Regulations 2011, reg 4(8); EIA Regulations 1999, reg 4(7).
[14]   This is correctly set out in the regulations applying to Wales: EIA Regulations 1999, reg 25(9). In England, however, the EIA Regulations 2011 contain an error. Whilst headed 'Appeal to the Secretary of State without a screening opinion or screening direction', reg 35(1) requires a screening direction regardless of whether an opinion or direction has been adopted.

ENVIRONMENTAL STATEMENTS IN ENFORCEMENT APPEALS

10.08 If the unlawful development or part of it is EIA development, then an environmental statement must be submitted by the appellant with the appeal or in a later period allowed by the Minister.[15] In that latter case the Minister would issue a notice within three weeks of receiving the appeal specifying a period for the submission of the environmental statement. A later period may subsequently be allowed. If no environmental statement is submitted within the period then the deemed planning application and any ground (a) appeal will lapse. These lapse in their entirety and an appeal seeking permission for part of the development (which might not require EIA) would therefore be lost. Putting together an environmental statement is a substantial exercise[16] and may require surveys to be carried out at particular times of the year or for long periods (such as ecological or groundwater surveys). There are practical reasons why an environmental statement may be considerably delayed. However, in deciding on the appropriate period to allow, the Minister is entitled to consider the extent of the need to resolve the enforcement appeal with reasonable expedition.

10.09 If an environmental statement is submitted, then the Minister will send a copy to the local planning authority.[17] The Minister or the Inspector may also require further information to be submitted if the statement does not meet the requirements for an environmental statement.[18] Publicity of the receipt of the environmental statement is given by:

(a) the Secretary of State or Welsh Ministers notifying the persons who received copies of the regulation 32 or 25 notices;[19] and

(b) the local planning authority advertising the environmental statement (and also any further information submitted).[20]

The advertisement will give a period of at least 21 days for inspection of the documents[21] although they have to be available with the planning register kept by the local planning authority in any event.[22] A further 14 days after the inspection period is then given for comments to be made to the Secretary of State or Welsh Ministers.[23] This consultation period will run independently of the periods under the various enforcement regulations and rules, although it is desirable for it to tie in with the six-week period from the starting date if the environmental statement is submitted with the appeal. These representations, along with all of the other submissions on the appeal, will be considered in determining the appeal. A reasoned decision is produced in an appeal in any event, but the Minister must ensure that the decision or a statement with it include information on public participation, the

---

[15] EIA Regulations 2011, reg 36; EIA Regulations 1999, reg 25(12).
[16] Local planning authorities and statutory consultees are required to co-operate in the statement preparation process if asked: EIA Regulations 2011, reg 34; EIA Regulations 1999, reg 25(7).
[17] EIA Regulations 2011, reg 37(a); EIA Regulations 1999, reg 25(13)(a).
[18] EIA Regulations 2011, regs 22(1), (10), 38; EIA Regulations 1999, regs 19(1), (10) and 25(14).
[19] EIA Regulations 2011, reg 37(b); EIA Regulations 1999, reg 25(13)(b).
[20] EIA Regulations 2011, reg 39; EIA Regulations 1999, reg 25(16).
[21] EIA Regulations 2011, reg 39(1)(e); EIA Regulations 1999, reg 25(16)(d).
[22] EIA Regulations 2011, reg 40; EIA Regulations 1999, reg 25(19).
[23] EIA Regulations 2011, reg 39(1)(f); EIA Regulations 1999, reg 25(16)(e). The period is therefore a minimum of 21 days plus 14 days.

main measures to address major adverse effects of the development and how to challenge the decision.[24]

ENVIRONMENTAL IMPACT ASSESSMENT OF REVOCATION, MODIFICATION AND DISCONTINUANCE ORDERS

10.10   If a modification order is made on a planning permission or a discontinuance order requires a use to be carried out or operational development altered, then it is the discontinuance order or the planning permission as modified which authorises the developer to proceed. This is consequently a development consent under the EIA Directive, a point which is more obvious when planning permission is granted in a discontinuance order. Neither the 2011 nor the 1999 EIA Regulations apply to discontinuance or modification orders but the EIA Directive applies by direct effect: see *Smout v Welsh Ministers*.[25] In *Smout* planning permissions for land filling had been modified to exclude an area which had been designated as a Special Area of Conservation because of the presence of great crested newts. This exclusion resulted in the phasing and final landform of the remainder of the site being changed and the claimant contended that the project could not proceed without the modification. The courts accepted that the Welsh Ministers had to consider whether EIA was required but they were entitled to find that it was not necessary in that case. The simple revocation of a planning permission could not require EIA as there would be no development consent remaining. A discontinuance order which required the removal of the entirety of a major development might require EIA if that demolition was likely to have significant environmental effect, although that is unlikely to arise.

WHETHER ENFORCEMENT PROCEEDINGS MUST BE TAKEN BECAUSE AN UNLAWFUL PROJECT WOULD OTHERWISE AVOID ENVIRONMENTAL IMPACT ASSESSMENT

10.11   A fundamental requirement of European Union law is that the member states take steps to enforce it effectively.[26] The environmental impact assessment regime requires detailed assessments of particular projects before they are authorised. If a project is constructed without the necessary planning permission and is not subsequently required to obtain planning permission then any EIA which would have been required for that scheme will not have been carried out. The time limits for taking enforcement action will ultimately mean that the development becomes lawful without having been subject to EIA. Whilst the Town and Country Planning Act 1990 provides for a discretionary system of enforcement, the courts have recognised that the need to enforce European law may compel a planning authority to enforce against a particular project. In *R (Prokopp) v London Underground Limited*[27] deemed planning permission had been granted for a railway line, the East London Line Northern Extension. That planning permission had lapsed because there had been a failure to comply with a condition on the permission. The local planning authorities concerned decided not to enforce against the development if planning obligations were entered into, replicating

---

[24]   EIA Regulations 2011, reg 40(3) applying reg 24; EIA Regulations 1999, reg 25(19) applying reg 21.
[25]   [2011] EWCA Civ 1750, upholding [2010] EWHC 3307 (Admin), [2011] Env LR 17.
[26]   See, for example, *Francovich* (C-6/90) [1993] 2 CMLR 66 and *R (Wells) v Secretary of State for Transport, Local Government and the Regions* (C-201/02) [2004] 1 CMLR 31.
[27]   [2003] EWCA Civ 961, [2004] Env LR 8.

the conditions on the expired permission. Ultimately the courts upheld the decision, considering that an adequate EIA had been carried out of the original approval and that the decision not to enforce was not a development consent. Schiemann LJ did consider the more general question of enforcement and EIA:[28]

> 'I would accept for the purposes of the present appeal that if a project which falls within the Directive goes ahead without there having been an Environmental Impact Assessment and the national authorities simply stand by and do nothing then this might well amount to a breach of our obligations under the Directive. But that is not this case.'

10.12   In *Commission v United Kingdom* (C-98/04) the Commission challenged the lawful development certificate system. Whilst the proceedings failed, as discussed further below, Advocate General Colomer discussed whether there might be a duty to enforce in EIA cases:[29]

> '27. Community law precludes implementation of such projects without prior authorisation and, if appropriate, without assessment of their impact, where implementation becomes irreversible with the passage of time.
>
> 28. That is precisely the effect of the United Kingdom system, which, as the case of the scrap yard over which these proceedings arose demonstrates, and as the defendant Government accepts, allows action to be taken in breach of the directive, without prior evaluation or impact assessment, and to be legitimised by the passage of time so that the situation can no longer be remedied.
>
> [...]
>
> 32. It is a matter of analysing whether, regardless of the passage of time, the U Kingdom legislation allows the possibility that activities included in the first two annexes to might be carried out without approval and without the required consent; as we have already seen, that question must be answered unequivocally in the affirmative.
>
> 33. If those responsible for monitoring the lawfulness of town planning do not react on learning that a facility is operating without an assessment of its effects on the environment having been carried out, or, where its scale is evident, do not require its assessment, they are tacitly consenting to it and, thereby, contravening the directive. ...
>
> 34. In short, the obligation on the Community Member States to adopt the rules necessary to achieve the result sought by the directive is binding on all public authorities under the third paragraph of Article 249 EC, so that national legislation which allows the administration to take no action and allow a project awaiting consent and assessment of its effects on the environment to be implemented without those assessments being made infringes Articles 2(1) and 4 of the directive, as the United Kingdom Government accepts.'

10.13   In *R (Ardagh Glass) v Chester City Council*[30] a rival glass manufacturer, Quinn Glass, had built a factory without planning permission, there having been permission for a smaller factory on the site. Ultimately planning permission was granted, quashed by the court and subsequent planning applications refused by the Secretary of State. By the time of the instant proceedings, the plant had been substantially complete for approaching four years. Having ordered the Council to take enforcement action on domestic grounds, HH Judge Mole QC held, commenting on *Prokopp*:[31]

---

[28]   *Prokopp* at para 38.
[29]   *Commission v UK*, AG's opinion at para 27–34
[30]   [2009] EWHC 745 (Admin), [2009] Env LR 34.
[31]   *Ardagh* at para 110.

'a purposive interpretation of art.2(1) strongly suggests that for the defendant councils to permit the Quinn Glass development to achieve immunity, whether by a positive decision not to take enforcement action or by mere inaction, would, as Schiemann L.J. contemplated, amount to a breach of the UK's obligations under the Directive.'

The Court of Appeal upheld the judge's refusal to order the authority to serve a stop notice, considering that the enforcement notice was sufficient to ensure the removal of the unauthorised EIA development if retrospective planning permission was refused.[32]

10.14   In *R (Baker) v Bath and North East Somerset Council*[33] HH Judge Birtles quashed defective EIA screening opinions on planning applications for unlawful waste sites but declined to order the Council to take enforcement action. He considered that it was not known whether the proposals were in fact for EIA development and EIA screening was being progressed.[34] The conclusion also appears to have been influenced by the absence of an imminent danger that the development would become lawful by the passage of time.[35] Even where EIA is required, there may be a degree of discretion as to the timing of any enforcement action, particularly where the developer is seeking to produce an adequate environmental statement.[36]

ENVIRONMENTAL IMPACT ASSESSMENT AND LAWFUL DEVELOPMENT CERTIFICATES

10.15   The European Commission's complaint about the lawful development certificate system in *Commission v United Kingdom* (C-98/04) was that it allowed 'by-passing of the procedures governing application for consent and environmental impact assessment'.[37] The European Court of Justice dismissed the claim as inadmissible as it failed to challenge the time limits on enforcement action and these were inseparable from the certificates. It is suggested that there can be no need for EIA of lawful development certificate applications as they simply identify what development is or has become lawful. The critical issue is that there may be a need to enforce to ensure that EIA is carried out, as the Advocate General identified.

ENVIRONMENTAL IMPACT ASSESSMENT OF STEPS REQUIRED OR DIRECT ACTION IN ENFORCEMENT MATTERS

10.16   In *R (McCarthy) v Basildon District Council*[38] the council proposed to take direct action under s 178 of the Town and Country Planning Act 1990 to remove travellers' caravans and tipped material from 54 plots on a former scrapyard at Dale Farm. The courts rejected arguments that the council's proposed physical works might constitute a project under the EIA Directive and so require EIA.[39]

---

[32]   [2010] EWCA Civ 172, [2010] Env LR 32 at para 22 per Sullivan LJ.
[33]   [2009] EWHC 3320 (Admin).
[34]   *Baker* at paras 36–40.
[35]   See the Council's submissions at *Baker,* para 32.
[36]   *R (Baker) v Bath and North East Somerset Council* [2013] EWHC 946 (Admin).
[37]   *Commission v UK,* judgment, at para 19.
[38]   *Sub nom R (Sheridan) v Basildon District Council.*
[39]   *Sheridan* [2011] EWHC 2938(Admin) at paras 127, 128 per Ouseley J ('absurd') and [2011] EWCA Civ 1374 at para 33 per Sullivan LJ ('far-fetched').

Chapter 11

Stop Notices

11.01   The enforcement notice procedure can be slow in securing compliance with planning control. An enforcement notice will take at least 28 days to take effect, and there is then a period to take the steps required. The process can be delayed by an appeal to the Secretary of State or Welsh Ministers and then to the High Court.

11.02   A stop notice allows the local planning authority to ban activity almost immediately. However, it may only be served with or after an enforcement notice dealing with that activity. If the planning authority wishes to prohibit activity before issuing an enforcement notice, then a temporary stop notice can be served, as discussed in Chapter 12 below. A stop notice cannot be appealed. Failure to comply with a stop notice is a criminal offence, although compensation may be payable if the enforcement notice is subsequently quashed or either notice is withdrawn. Stop notices are used to support relatively few enforcement notices. In 2011/2012, 122 stop notices were served as against 4,590 enforcement notices; 158 stop notices had been served in the previous year. As stop notices tend to be used against development which has just got started, they are more likely to be used during a construction boom (210 were served in 2005/2006). There is, however, a general decline in their use.[1] In part this may be due to the availability of temporary stop notices which may have caused the activities to cease before an enforcement notice is issued. Use of stop notices has varied from authority to authority. In 2011/2012 South Cambridgeshire District Council served 16 stop notices, which was more than the number served in the North East, the North West, Yorkshire and the Humber combined. The stop notice procedure was heavily amended by the 1991 reforms. Guidance on its exercise is provided by Annex 3 to Circular 10/97.

ISSUE OF A STOP NOTICE

11.03   The power to issue stop notices is in s 183(1) of the Town and Country Planning Act 1990. It provides:

> 'Where the local planning authority consider it expedient that any relevant activity should cease before the expiry of the period for compliance with an enforcement notice, they may, when they serve the copy of the enforcement notice or afterwards, serve a notice (in this Act referred to as a "stop notice") prohibiting the carrying out of that activity on the land to which the enforcement notice relates, or any part of that land specified in the stop notice.'

Stop notices are subject to the following restrictions:

(a)   they are dependent upon a copy of an enforcement notice being served with or before the stop notice;[2]

---

[1]   In 1993/4, 283 stop notices were served, with 247 used in the following year.
[2]   Town and Country Planning Act 1990, s 183(1).

(b) they can only prevent activity required to cease under the enforcement notice or activity which is part of that activity or associated with it;[3]

(c) they cannot require steps to be taken, for example, a stop notice can require building activity to cease, but not require the removal of the unauthorised development;

(d) they may not be served where the enforcement notice has taken effect,[4] although they may be served when taking effect is delayed by an enforcement notice appeal;

(e) they may not prevent the use of any building as a dwelling house;[5] and

(f) they may not 'prohibit the carrying out of any activity if the activity has been carried out without planning permission (whether continuously or not) for a period of more than four years ending with the service of the notice'[6] unless the activity is, or is incidental to, building, engineering, mining or other operations or the deposit of refuse or waste materials.[7] This period is less than the usual ten-year time limit for enforcement action against uses.

Stop notices can prohibit the use of land for residential caravans. Prior to 1991 stop notices could not prohibit the use of land for residential caravans but this prohibit was lifted on the recommendation of the Carnwath Report.[8] The Court of Appeal in *R (Wilson) v Wychavon District Council*[9] held that the ability to use stop notices against residential caravans but not against dwelling houses was compatible with the anti-discrimination provisions of the European Convention on Human Rights. The provision served a legitimate aim and there were differences between a dwelling house (where construction could be subject to a stop notice and, if constructed, the impact of the building would remain) and residential caravans, which could be brought onto land or removed rapidly.

THE DECISION TO SERVE

11.04 Circular 10/97 Annex 3, paras 3.19 to 3.23 provide guidance on deciding to serve a stop notice. Local planning authorities are advised to carry out a 'quick but thorough' cost/benefit assessment. The costs to the firm, operator or landowner prevented from carrying out the activity should be compared to the benefits to the amenity of the neighbourhood. The stop notice's requirements should:

> 'prohibit only what it is essential to safeguard amenity or public safety in the neighbourhood; or to prevent serious or irreversible harm to the environment in the surrounding area'.[10]

---

[3] Town and Country Planning Act 1990, s 183(2).
[4] Town and Country Planning Act 1990, s 183(3).
[5] Town and Country Planning Act 1990, s 183(4).
[6] Town and Country Planning Act 1990, s 183(5). The period can include any time that the activity is carried on with planning permission, for example, under a temporary planning permission: *Scott Markets Limited v Waltham Forest London Borough Council* (1979) 38 P & CR 597.
[7] Town and Country Planning Act 1990, s 183(5A).
[8] Robert Carnwath QC, *Enforcing Planning Control* at para 9.10.
[9] [2007] EWCA Civ 52, [2007] QB 801, paras 66–73 per Richards LJ.
[10] Circular 10/97 Annex 3, para 3.20.

If practicable, the local planning authority should discuss alternative means of production or operation with the person carrying on the activity.[11] The circular says that benefits to the amenity of the neighbourhood should be considered in terms of the number of people likely to benefit and how adversely affected their amenities would be without the stop notice.[12] There may of course be other benefits in addition to those mentioned in the circular, such as preventing harm to nature conservation interests or the historic environment. Circular 21/91 had said that possible compensatory liability was material in deciding whether to serve.[13] This text was omitted from the 1997 circular but the point is correct in the light of the Supreme Court's decision in *R (Health & Safety Executive) v Wolverhampton City Council*.[14]

11.05 The discretion to serve a stop notice was considered in *Elmbridge Borough Council v Wendy Fair Markets Ltd*.[15] The effect of an enforcement notice had been suspended whilst an application for leave to appeal to the High Court under s 289 was pursued. The LPA then served a stop notice on Wendy Fair Markets. Wendy Fair Markets then applied to quash the stop notice. Mr Justice Harrison dismissed this application. The note in the *Journal of Planning and Environment Law* on the Court of Appeal decision contains his main points:

(a) the contents of the Circular can be relevant;

(b) the Circular is advisory and not binding on the local planning authority;

(c) in the particular case, concerning the Green Belt, the planning issue was clear cut and there was no need to carry out a detailed cost/benefit analysis of the effect of serving the stop notice;[16]

(d) a stop notice can prevent unauthorised use in an important and sensitive part of the Green Belt and the delay to the enforcement notice taking effect was relevant by lengthening the period of unauthorised use;

(e) a purpose of preventing a profit being made from the unauthorised use would be unlawful; and

(f) the court should only interfere with a decision under s 183 if it is clear that the decision has been reached in an unlawful way.

The Court of Appeal granted leave to appeal against this decision. It considered arguable that there must be some reason to make discontinuance essential to safeguard the amenity of the area or public safety, to abate a nuisance or to prevent serious damage to the environment. The substantive appeal was not determined as the enforcement notice came into effect first when the Court of Appeal decided it could not consider an appeal against a refusal of leave under s 289.[17]

11.06 In *R v Hounslow London Borough Council ex p Dooley*, a travel agency had been converted without planning permission into a restaurant. The local planning

---

[11] Paragraph 3.21.
[12] Paragraph 3.22.
[13] Circular 21/91 Annex 3, para 24.
[14] [2012] UKSC 34; [2012] 1 WLR 2264.
[15] [1995] JPL 928, CA.
[16] For discussion of this point see Shona Emmett, 'Stop Notices and the Cost Benefit Assessment' [1996] JPL 3.
[17] *Wendy Fair Markets Ltd v Secretary of State for the Environment* [1996] JPL 649.

authority issued an enforcement notice against the entire use and a stop notice against evening use. The High Court considered that a cost/benefit analysis which simply said that there would be a potential financial impact on the operators from curtailing their activities was sufficient in that case.[18]

FORM OF THE STOP NOTICE

11.07 The stop notice must refer to the relevant enforcement notice, and specify the land and activities covered and the date on which it will take effect. There is no prescribed form for the stop notice but a model notice is provided as the Appendix to Annex 3 of Circular 10/97. The stop notice should precisely and unambiguously set out the activities prohibited. The enforcement notice cannot be relied upon to say what is or is not permitted.[19] In *Dhar,* an extension was being constructed in excess of that approved in a planning permission. The local planning authority issued an enforcement notice, which required the extension to be reduced to that permitted. It then served a stop notice, which in terms prohibited the carrying out of building operations in connection with the extensions generally and also annexed a copy of the enforcement notice. The Court of Appeal held that the stop notice was invalid because it should have been confined to works in breach of planning control. They disagreed with the argument that the enforcement notice could be considered. Russell LJ said:

> 'It is the stop notice which defines the extent of the prohibition: it is a contravention of the stop notice which was the subject matter of this prosecution, and in our judgment because of the penal consequences that flow from such a contravention, the terms of the stop notice must be strictly construed. If the meaning is unambiguous assistance is not to be derived from other documents.'

A different result might be reached if the stop notice incorporated the prohibition in the enforcement notice and was consistent with it. However, the better practice is to include all the requirements on the stop notice itself, rather than relying on the enforcement notice. This also reduces the risk of error in any site notice.

11.08 The circular's model notice suggests appending the enforcement notice to the stop notice which remains sensible, subject to the caution given above. Having identified the land by a description and a plan, the model suggests specifying the breach this way:

> '4. Activity To Which This Notice Relates
>
> [Specify the activity required by the enforcement notice to cease, and any activity carried out as part of that activity, or associated with it]
>
> 5. What You Are Required To Do
>
> Cease all the activity specified in this notice.'

A stop notice can only require activity to cease, so positive steps in an enforcement notice (such as demolishing a building) cannot be included in the stop notice. The stop notice might also be against only the part of the unlawful use that causes the

---

[18]   (2000) 80 P & CR 405 at 417 per George Bartlett QC.
[19]   *R v Dhar* [1993] 2 PLR 60, [1993] Crim LR 615, CA, cf *Bristol Stadium v Brown* [1980] JPL 107.

greatest harm. For example, the stop notices in *Dooley* restricted only the evening use of the unlawful restaurant.

SERVICE AND SITE NOTICES

11.09   A stop notice may be served by the local planning authority 'on any person who appears to them to have an interest in the land or to be engaged in any activity prohibited by the notice'.[20] This includes the owner. By s 184(1), '[T]he stop notice must refer to the enforcement notice to which it relates and have a copy of that notice annexed to it'. Additionally, the local planning authority may display a site notice after a stop notice has been served. The site notice is a notice:[21]

'(a)   stating that a stop notice has been served and that any person contravening it may be prosecuted for an offence under section 187,

(b)   giving the date when the stop notice takes effect, and

(c)   indicating its requirements.'

'Indicating' requirements is on its face a lesser requirement than setting out or specifying the requirements of the stop notice. However the context is of a site notice which gives rise to criminal liability if the underlying stop notice is not complied with. If a person is aware of the existence of the stop notice from a site notice and breaches the stop notice then he will have no defence to criminal proceedings even if he has not seen the stop notice itself. It follows that a site notice should indicate the stop notice's requirements in sufficient detail that a reader will know what activity is prohibited.

ENFORCEMENT REGISTER

11.10   Details of stop notices issued are required to be entered in the enforcement register.[22] The enforcement register shall contain:

'the date of service and, if applicable, of withdrawal of any stop notice referring to the enforcement notice, together with a statement or summary of the activity prohibited by any such stop notice'.[23]

The information shall be entered as soon as practicable and in any event within 14 days of the event.[24]

TAKING EFFECT

11.11   The stop notice must specify the date on which it will take effect: s 184(2). For clarity, the subsection provides that the stop notice cannot be contravened until

---

[20]   Town and Country Planning Act 1990, s 183(6).
[21]   Town and Country Planning Act 1990, s 184(6).
[22]   Town and Country Planning Act 1990, s 188(1)(c).
[23]   Town and Country Planning (Development Management Procedure) (England) Order 2010, Art 38;
       Town and Country Planning (Development Management Procedure) (Wales) Order 2012, Art 30.
[24]   DMPO, Art 38(8); DMPO Wales, Art 30(5).

that date. Usually that must be at least three days after the service of the notice, but notices can take effect in shorter periods, or even immediately, if special reasons are given. The date of taking effect:[25]

'(a) must not be earlier than three days after the date when the notice is served, unless the local planning authority consider that there are special reasons for specifying an earlier date and a statement of those reasons is served with the stop notice; and

(b) must not be later than twenty-eight days from the date when the notice is first served on any person.'

The three-day limitation gives the person served some time to end the activity. Three days after includes the date on which the notice takes effect, so a stop notice served on 3 November can take effect under the three-day limitation on 6 November.[26] The requirement for 'special reasons' for a shorter period means that there must be some particular justification for urgency. The overriding urgency of stopping the breach must justify a lesser period or an immediate halt to the activity. Circular 10/97 provides the example that:

'it may be considered essential to protect an area of special landscape value, or a conservation area, from operational development (such as buildings, roadways or other hard surfaces) which, if continued, would be especially harmful.'[27]

Although the example is of locally designated areas, a period of less than three days can be justified in areas without special designation if the harm is extensive or difficult to reverse. Commonplace examples include unlawful demolition of buildings or harm to nature conservation interests.

11.12 The maximum 28-day period from service before a stop notice takes effect matches the minimum period for an enforcement notice to take effect.[28] If a period for compliance with planning control of more than 28 days is acceptable, then an enforcement notice alone is appropriate. A stop notice can then be issued if the taking effect of the enforcement notice is delayed by an appeal. In practice the seriousness of the harm resulting from the breach will mean that stop notices come into effect in much less than 28 days.

WITHDRAWAL OF A STOP NOTICE AND CESSATION OF EFFECT

Withdrawal

11.13 The local planning authority may withdraw a stop notice by serving notice upon the persons served with it.[29] Additionally, if a site notice was displayed, they must display a notice of the withdrawal in its place.[30] Unlike enforcement notices withdrawal only takes effect on service rather than the decision to withdraw.[31] The local planning authority may serve a further stop notice on those persons or on others.[32]

---

[25] Town and Country Planning Act 1990, s 184(3).
[26] *R (Dooley) v Hounslow London Borough Council* (2000) 80 P & CR 405 at 409.
[27] Circular 10/97 Annex 3, para 3.29.
[28] Town and Country Planning Act 1990, s 172(3)(b).
[29] Town and Country Planning Act 1990, s 183(7).
[30] Town and Country Planning Act 1990, s 184(7).
[31] Cf Town and Country Planning Act 1990, s 173A(1).
[32] Town and Country Planning Act 1990, s 183(7).

Cessation of effect

11.14   A stop notice will cease to have effect under s 184(4) when:

'(a) the enforcement notice to which it relates is withdrawn or quashed; or

(b) the period for compliance with the enforcement notice expires; or

(c) notice of the withdrawal of the stop notice is first served under section 183(7).'

The different wording of paragraphs (a) and (c) is because withdrawal takes effect at different times: an enforcement notice is withdrawn on the decision to withdraw, whilst a stop notice requires service of the withdrawal. An enforcement notice is quashed when the Secretary of State or Inspector's decision is sent out to the parties. Where several people had been served with a stop notice, then the first service of notice of withdrawal of the stop notice occurs for the purposes of under paragraph (c) when one of those people is served.

11.15   Whilst a stop notice will remain in effect in the period between the decision to withdraw and service of the withdrawal, it is unlikely to be in the public interest to prosecute for a breach that occurred in that period. The Act does not explicitly say that posting a notice on site that the stop notice is withdrawn causes it to cease to have effect, but it is questionable whether it can have any legal effect in such circumstances. If an enforcement notice is quashed on appeal to the Secretary of State, the stop notice ceases to have effect immediately. It cannot be suspended or revived by an appeal to the High Court against the Secretary of State's decision.[33] Section 184(4)(b) emphasises the temporary nature of stop notices: they apply until the enforcement notice should have been complied with. Criminal liability is then applied by the enforcement notice. Where the time for the enforcement notice taking effect is delayed by an appeal, a stop notice would continue to have effect in that period as well as during the enforcement notice's compliance period.

VALIDITY AND CHALLENGE

11.16   The validity of a stop notice may be challenged by judicial review or as a defence to criminal proceedings. Such a notice cannot be appealed to the Secretary of State. Conversely, there are no statutory bars to challenge in the High Court or other legal proceedings. The decision to issue the notice can be challenged on normal judicial review grounds. In *R v Rochester upon Medway City Council ex p Hobday*,[34] a council decision to issue a stop notice was challenged (unsuccessfully) on *Wednesbury* unreasonableness grounds. A stop notice which prohibits acts, only some of which are in breach of planning control, is invalid.[35]

11.17   The approach to challenging stop notices has been complicated by relatively old case law. A challenge to the validity of a stop notice was considered by the Divisional Court, but rejected on its merits in *Bristol Stadium v Brown*.[36] In *R v Jenner*,[37] Mr Jenner had sought to argue in criminal proceedings that the activity

---

[33] *R v Secretary of State for the Environment ex p Hillingdon London Borough Council* [1992] 2 PLR 91.

[34] [1989] 2 PLR 38.

[35] *R v Dhar* [1993] 2 PLR 60, CA.

[36] [1980] JPL 107.

[37] [1983] 1 WLR 873.

had been carried on for more than the period within which a stop notice had to be served.[38] The Crown Court had ruled that it was not possible to challenge the validity of a stop notice by way of defence to a prosecution and so he could not run this point. Without upsetting that conclusion, the Court of Appeal in *Jenner* had said that a defendant could simply show that the activity had been carried on for so long that it cannot be prohibited by a stop notice. In those circumstances the notice did not apply to that activity. Walker LJ did observe that judicial review was not a suitable means of resolving those issues. In *R v Epping Forest District Council ex p Strandmill*,[39] it was again alleged that the activity had been carried out for more than the prescribed period. Whilst the committee could have rationally concluded that a notice could be served on the material they had, the applicant asked the Court to determine as a matter of fact whether the activity had been going on for that period. Nolan J considered that whilst *Wednesbury* review could be carried out, the period for which the activity had been carried out was left to any criminal proceedings.

11.18   *R (JRP Holdings Ltd) v Spelthorne Borough Council*[40] again concerned the submission that the activity had been carried on for more than the relevant period of four years. The Council accepted that this was likely to be the case, but that this did not invalidate the stop notice. Dyson LJ agreed saying:

> 'if the stop notice issued in respect of the change of use enforcement notice was served in breach of s 183(5) that would not be a ground for judicial review, although it would be a defence to a criminal prosecution'.[41]

However, the House of Lords in *Boddington v British Transport Police*[42] established that the lawfulness of a legal instrument or administrative decision could be challenged by way of defence to criminal proceedings unless the statutory context was clearly against such a challenge (eg *R v Wicks*[43]). The validity of a stop notice would be able to be raised in criminal proceedings. In those circumstances the *Jenner* distinction between the lawfulness of the stop notice and its scope (arising from the time limit on activities rather than the wording of the notice) becomes unnecessary. It is not difficult to say that a notice, which purports to prohibit activities that it is not able on the facts to prohibit, is unlawful or that the decision to issue it was irrational. The person served should not have to assume that the notice does not mean what it says.

11.19   The critical factors should be the nature of the argument raised and the ability to prove the respective contentions. Judicial review concerns the lawfulness of the authority's decision and the court's ability to review factual findings is limited, essentially to whether there was no evidence which could have supported that finding or the assessment was irrational. Conversely the criminal courts have to make findings of fact, such as whether the activity has been carried on for more than four years. A disputed question of fact is better resolved in criminal proceedings where witnesses can be called and cross-examined. Conversely, an issue as to the meaning of the General Permitted Development Order may be readily resolved by judicial review.

---

[38]   At the time the Town and Country Planning Act 1971, s 90(2) provided a 12-month period.
[39]   [1990] JPL 415. This was one of a number of enforcement cases involving Wendy Fair Markets.
[40]   [2007] EWCA Civ 1122, [2008] JPL 696. This is a decision on a permission application and so strictly ought not to be cited.
[41]   At para 7.
[42]   [1999] 2 AC 143.
[43]   [1998] AC 92.

COMPENSATION

11.20   Compensation may be payable for loss due to the service of a stop notice if the stop notice or its enforcement notice is withdrawn, varied or quashed and the activity prohibited was not in breach of planning control. Compensation may be payable if (s 186(1)):

> '(a) the enforcement notice is quashed on grounds other than those mentioned in paragraph (a) of section 174 [ie that planning permission should be given];
>
> (b) the enforcement notice is varied (otherwise than on the grounds mentioned in that paragraph) so that any activity the carrying out of which is prohibited by the stop notice ceases to be a relevant activity;
>
> (c) the enforcement notice is withdrawn by the local planning authority otherwise than in consequence of the grant by them of planning permission for the development to which the notice relates; or
>
> (d) the stop notice is withdrawn.'

No compensation is payable 'in respect of the prohibition in a stop notice of any activity which, at any time when the notice is in force, constitutes or contributes to a breach of planning control'.[44] This prevents the unmeritorious recovery of compensation where the stop notice or enforcement notice is quashed or withdrawn because of defects or for reasons of expediency. In considering in a compensation claim whether there is a breach of planning control, the Upper Tribunal (Lands Chamber) may be bound by earlier decisions as to lawfulness on the basis of *res judicata*.[45]

Claimants for compensation

11.21   Any person having an interest in or occupying the land subject to the stop notice when it is first served is entitled to claim compensation.[46] The interest may be legal or equitable but a mere right to use the land was insufficient: *International Ferry Traders Ltd v Adur District Council*.[47] In *International Ferry Traders* a stop notice had been served and an enforcement notice issued against the use of quays for the docking of ships and the loading and unloading of cargoes and the temporary storage of cargo. The controversy had arisen because the cargoes were live animals. The enforcement notice was subsequently quashed. The Court of Appeal agreed with the Lands Tribunal that licences to use the land which were expressed not to give a right to exclusive possession did not give rise to an interest in the land.[48] In *International Ferry Traders,* the Lands Tribunal held that an occupier of part of the land subject to a stop notice could claim compensation.[49] A contractual licensee may be, but is not necessarily, an occupier.[50] The exporters in that case had insufficient control of the land to be occupiers. A contractor carrying out the activity is not entitled to claim against the LPA unless he is also the occupier. He is left with contractual claims

---

44 Town and Country Planning Act 1990, s 186(5)(a).

45 *Payne v Caerphilly County Borough Council* [2009] RVR 66 (Lands Tribunal).

46 Town and Country Planning Act 1990, s 186(2).

47 [2004] EWCA Civ 288; [2004] JPL 1610.

48 At para 23, following *Stevens v Bromley London Borough Council* [1972] 1 Ch 400 and distinguishing *Pennine Raceway v Kirklees Metropolitan Borough Council* [1983] QB 382.

49 *International Ferry Traders* Court of Appeal at para 16.

50 *International Ferry Traders* Court of Appeal at para 24.

against the person employing him. A claimant may recover from the LPA sums payable by him for breach of contract in ceasing the activities.[51]

Entitlement to compensation

11.22   If the necessary conditions are satisfied, compensation is recoverable 'in respect of any loss or damage directly attributable to the prohibition contained in the notice' or, where the enforcement notice is varied, the activities which are no longer prohibited by the stop notice.[52] The loss or damage 'shall include any sum payable in respect of a breach of contract caused by the taking of action necessary to comply with the prohibition'.[53] In *Shopsearch UK Ltd v Greenwich London Borough Council*[54] the Lands Tribunal held that there was no power to award exemplary damages as s 186 is concerned with loss or damage directly attributable to the prohibition. In that case compensation was awarded to a freeholder for the loss of rent and abortive advertising costs following service of a temporary stop notice and a stop notice against an alleged use as a bar and lap-dancing club. Interest is payable from the date of service of the stop notice.[55] The stop notice need not have been served on the claimant for that person to be able to make a claim.

The effect of a failure to provide information to the local planning authority on compensation

11.23   If the claimant was statutorily required to provide information before the stop notice was served, compensation is not awarded if he failed to provide information or co-operate and had he done so the loss or damage could have been avoided. This applies if the claimant should have provided information that could have led to the stop notice not being served or it being varied. Compensation is not awarded if:

(a)   the claimant was required to provide information under:

    (i)   a planning contravention notice (see Town and Country Planning Act 1990, s 171C);

    (ii)   a section 330 Town and Country Planning Act notice; or

    (iii) a notice Local Government (Miscellaneous Provisions) Act 1976, under s 16; and

(b)   the loss or damage claimed could have been avoided if he had provided the information or otherwise co-operated with the local planning authority when responding to the notice.[56]

To rely on the proviso the local planning authority will have had to seek information under one of these statutory notice provisions. A failure of the claimant to reply, or reply fully, to correspondence does not protect the authority. Of course, if a stop

---

[51]   Town and Country Planning Act 1990, s 186(4).
[52]   Town and Country Planning Act 1990, s 186(2).
[53]   Town and Country Planning Act 1990, s 186(4).
[54]   [2009] RVR 198; [2009] JPL.1375 at para 41.
[55]   Planning and Compensation Act 1991, s 80 and Sch 18, Pt I.
[56]   Town and Country Planning Act 1990, s 186(5)(b).

notice has to be served urgently then the information-gathering notices may be too slow to be used for that notice.[57] The most obvious circumstance for this proviso to apply is where an explanation in response to a notice would have persuaded the planning authority that there was no breach of planning control. That is a matter of fact. The extent to which the local planning authority was willing to accept any later explanation that the activities were lawful may indicate whether service of the stop notice would have been avoided by a response to information-gathering notices.

The claims procedure

11.24   Compensation claims are made to the local planning authority.[58] The procedure is set out in the Town and Country Planning General Regulations 1992. The claim is made in writing, delivered or sent by pre-paid post, to the local planning authority.[59] The claim must be made within '12 months from the date of the decision in respect of which the claim or notice is made or given',[60] unless this period is extended by the Secretary of State in any particular case. Time runs from the date of the decision to vary, quash or withdraw the relevant notice. So where an enforcement notice is quashed on appeal, time runs from the appeal decision even if there is a subsequent appeal to the High Court against that decision.[61] The period cannot be extended after it has expired.[62] No particular form of claim is prescribed, but it must unequivocally state that a claim is being made.[63] In the *International Ferry Traders* case it was sufficient to say in a letter:[64]

'In the light of the decision of the Secretary of State dated January 28, 1998 we write to give you notice that it is the intention of our client company to claim compensation from your authority under s 186 of the Town and Country Planning Act 1990. Full details of the claim will be served on you in due course.'

There was no need to specify the heads of claim nor the sum sought. Pill LJ said in *International Ferry Traders*:[65]

'I accept [IFT's] submission that a claim was made and that the distinction claimed by the Council is not a real one. The inference that a claim was not being made in the letter could not properly be drawn from the terms of the letter. The future aspect upon a reading of the first paragraph as a whole goes to the "full details" of the claim and not the existence of the claim. Nor is it correct that the regulations require that the main heads of claim should have been indicated within the 12-month period. However, having reached that conclusion, I add that in order to avoid points like this being taken and in the interests of the administration of justice, claimants should make any claim they propose to make clearly and promptly, giving appropriate details as soon as they reasonably can.'

---

[57] The minimum compliance periods for planning contravention notices and section 330 notices are 21 days, see Chapter 5.
[58] Town and Country Planning Act 1990, s 186(3).
[59] Town and Country Planning General Regulations 1992, reg 12(1).
[60] Town and Country Planning General Regulations 1992, reg 12(2).
[61] See *International Ferry Traders Ltd v Adur District Council* [2004] EWCA Civ 288, [2004] JPL 1610 paras 1, 6, 7.
[62] *R v Secretary of State for the Environment ex p Hillingdon London Borough Council* (1992) 64 P & CR 105, [1992] 2 PLR 91.
[63] *Texas Homecare Ltd v Lewes District Council* (1985) 51 P & CR 205.
[64] *International Ferry Traders* at paras 38, 39.
[65] At para 39.

If the claim, or its amount, is not accepted, then the claim is referred to the Upper Tribunal (Lands Chamber),[66] which is still semi-officially referred to as the Lands Tribunal. The procedure is set out in Land Compensation Act 1961, ss 2 and 4 and the Tribunal Procedure (Upper Tribunal) (Lands Chamber) Rules 2010.

SERVICE OF STOP NOTICES BY THE SECRETARY OF STATE

11.25   Section 185 empowers the Secretary of State and Welsh Ministers to serve a stop notice in the same way as the local planning authority. The Secretary of State may serve a stop notice if it appears to him expedient that such a notice should be served in respect of any land.[67] The notice will have the same effect as if it had been served by the local planning authority.[68] He must consult the local planning authority before serving a stop notice.[69] Compensation required to be paid under s 186 in respect of a Secretary of State's stop notice is paid by the local planning authority named by the Secretary of State in the stop notice as the authority responsible for that matter in that area,[70] which might be thought to be a little unfair.

PROSECUTION FOR FAILING TO COMPLY WITH A STOP NOTICE

Prosecution by the local planning authority

11.26   Stop notices are imposed where there is an urgent need to stop the activity being carried on. If it were appropriate to serve the notice, failure to comply would cause substantial planning harm. In these circumstances, the local planning authority would expect to take criminal proceedings promptly if the notice is not complied with.

Prosecution by third parties

11.27   As with enforcement notices, prosecutions are usually brought by the local planning authority, but third parties may also prosecute.

THE OFFENCE

11.28   Failure to comply with a stop notice is an offence, subject to the same powers to fine as failure to comply with an enforcement notice. Much of the commentary and case law on enforcement notice prosecutions under s 179 is relevant to stop notice prosecutions.[71] Section 187(1) provides:

> 'If a person contravenes a stop notice after a site notice has been displayed or the stop notice has been served on him he shall be guilty of an offence.'

'Contravening' means carrying out the activity prohibited by the notice. It includes causing or permitting the stop notice's contravention.[72] A person does not need to

---

[66]   Town and Country Planning Act 1990, s 186(6).
[67]   Town and Country Planning Act 1990, s 185(1).
[68]   Town and Country Planning Act 1990, s 185(2).
[69]   Town and Country Planning Act 1990, s 185(3).
[70]   Town and Country Planning Act 1990, Sch 1, para 16(1), (2)(b).
[71]   See Chapter 9 above.
[72]   Town and Country Planning Act 1990, s 187(1B).

have knowledge of the existence of the notice before committing an offence: lack of knowledge is potentially a defence to be proved. It is possible for a person to be served with a notice without knowing of its existence: for example if the notice is left their usual or last known place of abode and they have either moved or were simply not there until after the offence has said to have been committed.[73] However, the stop notice must have taken effect before it can be contravened. A site notice cannot be displayed until the stop notice has been served on some person. The offence may be charged for a day or a longer period.[74] As with enforcement notices, a person may be convicted of a second or subsequent offence after the date of the preceding conviction.[75] In practice this will not occur unless the taking effect of the enforcement notice has been delayed by an appeal.

DEFENCES

11.29   The one statutory defence is provided by s 187(3):

'… it shall be a defence for the accused to prove—

(a)   that the stop notice was not served on him, and

(b)   that he did not know, and could not reasonably have been expected to know, of its existence.'

This defence is only applicable if the prosecution is because a site notice has been displayed (as otherwise the only defendants would have been served). Knowledge is tested at the time the offence is alleged to have been committed. A defendant who was present on the land after the site notice had been displayed would have been reasonably expected to know of its existence unless the notice had been removed or he was subject to some disability. It will depend on the circumstances whether a defendant who did not enter the land, such as the employer of building contractors or an absent owner could reasonably have been expected to have been told of the notice by any employee or other person on the land. The defence must be proved on the balance of probabilities.

SENTENCE

11.30   On summary conviction the maximum sentence is a fine of up to £20,000.[76] On conviction on indictment, the fine is unlimited.[77] In determining a fine the court shall particularly 'have regard to any financial benefit which has accrued or appears likely to accrue to [the defendant] in consequence of the offence'.[78] The financial benefit could be continuing a profitable use, or the payment received by building contractors, see Chapter 9 on enforcing enforcement notices. The confiscation provisions of the Proceeds of Crime Act 2003 could also be used against those convicted of breaches of stop notices.

---

[73]   See the modes of service in Town and Country Planning Act 1990, s 329.
[74]   Town and Country Planning Act 1990, s 187(1A).
[75]   Town and Country Planning Act 1990, s 187(1A).
[76]   The Legal Aid, Sentencing and Punishment of Offenders Act 2012, s 85 allows the sentence on summary conviction to be unlimited, but this provision is not yet in force.
[77]   Town and Country Planning Act 1990, s 187(2).
[78]   Town and Country Planning Act 1990, s 187(2A).

Chapter 12

Temporary Stop Notices

12.01   A temporary stop notice may be issued by a local planning authority to prohibit an activity which is in breach of planning control. The process is very similar to the stop notice procedure, except that a temporary stop notice can be served before an enforcement notice has been served and only has effect for 28 days. Temporary stop notices therefore provide a means of enforcement which does not have to await the drafting of an enforcement notice or the identification of who to serve with the enforcement notice.

12.02   A temporary stop notice would tend to be used in this way. The temporary stop notice would be issued and served and if the local planning authority was not satisfied that the activity restrained by the notice had ceased, the authority would issue an enforcement notice and serve a stop notice to continue the prohibition after the end of the 28-day period. An alternative course would be to use a temporary stop notice in conjunction with a breach of condition notice. 28 days must elapse before a breach of condition notice takes effect and a temporary stop notice could be used for that period. Whilst intended to be a quick enforcement mechanism, local planning authorities must still exercise care. The financial consequences for the person served may be substantial, and if the activity prohibited was in fact lawful, the authority will be liable to pay compensation for any loss caused.

12.03   Temporary stop notices were introduced by the Planning and Compulsory Purchase Act 2004 as ss 171E to 171H in Part VII of the Town and Country Planning Act 1990. Since their introduction, temporary stop notices have proved more popular that stop notices. From a high of 556 temporary stop notices having been served by English authorities in 2006/2007, numbers have settled down to under 300 per year (260 in 2011/2012). The use of temporary stop notices may reflect the level of development activity more than other enforcement mechanisms, as they are a quick way of bringing a developer to heel if works have started without complying with planning conditions. Guidance is given in ODPM Circular 02/2005 *Temporary Stop Notice*. The temporary stop notice powers have not been brought into force in Wales.

TEMPORARY STOP NOTICES

12.04   A temporary stop notice may be issued if the local planning authority thinks (s 171E(1)):

> '(a) that there has been a breach of planning control in relation to any land, and
>
> (b) that it is expedient that the activity (or any part of the activity) which amounts to the breach is stopped immediately.'

The notice must:[1]

'(a) specify the activity which the authority think amounts to the breach;

(b) prohibit the carrying on of the activity (or of so much of the activity as is specified in the notice);

(c) set out the authority's reasons for issuing the notice'

A temporary stop notice may therefore act against only the most troublesome part of the breach of control (such as restricting the hours on an unlawful use). The Circular expresses caution about confining a notice to part of a site if there is a risk that the activity will be moved to another part of the site.[2] However, the notice can only apply to the land in respect of which there is the breach of planning control and where a use is concerned; this depends upon the identification of the planning unit.[3] A model temporary stop notice is provided in the Annex to Circular 02/2005.

Issuing a temporary stop notice

12.05   Once a temporary stop notice has been issued, a copy must be displayed on the land along with a statement of the effect of the notice and of s 171G (which provides for criminal offences).[4] The copy notice and statement should be firmly fixed to a structure on the land that is the subject of the notice or put on a stake forced into the ground. It is insufficient to put the display on a structure next to the land, such as a lamp post. Section 171E(6) provides that a temporary stop notice 'has effect from the time a copy of it is first displayed in pursuance of subsection (5)'. The effect of the notice is therefore immediate (as subsection (1) also says); unlike many stop notices a temporary stop notice does not provide for a period for compliance. There is an issue as to whether a temporary stop notice has effect on an individual served with the notice but prior to the display of the notice on the site or where a display is not in accordance with the legislation. Subsection (6) relies on display to start the effect of the notice and, by subsection (7), display also determines when the notice ceases to have effect. However s171G(1) says that an offence is committed by a person who contravenes a temporary stop notice which has been served on him or which has been displayed. The implication of that provision is that a notice can be contravened before it has been displayed or if it has been never displayed.[5] However the prudent advice to a person served with a notice would usually be to stop the activity.

12.06   Subject to this point, an authority could give time for compliance by serving the notice and then delaying the display of the notice on the ground. However that would need to be explained to those served (as they are likely to stop immediately upon service otherwise) and any delay would need to be very short otherwise it would be inappropriate to use the temporary stop notice procedure. The notice may be served on any person who the authority thinks is carrying on the activity, is an occupier of, or has an interest in, the land.[6] There is no obligation to serve, reflecting

---

[1] Town and Country Planning Act 1990, s 171E(3).
[2] Circular 02/2005, para 10.
[3] See Chapter 2.
[4] Town and Country Planning Act 1990, s.171E(5).
[5] Circular 02/2005 para 5, 6 and 44 appear to assume this is the case.
[6] Town and Country Planning Act 1990, s.171E(4).

the fact that action might be taken before the authority have managed to find out who is involved in the breach of control. Similarly, any service would be on those the authority think are involved or have an interest. If they prove not to have been involved then that does not affect the operation of the notice. However, since the local planning authority will wish to shut down the breach as soon as possible, it is sensible to serve those who might be involved.

Duration of a temporary stop notice

12.07   A temporary stop notice ceases to have effect:[7]

'(a)   at the end of the period of 28 days starting on the day the copy notice is so displayed,

(b)   at the end of such shorter period starting on that day as is specified in the notice, or

(c)   if it is withdrawn by the local planning authority.'

Since the 28 day period starts on the day of display, a temporary stop notice displayed on a Monday will cease to have effect at the end of the Sunday just under four weeks later, unless an earlier date has been specified.

Whilst it might seem sensible to withdraw a temporary stop notice when a (permanent) stop notice takes effect, the withdrawal of a temporary notice gives rise to compensation. In those circumstances a temporary stop notice should be allowed to run its course even though there would be a period of overlap with a stop notice. Alternatively the stop notice could be drafted to come into effect as soon as the temporary notice expires.

Regularising the breach of planning control such as by the grant of planning permission or the approval of details under a planning permission does not terminate the effect of the notice, however there is some protection against compensation claims if the notice is then withdrawn, as discussed further below.

Exceptions to the use of temporary stop notices

Limitations on the ability to issue a temporary stop notice have been introduced in respect of dwelling houses, residential caravans, activities carried on for more than four years and concerning repeated use of temporary stop notices. The residential caravan exception was revoked in 2013.

Dwelling houses and residential caravans

12.08   Section 171F(1) of the 1990 Act provides:

'A temporary stop notice does not prohibit–

(a)   the use of a building as a dwelling house;

(b)   the carrying out of an activity of such description or in such circumstances as is prescribed.'

---

[7]   Town and Country Planning Act 1990, s 171E(7).

With respect to dwelling houses the provision reflects the stop notice regime. The Town and Country Planning (Temporary Stop Notice) (England) Regulations 2005 were made under sub-section (1) in respect of residential caravans. The stationing of a caravan could not be prohibited by a temporary stop notice in these circumstances (regulation 2(2)):

'(a) the caravan is stationed on the land immediately before the issue of the temporary stop notice; and

(b) the caravan is at that time occupied by a person as his main residence;

unless the local planning authority consider that the risk of harm to a compelling public interest arising from the stationing of the caravan is so serious so as to outweigh any benefit, to the occupier of the caravan, in the stationing of the caravan for the period for which the temporary stop notice has effect.'

The effect was that temporary stop notices could prohibit works to enable land to be used for caravans (such as laying hardstanding and installing water pipes) and could prevent further caravans from being brought onto the site, but could not require the removal of residential caravans unless the risk of harm proviso was satisfied. This limitation caused problems when caravans were moved onto a site over a weekend.[8] The difficulty was that unless the use was brought to an end very quickly – in a matter of days – it might in practice take years to resolve. No similar restriction had been applied to the use of stop notices but their service is delayed by the need to issue an enforcement notice. The restriction was unnecessary as a proportionate response, having regard to the effect on rights under Article 8 of the European Convention on Human Rights, was required in any event. The 2005 regulations were revoked in their entirety with effect from 4 May 2013, so this restriction no longer applies.[9]

Four years' activity
As for stop notices,[10] a temporary stop notice 'does not prohibit the carrying out of any activity which has been carried out (whether or not continuously) for a period of four years ending with the day on which the copy of the notice is first displayed'.[11] This restriction limits its effect against uses as the restriction does not apply to activity consisting of or incidental to building, engineering, mining or other operations or the deposit of refuse or waste materials.[12] The four year limit is applied ignoring any period during which the activity is authorised by a planning permission[13] This means that a notice can be issued if an activity started under a temporary planning permission and that temporary permission (or the final temporary permission) expired during the four year period. It is less clear whether ignoring the period of the temporary permission means that the four year period is extended back in time to see whether there were four years of activity which were not authorised.

The effect of the prohibition is that notwithstanding the terms of the notice, a temporary stop notice does not prohibit activity that has been carried on for more than four years.

---

[8] For example, see the facts of *Mid-Suffolk District Council v Upton* [2007] EWHC 2296 (QB).

[9] Town and Country Planning (Temporary Stop Notice) (England) (Revocation) Regulations 2013.

[10] See Town and Country Planning Act 1990, s 183(5),(5A).

[11] Town and Country Planning Act 1990, s 171F(2).

[12] Town and Country Planning Act 1990, s 171F(3).

[13] Town and Country Planning Act 1990, s 171F(4).

Second temporary stop notices

12.09 Only one temporary stop notice may 'be issued in respect of the same activity unless the local planning authority has first taken some other enforcement action in relation to the breach of planning control which is constituted by the activity.'[14] So the general rule is that a temporary stop notice can only be used once against a particular breach. The expectation is that the planning authority will have used the time given by the notice to take other action, if required. This generates a few issues. If a defective temporary stop notice is issued, a replacement notice cannot be issued unless it can be said that the first notice was not a temporary stop notice. Where the original notice has an error on its face such that it is a nullity (such as failing to contain a prohibition on the activity) then it can readily be said that there was no original notice. If the notice would have been found *ultra vires* then it is debatable whether a second notice can be issued before the High Court rules on the unlawfulness. Since the Court would not be able to determine the point very quickly, that is a practical problem. If the notice is lawful, but the Council wish to change the nature of the prohibition (against the same activity) then they cannot do so by a new notice.

Second temporary stop notices are allowed if the authority has issued an enforcement notice, served a breach of condition notice or obtained an injunction under section 187B.[15] This allows a prohibition to be imposed prior to an enforcement notice or breach of condition notice taking effect, although a stop notice may still have to be served in the event of an enforcement notice appeal. The rationale for allowing a temporary stop notice to be served when an injunction has been obtained is less clear. Enforcement is best left to the court order once it has to be complied with. The Court will have considered the appropriate period for compliance so it is not obvious why the planning authority should be able to institute an immediate ban (although they could use an enforcement notice and stop notice to do the same).

The decision to issue a temporary stop notice

12.10 Provided that there is a breach of planning control underway, the decision to issue a temporary stop notice is a matter of discretion. In reaching that decision the local planning authority must have regard to the nature and impact of the breach and the effect on the person carrying out the breach. Circular 02/2005 advises:[16]

> 'The effect of issuing a temporary stop notice will be to halt the breach of control, or the specified activity immediately. This can have immediate serious consequences on a business. Local planning authorities should therefore ensure that a quick but adequate assessment of the likely consequences of issuing a temporary stop notice is available to the officer who will authorise issue of the notice. It should not be necessary to carry out a detailed cost/benefit assessment but the assessment should examine the foreseeable costs to the company, operator or landowner against whose activities the stop notice is directed, and the benefit to amenity in the vicinity of the site which is likely to result from a temporary stop notice.'

---

[14] Town and Country Planning Act 1990, s 171F(5).
[15] The first two acts are defined as 'enforcement action' by section 171A(2) and for the purpose of this section only, enforcement action is extended to include the obtaining of an injunction [not merely making an application for an injunction] by s 171F(6), Town and Country Planning Act 1990.
[16] Circular 02/2005, para 36.

The Circular also gives guidance on a cost/benefit analysis in terms which are almost identical to the advice in Circular 10/97 on issuing stop notices.[17] Beyond editing out examples and omitting mention of the Wendy Fair litigation, the substantive change is that advice that the authority 'should' whenever possible discuss the matter with the person carrying on the activity before serving a stop notice is replaced by guidance that it 'may choose to discuss, whenever practicable', prior to service of a temporary stop notice.[18]

Offences

12.11   Section 171G(1) provides:

'A person commits an offence if he contravenes a temporary stop notice–

(a)   which has been served on him, or

(b)   a copy of which has been displayed in accordance with section 171E(5).'

A notice can only be contravened when it is in effect. Whether a temporary stop notice has effect following service but before display is discussed above. It could not be contravened after it has ceased to have effect.

The section establishes that contravention of a temporary stop notice includes causing or permitting the contravention of the notice[19] and an offence may be charged by reference to a day or a longer period of time.[20] By subsection (4) a person may be convicted of more than one offence under the same notice at different dates or times. The utility of this provision is perhaps limited to occasions when a person quickly accepts a caution and then contravenes the notice again. A court conviction within the 28 day period is not practical and multiple breaches can be dealt with as an offence over a period.

It is a defence for a person to prove, on the balance of probabilities:[21]

'(a)   that the temporary stop notice was not served on him, and

(b)   that he did not know, and could not reasonably have been expected to know, of its existence.'

The prosecution would need to prove that the temporary stop notice was in effect by showing beyond reasonable doubt that the notice had been displayed on the site (or if this was adequate on its own, that the notice had been served on the defendant). The defence might only arise if the notice was displayed but the defendant had not been served with it.

Reasonably, the penalties for contravention of a temporary stop notice are the same as for contravention of a stop notice. The offence is triable either way, with a maximum fine of £20,000 in the Magistrates' Court or an unlimited fine in the Crown Court.[22]

---

[17]   Compare Circular 02/2005 para 37 to 39 with Circular 10/97, Annex 3, para 3.20 to 3.22.
[18]   Compare Circular 02/2005 para 38 with Circular 10/97, Annex 3, para 3.21.
[19]   Town and Country Planning Act 1990, s 171G(2).
[20]   Town and Country Planning Act 1990, s 171G(3).
[21]   Town and Country Planning Act 1990, s 171G(5).
[22]   Town and Country Planning Act 1990, s 171G(6).

As with other planning offences, the presence or lack of financial benefit has to be taken into account in sentencing.[23]

Compensation

12.12   As with stop notices, compensation may be payable if a temporary stop notice is issued and the activity was at the time lawful.

A person who had an interest in the land 'at the time the notice is served … is entitled to be compensated by the local planning authority in respect of any loss or damage directly attributable to the prohibition effected by the notice'[24] in the following circumstances:

(a)   the activity which is specified in the notice is authorised by planning permission or by a development order, a local development order or a neighbourhood development order;'[25]

'Authorised by planning permission' would mean authorised to be carried out at the time in the light of conditions attaching to any permission. So activity which is in breach of a condition or where a permission is not implemented because of non-compliance with a condition cannot trigger compensation. Compensation is not payable if the planning permission is granted on or after the date on which a copy of the notice is first displayed under section 171E(6),[26] even if the notice is kept in force after the permission is granted.

(b)   a certificate in respect of the activity is issued under section 191 or granted under that section by virtue of section 195;'[27]

Section 191 certificates are certificates of lawfulness of proposed use or development ('CLEUD') and section 195 is the appeal provision for such certificates. The provision does not say when the certificate has to be issued. If the certificate pre-dates the temporary stop notice then it would be a major blunder for the authority to have issued the notice in the first place. A CLEUD certifies the lawfulness of activities at the date of the application, so it is possible for a CLEUD to be applied for before a temporary stop notice is issued and granted after that time. A CLEUD applied for after the notice is issued can only certify lawfulness at the date of the application, when circumstances might have changed, although that is catered for by the absence of compensation for unlawful activity, as discussed below. It may be appropriate to take a wide view of the certificates giving rise to compensation, in the light of safeguards for authorities in the legislation.

(c)   the authority withdraws the notice.

No compensation is payable 'respect of the prohibition in a temporary stop notice of any activity which, at any time when the notice is in force, constitutes or contributes to a breach of planning control'[28] and this provides important protection for local planning authorities. If the CLEUD arises from a consent issued after the notice

---

23   Town and Country Planning Act 1990, s 171G(7).
24   Town and Country Planning Act 1990, s 171H(4).
25   Town and Country Planning Act 1990, s 171H(1)(a)
26   Town and Country Planning Act 1990, s 171H(2).
27   Town and Country Planning Act 1990, s 171H(1)(b).
28   Town and Country Planning Act 1990, s 186(5)(a) as modified by s 171H(5).

or a notice is withdrawn because permission has been granted or for a technical defect, there will not be compensation payable if the notice attacked a breach of planning control. Other provisions governing stop notice compensation also apply to temporary stop notices and so compensation is not payable for losses that could have been avoided if the claimant had complied with requests for information under a planning contravention notice, section 330 notice or notice under section 16 of the Local Government (Miscellaneous Provisions) Act 1976.[29]

The claim procedure is as considered in chapter 11 on stop notices. The claim must be made within 12 months or any longer period allowed by Ministers and disputed claims are dealt with by the Upper Tribunal (Lands Chamber).[30]

---

[29]   Town and Country Planning Act 1990, s 186(5)(b) as modified by s 171H(5).
[30]   Town and Country Planning Act 1990, s 186, as applied by s 171H(5).

Chapter 13

Breach of Condition Notices

13.01 Whilst enforcement notices can be issued against breaches of conditions or limitations, a faster enforcement method was introduced in the Planning and Compensation Act 1991: the breach of condition notice. A breach of condition notice specifies steps to comply with a condition[1] giving a set period for compliance. Failure to comply with the conditions or to do the specified steps is an offence. The notice is served by the local planning authority. Unlike an enforcement notice, there is no ability to appeal to the Secretary of State. The planning merits of the condition are irrelevant, although the legality of it is not. Therefore, the delays (and safeguards) in the appeal process are not present. The validity of a breach of condition notice can be challenged by judicial review or as a defence to a prosecution.

SERVICE

13.02 A local planning authority 'may' serve a breach of condition notice if:

(a) planning permission has been granted subject to conditions;[2]

(b) the permission has been implemented;[3] and

(c) any of the conditions has not been complied with.[4]

The breach of condition notice may be served on any person who is, or has been, carrying out or causing or permitting another to carry out the development and anyone in control of the land.[5] By analogy with enforcement notices, permitting something includes giving express permission and failing to take reasonable steps to prevent it.[6] A breach of condition notice binds the person served with the notice, unlike an enforcement notice, which binds the land and so may affect persons who are not served.

13.03 A person in control can only be required to comply with conditions regulating the use of the land.[7] The view is that the person currently in control should not be made liable for the acts of a person who carried out development before he took control. The person in control when operational development was carried out would probably have permitted the development and so could be served

---

[1] This includes limitations: Town and Country Planning Act 1990, s 187A(13)(a).
[2] Town and Country Planning Act 1990, s 187A(1).
[3] See *Handoll v Warner Goodman & Streat* (1995) 70 P & CR 627.
[4] Town and Country Planning Act 1990, s 187A(2).
[5] Town and Country Planning Act 1990, s 187A(2).
[6] *Test Valley Investments Ltd v Tanner* (1964) 15 P & CR 279.
[7] Town and Country Planning Act 1990, s 187A(4).

with a breach of condition notice for that development. In *Davenport v London Borough of Hammersmith and Fulham*[8] a planning permission for a motor vehicle repairs on a site had included a condition prohibiting the parking of vehicles left with or under the control of the applicant on the public road leading up to the site. The site was being run by two brothers, one of whom had applied for the original consent. Breach of condition notices were served against the garage leaving customers' cars on the road. Whilst a notice could be served on the brother who had carried out the development, the conviction of the other brother was quashed. Richards J held that the condition regulated the use of the road and whilst the brother was in control of the garage site he did not have control of the public highway which was outside the site.

13.04   The time limits for taking enforcement action in s 171B apply.[9] For conditions, these are ten years unless the condition relates to a change of use of a building to use as a single dwelling house where a four-year period applies or a different period is available under a planning enforcement order. If an enforcement notice is in effect in respect of the breach, a breach of condition notice can be served at any time.[10] Annex 4 of Circular 10/97 gives specific guidance on breach of condition notices

13.05   Government guidance particularly recommends the use of a breach of condition notice when a valid condition has clearly been breached.[11] Where there is scope for argument about the interpretation, validity or enforceability of a condition, that guidance suggests that the local planning authority proceed by enforcement notice rather than breach of condition notice. There is no guidance as to whether to serve a notice when a condition is valid but there is dispute about its planning merits. Where for example, an application has been made for the lifting or varying of the condition or that issue is going to appeal, the local planning authority will need to balance their view of the harm to the public interest with the possibility of the condition being lifted on appeal.

13.06   The minimum period for compliance is not less than 28 days beginning with the date of service of the notice.[12] Circular 10/97 advises that the compliance period should be commensurate with the requirements of the notice.[13] It should reflect the time in which compliance can be achieved. The circular advises that normally a breach of condition notice is only served on one person[14] and this reflects the legislative structure of having a notice served on a person rather than a notice issued and copies served. Best practice is to serve notices each of which identifies who it is served on. Particularly where there are several companies or individuals involved with a site, and potentially several notices, it may be difficult to work out who has actually been served with a notice. It may be the case that separate notices are served on different developers or controllers of land which are identical in all respects except for the addressee.

---

[8]   (1999) 78 P & CR 421, [1999] JPL 1122.
[9]   See the discussion of time limits in Chapter 3 above.
[10]   171B(4)(a).
[11]   Circular 10/97 Annex 4, para 4.6.
[12]   Town and Country Planning Act 1990, s 187A(7)(a).
[13]   Circular 10/97 Annex 4 para 4.14.
[14]   Circular 10/97 Annex 4 para 4.13.

DRAFTING NOTICES

13.07   The notice will specify:

(a) the conditions which must be complied with;[15]

(b) 'the steps which the LPA consider ought to be taken, or the activities which ought to cease', to comply with these conditions;[16]

(c) the period, of not less than 28 days from the date of service, allowed for compliance.[17]

Several conditions may be specified in one notice, however, if there are to be different compliance periods, the circular advises that separate notices ought to be issued so there is no doubt as to which compliance period applies to which condition.[18] This might be over-cautious advice. It is not uncommon for notices to contain several different compliance (such as ceasing the activity, demolishing the building, removing the debris and laying topsoil and seeding). What matters is that is it clear to a recipient what has to be done and when it has to be done by. A model breach of condition notice is provided in the Appendix to Annex 4, Circular 10/97. This also specifies in the notice the subject land, the relevant planning permission, the consequences of noncompliance, the council officer responsible for enquiries and encourages the person served to seek professional advice.

THE ENFORCEMENT REGISTER

13.08   Details of breach of condition notices must be entered on the register of enforcement notices and stop notices.[19] The register entry shall include the address (or a location plan), the name of the serving authority the date of service, sufficient details of the planning permission to enable it to be identified, a statement or summary of the condition not complied with and the notice's requirements, including the compliance period.[20] The register entries are to be removed if the notice is withdrawn or quashed by a court.[21]

COMPLIANCE

13.09   The person served ('the person responsible')[22] is required to secure compliance with the notice. Failure to secure compliance is a criminal offence (subject to possible defences), even if the notice should not have been served. Therefore, a person wrongly served with a notice should promptly inform the local planning authority and ask them to withdraw it. If they do not, he should seek judicial review to have the notice quashed.

---

[15] Town and Country Planning Act 1990, s 187A(2).
[16] Town and Country Planning Act 1990, s 187A(5).
[17] Town and Country Planning Act 1990, s 187A(7).
[18] Circular 10/97 Annex 4, para 4.9.
[19] Town and Country Planning Act 1990, s 188(1).
[20] Town and Country Planning (Development Management Procedure) (England) Order 2010, art 38(3); Town and Country Planning (Development Management Procedure) (Wales) Order 2012, art 30(2).
[21] 2010 DMPO, art 38(4), 2012 DMPO, art 30(3).
[22] Town and Country Planning Act 1990, s 187A(3).

WITHDRAWAL OR EXTENSION OF TIME

13.10   The local planning authority may withdraw a breach of condition notice, whether or not the period for compliance has expired.[23] Withdrawal does not prevent the service of a further notice in respect of the conditions in that notice or other conditions. It should be remembered that the extension of the time limit to four years from the service of the notice (s 171B(4)(b)) will still apply where a notice is withdrawn. The period for compliance may be extended by the local planning authority.[24] That extension should be for a set period. Whilst the statute is not clear, more than one extension can probably be granted. Such withdrawals or extensions must be served by notice on the person responsible.[25] Unlike enforcement notices,[26] there is no power to waive or relax the requirements of the breach of condition notice. The local planning authority must withdraw and reissue if it intends to make such a change.

EFFECT OF PLANNING PERMISSION

13.11   Planning permission granted for development already carried out will disapply any inconsistent parts of a breach of condition notice.[27] This planning permission would be under s 73A (planning permission for development already carried out). If a condition to which a breach of condition notice relates is discharged, then that part of the breach of condition notice ceases to have effect.[28] This applies to planning permission under s 73A and a grant of planning permission to develop land without compliance with conditions previously attached.[29] If a condition in a breach of condition notice is superseded by a new permission pursuant to a section 73 application, then a new breach of condition notice would have to be served to force compliance with that new condition under the new consent. The breach of condition notice requires compliance with the conditions specified in the notice: a different, but replacement, condition is not covered. Criminal liability incurred before the grant of planning permission is unaffected.[30] However, the local planning authority would have to consider whether it was in the public interest to prosecute for an act which was now acceptable in planning terms. Any sentence is likely to be reduced as a result.

PROSECUTION

13.12   If the notice is not complied with then the person responsible is in breach of the notice and commits an offence.[31] Section 187A(8) provides:

'If at any time after the end of the period for compliance with the notice—

(a)   any of the conditions specified in the notice is not complied with; and

---

[23]   Town and Country Planning Act 1990, s 187A(6).
[24]   Town and Country Planning Act 1990, s 187A(7)(b).
[25]   Town and Country Planning Act 1990, s 187A(6), (7).
[26]   Town and Country Planning Act 1990, s 173A.
[27]   Town and Country Planning Act 1990, s 180(1).
[28]   Town and Country Planning Act 1990, s 180(2).
[29]   Town and Country Planning Act 1990, s 73.
[30]   Town and Country Planning Act 1990, s 180(3).
[31]   Town and Country Planning Act 1990, s 187A(8), (9).

(b) the steps specified in the notice have not been taken or, as the case may be, the activities specified in the notice have not ceased,

the person responsible is in breach of the notice.'

Relatively little guidance has been provided as to when prosecutions should be brought. The new revoked PPG18 considered it inappropriate to prosecute for a failure to comply with a limitation imposed on permitted development under the General Permitted Development Order unless the breach of condition notice included a full explanation of the allegedly unauthorised development and the householder has failed to take satisfactory steps to regularise it, despite being allowed adequate time.[32]

13.13   The prosecution must prove:

(a) that the defendant was served;

(b) any of the specified conditions are not complied with;

(c) the steps specified have not been taken, or the activities have not ceased; and

(d) the period for compliance has ended.

The Divisional Court in *Nourish v Adamson*[33] said that it was an essential element of the offence that the defendant should be the person having control of the land. This appears to be on the basis that the notice was served on the defendant as having control of the land under s 187A(2)(b) as distinct from having carried out the development under sub-paragraph (a). There may be a question whether this has to be proved by the prosecution or is a matter going to the validity of the notice, and so a point to be proved by the defence. In *Nourish,* the court considered that the magistrates had been entitled to find that the owner was in control, subject to the defendant being under an evidential burden to give a reason why he did not have control (such as having leased the land).

13.14   Failure both to comply with the conditions and to take the steps or cease the activities specified must be proven.[34] A responsible person is not in breach if he complies with the conditions, but in a different way to that specified in the notice. The offence is a continuing offence and may be charged for a day or a longer period. A second prosecution may be brought for any time after the date of a conviction if the notice is still breached.[35] The offence is tried summarily. A prosecution must be brought within six months of the offence last being committed, only covering breaches in those six months.

DEFENCES

13.15   Two statutory defences are provided.

(a) The defendant 'took all reasonable measures to secure compliance with the conditions specified in that notice'[36]

---

[32]   Paragraph 18
[33]   [1998] JPL 859.
[34]   *Quinton v North Cornwall District Council* [1994] CLY 4315, Truro Crown Court.
[35]   Town and Country Planning Act 1990, s187A(10).
[36]   Town and Country Planning Act 1990, s 187A(11)(a).

This defence is comparable to that of doing everything that could be expected to secure compliance with an enforcement notice.[37] The reasonable measures are to secure compliance with the condition and therefore need not be measures to carry out the steps specified.The provision is not explicit as to whether the measures are those that were reasonable after the notice was served or the developer must show that the condition could not have been complied with by reasonable measures when it was originally breached. This is particularly important for a developer who in carrying out the development failed to comply with conditions, but disposed of his interest and control of the site before the notice was served. In those circumstances he cannot comply with the notice. The former view, that reasonable measures are considered after the notice is served, is preferable. This defence may apply if the compliance period is unreasonable.

(b)   Where the defendant was served as having control of the land, that he longer had control on the date charged.[38]

The defences must be proven by the defendant on the balance of probabilities.

13.16   A Crown Court has held that s 187A(11) can only be relied upon if it is proven that it was not possible to comply with the steps specified in the notice.[39] This appears to apply too high a test.

SENTENCE

13.17   The maximum sentence for an offence committed in England is a level 4 fine, currently £2,500, but the maximum sentence in Wales is for a level 3 fine (£1,000).[40]

CHALLENGE TO THE VALIDITY OF A BREACH OF CONDITION NOTICE BY JUDICIAL REVIEW

13.18   The service of a breach of condition notice can be challenged by judicial review. The court can investigate whether a condition has not been complied with before the notice, is served as this goes to the jurisdiction of the local planning authority to serve the notice.[41] Another jurisdictional matter, allowing the court to determine the underlying facts, is whether the person served is carrying out or has been carrying out the development or has control of the land. The validity of the condition can be challenged, as can the reasonableness of serving the breach of condition notice. The notice could also fail to include the necessary details.

13.19   In *Trim v North Dorset District Council*,[42] a breach of condition notice had been served in January 2008 against breach of an equestrian occupancy condition on a house. Mr Trim commenced civil proceedings in December 2009, seeking a

---

[37]   Town and Country Planning Act 1990, s 179(3).
[38]   Town and Country Planning Act 1990, s 187A(11)(b).
[39]   *Quinton v North Cornwall District Council* [1994] CLY 4315.
[40]   Town and Country Planning Act 1990, s 187A(12) as substituted by the Localism Act 2011, s 126(2). For offences committed in England prior to 6 April 2012, the maximum sentence is a level 3 fine.
[41]   *R v Ealing London Borough Council ex p Zainuddin* [1995] JPL 925.
[42]   [2010] EWCA Civ 1446, [2011] 1 WLR 1901.

declaration that the notice had been served outside the 10-year period. The Court of Appeal held that it was an abuse of process to challenge the notice in private law proceedings: the appropriate means were judicial review or as a defence to a criminal prosecution. It also refused to extend time for bringing judicial review. One of Mr Trim's arguments was that he was left in limbo with a breach of condition notice in place but the local planning authority had not sought to prosecute. One potential route, not canvassed in the judgment, would have been to have asked the authority to withdraw the notice if they were unwilling to enforce it, and bring judicial review proceedings if they did not.

VALIDITY IN CRIMINAL PROCEEDINGS

13.20   The original enforcement circular following the 1991 reforms (Circular 17/92) considered that the validity of a breach of condition notice can be challenged in the magistrates' court by way of defence to a prosecution. This was revised in Circular 10/97 in the light of the Court of Appeal's judgment in *R v Wicks*,[43] which had taken a restrictive approach to defendants challenging in criminal proceedings notices which had been served on them. The circular therefore suggested that the validity of a notice could 'probably not be challenged by way of defence to a prosecution brought by an LPA if the notice is valid on its face'[44] However, the House of Lords judgment in *Wicks* took a narrower view, excluding collateral challenge to a notice because of the particularities of the enforcement notice regime. In *Diellito v Ealing London Borough Council*,[45] the Divisional Court considered that the absence of a right of appeal against a breach of condition notice, amongst other factors, permitted the validity of the notice to be challenged in criminal proceedings. The defendant was therefore entitled to contend that the notice was invalid as the 10-year period for taking enforcement action had expired and the condition being enforced was invalid. The court considered the merits of the condition point (rejecting it) and returned the case to the magistrates' court to consider the time limit. Similarly, it was possible to argue in *Davenport v London Borough of Hammersmith and Fulham*[46] that breach of condition notices were invalid because the underlying condition was unlawful and a notice was served on a person who was not the developer and did not have control of the land.

---

[43]   [1995] 93 LGR 377.
[44]   Circular 10/97 Annex 4, para 4.20.
[45]   [2000] QB 381.
[46]   (1999) 78 P & CR 421.

Chapter 14

Injunctions

14.01   Planning enforcement is principally concerned with:

• ending the contravention;

• ceasing the use; and

• restoring the land.

Criminal sanctions can only act indirectly. An owner or other interested person who fails to comply can be prosecuted and fined. If this stance is maintained after conviction then another prosecution can be brought. However, the criminal court cannot order compliance with planning control. Additionally, none of the enforcement, stop and breach of condition notice measures can be used in advance of a breach of planning control.

14.02   The civil courts, by means of an injunction, can order a person to obey the planning laws. If he fails to, he can then be imprisoned for contempt of court. The injunction jurisdiction in planning matters began hesitantly and in exceptional circumstances. It was put on an explicit statutory basis by the Planning and Compensation Act 1991 and has become a useful and effective tool for local planning authorities in planning enforcement. In 1994/1995, 91 injunctions were sought: all but two were granted. The use of injunctions peaked at 101 being sought in 2004/2005. In 2011/2012, 66 were obtained and two applications refused.[1] Local planning authorities are able to obtain injunctions for planning breaches under their general powers to bring proceedings in s 222 of the Local Government Act 1972 and under specific statutory provision. Section 187B of the Town and Country Planning Act 1990 allows for injunctions to be sought to restrain breaches of planning control and similar provisions apply for the trees, listed buildings and conservation areas, and hazardous substances regimes.[2] The same procedural approach applies to all injunctions under the Planning Acts and so these can be considered together. In this chapter they will be referred to as planning injunctions. The tests to obtain a planning injunction are more easily met and consequently s 222 is usually only employed for applications that fall outside those powers. Third parties cannot bring civil proceedings to enforce planning law directly against developers and landowners, but may be able to bring a relator action or seek an injunction to preserve the position whilst public law proceedings are brought against an authority.

SECTION 222 OF THE LOCAL GOVERNMENT ACT 1972

14.03   Local authorities have a general power to bring proceedings under s 222 of the Local Government Act 1972. This provides:

---

[1]   Department of Communities and Local Government figures.

[2]   Town and Country Planning Act 1990, s 214A; Planning (Listed Buildings and Conservation Areas) Act 1990, s 44A; or Planning (Hazardous Substances) Act 1990, s 26AA.

'Where a local authority consider it expedient for the promotion or protection of the interests of the inhabitants of their area—

(a) they may prosecute or defend or in the case of civil proceedings may institute them in their own name ...'.

This local authority power includes seeking injunctions to restrain breaches of the criminal law. It was frequently used to uphold the old Sunday trading laws.[3]

14.04   A breach of planning control does not give rise to a civil cause of action at common law, so s 222 was used in regulatory enforcement only where a criminal offence had been committed. An injunction could only be sought under s 222 for breaches of planning control if a criminal offence had been committed.[4] However, the local authority needed to go beyond showing simply a breach of the criminal law. It was said in one case that the breach had to be 'deliberate and flagrant'.[5] In *City of London Corporation v Bovis Construction Ltd*,[6] Bingham LJ laid down the following principles:

(a) that the jurisdiction is to be invoked and exercised exceptionally and with great caution;

(b) that there must certainly be something more than mere infringement of the criminal law before the assistance of civil proceedings can be invoked and accorded for the protection or promotion of the interests of the inhabitants of the area; and

(c) that the essential foundation for the exercise of the court's discretion to grant an injunction is not that the offender is deliberately and flagrantly flouting the law but the need to draw the inference that the defendant's unlawful operations will continue unless and until effectively restrained by the law and that nothing short of an injunction will be effective to restrain them.

This approach imposes severe limitations upon the injunction power under s 222. It is very difficult to seek an injunction unless criminal proceedings had been tried. Even then much more than the criminal offence needs to be shown for an injunction. These powers were applied in planning enforcement. In *Runnymede Borough Council v Ball*,[7] an injunction was obtained against gypsies to prevent the unlawful use of land as a caravan site in breach of enforcement and stop notices. This was justified because irreparable damage would occur which might not be preventable by issuing proceedings in the magistrates' court.

Defendants under section 222 injunctions

14.05   Because the injunction will be to enforce the criminal law, the order may only be sought against a person who had or would have committed the criminal offence in question.

---

[3]   For example, *Stoke-on-Trent City Council v B & Q (Retail) Ltd* [1984] AC 754.
[4]   *Runnymede Borough Council v Smith* [1986] JPL 592; *Doncaster Borough Council v Green* (1991) 64 P & CR 73; *East Hampshire District Council v Davies* [1991] 2 PLR 8.
[5]   *Stoke-on-Trent City Council v B & Q (Retail) Ltd* [1984] AC 754.
[6]   [1992] 3 All ER 697, CA.
[7]   [1986] JPL 288.

STATUTORY PLANNING INJUNCTIONS UNDER S 187B OF THE TOWN AND COUNTRY PLANNING ACT 1990

14.06   Following the report of Robert Carnwath QC, *Enforcing Planning Control*, the Planning and Compensation Act 1991 made substantial changes to planning enforcement. A major reform was the creation of specific injunction powers. Section 187B(1) provides:

> 'Where a local planning authority consider it necessary or expedient for any actual or apprehended breach of planning control to be restrained by injunction, they may apply to the court for an injunction, whether or not they have exercised or are proposing to exercise any of their other powers under this Part.'

On this application, 'the court may grant such an injunction as the court thinks appropriate for the purpose of restraining the breach'.[8] Similar powers are provided for protected trees, listed buildings, conservation area consent and hazardous substances.[9]

Scope of the section 187B power

14.07   The power is wide and not constrained to breaches of the criminal law.[10] Whilst injunctions will frequently be sought when an enforcement notice is not complied with, they can be an alternative to the existing procedures. To prevent an apprehended breach of planning control, a *qua timet* injunction can be sought. Mandatory injunctions can be obtained to compel the defendant to carry out works (*Croydon London Borough Council v Gladden*).[11] In this case the Order required the removal of a life-size model Spitfire from the garden of a suburban house. Injunctions can be obtained on an interim, and occasionally without warning, basis.

14.08   The operation of the power is generally wider than those under s 222 of the Local Government Act 1972 and should not be construed as impliedly limited by the restrictions in *Bovis* and other cases: see *Runnymede Borough Council v Harwood*.[12] One constraint though is that any injunction must be against a breach of planning control. Sullivan LJ pointed out in *Trott v Broadland District Council*:[13]

> 'While a failure to comply with a requirement of an enforcement notice may, in some circumstances, also amount to a failure to comply with a condition in a planning permission, it does not follow that there has been a failure to comply with a condition merely because there has been non-compliance with a requirement of an enforcement notice.'

A failure to comply with a requirement of an enforcement notice which is not based on a breach of planning control might be enforced against by an injunction

---

[8]   Town and Country Planning Act, s 187B(2).

[9]   Town and Country Planning Act 1990, s 214A; Planning (Listed Buildings and Conservation Areas) Act 1990, s 44A; Planning (Hazardous Substances) Act 1990, s 26AA respectively.

[10]   As made clear in *Doncaster Borough Council v Green* (1992) 64 P & CR 73, 83.

[11]   [1994] 1 PLR 30, 35.

[12]   [1994] 1 PLR 22, 24.

[13]   [2011] EWCA Civ 301 at para 24. In that case an Inspector had varied an enforcement notice to require access to a piece of land to be given to residents of a block of flats when the underlying planning permission did not require such access. The Council's section 187B injunction was therefore discharged.

under s 222 of the Local Government Act 1972.[14] The merits of such proceedings might require careful consideration, as the complaint might be technical rather than underpinned by planning merits.

The role of the court

14.09   The court in *Hambleton District Council v Bird,*[15] took a narrow view of the ability of the court in to do other than grant an injunction. Gypsies were using land at a farm for residential caravans in breach of an enforcement notice. A later application for planning permission had been refused. The Court of Appeal held that the essential test was whether nothing short of an injunction would be effective to restrain the defendants. Whilst this test is apparently tough, the local authority's powers to seek an injunction were viewed benevolently. Following *Mole Valley District Council v Smith*[16] the court held that whether it is necessary or expedient to seek an order was for the local planning authority alone. It determined the balance of the public interest. The possibility of planning permission being granted in the future was not a legitimate reason for refusing an injunction. Since there had been a consistent intention by the defendants to remain at the farm and break the law, the injunction was granted.

14.10   The *Hambleton* approach was followed in *Aylesbury Vale DC v Miller*[17] and *Tandridge DC v Delaney.*[18] In *Aylesbury,* the High Court accepted that it could consider whether the Council decision to seek an injunction was *Wednesbury* unreasonable, but said that matters previously considered by the Council were not to be revisited. In *Tandridge* it was found that the court could consider changes in planning circumstances since the last consideration of the matter in the planning process.

14.11   The *Hambleton* approach was overturned by the Court of Appeal in *South Bucks District Council v Porter.*[19] The case concerned the relationship of s 187B with the Human Rights Act 1998, in that case, Art 8 of the European Convention on Human Rights. The *Hambleton* approach relied upon whether the injunction was necessary to stop the contraventions, but did not include the other element of proportionality in Convention cases: that it does not impose an excessive burden on the individual. The introduction of this balance then opened out issues for the court's consideration. The Court of Appeal showed scepticism as to whether *Hambleton* was correct in a purely 'domestic law' context. Implicitly their proportionality approach is the same in property rights cases engaging Art 1 of the First Protocol, subject to the recognised differences between the two provisions. Virtually all planning injunction cases will engage Art 1, First Protocol or Art 8 rights. The exceptions would be certain trespasser cases where the court is unlikely to find much difficulty in making an order on any approach. So *Hambleton* has now been displaced. One further consequence is that Circular 10/97 *Enforcing Planning Control* no longer accurately reflects the law at para 5.10.

---

[14]   See *Trott* at para 32.
[15]   [1995] 3. PLR 8.
[16]   [1992] 3 PLR 22.
[17]   30 July 1999, unreported.
[18]   [2000] 1 PLR 11.
[19]   [2001] EWCA Civ 1549, [2002] JPL 608.

14.12   The House of Lords dismissed the local authorities' appeals in *Porter*.[20] Lord Bingham of Cornhill summarised the court's discretion as:[21]

'The court's discretion to grant or withhold relief is not however unfettered (and by quoting the word "absolute" from the 1991 circular in paragraph 41 of his judgment Simon Brown LJ cannot have intended to suggest that it was). The discretion of the court under section 187B, like every other judicial discretion, must be exercised judicially. That means, in this context, that the power must be exercised with due regard to the purpose for which the power was conferred: to restrain actual and threatened breaches of planning control. The power exists above all to permit abuses to be curbed and urgent solutions provided where these are called for. Since the facts of different cases are infinitely various, no single test can be prescribed to distinguish cases in which the court's discretion should be exercised in favour of granting an injunction from those in which it should not. Where it appears that a breach or apprehended breach will continue or occur unless and until effectively restrained by the law and that nothing short of an injunction will provide effective restraint (*City of London Corporation v Bovis Construction Ltd* [1992] 3 All ER 697, 714), that will point strongly towards the grant of an injunction. So will a history of unsuccessful enforcement and persistent non-compliance, as will evidence that the defendant has played the system by wilfully exploiting every opportunity for prevarication and delay, although section 187B(1) makes plain that a local planning authority, in applying for an injunction, need not have exercised nor propose to exercise any of its other enforcement powers under Part VII of the Act. In cases such as these the task of the court may be relatively straightforward. But in all cases the court must decide whether in all the circumstances it is just to grant the relief sought against the particular defendant.'

14.13   Lord Bingham also took this view on the relationship between sanctions and granting injunctions:

'Apprehension that a party may disobey an order should not deter the court from making an order otherwise appropriate: there is not one law for the law-abiding and another for the lawless and truculent. When making an order, the court should ordinarily be willing to enforce it if necessary. The rule of law is not well served if orders are made and disobeyed with impunity. These propositions however rest on the assumption that the order made by the court is just in all the circumstances and one with which the defendant can and reasonably ought to comply, an assumption which ordinarily applies both when the order is made and when the time for enforcement arises. Since a severe financial penalty may be imposed for failure to comply with an enforcement notice, the main additional sanction provided by the grant of an injunction is that of imprisonment. The court should ordinarily be slow to make an order which it would not at that time be willing, if need be, to enforce by imprisonment. But imprisonment in this context is intended not to punish but to induce compliance, reinforcing the requirement that the order be one with which the defendant can and reasonably ought to comply.'

A prior acquittal on an enforcement notice prosecution does not prevent an injunction being granted.[22]

Defendants

14.14   Section 187B injunctions can be sought against any person who is carrying out or permitting acts in breach of planning control or whom the court considers responsible to remedy a breach of planning control. The section does not itself say

---

[20]   *Wrexham County Borough Council v Berry* [2003] UKHL 26, [2003] JPL 1412.
[21]   Para 29.
[22]   *South Hams District Council v Halsey*, CA, [1996] JPL 761.

who the defendants can be but the purpose of the injunction is to restrain 'any actual or apprehended breach of planning control'.[23] An injunction can be granted against anyone if it is effective to achieve this. Possible defendants are as follows:

(a) those carrying on or instructing the carrying on of the activity in breach of planning control. This includes persons who could not be criminally liable if enforcement action was taken (eg persons not in control);

(b) those permitting the activity in breach of planning control. They must have the power to prevent the breach, either because of an interest in the land or control over the persons carrying out the activity;

(c) those with the power, whether as of right or in practice, to remedy the breach. Only an owner can be criminally liable for failing to take these steps. However, in *London Borough of Lambeth v Tooting Nursing Agency Limited*,[24] both the company owning a house and its current residents (one a former owner) were ordered to remove an extension;

(d) those criminally liable under an enforcement notice, a stop notice or a breach of condition notice.

Injunctions can be sought against persons whose identity is unknown[25] And the procedure is discussed further below.

SECTIONS 187B AND 222 COMPARED

14.15   In practice the section 187B power is much wider than the section 222 power. It is not restricted to enforcement against criminal offences and is granted more readily. It should therefore be used instead of s 222, unless there is doubt as to whether there is a breach of planning control or there is another, distinct, claim against the defendant. A good illustration of such a situation is a breach of advertising control, which may be a breach of planning control but is also a separate offence under s 224 of the Act. In these circumstances it may be appropriate to bring claims under both s 187B and s 222.

Procedure for obtaining an injunction

14.16   Applications for planning injunctions should be sought by bringing a Pt 8 claim in the Queen's Bench Division of the High Court or in the County Court.[26] Injunction applications under s 222 would usually be brought under Pt 8 as there tend not to be substantial disputes of fact. The Pt 8 procedure is quicker than bringing conventional proceedings by Pt 7 claim, as exchanges of pleadings and automatic disclosure does not apply. The Pt 8 claim form[27] will state that Pt 8 applies, the remedy sought and the enactment that the claim is made under.[28] The claim form

---

[23]   Town and Country Planning Act, s 187B(1).
[24]   1 May 1995, unreported
[25]   Town and Country Planning Act, s 187B(3).
[26]   CPR 8.1(6); Practice Direction 8A, Alternative Procedure for Claims, para 9.4. These are applications under Town and Country Planning Act 1990, ss 187B, 214A; Planning (Listed Buildings and Conservation Areas) Act 1990, s 44A; Planning (Hazardous Substances) Act 1990, s 26AA.
[27]   Form N208: see Practice Direction 8A, para 4.2.
[28]   CPR 8.2.

should be accompanied by evidence in the form of a witness statement or statements and exhibited documents.[29] Following the Civil Procedure Rules reforms there is no longer any need for evidence to be contained in an affidavit. There should be a witness statement from a planning officer. Witness statements from neighbours and other third parties are sometimes put in but this should only be to deal with points that council officers can not adequately deal with.

THE CONTENTS OF WITNESS STATEMENTS

14.17   The witness statements should detail:

- the property, with a plan exhibited;

- the current use of the property or the operational development complained of;

- in what way the development is in breach of planning control;

- when (as far as is known) the breach commenced;

- the harm in planning terms caused by the development (to be stated by the planning officer);

- any planning permissions or refusals relevant to the development;

- whether planning permission is likely to be granted if applied for;

- the defendant's role in the property;

- whether enforcement action has been taken;

- any criminal prosecutions of the defendant or connected persons in respect of planning matters on the property, unless they disclose spent convictions;[30]

- communications between the defendant and the local planning authority, including any showing knowledge of the breach of planning control and that the defendant will not voluntarily remedy the breach;

- the local planning authority's view that an injunction is necessary or expedient;

- if an interlocutory injunction is to be applied for, an explanation why such relief is necessary;

- if a without notice interim injunction is sought, its urgency must be explained as should any decision not to inform the defendant of the application.

EXHIBITS REQUIRED

14.18   The exhibits are likely to include:

- a plan of the property;

- evidence of title to the property and the defendant's role in the property – is that person able to comply with an order?

---

[29] Practice Direction 8A, para 7. The evidence could simply be in the claim form, but this is unlikely to be sufficient for a planning injunction.

[30] Rehabilitation of Offenders Act 1974, s 4(1).

- photographic evidence of the development complained of and breaches of any notices;

- any enforcement notice or other notice breached;

- planning contravention notices or section 330 notices which disclose useful information;

- any relevant inspector's report and Secretary of State's decision;

- committee or delegated reports setting out the local planning authority's view on the development;

- correspondence between the parties.

INJUNCTIONS AGAINST PERSONS UNKNOWN

14.19   A local planning authority may obtain a planning injunction against a person whose name is unknown to them.[31] This provides a remedy against persons who are uncooperative and refuse to give their names. It may also be used in emergency situations where there is not time to identify all the persons concerned. The claim form must describe the defendant by reference to:[32]

'(a) a photograph,

(b) a thing belonging to or in the possession of the defendant, or

(c) any other evidence'

with sufficient particularity to enable service to be effected[33] The claimant must file a witness statement stating:

'(a) that the applicant was unable to ascertain', the defendant's identity within the time reasonably available to him,

(b) the steps taken by him to ascertain the defendant's identity,

(c) the means by which the defendant has been described in the claim form;

and that the description is the best that the applicant is able to provide.'[34]

Given the normal requirement for personal service, the defendants should be identified individually. A collective identification, eg, 'all persons on the land and controlling certain vehicles', is inadequate.[35] A marked photograph is appropriate, as may be the use of nicknames. Identifying by possessions is more difficult; 'man in hard hat and fluorescent jacket' would not have sufficient particularity, especially on a building site.

THE DEFENDANT'S RESPONSE

14.20   A defendant must file an acknowledgment of service not more than 14 days after service of the claim form and serve it on the other parties.[36] The acknowledgment

---

[31]   CPR 8.2A, Practice Direction 8A, para 20.2.
[32]   Practice Direction 8A, para 20.4. These rules also apply to tree injunctions under s 214A and injunctions under s 44A Listed Buildings Act and s 26AA Hazardous Substances Act.
[33]   Practice Direction 8A, para 20.5.
[34]   Practice Direction 8A, para 20.6.
[35]   See [1996] JPL 91 for an (unnamed) example.
[36]   CPR 8.3, using form N210: Practice Direction 8A, para 5.2.

must state whether the claim is contested. The defendant is not required to file a defence.[37] If an acknowledgment is not filed in time then the defendant may only take part in the hearing of the claim with the court's permission.[38] The defendant's evidence should be filed and served with the acknowledgment of service.[39] The claimant has a further 14 days to file and serve any written evidence in reply to the defendant's evidence.[40]

INTERIM INJUNCTIONS

14.21   An interim injunction takes effect before the merits of the matter have been finally determined. A party seeking ex parte relief must make full and frank disclosure of anything known to it that might lead a court to refuse relief. If full and frank disclosure is not made, the injunction is liable to be discharged in an inter partes hearing regardless of the merits of the case. Interim orders can be obtained in a matter of days, or even hours. Injunctions can be obtained outside court hours, if need be over the telephone. An interim application should be made 'on notice' where possible. An application notice should be filed under CPR 23.3. Service must be made as soon as practicable after it is filed and at least three days before the court is to deal with the application, along with any witness statement and a draft order.[41] More urgent cases can arise and application can be made without notice 'if it appears to the Court that there are good reasons for not giving notice'.[42] Reasons for not giving notice must be included in the evidence.[43] 'Without notice' means without giving formal notice in accordance with the rules (ie within three days). The Practice Direction (Interim Injunctions) says that such applications should be filed two hours before the hearing if possible.[44]

14.22   Further, 'except in cases where secrecy is essential, the applicant should take steps to notify the respondent informally of the application.'[45] Even if an application is being made urgently – for example to stop demolition or prevent the laying of hardstanding at a potential caravan site – as much notice as possible should be given to the other side. Usually the court would want to know that a warning had been given and why it was thought that an injunction was necessary to stop the actual or apprehended breach. In the planning context, secrecy would only be required if there was good reason to believe that serious planning harm would result if warning were given (eg demolition of a listed building).

14.23   Applications for interim injunctions would be considered in the principles of *American Cyanamid v Ethicon*:[46] that there must be a serious question to be tried and then whether the balance of convenience lies in favour of granting or refusing the interlocutory relief sought. Where a breach has been allowed to continue for a long period, it may be appropriate to proceed straight to a permanent injunction.

---

[37]   CPR 8.9.
[38]   CPR 8.4.
[39]   CPR 8.5(3), (4).
[40]   CPR 8.5(5), (6).
[41]   CPR 23.7(1).
[42]   CPR 25.3(1).
[43]   CPR 25.3(3).
[44]   Practice Direction (Interim Injunctions), para 4.3(2).
[45]   Practice Direction (Interim Injunctions), para 4.3(3).
[46]   [1975] AC 396.

However, delay in applying for an interlocutory injunction is not a factor when there is no arguable case against the grant of a permanent injunction.[47]

CROSS-UNDERTAKING IN DAMAGES

14.24 In litigation generally, a private person seeking an interim injunction will normally have to give a cross-undertaking in damages. He will promise to pay damages to the person who is subject to the injunction if it is not confirmed at trial. It is settled that the Crown, when enforcing the law, will not normally, as a matter of the court's discretion, be required to give a cross-undertaking.[48] The same principle applies to local authorities and other public authorities which are seeking to enforce the law in the interests of the public generally.[49] As a matter of practice, cross-undertakings have not been required in planning injunctions.

THE FINAL HEARING

14.25 When the claim form is issued, the court will fix a hearing date.[50] Usually a date will be fixed relatively early but the parties will need to consider whether they can be ready for a final hearing in that time and the time allocated will be adequate. On the hearing date, the court will either finally dispose of the claim or give case management directions.[51] If the final hearing cannot take place on that date, it would be helpful to agree a refixing or directions to avoid the hearing. The final hearing of an injunction application will often simply be dealt with by oral submissions on the filed evidence. Evidence can only be considered if it has been filed in accordance with r 8.5, an extension of time has been granted for the evidence,[52] or the court gives permission. The parties may agree to extend time for the defendant's evidence by up to 14 days (if the agreement is filed with the acknowledgment of service) and extend time for a written response from the claimant by 28 days.[53] If there are disputes of fact or expert opinion that need to be resolved, then the court may require or permit a party to give oral evidence.[54] Usually the parties will attempt to resolve whether oral evidence is required and the court may give directions that a witness attend to be cross-examined.[55] Such directions will often identify the particular issues on which cross-examination may take place.

FORM OF INJUNCTIONS

14.26 The Court of Appeal gave guidance on the form of planning injunctions in *London Borough of Brent v Dowman*.[56] An enforcement notice had been upheld

---

[47] *Stoke-on-Trent City Council v W & J Wass* [1992] 2 PLR 22.
[48] *Hoffmann-La Roche & Co v Secretary of State for Trade and Industry* [1975] AC 295.
[49] *Kirklees Borough Council v Wickes Building Supplies Ltd* [1992] 3 All ER 717, HL; *Financial Services Authority v Sinaloa Gold* [2013] UKSC 11, [2013] 2 WLR 678.
[50] Practice Direction 8A, para 20.7. Notice of this date must be served by the claimant on or with the claim form: Practice Direction 8A, para 20.9.
[51] Practice Direction 8A, para 8, 20.10.
[52] Practice Direction 8A, para 7.4.
[53] The ability of the parties to agree an extension of the time limits under CPR 2.11 is constrained by Practice Direction 8A, para 7.5.
[54] CPR 8.6(2).
[55] CPR 8.6(3).
[56] [2003] EWCA Civ 920, [2004] JPL 195.

preventing the use of a shop as a repair workshop for cars. It was accepted that some work on cars was ancillary to the shop use. The court considered the *Mansi* principle, saying:[57]

> '[it] has implications for the exercise of a court's discretion when an injunction is sought under section 187B. If such an injunction is granted, it should not normally be so worded as to restrain the landowner from using his land in a way which is permitted development under the Act or the 1995 Order or is ancillary to the primary use of the land, that being a primary use which the enforcement notice does not seek to prevent. It would not normally be just for an owner to be at risk from an injunction for some use or activity for which he could not be successfully prosecuted under the enforcement notice.'

This is more properly a question of the jurisdiction of the court rather than a matter going to its discretion. The court only has power to grant an injunction to restrain an actual or apprehended breach of planning control.

14.27   Faced with a list of prohibited activities, the Court of Appeal preferred a more general formulation of the injunction preventing use:[58]

> 'as a repair workshop for vehicles, provided that the premises may be used for fitting to cars goods sold in the shop in a manner ancillary to the use of the premises as a retail shop.'

The court declined to order the removal of items, being uncertain what was appropriate for the permitted activities. Pill LJ gave a further reason:

> 'It does not necessarily follow from a finding that a business use is not permitted that an order should be made requiring equipment which could be used to carry out that use be removed from the premises. In some circumstances it may be necessary to order removal to give efficacy to the order of the Court but the burden is upon the party seeking the injunction to show that the order for removal is necessary in the particular circumstances. Interference with an owner's right to retain his goods on his premises would need to be justified.'

PENAL NOTICE

14.28   The local planning authority will undoubtedly wish to enforce a planning injunction by proceedings for contempt of court if it is breached. There must be:

> 'is prominently displayed, on the front of the copy of the judgment or order served in accordance with this Section, a warning to the person required to do or not do the act in question that disobedience to the order would be a contempt of court punishable by imprisonment, a fine or sequestration of assets'.[59]

The Practice Direction suggests:

> 'a penal notice endorsed on it as follows (or in words to substantially the same effect)—
>
> > "If you the within-named [ ] do not comply with this order you may be held to be in contempt of court and imprisoned or fined, or your assets may be seized."'[60]

---

[57]   Para 17. The *Mansi* principle is considered further in Chapter 6, above.
[58]   Para 41.
[59]   Civil Procedure Rules, r 81.9.
[60]   Practice Direction 81 para 1.

Where an undertaking is accepted from a defendant, the court may decline to allow contempt of court proceedings 'unless the party giving the undertaking has made a signed statement to the effect that that party understands the terms of the undertaking and the consequences of failure to comply with it'.[61]

COMMITTAL

14.29   An injunction is enforced by committal for contempt. The court that made the order may fine or imprison anyone subject to and in breach of the order. Failure to comply with a court order or an undertaking given to the court is contempt of court, punishable by an unlimited fine and up to two years' imprisonment.[62] The local planning authority would apply to the court for the defendant to be committed for contempt.[63] Procedural rules for committal applications are in Civil Procedure Rules Part 81 and the accompanying practice direction.[64]

THIRD PARTY INJUNCTIONS

14.30   The planning regime is a system of control exercised by public authorities in the public interest. The statutory powers to apply for injunctions are given to local planning authorities and in respect of breaches of historic environment controls, English Heritage. With limited exceptions, such as being a party to a planning obligation or becoming entitled to compensation, it does not create private rights. Contracts can require compliance with planning control (it is a common provision in a lease that a tenant complies with planning and other regulations). Agreements relating to proposed development will require one party or another to secure any necessary planning consent and rely on it. Some actions which are in breach of planning control might also give rise to a tortious claim: a noisy activity might constitute a private or public nuisance; or a new building might interfere with a right of light. However a breach of planning control does not in itself give rise to a private law cause of action. A third party, whether a neighbour, interest group or commercial rival who wishes to stop a breach of planning control has two ways of obtaining an injunction against the developer:

(a)   a relator action; or

(b)   obtaining an injunction (usually on an interim basis) in support of a challenge to the planning authority's approval of the scheme or failure to act.

Relator actions

14.31   The Attorney General is the guardian of the public interest on behalf of the Crown. He is entitled to bring actions to protect that interest, even if no private interest of the Crown is involved. This can include seeking injunctions to prevent breaches of

---

[61]   Practice Direction 81, para 2.2

[62]   Contempt of Court Act 1981, s 14(1), (2).

[63]   For committals on planning injunctions see *Guildford Borough Council v Smith* [1994] JPL 734 and *Broxbourne Borough Council v Robb* [2011] EWCA Civ 1355.

[64]   A useful discussion of committal in the planning context is in *Westminster City Council v Addbins Limited* [2012] EWHC 3716 (QB), [2013] JPL 654.

the law, but the power must be exercised with caution.[65] The Attorney General could decide to seek an injunction on behalf of the Crown to enforce planning control. He is very unlikely to do so unless the local planning authority is failing to act or he seeks to enforce an enforcement notice issued by the Secretary of State under s 182. It is this jurisdiction that is invoked by third parties by means of a relator action. The third party (the relator) must instruct solicitors and counsel who must certify that the action is proper for the Attorney General's acceptance and that the relator will be responsible for the costs. Once the Attorney General accepts the action he takes no further part in the proceedings and it continues as private litigation. It is entirely a matter for the Attorney General whether he will allow a relator action to be brought. The courts will not intervene if he declines.[66]

14.32 This procedure was used by local planning authorities in planning cases before the enactment of s 222 of the Local Government Act 1972. However, with the 1972 Act and the subsequent specific provisions it is now redundant for local authority purposes. Relator actions have been used by local residents in respect of planning matters.[67] In New Zealand a neighbour used the procedure to declare a planning permission void and obtain an injunction against the unauthorised use of the land.[68]

INTERIM INJUNCTIONS TO PREVENT WORKS PREJUDICING COURT PROCEEDINGS

14.33 The High Court has power to grant an interim injunction to prevent its proceedings being frustrated by subsequent events, such as the destruction of the subject matter of the case. So if a planning permission authorises the demolition of a historic building, then the High Court is able to grant an interim injunction preventing demolition pending the determination of a judicial review of that decision. Similarly, if a local planning authority is failing to act against an allegedly unlawful development then the court may grant an injunction to hold the line. In *R (Prokopp) v London Underground Limited,* two local authorities had agreed not to take enforcement action against the demolition of Bishopsgate Goods Yard and the construction of railway. An interim injunction was granted to prevent the demolition of the Goods Yard. Collins J explained the power at the later substantive hearing:[69]

> 'If a developer is about to take what may be irrevocable steps which are said to be unlawful but the [local planning authority] is not taking action, there must be a way in which the court can preserve the position. Thus I am satisfied that an individual can seek and, if appropriate, obtain interim relief to prevent such arguably unlawful action. His claim will initially be against the developer, but he must notify the [local planning authority] and add it (as has been done here) as defendant. The developer will then become an interested party and the claim will proceed against the [local planning authority]. The court will in such a case have imposed time limits on the [local planning authority] to ensure that it makes its decisions within a reasonable time. What a private individual cannot do, at least in a public law claim, is to obtain a permanent injunction the effect of which is to take the enforcement action which is the responsibility of the [local planning authority] and which

---

65   *Gouriet v Union of Post Office Workers* [1978] AC 435.
66   *London County Council v Attorney General* [1902] AC 165.
67   *Judicial Review of Administrative Action*, de Smith, Woolf and Jowell, 1995, para 2–100 [update].
68   *Attorney General v Codner* [1973] 1 NZLR 545.
69   [2003] EWHC 960 (Admin) at para 15.

contains safeguards for the developer in the form of rights of appeal on specific grounds. Clearly if an individual's private law rights (for example in nuisance) are being infringed, different considerations apply, but that claim would be in private and not in public law.'

14.34 Applications for interim injunctions would be considered in the principles of *American Cyanamid v Ethicon*:[70] that there must be a serious question to be tried and then whether the balance of convenience lies in favour of granting or refusing the interlocutory relief sought. As it is not possible to rebuild a historic building that is demolished, the balance of convenience will tend to lie in favour of granting an interim injunction. Reflecting the approach in environmental justice cases to ensuring that proceedings are not prohibitively expensive to members of the public and interest groups, claimants have tended not to be required to give a cross-undertaking that they will pay damages to the developer for losses caused by the interim injunction if the claim fails.[71] This approach has been formalised in respect of claims under the Aarhus Convention challenging 'acts and omissions by private persons and public authorities which contravene provisions of its national law relating to the environment'.[72] The practice direction on interim injunctions provides:[73]

'If in an Aarhus Convention claim the court is satisfied that an injunction is necessary to prevent significant environmental damage and to preserve the factual basis of the proceedings, the court will, in considering whether to require an undertaking by the applicant to pay any damages which the respondent or any other person may sustain as a result and the terms of any such undertaking –

(a) have particular regard to the need for the terms of the order overall not to be such as would make continuing with the claim prohibitively expensive for the applicant; and

(b) make such directions as are necessary to ensure that the case is heard promptly'

If the works or use is being carried out by a public authority in breach of planning control then the decision to carry on that activity may be susceptible to judicial review. So activity which is part of promoting a statutory role, such as providing car parking or housing clearance, would be reviewable, but that may be more debatable if the authority is acting purely like a private landowner.[74]

---

[70] [1975] AC 396.

[71] See the Aarhus Convention on Access to Information, Public Participation in Decision-Making and Access to Justice in Environmental Matters, Art 9; the Environmental Impact Assessment Directive, Art 11; and *Ensuring access to environmental justice in England and Wales* ('the Sullivan Report'), paras 73–83

[72] Aarhus Convention, Art 9(3).

[73] Practice Direction 25A – Interim Injunctions, para 5.1B(1).

[74] See consideration of the reviewability of decisions to sell property in *R (Pepper) v Bolsover District Council* [2001] JPL 804.

Chapter 15

Discontinuance, Revocation and Maintenance of Land

15.01   There is a range of powers for dealing with an undesirable use or condition of land which might not be a breach of planning control. This chapter focuses on three provisions in the Town and Country Planning Act 1990 and identifies a variety of environmental powers which might be useful. The Planning Act powers are:

(1) discontinuance – which requires the cessation or limitation of uses or the removal or alteration of buildings on land whether or not these are unlawful;

(2) revocation or modification – which eliminates or alters planning permissions insofar as they have not been carried out. This is not strictly enforcement, but is allied to those powers; and

(3) section 215 orders for the maintenance of land – this can require the clean-up of land which causes harm to the amenity of the area.

As there is an overlap with advertising enforcement, the removal of graffiti and other signs under s 225F of the Town and Country Planning Act 1990 is discussed in Chapter 18 on advertising control.

DISCONTINUANCE ORDERS

15.02   The local planning authority is empowered to require the discontinuance of any use of land or require that buildings should be altered or removed, whether the use or buildings are lawful or unlawful. Compensation may be payable for losses caused by discontinuance orders. Consequently orders tend to be used in a limited number of cases against lawful development as enforcement action can be taken without a compensation risk against unlawful development. The power is exercised in the interests of the proper planning of the area and if it appears (s 102(1)):

'(a) that any use of land should be discontinued, or that any conditions should be imposed on the continuance of a use of land; or

(b) that any buildings or works should be altered or removed,

[the local planning authority] may by order—

    (i) require the discontinuance of that use, or

    (ii) impose such conditions as may be specified in the order on the continuance of it, or

    (iii) require such steps as may be so specified to be taken for the alteration or removal of the buildings or works,

as the case may be.'

Similar provisions are made with respect to mineral workings in s 102(8) and Sch 9 (special minerals orders).

15.03 Compensation is payable if the development is lawful.[1] However, compensation is not recoverable if the use or development is contrary to law[2] and this includes a breach of planning control, which can still be the subject of enforcement action.[3] A discontinuance order may only take effect if confirmed by the Secretary of State or the Welsh Ministers.[4] Prior to confirmation, the owner or occupier of the land affected by the order and any other person affected by the order are entitled to a hearing.[5] A confirmed order may only be challenged by application to the High Court under s 288 of the Town and Country Planning Act 1990.[6] It is not possible for the local planning authority to withdraw a discontinuance order once they have given notice of its confirmation, even if an appreciation of the scale of likely compensation means that the authority now wish they had not made the order. The Secretary of State or Welsh Ministers are able to make a discontinuance order. Any compensation due as a result of a ministerial order is payable by the local planning authority.

15.04 It is an offence to use land in breach of a discontinuance order or to contravene a condition in such an order (s 189(1)(a)). Contravening the requirements of a minerals special order is also an offence under s 189. The offence is triable either way, being punishable with a statutory maximum fine in the magistrates' court (£5,000) and an unlimited fine in the Crown Court. The local planning authority can enter land and carry out the steps required under a discontinuance or special minerals order, recovering the cost from the owner (s 190).

15.05 Because of the potential liability for compensation and the fact that criminal sanctions are weaker than for enforcement notices, discontinuance orders are rarely used. The discontinuance process might be employed with enforcement notices where the undesirable activities consist of a mix of lawful and unlawful uses. Essentially the enforcement notices would deal with the unlawful uses and a discontinuance order would address the totality. That is a risky enterprise if the extent of the lawful uses is not correctly ascertained. In *Jefferey v First Secretary of State*:[7] a local authority had made a discontinuance order for the use of land for siting touring caravans and tents, believing that the touring caravan part of the use was limited by planning condition to a three-week period in the summer of 1999 to accommodate those attending the total solar eclipse. The authority were so shocked when the Secretary of State ruled that the condition was invalid and so the touring caravan use was permanent that they brought three sets of High Court proceedings, all of which failed.[8] The authority would not have made a discontinuance order if it had appreciated that a seven-figure compensation liability would result. Ultimately they granted permission for a permanent touring caravan use on the site.

---

[1] Town and Country Planning Act 1990, s 115.
[2] Land Compensation Act 1961, s 5, r 4.
[3] *Hughes v Doncaster Metropolitan Council* [1991] 1 AC 382.
[4] Town and Country Planning Act 1990, s 103.
[5] Town and Country Planning Act 1990, s 103(4).
[6] Town and Country Planning Act 1990, ss 284(2), 288.
[7] [2007] EWCA Civ 584, [2006] EWHC 2920, [2007] JPL 907.
[8] See *Teignbridge District Council v First Secretary of State* [2006] EWHC 2745 (Admin).

REVOCATION OR MODIFICATION

15.06   A planning permission may be revoked or modified under s 97 of the Town and Country Planning Act 1990. This is not strictly an enforcement mechanism as it does not seek to remedy any unlawful action but removes or alters a planning permission. It does, however, provide a means of exercising greater control or remedying erroneous planning decisions. Section 97(1) provides:

> 'If it appears to the local planning authority that it is expedient to revoke or modify planning permission to develop land granted on an application made under this Part, the authority may by order revoke or modify the permission to such an extent as they consider expedient.'

The authority shall have regard to the development plan and to other material considerations,[9] so the presumption in favour of the development plan applies.[10] Revocation and modification deals with development which has not yet taken place:[11]

> 'The power conferred by this section may be exercised
>
> (a)   where the planning permission relates to the carrying out of building or other operations, at any time before those operations have been completed;
>
> (b)   where the permission relates to a change of the use of any land, at any time before the change has taken place'

A revocation or modification order of a planning permission for building or other operations does not affect so much of those operations as has been carried out.[12] However, it may affect how that operational development is used (for example, by imposing conditions on hours of operation).

15.07   In a similar way to a discontinuance order, a revocation or modification order must be confirmed by the Secretary of State or Welsh Ministers, unless all the landowners and occupiers of the land subject to the order and any other person who in the local planning authority's opinion will be affected by the order have notified the authority in writing that they do not object to it.[13]

15.08   Compensation is payable for any loss caused by a revocation or modification order.[14] Care must be taken to establish that the order caused the loss. If the developer needs another consent (such as a species licence) which would not have been granted then any loss would not have been caused by the revocation or modification order.[15]

15.09   There is no provision relating to failure to comply with a revocation or modification order. As the order has prospective effect only, the question is whether what is then done is without a necessary planning permission having regard to the order or whether it is in breach of a condition on the relevant planning permission as modified by the order. Such a breach of planning control would then be enforced against in the usual way.

---

9   Town and Country Planning Act 1990, s 97(2).
10   Planning and Compulsory Purchase Act 2004, s 38(6).
11   Town and Country Planning Act 1990, s 97(3).
12   Town and Country Planning Act 1990, s 97(4).
13   Town and Country Planning Act 1990, ss 98, 99.
14   Town and Country Planning Act 1990, s 107.
15   *MWH Associates Ltd v Wrexham County Borough Council* [2012] EWCA Civ 1884, [2013] RVR 112.

SECTION 215 NOTICES REQUIRING PROPER MAINTENANCE OF LAND

15.10 Despoiled or badly kept land can affect the amenity of an area. Rubbish and scrap materials may be visually intrusive. They may also cause environmental problems. So, under s 215 of the Town and Country Planning Act 1990, the local planning authority may serve a notice requiring the land to be cleaned up.[16] The power is exercisable if it appears that 'the amenity of a part of [the local planning authority's] area, or of an adjoining area, is adversely affected by the condition of land in their area' (s 215(1)). The notice 'shall require such steps for remedying the condition of the land as may be specified in the notice to be taken within such period as may be so specified'.[17] It must be clear what is required. Leggatt J held in *Allsop v Derbyshire Dales District Council*:[18]

> 'as a matter of general principle, such notice in order to be valid must identify the condition of the land about which complaint is made and the steps required to remedy that condition with sufficient clarity to enable the recipient of the notice fairly to understand the nature of the complaint and exactly what it is that he must do in order to comply with the notice. That is a basic requirement of fairness and natural justice.'

Similarly in *Jolly v Fylde Borough Council*,[19] the Crown Court held that section 215 notices were subject to the same approach to nullity as enforcement notices.

15.11 Like enforcement notices, the section 215 notice only takes effect after a specified period. This must be at least 28 days after it has been served on the owner and occupier of the land.[20] It must be served on all such persons.[21] A section 215 notice may only apply to the land which adversely affects the amenity of the area and may not be served on any person who only owns or occupies other land. In *Toni & Guy (South) Limited v London Borough of Hammersmith and Fulham,* a section 215 notice had been served on all the occupiers a building when the council required the rendering of the first to third floors of the front elevation. The occupiers of the ground floor appealed and the Council accepted that they had no control over or rights in the parts of the building where the works were required. The notice was quashed with respect to the ground floor occupiers, as the Council had no power to serve them.

Appeal

15.12 A person served with a section 215 notice, or any other person interested in the land, has a right of appeal to the magistrates' court. The appeal must be made before the notice takes effect, and can be on any of the following grounds (s 217(1)):

---

[16] *Town and Country Planning Act 1990 Section 215 Best Practice Guidance* was issued by the Office of the Deputy Prime Minister in January 2005. English Heritage has given guidance on the use of s 215 in heritage cases in *Stopping the Rot.*

[17] Town and Country Planning Act 1990, s 215(2).

[18] [2012] EWHC 3562 (Admin).

[19] Case reference Preston A20120016.

[20] Town and Country Planning Act 1990, s 215(3), (4).

[21] *Toni & Guy (South) Limited v London Borough of Hammersmith and Fulham* [2009] EWHC 203 (Admin) at para 25.

'(a) that the condition of the land to which the notice relates does not adversely affect the amenity of any part of the area of the local planning authority who served the notice, or of any adjoining area;

(b) that the condition of the land to which the notice relates is attributable to, and such as results in the ordinary course of events from, the carrying on of operations or a use of land which is not in contravention of Part III [the requirement to have planning permission];

(c) that the requirements of the notice exceed what is necessary for preventing the condition of the land from adversely affecting the amenity of any part of the area of the local planning authority who served the notice, or of any adjoining area;

(d) that the period specified in the notice as the period within which any steps required by the notice are to be taken falls short of what should reasonably be allowed.'

15.13   The ground (b) appeal, and so the scope of section 215 notices, was considered in *Allsop v Derbyshire Dales District Council.*[22] A section 215 notice was served on a farmer requiring him to 'cease the use of the land for the storage of vehicles and trailers'. The storage had been of agricultural trailers but it became apparent in the course of the appeal that the Council's sole concern was a 'lurid face' painted on the side of one of the trailers. The Crown Court varied the notice to prohibit only vehicles or trailers with 'unorthodox livery'. On appeal by case stated, the High Court quashed the notice holding that a section 215 notice cannot require the cessation of a lawful use. Leggatt J said that 'the use of the land for storage of vehicles and trailers bearing unorthodox livery' did not contravene planning control and so 'the condition of the land to which the notice relates is attributable to, and such as results in the ordinary course of events from, a use of land which is not in contravention of Part III'.[23] Whilst the general principle is sound, its application to the circumstances may be more open to argument.

15.14   An appellant can also contend that the notice is unlawful.[24] The notice does not take effect until the appeal is finally determined or is withdrawn.[25] An appeal would be made by way of complaint.[26] The magistrates court may quash or vary the notice or correct any informality, defect or error if it is not material. They may also give directions,[27] which can be important if the appeal is brought by or is successful in relation to, only some of the persons served. The local planning authority or appellant may appeal the magistrates' decision to the Crown Court[28] or to the High Court by case stated[29] or challenge on a matter of court procedure by judicial review.

15.15   If the notice has been served on both the owner and occupier or that person has appealed under s 217, then the notice cannot be challenged in any other proceedings on grounds (a) or (b) above.[30] This is a similar bar to s 285(1) in respect of enforcement notices. However, a person who held an interest in the land when the notice was served, but was not himself served and did not appeal, is not subject to the statutory bar in s 216 (criminal) proceedings and so may raise the condition of the

[22] [2012] EWHC 3562 (Admin) at para 29.
[23] At para 27.
[24] *R v Oxford Crown Court ex p Smith* (1989) 154 JP 422.
[25] Town and Country Planning Act 1990, s 217(3).
[26] Magistrates' Court Rules 1981, r 34.
[27] Town and Country Planning Act 1990, s 217(5).
[28] Town and Country Planning Act 1990, s 218.
[29] Magistrates' Courts Act 1980, s 111(2).
[30] Town and Country Planning Act 1990, s 285(3).

land as a defence.[31] A person who appeals is treated in later proceedings as having been duly served with the notice.[32]

Prosecution

15.16   It is an offence for the owner or occupier to fail to take the steps required by the section 215 notice in the specified period (s 216(2)). A form of defence, which has been replaced in most planning law, still applies. If the owner or occupier have ceased to have that status before the end of the compliance period then they are entitled to have their successors brought before the court if prosecuted. If the failure to comply was attributable in whole or in part to the default of a successor then that person is also guilty. If the original defendant in addition proves that he took all reasonable steps to secure compliance with the notice, he will be acquitted.[33] The offence is summary only, and is punishable with a level 3 (£1,000) fine. After the first conviction, a subsequent offence is punishable by a daily fine of one-tenth of level 3, that is, £100.

Carrying out the works

15.17   If the notice is not complied with, the local planning authority is empowered to enter the land, carry out the works and recover the cost from the owner in a similar manner to carrying out works under an enforcement notice (s 219).

---

[31]   Town and Country Planning Act 1990, s 285(4).
[32]   Town and Country Planning Act, 1990, s 217(6).
[33]   Town and Country Planning Act 1990, s 216(5).

Chapter 16

Historic Environment

16.01   Protection of the historic environment of buildings, urban and rural landscapes, and the remains of the past is an important part of the planning process. Protection is offered by normal planning controls but special statutory controls are also provided for listed buildings, conservation areas and archaeological remains.[1] Policy on the historic environment is contained in England in the National Planning Policy Framework, particularly Section 12, the publications *Principles of Selection for Listed Buildings* and *Scheduled Monuments,* with further guidance in the *Historic Environment Planning Practice Guide.*[2] English Heritage produces a range of guidance, some of which deals with enforcement issues. Welsh heritage policy is in Planning Policy Wales and Welsh Office Circulars 60/96 *Planning and the Historic Environment: Archaeology* and 61/96 *Planning and the Historic Environment: Historic Buildings and Conservation Areas.*

LISTED BUILDING CONTROL

16.02   Buildings of architectural or historic interest may be listed under s 1 of the Planning (Listed Buildings and Conservation Areas) Act 1990 ('the Listed Buildings Act'). In England this power is exercised by the Secretary of State for Culture, Media and Sport, in Wales by the Welsh Ministers. In England there are presently about 375,000 listed building entries (which may cover more than one building, such as a terrace, or multiple entries may cover individual structures within an overall site, such as a stable block). As a matter of policy, listed buildings are classified in descending order of importance as Grade I (2 per cent of the total), Grade II* (5.5 per cent) and the remainder as Grade II.

16.03   'Building' in s 1 comprises the expanded definition of building in s 336 of the Town and Country Planning Act 1990 as including 'any structure or erection, and any part of a building, as so defined, but does not include plant or machinery comprised in a building'.[3] It is therefore possible for a listing to include only part of a building.[4] The definition of listed building is further expanded by s 1(5):[5]

'(a)   any object or structure fixed to the building;

(b)   any object or structure within the curtilage of the building which, although not fixed to the building, forms part of the land and has done so since before July 1, 1948,

shall be treated as part of the building.'

---

[1]   For a more detailed consideration of this legislation see Richard Harwood, *Historic Environment Law* (Institute of Art and Law, 2012).

[2]   The Practice Guide was produced to support the now revoked Planning Policy Statement 5: *Historic Environment.*

[3]   Town and Country Planning Act 1990, s 336(1) of the Act, as applied by Listed Buildings Act, s 91.

[4]   *Shimizu Ltd v Westminster City Council* [1997] 1 WLR 168 at 180 per Lord Hope of Craighead.

[5]   Listed Buildings Act, s 1(5).

'Fixed' has been considered as having the same meaning as in property law and depends upon the degree of annexation and the purpose of annexation of the object or structure.[6] However the property law cases are affected by their context (landlord and tenant, trusts, agreements for sale) and many are dated.[7] A curtilage comprises land and buildings which are 'part and parcel' of the land comprised with a building.[8]

16.04 Works affecting the listed building's character of special architectural or historic interest are banned unless authorised or excepted under the Listed Buildings Act. Section 7 provides:

> 'Subject to the following provisions of this Act, no person shall execute or cause to be executed any works for the demolition of a listed building or for its alteration or extension in any manner which would affect its character as a building of special architectural or historic interest, unless the works are authorised.'

Listed building control therefore applies to two elements:

(1) demolition of a listed building; and

(2) works for a listed building's alteration or extension which would affect its character as a building of special architectural or historic interest

16.05 Whilst only part of a building may be listed, in s 7 the expression 'listed building' means the whole of the listed building and does not include part of the building which : see *Shimizu Shimizu Ltd v Westminster City Council*.[9] Consequently, 'demolition' only occurs if there is demolition of the whole or the substantial part of the listed building. In *Shimizu,* the House of Lords considered that the demolition of a listed building except for its façade, chimney-breasts and chimney-stacks was demolition under s 7.[10] Whether the works affect the building's special architectural or historic interest is a matter of fact for the decision maker or court concerned, although this might apply to works which are limited in scale.[11] The effect of works must be judged in their totality, rather than the effect of incomplete works. In *East Riding of Yorkshire Council v Hobson* Keene LJ said:[12]

> 'If what is being done by way of works of alteration to a listed building involves both a stage of removal and dismantling and a stage of replacement or rebuilding, it cannot, in my judgment, be right to cease the assessment of the effect of these works of alteration in an artificial manner part of the way through.'

16.06 Listed building control is independent of any need for planning permission. Frequently, both listed building consent and planning permission is required. Listed

---

[6] *Debenhams plc v Westminster City Council* [1987] AC 396. High profile planning appeal decisions on the removal of works of art from buildings are *Time Life* [1999] JPL 292 and *Noseley Hall* [1999] JPL 1145.

[7] The most useful judgments are *Leigh v Taylor* [1902] AC 157; *Berkeley v Poulett* (1977) Real Property and Conveyancing 754; and *Elitestone v Morris* [1997] 1 WLR 687.

[8] The leading authority is *Skerritts of Nottingham Ltd v Secretary of State for the Environment, Transport and the Regions* [2001] QB 59. Land will remain within the curtilage if it was in the curtilage at the time of listing (*R v London Borough of Camden ex p Bellamy* [1992] JPL 255) but the curtilage may be able to expand (*R (Sumption) v London Borough of Greenwich* [2008] 1 P & CR 20, doubted at the permission hearing [2008] EWCA Civ 404).

[9] [1997] 1 WLR 168.

[10] Per Lord Hope at 185 and 187.

[11] See *Braun v First Secretary of State* [2002] EWHC 2767 (Admin) at para 29.

[12] [2008] EWHC 1003 (Admin); [2009] PTSR 561 at para 17.

building control also covers many works, such as internal works, which are not operational development under s 55 of the Town and Country Planning Act 1990. Listed building consent is granted on application by the local planning authority or on appeal or call-in by the Secretary of State for Communities and Local Government or Welsh Ministers. It may be granted subject to conditions.[13] Listed building consent is not required if the works should be covered by development consent for a nationally significant infrastructure project under the Planning Act 2008.[14]

AVAILABLE ENFORCEMENT MECHANISMS

16.07   The local planning authority has the following enforcement mechanisms available in the event of works being carried on without listed building consent or in breach of conditions on a listed building consent:

(a)   Criminal prosecution;

(b)   Issuing a listed building enforcement notice;

(c)   Injunctive proceedings.

Listed building prosecutions

16.08   Unlike a breach of planning control, criminal liability is incurred immediately upon a breach of listed building control. It is an offence to contravene s 7, as s 9(1) quite simply puts it:

'If a person contravenes section 7 he shall be guilty of an offence.'

Section 9(1), therefore, gives five questions to be answered in a prosecution:[15]

(1)   Was the building in question a listed building?

(2)   If so, were the works specified in each count executed for its alteration or demolition?

(3)   If so, did the defendant cause the works specified in each count to be executed?

(4)   If so, unless the works amounted to demolition were they executed in a manner which affected the character of the building as a building of special architectural or historic interest?

(5)   If so, were such works authorised?

It is also an offence 'if a person executing or causing to be executed any works in relation to a listed building under a listed building consent fails to comply with any condition attached to the consent' (s 9(2)). The two offences overlap, because works of demolition will only be authorised (and so avoid liability under s 9(1)) if they 'are executed in accordance with the terms of the consent and any conditions attached to it'.[16]

---

[13]   Listed Buildings Act 1990.
[14]   Listed Buildings Act, s 7(2). Similar exemptions mean that conservation area consent and scheduled monument consent are not required for such projects.
[15]   *R v Sandhu* [1997] JPL 853, adapted to encompass demolition.
[16]   Listed Buildings Act, s 8(2)(d).

16.09 A statutory defence of urgent necessity is provided if it is shown by the defendant on the balance of probabilities (s 9(3)):

> '(a)   that works to the building were urgently necessary in the interests of safety or health or for the preservation of the building;
>
> (b)   that it was not practicable to secure safety or health or, as the case may be, the preservation of the building by works of repair or works for affording temporary support or shelter;
>
> (c)   that the works carried out were limited to the minimum measures immediately necessary; and
>
> (d)   that notice in writing justifying in detail the carrying out of the works was given to the local planning authority as soon as reasonably practicable.'

The offence is one of strict liability. A person will be guilty of an offence if s 7 is breached (subject to the statutory defence), even if they were unaware that the building was listed or reasonably considered that listed building consent was not required. Evidence of the defendant's intention is irrelevant to guilt. In *R v Sandhu,* the Court of Appeal quashed a conviction for carrying out authorised alterations because inadmissible and prejudicial evidence had been admitted from the local authority's planning officer and the defendant's architect and joiner that he had ignored their warnings and chosen an incompetent builder to save costs.[17]

16.10 Section 9 offences are triable either way. The importance attached to protecting listed buildings is shown by the availability of a sentence of imprisonment: in the Crown Court, two years; in the magistrates' court, six months. Fines of up to £20,000 in summary trial and an unlimited amount on indictment are also available.[18] As with other planning offences, the court should have regard to financial benefit from the breach when determining the size of fines.[19] Sentencing for heritage offences is discussed further below.

16.11 *Best Practice Guidance on Listed Building Prosecutions* was published by the Department of Communities and Local Government in 2006. Whilst this guidance should be considered with caution,[20] it suggests the following public interest factors to consider in listed building prosecution decisions in addition to those in the Code for Crown Prosecutors:

- 'How long the building has been listed

- Whether the feature that was altered or destroyed was historically or architecturally important or unique

- Whether or not the feature can be replaced or replicated

- The extent to which the overall architectural or historic importance of the building has been affected

- The importance of the building as a whole

---

[17]   [1997] JPL 853.

[18]   Listed Buildings Act, s 9(4). The magistrates' court fine would become unlimited when the Legal Aid, Sentencing and Punishment of Offenders Act 2012, s 85 is brought into force.

[19]   Listed Buildings Act, s 9(5).

[20]   For example, the guidance includes a sample notice to be given to new owners of listed buildings which contain serious errors in summarising legislation. Lord Taylor's *External Review of Government Planning Practice Guidance* (2012) recommended its cancellation.

- Whether listed building consent was sought and the extent to which such consent was complied with

- The extent of compliance with any Listed Building Enforcement Notice (although this of itself does not automatically mean that a prosecution should not proceed)'.

The significance of the first point is not obvious.

16.12   Prosecutions are normally brought by the local planning authority. English Heritage can prosecute offences under the Listed Building Act in England,[21] although it has done so rarely: the most prominent example was for the demolition in 2003 of the Grade II listed Modern Movement house 'Greenside', which had overlooked the 17th green of the West Course at Wentworth in Surrey.

Listed building enforcement notices

16.13   A system of listed building enforcement notices is established by Part I, Chapter IV of the Listed Buildings Act on similar lines to enforcement notices for breach of planning control. These powers are exercised by local planning authorities, with English Heritage also having jurisdiction in Greater London.[22] The Secretary of State for Communities and Local Government can issue a listed building enforcement notice after consulting the relevant local planning authority and English Heritage.[23] The Welsh Ministers have the same power in Wales, subject to consultation with the local planning authority. If it appears to the local planning authority (s 38(1)):

'(a) that any works have been or are being executed to a listed building in their area; and

(b)   that the works are such as to involve a contravention of section 9(1) or (2),

they may, if they consider it expedient to do so having regard to the effect of the works on the character of the buildings as one of special architectural or historic interest, issue a listed building enforcement notice.'

As with enforcement notices, the test for the planning authority is one of expediency, so the authority must consider whether harm was caused by the works. There is, however, no requirement to have regard to the development plan, which means that the statutory presumption in favour of the development plan does not apply. However, development plan policies on the historic environment may be relevant to any decision to enforce.

16.14   The listed building enforcement notice will specify the alleged contravention and will require steps to be taken (s 38(2)):

'(a) for restoring the building to its former state;

(b)   if the authority consider that such restoration would not be reasonably practicable or would be undesirable, for executing such further works specified in the notice as they consider necessary to alleviate the effect of the works which were carried out without listed building consent; or

(c)   for bringing the building to the state in which it would have been if the terms and conditions of any listed building consent which has been granted for the works had been complied with.'

---

[21]   National Heritage Act 1983, s 33(2A).
[22]   Listed Buildings Act, s 45.
[23]   Listed Buildings Act, s 46.

A listed building enforcement notice can require parts of a building which have been unlawfully removed to be replaced.[24]

16.15 Unlike enforcement notices and breach of condition notices for breaches of planning control, there are no time limits for issuing a listed building enforcement notice. This can have serious consequences on the sale of a property or for a subsequent purchaser. A listed building enforcement notice may be issued in respect of works carried out by a previous owner of the building (as happened to the unfortunate Mr Braun in *Braun v First Secretary of State).*[25] A prospective purchaser should, therefore, seek to establish whether works have been carried out which needed, or might have needed, listed building consent and either did not have consent or conditions on the consents were not complied with. A judgment then has to be made whether to seek to regularise the position.

16.16 Listed building enforcement notice are subject to similar procedural rules to enforcement notices. There is right of appeal to the Secretary of State or the Welsh Ministers under s 39 of the Listed Buildings Act. Eleven grounds of appeal are allowed. These are:[26]

'(a) that the building is not of special architectural or historic interest;

(b) that the matters alleged to constitute a contravention of section 9(1) or (2) have not occurred;

(c) that those matters (if they occurred) do not constitute such a contravention;

(d) that works to the building were urgently necessary in the interests of safety or health or for the preservation of the building, that it was not practicable to secure safety or health or, as the case may be, the preservation of the building by works of repair or works for affording temporary support or shelter, and that the works carried out were limited to the minimum measures immediately necessary;

(e) that listed building consent ought to be granted for the works, or that any relevant condition of such consent which has been granted ought to be discharged, or different conditions substituted;

(f) that copies of the notice were not served as required by section 38(4);

(g) except in relation to such a requirement as in mentioned in section 38(2)(b) or (c), that the requirements of the notice exceed what is necessary for restoring the building to its condition before the works were carried out;

(h) that the period specified in the notice as the period within which any step required by the notice to be taken falls short of what should reasonably be allowed;

(i) that the steps required by the notice for the purpose of restoring the character of the building to its former state would not serve that purpose;

(j) that the steps required to be taken by virtue of section 38(2)(b) exceed what it is necessary to alleviate the effect of the works executed to the building;

(k) that steps required to be taken by virtue of section 38(2)(c) exceed what is necessary to bring the building to the state in which it would have been if the terms and conditions of the listed building consent had been complied with.'

---

[24] *R v Leominster District Council ex p Antique Country Buildings Ltd* (1987) 56 P & CR 240; *R (C & P Reinforcement Ltd) v East Hertfordshire District Council* [2009] EWHC 3128 (Admin).

[25] [2003] EWCA Civ 665, [2003] JPL 1536.

[26] Listed Buildings Act, s 39(1).

Most of the grounds of appeal replicate those for enforcement notices;[27] however, grounds (a), (d) and (i) raise different issues. Ground (a) allows a challenge to the listing of the building. If an appeal is allowed on that ground then the Secretary of State or Welsh Ministers will remove the building from the list.[28]

16.17   The appeal mechanism is essentially the same as enforcement notice appeals. Again, it is governed by the Town and Country Planning (Enforcement Notices and Appeals) (England) Regulations 2000 and the Town and Country Planning (Enforcement Notices and Appeals) (Wales) Regulations 2003. Appeals may be determined following inquiry or hearing or by a written representations procedure using the enforcement notice appeal rules and regulations.[29] The appellant or local planning authority are able to insist on an oral hearing.[30] The Planning Act 2008 proposes to introduce a new s 88D into the Listed Buildings Act to allow the Secretary of State to decide the mode of determination of the appeal.[31] As with enforcement notice appeals this would allow the Secretary of State to require an appeal to proceed by written representations against the parties' wishes. However that provision has not been brought into force for listed building enforcement notice appeals. Like enforcement notices, the effect of a listed building enforcement notice is suspended pending determination of an appeal.[32] But this does not affect criminal liability under s 9. Concurrent criminal and appeal proceedings in this situation would pose difficulties and one proceeding may need to be adjourned to avoid prejudicing the other.

Failure to comply with a listed building enforcement notice

16.18   The owner of the land commits an offence if he is in breach of a listed building enforcement notice (s 43(2)). Section 43(1) defines breach of the notice as follows:

> 'Where, at any time after the end of the period for compliance with the notice, any step required by a listed building enforcement notice to be taken has not been taken, the person who is then owner of the land is in breach of the notice.'

Other persons interested in or occupying the land are not criminally liable unless they aid or abet the commission of the offence by the owner. As a listed building enforcement notice is solely concerned with remedying unlawful works, rather than ceasing a use of land, an occupier of the land (who is not an owner) is not obliged to comply with the notice.

---

[27]   See Chapter 7 above.
[28]   Listed Buildings Act, s 41(6)(c).
[29]   Town and Country Planning (Enforcement) (Inquiries Procedure) (England) Rules 2002; Town and Country Planning (Enforcement) (Inquiries Procedure) (Determination by Inspectors) (England) Rules 2002; Town and Country Planning (Enforcement) (Written Representations Procedure) (England) Regulations 2002; Town and Country Planning (Enforcement) (Hearings Procedure) (England) Rules 2002; Town and Country Planning (Enforcement) (Inquiries Procedure) (Wales) Rules 2003; Town and Country Planning (Enforcement) (Inquiries Procedure) (Determination by Inspectors) (Wales) Rules 2003; Town and Country Planning (Enforcement) (Hearings Procedure) (Wales) Rules 2003; Town and Country Planning (Enforcement) (Written Representations Procedure) (Wales) Regulations 2003.
[30]   Listed Buildings Act, s 40(2).
[31]   Planning Act 2008, s 196 and consequential amendments in Sch 10.
[32]   Listed Buildings Act, s 39(3).

16.19   Two statutory defences are provided (s 43(4)):

'(a) that he did everything he could be expected to do to secure that all the steps required by the notice were taken; or

(b) that he was not personally served with a copy of the listed building enforcement notice and was not aware of its existence.'

The offence is triable either way with fines of up to £20,000 on summary trial or an unlimited fine on indictment.[33] Imprisonment is not available for this offence unlike the s 9 offence. The local planning authority may enter the subject land, carry out the steps specified in the listed building enforcement notice and recover the expenses from the owner. These powers, in s 42 of the Listed Buildings Act, replicate s 178 of the Town and Country Planning Act 1990, including the application of Public Health Act 1936 powers.

Whether to proceed by a listed building enforcement notice or prosecution under s 9

16.20   The issue of an listed building enforcement notice is dependent upon a breach of s 9 so the planning authorities, including the Secretary of State and Welsh Ministers, have a choice of measures. Some guidelines on deciding the action to take can be set out. A section 9 prosecution may be more justified if:

• work has been carried out in knowing breach of listed building control;

• a prison sentence may be justified; or

• the damage is irreversible and little can be done to alleviate it.

• A listed building enforcement notice may be more likely if:

• the breach of listed building control was innocent or by a previous owner; or

• there is argument as to whether a breach of listed building control occurred. It is harder to prove in a criminal court than before an appeal inspector. The breach does not have to be proved on a prosecution for failing to comply with a LBEN.

If the building can be restored and the owner will not do so willingly, a listed building enforcement notice is appropriate even if a section 9 prosecution is brought as a criminal court cannot compel restoration works.

CHALLENGES TO APPEAL DECISIONS

16.21   The appellant, the LPA and any person having an interest in the subject land may challenge the Secretary of State's decision on a listed building enforcement notice appeal by appeal to the High Court (under s 65 of the Listed Buildings Act, matching s 289 of the Town and Country Planning Act 1990). If listed building consent is granted on the LBEN appeal then this has to be challenged by two proceedings: an application to the High Court under s 64 of the Listed Buildings Act (which is similar to s 288 of the Town and Country Planning Act 1990); and a s 65 appeal.[34]

---

[33] Listed Buildings Act, s 43(5). The magistrates' court fine would become unlimited when the Legal Aid, Sentencing and Punishment of Offenders Act 2012, s 85 is brought into force.

[34] See Chapter 8 above.

VALIDITY OF LISTED BUILDING ENFORCEMENT NOTICES

16.22   Matching s 285(1) of the Town and Country Planning Act 1990, the validity of a listed building enforcement notice 'shall not, except by way of an appeal under section 39, be questioned in any proceedings whatsoever on any of the grounds on which such an appeal may be brought'.[35] The principles of *R v Wicks*[36] will apply to restrict challenge by way of defence to criminal proceedings on other grounds unless the LBEN is a nullity.

INJUNCTIONS TO SUPPORT LISTED BUILDING CONTROL

16.23   Injunctions are available to restrain breaches of listed building control in the same way as breach of planning control. The Planning and Compensation Act 1991 created a specific injunction power replicating that in s 187B of the Town and Country Planning Act 1990. It inserted s 44A(1) into the Listed Buildings Act, providing that:

> 'Where a LPA consider it necessary or expedient for any actual or apprehended contravention of section 9(1) or (2) to be restrained by injunction, they may apply to the court for an injunction, whether or not they have exercised or are proposing to exercise any of their other powers under this Part.'

The court may grant such order as it 'thinks appropriate for the purpose of restraining the contravention' [37] English Heritage is empowered to bring proceedings under s 44A.[38]

16.24   This injunction power should generally be applied and construed in the same way as s 187B injunctions.[39] It will only apply when a section 9 criminal offence has been committed or is anticipated. In *Derby City Council v Anthony*[40] an injunction was granted under s 44A to prevent the demolition of a Grade II listed theatre. The court was prepared to apply the s 9(3) defence of urgent necessity but found, as a matter for the court, that it did not apply. A more difficult example is *Fenland District Council v Reuben Rose (Properties) Limited,*[41] where listed building consent had been granted but without the local planning authority notifying the Secretary of State prior to issuing the decision. Four years after the error, the authority sought an injunction on the basis that the consent was invalid and that works in accordance with it would be unauthorised. The Court of Appeal held that an injunction could be granted. This case raises problems of a decision maker's ability to challenge their own final decisions other than by judicial review and is discussed further in Chapter 1. The Local Government Act 1972, s 222 jurisdiction to restrain breaches of the criminal law is applicable. Since criminal liability is immediate then, unlike breaches of planning control, s 222 is not dependent upon failure to comply with notices.

---

[35]   Listed Buildings Act, s 64.
[36]   [1998] AC 92. See Chapter 8 above.
[37]   Listed Buildings Act, s 44A(2).
[38]   Listed Buildings Act, s 44A(4); National Heritage Act 1983, s 33(2A).
[39]   see Chapter 14 above.
[40]   [2008] EWHC 895 (QB).
[41]   [2000] PLCR 376.

INTENTIONAL DAMAGE TO A LISTED BUILDING

16.25   If a stranger intentionally damages a listed building without permission from the owner, he will be liable under the Criminal Damage Act 1971 as if he had damaged any other building.[42] If the owner intentionally damages a listed building, even if it does not affect its character, he is guilty of an offence under s 59 subject to a level 3 (£1,000) fine [check]. This maximum sentence is therefore considerably lower than under s 9.

The section 59 offence is:[43]

> 'If, with the intention of causing damage to a listed building, any relevant person does or permits the doing of any act which causes or is likely to result in damage to the building.'

A person is a relevant person if, apart from s 59(1) he would be entitled to do or permit the act in question. This would include the owner of the building and anyone acting with his permission. Failure to take reasonable steps to prevent damage occurring from the offence after conviction is a further offence, subject to a daily fine of one-tenth of level 3 (ie £100).[44]

Building preservation notices

16.26   Unlisted buildings may receive temporary protection from demolition or alteration by service of a building preservation notice. A local planning authority may serve a building preservation notice on any building in their area if (s 3(1), (2) of the Listed Buildings Act):

(a)   it is not a listed building;

(b)   it appears to them to be of special architectural or historic interest and in danger of demolition or of alteration in such a way as to affect its character as a building of architectural or historic interest; and

(c)   they have requested the Secretary of State to list it.

The notice acts as temporary listing of the building, applying all the listed building provisions (except causing damage under s 59) to the building.[45]

16.27   It remains in force for six months or until the Secretary of State or Welsh Ministers list the building or notifies the local planning authority that it will not be listed, whichever is the earlier.[46] English Heritage may serve building preservation notices in London.[47] Building preservation notices are rarely served because if they are not confirmed then compensation is payable by the local planning authority for 'any loss or damage directly attributable to the effect of the notice'[48] which may include standing down contractors.

---

[42]   The maximum sentence is 10 years' imprisonment: Criminal Damage Act 1971, s 4(2).
[43]   Listed Buildings Act, s 59(1).
[44]   Listed Buildings Act, s 59(4).
[45]   Listed Buildings Act, s 3(5).
[46]   Listed Buildings Act, s 3(3), (4).
[47]   Listed Buildings Act, s 3(8).
[48]   Listed Buildings Act, s 29.

CONSERVATION AREA CONSENT

16.28   Buildings in conservation areas which are not listed may only be demolished if conservation area consent is obtained (s 74(1), Listed Buildings Act), subject to limited exceptions. This requirement pre-dates the Planning and Compensation Act 1991, which brought demolition of buildings specified by the Secretary of State within the meaning of operational development in s 55 of the Town and Country Planning Act 1990. This procedure is carried out by the listed buildings provisions of the Listed Buildings Act as amended by the Town and Country Planning (Listed Buildings and Conservation Areas) Regulations 1990 (in England) and the Town and Country Planning (Listed Buildings and Conservation Areas) (Wales) Regulations 2012. These regulations apply the section 9 offence and the injunctive powers to demolition in conservation areas and establish conservation area enforcement notices, equivalent to listed building enforcement notices. Conservation area consent is due to be abolished in England by the Enterprise and Regulatory Reform Act 2013 and such demolition dealt with by strengthened planning enforcement powers. This is discussed further below.

SCHEDULED MONUMENTS

16.29   The Secretary of State and Welsh Ministers may schedule monuments that he considers to be of national importance under s 1 of the Ancient Monuments and Archaeological Areas Act 1979 (AMAAA). Approximately 20,000 monuments are presently scheduled in England. Works[49] on a scheduled monument require scheduled monument consent, granted either expressly or under a class consent. Executing or causing or permitting to be executed works to a scheduled monument without authorisation is an offence (s 2(1) of the AMAAA).[50] This includes carrying out works which do not have consent, or carrying out works without complying with the terms of the consent[51] or any conditions attached to it.[52] The offence provides for the maximum fine in summary courts at level 5 (£5000) or an unlimited fine in the Crown Court.[53] Unlike listed building offences, no penalty of imprisonment is available.

AREAS OF ARCHAEOLOGICAL IMPORTANCE

16.30   Areas of archaeological importance can be designated by the Secretary of State, the Welsh Ministers, English Heritage or local authorities under Pt II of the Ancient Monuments and Archaeological Areas Act 1979. In these areas there are special notice and access provisions to facilitate rescue archaeology. Failure to comply creates criminal liability. There are presently five such areas: the historic town centres of Canterbury, Chester, Exeter, Hereford and York.

SENTENCING

16.31   The sentencing issues which arise on the various historic environment offences are similar. Various sentencing factors were discussed by the Court of

---

[49]   Defined by s 2 of the AMAAA.
[50]   AMAAA, s 2(1).
[51]   AMAAA, s 2(3)(b).
[52]   AMAAA, s 2(6) .
[53]   AMAAA, s 2(10).

Appeal in *R v Duckworth,* where a Grade II Elizabethan listed building had been demolished without any application for consent. Hobhouse LJ considered previous scheduled monument sentencing decisions in *Sims Ltd*[54] and *Simpson*[55] and said:[56]

> 'It will only be in exceptional circumstances that it will be appropriate to pass a prison sentence; indeed, the criteria in the Criminal Justice Act have to be satisfied before a prison sentence is passed.
>
> There may be cases where the blatancy of the defendant's conduct and the seriousness of his criminal behaviour do make such a course necessary. ...
>
> The factors relevant to the sentence must include the following.
>
> First, the degree of damage that has been done to the historic structure. The purpose of this leglisation is the preservation of the historic monuments and other similar structures that are protected by the legislation. The offence is an offence of damaging or altering those structures without the appropriate consent or permission. Therefore, the first factor in considering the seriousness of the offence is to consider the degree of damage that has been done.
>
> A second factor is the degree of financial gain that the defendant has attempted to achieve. In nearly all cases financial gain will have been the motive of the defendant. If he disregards the provisions of the Act, it will almost certainly have been with a view to saving himself money or to the gaining of profit for himself. Where a financial penalty is being imposed on the defendant, it must take into account the financial advantage which the defendant was attempting to achieve, otherwise the deterrent and punitive effect of the sentence may be lost.
>
> Thirdly, and in many respects most importantly, is the degree of culpability of the defendant. These offences can be committed in a number of circumstances. They are sometimes described as offences of strict liability whether or not that term is wholly accurate. But the offence may be committed through a lack of care on the part of the defendant or indeed through ignorance of his proper responsibilities in the relevant matter. On the other hand, it may be a case where the defendant has acted wilfully, in disregard of the need to obtain consent, or he has even acted wilfully, with an intent to damage or destroy an historic structure.'

16.32   In *R v Johnson,* the defendant had purchased a 160-year-old house of townscape merit in a conservation area in Twickenham, which he proceeded to demolish without consent. It was accepted that he was grossly negligent in not applying for consent. The agreed financial benefit was £109,000 mainly due to the absence of value added tax on new build works. The Court of Appeal referred to the Institute of Historic Buildings and Conservation's database of sentences for heritage offences, summarising it in this way:[57]

> 'First, of the 150 fines recorded on that database, all but 19 are below £15,000. Secondly, of those 19, listed buildings account for 15; and the highest fine relating to an unlisted building in a conservation area is £15,000 (imposed in 2005 for the demolition, acknowledged to be in good faith, of two adjoining properties by a very substantial developer). Thirdly, the next unlisted building is one in the curtilage of a listed building, where the developer was fined £21,000 in 1992. Fourthly, only two entries on the database exceed the fine imposed on the applicant: in 1998 McCarthy and Stone (a major developer) was fined £200,000

---

54   (1993) 14 Cr App R (S) 213. The magistrates' court fine would become unlimited when the Legal Aid, Sentencing and Punishment of Offenders Act 2012, s 85 is brought into force.

55   (1993) 14 Cr App R (S) 602.

56   [1995] 16 Cr App R (S) 529 at 531.

57   [2012] EWCA Crim 580, [2012] 2 Cr App R (S) 87.

for the demolition of Stelvio House, Newport, Gwent (a Grade II listed building); and in 2007 a developer was fined £95,000 on a total of 21 counts for unauthorised alterations to two Grade II* listed buildings in Park Street, Windsor. Fifthly, in 2007 an architectural practice was fined £25,000 and the contractor £20,000 for the substantial demolition of two Grade II Lodges by John Nash; they were listed buildings in Hanover House, Outer Circle, Regent's Park, London.'

In the *Johnson* appeal the sentence was reduced from an £80,000 fine to £33,000, making allowance for the early guilty plea.

16.33   *Johnson* was followed by the Court of Appeal in *R v Rance*.[58] Mr Rance had demolished a Victorian house in a conservation area in Fulham intending to rebuild a home for his family on the site.[59] He had not applied for conservation area consent. In the light of the deliberate attempt to disregard planning procedures the Court of Appeal considered that a fine of £50,000 was appropriate, a reduction from the £120,000 imposed by the Crown Court.

16.34   The Institute of Historic Buildings and Conservation's database[60] is a useful resource but like most such lists should be used with caution. Sentences imposed will reflect all the circumstances which cannot be fully recorded on the database. The database is drawn from voluntary reporting, usually by local planning authorities, and so is not comprehensive. It also not necessarily updated to reflect appeal decisions.

16.35   English Heritage has given guidance on the preparation of Heritage Crime Impact Statements. There will usually be a need in heritage cases to produce evidence relevant to sentence, dealing with the historic and architectural importance of the asset, the effect of the unlawful works, possible remediation and any profit made. This evidence would not be relevant to whether an offence was committed unless to prove that a building was listed or that its special historic or architectural interest was affected by works. Evidence that is irrelevant to guilt should not be produced to the jury or magistrates (in the latter case, prior to verdict).[61]

ENTERPRISE AND REGULATORY REFORM ACT 2013

16.36   The Enterprise and Regulatory Reform Act 2013 makes a series of changes to historic environment law in England. At the time of writing these are not yet in force.[62] The changes relevant to enforcement matters are the abolition of conservation area consent and the introduction of certificates of lawfulness of proposed works to listed buildings.

Abolition of conservation area consent

16.37   Since the vast majority of building demolition which required conservation area consent was part of a project involving new build which needed planning

---

[58]   [2012] EWCA Crim 2023.
[59]   Although not in issue in the Court of Appeal, the demolition had consisted of removing the spine and side walls of the house. The front elevation then became unstable and consent was granted for its demolition.
[60]   At http://www.ihbc.org.uk/resources/resources.html
[61]   See *R v Sandhu* [1997] JPL 853.
[62]   Draft fees regulations suggest that the abolition of conservation area consent will come into force on 1 October 2013.

permission then there was always a strong case for incorporating demolition in conservation areas within planning control and abolishing conservation area consent. Under the Town and Country Planning (Demolition – Description of Buildings) Direction 1995, planning permission was not required for demolition which needed conservation area consent so there was not a duplication of consent at that point. However, in March 2011, the Court of Appeal in *R (SAVE Britain's Heritage) v Secretary of State for Communities and Local Government*[63] declared that most of the Demolition Direction, including that part, was unlawful. Consequently planning permission was also required, although this would usually be granted by the Town and Country Planning (General Permitted Development) Order 1995. The case for abolishing conservation area consent and merging that control with the need for planning permission became overwhelming. Since conservation area consent gave rise to immediate criminal liability, whereas breach of planning control does not, a number of consequential changes were required to maintain the standard of protection.

16.38 Section 63 and Sch 17 of the Enterprise and Regulatory Reform Act 2013 introduce a series of amendments to bring about the abolition of conservation area consent and its replacement by planning control. The need for conservation area consent under s 74 of the Listed Buildings Act is confined to Wales. It will be an 'offence for a person to carry out or cause or permit to be carried out relevant demolition without the required planning permission': proposed s 196D(1) of the Town and Country Planning Act 1990. Similarly, it will also be 'an offence for a person to fail to comply with any condition or limitation subject to which planning permission for relevant demolition is granted'.[64] Relevant demolition defined as:[65]

> 'the demolition of a building that—
>
> (a) is situated in a conservation area in England; and
>
> (b) is not a building to which section 74 of the Planning (Listed Buildings and Conservation Areas) Act 1990 does not apply by virtue of section 75 of that Act (listed buildings, certain ecclesiastical buildings, scheduled monuments and buildings described in a direction of the Secretary of State under that section).'

The health and safety defence in s 9 of the Listed Buildings Act is applied to this provision, so replicating the present situation under conservation area consent:[66]

> 'It is a defence for a person accused of an offence under this section to prove the following matters—
>
> (a) that the relevant demolition was urgently necessary in the interests of safety or health;
>
> (b) that it was not practicable to secure safety or health by works of repair or works for affording temporary support or shelter;
>
> (c) that the relevant demolition was the minimum measure necessary; and
>
> (d) that notice in writing of the relevant demolition was given to the local planning authority as soon as reasonably practicable.'

---

[63] [2011] EWCA Civ 334, [2011] JPL 1016.
[64] Proposed Town and Country Planning Act 1990, s 196D(2).
[65] Proposed Town and Country Planning Act 1990, s 196D(3).
[66] Proposed Town and Country Planning Act 1990, s 196D(4).

The offence will be triable either way, with maximum sentences of 12 months' imprisonment in the magistrates' court, or two years' imprisonment in the Crown Court, or a fine in either court.[67] Any financial benefit must be taken into account in sentencing[68] and a subsequent grant of permission will not affect liability for an offence which has occurred.[69]

16.39 As planning permission is presently required for such demolition, the local planning authority has the usual range of enforcement provisions available to it. English Heritage would be given power to prosecute or seek a planning injunction in respect of relevant demolition.[70] A new ground of appeal against an enforcement notice would apply for relevant demolition which was urgently necessary in the interests of health and safety:[71]

'(2C) Where any breach of planning control constituted by the matters stated in the notice relates to relevant demolition (within the meaning of section 196D), an appeal may also be brought on the grounds that—

(a)   the relevant demolition was urgently necessary in the interests of safety or health;

(b)   it was not practicable to secure safety or health by works of repair or works for affording temporary support or shelter; and

(c)   the relevant demolition was the minimum measure necessary.'

There would be no time limit for taking enforcement action against relevant demolition, mirroring the current unlimited time for acting against conservation area consent breaches – see the proposed s 171B(2A):

'There is no restriction on when enforcement action may be taken in relation to a breach of planning control in respect of relevant demolition (within the meaning of section 196D).'

For these provisions to be effective, permitted development rights for relevant demolition would have to be removed from Pt 31 of the Town and Country Planning (General Permitted Development) Order 1995. Some transitional provision will also need to be made to allow relevant demolition to proceed under existing conservation area consents.

Certificates of lawfulness of proposed works to listed buildings

16.40 Another enforcement related change in the 2013 Act is to introduce certificates of lawfulness of proposed works to listed buildings. At present there is no formal mechanism for determining that listed building consent is not required short of doing the act and arguing the issue out in response to enforcement proceedings. A

---

[67]   Proposed Town and Country Planning Act 1990, s 196D(5). Until the Criminal Justice Act 2003, s 154(1) comes into force, the maximum sentence in the magistrates' court is six months' imprisonment: proposed Town and Country Planning Act 1990, s 196D(6). Similarly, until the Legal Aid, Sentencing and Punishment of Offenders Act 2012, s 85(1) comes into force, the maximum fine in the magistrates' court is £20,000: proposed Town and Country Planning Act 1990, s 196D(7).

[68]   Proposed Town and Country Planning Act 1990, s 196D(8).

[69]   Proposed Town and Country Planning Act 1990, s 196D(9).

[70]   By amending s 33, National Heritage Act 1983: see Enterprise and Regulatory Reform Act 2013, Sch 17, para 1.

[71]   Proposed Town and Country Planning Act 1990, s 174(2C).

local planning authority may give an informal view (which will usually suffice) or it may decline to take action on a listed building consent application if it considers that consent is not required.[72] A system of certificates will be introduced as a new s 26H of the Planning (Listed Buildings and Conservation Areas) Act 1990,[73] modelled on the lawful development certificate regime.[74] A certificate application may be made by 'a person who wishes to ascertain whether proposed works for the alteration or extension of a listed building in England would be lawful'.[75] They need not propose to carry out the works themselves. It is said that 'works would be lawful if they would not affect the character of the listed building as a building of special architectural or historic interest',[76] but that is not expressed to be exclusive. It may be that a certificate could also be granted if the works do not alter the building (such as the removal of a statue which is not part of the listed building) or the works are lawful under a listed building consent or development consent order.

16.41　The application must specify the building and describe the works and be in a form prescribed by regulations.[77] If the local planning authority are provided with 'information satisfying them that the works described in the application would be lawful at the time of the application, they must issue a certificate to that effect; and in any other case they must refuse the application'.[78] They are allowed to allow or refuse an application in part or modify the description. A certificate must:[79]

'(a)　specify the building to which it relates;

(b)　describe the works concerned;

(c)　give the reasons for determining that the works would be lawful; and

(d)　specify the date of issue of the certificate.'

The works in a certificate are 'conclusively presumed to be lawful' provided that they are carried out within 10 years beginning with the date of issue of the certificate and the certificate has not been revoked.[80] Revocation by the local planning authority is only possible:[81]

'if, on the application for the certificate—

(a)　a statement was made or document used which was false in a material particular; or

(b)　any material information was withheld.'

An offence is created in a similar manner to lawful development certificates:[82]

'A person is guilty of an offence if, for the purpose of procuring a particular decision on an application (whether or not by that person) for the issue of a certificate under section 26H, the person—

---

[72]　*Chambers v Guildford Borough Council* [2008] EWHC 826 (QB), [2008] JPL 1459.
[73]　Inserted by Enterprise and Regulatory Reform Act 2013, s 61.
[74]　Much of the case law and discussion in Chapter 23 below will apply to the listed building certificates.
[75]　Proposed Listed Buildings Act 1990, s 26H(1).
[76]　Proposed Listed Buildings Act 1990, s 26H(2).
[77]　Proposed Listed Buildings Act 1990, ss 26H(1), 26I(1).
[78]　Proposed Listed Buildings Act 1990, s 26H(3).
[79]　Proposed Listed Buildings Act 1990, s 26H(4).
[80]　Proposed Listed Buildings Act 1990, s 26H(5).
[81]　Proposed Listed Buildings Act 1990, s 26I(6).
[82]　Proposed Listed Buildings Act 1990, s 26J(1).

(a)   knowingly or recklessly makes a statement which is false or misleading in a material particular;

(b)   with intent to deceive, uses any document which is false or misleading in a material particular; or

(c)   with intent to deceive, withholds any material information.'

The offence is punishable by a fine up to the statutory maximum on summary conviction or imprisonment for up to two years or a fine on indictment.[83]

16.42   There will be a right of appeal to the Secretary of State against refusal of the application in whole or in part, modification or substitution of the description or a failure to determine the application within the prescribed period.[84] The appeal will be allowed if refusal was, or would not have been, well-founded.[85]

---

[83]   Proposed Listed Buildings Act 1990, s 26J(2). Proposed s 26J(3) is a provision disapplying the six-month period for bringing summary only proceedings, which is entirely redundant as the offence is triable either way and so has no time limit.

[84]   Proposed Listed Buildings Act 1990, s 26K(1), (7).

[85]   Proposed Listed Buildings Act 1990, s 26K(4).

Chapter 17

Trees and Hedgerows

17.01   Separate regimes protect certain trees and hedgerows from damage and removal.

TREES

17.02   Sections 197 to 214D of the Town and Country Planning Act 1990 make specific provision for trees. The Planning Act 2008 contained provisions to transfer more of the substance of the control to regulations by providing detailed regulation making powers (ss 202A to 202G) and omitting many of the substantive provisions in the primary legislation. This change was introduced in England with the detail of the regime in the Town and Country Planning (Tree Preservation) (England) Regulations 2012. Wales has not brought the 2008 Act amendments into force and still uses the Town and Country Planning (Trees) Regulations 1999.

17.03   Trees can be protected in three ways:

(a) tree preservation order;

(b) interim protection in conservation areas;

(c) conditions in planning permissions.

Conditions affecting trees in planning permissions are enforced in the usual way. There is a duty to include appropriate provision for the preservation or planting of trees in a planning permission.[1]

Tree preservation orders

17.04   Tree preservation orders ('TPOs') can be made by local planning authorities to protect individual trees, groups of trees or woodlands if it is 'expedient in the interests of amenity'.[2] A TPO shall be in the form set out in the Schedule to the Regulations or in a form substantially to the like effect.[3] The order must specify the trees, groups of trees or woodlands to which it relates and must indicate the position by reference to a map. On making a TPO the local planning authority must serve a copy on the owners and occupiers of the land affected.[4] Formally the TPO only

---

[1] Town and Country Planning Act 1990, s 197(a).
[2] Town and Country Planning Act 1990, s 198(1).
[3] Town and Country Planning (Tree Preservation) (England) Regulations 2012, reg 3(1), Town and Country Planning (Trees) Regulations 1999, reg 2(1).
[4] Town and Country Planning (Tree Preservation) (England) Regulations 2012, reg 5, Town and Country Planning (Trees) Regulations 1999, reg 3.

takes effect when it is confirmed by the local planning authority,[5] but English TPOs have provisional effect until a decision on confirmation or six months have expired (whichever is earlier).[6] In Wales there is a discretion to make a provisional TPO which has effect for six months pending confirmation.[7] Before deciding whether to confirm the TPO, the local planning authority will take account of objections or representations made within 28 days of service.[8] On confirming the TPO the LPA may modify it. However this power is limited, especially if further trees are to be covered.[9] The Secretary of State and Welsh Ministers have reserved power to make TPOs.[10]

17.05   The validity of a TPO may be challenged by an application to the High Court under s 288 of the Town and Country Planning Act 1990 within six weeks of its confirmation. There is no power to suspend the TPO by interim order under s 288 as the trees may then be cut down before the substantive hearing.[11] The validity of a TPO may not be challenged by judicial review, whether before or after confirmation.[12]

Tree preservation order consents and exemptions

17.06   Subject to exemptions, tree preservation area consent is required to cut down, top, lop, uproot or wilfully damage or destroy a tree or cause or permit the cutting down, topping, lopping, wilful damage or wilful destruction of a tree specified in a TPO.[13] There are various exemptions to the requirement for consent. In England these are contained in the regulations,[14] whilst in Wales they are in the Act and the form of order scheduled to the regulations.[15] These exemptions include: works to trees dying, dead or in a dangerous condition; compliance with the requirements of an Act of Parliament; preventing or abating a nuisance;[16] development authorised by a planning permission; cultivation of trees for fruit in the course of a business or trade; and felling authorised by a felling licence.

17.07   Tree preservation order consents are granted by the local planning authority (or on appeal, the Secretary of State or Welsh Ministers) and may be subject to conditions. If loss or damage is suffered by reason of the refusal of TPO consent, the grant of any consent subject to conditions or the refusal of consent under any conditions imposed on a consent, then compensation is recoverable under the terms

---

[5]   For Wales in the Town and Country Planning Act 1990, s 199(1); Town and Country Planning (Tree Preservation) (England) Regulations 2012, reg 4(1).

[6]   Town and Country Planning (Tree Preservation) (England) Regulations 2012, reg 4(2).

[7]   In Wales, Town and Country Planning Act 1990, s 201.

[8]   Town and Country Planning (Tree Preservation) (England) Regulations 2012, reg 7, Town and Country Planning (Trees) Regulations 1999, reg 5(1).

[9]   *Evans v Waverley Borough Council* [1995] 3 PLR 80.

[10]   Town and Country Planning Act 1990, s 202.

[11]   Town and Country Planning Act 1990, s 288(5), (6).

[12]   Town and Country Planning Act 1990, s 284(1), (2).

[13]   See Town and Country Planning (Tree Preservation) (England) Regulations 2012, reg 13 and the form in the Schedule at para 3 and in Town and Country Planning (Trees) Regulations 1999, Schedule form at para 4.

[14]   Town and Country Planning (Tree Preservation) (England) Regulations 2012, reg 14.

[15]   Town and Country Planning Act 1990, s 198(6) and Town and Country Planning (Trees) Regulations 1999, Schedule form at para 5.

[16]   In *Perrin v Northampton Borough Council* [2006] EWHC 2331 (TCC), [2007] Env LR 12 at para 44, 45 it was held that 'nuisance' means actionable nuisance in private or public nuisance.

of the TPO.[17] The compensation is payable by the authority which made the TPO and the claim should be lodged within 12 months. Disputes as to compensation may be referred to the Upper Tribunal (Lands Chamber).[18]

Breach of a tree preservation order

17.08   Two separate offences of contravening a TPO are created, depending upon the nature of the contravention. The first offence is under s 210(1):

> 'If any person, in contravention of a tree preservation order
>
> (a)   cuts down, uproots or wilfully destroys a tree; [or]
>
> (b)   wilfully damages, tops or lops a tree in such a manner as to be likely to destroy it.'

In England a paragraph (c) is added to subsection (1) that an offence is also committed if a person 'causes or permits the carrying out of any of the activities in paragraph (a) or (b)'. This is strictly unnecessary as a person who caused the acts would have carried them out and a person who permits is likely to be a secondary party as having aided or abetted, counselled or procured.

17.09   The prosecution must prove that:

(a)   the tree was subject to a TPO;

(b)   the defendant carried out the activities in s 210(1); and

(c)   the activities were in contravention of the order.

It is for the defendant to prove that any exemption, such as danger, applies.[19]

17.10   The subsection (1) offence is punishable on the same basis as breach of an enforcement notice: a £20,000 fine in the magistrates' court or an unlimited fine in the Crown Court.[20] As with many other enforcement offences, regard is to be had to any benefit accruing to the defendant.[21]

17.11   The second tree offence is under s 210(4) and arises:

> 'If any person contravenes the provisions of a tree preservation order otherwise than as mentioned in subsection (1), he shall be guilty of an offence and liable on summary conviction to a fine not exceeding level 4 on the standard scale.'

This includes topping, lopping and wilful damage not likely to destroy the tree. The time period for bringing prosecutions under subsection (4) is extended in England.

---

[17]   In England under Town and Country Planning (Tree Preservation) (England) Regulations 2012, reg 24; in Wales under Town and Country Planning Act 1990, s 203 and the Schedule form, para 9.

[18]   In England under Town and Country Planning (Tree Preservation) (England) Regulations 2012, reg 24(9); in Wales under Town and Country Planning Act 1990, s 205. For examples see *John Lyon Charity v Westminster City Council* [2012] UKUT 117 (LC), [2012] JPL 985; *Factorset Ltd v Selby District Council* [1995] 2 PLR 11.

[19]   *R v Alath Construction Ltd* [1990] 1 WLR 1255.

[20]   Town and Country Planning Act 1990, s 210(2). The magistrates' court fine would become unlimited when the Legal Aid, Sentencing and Punishment of Offenders Act 2012, s 85 is brought into force.

[21]   Town and Country Planning Act 1990, s 210(3).

The usual time limit for laying and information or a charge for a summary offence is 12 months. Proceedings may also be brought for the offence within six months of the date on which the prosecutor had sufficient evidence to justify the proceedings, provided the prosecution is brought within three years of the date of the offence.[22] The prosecutor may certify when sufficient information was known.[23] Whilst that certificate is expressed to be 'conclusive' it is subject to review by the magistrates' court on normal public law grounds, as an abuse of process or if there is fraud, additionally the certificate must comply in substance and form with the statutory requirements.[24] This extension to the time limit does not apply in Wales.[25] There is no statutory requirement to have regard to financial benefit when sentencing for the subsection (4) offence, and it may be that such a benefit is less likely, but the presence or absence of a financial benefit would be relevant to sentence in any event.

Replacement of trees

17.12   The replacement of trees subject to TPOs is governed by ss 206 and 207. This duty applies where a tree is unlawfully removed and in the case of certain lawful removals. A tree covered by a TPO must be replaced if:

(a) it was removed, uprooted or destroyed in contravention of tree preservation regulations (or in Wales, contravention of the TPO);[26]

(b) (in England) the tree, 'except in the case of a tree to which the order applies as part of a woodland, is removed, uprooted or destroyed or dies at a prescribed time'.[27] A prescribed time is when the tree is dead or if the works are done to remove an immediate risk of serious harm[28];

(c) 'except in the case of a tree to which the order applies as part of a woodland, is removed, uprooted or destroyed or dies at a time when its cutting down or uprooting is authorised only by virtue of section 198(6)(a)'.[29] Section 198(6) is the exception for trees which are dead, dying or dangerous; or

(d) conditions under a TPO consent require it.[30]

Subject to any different requirement in a condition, the duty of the owner of the land is 'to plant another tree of an appropriate size and species at the same place as soon as he reasonably can'.[31]

17.13   If the replacement requirements are not complied with, the local planning authority may serve a notice requiring the planting of specified trees in a specified time. Section 207(1) provides:

---

[22]   Town and Country Planning Act 1990, s 210(4A), (4B). These provisions were inserted by the Localism Act 2012 and only apply to offences committed on or after 6 April 2012.

[23]   Town and Country Planning Act 1990, s 210(4C), (4D).

[24]   *Burwell v Director of Public Prosecutions* [2009] EWHC 1069 (Admin). There is a degree of judgment involved in assessing what evidence justifies making the application: see *RSPCA v Johnson* [2009] EWHC 2702 (Admin).

[25]   Town and Country Planning Act 1990, s 210(4E).

[26]   Town and Country Planning Act 1990, s 206(1)(a).

[27]   Town and Country Planning Act 1990, s 206(1)(b) (as amended by the Planning Act 2008).

[28]   Town and Country Planning (Tree Preservation) (England) Regulations 2012, reg 25.

[29]   Town and Country Planning Act 1990, s 206(1)(b).

[30]   See Town and Country Planning Act 1990, s 207(1).

[31]   Town and Country Planning Act 1990, s 206(1).

'(1) If it appears to the local planning authority that—

(a)   the provisions of section 206, or

(b)   any conditions of a consent given under a tree preservation order which require the replacement of trees,

are not complied with in the case of any tree or trees, that authority may serve on the owner of the land a notice requiring him, within such period as may be specified in the notice, to plant a tree or trees of such size and species as may be so specified.'

This section 207 notice must be served within four years of the breach.[32] Like enforcement notices, the notice only takes effect from a time specified in the notice, at least 28 days from the date of service.[33] The s 207 notice can be appealed to the Secretary of State or Welsh Ministers. The grounds of appeal are (s 208(1)):

'(a)   that the provisions of s 206 or, as the case may be, the conditions mentioned in s 207(1)(b) are not applicable or have been complied with;

(aa) that in all the circumstances of the case the duty imposed by s 206(1) should be dispensed with in relation to any tree;

(b)   that the requirements of the notice are unreasonable in terms of period or the size or species of trees specified in it;

(c)   that the planting of a tree or trees in accordance with the notice is not required in the interests of amenity or would be contrary to the practice of good forestry;

(d)   that the place on which the tree or trees are required to be planted is unsuitable for that purpose.'

The procedure on appeal is set out in s 208 and Sch 6. This follows the procedure for enforcement notice appeals: see Chapter 7 above. The lawfulness of the Minister's decision on a s 208 appeal can be challenged on a point of law by an appeal to the High Court under s 289(2).[34]

17.14   In a similar manner to s178 direct action in respect of enforcement notices, the local planning authority can enter the land and plant the trees, recovering the cost from the owner, if a section 207 notice is not complied with.[35] It is an offence to obstruct a person exercising this power.[36] The replacement provisions are unusually constrained. The s 206 duty may only be enforced by a section 207 notice.[37] It is not an offence to fail to comply with the section 207 notice. However, the notice may have been issued following a breach of the TPO creating an offence under s 210 and so a prosecution may be brought or injunction sought.

Trees in conservation areas

17.15   Trees in conservation areas receive interim protection by a requirement that notice is served on the local planning authority before they are damaged or destroyed. The structure of the offence is unduly complex. Section 211 creates an offence to cut

---

[32]   Town and Country Planning Act 1990, s 207(2).
[33]   Town and Country Planning Act 1990, s 207(3), (4).
[34]   See Chapter 8 for discussion of these challenges.
[35]   Town and Country Planning Act 1990, s 209.
[36]   Town and Country Planning Act 1990, s 209(6).
[37]   Town and Country Planning Act 1990, s 207(5).

down, top, lop, uproot, wilfully damage or wilfully destroy a tree in a conservation area subject to various exceptions. In England s 211(1) provides:

'Subject to the provisions of this section and section 212, any person who, in relation to a tree to which this section applies, does any act which might by virtue of section 202C be prohibited by tree preservation regulations shall be guilty of an offence.'

The acts which might be prohibited by s 202C are cutting down, topping, lopping, uprooting, wilful damage or wilful destruction of trees and causing or permitting such acts. In Wales, s 211(1) refers to the identical list of acts in s 198(3)(a). Exceptions to the prohibition are:

(a) the act is authorised by an order granting development consent under the Planning Act 2008;[38]

(b) the tree is subject to a TPO (when that regime applies); and[39]

(c) the tree or the act is exempted by the tree regulations.[40] In England the exemptions are those in reg 14 and additional exemptions in reg 15.[41] In particular these include the cutting down, uprooting, topping or lopping of a tree whose diameter (or the diameter of any stem) does not exceed 75 millimetres at a point 1.5 metres above the natural ground level.[42]

17.16   If the act falls within s 211, it is then a defence:[43]

'(a) that he served notice of his intention to do the act in question (with sufficient particulars to identify the tree) on the local planning authority in whose area the tree is or was situated; and

(b) that he did the act in question—

(i) with the consent of the local planning authority in whose area the tree is or was situated, or

(ii) after the expiry of the period of six weeks from the date of the notice but before the expiry of the period of two years from that date.'

17.17   Section 210 applies to the offence. As discussed above this creates two separate offences: one triable either way (from s 210(1)) and one summary (from s 210(4)). A summons alleging wilful damage, topping or lopping must say it was likely to destroy the tree if the more serious offence is brought.

17.18   The six-week notice period gives the local planning authority time to decide whether to make a TPO to protect the tree or trees. Service of the notice on the authority ought to be in accordance with s 329.[44] The principal issue is whether the removal of the tree causes harm to the character and appearance of the conservation

[38]   Town and Country Planning Act 1990, s 211(1A).
[39]   Town and Country Planning Act 1990, s 211(2).
[40]   Town and Country Planning Act 1990, s 211(4) applying s 210.
[41]   Town and Country Planning (Tree Preservation) (England) Regulations 2012.
[42]   Town and Country Planning (Tree Preservation) (England) Regulations 2012, reg 15(1), (2); Town and Country Planning (Trees) Regulations 1999, reg 10. The diameter limit is increased to 100 mm if the cutting down or uprooting is solely to improve the growth of other trees. It is prudent for a landowner to take a photographic record of such diameters prior to works.
[43]   Town and Country Planning Act 1990, s 211(3).
[44]   There is no prescribed form, but a standard form is available on the Planning Portal website.

area.[45] The expiry of the six-week period does not prevent the local planning authority from making a TPO to protect the trees before they are cut down.[46]

17.19   If a tree is removed, uprooted or destroyed in contravention of s 211 or the act was only justified by the Regulations because the tree was dying, dead or dangerous or in compliance with statutory obligations or necessity for the prevention or abatement of a nuisance, the owner must replace it (s 213(1)). The owner may apply to the local planning authority for this obligation to be dispensed with.[47] If the obligation is not dispensed with and he fails to comply, the section 207 notice procedure applies.[48]

Tree injunctions

17.20   A specific injunction power is provided in s 214A. Section 214A(1) provides:

> 'Where a local planning authority consider it necessary or expedient for an actual or apprehended offence under section 210 or 211 to be restrained by injunction, they may apply to the court for an injunction, whether or not they have exercised or are proposing to exercise any of their other powers under this Chapter.'

This follows the wording of s 187B(1), and the remaining provisions of that section are applied by reference. The principles applicable to injunctions to restrain breaches of planning control generally apply to tree injunctions. The main points of emphasis would be that the destruction of a mature tree is hard to remedy except in decades so the balance of convenience may be more in favour of an interim injunction. However in *Kirklees Borough Council v Brook,*[49] the High Court held that removing branches, damaging bark, uprooting whole trees and depositing waste on the lower parts of trees was not in that case so serious as to justify an injunction.

Powers of entry in respect of trees

17.21   Persons authorised by the local planning authority are given powers of entry in connection with TPOs, section 210 and 211 offences and section 207 notices. These provisions, in ss 214B–214D, parallel the entry provisions in sections 196A–196C.

HEDGEROWS

17.22   The Environment Act 1995 empowered the Secretary of State to make regulations to protect important hedgerows.[50] The Hedgerows Regulations 1997[51] require consent from the local planning authority for the removal of 'important hedgerows' over 20 metres in length (or, if shorter, meeting other hedgerows at each

---

[45]   *Sherwood and Sherwood v Secretary of State for the Environment* [1996] JPL 925, following the approach in *South Lakeland District Council v Secretary of State for the Environment* [1992] 2 AC 141.

[46]   *R v North Hertfordshire District Council ex p Hyde* [1989] 3 PLR 89.

[47]   Town and Country Planning Act 1990, s 213(2).

[48]   Town and Country Planning Act 1990, s 213(3).

[49]   [2004] EWHC 2841 (Ch), [2005] 2 P & CR 17.

[50]   Environment Act 1995, s 97.

[51]   SI 1997/1160.

end) growing in, or adjacent to, any common land, designated nature reserve or site of special scientific interest, or land used for agriculture, forestry or the breeding or keeping of horses, ponies or donkeys, unless they are within or mark the boundary of the curtilage of a dwelling house.[52] Important hedgerows are those over 30 years old which meet one of the criteria in Pt II of Sch 1 to the regulations. These criteria cover archaeology and history and wildlife and landscape.

17.23   An important hedgerow may only be removed (subject to exceptions)[53] if the owner has served a hedgerow removal notice on the local planning authority and either consent has been given or a period of 42 days has passed without the authority serving a hedgerow retention notice.[54] Where a hedgerow retention notice has been given stating that work relating to a hedgerow may not be carried out, and that notice has not been withdrawn, removal of the hedgerow consisting of or including any such work is prohibited.[55]

17.24   The hedgerows regime is enforceable by criminal prosecution, notice and injunction. By reg 7(1):

'A person who intentionally or recklessly removes, or causes or permits another person to remove, a hedgerow in contravention of regulation 5(1) or (9) is guilty of an offence.'

Regulaton 5(1) is carrying out works without waiting for a consent or the time for a retention notice to pass. Regulation 5(9) is removal in contravention of a retention notice. The regulation 7(1) offence is triable either way, with a fine up to the statutory maximum (£5,000) in the magistrates' court or an unlimited fine in the Crown Court.[56]

17.25   One of the exceptions to needing to give notice is if the removal is required 'for making a new opening in substitution for an existing opening which gives access to land'.[57] This exception is subject to the requirement in reg 6(2) that:

'Where the removal of a hedgerow to which these Regulations apply is permitted by these Regulations only by paragraph (1)(a), the person removing it shall fill the existing opening by planting a hedge within 8 months of the making of the new opening.'

By reg 7(2):

'A person who contravenes or fails to comply with regulation 6(2) is guilty of an offence.'

This offence is punishable by a fine not exceeding level 3 (£1,000) in the magistrates' court.[58] For both hedgerows offences, the court shall have regard to any financial benefit which has accrued or appears likely to accrue to the defendant when sentencing.[59] Company directors may be liable if their companies are in breach.[60]

---

[52]   Hedgerows Regulations, reg 3.
[53]   The exceptions are in the Hedgerows Regulations, reg 6.
[54]   Hedgerows Regulations, reg 5(1).
[55]   Hedgerows Regulations, reg 5(9).
[56]   Hedgerows Regulations, reg 7(4). The magistrates' court fine would become unlimited when the Legal Aid, Sentencing and Punishment of Offenders Act 2012, s 85 is brought into force.
[57]   Hedgerows Regulations, reg 6(1).
[58]   Hedgerows Regulations, reg 7(5).
[59]   Hedgerows Regulations, reg 7(6).
[60]   Hedgerows Regulations, reg 7(7), applying Town and Country Planning Act 1990, s 331.

17.26   If a hedgerow has been removed in breach of reg 5, the local planning authority may serve a hedgerow replacement notice on the owner of the land (or if removed by a utility operator, on that operator) requiring another hedgerow to be planted.[61] The notice shall state the species and position of the shrubs, or trees and shrubs, to be planted and the period within which the planting is to be carried out.[62] The authority may carry out the works in default and recover the cost from the owner as under the tree preservation order regime.[63]

17.27   A hedgerow retention notice or a hedgerow replacement notice may be appealed to the Secretary of State or Welsh Ministers within 28 days of the notice being given to the appellant, or any longer period allowed by the Minister.[64] Grounds of appeal must be stated in the notice of appeal.[65] Appeals may be determined by written representations, hearing or inquiry, with the appellant and local planning authority having a right to be heard.[66] The usual powers on evidence and costs apply.[67] The Minister or an inspector may allow or dismiss the appeal in whole or in part and give directions, including directing the quashing or modification of the notice.[68]

17.28   In similar terms to planning injunctions, the local planning authority may apply for an injunction to restrain an actual or apprehended breach of the Hedgerow Regulations:[69]

'(1)   Where a local planning authority consider it necessary or expedient for an actual or apprehended offence under these Regulations to be restrained by injunction, they may apply to the court for an injunction, whether or not they have exercised or are proposing to exercise any of their other powers under these Regulations.

(2)   On an application under paragraph (1) the court may grant such an injunction as the court thinks appropriate for the purpose of restraining the offence.'

Rights of entry with and without warrants are also provided.[70]

---

[61]   Hedgerows Regulations, reg 8(1).
[62]   Hedgerows Regulations, reg 8(2).
[63]   Hedgerows Regulations, reg 8(3).
[64]   Hedgerows Regulations, reg 9(1).
[65]   Hedgerows Regulations, reg 9(2). An appeal form is on the Planning Portal website, although its use is not obligatory.
[66]   Hedgerows Regulations, reg 9(4).
[67]   Hedgerows Regulations, reg 9(5).
[68]   Hedgerows Regulations, reg 9(3).
[69]   Hedgerow Regulations, reg 11.
[70]   Hedgerow Regulations, regs 12, 13.

Chapter 18

Advertising Control

18.01 Advertising control is subject to a special statutory regime. This provides a separate system of advertising consent, replacing planning permission, with its own enforcement mechanism, but if advertising consent is not obtained, conventional planning enforcement remedies apply in addition to advertising offences. The advertising regime is principally contained in ss 220 to 225E of the Town and Country Planning Act 1990. The detail of this control is in the Town and Country Planning (Control of Advertisements) (England) Regulations 2007 ('the 2007 Advertising Regulations'). These replaced, with amendments, the Town and Country Planning (Control of Advertisements) Regulations 1992 ('the 1992 Advertising Regulations'). The relevant secondary legislation in Wales remains the 1992 Regulations.

18.02 Advertisement is comprehensively and exhaustively defined by s 336(1) of the 1990 Act as follows:

> 'any word, letter, model, sign, placard, board, notice, awning, blind, device or representation, whether illuminated or not, in the nature of, and employed wholly or partly for the purposes of, advertisement, announcement or direction, and (without prejudice to the previous provisions of this definition) includes any hoarding or similar structure used, or designed, or adapted for use and anything else principally used, or designed or adapted principally for use, for the display of advertisements, and references to the display of advertisements shall be construed accordingly.'

The definition is somewhat circular as the advertisement must be 'in the nature of, and employed wholly or partly for the purposes of advertisement, announcement or direction', but announcement or direction gives it a very broad meaning. Whilst there may be debate whether a sign which merely contained a statement of political opinion would be an advertisement, one which included the website details of a political organisation would be.[1] Similarly, faded advertisements for newspapers which had ceased publication in 1921 and which had not been maintained since were not 'employed … for the purposes of advertisement' in 2004.[2] However advertisements include signage giving the name or number of a building.

18.03 The objectives of the advertising regime are in s 220(1) of the Town and Country Planning Act 1990 which enables the Secretary of State or Welsh Ministers to make regulations regulating the display of advertisements 'so far as appears … expedient in the interests of amenity or public safety'. The concern is with the presence of the advertisement on the site, rather than the tastefulness (or otherwise) of the individual advertisement. However, the purpose of an advertisement and its relationship with the use of the land is often critical to acceptability. Signage which gives the address of a building or explains its use may be seen as permissible when

---

[1] See *Butler v Derby City Council* [2005] EWHC 2835 (Admin), [2006] 1 WLR 1346.
[2] *Wandsworth London Borough Council v South Western Magistrates' Court* [2007] EWHC 1079 (Admin).

more general commercial advertising would not be. Consequently the categories of advertisements which do not need an express application are closely related to their purposes.

18.04   The 2007 Advertising Regulations require local planning authorities to exercise their powers under the Regulations 'in the interests of amenity and public safety' taking into account the development plan, so far as material, and any other relevant factors.[3] Some relevant factors are set out:[4]

'(a) factors relevant to amenity include the general characteristics of the locality, including the presence of any feature of historic, architectural, cultural or similar interest;

(b) factors relevant to public safety include—

(i)   the safety of persons using any highway, railway, waterway, dock, harbour or aerodrome (civil or military);

(ii) whether the display of the advertisement in question is likely to obscure, or hinder the ready interpretation of, any traffic sign, railway signal or aid to navigation by water or air;

(iii) whether the display of the advertisement in question is likely to hinder the operation of any device used for the purpose of security or surveillance or for measuring the speed of any vehicle.'

18.05   The 1992 Advertising Regulations refer to the interests of amenity and public safety but not to the development plan. The non-exclusive list of material factors for local planning authorities in Wales is:[5]

'(a) in the case of amenity, the general characteristics of the locality, including the presence of any feature of historic, architectural, cultural or similar interest, disregarding, if they think fit, any advertisement being displayed there;

(b) in the case of public safety—

(i)   the safety of any person who may use any road, railway, waterway, dock, harbour or aerodrome;

(ii) whether any display of advertisements is likely to obscure, or hinder the ready interpretation of, any road traffic sign, railway signal or aid to navigation by water or air.'

18.06   An injunction obtained by the London Borough of Hounslow in 1995 illustrates public safety concerns. A large advertisement was displayed on a building so as to be visible from the M4. There were too many distractions to drivers on that part of the motorway and the advertisement made the road even more unsafe so an order was made for its removal.

18.07   Guidance on advertising control is given in Communities and Local Government Circular 03/2007 *Town and Country Planning (Control of Advertisements) (England) Regulations 2007*. Planning Policy Guidance Note 19 on advertising control was revoked by the National Planning Policy Framework. The NPPF's policy on advertising is brief:

---

[3]   2007 Advertising Regulations, reg 3(1).
[4]   2007 Advertising Regulations, reg 3(2).
[5]   1992 Advertising Regulations, reg 4(1).

'67.   Poorly placed advertisements can have a negative impact on the appearance of the built and natural environment. Control over outdoor advertisements should be efficient, effective and simple in concept and operation. Only those advertisements which will clearly have an appreciable impact on a building or on their surroundings should be subject to the local planning authority's detailed assessment. Advertisements should be subject to control only in the interests of amenity and public safety, taking account of cumulative impacts.'

Welsh guidance is in *Planning Policy Wales*, Circular 14/92 and Technical Advice Note 7: *Outdoor Advertisement Control. Planning Policy Wales* advises:

'3.5.1 The statutory provisions enable local planning authorities to control the display of advertisements when justified in the interests of public safety and amenity. The control regime does not enable the authority to regulate the subject matter of any advertisement. The test in assessing an advertisement's impact on public safety is whether the advertisement itself, or the exact location proposed for its display, is likely to be so distracting or confusing that it creates a hazard to, or endangers, people in the vicinity who are taking reasonable care for their own and others' safety.

3.5.2   The test in considering an advertisement's impact on amenity is whether it will adversely affect the appearance of the building, or of the immediate neighbourhood, where it is to be displayed. Local planning authorities should therefore consider the local characteristics of the neighbourhood, including its scenic, historic, architectural or cultural features. Because assessment of these factors may appear to involve some subjective judgement, authorities should be consistent in their assessment of visual impact in similar or comparable neighbourhoods or surroundings.'

THE CATEGORIES OF ADVERTISEMENTS

18.08   In England advertisements fall under three categories under the 2007 Regulations:

(1)   advertisements which do not need consent, which are identified in Sch 1 of the 2007 Advertising Regulations;[6]

(2)   advertisements with deemed consent under Sch 3 of the 2007 Advertising Regulations;[7] and

(3)   advertisements requiring express consent by the approval of an application by the local planning authority or the Secretary of State.[8]

In Wales, advertisements which do not need consent are identified in Sch 2 of the 1992 Advertising Regulations, subject to requirements in regs 3(2) and 5(2). Categories of deemed consent are also set out in Sch 3 of those earlier regulations but they differ, as to detail, with the English deemed consent provisions.

18.09   Subject to limited exceptions, advertisements require express or deemed consent. Regulation 4(1) of the 2007 regulations provides:

---

[6]   Regulations 1(3), 4(2) of the 2007 Advertising Regulations. Under the 1992 Advertising Regulations this category are known as exempt advertisements and are in Sch 2.
[7]   Regulation 6.
[8]   Regulation 4(1).

'Subject to paragraph (2), no advertisement may be displayed unless consent for its display has been granted—

(a) by the local planning authority or the Secretary of State on an application in that behalf (referred to in these Regulations as 'express consent'); or

(b) by regulation 6 (referred to in these Regulations as 'deemed consent').'

The paragraph (2) exception is for the Schedule 1 advertisements. These advertisements include advertisements on enclosed land,[9] vehicles,[10] items for sale, election posters, traffic signs, and the flags of nations, the European Union, the United Nations, international organisations (of which the UK is a member), St Patrick, St David, armed forces and administrative areas.[11] A more general category is an exemption for non-illuminated advertisements inside buildings which may be visible externally, provided '[N]o part of the advertisement may be within 1 metre of any external door, window or other opening, through which it is visible from outside the building'.[12]

18.10   In both regulations, reg 6 grants deemed consent for advertisements within classes in Sch 3. This deemed consent is subject to conditions and limitations in the particular class. Express consent is obtained by application to the local planning authority in a similar way to seeking planning permission. If the application is refused, granted subject to conditions or not determined, then an appeal may be brought to the Secretary of State or Welsh Ministers. Such appeals are normally determined by written representations or informal hearing.

STANDARD CONDITIONS

18.11   Standard conditions must be complied with for all advertisements.[13] In England these conditions are:[14]

'1. No advertisement is to be displayed without the permission of the owner of the site or any other person with an interest in the site entitled to grant permission.

1   No advertisement shall be sited or displayed so as to—

(a) endanger persons using any highway, railway, waterway, dock, harbour or aerodrome (civil or military);

---

[9]   Including railway and bus stations but all subject to the requirement that 'is not readily visible from outside the enclosed land or from any place to which the public have a right of access': 2007 Advertising Regulations, Schedule 1, table, para 1.

[10]   The vehicle must not be used principally for the display of advertisements. This relates to use at the time of the alleged advertising: see *Tile Wise Ltd v South Somerset District Council* [2010] EWHC 1618 (Admin), [2011] PTSR 381; *Calderdale Metropolitan Borough Council v Windy Bank Dairy Farm Limited* [2010] EWHC 2929 (Admin), [2011] JPL 754.

[11]   The extended list of flags came into force in England in 2012. Administrative areas whose flags may be flown are any island, county, district, borough, burgh, parish, city, town or village within the United Kingdom and the Black Country, East Anglia, Wessex, any part of Lincolnshire, any Riding of Yorkshire and any historic county. The flags of St George and St Andrew are national flags. In Wales the only exempt flags are national flags. The Secretary of State has published the *Plain English guide to flying flags* (November 2012).

[12]   2007 Advertising Regulations, Sch 1, Class I. Schedule 2, Class J of the Welsh legislation is in similar terms but the exemption does not apply to buildings used principally for the display of advertisements.

[13]   Except that advertisements displayed pursuant to standing orders of the Houses of Parliament do not have to be maintained under standard condition 4: reg 1(3)(b), (c).

[14]   2007 Advertising Regulations, Sch 2.

(b)   obscure, or hinder the ready interpretation of, any traffic sign, railway signal or aid to navigation by water or air; or

(c)   hinder the operation of any device used for the purpose of security or surveillance or for measuring the speed of any vehicle.

2   Any advertisement displayed, and any site used for the display of advertisements, shall be maintained in a condition that does not impair the visual amenity of the site.

3   Any structure or hoarding erected or used principally for the purpose of displaying advertisements shall be maintained in a condition that does not endanger the public.

4   Where an advertisement is required under these Regulations to be removed, the site shall be left in a condition that does not endanger the public or impair visual amenity.'

The Welsh standard conditions are:[15]

'1.   Any advertisements displayed, and any site used for the display of advertisements, shall be maintained in a clean and tidy condition to the reasonable satisfaction of the local planning authority.

2.   Any advertisements displayed, and any site used for the display of advertisements, shall be maintained in a clean and tidy condition to the reasonable satisfaction of the local planning authority.

3.   Where an advertisement is required under these Regulations to be removed, the removal shall be carried out to the reasonable satisfaction of the local planning authority.

4.   No advertisement is to be displayed without the permission of the owner of the site or any other person with an interest in the site entitled to grant permission.

5.   No advertisement shall be sited or displayed so as to obscure, or hinder the ready interpretation of, any road traffic sign, railway signal or aid to navigation by water or air, or so as otherwise to render hazardous the use of any highway, railway, waterway or aerodrome (civil or military).'

DEEMED CONSENT

18.12   Almost every building carries an advertisement, even if it is only a house number or details of the owner of a piece of street furniture. There is a great deal of advertising that is treated as routine. For example, most businesses will want their premises to show what they do. There will also be a variety of temporary advertisements, for events or around construction sites, which most people would expect to see. For much of the smaller scale or routine advertising, the costs of applying for consent would be disproportionate to the value of the particular advertisement and consent would usually not be refused. Consequently wide categories of deemed consent are allowed, but subject to very technical conditions. These must be considered in detail and with care. The application of case law on different versions of the regulations also needs careful consideration. Local planning authorities are able to require the removal of individual deemed consent advertisements by serving a discontinuance notice.

---

[15]   1992 Advertising Regulations, Sch 1.

18.13 Some deemed consent categories are capable of permitting lucrative advertisements and have resulted in extensive litigation, particularly involving sites in central and west London. The classes of deemed consent are:[16]

Class 1   Functional advertisements of government departments and their agencies, local authorities, public transport undertakers, statutory undertakers and Transport for London

Class 2   Miscellaneous advertisements relating to the premises on which they are displayed

Class 3   Miscellaneous temporary advertisements

Class 4   Illuminated advertisements on business premises

Class 5   Other advertisements on business premises[17]

Class 6   An advertisement on a forecourt of business premises

Class 7   Flag advertisements

Class 8   Advertisements on hoardings[18]

Class 9   Advertisements on highway structures

Class 10   Advertisements for neighbourhood watch and similar schemes

Class 11   Directional advertisement

Class 12   Advertisements inside buildings

Class 13   Advertisements on sites used for preceding 10 years for display of advertisements without express consent

Class 14   Advertisements displayed after expiry of express consent

Class 15   Advertisements on balloons

Class 16   Advertisements on telephone kiosks

Class 17   Advertisements on a charging point for electric vehicles

18.14 Deemed consent after a period of time is provided by Class 13. The English provision gives deemed consent where '[A]n advertisement displayed on a site that has been used continually for the preceding ten years for the display of advertisements without express consent.' This is subject to a variety of conditions and limitations including that there has been no material increase in the extent to which the site has been used for the display of advertisements or a material alteration in the manner in which it has been so used. The 1992 Advertising Regulations in Wales give the equivalent deemed consent to sites used without express consent since 1 April 1974.[19]

---

[16]   2007 Advertising Regulations, Sch 3. The Welsh regulations are structured the same way but do not include Classes 15 to 17.

[17]   See in particular *Addison Lee Ltd v Westminster City Council* [2012] EWHC 152 (Admin), [2012] JPL 969 and *Berridge v Vision Posters Ltd* (1995) 159 JPN 163.

[18]   See *R (Cal Brown Ltd (t/a CB Advertising Ltd) v Hounslow London Borough Council* [2001] EWHC Admin 864, [2002] JPL 867; *Postermobile Plc v Kensington and Chelsea Royal London Borough Council* [2001] JPL 196; *Brent London Borough Council v Maiden Outdoor Advertising Ltd* [2002] EWHC 1240 (Admin), [2003] JPL 192.

[19]   Class 13 in its different versions has given rise to substantial litigation. Under the 2007 Regulations see *Winfield v Secretary of State for Communities and Local Government* [2012] EWCA Civ 1415, [2013] 1 WLR 948; *R(Clear Channel UK Ltd) v Hammersmith and Fulham London Borough Council* [2009] EWCA Civ 2142, [2010] JPL 751 and *Wandsworth London Borough Council v Adrenalin Advertising Ltd* [2011] EWHC 1040 (Admin), [2011] JPL 1308. For the 1992 and earlier regulations see *R(Maiden Outdoor Advertising Ltd) v Lambeth London Borough Council* [2003] EWHC 1224 (Admin), [2004] JPL 820; *Arthur Maiden Ltd v Lanark County Council* [1958] JPL 417; *Mills & Allen Ltd v City of Glasgow District Council* [1980] JPL 409.

18.15   If an express consent expires, the advertisement may be continued to be displayed unless a condition requires its removal or a renewal of consent has been refused (Class 14). The Minister is empowered to issue directions restricting deemed consent in any particular area or case upon application by the local planning authority.[20] The local planning authority is expected to show that the direction would improve visual amenity and there is no other way of effectively controlling the display of that particular class of advertisement.[21]

18.16   The local planning authority can themselves issue a discontinuance notice against the display of an advertisement with deemed consent if they consider that it is 'necessary to do so to remedy a substantial injury to the amenity of the locality or a danger to members of the public'.[22] There is a right of appeal to the Minister.[23] Compensation is payable if the site has been used for the display of advertisements since 1 August 1948.[24] A discontinuance notice cannot be used against an advertisement which falls within Sch 1 of the 2007 regulations (or the exempt category in Sch 2 of the 1992 regulations) as it does not need any consent at all.

AREAS OF SPECIAL CONTROL ORDERS

18.17   Some areas require special protection against advertisements in the interests of amenity. The Minister can approve area of special control orders, after being made by the local planning authority.[25] These not only restrict deemed consent but also the ability to grant express consent to certain advertisements such as hoardings not relating to local events or which are illuminated. These orders are normally granted in largely or wholly rural areas. They will be granted in other situations where additional protection beyond the planning authority's normal powers is necessary. This may be because of conservation area status or important architectural, archaeological, historical or visual characteristics. The National Planning Policy Framework advises:

> '68. Where an area justifies a degree of special protection on the grounds of amenity, an Area of Special Control Order may be approved. Before formally proposing an Area of Special Control, the local planning authority is expected to consult local trade and amenity organisations about the proposal. Before a direction to remove deemed planning consent is made for specific advertisements, local planning authorities will be expected to demonstrate that the direction would improve visual amenity and there is no other way of effectively controlling the display of that particular class of advertisement. The comments of organisations, and individuals, whose interests would be affected by the direction should be sought as part of the process.'

PROSECUTION

18.18   Immediate criminal liability is imposed for breaches of the Advertising Regulations. It is a summary offence if 'any person displays an advertisement in

---

[20]   2007 Advertising Regulations and 1992 Advertising Regulations, both reg 7.
[21]   TAN 7, para 22 and in the revoked PPG 19, para 28
[22]   2007 Advertising Regulations and 1992 Advertising Regulations, reg 8.
[23]   2007 Advertising Regulations, reg 17; 1992 Advertising Regulations, reg 15.
[24]   Town and Country Planning Act 1990, s 223.
[25]   2007 Advertising Regulations, regs 20, 21; 1992 Advertising Regulations, regs 18, 19.

contravention of the regulations he shall be guilty of an offence'.[26] The person or company that sets up the advertising hoarding would be displaying it. A person is deemed to display an advertisement if:[27]

'(a) he is the owner or occupier of the land on which the advertisement is displayed; or

(b) the advertisement gives publicity to his goods, trade, business or other concerns.'

A person is not guilty by reason of these deemed display provisions if he proves:[28]

'(a) the advertisement was displayed without his knowledge; or

(b) he took all reasonable steps to prevent the display or, after the advertisement had been displayed, to secure its removal.'

18.19   The offence is only triable before the magistrates' court on a summary basis.[29] The six-month period for bringing a prosecution[30] may be extended (in England) as proceedings may also be brought within six months of sufficient evidence to justify the proceedings coming to the prosecutor's knowledge.[31] In such cases, the prosecution must still be brought within three years of the offence being committed.[32] Since advertisements will be in plain sight, the circumstances in which an extended time period can be justified will be limited, perhaps relating to knowledge of the facts concerning deemed consent. The display of different advertisements on different dates on the same hoarding creates separate offences for each advertisement rather than a continuing offence.[33]

18.20   The normal contravention of the Advertising Regulations alleged is a breach of reg 4 in England or reg 5 in Wales: display of an advertisement without express or deemed consent. Additionally, reg 30 (2007) and reg 27 (1992) state that it is an offence under s 224(3) to display an advertisement contravening the regulations.[34] If a condition in a deemed consent is not complied with then the deemed consent does not apply to the advertisement in question.

SENTENCE

18.21   The sentence is a maximum fine at level 4 (£2,500).[35] If the contravention continues a further offence carries a daily fine of £250 (one-tenth of the level 3 fine) for each day in which the offence continues after the original conviction.

---

[26]   Town and Country Planning Act 1990, s 224(3).
[27]   Town and Country Planning Act 1990, s 224(4).
[28]   Town and Country Planning Act 1990, s 224(5), (6).
[29]   Town and Country Planning Act 1990, s 224(3).
[30]   Magistrates' Courts Act 1980, s 127.
[31]   Town and Country Planning Act 1990, s 224(7).
[32]   Town and Country Planning Act 1990, s 224(8). To rely on this additional period, the offence must also have been committed after the provision came into force (6 April 2012). For the approach to certification of this period, see *Burwell v Director of Public Prosecutions* [2009] EWHC 1069 (Admin). There is a degree of judgment involved in assessing what evidence justifies making the application: see *RSPCA v Johnson* [2009] EWHC 2702 (Admin).
[33]   *Royal Borough of Kingston upon Thames v National Solus Sites Ltd* [1994] JPL 251.
[34]   These provisions also exempt the Crown from committing the offence.
[35]   Town and Country Planning Act 1990, s 224(3). The fine was increased by the Anti-Social Behaviour Act 2003, s 53.

POWER TO REMOVE OR OBLITERATE PLACARDS AND POSTERS

18.22   The local planning authority can remove or obliterate any placard or poster that, in their opinion, is displayed in contravention of the Advertising Regulations.[36] If the person displaying or causing to be displayed the advertisement is identified on it then the local planning authority must give him notice if they know or can ascertain his address after reasonable enquiry.[37] If they cannot identify or find the address of this person, then the notice provisions apply to any identifiable person whose 'goods, services or concerns' are publicised by the placard or poster.[38] The notice must state that in the authority's opinion the advertisement is displayed in contravention of the Advertising Regulations and 'that they intend to remove or obliterate it on the expiry of a period specified in the notice and recover from [the advertiser] the costs they may reasonably incur in doing so'.[39] The period specified must not be less than two days from the date of service of the notice.[40]

18.23   Where any damage is caused to land or chattels by an authority removing or obliterating advertisements under this power, then compensation is payable by anyone suffering damage other than the person displayed the advertisement or caused its display.[41] This is to protect the owner of a building which is fly-posted. The local planning authority may enter land at a reasonable time to exercise this power if the land is unoccupied and it is impossible to exercise the power otherwise.[42] Section 225 gives a power to obliterate or remove: it does not give a power to put another advertisement over the placard or poster. The practice of some local authorities of putting a sticker stating in large letters 'CANCELLED' (sometime with an explanation in very small print that the advertisement is cancelled by the local authority) with the effect of misleading casual readers that the event or product being advertised is cancelled is not authorised under s 225.

18.24   The powers to remove or obliterate advertisements are subject to judicial review. Whether an advertisement is displayed in contravention of the Advertising Regulations is a matter of law and fact to be determined by the court.[43] An advertiser resisting a notice should challenge it by judicial review proceedings in the Administrative Court, seeking an interim injunction under the urgency procedure, rather than by bringing civil proceedings for threatened trespass as the disput[e is essentially a public rather than private law matter.

POWER TO REMOVE STRUCTURES USED FOR UNAUTHORISED DISPLAYS

18.25   The London Local Authorities Act 1995 had included powers to remove unlawful advertising hoardings and the defacement of buildings. These provisions

---

[36]   Town and Country Planning Act 1990, s 225(1). The power does not allow the removal or obliteration of placards or posters displayed within a building to which there is no public right of way (s 225(2)).
[37]   Town and Country Planning Act 1990, s 225(3).
[38]   Town and Country Planning Act 1990, s 225(7), (8).
[39]   Town and Country Planning Act, s 225(3).
[40]   Town and Country Planning Act, s 225(5).
[41]   Town and Country Planning Act, s 225(9), (10). Disputed compensation claims can be referred to the Upper Tribunal (Lands Chamber): Town and Country Planning Act, s 225(11) applying s 118.
[42]   Town and Country Planning Act 1990, s 324(3).
[43]   *R (Maiden Outdoor Advertising Ltd) v London Borough of Lambeth* [2003] EWHC 1224 (Admin), [2004] JPL 820 at paras 35, 36.

were used as the basis for nationwide provisions introduced by the Localism Act 2011. Sections 225A to 225E were inserted into the 1990 Act by the Localism Act and the London legislation repealed.[44] Section 225A applies to display structures which are used for the display of advertisements in breach of the Advertising Regulations. A display structure is:[45]

(a) a hoarding or similar structure used, or designed or adapted for use, for the display of advertisements;

(b) anything (other than a hoarding or similar structure) principally used, or designed or adapted principally for use, for the display of advertisements;

(c) a structure that is itself an advertisement; or

(d) fitments used to support anything within any of paragraphs (a) to (c)

which is used for the display of advertisements which require, but do not have, consent under the Advertising Regulations.

18.26   The authority must first serve a removal notice upon 'a person who appears to the local planning authority to be responsible for the erection or maintenance of the display structure'.[46] This is the person who appear to the local planning authority to be responsible for the erection or maintenance of the display and whose name and address is known by the authority or could be found after reasonable enquiry.[47] The name of the outdoor advertising company is usually displayed on hoardings, otherwise the authority should notify the owner or occupier of the land if they can be found. If no person responsible can be found then the authority must fix a removal notice to the display structure or in the vicinity of the structure and serve a copy on the occupier of the land if they can be identified.[48] A removal notice will state that the display structure is used for advertising in breach of the Advertising Regulations, the authority intend 'after a time specified in the notice to remove the display structure' and that they may recover expenses from a person served with the removal notice unless they show that they were not responsible for the erection or maintenance of the display structure.[49] The time given must be not less than 22 days beginning with the date of the notice[50] (so if a notice is dated Tuesday then last day is Tuesday three weeks later). If the display structure is not removed within the period then the local planning authority may remove and then dispose of the display structure.[51] Compensation is payable for damage caused to land or chattels from the removal, except for damage to the display structure itself and 'damage reasonably caused in removing the display structure'.[52]

---

[44] For the repeal see Localism Act 2011, Sch 25, Pt 19. The new provisions contain a great number of drafting difficulties and uncertainties and would be ripe for an early review and revision by an order under the Legislative and Regulatory Reform Act 2006.

[45] Town and Country Planning Act 1990, s 225A(13),(14). The definition includes moveable structures: s 225A(15).

[46] Town and Country Planning Act 1990, s 225A(3).

[47] Town and Country Planning Act 1990, s 225A(4).

[48] Town and Country Planning Act 1990, s 225A(5), (6).

[49] Town and Country Planning Act 1990, s 225A(11). The notice must state the effect of s 225A(7), (8) which deal with recovery of expenses.

[50] Town and Country Planning Act 1990, s 225A(12).

[51] Town and Country Planning Act 1990, s 225A(1). There is no power to remove a display structure 'in a building to which there is no public right of access': Town and Country Planning Act 1990, s 225A(2).

[52] Town and Country Planning Act 1990, s 225A(9). Compensation is determined by the Upper Tribunal (Lands Chamber): Town and Country Planning Act 1990, s 225A(10), applying s 118.

18.27　A right of appeal to the magistrates' court is introduced by s 225B.[53] This is a change from the London legislation which provided no right of appeal. A person who has been served with a removal notice may appeal on the grounds:[54]

'(a) that the display structure concerned is not used for the display of advertisements in contravention of regulations under section 220;

(b) that there has been some informality, defect or error in, or in connection with, the notice;

(c) that the period between the date of the notice and the time specified in the notice is not reasonably sufficient for the removal of the display structure;

(d) that the notice should have been served on another person.'

In addition, the owner or occupier of the land may appeal, if the notice has been fixed to the structure or exhibited in its vicinity and they were not served with a removal notice, on the grounds that:[55]

'(a) that the display structure concerned is not used for the display of advertisements in contravention of regulations under section 220;

(b) that there has been some informality, defect or error in, or in connection with, the notice;

(c) that the period between the date of the notice and the time specified in the notice is not reasonably sufficient for the removal of the display structure.'

18.28　Section 225B does not state the court's powers on an appeal. Implicitly if the appeal is allowed then the authority has no power to remove the display structure, but no power is given to vary the notice. Appeal grounds (a) ask the court to determine whether the structure is used for the display of advertisements and whether these are in breach of the Advertising Regulations. If the 'informality, defect or error in, or in connection with' the notice is not material then the court must dismiss the appeal on that ground.[56] The absence of an express power to vary causes difficulties if there is a material error which could be corrected or the period for compliance is too short. An appellant who contends that the removal notice should have been served on another person must serve a copy of the notice of appeal on that other person.[57] The court is not given a power to treat that other person as if they have been served, so presumably a successful appeal on this ground will simply identify the right person for the authority to serve notice upon in the future.

18.29　The power to remove a display structure is subject to the right of appeal.[58] Whilst not expressed, the implication is that removal cannot take place whilst an appeal is underway, although unlike most powers, which are suspended in the event of an appeal, this is not on the face of the statute.[59] No time for bringing an appeal is set out, leaving open the questions whether an appeal can be brought after the 22-

---

[53] An appeal would be by way of a complaint: Magistrates' Courts Rules 1981, r 34.

[54] Town and Country Planning Act 1990, s 225B(1).

[55] Town and Country Planning Act 1990, s 225B(3). Such persons are called 'permitted appellants'.

[56] Town and Country Planning Act 1990, s 225B(4). Similar provision is made on other appeals, such as against Town and Country Planning Act 1990 section 215 notices to clear up land.

[57] Town and Country Planning Act 1990, s 225B(5).

[58] Town and Country Planning Act 1990, s 225A(1).

[59] If the removal power is not suspended, then an appellant would need to seek an order under judicial review preventing enforcement whilst the appeal proceeds.

day period has expired and if so, whether such an appeal will suspend the power to remove the structure. If an appeal suspends the power to remove, another uncertainty is whether the power will remain suspended on a further appeal by case stated. If the local planning authority seek to recover the costs of removal from a person served with a removal notice, they may not resist the claim on any of the grounds on which they could have appealed.[60]

REMEDYING PERSISTENT PROBLEMS WITH UNAUTHORISED ADVERTISEMENTS

18.30   Section 225C allows steps to be taken to make it harder for unauthorised advertisements to be displayed on sites where there is a persistent problem. This is intended to be used against buildings and structures that are frequently flyposted. These measures might include the application of coatings to make it harder to affix advertisements or securing a site so it is harder to access. The powers apply:[61]

> 'if the local planning authority for an area in England have reason to believe that there is a persistent problem with the display of unauthorised advertisements on a surface of—
>
> (a)   any building, wall, fence or other structure or erection; or
>
> (b)   any apparatus or plant.'

'Persistent problem' is not defined in the legislation. Persistent would have its normal meaning and would involve some degree of continuing or frequent activity. An issue is what 'problem' is intended to add. It might be said that persistent flyposting is not a problem for the public interest which the planning authority represents, if the advertisements are swiftly removed by the site owner or occupier. An unauthorised advertisement is one in breach of s 224(3) of the Town and Country Planning Act 1990 or s 132 of the Highways Act 1980.[62] The breach must have occurred after the coming into force of this provision on 6 April 2012.[63] The power is concerned with a surface on any building (and so on) so appears to relate to a particular building or structure rather than a type of buildings or structures.

18.31   The authority is empowered to serve an action notice 'requiring the owner or occupier of the land in or on which the surface is situated to carry out the measures specified in the notice by a time specified in the notice'.[64] The measures must be 'reasonable measures to prevent or reduce the frequency of the display of unauthorised advertisements on the surface concerned'.[65] A time period for taking the action must be specified of at least 28 days beginning with the date of the notice.[66] This time may be 'postponed' by the local planning authority, which presumably means a later time for compliance being set. If compliance is to be postponed without setting a new period then the notice ought to be withdrawn. The notice must be served on the

---

[60]   Town and Country Planning Act 1990, s 225B(6).

[61]   Town and Country Planning Act 1990, s 225C(1).

[62]   Highways Act 1980, s 132(1) makes it an offence if a person 'without either the consent of the highway authority for the highway in question or an authorisation given by or under an enactment or a reasonable excuse, paints or otherwise inscribes or affixes any picture, letter, sign or other mark upon the surface of a highway or upon any tree, structure or works on or in a highway'.

[63]   Town and Country Planning Act 1990, s 225C(16).

[64]   Town and Country Planning Act 1990, s 225C(4).

[65]   Town and Country Planning Act 1990, s 225C(6).

[66]   Town and Country Planning Act 1990, s 225C(4), (5).

owner or occupier of the land or, if their name and address cannot be ascertained after reasonable enquiry, fixed to the surface.[67]

18.32　Section 225C has effect subject to the other provisions of town and country planning, historic buildings and ancient monuments legislation and Pt 2 of the Food and Environment Protection Act 1985.[68] Consequently action cannot be taken unless and until it has any necessary planning, listed building or scheduled monument consent. The extent to which an action notice can interfere with rights under planning law which could normally only be removed by a discontinuance order is questionable.[69] Part 2 of the Food and Environment Protection Act 1985 relates to the licensing of deposits at sea and it is not apparent how this might be relevant to an action notice. Since 2011, this regime has been replaced in England and Wales by the Marine and Coastal Access Act 2009.

18.33　If an action notice is served on a statutory undertaker in respect of its operational land, the undertaker may serve a counter-notice within 28 days, being within the date of service of the action notice, 'specifying alternative measures which will in the statutory undertaker's reasonable opinion have the effect of preventing or reducing the frequency of the display of unauthorised advertisements on the surface to at least the same extent as the measures specified in the notice.'[70] A counter-notice has the effect of requiring those measures to be carried out.[71] The council has no right of appeal if it does not accept the counter-notice, but can decline to take any action if the counter-notice is not complied with. If the measures are not carried out in the specified time then the local planning authority may carry out the measures[72] subject to the right of appeal to the magistrates' court.

18.34　Local planning authorities may recover the expense of carrying out the measures from the person who is subject to the action notice unless the surface is part of a flat or dwelling house or is within or part of the boundary of the curtilage of a dwelling house.[73] Dwelling house does not include flats under this provision,[74] so expenses can be recovered in respect of the boundary of a block of flats. The intention is to protect home owners or occupiers from bearing the cost of the authority's works. Compensation is payable for damage caused to the land or chattels by the authority carrying out the measures, except for damage which is reasonably caused.[75]

18.35　A person served with an action notice has a right of appeal to the magistrates' court on the grounds:[76]

---

[67]　Town and Country Planning Act 1990, s 225C(2), (3).

[68]　Town and Country Planning Act 1990, s 225C(8).

[69]　See on section 215 derelict land notices, *Allsop v Derbyshire Dales District Council* [2012] EWHC 3562 (Admin), discussed in Chapter 15.

[70]　Town and Country Planning Act 1990, s 225E(2).

[71]　Town and Country Planning Act 1990, s 225E(3).

[72]　Town and Country Planning Act 1990, s 225C(10).

[73]　Town and Country Planning Act 1990, s 225C(10)(b), (14). The Public Health Act 1875, sections 275 and 291 provisions on recovery of expenses apply: Town and Country Planning Act 1990, s 225C(15). In proceedings for the recovery of expenses from a person served with an action notice, that person may not raise any question which could have been raised on appeal: Town and Country Planning Act 1990, s 225D(5).

[74]　Town and Country Planning Act 1990, s 225C(16)

[75]　Town and Country Planning Act 1990, s 225C(12). Compensation is determined by the Upper Tribunal (Lands Chamber): Town and Country Planning Act 1990, s 225C(13), applying s 118.

[76]　Town and Country Planning Act 1990, s 225D(1).

'(a) that there is no problem with the display of unauthorised advertisements on the surface concerned or any such problem is not a persistent one;

(b) that there has been some informality, defect or error in, or in connection with, the notice;

(c) that the time within which the measures specified in the notice are to be carried out is not reasonably sufficient for the purpose;

(d) that the notice should have been served on another person.'

The owner or occupier of premises including the surface on which an action notice has been fixed may appeal on these grounds:[77]

'(a) that there is no problem with the display of unauthorised advertisements on the surface concerned or any such problem is not a persistent one;

(b) that there has been some informality, defect or error in, or in connection with, the notice;

(c) that the time within which the measures specified in the notice are to be carried out is not reasonably sufficient for the purpose.'

18.36   It is not a ground of appeal that no action should have been taken even though there was a persistent problem or that other steps should have been required, although the lawfulness of the notice can be challenged in the appeal.[78] There are similarities with s 225B appeals, discussed above. An appeal would only succeed against a material informality, defect or error.[79] On a ground (d) appeal, the appellant has to serve the person they consider ought to have been served with the notice.[80]

DEFACEMENT OF PREMISES

18.37   An advertisement has a purpose of advertising something, whether it is authorised by the owner of the site or is fly-posted without consent. Graffiti will only occasionally be an advertisement but is more harmful to visual amenity. Property owners will sometimes lack the energy to clean off graffiti. The Localism Act 2011 introduced new powers in England to require 'signs' to be removed from premises in ss 225F to 225I. 'Signs' are defined as:[81]

'(a) includes any writing, letter, picture, device or representation, but

(b) does not include an advertisement'.

The definition is both non-exclusive ('includes') and exclusionary (not including an advertisement). Graffiti would be a sign, as would be a message which was not an advertisement.

18.38   Section 225F provides powers to local planning authorities where a sign is on a 'surface that is readily visible from a place to which the public have access' and

---

[77]   Town and Country Planning Act 1990, s 225D(2).
[78]   As with section 215 derelict land notices: *R v Oxford Crown Court ex p Smith* (1990) 154 JP 422.
[79]   Town and Country Planning Act 1990, s 225D(3).
[80]   Town and Country Planning Act 1990, s 225D(4).
[81]   Town and Country Planning Act 1990, s 225F(12).

they 'consider the sign to be detrimental to the amenity of the area or offensive'.[82] Offensive must be understood in a way which is compatible with the right to freedom of expression under Art 10 of the European Convention on Human Rights. The authority may then serve a notice on the occupier of the premises[83] requiring the sign to be removed or obliterated within a period of not less than 15 days beginning with the date of service of the notice.[84] If there appears to be no occupier, then a notice can be fixed to the surface, requiring the owner or occupier to remove or obliterate the sign within the same period.[85] There is no prescribed form for a notice, but it must identify the surface and the sign, the statutory powers relied upon, who has served or fixed the notice, who is required to remove or obliterate the sign and the period within which to do it. Whilst not a statutory requirement, contact details for the authority should be included, along with an explanation of the right of appeal. If the work is not done within the time specified then the authority may remove or obliterate the sign, subject to a right of appeal, and recover the cost from the person required by the notice to do the work.[86] However the cost cannot be recovered were the surface forms part of a flat or dwelling house, is within the curtilage of or is part of the boundary of a dwelling house.[87]

18.39   Statutory undertakers have a considerable number of buildings and structures that are unoccupied and so particularly vulnerable to graffiti, such as sub-stations and telecommunications cabinet boxes in streets.[88] Special provision is made to limit their responsibilities. First, s 225F only applies if the surface 'abuts on, or is one to which access is given directly from, either (a) a street; or (b) any place, other than a street, to which the public have access as of right'.[89] Specific protection is given to universal postal service providers (in practice, Royal Mail). They are treated as being the occupier of any universal postal service letter box or a universal postal service pouch box which belongs to them.[90] Consequently notice must be served on the provider,[91] rather than simply affixed to the surface. A letter box is what is ordinarily referred to as a post box, where people put letters to be sent through the post. A pouch box is a fixed box where post is left by Royal Mail for their staff to replenish their bags whilst delivering the post. A minimum 28-day period is given for universal postal service providers to remove or obliterate signs.[92]

18.40   Similarly, notice must be given to statutory undertakers in respect of their bus shelters or other street furniture that is not on their operational land (so usually on the highway).[93] Again, they have a period of 28 days to remove or obliterate any identified sign.[94] These notices may be appealed to the magistrates' court: s 225(1).

---

[82]   Town and Country Planning Act 1990, s 225F(1).
[83]   Premises is defined widely as 'building, wall, fence or other structure or erection, or apparatus or plan': Town and Country Planning Act 1990, s 225F(12).
[84]   Town and Country Planning Act 1990, s 225F(2), (4).
[85]   Town and Country Planning Act 1990, s 225F(3), (4).
[86]   Town and Country Planning Act 1990, s 225F(6).
[87]   Town and Country Planning Act 1990, s 225F(8).
[88]   Statutory undertakers are defined as 'enactment to carry on any railway, light railway, tramway, road transport, water transport, canal, inland navigation, dock, harbour, pier or lighthouse undertaking or any undertaking for the supply of hydraulic power and a relevant airport operator' and universal postal service providers for these purposes: Town and Country Planning Act 1990, s 262(1), (5B).
[89]   Town and Country Planning Act 1990, s 225F(11).
[90]   Town and Country Planning Act 1990, s 225F(10).
[91]   Town and Country Planning Act 1990, s 225G(1).
[92]   Town and Country Planning Act 1990, s 225G(1)(b).
[93]   Town and Country Planning Act 1990, s 225H(1).
[94]   Town and Country Planning Act 1990, s 225H(1)(c).

A person served with a notice, or the owner or occupier where the notice has been fixed to the surface may appeal on the following grounds:[95]

'(a) that the sign concerned is neither detrimental to the amenity of the area nor offensive;

(b) that there has been some informality, defect or error in, or in connection with, the notice;

(c) that the time within which the sign concerned is to be removed or obliterated is not reasonably sufficient for the purpose;'

Additionally a person served may appeal on ground (d) 'that the notice should have been served on another person'. The appellant must serve a copy of the notice of appeal on that person.[96] Appeals on the basis of an informality, defect or error will not succeed if the error was not material.[97] In responding to a claim for the recovery of expenses, a person may not raise matters that could have been raised on an appeal.[98]

Removal of signs at the owner or occupier's request

18.41   Local planning authorities are empowered to remove or obliterate signs at the request of the owner or occupier of the premises and recover the expense of doing so: s 225J. The power applies to signs that are readily visible from a place to which the public have access.[99] Premises means building, wall, fence or other structure or erection, or apparatus or plant.[100] The definition of 'sign' is wider than in s 225F. Sign includes 'any writing, letter, picture, device or representation' and any advertisement, except an advertisement which has express or deemed consent.[101]

Powers of entry onto operational land

18.42   The local authority powers to enter land to remove display structures (s 225A), take steps to discourage unlawful advertisements (s 225C) and remove or obliterate signs (s 225F) are restricted with respect to the operational land of statutory undertakers.[102] These restrictions also apply to the right of entry to investigate the possible use of these powers.[103] The powers of entry may only be exercised if:[104]

'(a) the authority has served on the statutory undertaker notice of the authority's intention to do so;

(b) the notice specified the display structure, surface or sign concerned and its location; and

(c) the period of 28 days beginning with the date of service of the notice has ended.'

---

[95]   Town and Country Planning Act 1990, s 225I(1) (for persons served), (2) (when the notice is fixed).
[96]   Town and Country Planning Act 1990, s 225I(4).
[97]   Town and Country Planning Act 1990, s 225I(3).
[98]   Town and Country Planning Act 1990, s 225I(5).
[99]   Town and Country Planning Act 1990, s 225J(1).
[100]   Town and Country Planning Act 1990, s 225J(3).
[101]   Town and Country Planning Act 1990, s 225J(4).
[102]   This protection for statutory undertakers does not apply to airport operators: Town and Country Planning Act 1990, s 225K(7).
[103]   The right of entry will be under the Town and Country Planning Act 1990, s 324(3).
[104]   Town and Country Planning Act 1990, s 225K(2).

The statutory undertaker may serve a counternotice within that period prohibiting the entry or specifying conditions under which the entry may be carried out.[105] Entry may be prohibited if:[106]

'the statutory undertaker has reasonable grounds to believe, for reasons connected with the operation of its undertaking, that the power cannot be exercised under the circumstances in question—

(a) without risk to the safety of any person; or

(b) without unreasonable risk to the efficient and economic operation of the statutory undertaker's undertaking.'

The undertaker may impose conditions which are:[107]

'(a) necessary or expedient in the interests of safety or the efficient and economic operation of the undertaking concerned; or

(b) for the protection of any works, apparatus or other property not vested in the statutory undertaker which are lawfully present on, in, under or over the land upon which entry is proposed to be made.'

ADVERTISING CONTROL ENFORCEMENT

18.43 The Secretary of State is empowered to provide in the Advertising Regulations for the removal of advertisements, or the discontinuance of a use for advertisements, which are in breach of the regulations.[108] This power can include applying the enforcement notice and stop notice provisions to advertising control. These powers have not been exercised, presumably because the enforcement powers in Pt VII of the Act are generally applicable in any event.

ENFORCEMENT REMEDIES

18.44 The conventional planning enforcement remedies in Pt VII apply to most breaches of advertising control. The erection or fixing of an advertising hoarding or sign may amount to a building operation.[109] Use of land for the display of advertisements may amount to a material change of use. It is specifically provided in s 55(5) of the 1990 Act that:

'the use for the display of advertisements of any external part of a building which is not normally used for that purpose shall be treated for the purposes of this section as involving a material change in the use of that part of the building'.

Where the display of advertisements is in accordance with the Advertising Regulations, planning permission is deemed to be granted.[110] Consequentially, enforcement and stop notices can be served where advertising consent is not obtained

---

[105] Town and Country Planning Act 1990, s 225K(5) and (3) respectively.
[106] Town and Country Planning Act 1990, s 225K(6).
[107] Town and Country Planning Act 1990, s 225K(4).
[108] Town and Country Planning Act 1990, s 224.
[109] *Howell v Sunbury-on-Thames Urban District Council* (1963) 62 LGR 119.
[110] Town and Country Planning Act 1990, s 222.

and development has taken place. Once an advertisement contravenes the Advertising Regulations the question is whether there is a breach of planning control, which has not become lawful by passage of time. In this context it should be noted that the display of a different form of advertising (eg three-sided revolving displays rather than flat hoardings) can amount to a different activity for a stop notice.[111]

INJUNCTIONS

18.45   Injunctions are available under s 222 of the Local Government Act 1972 to restrain breaches of the Advertising Regulations. These are subject to the limitations *in City of London Corporation v Bovis Constructions Ltd*[112] discussed in Chapter 14 above. If the advertising contravention is also a breach of planning control, then injunctions can be obtained under s 187B of the 1990 Act. Due to the overlapping jurisdictions, it may be appropriate to seek an injunction under both sections.

---

[111]   *Arora v Hackney London Borough Council* (1991) 155 JP 808.
[112]   [1992] 3 All ER 697, CA.

Chapter 19

Planning Obligations

19.01   Planning obligations are made by persons to impose obligations on their interests in land for planning purposes. These are normally entered into by developers to resolve problems connected with a development and so get planning permission. For example, they may provide for the setting out of open space or the provision of affordable housing as part of a private housing development. Alternatively money could be paid to the local authority to subsidise a bus service to reduce car travel to a new shopping development. Planning obligations are made under s 106 of the Town and Country Planning Act 1990 and are also commonly referred to as section 106 obligations. These provisions were substantially recast by the Planning and Compensation Act 1991.

OLD PLANNING AGREEMENTS

19.02   The first form of planning obligation was agreements made under s 34 of the Town and Country Planning Act 1932. The effect of these agreements has been preserved[1] and despite their considerable antiquity some remain in force. The 1947 Town and Country Planning Act introduced a form of planning agreement which remained essentially unchanged until 1992. These agreements are most commonly section 52 agreements under the Town and Country Planning Act 1971. Section 106 agreements made prior to 25 October 1991 are under the original form of legislation and are changed and enforced in the same way as section 52 agreements. These old planning agreements are enforceable by normal contractual remedies. Normally the appropriate remedy is an injunction although specific performance or damages might be appropriate in some cases.[2] The local planning authority need not use other planning enforcement powers (if any are available) before seeking to use contractual remedies.[3] These earlier agreements do run with the land so can be enforced against successors in title. There are no statutory remedies available to the local planning authority.

POST-1991 ACT PLANNING OBLIGATIONS

19.03   A planning obligation can be entered into by persons interested in land unilaterally or by agreement with a local planning authority for the area. An obligation is made by deed and is:[4]

---

[1]   Town and Country Planning Act 1971, Sch 24, para 88; Planning (Consequential Provisions) Act 1990, Sch 3, para 3.
[2]   Such agreements could not provide for the payment of money so concerned something happening or not happening on the land.
[3]   *Avon County Council v Millard* (1985) 50 P & CR 275.
[4]   Town and Country Planning Act 1990, s 106(1). For the scope of planning obligations see *Westminster City Council v Secretary of State for Communities and Local Government* [2013] EWHC 690 (Admin) and *R (Holder) v Gedling Borough Council* [2013] EWHC 1611 (Admin).

'(a) restricting the development or use of the land in any specified way;

(b) requiring specified operations or activities to be carried out in, on, under or over the land;

(c) requiring the land to be used in any specified way; or

(d) requiring a sum or sums to be paid to the authority (or, in a case where section 2E applies, to the Greater London Authority) on a specified date or dates or periodically.'

The obligation is enforceable by the relevant local planning authority against the person entering into the obligation and any person deriving title from him.[5] Enforcement can take place under statutory powers in s 106 and by contractual rights. The obligation is subject to the normal legal remedies for enforcing contracts and deeds. Additionally, 'a restriction or requirement imposed under a planning obligation is enforceable by injunction'.[6] Unless significant factual disputes are anticipated, proceedings would usually be brought by a Pt 8 claim form. An interim injunction was sought by the local planning authority under this subsection in *Hertsmere Borough Council v Brent Walker Group plc.*[7] The court accepted an equivalent undertaking from the defendants.

19.04 If any requirement in a planning obligation to carry out operations in, on, under or over the subject land is breached, the local planning authority may (s 106(6)):

'(a) enter the land and carry out the operations; and

(b) recover from the person or persons against whom the obligation is enforceable any expenses reasonably incurred by them in doing so.'

The power to enter is exercisable on 21 days' notice.[8] It is an offence, punishable by a level 3 (£1,000) fine on summary conviction to obstruct a person exercising this power.[9] Regulations may provide for charging on the land of sums required to be paid under a planning obligation or expenses recoverable under subsection (6)(b), but these have never been made.[10]

THE LANDOWNER'S RESPONSE TO PLANNING OBLIGATION PROCEEDINGS

19.05 The landowner's response to actual or threatened proceedings or direct action on a planning obligation or agreement may involve the following aspects:

(a) consideration of whether the obligation has been breached. The timing or conditions for carrying out obligations may be complex. Some obligations provide that the payment of money is only required if there is a particular need – there may be a question whether such a need arises;

---

[5] Town and Country Planning Act 1990, s 106(3).
[6] Town and Country Planning Act 1990, s 106(5).
[7] [1994] 1 PLR 1.
[8] Town and Country Planning Act 1990, s 106(7).
[9] Town and Country Planning Act 1990, s 106(8).
[10] Town and Country Planning Act 1990, s 106(12).

(b) any dispute resolution procedure (such as arbitration or expert determination) and whether it can be insisted upon;[11]

(c) whether to bring civil proceedings to enforce obligations owing to the owner (such as the repayment of unspent sums) or to seek a declaration that there is no breach;

(d) a challenge by judicial review to the exercise of the discretion to enforce the obligation, although the record of such challenges is not good;[12] and

(e) if the concern is that there is a breach but it is considered that the obligation ought not to apply or be changed, then the best route for a landowner is to try to have the obligation changed. A person subject to an obligation can apply to the local planning authority for the obligation's modification or discharge subject to certain time limits before the application can be made.[13] If refused, the application may be appealed to the Secretary of State or Welsh Ministers.[14] Where it is too early to make an application, the person may ask the local planning authority (and any other parties) to agree to change the obligation. A refusal by the authority to agree is subject to judicial review on the usual public law grounds.[15]

THIRD PARTIES

19.06   A planning obligation does not give any rights to persons who are not parties to it or against whom it is not enforceable. If such a person, such as a neighbouring landowner, considers that an obligation is not being enforced when it ought to be, their remedy is to seek judicial review of the local planning authority's failure to act rather than a declaration in ordinary civil proceedings.[16] Whilst an authority has a discretion whether and how to enforce, there will often be an underlying disagreement about the meaning of the obligation or the approach to enforcement which can be determined by the Administrative Court.

---

[11]   Local planning authorities will often (quite reasonably) insist that alternative dispute resolution clauses are without prejudice to their powers to bring proceedings or take direct action under s 106.

[12]   *R (Renaissance Habitat Ltd) v West Berkshire Council* [2011] EWHC 242 (Admin), [2011] JPL 1209; *R (Millgate Developments Ltd) v Wokingham Council* [2011] EWCA Civ 1062, [2012] JPL 258.

[13]   Town and Country Planning Act, s 106A. Applications can be made after five years from the making of the obligation (s 106A(4)(b)) and applications in respect of pre-7 April 2010 obligations can be made at any time in England: Town and Country Planning (Modification and Discharge of Planning Obligations) Regulations 1992, reg 2A.

[14]   Town and Country Planning Act 1990, s 106B. An application to the High Court can be made against the appeal decision by judicial review.

[15]   *R (Batchelor Enterprises Ltd) v North Dorset District Council* [2003] EWHC 3006 (Admin), [2004] JPL 1222.

[16]   *Milebush Properties Ltd v Tameside Metropolitan Borough Council* [2010] EWHC 1022 (Ch), [2010] JPL 1303.

Chapter 20

Hazardous Substances

20.01　The hazardous substances regime in the planning process is unusual and to a degree, anomalous. It requires consent for the presence of particular hazardous substances above the relevant controlled quantity. It is separate from planning control over the use of the land involving those substances or the construction of stores or manufacturing equipment to use the substances. It is also separate from the various environmental regimes, such as environmental permitting or the Control of Major Accident Hazards, which may also relate to the substance and its use. It is the presence of the hazardous substance on, over or under land that requires the consent of the hazardous substances authority: s 4 of the Planning (Hazardous Substances) Act 1990 ('the Hazardous Substances Act'). Various exceptions apply, such as the temporary presence of substances being transported.

20.02　The hazardous substances authority is the relevant district or unitary council, except for land which is used for the winning or working of minerals or for waste disposal when any county council for the area is the hazardous substances authority. The Broads Authority, urban development corporations, Mayoral development corporations, housing action trusts and the Homes and Communities Agency are hazardous substances authorities for their areas subject to a country council having responsibility for a minerals or waste site.[1] National park authorities are hazardous substances authorities for all matters within their areas.[2] Hazardous substances are prescribed by the Planning (Hazardous Substances) Regulations 1992[3] and include ammonia, sulphur dioxide and hydrogen. Guidance is given by Circular 04/00 *Planning Controls for Hazardous Substances*.

ENFORCEMENT OF THE HAZARDOUS SUBSTANCES REGIME

20.03　The hazardous substances regime can be enforced by prosecution, injunction or requiring steps to be taken under contravention notices.

Prosecution

20.04　Breach of the hazardous substances regime gives rise to immediate criminal liability. The offence occurs when there is a 'contravention of hazardous substances control',[4] which is defined as:[5]

---

[1]　Hazardous Substances Act, s 3.
[2]　Environment Act 1995, Sch 9 para 14.
[3]　SI 1992/656
[4]　Hazardous Substances Act, s 23(1).
[5]　Hazardous Substances Act, s 23(2).

'(a) if a quantity of a hazardous substances equal to or exceeding the controlled quantity is or has been present on, over or under land and either—

  (i) there is no hazardous substances consent for the presence of the substance; or

  (ii) there is hazardous substances consent for its presence but the quantity present exceeds the maximum quantity permitted by the consent;

(b) if there is or has been a failure to comply with a condition subject to which a hazardous substances consent was granted.'

An offence would be committed by 'the appropriate person'. If the contravention is having too much hazardous substance on the site (the para (a) contravention), then an offence is committed by any person 'knowingly causing the substance to be present on, over or under the land' or 'allowing it to be so present' as well as by the person in control of the land.[6] The person in control of the land is also guilty of an offence if there is a failure to comply with a condition attached to a hazardous substances consent (para (b)).

20.05 There are several defences, which must be proved by the defendant on the balance of probabilities. Defences which are applicable to either contravention are:[7]

'(a) that he took all reasonable precautions and exercised all due diligence to avoid commission of the offence, or

(b) that commission of the offence could be avoided only by the taking of action amounting to a breach of a statutory duty'.

Where the allegation is that there was no hazardous substances consent it is a defence to prove:

'that at the time of the alleged commission of the offence he did not know, and had no reason to believe ... that the substance was present; or ... that it was present in a quantity equal to or exceeding the controlled quantity'.[8]

If the quantity of the hazardous substance exceeded that allowed by a consent then it is a defence to show that there was no knowledge or reason to believe that 'the substance was present in a quantity exceeding the maximum quantity permitted by the consent'.[9] Where a failure to comply with a condition is alleged, then it is defence to:

'prove that he did not know, and had no reason to believe, that there was a failure to comply with a condition subject to which hazardous substances consent had been granted'.[10]

The offence is punishable by a fine of up to £20,000 on summary conviction and an unlimited fine on indictment.[11] As with other planning offences, the court is required to have regard to any financial benefit from the offence.[12]

---

[6]   Hazardous Substances Act, s 23(3).
[7]   Hazardous Substances Act, s 23(5).
[8]   Hazardous Substances Act, s 23(6)(a).
[9]   Hazardous Substances Act, s 23(6)(b).
[10] Hazardous Substances Act, s 23(7).
[11] Hazardous Substances Act, s 23(4).
[12] Hazardous Substances Act, s 23(4A).

Hazardous substances contravention notices

20.06   The hazardous substances authority is provided with an equivalent mechanism to enforcement notices by issuing hazardous substances contravention notices under s 24.The notice will specify the alleged contravention of hazardous substance control and the steps required to remedy it in whole or part.[13] These may include requiring that the hazardous substances be removed from the land or directing that a hazardous substances consent shall cease to have effect either generally or in respect of particular substances at the end of a specified period.[14] The notice can, therefore, terminate a consent without compensation. As with enforcement notices, the contravention notice has to contain a period in which to take effect and a period from that point for compliance with each of its steps.[15] Notices are required to identify the land to which they relate.[16] A copy of a notice is required to be served on the owner of the land, any other person who appears to be in control of the land and any other person having an interest in the land that the authority considers to be materially affected by the notice.[17] A statement of the reasons for issuing the notice and the right of appeal must accompany any copy of the notice.[18]

20.07   An appeal may be brought to the Secretary of State under s 174 of the Town and Country Planning Act 1990 as modified for hazardous substances.[19] The grounds of appeal are:

(a) that, in respect of any contravention of hazardous substances control specified in the notice, hazardous substances consent ought to be granted for the quantity of the hazardous substance present on, over or under the land or, as the case may be, the condition concerned ought to be discharged;

(b) that the matters alleged to constitute a contravention of hazardous substances control have not occurred;

(c) that those matters (if they occurred) do not constitute a contravention of hazardous substances control;

(d) that copies of the hazardous substances contravention notice were not served as required by or under s 24(4) of the Planning (Hazardous Substances) Act 1990;

(e) that the steps required by the notice to be taken exceed what is necessary to remedy any contravention of hazardous substances control;

(f) that any period specified in the notice in accordance with s 24(5)(b) of that Act falls short of what should reasonably be allowed.

There is no recommended appeal form.[20] The appellant has to send the notice of appeal with grounds and submissions to the Secretary of State or Welsh Ministers

---

[13] Hazardous Substances Act, s 24(1).
[14] Hazardous Substances Act, s 24(6), (7).
[15] Hazardous Substances Act, s 24(5).
[16] Planning (Hazardous Substances) Regulations 1992, reg 17(1).
[17] Hazardous Substances Act, s 24(4); Planning (Hazardous Substances) Regulations 1992, reg 17(2). The authority is also encouraged to liaise with the Health and Safety Executive prior to issuing a notice and so send a copy to the HSE Area Office for information: Circular 04/00, para 108.
[18] Planning (Hazardous Substances) Regulations 1992, reg 17(3).
[19] Modified by the Planning (Hazardous Substances) Regulations 1992, reg 18 and Sch 4.
[20] There is no specific guidance on hazardous substance contravention notice appeals, beyond brief text in Circular 04/00 at paras 107 and 112.

and copy this to the hazardous substances authority.[21] The appeal notice should be sent to the Bristol or Cardiff office of the Planning Inspectorate, as appropriate. The authority have 28 days to respond with their submissions on each ground of appeal and say whether consent should be granted and any conditions which ought to be applied to any consent.[22] Within that period the authority has to give notice of the appeal to occupiers of properties in the locality of the site.[23]

20.08　The provisions in the Town and Country Planning Act 1990 on direction action by authorities, prosecution for failure to comply with an enforcement notice and the effect of subsequent consents or breaches are applied with modifications to hazardous substances contravention notices.[24]

Injunctions

20.09　An equivalent injunction power to s 187B of the Town and Country Planning Act 1990 is provided for actual or apprehended contraventions of hazardous substances control: s 26AA. An injunction may be sought:[25]

> 'Where a hazardous substances authority consider it necessary or expedient for any actual or apprehended contravention of hazardous substances control to be restrained by injunction, they may apply to the court for an injunction, whether or not they have exercised or are proposing to exercise any of their other powers under this Act.'

The court may grant such an injunction as it thinks appropriate for the purpose of restraining the contravention.[26] An application would be considered on the same principles,[27] although interim applications are more likely to be treated as urgent and thus made without notice.

---

[21]　Town and Country Planning Act 1990, s 174(3),(4) (as modified) and Planning (Hazardous Substances) Regulations 1992, reg 19(1).
[22]　Planning (Hazardous Substances) Regulations 1992, reg 19(2).
[23]　Planning (Hazardous Substances) Regulations 1992, reg 19(3).
[24]　Town and Country Planning Act 1990, ss178–181, modified by Planning (Hazardous Substances) Regulations 1992, reg 20 and Sch 4, Pt 2.
[25]　Hazardous Substances Act, s 26AA(1).
[26]　Hazardous Substances Act, s 26AA(2).
[27]　See Chapter 14 above.

Chapter 21

Nationally Significant Infrastructure Projects

OUTLINE OF THE DEVELOPMENT CONSENT REGIME

21.01   The Planning Act 2008 introduced a new development consent regime for certain major infrastructure projects, such as large power stations, power lines, very substantial highways works, railways, harbours, airports and hazardous waste facilities. Nationally significant infrastructure projects are defined.[1] These replaced, at least to a degree, approval by various specialist consent regimes and deemed planning permission, or the grant of planning permission on an express application. For schemes falling within the categories in the Planning Act 2008, 'development consent' is required 'for development to the extent that the development is or forms part of a nationally significant infrastructure project'.[2] Development has the same definition as in s 55 of the Town and Country Planning Act 1990 with several specific additions, in particular (to the extent that they would not be otherwise) the conversion of a power station, underground gas storage, increases in the permitted use of an airport and:[3]

'(a)   works for the demolition of a listed building or its alteration or extension in a manner which would affect its character as a building of special architectural or historic interest;

(b)   demolition of a building in a conservation area;

(c)   works resulting in the demolition or destruction of or any damage to a scheduled monument;

(d)   works for the purpose of removing or repairing a scheduled monument or any part of it;

(e)   works for the purpose of making any alterations or additions to a scheduled monument;

(f)   flooding or tipping operations on land in, on or under which there is a scheduled monument.'

If development consent is required under the Planning Act 2008, then there is no requirement for planning permission, various specialist consents[4] and (in England) listed building, conservation area or scheduled monument consent.[5] Approval is given in the form of an 'order granting development consent',[6] which is more usually referred to as a development consent order.

---

[1]   Planning Act 2008, Pt 3, as amended by the Growth and Infrastructure Act 2013, ss 26, 27.
[2]   Planning Act 2008, s 31.
[3]   Planning Act 2008, s 32(2), (3).
[4]   Such as constructing generating stations under the Electricity Act 1989, s 36.
[5]   Planning Act 2008, s 33(1).
[6]   See Planning Act 2008, Pt 7.

ENFORCEMENT OF THE DEVELOPMENT CONSENT REGIME

21.02   The development consent regime is enforced by mechanisms which are reasonably similar to those used in the rest of the planning system. The main changes are:

(a) immediate criminal liability applies to any breaches; and

(b) a notice requiring compliance may only be served after conviction, cannot be appealed but does not lead to fresh criminal liability.

Enforcement is the responsibility of the district planning authority unless any of the relevant development is the construction or alteration of a hazardous waste facility within the development consent regime, in which case the county planning authority has enforcement powers.[7]

Criminal offences

21.03   It is an offence to carry out development without development consent. Section 160(1) provides:

'A person commits an offence if the person carries out, or causes to be carried out, development for which development consent is required at a time when no development consent is in force in respect of the development.'

Breach of a development consent order is dealt with by s 161(1):

'A person commits an offence if without reasonable excuse the person—

(a) carries out, or causes to be carried out, development in breach of the terms of an order granting development consent, or

(b) otherwise fails to comply with the terms of an order granting development consent.'

This offence does not apply to conditions applied to deemed marine licences contained within a development consent order.[8] A reasonable excuse defence therefore applies. It is also a defence to a breach of a development consent order to prove that 'the breach or failure to comply occurred only because of an error or omission in the order' and that error or omission has been corrected by notice.[9] The section 160 and 161 offences are triable either way, so in the magistrates' court or the Crown Court.[10]

21.04   Time limits for taking action are imposed and these are derived from the approach in the Town and Country Planning Act 1990. However as control is imposed by the criminal law, offences operate in an unusual fashion. Ordinarily there is no time limit for bringing a prosecution for an either way offence. However for these offences any charge must be brought within 'the relevant 4-year period' or any 'extended period' which applies.[11] The relevant four-year period means:[12]

---

[7] Planning Act 2008, s 173.
[8] Planning Act 2008, ss 145(4), 161(2).
[9] Planning Act 2008, s 161(3). Implicitly the defence arises where the correction will have been made after the offence is alleged to have been committed. There would be no breach of the order if the correction had taken place beforehand.
[10] Planning Act 2008, ss 160(2) and 161(3) respectively.
[11] Planning Act 2008, s 162(1).
[12] Planning Act 2008, s 162(2).

'(a) in the case of an offence under section 160, the period of 4 years beginning with the date on which the development was substantially completed;

(b) in the case of an offence under section 161, the period of 4 years beginning with the later of—

(i) the date on which the development was substantially completed, and

(ii) the date on which the breach or failure to comply occurred.'

'Substantially completed' echoes the four-year time limit from when 'operations were substantially completed' in s 171B(1) of the Town and Country Planning Act 1990,[13] but the development consent time limit applies to substantial completion of the development rather than the operations. Where the development has a period between the completion of physical works and the full bringing into use of the facility then the paragraph (a) or (b)(i) time limit might expire four years from the later date. Paragraph (b)(ii) raises questions if there is a continuing breach: whether any prosecution has to be brought within four years of the start of the breach or merely relates to the elements of the breach within the four year period. Depending upon the particular circumstances, a breach may be a single event that is then unremediated, a continuous breach or a series of individual breaches.

21.05 The extended period applies:[14]

'if during the relevant 4-year period—

(a) an information notice has been served under section 167, or

(b) an injunction has been applied for under section 171.'

The extended period is a four-year period from the later of the service of the information notice or the application for the injunction.[15] The section is silent as to what the information notice or injunction must relate. Logically it must relate to the particular development or development consent order. The question then is how precisely it must relate to the particular offence. Action in respect of an entirely separate breach of an order does not appear to be a sound basis for extending time, yet an information notice may be in broad terms. The maximum sentence for either offence is on summary conviction a £50,000 fine, or an unlimited fine on indictment.[16]

OBTAINING INFORMATION

Right to enter land

21.06 The local planning authority has a right to enter land without a warrant, at any reasonable hour, if it has reasonable grounds for suspecting that an offence under ss 160 or 161 is being, or has been, committed on the land.[17] The breach must be

---

[13] See Chapter 3 and *Sage v Secretary of State for the Environment, Transport and the Regions* [2003] UKHL 22, [2003] 1 WLR 983.

[14] Planning Act 2008, s 162(3).

[15] Planning Act 2008, s 162(4).

[16] Planning Act 2008, ss 160(2) and 161(3) respectively. The magistrates' court fine would become unlimited when the Legal Aid, Sentencing and Punishment of Offenders Act 2012, s 85 is brought into force.

[17] Planning Act 2008, s 163(1), (2). There are separate powers of entry for surveying in connection with proposed orders: Planning Act 2008, s 53.

suspected on the land that is being entered. The occupier has to be given 24 hours' notice before entry into a building used as a dwelling house.[18] A warrant may be obtained from a justice of the peace if it is shown on a sworn information that there are reasonable grounds for suspecting an offence and admission to the land has been refused, or a refusal is reasonably apprehended, or the case is one of urgency.[19] There is a statutory assumption that 'admission to land is to be regarded as having been refused if no reply is received to a request for admission within a reasonable period'.[20]

21.07   A warrant authorises entry on one occasion only, within a month of the issue of the warrant, and at a reasonable hour (except in an urgent case).[21] A person authorised to enter (with or without a warrant) must be able to produce evidence of authority and must state the purpose of the entry if required. They may take onto the land such other persons as may be necessary. If no owner or occupier was present at the time, the land must be left as secure against trespassers as it was.[22] It is an offence, punishable by a level 3 (£1,000) fine on summary conviction, if a person 'wilfully obstructs a person acting in the exercise of a relevant right of entry'.[23] The local planning authority are liable to pay compensation for any damage caused to land or chattels in the exercise of a right of entry.[24] These rights of entry do not apply to Crown land.[25]

POWER TO REQUIRE INFORMATION

21.08   The local planning authority can serve 'information notices' to require answers to questions. These are similar to planning contravention notices.[26] An information notice may be served 'in relation to any land if it appears to the relevant local planning authority that an offence under section 160 or 161 may have been committed on or in respect of the land': Planning Act 2008, s 167(1), (2). The notice may be served on the owner or occupier of the land or a person with any other interest in it or a person carrying out operations on the land or using it for any purpose.[27] Required information will be specified in the notice within the categories of:[28]

'(a) information about any operations being carried out in, on, over or under the land, any use of the land and any other activities being carried out in, on, over or under the land, and

(b) information about the provisions of any order granting development consent for development of the land.'

Compliance with the notice would be by giving the required information to the authority in writing.[29] It is a summary offence 'if without reasonable excuse the

---

[18] Planning Act 2008, s 163(3).
[19] Planning Act 2008, s 164(1), (2).
[20] Planning Act 2008, s 164(4).
[21] Planning Act 2008, s 164(5).
[22] Planning Act 2008, s 165(1).
[23] Planning Act 2008, s 165(2), (3).
[24] Planning Act 2008, s 165(4). Disputes about compensation are to be resolved by the Upper Tribunal (Lands Chamber): Planning Act 2008, s 165(5), (6).
[25] Planning Act 2008, s 166. Crown land is defined in Planning Act 2008, s 227 in similar manner to the Town and Country Planning Act 1990 definition.
[26] See Chapter 5 above.
[27] Planning Act 2008, s 167(3).
[28] Planning Act 2008, s 167(4).
[29] Planning Act 2008, s 167(6)

person fails to comply with any requirement of an information notice' before 'the end of the period of 21 days beginning with the day on which the information notice is served'.[30] It is implicit that the person required to comply with the notice is the person on whom it was served.[31]

21.09   Section 167(4) says that an information notice 'may' require the information listed above. However it can hardly be an information notice if it does not require information. Since a notice will compel the provision of information under pain of criminal sanction, the powers are probably confined to seeking such information, although those categories are themselves broad. The purpose of an information notice must be in connection with enforcement of the development consent regime, as that is the trigger for the power arising. Notwithstanding the breadth of development or use, it would be acting for an improper purpose to use information notices to investigate breaches of other regimes. The relationship of information notices with the privilege against self-incrimination will need to be considered. Self-incrimination is not addressed in the legislation, although the reasonable excuse defence exists. In *R v Hertfordshire County Council ex p Green Environmental Industries Ltd,*[32] a company was required to provide answers under an Environmental Protection Act 1990 notice as they requested factual information rather than sought an admission of wrongdoing. Whether the information would have been admitted in a criminal prosecution for breach of the underlying regulatory control depended upon whether 'the admission of the evidence would have such an adverse effect on the fairness of the proceedings that the court ought not to admit it' under s 78 of the Police and Criminal Evidence Act 1984.

21.10   As with planning contravention notices, it is an offence if a person:[33]

'(a) makes any statement purporting to comply with a requirement of an information notice which he knows to be false or misleading in a material respect, or

(b) recklessly makes such a statement which is false or misleading in a material respect.'

Such an offence is punishable summarily, by a fine not exceeding level 5 (£5,000).[34]

NOTICE OF UNAUTHORISED DEVELOPMENT AND DIRECT ACTION

21.11   The local planning authority may serve a 'notice of unauthorised development', but this is solely concerned with enabling it to take direct action following a conviction.[35] Unlike the enforcement notice regimes under the various Planning Acts, these notices are not freestanding enforcement mechanisms. A notice of unauthorised development may only be served on a person who has been convicted of an offence under ss 160 or 161: s 169(1), (3). If development has been carried out without a development consent order (in breach of s 160) then the notice will specify steps to remove the development and to restore the land on which the

---

[30] Planning Act 2008, s 168(1), (2).
[31] See Planning Act 2008, s 167(4).
[32] [2000] 2 AC 412.
[33] Planning Act 2008, s 168(4).
[34] Planning Act 2008, s 168(5). This fine would become unlimited when the Legal Aid, Sentencing and Punishment of Offenders Act 2012, s 85 is brought into force.
[35] For a discussion of direct action under s 178 of the Town and Country Planning Act 1990, see Chapter 9.

development has been carried out to its previous condition.[36] If there has been a breach of a development consent order then the notice would require the person to remedy the breach or failure to comply.[37] Unlike planning enforcement notices, the regime does not refer to notices requiring remediation of the harm caused. A period or periods for taking the steps must be specified in the notice.[38]

21.12   No offence is committed if a notice is not complied with. The sole effect of non-compliance is that the local planning authority is able to take direct action to carry out steps in a notice if they have not been taken before the end of the specified period: s 170(1). The authority would be empowered to enter the land on which the development has been carried out and to take those steps. Expenses can be recovered by the authority from the owner of the land, regardless of whether the owner was served with the notice. The notice would be served on a convicted defendant. Whilst the owner would have a statutory cause of action to recover the expenses paid to the authority (and the owner's own expenses) from the person convicted,[39] that might or might not protect their position.[40] The costs recovery provisions in ss 276, 289 and 294 of the Public Health Act 1936 are applied to this direct action.[41] It is an offence, punishable by a level 3 fine (£1,000) to obstruct a person exercising the direct action powers.[42]

INJUNCTION

21.13   The local planning authority may apply to the High Court or county court for an injunction 'if it considers it necessary or expedient for any actual or apprehended prohibited activity to be restrained by injunction': s 171(1). Prohibited activity means:[43]

> 'activity that constitutes an offence under section 160 or 161 in relation to land in the area of the local planning authority.'

The court 'may grant such an injunction as the court thinks fit for the purpose of restraining the prohibited activity'.[44] The language of this section is very closely modelled on s 187B of the Town and Country Planning Act 1990, which is discussed in Chapter 14 above.

---

[36]   Planning Act 2008, s 169(2).
[37]   Planning Act 2008, s 169(4).
[38]   Planning Act 2008, s 169(5). Further requirements may be prescribed, but this power has not been exercised.
[39]   Whilst not stated, it is implicit that the person found guilty of the offence has been served with the relevant notice of unauthorised development.
[40]   The occupier can also recover his expenses from the person convicted: Planning Act 2008, s 170(2)(a).
[41]   Infrastructure Planning (Miscellaneous Prescribed Provisions) Regulations 2010, reg 5.
[42]   Planning Act 2008, s 170(6), (7).
[43]   Planning Act 2008, s 171(2).
[44]   Planning Act 2008, s 171(3).

Chapter 22

Community Infrastructure Levy

22.01   The overall purpose of the Community Infrastructure Levy (CIL):[1]

'is to ensure that costs incurred in supporting the development of an area can be funded (wholly or partly) by owners or developers of land in a way that does not make development of the area economically unviable.'

The framework powers for CIL are in Pt 11 of the Planning Act 2008, with the detail set out in the Community Infrastructure Levy Regulations 2010.[2] Section 218 of the Planning Act 2008 requires the regulations to deal with the enforcement of CIL.

22.02   Under CIL, charging authorities (which are local planning authorities and the Mayor of London[3]) are able to adopt a schedule of charges to be applied to new development in their area. This schedule will be devised having regard to infrastructure proposals in the area, the amount of development that is likely to take place and its ability to contribute to those infrastructure costs. Schedules have typically set the charge as an amount per square metre of floorspace for defined uses of land. Chargeable development is development for which planning permission has been granted,[4] including development under a 'general consent' – the Town and Country Planning (General Permitted Development) Order 1995 – or a local consent such as a local development order or neighbourhood development order.[5] Charging authorities are also collecting authorities, except that the Mayor of London's CIL is collected by the London borough councils.[6] Enforcement powers are given to collecting authorities, including a power to prosecute for offences under the CIL Regulations.[7]

22.03   Commonly, agreements between landowners and developers will identify who is liable to pay CIL and the paying party would then send an assumption of liability notice to the collecting authority.[8] Otherwise liability is apportioned between those with material interests in the land (meaning a freehold estate or a leasehold estate with more than seven years remaining when planning permission first permits the chargeable development).[9] CIL is payable at the end of the period of 60 days beginning with the intended date of commencement of the development, unless the charging authority has adopted an instalment policy.[10]

---

[1]   Planning Act 2008, s 205(2).
[2]   Which have been frequently amended.
[3]   Planning Act 2008, s 206.
[4]   Community Infrastructure Levy Regulations 2010, reg 9.
[5]   Community Infrastructure Levy Regulations 2010, reg 5(3).
[6]   Community Infrastructure Levy Regulations 2010, reg 10.
[7]   Community Infrastructure Levy Regulations 2010, reg 111.
[8]   Community Infrastructure Levy Regulations 2010, reg 31.
[9]   Community Infrastructure Levy Regulations 2010, reg 4. Planning permission first permits development when the final pre-commencement condition is discharged or for a general consent when notice of chargeable development is given: reg 8.
[10]   Community Infrastructure Levy Regulations 2010, reg 70.

ENFORCEMENT OF CIL

22.04   CIL may be enforced by CIL stop notices preventing activity on the site, liability orders (leading to the levying of distress, imprisonment and charging orders), local land charges and civil proceedings. Surcharges and interest can also be levied.

CIL stop notices

22.05   CIL stop notices are a means of preventing the continuation of development until sums are paid under the Community Infrastructure Levy. They may be served by the collecting authority and it is a criminal offence to contravene a CIL stop notice. The use of CIL stop notices is discretionary. There is no guidance on their use and their purpose is different from temporary stop notices and stop notices served against breaches of planning control. If the proposed development has planning permission (which it usually will have), then the CIL stop notice is concerned with recovering revenue on an otherwise desirable development. That points towards its use when obtaining the payment proves difficult, rather than as an early response to non-payment.

22.06   The collecting authority must issue a warning notice before it issues a CIL stop notice. A warning notice would be served if an amount has become payable and the authority 'considers it expedient that development should stop until the amount has been paid'.[11] The warning notice must be served on the person liable for the unpaid amount, every owner and occupier of the land known to the authority and any other person that the authority considers will be materially affected by a CIL stop notice.[12] The warning notice will be dated and will set out the authority's reasons for issuing the notice, the unpaid amount and that it is due in full immediately, the period after which the CIL stop notice may be issued and the effect of, and possible consequences of a failure to comply with, a CIL stop notice.[13] The period between the issue of a warning notice and issue of a CIL stop notice must be between 3 and 28 days.[14] A copy of the notice must be displayed on the land by the authority.[15]

22.07   A CIL stop notice may be served if the collecting authority 'has issued a warning notice' and the amount specified in the notice is unpaid (in whole or in part) at the end of the period specified.[16] The regulations refer to the warning notice having been issued rather than served in accordance with reg 89. It would be difficult to see how a CIL stop notice might be lawful if the underlying warning notice was not served in breach of the regulations. There may though be a different outcome if the person complaining was served with the warning notice but wished to contend that someone else should also have been served. The notice is to be served on the person liable to pay, each person known to be an owner or occupier of the land and any other person the authority considers may be materially affected by the notice.[17]

---

[11]   Community Infrastructure Levy Regulations 2010, reg 89(1), (2).
[12]   Community Infrastructure Levy Regulations 2010, reg 89(3).
[13]   Community Infrastructure Levy Regulations 2010, reg 89(4).
[14]   Community Infrastructure Levy Regulations 2010, reg 89(4)(e).
[15]   Community Infrastructure Levy Regulations 2010, reg 89(5).
[16]   Community Infrastructure Levy Regulations 2010, reg 90(1), (2).
[17]   Community Infrastructure Levy Regulations 2010, reg 90(3).

22.08   A CIL stop notice must contain the date on which it takes effect, the reasons for issuing the notice, the unpaid amount and that is it due in full immediately, specify the relevant activity which must cease and the possible consequences of a failure to comply.[18] Relevant activity means:[19]

> 'any activity connected with the chargeable development which is specified in the CIL stop notice as an activity which the collecting authority requires to cease, and any activity carried out as part of that activity or associated with that activity'.

The prohibition might therefore be in respect of particular aspects of the development or against the works in their entirety. The notice must be displayed by the authority on the relevant land.[20]

22.09   Regulation 90(8) says that a CIL stop notice has effect from the date in the notice, which might be immediate. However a person only commits an offence if he:[21]

> 'contravenes a CIL stop notice—
>
> (a)   which has been served on that person; or
>
> (b)   a copy of which has been displayed in accordance with regulation 90(6).'

In practical terms, therefore, a CIL stop notice will not have effect before it is served or displayed on the site.

22.10   The CIL stop notice offence is similar to other planning offences. Contravention includes causing or permitting the contravention,[22] but is not further defined. It means the carrying out of the relevant activity which is required to cease after the notice has taken effect.[23] For the avoidance of doubt, an offence may be charged for a day or over a longer period and a person may be convicted more than once on the same notice.[24]

22.11   It is a defence:[25]

> 'to prove that—
>
> (a)   the CIL stop notice was not served on the person; and
>
> (b)   the person did not know, and could not reasonably have been expected to know, of its existence.'

The validity of the notice can also be challenged by judicial review or as a defence to a prosecution.

---

[18]   Community Infrastructure Levy Regulations 2010, reg 90(4).
[19]   Community Infrastructure Levy Regulations 2010, reg 90(5). The notice cannot prohibit works which are necessary in the interests of health and safety: reg 90(7).
[20]   Community Infrastructure Levy Regulations 2010, reg 90(6).
[21]   Community Infrastructure Levy Regulations 2010, reg 93(1).
[22]   Community Infrastructure Levy Regulations 2010, reg 93(2).
[23]   Community Infrastructure Levy Regulations 2010, reg 90(5).
[24]   Community Infrastructure Levy Regulations 2010, reg 93(3), (4).
[25]   Community Infrastructure Levy Regulations 2010, reg 93(5).

22.12   The offence is triable either way, with a maximum fine on summary conviction of £20,000 and an unlimited fine on indictment.[26] Any financial benefit from the breach of the notice must be taken into account in sentencing.[27]

22.13   A CIL stop notice can be withdrawn by serving written notice on the persons served with the original notice.[28] The notice must be withdrawn when the unpaid amount is paid in full.[29] A notice ceases to have effect when notice of the withdrawal is served.[30] There is no period set out in the regulations between the obligation to withdraw arising when payment is made and notice of the withdrawal being served. The obligation appears to be immediate and there is no reason why the development should be delayed any further once the liability has been discharged. An email may suffice. Whilst all persons who received the CIL stop notice must be served with notice of the withdrawal, it is a reasonable interpretation that the stop notice ceases to have effect once the first person is served. Notice of withdrawal of the notice must also be displayed on the land.[31]

22.14   Regulation 94 provides an injunction power in respect of breaches of CIL stop notices, modelled on the planning injunction provisions in s 187B of the Town and Country Planning Act 1990:[32]

'(1) A collecting authority may apply to the court for an injunction if it considers it necessary or expedient for any actual or apprehended breach of a CIL stop notice to be restrained by injunction.

(2) On an application under this regulation the court may grant such an injunction as the court thinks fit for the purpose of restraining the breach.'

Such an injunction will restrain a breach of a CIL stop notice and so cannot be sought simply because there is non-payment – the notice needs to come first. The order will be concerned with restraining the breach – stopping the works on site – but if no liability order has been made then a civil claim for the recovery of the sum can be made in those proceedings under reg 106. It is not apparent when an application for an injunction against an apprehended breach of a CIL stop notice would be justified. The CIL stop notice would set a date for compliance which could be immediate, so would be breached or not breached.

22.15   Details of CIL stop notices are to be contained on the enforcement and stop notices register kept by the local planning authority. The register must detail:[33]

'(a) the address of the land to which the notice relates or a plan by reference to which its location can be ascertained;

(b) details of the relevant planning permission sufficient to enable it to be identified;

---

[26] Community Infrastructure Levy Regulations 2010, reg 93(6). The magistrates' court fine would become unlimited when the Legal Aid, Sentencing and Punishment of Offenders Act 2012, s 85 is brought into force.

[27] Community Infrastructure Levy Regulations 2010, reg 93(7).

[28] Community Infrastructure Levy Regulations 2010, reg 91(1).

[29] Community Infrastructure Levy Regulations 2010, reg 91(2).

[30] Community Infrastructure Levy Regulations 2010, reg 91(4).

[31] Community Infrastructure Levy Regulations 2010, reg 91(3).

[32] Community Infrastructure Levy Regulations 2010, reg 94. An application can be made in a county court or the High Court: reg 94(3).

[33] Community Infrastructure Levy Regulations 2010, reg 92(1).

(c)   the name of the collecting authority;

(d)   the date of issue of the notice;

(e)   the date of service of the notice;

(f)   the date specified in the notice as the date on which it is to take effect; and

(g)   a statement or summary of the activity prohibited by the notice.'

The entries must be removed if the notice is withdrawn or quashed.[34]

Reminder notices and liability orders

22.16   Various civil enforcement powers are available to seek to recover CIL charges. The starting point is for the collecting authority to serve a reminder notice after a sum has become due.[35] The notice must state the amount in respect of which the authority will seek a liability order.[36] If the amount in the reminder notice is wholly or partly unpaid seven days after service of the notice, then the authority may apply to the magistrates' court for a liability order.[37] The application is made by a complaint to a justice of the peace leading to the issue of a summons.[38] Applications can be made within six years of the amount becoming due,[39] so following the Limitation Act 1980 time limit for civil actions. At least 14 days must elapse between the service of the summons and the making of a liability order.[40]

22.17   The regulations provide that a liability order must be made by the court if it is satisfied that the amount has become payable by the defendant and has not been paid.[41] However this provision does not address the requirement for a reminder notice to be served and a week to pass before a liability order is applied for. A liability order will be for the amount outstanding and the reasonable costs of obtaining the order.[42] If the outstanding amount is paid after the application is made, then the court must make a liability order for the collecting authority's reasonable costs, if so requested.[43] A single liability order may deal with more than one person or more than one amount due,[44] but these must all have been subject to reminder notices before the application is made. A liability order may be enforced by distress and sale of goods, a charging order or imprisonment. It is also a debt for the purpose of a creditor's petition or winding up order against a company.[45]

Distress

22.18   The levying of distress is having bailiffs seize a debtor's goods and those goods can then be sold to pay the debt and the costs of distress. Under the CIL

---

[34]   Community Infrastructure Levy Regulations 2010, reg 92(2).
[35]   Community Infrastructure Levy Regulations 2010, reg 96.
[36]   Community Infrastructure Levy Regulations 2010, reg 96(1).
[37]   Community Infrastructure Levy Regulations 2010, reg 97(1).
[38]   Community Infrastructure Levy Regulations 2010, reg 97(2).
[39]   Community Infrastructure Levy Regulations 2010, reg 97(3).
[40]   Community Infrastructure Levy Regulations 2010, reg 97(9).
[41]   Community Infrastructure Levy Regulations 2010, reg 97(5).
[42]   Community Infrastructure Levy Regulations 2010, reg 97(6).
[43]   Community Infrastructure Levy Regulations 2010, reg 97(7).
[44]   Community Infrastructure Levy Regulations 2010, reg 97(8).
[45]   Community Infrastructure Levy Regulations 2010, reg 105.

Regulations, distress and sale of goods may take place following the making of a liability order.[46] The levying of distress, or at the later stage the sale of the goods, can be avoiding by paying or tendering the sums due.[47] The amount due will be whatever remains due under the liability order and a charge for distress.[48] A person aggrieved by the levy of, or an attempt to levy, a distress may appeal to the magistrates' court by complaint. The court may require seized goods to be released or compensation paid for goods sold.[49]

Charging orders

22.19   Where a liability order or orders have been made against a debtor and at least £2,000 remains outstanding then an application can be made to the county court.[50] Written notification of the intention to seek the charging order must be given to the debtor and to any person the authority considers may be prejudiced by the making of the order. The notification will set out the reasons for seeking a charging order, its effect, the amount due and the steps the authority will take if it is not paid.[51] If the charge is to be imposed on land then the notification must be displayed on that land.[52] The application for the order may be made if payment is not received within 21 days of the notification.[53] The court has a discretion whether to make a charge and must consider any evidence of the personal circumstances of the debtor and whether any other person would be likely to be unduly prejudiced by the order.[54] An order will specify the interest charged and any conditions imposed by the court.[55] Such a charge may be enforced as an equitable charge and may be protected by an entry on the Land Register or as a local land charge.

Imprisonment

22.20   A collecting authority may apply to the magistrates' court for a warrant to commit an individual debtor to prison where it has sought to levy distress and the bailiff reports that they have been unable to find sufficient goods and the authority shows that it is unable to recover the sum under a charging order.[56] If the court finds that the failure to pay was due to the debtor's 'wilful refusal or culpable neglect' then it may issue a warrant of commitment or fix a term of imprisonment (up to three months) and postpone the issue of the warrant until such time and subject to any conditions it thinks just.[57] The warrant will be for the sums outstanding under the liability order, attempted distress and the costs of the warrant.[58] If the sums due

---

46   Community Infrastructure Levy Regulations 2010, reg 98.

47   Community Infrastructure Levy Regulations 2010, reg 98(5), (6).

48   The latter sum is calculated under the Non-Domestic Rating (Collection and Enforcement) (Local Lists) Regulations 1989, Sch 3: see Community Infrastructure Levy Regulations 2010, reg 98(3), (4).

49   Community Infrastructure Levy Regulations 2010, reg 99.

50   Community Infrastructure Levy Regulations 2010, reg 103. This is the appropriate court under the Charging Orders Act 1979, s 1.

51   Community Infrastructure Levy Regulations 2010, reg 103(4).

52   Community Infrastructure Levy Regulations 2010, reg 103(6).

53   Community Infrastructure Levy Regulations 2010, reg 103(7).

54   Community Infrastructure Levy Regulations 2010, reg 104(1).

55   Community Infrastructure Levy Regulations 2010, reg 104(2).

56   Community Infrastructure Levy Regulations 2010, reg 100(1).

57   Community Infrastructure Levy Regulations 2010, reg 100(3), (8).

58   Community Infrastructure Levy Regulations 2010, reg 100(4), (5).

(including any further costs incurred by the authority) are paid, then no further steps are taken and, if imprisoned, the debtor is released.[59]

Local land charges

22.21 The chargeable amount is a local land charge.[60] If the collection authority wishes to enforce the charge (with the powers of a mortgagee)[61] then it must give notice to the owners of the land, any other person who may be prejudiced by enforcement and display notice on the land.[62] The notice must explain the reasons for seeking to enforce, set out the outstanding amounts due and explain what steps the authority will take.[63] If the payment is not received within 21 days of notice being given, then the authority may apply to the county court for consent to enforce the charge.[64] The court must consider all the circumstances of the case including any evidence that a person will be unduly prejudiced by enforcement of the charge.[65] A local land charge can only be imposed if the sum outstanding is £2,000 or more. Similarly it can only be enforced if £2,000 or more remains outstanding.[66]

Civil liability

22.22 An amount that has become due under CIL may be recovered in civil proceedings provided that a liability order has not been made in respect of it.[67]

Interest

22.23 Interest is charged on amounts that are overdue at a rate of 2.5 per cent above the Bank of England base rate.[68] This is charged as simple rather than compound interest.[69]

Surcharges

22.24 Surcharges are payable for various defaults under the CIL regime. These are essentially penalties, which are added to the liability.[70] Collecting authorities have a discretion whether to impose a surcharge. The following surcharges may be payable:

(a) if nobody has assumed liability to pay CIL in respect of chargeable development and that development has commenced: £50;[71]

---

[59] Community Infrastructure Levy Regulations 2010, reg 100(6). Partial payment gives rise to a pro rata reduction in length of imprisonment.
[60] Community Infrastructure Levy Regulations 2010, reg 66.
[61] With a mortgagee's powers under the Law of Property Act 1925: Community Infrastructure Levy Regulations 2010, reg 107(7).
[62] Community Infrastructure Levy Regulations 2010, reg 107(2), (3).
[63] Community Infrastructure Levy Regulations 2010, reg 107(3).
[64] Community Infrastructure Levy Regulations 2010, reg 107(4).
[65] Community Infrastructure Levy Regulations 2010, reg 107(5).
[66] Community Infrastructure Levy Regulations 2010, reg 107(6).
[67] Community Infrastructure Levy Regulations 2010, reg 106.
[68] Community Infrastructure Levy Regulations 2010, reg 87(1).
[69] Community Infrastructure Levy Regulations 2010, reg 87(3).
[70] Community Infrastructure Levy Regulations 2010, reg 88.
[71] Community Infrastructure Levy Regulations 2010, reg 80.

(b) where the material interests require the authority to apportion liability between them (presumably when they have not agreed themselves): £500 for each interest;[72]

(c) where chargeable development takes place under a general consent before the collecting authority has received a notice of chargeable development: 20 per cent of the chargeable amount or £2,500, whichever is lower.[73] One surcharge would be payable for the development, to be apportioned between the interests pro rata to the apportionment of the liability;[74]

(d) where chargeable development takes place before the collecting authority has received a commencement notice: 20 per cent of the chargeable amount or £2,500, whichever is lower.[75] Again there would be one surcharge for the development, to be apportioned between the interests pro rata to the apportionment of the liability;[76]

(e) if a person is required to notify the collecting authority of a disqualifying event fails to do so within 14 days of the event: 20 per cent of the chargeable amount payable or £2500, whichever is the lower amount.[77] Disqualifying events are the withdrawal of charitable, social housing or exceptional circumstances reliefs;[78]

(f) where an amount due is not paid in full within 30 days beginning with the date on which it is due: 5 per cent of the amount due (not the amount outstanding) or £200, whichever is the greater. If the sum is not paid in full within six months then a further surcharge of 5 per cent of the unpaid amount or £200 (which is greater) may be imposed. The same surcharge can additionally be applied at the 12-month mark;[79] and

(g) a failure to comply with any requirement of an information notice[80] within 14 days, beginning with the date of service: 20 per cent of the amount of CIL the person is liable to pay or £1,000, whichever is the lower.[81]

Information requirements for general consents

22.25   Where development might be carried out under a general consent, the collecting authority may require an owner to provide it with information, documents or materials that the authority considers relevant to ascertain whether a notice of chargeable development (so initiating the date for liability) must be submitted.[82] If a notice of chargeable development has been submitted, the authority may request further information to enable it to calculate the chargeable amount.[83] No timescale is provided for complying with the requirement nor is there any sanction for failing

---

[72] Community Infrastructure Levy Regulations 2010, reg 81. There is no surcharge for apportioning a surcharge: reg 81(3).

[73] Community Infrastructure Levy Regulations 2010, reg 82(1).

[74] Community Infrastructure Levy Regulations 2010, reg 82(2).

[75] Community Infrastructure Levy Regulations 2010, reg 83(1).

[76] Community Infrastructure Levy Regulations 2010, reg 83(2).

[77] Community Infrastructure Levy Regulations 2010, reg 84.

[78] Community Infrastructure Levy Regulations 2010, regs 2(1), 48, 53 and 57.

[79] Community Infrastructure Levy Regulations 2010, reg 85.

[80] An information notice would be served by the collecting authority seeking information to enable it to apportion liability (reg 35) or determine whether social housing relief applies (reg 54).

[81] Community Infrastructure Levy Regulations 2010, reg 86.

[82] Community Infrastructure Levy Regulations 2010, reg 108A.

[83] Community Infrastructure Levy Regulations 2010, reg 64(8).

to do so, although a request is a prerequisite of exercising powers of entry under regulation 109(1)(e) or (f) below.[84]

Power of entry

22.26   Powers of entry are provided to the collecting authority under reg 109:[85]

'(a) to ascertain whether a chargeable development has been commenced;

(b) to determine whether any of the powers conferred on a collecting authority by this Part should be exercised in relation to a chargeable development or the relevant land;

(c) to ascertain whether there has been compliance with any requirement imposed as a result of any such power having been exercised in relation to a chargeable development or the relevant land;

(d) to display any notice required to be displayed on land in accordance with these Regulations;

(e) where a person has submitted a notice of chargeable development, for the purposes of gathering information required by the collecting authority in order for it to calculate the chargeable amount payable in respect of the chargeable development; or

(f) where no notice of chargeable development has been submitted, for the purposes of gathering information required by the collecting authority in order for it to ascertain whether a notice of chargeable development must be submitted under regulation 64(2).'

Entry to a private dwelling may only be required under a warrant issued by a justice of the peace.[86] A warrant may only be issued if there is good reason to believe that the authority will not be able to enforce CIL without it.[87] As with similar provisions elsewhere in planning law, it is an offence to wilfully obstruct a person exercising entry powers, punishable on summary conviction by a level 3 (£1,000) fine.[88]

False information

22.27   By reg 110(1):

'It is an offence for a person, knowingly or recklessly, to supply information which is false or misleading in a material respect to a charging authority or a collecting authority in response to a requirement under these Regulations.'

The offence is triable either way and is punishable by a fine of up to £20,000 on summary conviction or on indictment an unlimited fine or up to two years' imprisonment.[89]

---

[84]   Community Infrastructure Levy Regulations 2010, reg 109(3), (3A).
[85]   Community Infrastructure Levy Regulations 2010, reg 109(1).
[86]   Community Infrastructure Levy Regulations 2010, reg 109(4).
[87]   Community Infrastructure Levy Regulations 2010, reg 109(5). A warrant remains in force for one month or until its purpose has been fulfilled, whichever is sooner: reg 109(6).
[88]   Community Infrastructure Levy Regulations 2010, reg 109(7), (8).
[89]   Community Infrastructure Levy Regulations 2010, reg 110(2).

Chapter 23

Lawful Development Certificates

23.01   Existing uses, past development and time limits on enforcement action may create lawful planning uses of land that are not covered by an existing planning permission. Alternatively, a developer may not be certain whether a planning permission has been implemented and so whether further development can be carried out, or whether a proposed development amounts to a material change of use. Those issues can be fought over in an enforcement notice appeal or as a defence to proceedings, but most people would prefer to avoid such battles. The local planning authority may be willing to give a view informally, but that should still be in writing. Such a written opinion has the advantage of speed and little cost. Where the issues are reasonably straightforward, an informal opinion may be easy to obtain. However, such an opinion is not binding on the authority: it will not give rise to an estoppel – see *R (Reprotech (Pebsham) Limited) v East Sussex County Council,*[1] which is discussed further in Chapter 1.

23.02   There may be very rare circumstances where it would be irrational or unfair for a local planning authority to resile from an informal expression of opinion. If a use is temporary, the court may be more willing to protect the landowner as the planning impact would be more limited when set against the damage to the landowner. In *Postermobile v London Borough of Brent,*[2] it was an abuse of process to prosecute an advertiser who had relied upon advice from planning officers that a temporary display was lawful. An informal opinion might be of more limited value (and positively dangerous) if relevant information is omitted from the request or there is dispute as to what proposal an officer was considering. For example, an officer might advise whether a proposed side extension to a house had permitted development rights, unaware that the side of the house faced onto a highway.

23.03   A Lawful Development Certificate is a mechanism for providing certainty. A LDC is conclusive that what it says was or would have been lawful at the date of the application. Conversely, refusal of a certificate, or a grant in more limited terms, does not determine conclusively that those matters refused or omitted were unlawful. There are two types of Lawful Development Certificates: Certificates of Lawfulness of Existing Use or Development (CLEUDs) and Certificate of Lawfulness of Proposed Use or Development (CLOPUDs). The planning merits of an actual or proposed development are irrelevant. Guidance is provided by Annex 8 of Circular 10/97, although some of this advice is now dated.

---

[1]   [2002] UKHL 8, [2003] 1 WLR 348.
[2]   (1997) *The Times,* 8 December.

CLEUD – CERTIFICATE OF LAWFULNESS OF EXISTING USE OR DEVELOPMENT

23.04   The provisions relating to Certificates of Lawfulness of Existing Use or Developments (CLEUDs) in the Planning and Compensation Act 1991 reforms replaced Established Use Certificates. Established Use Certificates related solely to uses which had become 'established' either because of their continuance since 1963 or because they did not need planning permission.[3] They did not make the use of the land lawful, but were expressed to be conclusive in enforcement notice appeals to the Secretary of State.[4] On the contrary, CLEUDs establish the use as lawful. They determine whether (s 191(1) of the Town and Country Planning Act 1990):

'(a)   any existing use of buildings or other land is lawful;

(b)   any operations which have been carried out in, on, over or under land are lawful; or

(c)   any other matter constituting a failure to comply with any condition or limitation subject to which planning permission has been granted is lawful.'

Uses and operations are lawful if (s 191(2)):

'(a)   no enforcement action may then be taken in respect of them (whether because they did not involve development or require planning permission or because the time for enforcement action has expired or for any other reason); and

(b)   they do not constitute a contravention of any of the requirements of any enforcement notice then in force.'

Failure to comply with any condition or limitation is lawful if (s 191(3)):

'(a)   the time for taking enforcement action in respect of the failure has then expired; and

(b)   it does not constitute a contravention of any of the requirements of any enforcement notice or breach of condition notice then in force.'

The time for taking enforcement action has not expired if the time limits in s 171B have not passed or any extended time period because of a potential or actual planning enforcement order has not expired. Where there is or may be a planning enforcement order because a breach has been deliberately concealed, then time has not expired if:[5]

'(a)   the time for applying for an order under section 171BA(1) (a "planning enforcement order") in relation to the matter has not expired,

(b)   an application has been made for a planning enforcement order in relation to the matter and the application has neither been decided nor been withdrawn, or

(c)   a planning enforcement order has been made in relation to the matter, the order has not been rescinded and the enforcement year for the order (whether or not it has begun) has not expired.'

---

[3]   Town and Country Planning Act 1990, s 191, (before amendment by the 1991 Act).

[4]   The status of a use as established (and incapable of being subject to enforcement) but not lawful generated anomalies.

[5]   The planning enforcement order periods are referred to by s 191(3A). For time limits generally, see Chapter 3.

23.05   A CLEUD may be issued if the use or operations did not require planning permission, for example because of permitted development rights or because a change of use was not material. More commonly, they are issued if the time limits in s 171B have been satisfied. These are based upon the time for which the breach of planning control continued after it occurred. For material changes of use, the issue is whether it continued for four or ten years (as appropriate) after the original breach. If the use ceased after it became lawful, a CLEUD application should only be refused if the use was then abandoned.[6] If the local planning authority 'are provided with information' satisfying them of the lawfulness of the use, operation of other matter, or that description as modified or substituted by the authority, they must issue a certificate to that effect. If not, they must refuse the application.[7] Judgment is therefore involved in determining the application but once that judgment is formed, there is no discretion. The authority is able to grant a certificate with a completely different use from that applied for.[8]

CLOPUD – CERTIFICATE OF LAWFULNESS OF PROPOSED USE OR DEVELOPMENT

23.06   A Certificate of Lawfulness of Proposed Use or Development addresses prospective development. These provisions replaced and extended determinations as to whether planning permission was required under s 64 of the Town and Country Planning Act 1990.

CLOPUDs determine whether (s 192(1)):

'(a) any proposed use of buildings or other land; or

(b)   any operations proposed to be carried out in, on, over or under land,

would be lawful.'

If the local planning authority are provided with information satisfying them that the use or operations would be lawful if begun at the time of the application, they shall issue a certificate – if not, they shall refuse the application.[9] There are, therefore, two practical differences from CLEUDs. CLOPUDs cover specific proposals: they do not purport to identify every development that would be lawful. A CLOPUD can only be granted for the development applied for so the authority cannot issue a certificate to the effect that a scheme smaller than the proposal would be lawful. In some circumstances it might add a note to the decision that certain elements applied for would be lawful or mention this in correspondence. The factors to consider on a CLOPUD application include:

(a) whether the use or operations constitute development;

(b) whether it is permitted by any planning permission, including permitted development rights;

---

6   *Smith v Secretary of State for the Environment* [1994] JPL 640. The test of abandonment is contained in *Jennings Motors Ltd v Secretary of State for the Environment* [1982] QB 541.
7   Town and Country Planning Act 1990, s 191(4).
8   Town and Country Planning Act 1990, s 191(7).
9   Town and Country Planning Act 1990, s 192(2).

(c) the lawfulness of existing uses or operational development, as the ability to make a change of use or to exercise permitted development rights may depend upon this;[10] and

(d) whether conditions or limitations in any existing permission would be contravened.

THE APPLICATION FOR A CLEUD OR CLOPUD

23.07   The applicant does not need to have an interest in the land to make an application. The application is made to the local planning authority or county council (if it is a county matter – such as minerals or waste).[11] The application 'shall be made on a form published by the Secretary of State (or a form substantially to the like effect)': see Art 35 of the Town and Country Planning (Development Management Procedure) (England) Order 2010 ('the DMPO'). A similar requirement for use of a Welsh Ministers' form (or one substantially to the like effect) applies in Wales: see Art 28(1) of the Town and Country Planning (Development Management Procedure) (Wales) Order 2012 ('the DMPO (Wales)).[12] Standard forms are now available on the Planning Portal website or an application may be submitted online via that website. The model application forms appended to Annex 8 of Circular 10/97 are now out of date and should not be used. The application must specify the land and describe the use, operations or other matter in question in accordance with ss 191 or 192. Specific information is also required under those sections for various applications:

s 191(1)(a)	Any applicable Use Class
s 191(1)(c)	Sufficient details to identify the planning permission (ideally including the reference number)
S 192(1)(a)	Use at the date of application and any applicable Use Class

23.08   The particulars specified or referred to in the form must be provided.[13] The development orders require the application to be accompanied by:[14]

'(a) a plan identifying the land to which the application relates drawn to an identified scale and showing the direction of North;

(b) such evidence verifying the information included in the application as the applicant can provide; and

(c) a statement setting out the applicant's interest in the land, the name and address of any other person known to the applicant to have an interest in the land and whether any such other person has been notified of the application.'

23.09   Where the application is in respect of 'two or more uses, operations or other matters' the plan shall show where these are or will be.[15] The evidence is often

---

[10]   Consequently the determination of a CLOPUD application may involve consideration of time limits for enforcement action against existing development and planning enforcement orders.

[11]   Town and Country Planning (Development Management Procedure) (England) Order 2010, Art 10(1), 35(6), although if the local planning authority is a development corporation, enterprise zone or housing action trust outside Greater London or the former metropolitan counties, the application is made to the district council.

[12]   Made under Town and Country Planning Act 1990, s 193(1).

[13]   DMPO, Art 35(1), DMPO (Wales), Art 28(1).

[14]   DMPO, Art 35(2), DMPO (Wales), Art 28(2).

[15]   DMPO, Art 35(4), DMPO (Wales), Art 28(4).

given in the form of statutory declarations,[16] although statements can be given by affidavit or unsworn. Since witness statements in court proceedings no longer have to be sworn, it is not so apparent why greater formality would be required for LDC applications. Relevant documents, if available, should be provided. The applicant must also state his interest in the land, the name and address of any other person known to be interested in the land and whether that person has been notified of the application.[17]

23.10   A CLOPUD application in respect of Crown land shall include:[18]

'(a) a statement that the application is made in respect of Crown land; and

(b) where the application is made by a person authorised in writing by the appropriate authority, a copy of that authorisation.'

23.11   The local planning authority shall acknowledge the application, and if they later determine that the application was invalid, they shall notify the applicant as soon as practicable.[19] The local planning authority may require further information in writing.[20] They must determine the application within eight weeks unless the period is extended by agreement in writing.[21]

Practical points in applications

23.12   Applications usually turn on either factual matters (eg when the use began) or matters of law and judgment (eg whether a proposed operation has permitted development rights). Evidence on factual issues can be obtained from persons involved in the land at the relevant time, available documents and the local planning authority 's records. Local planning authorities should co-operate with applicants by making records available.[22] The burden of proof is on the applicant.[23] The standard of proof is the balance of probabilities. The applicant's evidence does not need to be corroborated by independent evidence,[24] although that usually helps if the passage of time is relied upon for the development or use to be lawful. Applications should state the precise use or operations which are sought to be covered. On CLOPUD applications there should be sufficient information for the local planning authority to understand exactly what is involved in the proposal.[25] If the lawfulness of an existing use is relied upon in a CLOPUD application (for example for proposed permitted development which depends on the existing use being lawful), sufficient evidence (which may be a CLEUD) must be produced to show its lawfulness. Formally CLEUDs and CLOPUDs are separate documents and an applicant should be clear what is being applied for. There may in some cases be a choice: for example, if it is said that a planning permission has been implemented by the carrying out of works, but not yet completed, and application could be made for a CLEUD in respect of those works or for a CLOPUD for the ability to develop under the planning permission.

---

[16]   Made under the Statutory Declarations Act 1835.
[17]   DMPO, Art 35(2)(c), DMPO (Wales), Art 28(2)(c).
[18]   DMPO, Art 35(3), DMPO (Wales), Art 28(3).
[19]   DMPO, Art 35(7), DMPO (Wales), Art 28(7).
[20]   DMPO, Art 35(9), DMPO (Wales), Art 28(9).
[21]   DMPO, Art 35(10), DMPO (Wales), Art 28(10).
[22]   Circular 10/97, Annex 8, para 8.12.
[23]   Circular 10/97, Annex 8, paras 8.12, 8.26.
[24]   see *F W Gabbitas v Secretary of State for the Environment* [1985] JPL 630 on enforcement appeals.
[25]   Circular 10/97, Annex 8, para 8.26.

Fees

23.13 In England the fees for LDC applications are set out under reg 11 of the Town and Country Planning (Fees for Applications, Deemed Applications, Requests and Site Visits) (England) Regulations 2012 ('2012 Fees Regulations'). In Wales fees are payable under Regulation 10A of the Town and Country Planning (Fees for Applications and Deemed Applications) Regulations 1989 ('the 1989 Fees Regulations'). Applications for CLEUDs under s 191(1)(a) and/or (b) for any existing use or operations pay the planning application fee for that development.[26] Section 191(c) applications to determine the lawfulness of failures to comply with conditions or limitations are subject to a £195 fee in England or £166 in Wales. If an application is made under subsection (a) or (b) (or both) and also (c), then the fees are added together.[27] Applications for CLOPUDs cost half the planning application fee.[28] A 'free go' is allowed for a second application made within 12 months of (a) the receipt of an earlier application which was later withdrawn, (b) the expiry of the eight-week period for the determination of an application which was subsequently appealed or (c) the refusal of the earlier application.[29] The application must be for the same site and relate to the same matter. Various exemptions and reductions are available to the disabled and parish councils.

Consultation on applications

23.14 Whilst the applicant must state whether all persons interested in the land have been notified, there is no statutory obligation on the applicant or the local planning authority to inform them. However, they should be informed and given an opportunity to comment. Since certificates are conclusive of the matters they contain, they can directly affect the legal rights of owners and tenants, and to fail to consult would be unfair. The refusal of a certificate, whilst not conclusive, may be highly prejudicial to existing interests. Similarly there is no statutory obligation on the local planning authority to consult the public or neighbours on an LDC application. There are however two good reasons to consult:

(1) Persons in the locality may have factual information which can assist in determining the application. This will particularly be the case where the application relies on the period and extent of a use.

(2) People may be interested to know of the application. Even without being able to add to the factual material, they may have submissions to make on the law or the judgment that should be made on the material. If they find out after the certificate is granted they may simply judicially review the decision. If they were unaware of the application because of the absence of consultation or publicity then an extension of time for bringing proceedings beyond the usual promptly and within three months period is likely to be granted. An extension of time was readily granted by the High Court in *R (Sumption) v London Borough of*

---

[26] 2012 Fees Regulations, reg 11(3)(a). Subject to specific provision for the use of dwellinghouses, where in the fee is £385 (£330 in Wales) per dwelling house if there are under 50 dwelling houses or £19,049 plus £115 per additional dwelling house over 50 units (£16,464 and £84 per additional dwelling in Wales), up to a maximum of £250,000: 2012 Fees Regulations, reg 11(6), 1989 Fees Regulations, reg 10A(6).

[27] 2012 Fees Regulations, reg 11(7), 1989 Fees Regulations, reg 10A(8)

[28] 2012 Fees Regulations, reg 11(3)(c), 1989 Fees Regulations, reg 10A(5)(c).

[29] 2012 Fees Regulations, reg 11(4), (5), 1989 Fees Regulations, reg 10A(3), (4).

Greenwich where a neighbour only became aware that a CLOPUD had been applied for or approved when investigating the start of works on the site.[30] In that case Mr Justice Collins suggested that consideration be given to requiring publicity or notification of LDC applications, but that suggestion has not been pursued by government.

LDC decision-making

23.15 Local planning authorities will need to consider the information in the application, any third party representations and the information in their own possession. Where an application relies on long user, the authority must be particularly careful when evaluating the strength and reliability of evidence. For example a person might assert in a statement that they had been using the site for a particular purpose for a certain number of years, but what does the statement actually say? Does it seem credible? Does it include or omit helpful detail? Should contemporaneous records be able to cast light on the matter? If so, have they been produced and what do they show? Should third parties have been aware of the activity and were they? It is a useful approach to ask how would the evidence stand up to cross-examination? The authority will need to identify the questions of fact and law which arise and work through those issues.

23.16 Since the planning merits of the proposal are not relevant, LDC decisions are generally taken by officers. However there will be LDC applications which raise important issues for the area or which would benefit from more open consideration. Local planning authority schemes of delegation can allow LDC applications to be considered by their planning committee, and it is prudent to have a constitutional mechanism for such applications to be taken to committee. Delegation arrangements vary as to whether an officer decision is taken by the authority's legal or planning officers but it is important for both parts of the council to work in cooperation on LDC issues.

FORM OF THE LDC DECISION

23.17 If the local planning authority decide to grant the application, in whole or part, they are required to issue a certificate. If the application is refused, then a decision notice will be issued. If the application is allowed in part, or as modified by the authority, then a certificate will be issued and the authority would also have to set out its decision not to accept the whole application and provide reasons. This might be on the certificate or in a separate decision notice. A Lawful Development Certificate shall:[31]

(a) specify the land to which it relates;

(b) describe the use, operations or other matter in question (specifying any Use Class);

---

[30] [2007] EWHC 2776 (Admin), [2008] 1 P & CR 336 at para 6, 7. It was the developer's misfortune for these purposes that the neighbour (who appeared in person in the proceedings) was Jonathan Sumption QC, later the first person to be appointed directly from the Bar to the Supreme Court.

[31] Town and Country Planning Act 1990, s 191(5) (for CLEUDs) and s 192(3) (for CLOPUDs).

(c) give the reasons for determining the use, operations or other matters to be lawful; and

(d) specify the date of the application for the certificate.

The CLEUD or CLOPUD shall be in the form provided in the relevant development management procedure order, or a form substantially to the like effect.[32] A document which was not a certificate was the 'Permission for Development' issued in response to an LDC application in *James Hay Pension Trustees Ltd v First Secretary of State*.[33] Ward LJ put the point emphatically:

> 'the Council used the wrong piece of paper. That, in my judgment, is an end to the matter.
> …
>
> Looking at this certificate, one is totally at a loss to know whether it is a grant of permission or a Certificate of Lawfulness of proposed use. An interested party should not be expected to trawl through the file to discover what may have been intended. The Act specifies more precision. This certificate did not provide it.'[34]

23.18   The certificate may incorporate by reference the application description or plans. The date of the application is important, as the certificate is conclusive as to lawfulness on that date and changes in circumstances might mean that the matter would be unlawful at a later date. As examples, the LDC may rely on a planning permission which later expires through lack of implementation or on a temporary permission.[35] A certification that actual or proposed development is lawful under a planning permission does not affect any failure to comply with a condition or limitation unless stated expressly.[36]

23.19   Circular 10/97 emphasises that a CLEUD must be precise as to the area of land to which it relates and the use, operations or breach which is lawful at the time.[37] For example, the number and type of caravans, the hours of works or height of stored materials can be specified. The circular explains this as providing a yardstick against which to judge any future intensification of use. This advice must be considered with caution. If an existing use is within a Use Class then any other use within that Use Class will also be lawful, subject to any planning conditions,

---

[32] DMPO 2010, Art 35(14) and Sch 8 in England; DMPO 2012, Art 28(14) and Sch 7 in Wales.
[33] [2006] EWCA Civ 1387, [2007] 1 P & CR 23. The document read:
'South Gloucestershire Council in pursuance of powers under the above-mentioned Act hereby PERMIT the details included in the first schedule on 13th July 2001 in accordance with the application and accompanying plans.
Area Planning Manager
On behalf of South Gloucestershire Council
Date: 19th November 2001
First Schedule
(1) That the 1964 planning permission (SG 7789) is not a personal consent to the Bristol Avon River Board; and
(2) that the store and class X use referred to in the planning permission SG 7789 is now covered by the reference to storage in the Use Class B8.
Second Schedule
Land at Winterbourne Station Yard …'
[34] *James Hay* at paras 27 and 31.
[35] In the event that the proposal was lawful at the date of application but the authority were satisfied that it became unlawful before the certificate was issued, it might include a note to that effect on the decision.
[36] Town and Country Planning Act 1990, s 193(5).
[37] Circular 10/97, Annex 8, para 8.16

so the use can be less precise. The Use Class, if relevant, should always be given.[38] Uses are also reasonably general: a detailed description cannot be more precise than the use itself. In *Westminster City Council v Secretary of State for Communities and Local Government,*[39] a CLEUD for the placing of tables and chairs as pavement furniture in connection with a restaurant was adequate, it was not required to try to spell out hours, days and times of year or numbers of chairs and tables. A certificate is not a way of imposing restrictions, which would have been in conditions if a planning permission had been granted. The Circular provides examples of particular situations where care should be taken in the description of the lawful development in a CLEUD.[40] In refusing, or refusing in part, an application the local planning authority must give clearly and precisely the full reasons for its decision and tell the applicant of his right to appeal.[41]

THE EFFECT OF A LDC

23.20   A LDC is conclusive as to what it describes as being lawful at the date of the application for the certificate. When a CLEUD is in force the lawfulness of the matters it covers is conclusively presumed.[42] A CLEUD also takes effect as if it was a grant of planning permission for the purposes of s 3(3) of the Caravan Sites and Control of Development Act 1960 (eligibility for caravan site licences).[43] The 1990 Act also treats it as a planning permission for certain, now redundant, waste consent provisions.[44] A CLEUD is treated as a planning permission for the purpose of the requirement to have planning permission for an environmental permit to be granted for certain waste operations.[45] A CLEUD is determinative at the time of the application and subsequent changes may mean that the use or development described in the certificate ceases to be lawful. For example, there may be a material change of use from that use, the structure may be demolished, the relevant planning permission quashed[46] or a discontinuance order made. An existing use described in a CLEUD can be abandoned where the use became lawful through passage of time.[47] The lawfulness of the matters contained in the CLOPUD shall be conclusively presumed 'unless there is a material change, before the use is instituted or the operations are begun, in any of the matters relevant to determining such lawfulness'.[48] Material changes could include changes to permitted development rights, the revocation or expiry of a planning permission, or an abandonment of a use.

---

[38]   Town and Country Planning Act 1990, ss 191(5)(b), 191(3)(b).

[39]   [2013] EWHC 23 (Admin) at para 76.

[40]   Circular 10/97, Annex 8, paras 8.22.

[41]   Town and Country Planning (Development Management Procedure) (England) Order 2010, Art 35(13); Town and Country Planning (Development Management Procedure) (Wales) Order 2010, Art 28(13).

[42]   Town and Country Planning Act 1990, s 191(6).

[43]   Town and Country Planning Act 1990, s 191(7).

[44]   Town and Country Planning Act 1990, s 191(7) applying to Control of Pollution Act 1974, s 5(2) and Environment Protection Act 1990, s 36(2)(a).

[45]   Environmental Permitting (England and Wales) Regulations 2010, Sch 9, para 3(2).

[46]   If a permission is quashed in legal proceedings then the likelihood is that proceedings would be brought against a related LDC in any event.

[47]   *M & M (Land) Ltd v Secretary of State for Communities and Local Government* [2007] EWHC 489 (Admin), [2007] 2 P & CR 18.

[48]   Town and Country Planning Act 1990, s 192(4).

THE PLANNING REGISTER

23.21   Applications for LDCs are included in the register of planning applications maintained by the local planning authority. The register will include the name and address of the applicant, the date of the application, the address or location of the application site, the description in the application, any decisions of the local planning authority or Minister and their date.[49]

LAWFUL DEVELOPMENT CERTIFICATES AND PLANNING OBLIGATIONS

23.22   Lawful development certificates do not deal with whether there has been or would be compliance with planning obligations. Sections 191 and 192 are solely concerned with whether the action or use is without planning permission or a breach of a planning condition. An LDC application that seeks to demonstrate compliance with a planning obligation would be entirely misconceived. A local planning authority may have to consider how to respond to an LDC application which intentionally or otherwise involves a planning obligation. It will have to consider whether the application falls within ss 191 or 192, and if so, determine those aspects. It might wish to add an informative explaining that the certificate does not cover planning obligations. Any view on compliance with an obligation should not be included in the operative part of the certificate.[50] The authority might wish to give a view on the obligation in an informative. Such a view would not be statutorily binding, but would be a legal decision capable of being subject to judicial review.

APPEALS

23.23   There is a right of appeal to the Secretary of State or Welsh Ministers. If the application is refused, or refused in part, or the local planning authority fail to determine the application in eight weeks or any extended period agreed in writing with the applicant, the applicant may by notice appeal to the Secretary of State or Welsh Ministers.[51] A partial refusal includes a modification or substitution of the description in the application.[52] As originally enacted in 1991, the legislation provided a right to appeal but no mechanism for imposing a time limit on when an appeal could be brought. An appeal could be brought many years after the decision was taken although appellants would usually wish to get on with the appeal. The Planning Act 2008 allowed a time period to be prescribed by development order.[53] Appeals are usually dealt with by Inspectors under delegated powers.[54] The rules and regulations governing written representations, hearings and inquiries in enforcement notice appeals apply to lawful development certificate appeals. These are discussed in Chapter 7.

---

[49]   2010 DMPO, Art 36(7), 2012 DMPO, Art 29(9).
[50]   In *R (Prudential Assurance Co Ltd) v Sunderland City Council* [2010] EWHC 1771 (Admin), [2011] JPL 322 LDCs were applied for a granted ruling as to whether a planning agreement applied. The Council accepted that an LDC could not deal with that issue, although the applicant for the certificates disagreed and the point was ultimately not resolved by the Court.
[51]   Town and Country Planning Act 1990, s 195(1); DMPO, Art 35(10), DMPO (Wales), Art 28(10).
[52]   Town and Country Planning Act 1990, s 195(4).
[53]   Town and Country Planning Act 1990, s 195(1B) to (1F).
[54]   Town and Country Planning Act 1990, Sch 6, para 1; Town and Country Planning (Determination of Appeals by Appointed Persons) (Prescribed Classes) Regulations 1997, reg 3.

23.24   The minister will issue or modify a CLEUD or CLOPUD, as appropriate, if he considers that the refusal or partial refusal is 'not well-founded', or in the event of a failure to determine, a refusal would not have been well-founded.[55] If he considers that a refusal was or would have been well-founded, he shall dismiss the appeal.[56] 'Not well-founded' is not defined in the Act. The effect of a local planning authority decision not being well-founded is that the Secretary of State or Welsh Ministers will issue a certificate. The local planning authority only issues a certificate if it is satisfied that the necessary matters are lawful. The Secretary of State should be similarly satisfied before issuing the certificate. A decision is not 'not well-founded' simply because of a flaw in the reasoning or other matter which would render it ultra vires, it must be shown to be the wrong result. The test for issuing a certificate should be same for the Secretary of State and the local planning authority.

CHALLENGE TO APPEAL DECISIONS

23.25   The decision of the Secretary of State, Welsh Ministers or an Inspector on an appeal under s 195 in respect of a CLEUD or CLOPUD may only be challenged by an application to the High Court under s 288 of the Act.[57] These applications are discussed in Chapter 8. A costs award in a lawful development certificate appeal can be challenged by judicial review, as with a costs decision on a planning appeal.

REVOCATION

23.26   A lawful development certificate may be revoked by the local planning authority if it transpires that:[58]

> 'on the application for the certificate:
>
> (a)   a statement was made or document used which was false in a material particular; or
>
> (b)   any material information was withheld'.

The false statement or withholding need not be by the applicant. Nor need the statement or document be provided with the application: the language of the statute is 'on the application' rather than with or in the application. The subsection applies to information provided later but in connection with the application. The default may even be by a person unconnected to the applicant who made a representation, although that is unlikely to justify revocation. 'Material' in 'material particular' and 'material information' must mean material to the decision on the application in a way which might have adversely affected the certificate granted. An entirely collateral or trivial point would not be material. However, the assessment of an LDC application involves judgments as to the credibility of evidence provided in the absence at the local planning authority stage of cross-examination. A false statement which affects

---

[55]   Town and Country Planning Act 1990, s 195(2).

[56]   Town and Country Planning Act 1990, s 195(3).

[57]   Town and Country Planning Act 1990, s 284(3)(g). An example of a Secretary of State's decision on a CLOPUD appeal was unsuccessfully challenged is *Church Commissioners for England v Secretary of State for the Environment* [1995] 2 PLR 99.

[58]   Town and Country Planning Act 1990, s 193(7).

the credibility of information provided may be material for revocation purposes (for example, if a statement supporting a CLEUD application on the basis of long use asserted that the observer had lived at a nearby property throughout the 10-year period when the person had lived there for only part of the period but had remained in the local area).

23.27 The potential effect of the false statement or withholding must have been potentially adverse to the certificate. This will be affected by the terms of the certificate: if it identifies a use within a particular use class (unconstrained by planning conditions) then debates about the frequency, precise type or operating hours of the use would be irrelevant because the use merely needed to be carried on within the use class.[59] Revocation would not be justified because the certificate ought to have been wider. If an LDC was granted on the basis that a business had operated from a site for 10 years, information would not have been withheld if the applicant had failed to put in all its business records which were confirmatory of that use. There is no obligation to deluge the authority with paper. However, a failure to produce records that indicated gaps in the operations or a scale or area of use less than that in the resulting certificate may be a material withholding. There may be an issue as to what is meant by 'withheld'. In ordinary language, withholding requires a positive decision to refrain from providing something when there is an opportunity to provide it. In those terms a person would not 'withhold' information if they appreciate its materiality.

23.28 Notice must be given when the local planning authority proposes to revoke a certificate. The owner and occupier of the land, any other person who would in the authority's opinion be affected by the revocation and, in the case of a certificate issued on appeal, the Secretary of State or Welsh Ministers, should be informed.[60] The persons notified have 14 days from the date they are served to make representations on the proposed revocation.[61] The notice must enable proper consultation to take place. In particular it must identify the claimed false statement or material information withheld before beginning the consultation, as the consultees must know the case they are being asked to meet.[62] The local planning authority must consider the representations before revoking the certificate. Written notice of the revocation must be given to those notified of the proposal, although legislation does not require notice to be given of a decision, following consultation, not to revoke.[63]

23.29 A decision to begin to revoke a lawful development certificate requires the Council to conclude that a false statement was made or material information withheld; and that it should exercise its discretion to revoke. The first is a conclusion of as to the facts in the correct legal context. The second is an exercise of discretion, which must be exercised reasonably. The crucial test would appear to be whether the decision on the certificate might have been different. There is no point in revoking a certificate if an identical certificate would be issued on a subsequent application. If the local planning authority knew of the false statement when making its decision,

---

[59] *R (Russman) v Hounslow London Borough Council* [2011] EWHC 931 (Admin).
[60] Town and Country Planning (Development Management Procedure) Order 2010, Art 35(15); Town and Country Planning (Development Management Procedure) (Wales) Order 2012, Art 28(15).
[61] DMPO, Art 35(16); DMPO (Wales), Art 28(16).
[62] *R v Surrey County Council ex p Bridge Court Holdings Ltd* [2000] 4 PLR 30 at p 45.
[63] DMPO, Art 35(17), DMPO (Wales), Art 28(17).

revocation would not be justified. The revocation can be challenged by judicial review and does not prevent the submission of a further LDC application.

PROSECUTION FOR PROVIDING MISLEADING INFORMATION

23.30   The provision of false information about an LDC application is an offence. An offence is committed:[64]

'if any person, for the purpose of procuring a particular decision on an application (whether by himself or another) for the issue of a certificate under section 191 or 192—

(a)   knowingly or recklessly makes a statement which is false or misleading in a material particular;

(b)   with intent to deceive, uses any document which is false or misleading in a material particular; or

(c)   with intent to deceive, withholds any material information.'

The offence applies to all persons concerned, including third parties, council officers and members. It also applies to persons attempting to procure a refusal or partial refusal of the application. Since no positive obligation to supply information is provided and an intention to deceive is required, a person can only be guilty of withholding material information if that act was designed to lead the local planning authority to the wrong conclusion on an issue.

THIRD PARTY CHALLENGE TO THE VALIDITY OF A LAWFUL DEVELOPMENT CERTIFICATE

23.31   The decision of the local planning authority to issue a lawful development certificate may be challenged by third parties by judicial review. They are likely to have standing because a certificate wider than is correct effectively grants planning permission. If a planning application had been made third parties would have been entitled to object. Since the only way they could challenge the certificate is by judicial review, they have a sufficient interest.[65] An applicant for a certificate has a right to appeal to the minister and would be expected to pursue that remedy before going to the court, except in an exceptional case. A third party challenge to a Secretary of State or Welsh Ministers decision on a lawful development certificate appeal would be by an application under s 288 of the Town and Country Planning Act 1990.

DECLARATION BY THE HIGH COURT OF THE LAWFULNESS OF PROPOSED ACTIONS

23.32   In *Reprotech,* the House of Lords has rejected the previous practice of the High Court making declarations as to the lawfulness of proposed actions. The

---

[64]   Town and Country Planning Act 1990, s 194(1).
[65]   *R v Sheffield City Council ex p Russell* (1994) 68 P & CR 331. For another example, see *R v Kensington and Chelsea Royal London Borough Council ex p Europa Foods Ltd* [1996] ECGS 5 (15 January 1996).

practice had been endorsed by the House of Lords in *Pyx Granite Co Ltd v Ministry of Housing and Local Government,*[66] who considered that:

> 'It is a principle not by any means to be whittled down that the subject's recourse to Her Majesty's courts for the determination of his rights is not to be excluded except by clear words'.[67]

In the past there have been a number of decisions where courts have considered applications for declaration.[68] In *Thames Heliport v London Borough of Tower Hamlets*[69] the Court of Appeal expressed concerns about the utility of such applications and the danger of setting the judge an examination paper rather than addressing the real points of concern (whilst considering that in certain respects those proceedings were justified).

23.33   In *R (Reprotech (Pebsham) Ltd) v East Sussex County Council,* the court had been asked to rule whether the generation of electricity at a waste disposal site was a material change of use. Giving the leading speech Lord Hoffmann said:[70]

> '37 ... I doubt whether the judge would have had jurisdiction to give such a ruling. In *Pyx Granite Co Ltd v Ministry of Housing and Local Government* [1960] AC 260 the House of Lords decided that, as an alternative to seeking a determination that no planning permission was required, a landowner could apply to the court for a declaration which would be binding upon the planning authority in enforcement proceedings. But the law was changed by section 33 of the Caravan Sites and Control of Development Act 1960, which made an appeal to the Secretary of State the sole method by which a landowner could challenge an enforcement notice on the ground that he does not need planning permission. So Lord Bridge of Harwich said in *Thrasyvoulou v Secretary of State for the Environment* [1990] 2 AC 273, 292:
>
> > "the effect of the changes made by section 33 of the 1960 Act was to substitute for the jurisdiction under section 23(4) of the Act of 1947 [an appeal against an enforcement notice to the justices on the ground that no permission was required] and for the jurisdiction of the High Court in proceedings for a declaration directed to the determination of legal rights in existing buildings or uses of land a new jurisdiction conferred exclusively on the minister."
>
> 38   Mr Porten[71] says that the exclusive procedure is concerned with challenges to enforcement notices. No enforcement notice has been issued and in seeking a declaration from Tucker J, Reprotech was not attempting to challenge one. It seems to me, however, that the only value of such a declaration would be to serve as an answer to enforcement proceedings if Reprotech proceed to generate electricity without planning permission. If, as the *Thrasyvoulou* case establishes, it cannot be used for this purpose, it has no point and should not be made.'

The practice of seeking declarations in support of the lawfulness of activities appears to have almost, and perhaps, entirely, died out since the *Reprotech* decision.

---

[66]   [1960] AC 260.

[67]   At 286 per Viscount Simonds.

[68]   Eg *St. Hermans Estate Co Ltd v Havant and Waterloo Urban District Council* (1970) 69 LGR 286, *Pedgrift v Oxfordshire County Council* (1992) 63 P & CR 246; *Burroughs Day v Bristol City Council* [1996] 1 EGLR 167; *Tesco Stores Limited v North Norfolk District Council* (1999) 78 P & CR 359.

[69]   (1997) 74 P & CR 164.

[70]   At 358, 359.

[71]   Author's note: leading counsel for Reprotech.

23.34   Declarations of the lawfulness or otherwise of activities may arise collaterally in court proceedings. If a planning injunction is sought then the court will have to decide whether there is a breach of planning control. As another example, judicial review of the failure to take enforcement action may consider the local planning authority's approach to lawfulness. However, the Administrative Court is concerned with whether the authority considered the matter lawfully in public law terms, and unless there could only be one correct conclusion on the facts, would not reach a conclusion whether the matters were lawful.[72] These instances tend to involve a complaint by a claimant that various matters are unlawful. A developer or landowner who wishes to establish that something is or would be lawful would be expected to apply for a lawful development certificate.

---

[72]   See *R (Save Woolley Valley Action Group Ltd) v Bath and North East Somerset Council* [2012] EWHC 2161 (Admin), [2013] Env LR 8 at para 65 per Lang J.

Appendix 1

Town and Country Planning Act 1990

PART III CONTROL OVER DEVELOPMENT

Meaning of development

55 Meaning of 'development' and 'new development'

(1) Subject to the following provisions of this section, in this Act, except where the context otherwise requires, 'development,' means the carrying out of building, engineering, mining or other operations in, on, over or under land, or the making of any material change in the use of any buildings or other land.

(1A) For the purposes of this Act 'building operations' includes—

(a) demolition of buildings;

(b) rebuilding;

(c) structural alterations of or additions to buildings; and

(d) other operations normally undertaken by a person carrying on business as a builder.

(2) The following operations or uses of land shall not be taken for the purposes of this Act to involve development of the land—

(a) the carrying out for the maintenance, improvement or other alteration of any building of works which—

(i) affect only the interior of the building, or

(ii) do not materially affect the external appearance of the building,

and are not works for making good war damage or works begun after 5th December 1968 for the alteration of a building by providing additional space in it underground;

(b) the carrying out on land within the boundaries of a road by a . . . highway authority of any works required for the maintenance or improvement of the road but, in the case of any such works which are not exclusively for the maintenance of the road, not including any works which may have significant adverse effects on the environment;

(c) the carrying out by a local authority or statutory undertakers of any works for the purpose of inspecting, repairing or renewing any sewers, mains, pipes, cables or other apparatus, including the breaking open of any street or other land for that purpose;

(d) the use of any buildings or other land within the curtilage of a dwellinghouse for any purpose incidental to the enjoyment of the dwellinghouse as such;

(e) the use of any land for the purposes of agriculture or forestry (including afforestation) and the use for any of those purposes of any building occupied together with land so used;

(f) in the case of buildings or other land which are used for a purpose of any class specified in an order made by the Secretary of State under this section, the use of the buildings or other land or, subject to the provisions of the order, of any part of the buildings or the other land, for any other purpose of the same class.

(g) the demolition of any description of building specified in a direction given by the Secretary of State to local planning authorities generally or to a particular local planning authority.

(2A) The Secretary of State may in a development order specify any circumstances or description of circumstances in which subsection (2) does not apply to operations mentioned in paragraph (a) of that subsection which have the effect of increasing the gross floor space of the building by such amount or percentage amount as is so specified.

(2B) The development order may make different provision for different purposes.

(3) For the avoidance of doubt it is hereby declared that for the purposes of this section—

(a) the use as two or more separate dwellinghouses of any building previously used as a single dwellinghouse involves a material change in the use of the building and of each part of it which is so used;

(b) the deposit of refuse or waste materials on land involves a material change in its use, notwithstanding that the land is comprised in a site already used for that purpose, if—

(i) the superficial area of the deposit is extended, or

(ii) the height of the deposit is extended and exceeds the level of the land adjoining the site.

(4) For the purposes of this Act mining operations include—

(a) the removal of material of any description—

(i) from a mineral-working deposit;

(ii) from a deposit of pulverised fuel ash or other furnace ash or clinker; or

(iii) from a deposit of iron, steel or other metallic slags; and

(b) the extraction of minerals from a disused railway embankment.

(4A) Where the placing or assembly of any tank in any part of any inland waters for the purpose of fish farming there would not, apart from this subsection, involve development of the land below, this Act shall have effect as if the tank resulted from carrying out engineering operations over that land; and in this subsection—

'fish farming' means the breeding, rearing or keeping of fish or shellfish (which includes any kind of crustacean and mollusc);

'inland waters' means waters which do not form part of the sea or of any creek, bay or estuary or of any river as far as the tide flows; and

'tank' includes any cage and any other structure for use in fish farming.

(5)   Without prejudice to any regulations made under the provisions of this Act relating to the control of advertisements, the use for the display of advertisements of any external part of a building which is not normally used for that purpose shall be treated for the purposes of this section as involving a material change in the use of that part of the building.

[…]

Requirement for planning permission

57 Planning permission required for development

(1)   Subject to the following provisions of this section, planning permission is required for the carrying out of any development of land.

(1A)   Subsection (1) is subject to section 33(1) of the Planning Act 2008 (exclusion of requirement for planning permission etc. for development for which development consent required).

(2)   Where planning permission to develop land has been granted for a limited period, planning permission is not required for the resumption, at the end of that period, of its use for the purpose for which it was normally used before the permission was granted.

(3)   Where by a development order, a local development order or a neighbourhood development order planning permission to develop land has been granted subject to limitations, planning permission is not required for the use of that land which (apart from its use in accordance with that permission) is its normal use.

(4)   Where an enforcement notice has been issued in respect of any development of land, planning permission is not required for its use for the purpose for which (in accordance with the provisions of this Part of this Act) it could lawfully have been used if that development had not been carried out.

(5)   In determining for the purposes of subsections (2) and (3) what is or was the normal use of land, no account shall be taken of any use begun in contravention of this Part or of previous planning control.

(6)   For the purposes of this section a use of land shall be taken to have been begun in contravention of previous planning control if it was begun in contravention of Part III of the 1947 Act, Part III of the 1962 Act or Part III of the 1971 Act.

(7)   Subsection (1) has effect subject to Schedule 4 (which makes special provision about use of land on 1st July 1948).

[…]

Other controls over development

106 Planning obligations

(1)   Any person interested in land in the area of a local planning authority may, by agreement or otherwise, enter into an obligation (referred to in this section and sections 106A and 106B as 'a planning obligation'), enforceable to the extent mentioned in subsection (3)—

(a) restricting the development or use of the land in any specified way;

(b) requiring specified operations or activities to be carried out in, on, under or over the land;

(c) requiring the land to be used in any specified way; or

(d) requiring a sum or sums to be paid to the authority (or, in a case where section 2E applies, to the Greater London Authority) on a specified date or dates or periodically.

(1A) In the case of a development consent obligation, the reference to development in subsection (1)(a) includes anything that constitutes development for the purposes of the Planning Act 2008.

(2) A planning obligation may—

(a) be unconditional or subject to conditions;

(b) impose any restriction or requirement mentioned in subsection (1)(a) to (c) either indefinitely or for such period or periods as may be specified; and

(c) if it requires a sum or sums to be paid, require the payment of a specified amount or an amount determined in accordance with the instrument by which the obligation is entered into and, if it requires the payment of periodical sums, require them to be paid indefinitely or for a specified period.

(3) Subject to subsection (4) a planning obligation is enforceable by the authority identified in accordance with subsection (9)(d)—

(a) against the person entering into the obligation; and

(b) against any person deriving title from that person.

(4) The instrument by which a planning obligation is entered into may provide that a person shall not be bound by the obligation in respect of any period during which he no longer has an interest in the land.

(5) A restriction or requirement imposed under a planning obligation is enforceable by injunction.

(6) Without prejudice to subsection (5), if there is a breach of a requirement in a planning obligation to carry out any operations in, on, under or over the land to which the obligation relates, the authority by whom the obligation is enforceable may—

(a) enter the land and carry out the operations; and

(b) recover from the person or persons against whom the obligation is enforceable any expenses reasonably incurred by them in doing so.

(7) Before an authority exercise their power under subsection (6)(a) they shall give not less than twenty-one days' notice of their intention to do so to any person against whom the planning obligation is enforceable.

(8) Any person who wilfully obstructs a person acting in the exercise of a power under subsection (6)(a) shall be guilty of an offence and liable on summary conviction to a fine not exceeding level 3 on the standard scale.

(9)   A planning obligation may not be entered into except by an instrument executed as a deed which—

(a) states that the obligation is a planning obligation for the purposes of this section;

(aa) if the obligation is a development consent obligation, contains a statement to that effect;

(b) identifies the land in which the person entering into the obligation is interested;

(c) identifies the person entering into the obligation and states what his interest in the land is; and

(d) identifies the local planning authority by whom the obligation is enforceable, and, in a case where section 2E applies, identifies the Mayor of London as an authority by whom the obligation is also enforceable

(10) A copy of any such instrument shall be given to the local planning authority so identified and, in a case where section 2E applies, to the Mayor of London.

(11) A planning obligation shall be a local land charge and for the purposes of the Local Land Charges Act 1975 the authority by whom the obligation is enforceable shall be treated as the originating authority as respects such a charge.

(12) Regulations may provide for the charging on the land of—

(a) any sum or sums required to be paid under a planning obligation; and

(b) any expenses recoverable by a local planning authority or the Mayor of London under subsection (6)(b),

and this section and sections 106A to 106BC shall have effect subject to any such regulations.

(13) In this section 'specified' means specified in the instrument by which the planning obligation is entered into and in this section and section 106A 'land' has the same meaning as in the Local Land Charges Act 1975.

(14) In this section and section 106A 'development consent obligation' means a planning obligation entered into in connection with an application (or a proposed application) for an order granting development consent.

PART VII ENFORCEMENT

171A Expressions used in connection with enforcement

(1) For the purposes of this Act—

(a) carrying out development without the required planning permission; or

(b) failing to comply with any condition or limitation subject to which planning permission has been granted, constitutes a breach of planning control.

(2) For the purposes of this Act—

(a) the issue of an enforcement notice (defined in section 172); or

(b) the service of a breach of condition notice (defined in section 187A),

constitutes taking enforcement action.

(3)   In this Part 'planning permission' includes permission under Part III of the 1947 Act, of the 1962 Act or of the 1971 Act.

171B Time limits

(1)   Where there has been a breach of planning control consisting in the carrying out without planning permission of building, engineering, mining or other operations in, on, over or under land, no enforcement action may be taken after the end of the period of four years beginning with the date on which the operations were substantially completed.

(2)   Where there has been a breach of planning control consisting in the change of use of any building to use as a single dwellinghouse, no enforcement action may be taken after the end of the period of four years beginning with the date of the breach.

(2A) There is no restriction on when enforcement action may be taken in relation to a breach of planning control in respect of relevant demolition (within the meaning of section 196D).[1]

(3)   In the case of any other breach of planning control, no enforcement action may be taken after the end of the period of ten years beginning with the date of the breach.

(4)   The preceding subsections do not prevent—

(a) the service of a breach of condition notice in respect of any breach of planning control if an enforcement notice in respect of the breach is in effect; or

(b) taking further enforcement action in respect of any breach of planning control if, during the period of four years ending with that action being taken, the local planning authority have taken or purported to take enforcement action in respect of that breach.

171BA Time limits in cases involving concealment

(1)   Where it appears to the local planning authority that there may have been a breach of planning control in respect of any land in England, the authority may apply to a magistrates' court for an order under this subsection (a 'planning enforcement order') in relation to that apparent breach of planning control.

(2)   If a magistrates' court makes a planning enforcement order in relation to an apparent breach of planning control, the local planning authority may take enforcement action in respect of—

(a) the apparent breach, or

(b) any of the matters constituting the apparent breach,

at any time in the enforcement year.

---

[1] Prospective amendment by Enterprise and Regulatory Reform Act 2013 in England.

(3)   'The enforcement year' for a planning enforcement order is the year that begins at the end of 22 days beginning with the day on which the court's decision to make the order is given, but this is subject to subsection (4).

(4)   If an application under section 111(1) of the Magistrates' Courts Act 1980 (statement of case for opinion of High Court) is made in respect of a planning enforcement order, the enforcement year for the order is the year beginning with the day on which the proceedings arising from that application are finally determined or withdrawn.

(5)   Subsection (2)—

    (a) applies whether or not the time limits under section 171B have expired, and

    (b) does not prevent the taking of enforcement action after the end of the enforcement year but within those time limits.

171BB Planning enforcement orders: procedure

(1)   An application for a planning enforcement order in relation to an apparent breach of planning control may be made within the 6 months beginning with the date on which evidence of the apparent breach of planning control sufficient in the opinion of the local planning authority to justify the application came to the authority's knowledge.

(2)   For the purposes of subsection (1), a certificate—

    (a) signed on behalf of the local planning authority, and

    (b) stating the date on which evidence sufficient in the authority's opinion to justify the application came to the authority's knowledge,

is conclusive evidence of that fact.

(3)   A certificate stating that matter and purporting to be so signed is to be deemed to be so signed unless the contrary is proved.

(4)   Where the local planning authority apply to a magistrates' court for a planning enforcement order in relation to an apparent breach of planning control in respect of any land, the authority must serve a copy of the application—

    (a) on the owner and on the occupier of the land, and

    (b) on any other person having an interest in the land that is an interest which, in the opinion of the authority, would be materially affected by the taking of enforcement action in respect of the apparent breach.

(5)   The persons entitled to appear before, and be heard by, the court hearing an application for a planning enforcement order in relation to an apparent breach of planning control in respect of any land include—

    (a) the applicant,

    (b) any person on whom a copy of the application was served under subsection (4), and

    (c) any other person having an interest in the land that is an interest which, in the opinion of the court, would be materially affected by the taking of enforcement action in respect of the apparent breach.

(6)   In this section 'planning enforcement order' means an order under section 171BA(1).

171BC Making a planning enforcement order

(1)   A magistrates' court may make a planning enforcement order in relation to an apparent breach of planning control only if—

(a)   the court is satisfied, on the balance of probabilities, that the apparent breach, or any of the matters constituting the apparent breach, has (to any extent) been deliberately concealed by any person or persons, and

(b)   the court considers it just to make the order having regard to all the circumstances.

(2)   A planning enforcement order must—

(a)   identify the apparent breach of planning control to which it relates, and

(b)   state the date on which the court's decision to make the order was given.

(3)   In this section 'planning enforcement order' means an order under section 171BA(1).

Planning contravention notices

171C Power to require information about activities on land

(1)   Where it appears to the local planning authority that there may have been a breach of planning control in respect of any land, they may serve notice to that effect (referred to in this Act as a 'planning contravention notice') on any person who—

(a)   is the owner or occupier of the land or has any other interest in it; or

(b)   is carrying out operations on the land or is using it for any purpose.

(2)   A planning contravention notice may require the person on whom it is served to give such information as to—

(a)   any operations being carried out on the land, any use of the land and any other activities being carried out on the land; and

(b)   any matter relating to the conditions or limitations subject to which any planning permission in respect of the land has been granted,

as may be specified in the notice.

(3)   Without prejudice to the generality of subsection (2), the notice may require the person on whom it is served, so far as he is able—

(a)   to state whether or not the land is being used for any purpose specified in the notice or any operations or activities specified in the notice are being or have been carried out on the land;

(b)   to state when any use, operations or activities began;

(c)   to give the name and postal address of any person known to him to use or have used the land for any purpose or to be carrying out, or have carried out, any operations or activities on the land;

(d) to give any information he holds as to any planning permission for any use or operations or any reason for planning permission not being required for any use or operations;

(e) to state the nature of his interest (if any) in the land and the name and postal address of any other person known to him to have an interest in the land.

(4) A planning contravention notice may give notice of a time and place at which—

(a) any offer which the person on whom the notice is served may wish to make to apply for planning permission, to refrain from carrying out any operations or activities or to undertake remedial works; and

(b) any representations which he may wish to make about the notice,

will be considered by the authority, and the authority shall give him an opportunity to make in person any such offer or representations at that time and place.

(5) A planning contravention notice must inform the person on whom it is served—

(a) of the likely consequences of his failing to respond to the notice and, in particular, that enforcement action may be taken; and

(b) of the effect of section 186(5)(b).

(6) Any requirement of a planning contravention notice shall be complied with by giving information in writing to the local planning authority.

(7) The service of a planning contravention notice does not affect any other power exercisable in respect of any breach of planning control.

(8) In this section references to operations or activities on land include operations or activities in, under or over the land.

171D Penalties for non-compliance with planning contravention notice

(1) If, at any time after the end of the period of twenty-one days beginning with the day on which a planning contravention notice has been served on any person, he has not complied with any requirement of the notice, he shall be guilty of an offence.

(2) An offence under subsection (1) may be charged by reference to any day or longer period of time and a person may be convicted of a second or subsequent offence under that subsection by reference to any period of time following the preceding conviction for such an offence.

(3) It shall be a defence for a person charged with an offence under subsection (1) to prove that he had a reasonable excuse for failing to comply with the requirement.

(4) A person guilty of an offence under subsection (1) shall be liable on summary conviction to a fine not exceeding level 3 on the standard scale.

(5) If any person—

(a) makes any statement purporting to comply with a requirement of a planning contravention notice which he knows to be false or misleading in a material particular; or

(b) recklessly makes such a statement which is false or misleading in a material particular,

he shall be guilty of an offence.

(6) A person guilty of an offence under subsection (5) shall be liable on summary conviction to a fine not exceeding level 5 on the standard scale.

171E Temporary stop notice

(1) This section applies if the local planning authority think—

    (a) that there has been a breach of planning control in relation to any land, and

    (b) that it is expedient that the activity (or any part of the activity) which amounts to the breach is stopped immediately.

(2) The authority may issue a temporary stop notice.

(3) The notice must be in writing and must—

    (a) specify the activity which the authority think amounts to the breach;

    (b) prohibit the carrying on of the activity (or of so much of the activity as is specified in the notice);

    (c) set out the authority's reasons for issuing the notice.

(4) A temporary stop notice may be served on any of the following—

    (a) the person who the authority think is carrying on the activity;

    (b) a person who the authority think is an occupier of the land;

    (c) a person who the authority think has an interest in the land.

(5) The authority must display on the land—

    (a) a copy of the notice;

    (b) a statement of the effect of the notice and of section 171G.

(6) A temporary stop notice has effect from the time a copy of it is first displayed in pursuance of subsection (5).

(7) A temporary stop notice ceases to have effect—

    (a) at the end of the period of 28 days starting on the day the copy notice is so displayed,

    (b) at the end of such shorter period starting on that day as is specified in the notice, or

    (c) if it is withdrawn by the local planning authority.

171F Temporary stop notice: restrictions

(1) A temporary stop notice does not prohibit—

    (a) the use of a building as a dwelling house;

    (b) the carrying out of an activity of such description or in such circumstances as is prescribed.

(2)   A temporary stop notice does not prohibit the carrying out of any activity which has been carried out (whether or not continuously) for a period of four years ending with the day on which the copy of the notice is first displayed as mentioned in section 171E(6).

(3)   Subsection (2) does not prevent a temporary stop notice prohibiting—

(a) activity consisting of or incidental to building, engineering, mining or other operations, or

(b) the deposit of refuse or waste materials.

(4)   For the purposes of subsection (2) any period during which the activity is authorised by planning permission must be ignored.

(5)   A second or subsequent temporary stop notice must not be issued in respect of the same activity unless the local planning authority has first taken some other enforcement action in relation to the breach of planning control which is constituted by the activity.

(6)   In subsection (5) enforcement action includes obtaining the grant of an injunction under section 187B.

171G Temporary stop notice: offences

(1)   A person commits an offence if he contravenes a temporary stop notice—

(a) which has been served on him, or

(b) a copy of which has been displayed in accordance with section 171E(5).

(2)   Contravention of a temporary stop notice includes causing or permitting the contravention of the notice.

(3)   An offence under this section may be charged by reference to a day or a longer period of time.

(4)   A person may be convicted of more than one such offence in relation to the same temporary stop notice by reference to different days or periods of time.

(5)   A person does not commit an offence under this section if he proves—

(a) that the temporary stop notice was not served on him, and

(b) that he did not know, and could not reasonably have been expected to know, of its existence.

(6)   A person convicted of an offence under this section is liable—

(a) on summary conviction, to a fine not exceeding £20,000;

(b) on conviction on indictment, to a fine.

(7)   In determining the amount of the fine the court must have regard in particular to any financial benefit which has accrued or has appeared to accrue to the person convicted in consequence of the offence.

171H Temporary stop notice: compensation

(1)   This section applies if and only if a temporary stop notice is issued and at least one of the following paragraphs applies—

(a) the activity which is specified in the notice is authorised by planning permission or by a development order, a local development order or a neighbourhood development order;

(b) a certificate in respect of the activity is issued under section 191 or granted under that section by virtue of section 195;

(c) the authority withdraws the notice.

(2) Subsection (1)(a) does not apply if the planning permission is granted on or after the date on which a copy of the notice is first displayed as mentioned in section 171E(6).

(3) Subsection (1)(c) does not apply if the notice is withdrawn following the grant of planning permission as mentioned in subsection (2).

(4) A person who at the time the notice is served has an interest in the land to which the notice relates is entitled to be compensated by the local planning authority in respect of any loss or damage directly attributable to the prohibition effected by the notice.

(5) Subsections (3) to (7) of section 186 apply to compensation payable under this section as they apply to compensation payable under that section; and for that purpose references in those subsections to a stop notice must be taken to be references to a temporary stop notice.

Enforcement notices

172 Issue of enforcement notice

(1) The local planning authority may issue a notice (in this Act referred to as an 'enforcement notice') where it appears to them—

(a) that there has been a breach of planning control; and

(b) that it is expedient to issue the notice, having regard to the provisions of the development plan and to any other material considerations.

(2) A copy of an enforcement notice shall be served—

(a) on the owner and on the occupier of the land to which it relates; and

(b) on any other person having an interest in the land, being an interest which, in the opinion of the authority, is materially affected by the notice.

(3) The service of the notice shall take place—

(a) not more than twenty-eight days after its date of issue; and

(b) not less than twenty-eight days before the date specified in it as the date on which it is to take effect.

172A Assurance as regards prosecution for person served with notice

(1) When, or at any time after, an enforcement notice is served on a person, the local planning authority may give the person a letter—

(a) explaining that, once the enforcement notice had been issued, the authority was required to serve the notice on the person,

    (b) giving the person one of the following assurances—

        (i) that, in the circumstances as they appear to the authority, the person is not at risk of being prosecuted under section 179 in connection with the enforcement notice, or

        (ii) that, in the circumstances as they appear to the authority, the person is not at risk of being prosecuted under section 179 in connection with the matters relating to the enforcement notice that are specified in the letter,

    (c) explaining, where the person is given the assurance under paragraph (b)(ii), the respects in which the person is at risk of being prosecuted under section 179 in connection with the enforcement notice, and

    (d) stating that, if the authority subsequently wishes to withdraw the assurance in full or part, the authority will first give the person a letter specifying a future time for the withdrawal that will allow the person a reasonable opportunity to take any steps necessary to avoid any risk of prosecution that is to cease to be covered by the assurance.

(2)   At any time after a person has under subsection (1) been given a letter containing an assurance, the local planning authority may give the person a letter withdrawing the assurance (so far as not previously withdrawn) in full or part from a time specified in the letter.

(3)   The time specified in a letter given under subsection (2) to a person must be such as will give the person a reasonable opportunity to take any steps necessary to avoid any risk of prosecution that is to cease to be covered by the assurance.

(4)   Withdrawal under subsection (2) of an assurance given under subsection (1) does not withdraw the assurance so far as relating to prosecution on account of there being a time before the withdrawal when steps had not been taken or an activity had not ceased.

(5)   An assurance given under subsection (1) (so far as not withdrawn under subsection (2)) is binding on any person with power to prosecute an offence under section 179.

173 Contents and effect of notice

(1)   An enforcement notice shall state—

    (a) the matters which appear to the local planning authority to constitute the breach of planning control; and

    (b) the paragraph of section 171A(1) within which, in the opinion of the authority, the breach falls.

(2)   A notice complies with subsection (1)(a) if it enables any person on whom a copy of it is served to know what those matters are.

(3)   An enforcement notice shall specify the steps which the authority require to be taken, or the activities which the authority require to cease, in order to achieve, wholly or partly, any of the following purposes.

(4)   Those purposes are—

    (a) remedying the breach by making any development comply with the terms (including conditions and limitations) of any planning permission which has been granted in respect of the land, by discontinuing any use of the land or by restoring the land to its condition before the breach took place; or

(b) remedying any injury to amenity which has been caused by the breach.

(5) An enforcement notice may, for example, require—

(a) the alteration or removal of any buildings or works;

(b) the carrying out of any building or other operations;

(c) any activity on the land not to be carried on except to the extent specified in the notice; or

(d) the contour of a deposit of refuse or waste materials on land to be modified by altering the gradient or gradients of its sides.

(6) Where an enforcement notice is issued in respect of a breach of planning control consisting of demolition of a building, the notice may require the construction of a building (in this section referred to as a 'replacement building') which, subject to subsection (7), is as similar as possible to the demolished building.

(7) A replacement building—

(a) must comply with any requirement imposed by any enactment applicable to the construction of buildings;

(b) may differ from the demolished building in any respect which, if the demolished building had been altered in that respect, would not have constituted a breach of planning control;

(c) must comply with any regulations made for the purposes of this subsection (including regulations modifying paragraphs (a) and (b)).

(8) An enforcement notice shall specify the date on which it is to take effect and, subject to sections 175(4) and 289(4A), shall take effect on that date.

(9) An enforcement notice shall specify the period at the end of which any steps are required to have been taken or any activities are required to have ceased and may specify different periods for different steps or activities; and, where different periods apply to different steps or activities, references in this Part to the period for compliance with an enforcement notice, in relation to any step or activity, are to the period at the end of which the step is required to have been taken or the activity is required to have ceased.

(10) An enforcement notice shall specify such additional matters as may be prescribed, and regulations may require every copy of an enforcement notice served under section 172 to be accompanied by an explanatory note giving prescribed information as to the right of appeal under section 174.

(11) Where—

(a) an enforcement notice in respect of any breach of planning control could have required any buildings or works to be removed or any activity to cease, but does not do so; and

(b) all the requirements of the notice have been complied with,

then, so far as the notice did not so require, planning permission shall be treated as having been granted by virtue of section 73A in respect of development consisting of the construction of the buildings or works or, as the case may be, the carrying out of the activities.

(12) Where—

    (a) an enforcement notice requires the construction of a replacement building; and

    (b) all the requirements of the notice with respect to that construction have been complied with,

planning permission shall be treated as having been granted by virtue of section 73A in respect of development consisting of that construction.

173A Variation and withdrawal of enforcement notices

(1) The local planning authority may—

    (a) withdraw an enforcement notice issued by them; or

    (b) waive or relax any requirement of such a notice and, in particular, may extend any period specified in accordance with section 173(9).

(2) The powers conferred by subsection (1) may be exercised whether or not the notice has taken effect.

(3) The local planning authority shall, immediately after exercising the powers conferred by subsection (1), give notice of the exercise to every person who has been served with a copy of the enforcement notice or would, if the notice were re-issued, be served with a copy of it.

(4) The withdrawal of an enforcement notice does not affect the power of the local planning authority to issue a further enforcement notice.

174 Appeal against enforcement notice

(1) A person having an interest in the land to which an enforcement notice relates or a relevant occupier may appeal to the Secretary of State against the notice, whether or not a copy of it has been served on him.

(2) An appeal may be brought on any of the following grounds—

    (a) that, in respect of any breach of planning control which may be constituted by the matters stated in the notice, planning permission ought to be granted or, as the case may be, the condition or limitation concerned ought to be discharged;

    (b) that those matters have not occurred;

    (c) that those matters (if they occurred) do not constitute a breach of planning control;

    (d) that, at the date when the notice was issued, no enforcement action could be taken in respect of any breach of planning control which may be constituted by those matters;

    (e) that copies of the enforcement notice were not served as required by section 172;

    (f) that the steps required by the notice to be taken, or the activities required by the notice to cease, exceed what is necessary to remedy any breach of planning control which may be constituted by those matters or, as the case may be, to remedy any injury to amenity which has been caused by any such breach;

(g) that any period specified in the notice in accordance with section 173(9) falls short of what should reasonably be allowed.

(2A) An appeal may not be brought on the ground specified in subsection (2)(a) if—

(a) the land to which the enforcement notice relates is in England, and

(b) the enforcement notice was issued at a time—

(i) after the making of a related application for planning permission, but

(ii) before the end of the period applicable under section 78(2) in the case of that application.

(2B) An application for planning permission for the development of any land is, for the purposes of subsection (2A), related to an enforcement notice if granting planning permission for the development would involve granting planning permission in respect of the matters specified in the enforcement notice as constituting a breach of planning control.

(2C) Where any breach of planning control constituted by the matters stated in the notice relates to relevant demolition (within the meaning of section 196D), an appeal may also be brought on the grounds that—

(a) the relevant demolition was urgently necessary in the interests of safety or health;

(b) it was not practicable to secure safety or health by works of repair or works for affording temporary support or shelter; and

(c) the relevant demolition was the minimum measure necessary.[2]

(3) An appeal under this section shall be made—

(a) by giving written notice of the appeal to the Secretary of State before the date specified in the enforcement notice as the date on which it is to take effect; or

(b) by sending such notice to him in a properly addressed and pre-paid letter posted to him at such time that, in the ordinary course of post, it would be delivered to him before that date; or

(c) by sending such notice to him using electronic communications at such time that, in the ordinary course of transmission, it would be delivered to him before that date.

(4) A person who gives notice under subsection (3) shall submit to the Secretary of State, either when giving the notice or within the prescribed time, a statement in writing—

(a) specifying the grounds on which he is appealing against the enforcement notice; and

(b) giving such further information as may be prescribed.

---

[2]   Prospective amendment by Enterprise and Regulatory Reform Act 2013 in England.

(5)   If, where more than one ground is specified in that statement, the appellant does not give information required under subsection (4)(b) in relation to each of those grounds within the prescribed time, the Secretary of State may determine the appeal without considering any ground as to which the appellant has failed to give such information within that time.

(6)   In this section 'relevant occupier' means a person who—

(a)   on the date on which the enforcement notice is issued occupies the land to which the notice relates by virtue of a licence; and

(b)   continues so to occupy the land when the appeal is brought.

175 Appeals: supplementary provisions

(1)   The Secretary of State may by regulations prescribe the procedure which is to be followed on appeals under section 174 and, in particular, but without prejudice to the generality of this subsection, may—

(a)   require the local planning authority to submit, within such time as may be prescribed, a statement indicating the submissions which they propose to put forward on the appeal;

(b)   specify the matters to be included in such a statement;

(c)   require the authority or the appellant to give such notice of such an appeal as may be prescribed;

(d)   require the authority to send to the Secretary of State, within such period from the date of the bringing of the appeal as may be prescribed, a copy of the enforcement notice and a list of the persons served with copies of it.

(2)   The notice to be prescribed under subsection (1)(c) shall be such notice as in the opinion of the Secretary of State is likely to bring the appeal to the attention of persons in the locality in which the land to which the enforcement notice relates is situated.

(3)   Subject to section 176(4), the Secretary of State shall, if either the appellant or the local planning authority so desire, give each of them an opportunity of appearing before and being heard by a person appointed by the Secretary of State for the purpose.

(3A)   Subsection (3) does not apply to an appeal against an enforcement notice issued by a local planning authority in England.

(4)   Where an appeal is brought under section 174 the enforcement notice shall subject to any order under section 289(4A) be of no effect pending the final determination or the withdrawal of the appeal.

(5)   Where any person has appealed to the Secretary of State against an enforcement notice, no person shall be entitled, in any other proceedings instituted after the making of the appeal, to claim that the notice was not duly served on the person who appealed.

(6)   Schedule 6 applies to appeals under section 174, including appeals under that section as applied by regulations under any other provisions of this Act.

176 General provisions relating to determination of appeals

(1)   On an appeal under section 174 the Secretary of State may—

   (a) correct any defect, error or misdescription in the enforcement notice; or

   (b) vary the terms of the enforcement notice,

if he is satisfied that the correction or variation will not cause injustice to the appellant or the local planning authority.

(2)   Where the Secretary of State determines to allow the appeal, he may quash the notice.

(2A) The Secretary of State shall give any directions necessary to give effect to his determination on the appeal.

(3)   The Secretary of State—

   (a) may dismiss an appeal if the appellant fails to comply with section 174(4) within the prescribed time; and

   (b) may allow an appeal and quash the enforcement notice if the local planning authority fail to comply with any requirement of regulations made by virtue of paragraph (a), (b), or (d) of section 175(1) within the prescribed period.

(4)   If section 175(3) would otherwise apply and the Secretary of State proposes to dismiss an appeal under paragraph (a) of subsection (3) of this section or to allow an appeal and quash the enforcement notice under paragraph (b) of that subsection, he need not comply with section 175(3).

(5)   Where it would otherwise be a ground for determining an appeal under section 174 in favour of the appellant that a person required to be served with a copy of the enforcement notice was not served, the Secretary of State may disregard that fact if neither the appellant nor that person has been substantially prejudiced by the failure to serve him.

177 Grant or modification of planning permission on appeals against enforcement notices

(1)   On the determination of an appeal under section 174, the Secretary of State may—

   (a) grant planning permission in respect of the matters stated in the enforcement notice as constituting a breach of planning control, whether in relation to the whole or any part of those matters or in relation to the whole or any part of the land to which the notice relates;

   (b) discharge any condition or limitation subject to which planning permission was granted;

   (c) determine whether, on the date on which the appeal was made, any existing use of the land was lawful, any operations which had been carried out in, on, over or under the land were lawful or any matter constituting a failure to comply with any condition or limitation subject to which planning permission was granted was lawful and, if so, issue a certificate under section 191.

(1A) The provisions of sections 191 to 194 mentioned in subsection (1B) shall apply for the purposes of subsection (1)(c) as they apply for the purposes of section 191, but as if—

(a) any reference to an application for a certificate were a reference to the appeal and any reference to the date of such an application were a reference to the date on which the appeal is made; and

(b) references to the local planning authority were references to the Secretary of State.

(1B) Those provisions are: sections 191(5) to (7), 193(4) (so far as it relates to the form of the certificate), (6) and (7) and 194.

(1C) If the land to which the enforcement notice relates is in England, subsection (1)(a) applies only if the statement under section 174(4) specifies the ground mentioned in section 174(2)(a).

(2) In considering whether to grant planning permission under subsection (1), the Secretary of State shall have regard to the provisions of the development plan, so far as material to the subject matter of the enforcement notice, and to any other material considerations.

(3) The planning permission that may be granted under subsection (1) is any planning permission that might be granted on an application under Part III.

(4) Where under subsection (1) the Secretary of State discharges a condition or limitation, he may substitute another condition or limitation for it, whether more or less onerous.

(5) Where an appeal against an enforcement notice is brought under section 174 and—

(a) the land to which the enforcement notice relates is in Wales, or

(b) that land is in England and the statement under section 174(4) specifies the ground mentioned in section 174(2)(a),

the appellant shall be deemed to have made an application for planning permission in respect of the matters stated in the enforcement notice as constituting a breach of planning control.

(5A) Where—

(a) the statement under subsection (4) of section 174 specifies the ground mentioned in subsection (2)(a) of that section;

(b) any fee is payable under regulations made by virtue of section 303 in respect of the application deemed to be made by virtue of the appeal; and

(c) the Secretary of State gives notice in writing to the appellant specifying the period within which the fee must be paid,

then, if that fee is not paid within that period, the appeal, so far as brought on that ground, and the application shall lapse at the end of that period.

(6) Any planning permission granted under subsection (1) on an appeal shall be treated as granted on the application deemed to have been made by the appellant.

(7) In relation to a grant of planning permission or a determination under subsection (1) the Secretary of State's decision shall be final.

(8) For the purposes of section 69 the Secretary of State's decision shall be treated as having been given by him in dealing with an application for planning permission made to the local planning authority.

178 Execution and cost of works required by enforcement notice

(1) Where any steps required by an enforcement notice to taken are not taken within the period for compliance with the notice, the local planning authority may—

   (a) enter the land and take the steps; and

   (b) recover from the person who is then the owner of the land any expenses reasonably incurred by them in doing so.

(2) Where a copy of an enforcement notice has been served in respect of any breach of planning control—

   (a) any expenses incurred by the owner or occupier of any land for the purpose of complying with the notice, and

   (b) any sums paid by the owner of any land under subsection (1) in respect of expenses incurred by the local planning authority in taking steps required by such a notice to be taken,

   shall be deemed to be incurred or paid for the use and at the request of the person by whom the breach of planning control was committed.

(3) Regulations made under this Act may provide that—

   (a) section 276 of the Public Health Act 1936, (power of local authorities to sell materials removed in executing works under that Act subject to accounting for the proceeds of sale);

   (b) section 289 of that Act (power to require the occupier of any premises to permit works to be executed by the owner of the premises); and

   (c) section 294 of that Act (limit on liability of persons holding premises as agents or trustees in respect of the expenses recoverable under that Act),

   shall apply, subject to such adaptations and modifications as may be specified in the regulations, in relation to any steps required to be taken by an enforcement notice.

(4) Regulations under subsection (3) applying section 289 of the Public Health Act 1936 may include adaptations and modifications for the purpose of giving the owner of land to which an enforcement notice relates the right, as against all other persons interested in the land, to comply with the requirements of the enforcement notice.

(5) Regulations under subsection (3) may also provide for the charging on the land of any expenses recoverable by a local planning authority under subsection (1).

(6) Any person who wilfully obstructs a person acting in the exercise of powers under subsection (1) shall be guilty of an offence and liable on summary conviction to a fine not exceeding level 3 on the standard scale.

179   Offence where enforcement notice not complied with

(1) Where, at any time after the end of the period for compliance with an enforcement notice, any step required by the notice to be taken has not been taken or any activity required by the notice to cease is being carried on, the person who is then the owner of the land is in breach of the notice.

(2)   Where the owner of the land is in breach of an enforcement notice he shall be guilty of an offence.

(3)   In proceedings against any person for an offence under subsection (2), it shall be a defence for him to show that he did everything he could be expected to do to secure compliance with the notice.

(4)   A person who has control of or an interest in the land to which an enforcement notice relates (other than the owner) must not carry on any activity which is required by the notice to cease or cause or permit such an activity to be carried on.

(5)   A person who, at any time after the end of the period for compliance with the notice, contravenes subsection (4) shall be guilty of an offence.

(6)   An offence under subsection (2) or (5) may be charged by reference to any day or longer period of time and a person may be convicted of a second or subsequent offence under the subsection in question by reference to any period of time following the preceding conviction for such an offence.

(7)   Where—

(a) a person charged with an offence under this section has not been served with a copy of the enforcement notice; and

(b) the notice is not contained in the appropriate register kept under section 188,

it shall be a defence for him to show that he was not aware of the existence of the notice.

(8)   A person guilty of an offence under this section shall be liable—

(a) on summary conviction, to a fine not exceeding £20,000; and

(b) on conviction on indictment, to a fine.

(9)   In determining the amount of any fine to be imposed on a person convicted of an offence under this section, the court shall in particular have regard to any financial benefit which has accrued or appears likely to accrue to him in consequence of the offence.

180 Effect of planning permission, etc, on enforcement or breach of condition notice

(1)   Where, after the service of—

(a) a copy of an enforcement notice; or

(b) a breach of condition notice,

planning permission is granted for any development carried out before the grant of that permission, the notice shall cease to have effect so far as inconsistent with that permission.

(2)   Where after a breach of condition notice has been served any condition to which the notice relates is discharged, the notice shall cease to have effect so far as it requires any person to secure compliance with the condition in question.

(3)   The fact that an enforcement notice or breach of condition notice has wholly or partly ceased to have effect by virtue of this section shall not affect the

liability of any person for an offence in respect of a previous failure to comply, or secure compliance, with the notice.

181 Enforcement notice to have effect against subsequent development

(1) Compliance with an enforcement notice, whether in respect of—

(a) the completion, removal or alteration of any buildings or works;

(b) the discontinuance of any use of land; or

(c) any other requirements contained in the notice,

shall not discharge the notice.

(2) Without prejudice to subsection (1), any provision of an enforcement notice requiring a use of land to be discontinued shall operate as a requirement that it shall be discontinued permanently, to the extent that it is in contravention of Part III; and accordingly the resumption of that use at any time after it has been discontinued in compliance with the enforcement notice shall to that extent be in contravention of the enforcement notice.

(3) Without prejudice to subsection (1), if any development is carried out on land by way of reinstating or restoring buildings or works which have been removed or altered in compliance with an enforcement notice, the notice shall, notwithstanding that its terms are not apt for the purpose, be deemed to apply in relation to the buildings or works as reinstated or restored as it applied in relation to the buildings or works before they were removed or altered; and, subject to subsection (4), the provisions of section 178(1) and (2) shall apply accordingly.

(4) Where, at any time after an enforcement notice takes effect—

(a) any development is carried out on land by way of reinstating or restoring buildings or works which have been removed or altered in compliance with the notice; and

(b) the local planning authority propose, under section 178(1), to take any steps required by the enforcement notice for the removal or alteration of the buildings or works in consequence of the reinstatement or restoration,

the local planning authority shall, not less than 28 days before taking any such steps, serve on the owner and occupier of the land a notice of their intention to do so.

(5) Where without planning permission a person carries out any development on land by way of reinstating or restoring buildings or works which have been removed or altered in compliance with an enforcement notice—

(a) he shall be guilty of an offence and shall be liable on summary conviction to a fine not exceeding level 5 on the standard scale, and

(b) no person shall be liable under section 179(2) for failure to take any steps required to be taken by an enforcement notice by way of removal or alteration of what has been so reinstated or restored.

182 Enforcement by the Secretary of State

(1) If it appears to the Secretary of State to be expedient that an enforcement notice should be issued in respect of any land, he may issue such a notice.

317

(2)   The Secretary of State shall not issue such a notice without consulting the local planning authority.

(3)   An enforcement notice issued by the Secretary of State shall have the same effect as a notice issued by the local planning authority.

(4)   In relation to an enforcement notice issued by the Secretary of State, sections 178 and 181 shall apply as if for any reference in those sections to the local planning authority there were substituted a reference to the Secretary of State.

Stop notices

183 Stop notices

(1)   Where the local planning authority consider it expedient that any relevant activity should cease before the expiry of the period for compliance with an enforcement notice, they may, when they serve the copy of the enforcement notice or afterwards, serve a notice (in this Act referred to as a 'stop notice') prohibiting the carrying out of that activity on the land to which the enforcement notice relates, or any part of that land specified in the stop notice.

(2)   In this section and sections 184 and 186 'relevant activity' means any activity specified in the enforcement notice as an activity which the local planning authority require to cease and any activity carried out as part of that activity or associated with that activity.

(3)   A stop notice may not be served where the enforcement notice has taken effect.

(4)   A stop notice shall not prohibit the use of any building as a dwellinghouse.

(5)   A stop notice shall not prohibit the carrying out of any activity if the activity has been carried out (whether continuously or not) for a period of more than four years ending with the service of the notice; and for the purposes of this subsection no account is to be taken of any period during which the activity was authorised by planning permission.

(5A) Subsection (5) does not prevent a stop notice prohibiting any activity consisting of, or incidental to, building, engineering, mining or other operations or the deposit of refuse or waste materials.

(6)   A stop notice may be served by the local planning authority on any person who appears to them to have an interest in the land or to be engaged in any activity prohibited by the notice.

(7)   The local planning authority may at any time withdraw a stop notice (without prejudice to their power to serve another) by serving notice to that effect on persons served with the stop notice.

184 Stop notices: supplementary provisions

(1)   A stop notice must refer to the enforcement notice to which it relates and have a copy of that notice annexed to it.

(2)   A stop notice must specify the date on which it will take effect (and it cannot be contravened until that date).

(3)   That date—

(a) must not be earlier than three days after the date when the notice is served, unless the local planning authority consider that there are special reasons for specifying an earlier date and a statement of those reasons is served with the stop notice; and

(b) must not be later than twenty-eight days from the date when the notice is first served on any person.

(4) A stop notice shall cease to have effect when—

(a) the enforcement notice to which it relates is withdrawn or quashed; or

(b) the period for compliance with the enforcement notice expires; or

(c) notice of the withdrawal of the stop notice is first served under section 183(7).

(5) A stop notice shall also cease to have effect if or to the extent that the activities prohibited by it cease, on a variation of the enforcement notice, to be relevant activities.

(6) Where a stop notice has been served in respect of any land, the local planning authority may display there a notice (in this section and section 187 referred to as a 'site notice')—

(a) stating that a stop notice has been served and that any person contravening it may be prosecuted for an offence under section 187,

(b) giving the date when the stop notice takes effect, and

(c) indicating its requirements.

(7) If under section 183(7) the local planning authority withdraw a stop notice in respect of which a site notice was displayed, they must display a notice of the withdrawal in place of the site notice.

(8) A stop notice shall not be invalid by reason that a copy of the enforcement notice to which it relates was not served as required by section 172 if it is shown that the local planning authority took all such steps as were reasonably practicable to effect proper service.

185 Service of stop notices by Secretary of State

(1) If it appears to the Secretary of State to be expedient that a stop notice should be served in respect of any land, he may himself serve such a notice.

(2) A notice served by the Secretary of State under subsection (1) shall have the same effect as if it had been served by the local planning authority.

(3) The Secretary of State shall not serve such a notice without consulting the local planning authority.

186 Compensation for loss due to stop notice

(1) Where a stop notice is served under section 183 compensation may be payable under this section in respect of a prohibition contained in the notice only if—

(a) the enforcement notice is quashed on grounds other than those mentioned in paragraph (a) of section 174(2);

(b) the enforcement notice is varied (otherwise than on the grounds mentioned in that paragraph) so that any activity the carrying out of which is prohibited by the stop notice ceases to be a relevant activity;

(c) the enforcement notice is withdrawn by the local planning authority otherwise than in consequence of the grant by them of planning permission for the development to which the notice relates; or

(d) the stop notice is withdrawn.

(2) A person who, when the stop notice is first served, has an interest in or occupies the land to which the notice relates shall be entitled to be compensated by the local planning authority in respect of any loss or damage directly attributable to the prohibition contained in the notice or, in a case within subsection (1)(b), the prohibition of such of the activities prohibited by the stop notice as cease to be relevant activities.

(3) A claim for compensation under this section shall be made to the local planning authority within the prescribed time and in the prescribed manner.

(4) The loss or damage in respect of which compensation is payable under this section in respect of a prohibition shall include any sum payable in respect of a breach of contract caused by the taking of action necessary to comply with the prohibition.

(5) No compensation is payable under this section—

(a) in respect of the prohibition in a stop notice of any activity which, at any time when the notice is in force, constitutes or contributes to a breach of planning control; or

(b) in the case of a claimant who was required to provide information under section 171C or 330 or section 16 of the Local Government (Miscellaneous Provisions) Act 1976, in respect of any loss or damage suffered by him which could have been avoided if he had provided the information or had otherwise co-operated with the local planning authority when responding to the notice.

(6) Except in so far as may be otherwise provided by any regulations made under this Act, any question of disputed compensation under this Part shall be referred to and determined by the Upper Tribunal.

(7) In relation to the determination of any such question, the provisions of section 4 of the Land Compensation Act 1961 shall apply subject to any necessary modifications and to the provisions of any regulations made under this Act.

187 Penalties for contravention of stop notice

(1) If any person contravenes a stop notice after a site notice has been displayed or the stop notice has been served on him he shall be guilty of an offence.

(1A) An offence under this section may be charged by reference to any day or longer period of time and a person may be convicted of a second or subsequent offence under this section by reference to any period of time following the preceding conviction for such an offence.

(1B) References in this section to contravening a stop notice include causing or permitting its contravention.

(2) A person guilty of an offence under this section shall be liable—

(a) on summary conviction, to a fine not exceeding £20,000; and

(b) on conviction on indictment, to a fine.

(2A) In determining the amount of any fine to be imposed on a person convicted of an offence under this section, the court shall in particular have regard to any financial benefit which has accrued or appears likely to accrue to him in consequence of the offence.

(3) In proceedings for an offence under this section it shall be a defence for the accused to prove—

(a) that the stop notice was not served on him, and

(b) that he did not know, and could not reasonably have been expected to know, of its existence.

187A Enforcement of conditions

(1) This section applies where planning permission for carrying out any development of land has been granted subject to conditions.

(2) The local planning authority may, if any of the conditions is not complied with, serve a notice (in this Act referred to as a 'breach of condition notice') on—

(a) any person who is carrying out or has carried out the development; or

(b) any person having control of the land,

requiring him to secure compliance with such of the conditions as are specified in the notice.

(3) References in this section to the person responsible are to the person on whom the breach of condition notice has been served.

(4) The conditions which may be specified in a notice served by virtue of subsection (2)(b) are any of the conditions regulating the use of the land.

(5) A breach of condition notice shall specify the steps which the authority consider ought to be taken, or the activities which the authority consider ought to cease, to secure compliance with the conditions specified in the notice.

(6) The authority may by notice served on the person responsible withdraw the breach of condition notice, but its withdrawal shall not affect the power to serve on him a further breach of condition notice in respect of the conditions specified in the earlier notice or any other conditions.

(7) The period allowed for compliance with the notice is—

(a) such period of not less than twenty-eight days beginning with the date of service of the notice as may be specified in the notice; or

(b) that period as extended by a further notice served by the local planning authority on the person responsible.

(8) If, at any time after the end of the period allowed for compliance with the notice—

(a) any of the conditions specified in the notice is not complied with; and

(b) the steps specified in the notice have not been taken or, as the case may be, the activities specified in the notice have not ceased,

the person responsible is in breach of the notice.

(9) If the person responsible is in breach of the notice he shall be guilty of an offence.

(10) An offence under subsection (9) may be charged by reference to any day or longer period of time and a person may be convicted of a second or subsequent offence under that subsection by reference to any period of time following the preceding conviction for such an offence.

(11) It shall be a defence for a person charged with an offence under subsection (9) to prove—

(a) that he took all reasonable measures to secure compliance with the conditions specified in the notice; or

(b) where the notice was served on him by virtue of subsection (2)(b), that he no longer had control of the land.

(12) A person who is guilty of an offence under subsection (9) shall be liable on summary conviction to a fine—

(a) not exceeding level 4 on the standard scale if the land is in England;

(b) not exceeding level 3 on the standard scale if the land is in Wales.

(13) In this section—

(a) 'conditions' includes limitations; and

(b) references to carrying out any development include causing or permitting another to do so.

Injunctions

187B Injunctions restraining breaches of planning control

(1) Where a local planning authority consider it necessary or expedient for any actual or apprehended breach of planning control to be restrained by injunction, they may apply to the court for an injunction, whether or not they have exercised or are proposing to exercise any of their other powers under this Part.

(2) On an application under subsection (1) the court may grant such an injunction as the court thinks appropriate for the purpose of restraining the breach.

(3) Rules of court may provide for such an injunction to be issued against a person whose identity is unknown.

(4) In this section 'the court' means the High Court or the county court.

Registers

188 Register of enforcement and stop notices

(1) Every district planning authority, every local planning authority for an area in Wales and the council of every metropolitan district or London borough shall

keep, in such manner as may be prescribed by a development order, a register containing such information as may be so prescribed with respect—

(za) to planning enforcement orders,

(a) to enforcement notices;

(b) to stop notices, and

(c) to breach of condition notices

which relate to land in their area.

(2) A development order may make provision—

(a) for the entry relating to any planning enforcement order, enforcement notice, stop notice or breach of condition notice, and everything relating to any planning enforcement order or any such notice, to be removed from the register in such circumstances as may be specified in the development order; and

(b) for requiring a county planning authority to supply to a district planning authority such information as may be so specified with regard to enforcement notices issued and stop notices and breach of condition notices served by, and planning enforcement orders made on applications made by, the county planning authority.

(3) Every register kept under this section shall be available for inspection by the public at all reasonable hours.

(4) In this section 'planning enforcement order' means an order under section 171BA(1).

Enforcement of orders for discontinuance of use, etc

189 Penalties for contravention of orders under s 102 and Schedule 9

(1) Any person who without planning permission—

(a) uses land, or causes or permits land to be used—

   (i) for any purpose for which an order under section 102 or paragraph 1 of Schedule 9 has required that its use shall be discontinued; or

   (ii) in contravention of any condition imposed by such an order by virtue of subsection (1) of that section or, as the case may be, sub-paragraph (1) of that paragraph; or

(b) resumes, or causes or permits to be resumed, development consisting of the winning and working of minerals or involving the depositing of mineral waste the the resumption of which an order under paragraph 3 of that Schedule has prohibited; or

(c) contravenes, or causes or permits to be contravened, any such requirement as is specified in sub-paragraph (3) or (4) of that paragraph,

shall be guilty of an offence.

(2) Any person who contravenes any requirement of an order under paragraph 5 or 6 of that Schedule or who causes or permits any requirement of such an order to be contravened shall be guilty of an offence.

(3)   Any person guilty of an offence under this section shall be liable—

    (a) on summary conviction, to a fine not exceeding the statutory maximum; and

    (b) on conviction on indictment, to a fine.

(4)   It shall be a defence for a person charged with an offence under this section to prove that he took all reasonable measures and exercised all due diligence to avoid commission of the offence by himself or by any person under his control.

(5)   If in any case the defence provided by subsection (4) involves an allegation that the commission of the offence was due to the act or default of another person or due to reliance on information supplied by another person, the person charged shall not, without the leave of the court, be entitled to rely on the defence unless, within a period ending seven clear days before the hearing, he has served on the prosecutor a notice in writing giving such information identifying or assisting in the identification of the other person as was then in his possession.

190   Enforcement of orders under s 102 and Schedule 9

(1)   This section applies where—

    (a) any step required by an order under section 102 or paragraph 1 of Schedule 9 to be taken for the alteration or removal of any buildings or works or any plant or machinery;

    (b) any step required by an order under paragraph 3 of that Schedule to be taken—

        (i)   for the alteration or removal of plant or machinery; or

        (ii) for the removal or alleviation of any injury to amenity; or

    (c) any step for the protection of the environment required to be taken by an order under paragraph 5 or 6 of that Schedule,

has not been taken within the period specified in the order or within such extended period as the local planning authority or, as the case may be, the mineral planning authority may allow.

(2)   Where this section applies the local planning authority or, as the case may be, the mineral planning authority may enter the land and take the required step.

(3)   Where the local planning authority or, as the case may be, the mineral planning authority have exercised their power under subsection (2) they may recover from the person who is then the owner of the land any expenses reasonably incurred by them in doing so.

(4)   [...]

(5)   Section 276 of the Public Health Act 1936 shall apply in relation to any works executed by an authority under subsection (2) as it applies in relation to works executed by a local authority under that Act.

Certificate of lawful use or development

191 Certificate of lawfulness of existing use or development

(1)   If any person wishes to ascertain whether—

(a) any existing use of buildings or other land is lawful;

(b) any operations which have been carried out in, on, over or under land are lawful; or

(c) any other matter constituting a failure to comply with any condition or limitation subject to which planning permission has been granted is lawful,

he may make an application for the purpose to the local planning authority specifying the land and describing the use, operations or other matter.

(2) For the purposes of this Act uses and operations are lawful at any time if—

(a) no enforcement action may then be taken in respect of them (whether because they did not involve development or require planning permission or because the time for enforcement action has expired or for any other reason); and

(b) they do not constitute a contravention of any of the requirements of any enforcement notice then in force.

(3) For the purposes of this Act any matter constituting a failure to comply with any condition or limitation subject to which planning permission has been granted is lawful at any time if—

(a) the time for taking enforcement action in respect of the failure has then expired; and

(b) it does not constitute a contravention of any of the requirements of any enforcement notice or breach of condition notice then in force.

(3A) In determining for the purposes of this section whether the time for taking enforcement action in respect of a matter has expired, that time is to be taken not to have expired if—

(a) the time for applying for an order under section 171BA(1) (a 'planning enforcement order') in relation to the matter has not expired,

(b) an application has been made for a planning enforcement order in relation to the matter and the application has neither been decided nor been withdrawn, or

(c) a planning enforcement order has been made in relation to the matter, the order has not been rescinded and the enforcement year for the order (whether or not it has begun) has not expired.

(4) If, on an application under this section, the local planning authority are provided with information satisfying them of the lawfulness at the time of the application of the use, operations or other matter described in the application, or that description as modified by the local planning authority or a description substituted by them, they shall issue a certificate to that effect; and in any other case they shall refuse the application.

(5) A certificate under this section shall—

(a) specify the land to which it relates;

(b) describe the use, operations or other matter in question (in the case of any use falling within one of the classes specified in an order under section 55(2)(f), identifying it by reference to that class);

325

(c) give the reasons for determining the use, operations or other matter to be lawful; and

(d) specify the date of the application for the certificate.

(6) The lawfulness of any use, operations or other matter for which a certificate is in force under this section shall be conclusively presumed.

(7) A certificate under this section in respect of any use shall also have effect, for the purposes of the following enactments, as if it were a grant of planning permission—

(a) section 3(3) of the Caravan Sites and Control of Development Act 1960;

(b) section 5(2) of the Control of Pollution Act 1974; and

(c) section 36(2)(a) of the Environmental Protection Act 1990.

192 Certificate of lawfulness of proposed use or development

(1) If any person wishes to ascertain whether—

(a) any proposed use of buildings or other land; or

(b) any operations proposed to be carried out in, on, over or under land,

would be lawful, he may make an application for the purpose to the local planning authority specifying the land and describing the use or operations in question.

(2) If, on an application under this section, the local planning authority are provided with information satisfying them that the use or operations described in the application would be lawful if instituted or begun at the time of the application, they shall issue a certificate to that effect; and in any other case they shall refuse the application.

(3) A certificate under this section shall—

(a) specify the land to which it relates;

(b) describe the use or operations in question (in the case of any use falling within one of the classes specified in an order under section 55(2)(f), identifying it by reference to that class);

(c) give the reasons for determining the use or operations to be lawful; and

(d) specify the date of the application for the certificate.

(4) The lawfulness of any use or operations for which a certificate is in force under this section shall be conclusively presumed unless there is a material change, before the use is instituted or the operations are begun, in any of the matters relevant to determining such lawfulness.

193 Certificates under sections 191 and 192: supplementary provisions

(1) An application for a certificate under section 191 or 192 shall be made in such manner as may be prescribed by a development order and shall include such particulars, and be verified by such evidence, as may be required by such an order or by any directions given under such an order or by the local planning authority.

(2)   Provision may be made by a development order for regulating the manner in which applications for certificates under those sections are to be dealt with by local planning authorities.

(3)   In particular, such an order may provide for requiring the authority—

(a)   to give to any applicant within such time as may be prescribed by the order such notice as may be so prescribed as to the manner in which his application has been dealt with; and

(b)   to give to the Secretary of State and to such other persons as may be prescribed by or under the order, such information as may be so prescribed with respect to such applications made to the authority, including information as to the manner in which any application has been dealt with.

(4)   A certificate under either of those sections may be issued—

(a)   for the whole or part of the land specified in the application; and

(b)   where the application specifies two or more uses, operations or other matters, for all of them or some one or more of them;

and shall be in such form as may be prescribed by a development order.

(5)   A certificate under section 191 or 192 shall not affect any matter constituting a failure to comply with any condition or limitation subject to which planning permission has been granted unless that matter is described in the certificate.

(6)   In section 69 references to applications for planning permission shall include references to applications for certificates under section 191 or 192.

(7)   A local planning authority may revoke a certificate under either of those sections if, on the application for the certificate—

(a)   a statement was made or document used which was false in a material particular; or

(b)   any material information was withheld.

(8)   Provision may be made by a development order for regulating the manner in which certificates may be revoked and the notice to be given of such revocation.

194 Offences

(1)   If any person, for the purpose of procuring a particular decision on an application (whether by himself or another) for the issue of a certificate under section 191 or 192—

(a)   knowingly or recklessly makes a statement which is false or misleading in a material particular;

(b)   with intent to deceive, uses any document which is false or misleading in a material particular; or

(c)   with intent to deceive, withholds any material information,

he shall be guilty of an offence.

(2)   A person guilty of an offence under subsection (1) shall be liable—

(a)   on summary conviction, to a fine not exceeding the statutory maximum; or

(b) on conviction on indictment, to imprisonment for a term not exceeding two years, or a fine, or both.

(3) Notwithstanding section 127 of the Magistrates' Courts Act 1980, a magistrates' court may try an information in respect of an offence under subsection (1) whenever laid

195 Appeals against refusal or failure to give decision on application

(1) Where an application is made to a local planning authority for a certificate under section 191 or 192 and—

(a) the application is refused or is refused in part, or

(b) the authority do not give notice to the applicant of their decision on the application within such period as may be prescribed by a development order or within such extended period as may at any time be agreed upon in writing between the applicant and the authority,

the applicant may by notice appeal to the Secretary of State.

(1B) A notice of appeal under this section must be—

(a) served within such time and in such manner as may be prescribed by a development order;

(b) accompanied by such information as may be prescribed by such an order.

(1C) The time prescribed for the service of a notice of appeal under this section must not be less than—

(a) 28 days from the date of notification of the decision on the application; or

(b) in the case of an appeal under subsection (1)(b), 28 days from—

(i) the end of the period prescribed as mentioned in subsection (1)(b), or

(ii) as the case may be, the extended period mentioned in subsection (1)(b).

(1D) The power to make a development order under subsection (1B) is exercisable by—

(a) the Secretary of State, in relation to England;

(b) the Welsh Ministers, in relation to Wales.

(1E) Section 333(5) does not apply in relation to a development order under subsection (1B) made by the Welsh Ministers.

(1F) A development order under subsection (1B) made by the Welsh Ministers is subject to annulment in pursuance of a resolution of the National Assembly for Wales.

(2) On any such appeal, if and so far as the Secretary of State is satisfied—

(a) in the case of an appeal under subsection (1)(a), that the authority's refusal is not well-founded, or

(b) in the case of an appeal under subsection (1)(b), that if the authority had refused the application their refusal would not have been well-founded, he shall grant the appellant a certificate under section 191 or, as the case may be, 192 accordingly or, in the case of a refusal in part, modify the certificate granted by the authority on the application.

(3)   If and so far as the Secretary of State is satisfied that the authority's refusal is or, as the case may be, would have been well-founded, he shall dismiss the appeal.

(4)   References in this section to a refusal of an application in part include a modification or substitution of the description in the application of the use, operations or other matter in question.

(5)   For the purposes of the application of section 288(10)(b) in relation to an appeal in a case within subsection (1)(b) it shall be assumed that the authority decided to refuse the application in question.

(6)   Schedule 6 applies to appeals under this section.

196 Further provisions as to references and appeals to the Secretary of State

(1)   Before determining an appeal to him under section 195(1), the Secretary of State shall, if either the appellant or the local planning authority so wish, give each of them an opportunity of appearing before, and being heard by, a person appointed by the Secretary of State for the purpose.

(2)   Where the Secretary of State grants a certificate under section 191 or 192 on such a reference or such an appeal, he shall give notice to the local planning authority of that fact.

(3)   The decision of the Secretary of State on such appeal shall be final.

(4)   The information which may be prescribed as being required to be contained in a register kept under section 69 shall include information with respect to certificates under section 191 or 192 granted by the Secretary of State.

(5)   […]

(6)   […]

(7)   […]

(8)   Subsection (5) of section 250 of the Local Government Act 1972 (which authorises a Minister holding an inquiry under that section to make orders with respect to the costs of the parties) shall apply in relation to any proceedings before the Secretary of State on an appeal under section 195 as if those proceedings were an inquiry held by the Secretary of State under section 250.

Rights of entry for enforcement purposes

196A Rights to enter without warrant

(1)   Any person duly authorised in writing by a local planning authority may at any reasonable hour enter any land—

    (a) to ascertain whether there is or has been any breach of planning control on the land or any other land;

    (b) to determine whether any of the powers conferred on a local planning authority by this Part should be exercised in relation to the land or any other land;

(c) to determine how any such power should be exercised in relation to the land or any other land;

(d) to ascertain whether there has been compliance with any requirement imposed as a result of any such power having been exercised in relation to the land or any other land,

if there are reasonable grounds for entering for the purpose in question.

(2) Any person duly authorised in writing by the Secretary of State may at any reasonable hour enter any land to determine whether an enforcement notice should be issued in relation to the land or any other land, if there are reasonable grounds for entering for that purpose.

(3) The Secretary of State shall not so authorise any person without consulting the local planning authority.

(4) Admission to any building used as a dwellinghouse shall not be demanded as of right by virtue of subsection (1) or (2) unless twenty-four hours' notice of the intended entry has been given to the occupier of the building.

196B Right to enter under warrant

(1) If it is shown to the satisfaction of a justice of the peace on sworn information in writing—

(a) that there are reasonable grounds for entering any land for any of the purposes mentioned in section 196A(1) or (2); and

(b) that—

(i) admission to the land has been refused, or a refusal is reasonably apprehended; or

(ii) the case is one of urgency,

the justice may issue a warrant authorising any person duly authorised in writing by a local planning authority or, as the case may be, the Secretary of State to enter the land.

(2) For the purposes of subsection (1)(b)(i) admission to land shall be regarded as having been refused if no reply is received to a request for admission within a reasonable period.

(3) A warrant authorises entry on one occasion only and that entry must be—

(a) within one month from the date of the issue of the warrant; and

(b) at a reasonable hour, unless the case is one of urgency.

196C Rights of entry: supplementary provisions

(1) A person authorised to enter any land in pursuance of a right of entry conferred under or by virtue of section 196A or 196B (referred to in this section as 'a right of entry')—

(a) shall, if so required, produce evidence of his authority and state the purpose of his entry before so entering;

(b) may take with him such other persons as may be necessary; and

(c) on leaving the land shall, if the owner or occupier is not then present, leave it as effectively secured against trespassers as he found it.

(2) Any person who wilfully obstructs a person acting in the exercise of a right of entry shall be guilty of an offence and liable on summary conviction to a fine not exceeding level 3 on the standard scale.

(3) If any damage is caused to land or chattels in the exercise of a right of entry, compensation may be recovered by any person suffering the damage from the authority who gave the written authority for the entry or, as the case may be, the Secretary of State.

(4) The provisions of section 118 shall apply in relation to compensation under subsection (3) as they apply in relation to compensation under Part IV.

(5) If any person who enters any land, in exercise of a right of entry, discloses to any person any information obtained by him while on the land as to any manufacturing process or trade secret, he shall be guilty of an offence.

(6) Subsection (5) does not apply if the disclosure is made by a person in the course of performing his duty in connection with the purpose for which he was authorised to enter the land.

(7) A person who is guilty of an offence under subsection (5) shall be liable on summary conviction to a fine not exceeding the statutory maximum or on conviction on indictment to imprisonment for a term not exceeding two years or a fine or both.

(8) In sections 196A and 196B and this section references to a local planning authority include, in relation to a building situated in Greater London, a reference to the Historic Buildings and Monuments Commission for England.

196D Offence of failing to obtain planning permission for demolition of unlisted etc buildings in conservation areas in England[3]

(1) It is an offence for a person to carry out or cause or permit to be carried out relevant demolition without the required planning permission.

(2) It is also an offence for a person to fail to comply with any condition or limitation subject to which planning permission for relevant demolition is granted.

(3) In this section 'relevant demolition' means the demolition of a building that—

(a) is situated in a conservation area in England; and

(b) is not a building to which section 74 of the Planning (Listed Buildings and Conservation Areas) Act 1990 does not apply by virtue of section 75 of that Act (listed buildings, certain ecclesiastical buildings, scheduled monuments and buildings described in a direction of the Secretary of State under that section).

(4) It is a defence for a person accused of an offence under this section to prove the following matters—

---

[3] Prospective amendment by Enterprise and Regulatory Reform Act 2013 in England. This section is not yet in force as at 1 July 2013.

    (a) that the relevant demolition was urgently necessary in the interests of safety or health;

    (b) that it was not practicable to secure safety or health by works of repair or works for affording temporary support or shelter;

    (c) that the relevant demolition was the minimum measure necessary; and

    (d) that notice in writing of the relevant demolition was given to the local planning authority as soon as reasonably practicable.

(5)   A person guilty of an offence under this section is liable—

    (a) on summary conviction, to imprisonment for a term not exceeding 12 months or a fine or both;

    (b) on conviction on indictment, to imprisonment for a term not exceeding 2 years or a fine or both.

(6)   In relation to an offence committed before the coming into force of section 154(1) of the Criminal Justice Act 2003, subsection (5)(a) has effect as if the reference to 12 months were to 6 months.

(7)   In relation to an offence committed before the coming into force of section 85(1) of the Legal Aid, Sentencing and Punishment of Offenders Act 2012, subsection (5)(a) has effect as if the reference to a fine were a reference to a fine not exceeding £20,000.

(8)   In determining the amount of any fine to be imposed on a person convicted of an offence under this section, the court must in particular have regard to any financial benefit which has accrued or appears likely to accrue to that person in consequence of the offence.

(9)   Where, after a person commits an offence under this section, planning permission is granted for any development carried out before the grant of the permission, that grant does not affect the person's liability for the offence.

PART VIII SPECIAL CONTROLS

CHAPTER I TREES

General duty of planning authorities as respects trees

197 Planning permission to include appropriate provision for preservation and planting of trees

It shall be the duty of the local planning authority—

    (a) to ensure, whenever it is appropriate, that in granting planning permission for any development adequate provision is made, by the imposition of conditions, for the preservation or planting of trees; and

    (b) to make such orders under section 198 as appear to the authority to be necessary in connection with the grant of such permission, whether for giving effect to such conditions or otherwise.

Nothing in this section applies in relation to neighbourhood development orders.

Tree preservation orders

198 Power to make tree preservation orders [England]

(1)   If it appears to a local planning authority that it is expedient in the interests of amenity to make provision for the preservation of trees or woodlands in their area, they may for that purpose make an order with respect to such trees, groups of trees or woodlands as may be specified in the order.

(2)   An order under subsection (1) is in this Act referred to as a 'tree preservation order'.

(5)   A tree preservation order may be made so as to apply, in relation to trees to be planted pursuant to any such conditions as are mentioned in section 197(a), as from the time when those trees are planted.

(7)   Tree preservation regulations shall have effect subject to—

(a)   section 39(2) of the Housing and Planning Act 1986 (saving for effect of section 2(4) of the Opencast Coal Act 1958 on land affected by a tree preservation order despite its repeal); and

(b)   section 15 of the Forestry Act 1967 (licences under that Act to fell trees comprised in a tree preservation order).

198 Power to make tree preservation orders [Wales]

(1)   If it appears to a local planning authority that it is expedient in the interests of amenity to make provision for the preservation of trees or woodlands in their area, they may for that purpose make an order with respect to such trees, groups of trees or woodlands as may be specified in the order.

(2)   An order under subsection (1) is in this Act referred to as a 'tree preservation order'.

(3)   A tree preservation order may, in particular, make provision—

(a)   for prohibiting (subject to any exemptions for which provision may be made by the order) the cutting down, topping, lopping, uprooting, wilful damage or wilful destruction of trees except with the consent of the local planning authority, and for enabling that authority to give their consent subject to conditions;

(b)   for securing the replanting, in such manner as may be prescribed by or under the order, of any part of a woodland area which is felled in the course of forestry operations permitted by or under the order;

(c)   for applying, in relation to any consent under the order, and to applications for such consent, any of the provisions of this Act mentioned in subsection (4), subject to such adaptations and modifications as may be specified in the order.

(4)   The provisions referred to in subsection (3)(c) are—

(a)   the provisions of Part III relating to planning permission and to applications for planning permission, except sections 56, 62, 65, 69(3) and (4), 71 91 to 96, 100 and 101 and Schedule 8; and

(b) sections 137 to 141, 143 and 144 (except so far as they relate to purchase notices served in consequence of such orders as are mentioned in section 137(1)(b) or (c));

(c) section 316.

(5) A tree preservation order may be made so as to apply, in relation to trees to be planted pursuant to any such conditions as are mentioned in section 197(a), as from the time when those trees are planted.

(6) Without prejudice to any other exemptions for which provision may be made by a tree preservation order, no such order shall apply—

(a) to the cutting down, uprooting, topping or lopping of trees which are dying or dead or have become dangerous, or

(b) to the cutting down, uprooting, topping or lopping of any trees in compliance with any obligations imposed by or under an Act of Parliament or so far as may be necessary for the prevention or abatement of a nuisance.

(7) This section shall have effect subject to—

(a) section 39(2) of the Housing and Planning Act 1986 (saving for effect of section 2(4) of the Opencast Coal Act 1958 on land affected by a tree preservation order despite its repeal); and

(b) section 15 of the Forestry Act 1967 (licences under that Act to fell trees comprised in a tree preservation order).

(8) In relation to an application for consent under a tree preservation order the appropriate authority may by regulations make provision as to—

(a) the form and manner in which the application must be made;

(b) particulars of such matters as are to be included in the application;

(c) the documents or other materials as are to accompany the application.

(9) The appropriate authority is—

(a) the Secretary of State in relation to England;

(b) the National Assembly for Wales in relation to Wales,

and in the case of regulations made by the National Assembly for Wales section 333(3) must be ignored.

199 Form of and procedure applicable to orders [England]

[...]

199 Form of and procedure applicable to orders [Wales]

(1) A tree preservation order shall not take effect until it is confirmed by the local planning authority and the local planning authority may confirm any such order either without modification or subject to such modifications as they consider expedient.

(2) Provision may be made by regulations under this Act with respect—

(a) to the form of tree preservation orders, and

(b) to the procedure to be followed in connection with the making and confirmation of such orders.

(3) Without prejudice to the generality of subsection (2), the regulations may make provision—

(a) that, before a tree preservation order is confirmed by the local planning authority, notice of the making of the order shall be given to the owners and occupiers of land affected by the order and to such other persons, if any, as may be specified in the regulations;

(b) that objections and representations with respect to the order, if duly made in accordance with the regulations, shall be considered before the order is confirmed by the local planning authority; and

(c) that copies of the order, when confirmed by the authority, shall be served on such persons as may be specified in the regulations.

200 Tree preservation orders: Forestry Commissioners and Natural Resources Body for Wales [England]

(1) A tree preservation order does not have effect in respect of anything done—

(a) by or on behalf of the Forestry Commissioners or the Natural Resources Body for Wales on land placed at their disposal in pursuance of the Forestry Act 1967 or otherwise under their management or supervision;

(b) by or on behalf of any other person in accordance with a relevant plan which is for the time being in force.

(2) A relevant plan is a plan of operations or other working plan approved by the Forestry Commissioners or the Natural Resources Body for Wales under—

(a) a forestry dedication covenant within the meaning of section 5 of the Forestry Act 1967, or

(b) conditions of a grant or loan made by the Forestry Commissioners under section 1 of the Forestry Act 1979 or made by the Natural Resources Body for Wales under article 10b of the Natural Resources Body for Wales (Establishment) Order 2012 (SI 2012/1903) for or in connection with the use or management of land for forestry purposes.

(3) A reference to a provision of the Forestry Act 1967 or the Forestry Act 1979 includes a reference to a corresponding provision replaced by that provision or any earlier corresponding provision.

200 Tree preservation orders: Forestry Commissioners and Natural Resources Body for Wales [Wales]

(1) A tree preservation order does not have effect in respect of anything done—

(a) by or on behalf of the Forestry Commissioners or the Natural Resources Body for Wales on land placed at their disposal in pursuance of the Forestry Act 1967 or otherwise under their management or supervision;

(b) by or on behalf of any other person in accordance with a relevant plan which is for the time being in force.

(2) A relevant plan is a plan of operations or other working plan approved by the Forestry Commissioners under—

    (a) a forestry dedication covenant within the meaning of section 5 of the Forestry Act 1967, or

    (b) conditions of a grant or loan made by the Forestry Commissioners under section 1 of the Forestry Act 1979 or made by the Natural Resources Body for Wales under article 10b of the Natural Resources Body for Wales (Establishment) Order 2012 (SI 2012/1903) for or in connection with the use or management of land for forestry purposes.

(3) A reference to a provision of the Forestry Act 1967 or the Forestry Act 1979 includes a reference to a corresponding provision replaced by that provision or any earlier corresponding provision.

201 Provisional tree preservation orders [England]

[…]

201 Provisional tree preservation orders [Wales]

(1) If it appears to a local planning authority that a tree preservation order proposed to be made by that authority should take effect immediately without previous confirmation, they may include in the order as made by them a direction that this section shall apply to the order.

(2) Notwithstanding section 199(1), an order which contains such a direction—

    (a) shall take effect provisionally on such date as may be specified in it, and

    (b) shall continue in force by virtue of this section until—

        (i) the expiration of a period of six months beginning with the date on which the order was made; or

        (ii) the date on which the order is confirmed,

    whichever first occurs.

202 Power for Secretary of State to make tree preservation orders [England]

(1) If it appears to the Secretary of State, after consultation with the local planning authority, to be expedient that a tree preservation order or an order amending or revoking such an order should be made, he may himself make such an order.

(2) Any order so made by the Secretary of State shall have the same effect as if it had been made by the local planning authority and confirmed by them under this Chapter.

(3) […]

202 Power for Secretary of State to make tree preservation orders [Wales]

(1) If it appears to the Secretary of State, after consultation with the local planning authority, to be expedient that a tree preservation order or an order amending or revoking such an order should be made, he may himself make such an order.

(2) Any order so made by the Secretary of State shall have the same effect as if it had been made by the local planning authority and confirmed by them under this Chapter.

(3) The provisions of this Chapter and of any regulations made under it with respect to the procedure to be followed in connection with the making and confirmation of any order to which subsection (1) applies and the service of copies of it as confirmed shall have effect, subject to any necessary modifications—

    (a) in relation to any proposal by the Secretary of State to make such an order,

    (b) in relation to the making of it by the Secretary of State, and

    (c) in relation to the service of copies of it as so made.

202A Tree preservation regulations: general [England and Wales][4]

(1) The appropriate national authority may by regulations make provision in connection with tree preservation orders.

(2) Sections 202B to 202G make further provision about what may, in particular, be contained in regulations under subsection (1).

(3) In this section and those sections 'tree preservation order' includes an order under section 202(1).

(4) In this Act 'tree preservation regulations' means regulations under subsection (1).

(5) In subsection (1) 'the appropriate national authority'—

    (a) in relation to England means the Secretary of State, and

    (b) in relation to Wales means the Welsh Ministers.

(6) Section 333(3) does not apply in relation to tree preservation regulations made by the Welsh Ministers.

(7) Tree preservation regulations made by the Welsh Ministers are subject to annulment in pursuance of a resolution of the National Assembly for Wales.

202B Tree preservation regulations: making of tree preservation orders [England and Wales][5]

(1) Tree preservation regulations may make provision about—

    (a) the form of tree preservation orders;

    (b) the procedure to be followed in connection with the making of tree preservation orders;

    (c) when a tree preservation order takes effect.

(2) If tree preservation regulations make provision for tree preservation orders not to take effect until confirmed, tree preservation regulations may—

    (a) make provision for tree preservation orders to take effect provisionally until confirmed;

---

[4] Not yet in force in Wales as of 1 July 2013.
[5] Not yet in force in Wales as of 1 July 2013.

    (b) make provision about who is to confirm a tree preservation order;

    (c) make provision about the procedure to be followed in connection with confirmation of tree preservation orders.

202C Tree preservation regulations: prohibited activities [England and Wales][6]

(1)   Tree preservation regulations may make provision for prohibiting all or any of the following—

    (a) cutting down of trees;

    (b) topping of trees;

    (c) lopping of trees;

    (d) uprooting of trees;

    (e) wilful damage of trees;

    (f) wilful destruction of trees.

(2)   A prohibition imposed on a person may (in particular) relate to things whose doing the person causes or permits (as well as to things the person does).

(3)   A prohibition may be imposed subject to exceptions.

(4)   In particular, provision may be made for a prohibition not to apply to things done with consent.

(5)   In this section 'tree' means a tree in respect of which a tree preservation order is in force.

202D Tree preservation regulations: consent for prohibited activities [England and Wales][7]

(1)   This section applies if tree preservation regulations make provision under section 202C(4).

(2)   Tree preservation regulations may make provision—

    (a) about who may give consent;

    (b) for the giving of consent subject to conditions;

    (c) about the procedure to be followed in connection with obtaining consent.

(3)   The conditions for which provision may be made under subsection (2)(b) include—

    (a) conditions as to planting of trees;

    (b) conditions requiring approvals to be obtained from the person giving the consent;

    (c) conditions limiting the duration of the consent.

(4)   The conditions mentioned in subsection (3)(a) include—

    (a) conditions requiring trees to be planted;

---

[6]   Not yet in force in Wales as of 1 July 2013.
[7]   Not yet in force in Wales as of 1 July 2013.

(b) conditions about the planting of any trees required to be planted by conditions within paragraph (a), including conditions about how, where or when planting is to be done;

(c) conditions requiring things to be done, or installed, for the protection of any trees planted in pursuance of conditions within paragraph (a).

(5) In relation to any tree planted in pursuance of a condition within subsection (4)(a), tree preservation regulations may make provision—

(a) for the tree preservation order concerned to apply to the tree;

(b) authorising the person imposing the condition to specify that the tree preservation order concerned is not to apply to the tree.

(6) 'The tree preservation order concerned' is the order in force in relation to the tree in respect of which consent is given under tree preservation regulations.

(7) The provision that may be made under subsection (2)(c) includes provision about applications for consent, including provision as to—

(a) the form or manner in which an application is to be made;

(b) what is to be in, or is to accompany, an application.

(8) Tree preservation regulations may make provision for appeals—

(a) against refusal of consent;

(b) where there is a failure to decide an application for consent;

(c) against conditions subject to which consent is given;

(d) against refusal of an approval required by a condition;

(e) where there is a failure to decide an application for such an approval.

(9) Tree preservation regulations may make provision in connection with appeals under provision made under subsection (8), including—

(a) provision imposing time limits;

(b) provision for further appeals;

(c) provision in connection with the procedure to be followed on an appeal (or further appeal);

(d) provision about who is to decide an appeal (or further appeal);

(e) provision imposing duties, or conferring powers, on a person deciding an appeal (or further appeal).

202E Tree preservation regulations: compensation [England and Wales][8]

(1) Tree preservation regulations may make provision for the payment of compensation—

(a) where any consent required under tree preservation regulations is refused;

(b) where any such consent is given subject to conditions;

(c) where any approval required under such a condition is refused.

---

[8] Not yet in force in Wales as of 1 July 2013.

(2)   Tree preservation regulations may provide for entitlement conferred under subsection (1) to apply only in, or to apply except in, cases specified in tree preservation regulations.

(3)   Tree preservation regulations may provide for entitlement conferred by provision under subsection (1) to be subject to conditions, including conditions as to time limits.

(4)   Tree preservation regulations may, in relation to compensation under provision under subsection (1), make provision about—

(a)   who is to pay the compensation;

(b)   who is entitled to the compensation;

(c)   what the compensation is to be paid in respect of;

(d)   the amount, or calculation of, the compensation.

(5)   Tree preservation regulations may make provision about the procedure to be followed in connection with claiming any entitlement conferred by provision under subsection (1).

(6)   Tree preservation regulations may make provision for the determination of disputes about entitlement conferred by provision under subsection (1), including provision for and in connection with the referral of any such disputes to, and their determination by the First-tier Tribunal or the Upper Tribunal.

202F Tree preservation regulations: registers [England and Wales][9]

Tree preservation regulations may make provision for the keeping of, and public access to, registers containing information related to tree preservation orders.

202G Tree preservation regulations: supplementary [England and Wales]

(1)   Tree preservation regulations may provide for the application (with or without[10] modifications) of, or make provision comparable to, any provision of this Act mentioned in subsection (2).

(2)   The provisions are any provision of Part 3 relating to planning permission or applications for planning permission, except sections 56, 62, 65, 69(3) and (4), 71, 91 to 96, 100 and 101 and Schedule 8.

(3)   Tree preservation regulations may make provision comparable to—

(a)   any provision made by the Town and Country Planning (Tree Preservation Order) Regulations 1969 or the Town and Country Planning (Trees) Regulations 1999;

(b)   any provision that could have been made under section 199(2) and (3).

(4)   Tree preservation regulations may contain incidental, supplementary, consequential, transitional and transitory provision and savings.

---

[9]   Not yet in force in Wales as of 1 July 2013.
[10]   Not yet in force in Wales as of 1 July 2013.

Compensation for loss or damage caused by orders, etc

203 Compensation in respect of tree preservation orders [England]

[...]

203 Compensation in respect of tree preservation orders [Wales]

A tree preservation order may make provision for the payment by the local planning authority, subject to such exceptions and conditions as may be specified in the order, of compensation in respect of loss or damage caused or incurred in consequence—

(a) of the refusal of any consent required under the order, or

(b) of the grant of any such consent subject to conditions.

204 Compensation in respect of requirement as to replanting of trees [England]

[...]

204 Compensation in respect of requirement as to replanting of trees [Wales]

(1) This section applies where—

(a) in pursuance of provision made by a tree preservation order, a direction is given by the local planning authority or the Secretary of State for securing the replanting of all or any part of a woodland area which is felled in the course of forestry operations permitted by or under the order; and

(b) the Forestry Commissioners decide not to make any grant or loan under section 1 of the Forestry Act 1979 in respect of the replanting by reason that the direction frustrates the use of the woodland area for the growing of timber or other forest products for commercial purposes and in accordance with the rules or practice of good forestry.

(2) Where this section applies, the local planning authority exercising functions under the tree preservation order shall be liable, on the making of a claim in accordance with this section, to pay compensation in respect of such loss or damage, if any, as is caused or incurred in consequence of compliance with the direction.

(3) The Forestry Commissioners shall, at the request of the person under a duty to comply with such a direction as is mentioned in subsection (1)(a), give a certificate stating—

(a) whether they have decided not to make such a grant or loan as is mentioned in subsection (1)(b), and

(b) if so, the grounds for their decision.

(4) A claim for compensation under this section must be served on the local planning authority—

(a) within 12 months from the date on which the direction was given, or

(b) where an appeal has been made to the Secretary of State against the decision of the local planning authority, within 12 months from the date of the decision of the Secretary of State on the appeal, but subject in either case to such extension of that period as the local planning authority may allow.

205 Determination of compensation claims [England]

[...]

205 Determination of compensation claims [Wales]

(1)   Except in so far as may be otherwise provided by any tree preservation order or any regulations made under this Act, any question of disputed compensation under section 203 or 204 shall be referred to and determined by the Upper Tribunal.

(2)   In relation to the determination of any such question, the provisions of section 4 of the Land Compensation Act 1961 shall apply subject to any necessary modifications and to the provisions of any regulations made under this Act.

Consequences of tree removal, etc

206 Replacement of trees [England]

(1)   If any tree in respect of which a tree preservation order is for the time being in force—

(a) is removed, uprooted or destroyed in contravention of the order, or

(b) except in the case of a tree to which the order applies as part of a woodland, is removed, uprooted or destroyed or dies at a prescribed time,

it shall be the duty of the owner of the land to plant another tree of an appropriate size and species at the same place as soon as he reasonably can.

(2)   The duty imposed by subsection (1) does not apply to an owner if on application by him the local planning authority dispense with it.

(3)   In respect of trees in a woodland it shall be sufficient for the purposes of this section to replace the trees removed, uprooted or destroyed by planting the same number of trees—

(a) on or near the land on which the trees removed, uprooted or destroyed stood, or

(b) on such other land as may be agreed between the local planning authority and the owner of the land,

and in such places as may be designated by the local planning authority.

(4)   In relation to any tree planted pursuant to this section, the relevant tree preservation order shall apply as it applied to the original tree.

(5)   The duty imposed by subsection (1) on the owner of any land shall attach to the person who is from time to time the owner of the land.

206 Replacement of trees [Wales]

(1)   If any tree in respect of which a tree preservation order is for the time being in force—

(a) is removed, uprooted or destroyed in contravention of the order, or

(b) except in the case of a tree to which the order applies as part of a woodland, is removed, uprooted or destroyed or dies at a time when its cutting down or uprooting is authorised only by virtue of section 198(6)(a),

it shall be the duty of the owner of the land to plant another tree of an appropriate size and species at the same place as soon as he reasonably can.

(2) The duty imposed by subsection (1) does not apply to an owner if on application by him the local planning authority dispense with it.

(3) In respect of trees in a woodland it shall be sufficient for the purposes of this section to replace the trees removed, uprooted or destroyed by planting the same number of trees—

(a) on or near the land on which the trees removed, uprooted or destroyed stood, or

(b) on such other land as may be agreed between the local planning authority and the owner of the land,

and in such places as may be designated by the local planning authority.

(4) In relation to any tree planted pursuant to this section, the relevant tree preservation order shall apply as it applied to the original tree.

(5) The duty imposed by subsection (1) on the owner of any land shall attach to the person who is from time to time the owner of the land.

207 Enforcement of duties as to replacement of trees [England and Wales]

(1) If it appears to the local planning authority that—

(a) the provisions of section 206, or

(b) any conditions of a consent given under a tree preservation order which require the replacement of trees,

are not complied with in the case of any tree or trees, that authority may serve on the owner of the land a notice requiring him, within such period as may be specified in the notice, to plant a tree or trees of such size and species as may be so specified.

(2) A notice under subsection (1) may only be served within four years from the date of the alleged failure to comply with those provisions or conditions.

(3) A notice under subsection (1) shall specify a period at the end of which it is to take effect.

(4) The specified period shall be a period of not less than twenty-eight days beginning with the date of service of the notice.

(5) The duty imposed by section 206(1) may only be enforced as provided by this section and not otherwise.

208 Appeals against s 207 notices

(1) A person on whom a notice under section 207(1) is served may appeal to the Secretary of State against the notice on any of the following grounds—

(a) that the provisions of section 206 or, as the case may be, the conditions mentioned in section 207(1)(b) are not applicable or have been complied with;

(aa) that in all the circumstances of the case the duty imposed by section 206(1) should be dispensed with in relation to any tree;

(b) that the requirements of the notice are unreasonable in respect of the period or the size or species of trees specified in it;

(c) that the planting of a tree or trees in accordance with the notice is not required in the interests of amenity or would be contrary to the practice of good forestry;

(d) that the place on which the tree is or trees are required to be planted is unsuitable for that purpose.

(2) An appeal under subsection (1) shall be made either—

(a) by giving written notice of the appeal to the Secretary of State before the end of the period specified in accordance with section 207(3); or

(b) by sending such notice to him in a properly addressed and pre-paid letter posted to him at such time that, in the ordinary course of post, it would be delivered to him before the end of that period.

(4) The notice shall—

(a) indicate the grounds of the appeal,

(b) state the facts on which the appeal is based, and

(c) be accompanied by such information as may be prescribed.

(4A) The power to make regulations under subsection (4)(c) is exercisable by—

(a) the Secretary of State, in relation to England;

(b) the Welsh Ministers, in relation to Wales.

(4B) Section 333(3) does not apply in relation to regulations under subsection (4)(c) made by the Welsh Ministers.

(4C) Regulations under subsection (4)(c) made by the Welsh Ministers are subject to annulment in pursuance of a resolution of the National Assembly for Wales.

(5) On an appeal under subsection (1) the Secretary of State shall, if either the appellant or the local planning authority so desire, give each of them an opportunity of appearing before and being heard by a person appointed by the Secretary of State for the purpose.

(6) Where such an appeal is brought , the notice under section 207(1) shall be of no effect pending the final determination or the withdrawal of the appeal.

(7) On such an appeal the Secretary of State may—

(a) correct any defect, error or misdescription in the notice; or

(b) vary any of its requirements,

if he is satisfied that the correction or variation will not cause injustice to the appellant or the local planning authority.

(8)   Where the Secretary of State determines to allow the appeal, he may quash the notice.

(8A) The Secretary of State shall give any directions necessary to give effect to his determination on the appeal.

(9)   Schedule 6 applies to appeals under this section.

(10) Where any person has appealed to the Secretary of State under this section against a notice, neither that person nor any other shall be entitled, in any other proceedings instituted after the making of the appeal, to claim that the notice was not duly served on the person who appealed.

(11) Subsection (5) of section 250 of the Local Government Act 1972 (which authorises a Minister holding an inquiry under that section to make orders with respect to the costs of the parties) shall apply in relation to any proceedings before the Secretary of State on an appeal under this section as if those proceedings were an inquiry held by the Secretary of State under section 250.

209 Execution and cost of works required by s 207 notice

(1)   If, within the period specified in a notice under section 207(1) for compliance with it, or within such extended period as the local planning authority may allow, any trees which are required to be planted by a notice under that section have not been planted, the local planning authority may—

(a)   enter the land and plant those trees, and

(b)   recover from the person who is then the owner of the land any expenses reasonably incurred by them in doing so.

(2)   Where such a notice has been served—

(a)   any expenses incurred by the owner of any land for the purpose of complying with the notice, and

(b)   any sums paid by the owner of any land under subsection (1) in respect of expenses incurred by the local planning authority in planting trees required by such a notice to be planted,

shall be deemed to be incurred or paid for the use and at the request of any person, other than the owner, responsible for the cutting down, destruction or removal of the original tree or trees.

(3)   Regulations made under this Act may provide that—

(a)   section 276 of the Public Health Act 1936 (power of local authorities to sell materials removed in executing works under that Act subject to accounting for the proceeds of sale);

(b)   section 289 of that Act (power to require the occupier of any premises to permit works to be executed by the owner of the premises); or

(c)   section 294 of that Act (limit on liability of persons holding premises as agents or trustees in respect of the expenses recoverable under that Act),

shall apply, subject to such adaptations and modifications as may be specified in the regulations, in relation to any steps required to be taken by a notice under section 207(1).

(4)   Regulations under subsection (3) applying section 289 of the Public Health Act 1936 may include adaptations and modifications for the purpose of giving the owner of land to which such a notice relates the right, as against all other persons interested in the land, to comply with the requirements of the notice.

(5)   Regulations under subsection (3) may also provide for the charging on the land of any expenses recoverable by a local authority or National Park authority under subsection (1).

(6)   Any person who wilfully obstructs a person acting in the exercise of the power under subsection (1)(a) shall be guilty of an offence and liable on summary conviction to a fine not exceeding level 3 on the standard scale.

210 Penalties for non-compliance with tree preservation order [England and Wales]

(1)   If any person, in contravention of a tree preservation order—

(a) cuts down, uproots or wilfully destroys a tree, or

(b) wilfully damages, tops or lops a tree in such a manner as to be likely to destroy it,

he shall be guilty of an offence.

(2)   A person guilty of an offence under subsection (1) shall be liable—

(a) on summary conviction to a fine not exceeding £20,000; or

(b) on conviction on indictment, to a fine.

(3)   In determining the amount of any fine to be imposed on a person convicted of an offence under subsection (1), the court shall in particular have regard to any financial benefit which has accrued or appears likely to accrue to him in consequence of the offence.

(4)   If any person contravenes the provisions of a tree preservation order otherwise than as mentioned in subsection (1), he shall be guilty of an offence and liable on summary conviction to a fine not exceeding level 4 on the standard scale.

(4A) Proceedings for an offence under subsection (4) may be brought within the period of 6 months beginning with the date on which evidence sufficient in the opinion of the prosecutor to justify the proceedings came to the prosecutor's knowledge.

(4B) Subsection (4A) does not authorise the commencement of proceedings for an offence more than 3 years after the date on which the offence was committed.

(4C) For the purposes of subsection (4A), a certificate—

(a) signed by or on behalf of the prosecutor, and

(b) stating the date on which evidence sufficient in the prosecutor's opinion to justify the proceedings came to the prosecutor's knowledge,

is conclusive evidence of that fact.

(4D) A certificate stating that matter and purporting to be so signed is to be deemed to be so signed unless the contrary is proved.

(4E) Subsection (4A) does not apply in relation to an offence in respect of a tree in Wales.

Trees in conservation areas

211 Preservation of trees in conservation areas [England and Wales]

(1)   Subject to the provisions of this section and section 212, any person who, in relation to a tree to which this section applies, does any act which might by virtue of section 198(3)(a) be prohibited by a tree preservation order shall be guilty of an offence.

(1A) Subsection (1) does not apply so far as the act in question is authorised by an order granting development consent.

(2)   Subject to section 212, this section applies to any tree in a conservation area in respect of which no tree preservation order is for the time being in force.

(3)   It shall be a defence for a person charged with an offence under subsection (1) to prove—

(a)   that he served notice of his intention to do the act in question (with sufficient particulars to identify the tree) on the local planning authority in whose area the tree is or was situated; and

(b)   that he did the act in question—

(i)   with the consent of the local planning authority in whose area the tree is or was situated, or

(ii) after the expiry of the period of six weeks from the date of the notice but before the expiry of the period of two years from that date.

(4)   Section 210 shall apply to an offence under this section as it applies to a contravention of a tree preservation order.

(5)   An emanation of the Crown must not, in relation to a tree to which this section applies, do an act mentioned in subsection (1) above unless—

(a)   the first condition is satisfied, and

(b)   either the second or third condition is satisfied.

(5A) Subsection (5) does not apply so far as the act in question is authorised by an order granting development consent.

(6)   The first condition is that the emanation serves notice of an intention to do the act (with sufficient particulars to identify the tree) on the local planning authority in whose area the tree is situated.

(7)   The second condition is that the act is done with the consent of the authority.

(8)   The third condition is that the act is done—

(a)   after the end of the period of six weeks starting with the date of the notice, and

(b)   before the end of the period of two years starting with that date.

212 Power to disapply s 211 [England]

(1)   The Secretary of State may by regulations direct that section 211 shall not apply in such cases as may be specified in the regulations.

(2)   Without prejudice to the generality of subsection (1), the regulations may be framed so as to exempt from the application of that section cases defined by reference to all or any of the following matters—

   (a)   acts of such descriptions or done in such circumstances or subject to such conditions as may be specified in the regulations;

   (b)   trees in such conservation areas as may be so specified;

   (c)   trees of a size or species so specified; or

   (d)   trees belonging to persons or bodies of a description so specified.

(3)   The regulations may, in relation to any matter by reference to which an exemption is conferred by them, make different provision for different circumstances.

212 Power to disapply s 211 [Wales]

(1)   The Secretary of State may by regulations direct that section 211 shall not apply in such cases as may be specified in the regulations.

(2)   Without prejudice to the generality of subsection (1), the regulations may be framed so as to exempt from the application of that section cases defined by reference to all or any of the following matters—

   (a)   acts of such descriptions or done in such circumstances or subject to such conditions as may be specified in the regulations;

   (b)   trees in such conservation areas as may be so specified;

   (c)   trees of a size or species so specified; or

   (d)   trees belonging to persons or bodies of a description so specified.

(3)   The regulations may, in relation to any matter by reference to which an exemption is conferred by them, make different provision for different circumstances.

(4)   Regulations under subsection (1) may in particular, but without prejudice to the generality of that subsection, exempt from the application of section 211 cases exempted from section 198 by subsection (6) of that section.

213 Enforcement of controls as respects trees in conservation areas [England]

(1)   If any tree to which section 211 applies—

   (a)   is removed, uprooted or destroyed in contravention of that section; or

   (b)   is removed, uprooted or destroyed or dies at a prescribed time,

   it shall be the duty of the owner of the land to plant another tree of an appropriate size and species at the same place as soon as he reasonably can.

(2)   The duty imposed by subsection (1) does not apply to an owner if on application by him the local planning authority dispense with it.

(3)   The duty imposed by subsection (1) on the owner of any land attaches to the person who is from time to time the owner of the land and may be enforced as provided by section 207 and not otherwise.

213 Enforcement of controls as respects trees in conservation areas [Wales]

(1)   If any tree to which section 211 applies—

   (a) is removed, uprooted or destroyed in contravention of that section; or

   (b) is removed, uprooted or destroyed or dies at a time when its cutting down or uprooting is authorised only by virtue of the provisions of such regulations under subsection (1) of section 212 as are mentioned in subsection (4) of that section,

   it shall be the duty of the owner of the land to plant another tree of an appropriate size and species at the same place as soon as he reasonably can.

(2)   The duty imposed by subsection (1) does not apply to an owner if on application by him the local planning authority dispense with it.

(3)   The duty imposed by subsection (1) on the owner of any land attaches to the person who is from time to time the owner of the land and may be enforced as provided by section 207 and not otherwise.

214 Registers of s 211 notices.

   It shall be the duty of a local planning authority to compile and keep available for public inspection free of charge at all reasonable hours and at a convenient place a register containing such particulars as the Secretary of State may determine of notices under section 211 affecting trees in their area.

Injunctions

214A Injunctions

(1)   Where a local planning authority consider it necessary or expedient for an actual or apprehended offence under section 210 or 211 to be restrained by injunction, they may apply to the court for an injunction, whether or not they have exercised or are proposing to exercise any of their other powers under this Chapter.

(2)   Subsections (2) to (4) of section 187B apply to an application under this section as they apply to an application under that section.

Rights of entry

214B Rights to enter without warrant

(1)   Any person duly authorised in writing by a local planning authority may enter any land for the purpose of—

   (a) surveying it in connection with making or confirming a tree preservation order with respect to the land;

   (b) ascertaining whether an offence under section 210 or 211 has been committed on the land; or

   (c) determining whether a notice under section 207 should be served on the owner of the land,

   if there are reasonable grounds for entering for the purpose in question.

(2)   Any person duly authorised in writing by the Secretary of State may enter any land for the purpose of surveying it in connection with making, amending or revoking a tree preservation order with respect to the land, if there are reasonable grounds for entering for that purpose.

(3)   Any person who is duly authorised in writing by a local planning authority may enter any land in connection with the exercise of any functions conferred on the authority by or under this Chapter.

(4)   Any person who is an officer of the Valuation Office may enter any land for the purpose of surveying it, or estimating its value, in connection with a claim for compensation in respect of any land which is payable by the local planning authority under this Chapter (other than section 204).

(5)   Any person who is duly authorised in writing by the Secretary of State may enter any land in connection with the exercise of any functions conferred on the Secretary of State by or under this Chapter.

(6)   The Secretary of State shall not authorise any person as mentioned in subsection (2) without consulting the local planning authority.

(7)   Admission shall not be demanded as of right—

   (a) by virtue of subsection (1) or (2) to any building used as a dwellinghouse; or

   (b) by virtue of subsection (3), (4) or (5) to any land which is occupied,

   unless twenty-four hours' notice of the intended entry has been given to the occupier.

(8)   Any right to enter by virtue of this section shall be exercised at a reasonable hour.

214C Right to enter under warrant

(1)   If it is shown to the satisfaction of a justice of the peace on sworn information in writing—

   (a) that there are reasonable grounds for entering any land for any of the purposes mentioned in section 214B(1) or (2); and

   (b) that—

      (i)   admission to the land has been refused, or a refusal is reasonably apprehended; or

      (ii) the case is one of urgency,

   the justice may issue a warrant authorising any person duly authorised in writing by a local planning authority or, as the case may be, the Secretary of State to enter the land.

(2)   For the purposes of subsection (1)(b)(i) admission to land shall be regarded as having been refused if no reply is received to a request for admission within a reasonable period.

(3)   A warrant authorises entry on one occasion only and that entry must be—

   (a) within one month from the date of the issue of the warrant; and

   (b) at a reasonable hour, unless the case is one of urgency.

214D Rights of entry: supplementary provisions

(1)   Any power conferred under or by virtue of section 214B or 214C to enter land (referred to in this section as 'a right of entry') shall be construed as including power to take samples from any tree and samples of the soil.

(2)   A person authorised to enter land in the exercise of a right of entry—

(a) shall, if so required, produce evidence of his authority and state the purpose of his entry before so entering;

(b) may take with him such other persons as may be necessary; and

(c) on leaving the land shall, if the owner or occupier is not then present, leave it as effectively secured against trespassers as he found it.

(3)   Any person who wilfully obstructs a person acting in the exercise of a right of entry shall be guilty of an offence and liable on summary conviction to a fine not exceeding level 3 on the standard scale.

(4)   If any damage is caused to land or chattels in the exercise of a right of entry, compensation may be recovered by any person suffering the damage from the authority who gave the written authority for the entry or, as the case may be, the Secretary of State.

(5)   The provisions of section 118 shall apply in relation to compensation under subsection (4) as they apply in relation to compensation under Part IV.

CHAPTER II LAND ADVERSELY AFFECTING AMENITY OF NEIGHBOURHOOD

215 Power to require proper maintenance of land

(1)   If it appears to the local planning authority that the amenity of a part of their area, or of an adjoining area, is adversely affected by the condition of land in their area, they may serve on the owner and occupier of the land a notice under this section.

(2)   The notice shall require such steps for remedying the condition of the land as may be specified in the notice to be taken within such period as may be so specified.

(3)   Subject to the following provisions of this Chapter, the notice shall take effect at the end of such period as may be specified in the notice.

(4)   That period shall not be less than 28 days after the service of the notice.

216 Penalty for non-compliance with s 215 notice

(1)   The provisions of this section shall have effect where a notice has been served under section 215.

(2)   If any owner or occupier of the land on whom the notice was served fails to take steps required by the notice within the period specified in it for compliance with it, he shall be guilty of an offence and liable on summary conviction to a fine not exceeding level 3 on the standard scale.

(3)   Where proceedings have been brought under subsection (2) against a person as the owner of the land and he has, at some time before the end of the compliance period, ceased to be the owner of the land, if he—

351

(a) duly lays information to that effect, and

(b) gives the prosecution not less than three clear days' notice of his intention,

he shall be entitled to have the person who then became the owner of the land brought before the court in the proceedings.

(4) Where proceedings have been brought under subsection (2) against a person as the occupier of the land and he has, at some time before the end of the compliance period, ceased to be the occupier of the land, if he—

(a) duly lays information to that effect, and

(b) gives the prosecution not less than three clear days' notice of his intention,

he shall be entitled to have brought before the court in the proceedings the person who then became the occupier of the land or, if nobody then became the occupier, the person who is the owner at the date of the notice.

(5) Where in such proceedings—

(a) it has been proved that any steps required by the notice under section 215 have not been taken within the compliance period, and

(b) the original defendant proves that the failure to take those steps was attributable, in whole or in part, to the default of a person specified in a notice under subsection (3) or (4),

then—

(i) that person may be convicted of the offence; and

(ii) if the original defendant also proves that he took all reasonable steps to ensure compliance with the notice, he shall be acquitted of the offence.

(6) If, after a person has been convicted under the previous provisions of this section, he does not as soon as practicable do everything in his power to secure compliance with the notice, he shall be guilty of a further offence and liable on summary conviction to a fine not exceeding one-tenth of level 3 on the standard scale for each day following his first conviction on which any of the requirements of the notice remain unfulfilled.

(7) Any reference in this section to the compliance period, in relation to a notice, is a reference to the period specified in the notice for compliance with it or such extended period as the local planning authority who served the notice may allow for compliance.

217 Appeal to magistrates' court against s 215 notice

(1) A person on whom a notice under section 215 is served, or any other person having an interest in the land to which the notice relates, may, at any time within the period specified in the notice as the period at the end of which it is to take effect, appeal against the notice on any of the following grounds—

(a) that the condition of the land to which the notice relates does not adversely affect the amenity of any part of the area of the local planning authority who served the notice, or of any adjoining area;

(b) that the condition of the land to which the notice relates is attributable to, and such as results in the ordinary course of events from, the carrying on of operations or a use of land which is not in contravention of Part III;

(c) that the requirements of the notice exceed what is necessary for preventing the condition of the land from adversely affecting the amenity of any part of the area of the local planning authority who served the notice, or of any adjoining area;

(d) that the period specified in the notice as the period within which any steps required by the notice are to be taken falls short of what should reasonably be allowed.

(2) Any appeal under this section shall be made to a magistrates' court.

(3) Where such an appeal is brought, the notice to which it relates shall be of no effect pending the final determination or withdrawal of the appeal.

(4) On such an appeal the magistrates' court may correct any informality, defect or error in the notice if satisfied that the informality, defect or error is not material.

(5) On the determination of such an appeal the magistrates' court shall give directions for giving effect to their determination, including, where appropriate, directions for quashing the notice or for varying the terms of the notice in favour of the appellant.

(6) Where any person has appealed to a magistrates' court under this section against a notice, neither that person nor any other shall be entitled, in any other proceedings instituted after the making of the appeal, to claim that the notice was not duly served on the person who appealed.

218 Further appeal to the Crown Court

Where an appeal has been brought under section 217, an appeal against the decision of the magistrates' court on that appeal may be brought to the Crown Court by the appellant or by the local planning authority who served the notice in question under section 215.

219 Execution and cost of works required by s 215 notice

(1) If, within the period specified in a notice under section 215 in accordance with subsection (2) of that section, or within such extended period as the local planning authority who served the notice may allow, any steps required by the notice to be taken have not been taken, the local planning authority who served the notice may—

(a) enter the land and take those steps, and

(b) recover from the person who is then the owner of the land any expenses reasonably incurred by them in doing so.

(2) Where a notice has been served under section 215—

(a) any expenses incurred by the owner or occupier of any land for the purpose of complying with the notice, and

(b) any sums paid by the owner of any land under subsection (1) in respect of expenses incurred by the local planning authority in taking steps required by such a notice, shall be deemed to be incurred or paid for the use and at the request of the person who caused or permitted the land to come to be in the condition in which it was when the notice was served.

(3)   Regulations made under this Act may provide that—

(a)   section 276 of the Public Health Act 1936 (power of local authorities to sell materials removed in executing works under that Act subject to accounting for the proceeds of sale);

(b)   section 289 of that Act (power to require the occupier of any premises to permit works to be executed by the owner of the premises); or

(c)   section 294 of that Act (limit on liability of persons holding premises as agents or trustees in respect of the expenses recoverable under that Act),

shall apply, subject to such adaptations and modifications as may be specified in the regulations, in relation to any steps required to be taken by a notice under section 215.

(4)   Regulations under subsection (3) applying section 289 of the Public Health Act 1936 may include adaptations and modifications for the purpose of giving the owner of land to which a notice under section 215 relates the right, as against all other persons interested in the land, to comply with the requirements of the enforcement notice.

(5)   Regulations under subsection (3) may also provide for the charging on the land of any expenses recoverable by a local authority under subsection (1).

(6)   [...]

CHAPTER III ADVERTISEMENTS

Advertisement regulations

220 Regulations controlling display of advertisements

(1)   Regulations under this Act shall make provision for restricting or regulating the display of advertisements so far as appears to the Secretary of State to be expedient in the interests of amenity or public safety.

(2)   Without prejudice to the generality of subsection (1), any such regulations may provide—

(a)   for regulating the dimensions, appearance and position of advertisements which may be displayed, the sites on which advertisements may be displayed and the manner in which they are to be affixed to the land;

(b)   for requiring the consent of the local planning authority to be obtained for the display of advertisements, or of advertisements of any class specified in the regulations;

(c)   for applying, in relation to any such consent and to applications for such consent, any of the provisions mentioned in subsection (3), subject to such adaptations and modifications as may be specified in the regulations;

(d) for the constitution, for the purposes of the regulations, of such advisory committees as may be prescribed by the regulations, and for determining the manner in which the expenses of any such committee are to be defrayed.

(2A) The regulations may also make provision as to—

(a) the form and manner in which an application for consent must be made;

(b) particulars of such matters as are to be included in the application;

(c) any documents or other materials which must accompany the application.

(3) The provisions referred to in subsection (2)(c) are—

(a) the provisions of Part III relating to planning permission and to applications for planning permission, except sections 56, 62 , 65, 69(3) and (4), 71, 91 to 98, 100 and 101 and Schedule 8;

(b) sections 137 to 141, 143 and 144 (except so far as they relate to purchase notices served in consequence of such orders as are mentioned in section 137(1)(b) or (c));

(c) section 316.

(4) Without prejudice to the generality of the powers conferred by this section, regulations made for the purposes of this section may provide that any appeal from the decision of the local planning authority, on an application for their consent under the regulations, shall be to an independent tribunal constituted in accordance with the regulations, instead of being an appeal to the Secretary of State.

(5) If any tribunal is so constituted, the Secretary of State may pay to the chairman and members of the tribunal such remuneration, whether by way of salaries or by way of fees, and such reasonable allowances in respect of expenses properly incurred in the performance of their duties, as he may with the consent of the Treasury determine.

221 Power to make different advertisement regulations for different areas

(1) Regulations made for the purposes of section 220 may make different provision with respect to different areas, and in particular may make special provision—

(a) with respect to conservation areas;

(b) with respect to areas defined for the purposes of the regulations as experimental areas, and

(c) with respect to areas defined for the purposes of the regulations as areas of special control.

(2) An area may be defined as an experimental area for a prescribed period for the purpose of assessing the effect on amenity or public safety of advertisements of a prescribed description.

(3) An area may be defined as an area of special control if it is—

(a) a rural area, or

(b) an area which appears to the Secretary of State to require special protection on grounds of amenity.

(4)   Without prejudice to the generality of subsection (1), the regulations may prohibit the display in an area of special control of all advertisements except advertisements of such classes (if any) as may be prescribed.

(5)   Areas of special control for the purposes of regulations under this section may be defined by means of orders made or approved by the Secretary of State in accordance with the provisions of the regulations.

(6)   Where the Secretary of State is authorised by the regulations to make or approve any such order as is mentioned in subsection (5), the regulations shall provide—

(a) for the publication of notice of the proposed order in such manner as may be prescribed,

(b) for the consideration of objections duly made to it, and

(c) for the holding of such inquiries or other hearings as may be prescribed,

before the order is made or approved.

(7)   Subject to subsection (8), regulations made under section 220 may be made so as to apply—

(a) to advertisements which are being displayed on the date on which the regulations come into force, or

(b) to the use for the display of the advertisements of any site which was being used for that purpose on that date.

(8)   Any regulations made in accordance with subsection (7) shall provide for exempting from them—

(a) the continued display of any such advertisements as there mentioned; and

(b) the continued use for the display of advertisements of any such site as there mentioned,

during such period as may be prescribed.

(9)   Different periods may be prescribed under subsection (8) for the purposes of different provisions of the regulations.

222 Planning permission not needed for advertisements complying with regulations

Where the display of advertisements in accordance with regulations made under section 220 involves development of land—

(a) planning permission for that development shall be deemed to be granted by virtue of this section, and

(b) no application shall be necessary for that development under Part III.

223 Repayment of expense of removing prohibited advertisements

(1)   Where, for the purpose of complying with any regulations made under section 220, works are carried out by any person—

(a) for removing an advertisement which was being displayed on 1st August 1948; or

(b) for discontinuing the use for the display of advertisements of a site used for that purpose on that date,

that person shall, on a claim made to the local planning authority within such time and in such manner as may be prescribed, be entitled to recover from that authority compensation in respect of any expenses reasonably incurred by him in carrying out those works.

(2) Except in so far as may be otherwise provided by any regulations made under this Act, any question of disputed compensation under this section shall be referred to and determined by the Upper Tribunal.

(3) In relation to the determination of any such question, the provisions of section 4 of the Land Compensation Act 1961 shall apply subject to any necessary modifications and to the provisions of any regulations made under this Act.

Enforcement of control over advertisements

224 Enforcement of control as to advertisements

(1) Regulations under section 220 may make provision for enabling the local planning authority to require—

(a) the removal of any advertisement which is displayed in contravention of the regulations, or

(b) the discontinuance of the use for the display of advertisements of any site which is being so used in contravention of the regulations.

(2) For that purpose the regulations may apply any of the provisions of Part VII with respect to enforcement notices or the provisions of section 186, subject to such adaptations and modifications as may be specified in the regulations.

(3) Without prejudice to any provisions included in such regulations by virtue of subsection (1) or (2), if any person displays an advertisement in contravention of the regulations he shall be guilty of an offence and liable on summary conviction to a fine of such amount as may be prescribed, not exceeding level 4 on the standard scale and, in the case of a continuing offence, one-tenth of level 4 on the standard scale for each day during which the offence continues after conviction.

(4) Without prejudice to the generality of subsection (3), a person shall be deemed to display an advertisement for the purposes of that subsection if—

(a) he is the owner or occupier of the land on which the advertisement is displayed; or

(b) the advertisement gives publicity to his goods, trade, business or other concerns.

(5) A person shall not be guilty of an offence under subsection (3) by reason only—

(a) of his being the owner or occupier of the land on which an advertisement is displayed, or

(b) of his goods, trade, business or other concerns being given publicity by the advertisement,

if he proves either of the matters specified in subsection (6).

(6) The matters are that—

(a) the advertisement was displayed without his knowledge; or

(b) he took all reasonable steps to prevent the display or, after the advertisement had been displayed, to secure its removal.

(7) Proceedings for an offence under subsection (3) may be brought within the period of 6 months beginning with the date on which evidence sufficient in the opinion of the prosecutor to justify the proceedings came to the prosecutor's knowledge.

(8) Subsection (7) does not authorise the commencement of proceedings for an offence more than 3 years after the date on which the offence was committed.

(9) For the purposes of subsection (7), a certificate—

(a) signed by or on behalf of the prosecutor, and

(b) stating the date on which evidence sufficient in the prosecutor's opinion to justify the proceedings came to the prosecutor's knowledge,

is conclusive evidence of that fact.

(10) A certificate stating that matter and purporting to be so signed is to be deemed to be so signed unless the contrary is proved.

(11) Subsection (7) does not apply in relation to an offence in respect of an advertisement in Wales.

225 Power to remove or obliterate placards and posters

(1) Subject to subsections (2) and (3), the local planning authority may remove or obliterate any placard or poster—

(a) which is displayed in their area; and

(b) which in their opinion is so displayed in contravention of regulations made under section 220.

(2) Subsection (1) does not authorise the removal or obliteration of a placard or poster displayed within a building to which there is no public right of access.

(3) Subject to subsection (4), where a placard or poster identifies the person who displayed it or caused it to be displayed, the local planning authority shall not exercise any power conferred by subsection (1) unless they have first given him notice in writing—

(a) that in their opinion it is displayed in contravention of regulations made under section 220; and

(b) that they intend to remove or obliterate it on the expiry of a period specified in the notice and recover from him the costs they may reasonably incur in doing so.

(4) Subsection (3) does not apply if—

(a) the placard or poster does not give his address, and

(b) the authority do not know it and are unable to ascertain it after reasonable inquiry.

(5)   The period specified in a notice under subsection (3) must be not less than two days from the date of service of the notice.

(6)   Where—

(a)   a local planning authority serve a notice on a person under subsection (3) in relation to a placard or poster, and

(b)   the person fails to remove or obliterate it within the period specified in the notice,

the authority may recover from that person the costs they may reasonably incur in exercising their power under subsection (1).

(7)   This subsection applies in relation to a placard or poster where—

(a)   the placard or poster does not identify the person who displayed it or caused it to be displayed, or

(b)   it does do so, but subsection (3) does not apply by reason of subsection (4), and

the placard or poster publicises the goods, services or concerns of an identifiable person.

(8)   Where subsection (7) applies, subsections (3) to (6) have effect as if the reference in subsection (3) to the person who displayed the placard or poster or caused it to be displayed were a reference to the person whose goods, services or concerns are publicised.

(9)   Where any damage is caused to land or chattels in the exercise of the power under subsection (1) in relation to a placard or poster, compensation may be recovered by any person suffering the damage from the local planning authority exercising the power.

(10) Subsection (9) does not permit the recovery of compensation by the person who displayed the placard or poster or caused it to be displayed.

(11) The provisions of section 118 apply in relation to compensation under subsection (9) as they apply in relation to compensation under Part 4.

[…]

225A Power to remove structures used for unauthorised display

(1)   Subject to subsections (2), (3) and (5) and the right of appeal under section 225B, the local planning authority for an area in England may remove, and then dispose of, any display structure—

(a)   which is in their area; and

(b)   which, in the local planning authority's opinion, is used for the display of advertisements in contravention of regulations under section 220.

(2)   Subsection (1) does not authorise the removal of a display structure in a building to which there is no public right of access.

(3)   The local planning authority may not under subsection (1) remove a display structure unless the local planning authority have first served a removal notice on a person who appears to the local planning authority to be responsible for the erection or maintenance of the display structure.

(4)   Subsection (3) applies only if there is a person—

    (a) who appears to the local planning authority to be responsible for the erection or maintenance of the display structure; and

    (b) whose name and address are either known by the local planning authority or could be ascertained by the local planning authority after reasonable enquiry.

(5)   If subsection (3) does not apply, the local planning authority may not under subsection (1) remove a display structure unless the local planning authority have first—

    (a) fixed a removal notice to the display structure or exhibited a removal notice in the vicinity of the display structure; and

    (b) served a copy of that notice on the occupier of the land on which the display structure is situated.

(6)   Subsection (5)(b) applies only if the local planning authority know who the occupier is or could identify the occupier after reasonable enquiry.

(7)   Where—

    (a) the local planning authority has served a removal notice in accordance with subsection (3) or (5)(b), and

    (b) the display structure is not removed by the time specified in the removal notice,

the local planning authority may recover, from any person on whom the removal notice has been served under subsection (3) or (5)(b), expenses reasonably incurred by the local planning authority in exercising the local planning authority's power under subsection (1).

(8)   Expenses are not recoverable under subsection (7) from a person if the person satisfies the local planning authority that the person was not responsible for the erection of the display structure and is not responsible for its maintenance.

(9)   Where in the exercise of power under subsection (1) any damage is caused to land or chattels, compensation may be recovered by any person suffering the damage from the local planning authority exercising the power, but compensation is not recoverable under this subsection or section 325(6)—

    (a) for damage caused to the display structure; or

    (b) for damage reasonably caused in removing the display structure.

(10)   The provisions of section 118 apply in relation to compensation under subsection (9) as they apply in relation to compensation under Part 4.

(11)   In this section 'removal notice', in relation to a display structure, means notice—

    (a) stating that in the local planning authority's opinion the display structure is used for the display of advertisements in contravention of regulations under section 220;

    (b) stating that the local planning authority intend after a time specified in the notice to remove the display structure; and

    (c) stating the effect of subsections (7) and (8).

(12) A time specified under subsection (11)(b) may not be earlier than the end of 22 days beginning with the date of the notice.

(13) In this section 'display structure' means (subject to subsection (14))—

    (a) a hoarding or similar structure used, or designed or adapted for use, for the display of advertisements;

    (b) anything (other than a hoarding or similar structure) principally used, or designed or adapted principally for use, for the display of advertisements;

    (c) a structure that is itself an advertisement; or

    (d) fitments used to support anything within any of paragraphs (a) to (c).

(14) Something is a 'display structure' for the purpose of this section only if—

    (a) its use for the display of advertisement requires consent under this Chapter, and

    (b) that consent has not been granted and is not deemed to have been granted.

(15) In subsection (13) 'structure' includes movable structure.

225B Appeal against notice under section 225A

(1) A person on whom a removal notice has been served in accordance with section 225A(3) or (5)(b) may appeal to a magistrates' court on any of the following grounds—

    (a) that the display structure concerned is not used for the display of advertisements in contravention of regulations under section 220;

    (b) that there has been some informality, defect or error in, or in connection with, the notice;

    (c) that the period between the date of the notice and the time specified in the notice is not reasonably sufficient for the removal of the display structure;

    (d) that the notice should have been served on another person.

(2) For the purposes of subsection (3), a person is a 'permitted appellant' in relation to a removal notice if—

    (a) the removal notice has been fixed or exhibited in accordance with section 225A(5)(a);

    (b) the person is an owner or occupier of the land on which the display structure concerned is situated; and

    (c) no copy of the removal notice has been served on the person in accordance with section 225A(5)(b).

(3) A person who is a permitted appellant in relation to a removal notice may appeal to a magistrates' court on any of the following grounds—

    (a) that the display structure concerned is not used for the display of advertisements in contravention of regulations under section 220;

    (b) that there has been some informality, defect or error in, or in connection with, the notice;

(c) that the period between the date of the notice and the time specified in the notice is not reasonably sufficient for the removal of the display structure.

(4) So far as an appeal under this section is based on the ground mentioned in subsection (1)(b) or (3)(b), the court must dismiss the appeal if it is satisfied that the informality, defect or error was not a material one.

(5) If an appeal under subsection (1) is based on the ground mentioned in subsection (1)(d), the appellant must serve a copy of the notice of appeal on each person who the appellant considers is a person on whom the removal notice should have been served in accordance with section 225A(3) or (5)(b).

(6) If—

(a) a removal notice is served on a person in accordance with section 225A(3) or (5)(b), and

(b) the local planning authority bring proceedings against the person for the recovery under section 225A(7) of any expenses,

it is not open to the person to raise in the proceedings any question which the person could have raised in an appeal under subsection (1).

(7) In this section 'removal notice' and 'display structure'have the same meaning as in section 225A.

225C Remedying persistent problems with unauthorised advertisements

(1) Subsections (2) and (3) apply if the local planning authority for an area in England have reason to believe that there is a persistent problem with the display of unauthorised advertisements on a surface of—

(a) any building, wall, fence or other structure or erection; or

(b) any apparatus or plant.

(2) The local planning authority may serve an action notice on the owner or occupier of the land in or on which the surface is situated.

(3) If after reasonable enquiry the local planning authority—

(a) are unable to ascertain the name and address of the owner, and

(b) are unable to ascertain the name and address of the occupier,

the local planning authority may fix an action notice to the surface.

(4) For the purposes of this section 'an action notice', in relation to a surface, is a notice requiring the owner or occupier of the land in or on which the surface is situated to carry out the measures specified in the notice by a time specified in the notice.

(5) A time may be specified in an action notice if it is a reasonable time not earlier than the end of 28 days beginning with the date of the notice.

(6) Measures may be specified in an action notice if they are reasonable measures to prevent or reduce the frequency of the display of unauthorised advertisements on the surface concerned.

(7) The time by which an owner or occupier must comply with an action notice may be postponed by the local planning authority.

(8) This section has effect subject to—

    (a) the other provisions of the enactments relating to town and country planning;

    (b) the provisions of the enactments relating to historic buildings and ancient monuments; and

    (c) Part 2 of the Food and Environmental Protection Act 1985 (which relates to deposits in the sea).

(9) Subsection (10) applies if—

    (a) an action notice is served under subsection (2) or fixed under subsection (3); and

    (b) the measures specified in the notice are not carried out by the time specified in the notice.

(10) The local planning authority may—

    (a) carry out the measures; and

    (b) recover expenses reasonably incurred by the local planning authority in doing that from the person required by the action notice to do it.

(11) Power under subsection (10)(a) is subject to the right of appeal under section 225D.

(12) Where in the exercise of power under subsection (10)(a) any damage is caused to land or chattels, compensation may be recovered by any person suffering the damage from the local planning authority exercising the power, but compensation is not recoverable under this subsection for damage reasonably caused in carrying out the measures.

(13) The provisions of section 118 apply in relation to compensation under subsection (12) as they apply in relation to compensation under Part 4.

(14) The local planning authority may not recover expenses under subsection (10)(b) in respect of a surface that—

    (a) forms part of a flat or a dwellinghouse;

    (b) is within the curtilage of a dwellinghouse; or

    (c) forms part of the boundary of the curtilage of a dwellinghouse.

(15) Each of sections 275 and 291 of the Public Health Act 1936 (provision for authority to agree to take the required measures at expense of owner or occupier, and provision for expenses to be recoverable also from owner's successor or from occupier and to be charged on premises concerned) applies as if the reference in that section to that Act included a reference to this section.

(16) In this section—

    'dwellinghouse'does not include a building containing one or more flats, or a flat contained within such a building;

    'flat' means a separate and self-contained set of premises constructed or adapted for use as a dwelling and forming part of a building from some other part of which it is divided horizontally;

'unauthorised advertisement' means an advertisement in respect of which an offence—

(a) under section 224(3), or

(b) under section 132 of the Highways Act 1980 (unauthorised marks on highway),

is committed after the coming into force of this section.

225D Right to appeal against notice under section 225C

(1) A person on whom notice has been served under section 225C(2) may appeal to a magistrates' court on any of the following grounds—

(a) that there is no problem with the display of unauthorised advertisements on the surface concerned or any such problem is not a persistent one;

(b) that there has been some informality, defect or error in, or in connection with, the notice;

(c) that the time within which the measures specified in the notice are to be carried out is not reasonably sufficient for the purpose;

(d) that the notice should have been served on another person.

(2) The occupier or owner of premises which include a surface to which a notice has been fixed under section 225C(3) may appeal to a magistrates' court on any of the following grounds—

(a) that there is no problem with the display of unauthorised advertisements on the surface concerned or any such problem is not a persistent one;

(b) that there has been some informality, defect or error in, or in connection with, the notice;

(c) that the time within which the measures specified in the notice are to be carried out is not reasonably sufficient for the purpose.

(3) So far as an appeal under this section is based on the ground mentioned in subsection (1)(b) or (2)(b), the court must dismiss the appeal if it is satisfied that the informality, defect or error was not a material one.

(4) If an appeal under subsection (1) is based on the ground mentioned in subsection (1)(d), the appellant must serve a copy of the notice of appeal on each person who the appellant considers is a person on whom the notice under section 225C(2) should have been served.

(5) If—

(a) notice under section 225C(2) is served on a person, and

(b) the local planning authority bring proceedings against the person for the recovery under section 225C(10)(b) of any expenses,

it is not open to the person to raise in the proceedings any question which the person could have raised in an appeal under subsection (1).

225E Applying section 225C to statutory undertakers' operational land

(1) Subsection (2) and (3) apply where the local planning authority serves a notice under section 225C(2) requiring a statutory undertaker to carry out measures

in respect of the display of unauthorised advertisements on a surface on its operational land.

(2) The statutory undertaker may, within 28 days beginning with the date of service of the notice, serve a counter-notice on the local planning authority specifying alternative measures which will in the statutory undertaker's reasonable opinion have the effect of preventing or reducing the frequency of the display of unauthorised advertisements on the surface to at least the same extent as the measures specified in the notice.

(3) Where a counter-notice is served under subsection (2), the notice under section 225C(2) is to be treated—

    (a) as requiring the alternative measures specified in the counternotice to be carried out (instead of the measures actually required by the notice under section 225C(2)); and

    (b) as having been served on the date on which the counter-notice is served.

(4) The time by which a statutory undertaker must carry out the measures specified in a counter-notice served under subsection (2) may be postponed by the local planning authority.

CHAPTER IV REMEDYING DEFACEMENT OF PREMISES

225F Power to remedy defacement of premises

(1) Subsections (2) and (3) apply if—

    (a) premises in England include a surface that is readily visible from a place to which the public have access;

    (b) either—

        (i) the surface does not form part of the operational land of a statutory undertaker, or

        (ii) the surface forms part of the operational land of a statutory undertaker and subsection (11) applies to the surface;

    (c) there is a sign on the surface; and

    (d) the local planning authority consider the sign to be detrimental to the amenity of the area or offensive.

(2) The local planning authority may serve on the occupier of the premises a notice requiring the occupier to remove or obliterate the sign by a time specified in the notice.

(3) If it appears to the local planning authority that there is no occupier of the premises, the local planning authority may fix to the surface a notice requiring the owner or occupier of the premises to remove or obliterate the sign by a time specified in the notice.

(4) A time specified under subsection (2) or (3) may not be earlier than the end of 15 days beginning the date of service or fixing of the notice.

(5) Subsection (6) applies if—

    (a) a notice is served under subsection (2) or fixed under subsection (3); and

    (b) the sign is neither removed nor obliterated by the time specified in the notice.

(6) The local planning authority may—

    (a) remove or obliterate the sign; and

    (b) recover expenses reasonably incurred by the local planning authority in doing that from the person required by the notice to do it.

(7) Power under subsection (6)(a) is subject to the right of appeal under section 225I.

(8) Expenses may not be recovered under subsection (6)(b) if the surface—

    (a) forms part of a flat or a dwellinghouse;

    (b) is within the curtilage of a dwellinghouse; or

    (c) forms part of the boundary of the curtilage of a dwellinghouse.

(9) Section 291 of the Public Health Act 1936 (provision for expenses to be recoverable also from owner's successor or from occupier and to be charged on premises concerned) applies as if the reference in that section to that Act included a reference to this section.

(10) For the purposes of this section, a universal postal service provider is treated as being the occupier of any plant or apparatus that consists of a universal postal service letter box or a universal postal service pouchbox belonging to it.

(11) This subsection applies to a surface if the surface abuts on, or is one to which access is given directly from, either—

    (a) a street; or

    (b) any place, other than a street, to which the public have access as of right.

(12) In this section—

    'dwellinghouse' does not include a building containing one or more flats, or a flat contained within such a building;

    'flat' means a separate and self-contained set of premises constructed or adapted for use as a dwelling and forming part of a building from some other part of which it is divided horizontally;

    'premises' means building, wall, fence or other structure or erection, or apparatus or plant;

    'sign'—

    (a) includes any writing, letter, picture, device or representation, but

    (b) does not include an advertisement;

    'statutory undertaker' does not include a relevant airport operator (within the meaning of Part 5 of the Airports Act 1986);

    'street' includes any highway, any bridge carrying a highway and any road, lane, mews, footway, square, court, alley or passage, whether a thoroughfare or not;

    'universal postal service letter box' has the meaning given in section 86(4) of the Postal Services Act 2000;

'universal postal service pouch-box' has the meaning given in paragraph 1(10) of Schedule 6 to that Act.

225G Notices under section 225F in respect of post boxes

(1) The local planning authority may serve a notice under section 225F(2) on a universal postal service provider in respect of a universal postal service letter box, or universal postal service pouch-box, belonging to the provider only if—

   (a) the authority has served on the provider written notice of the authority's intention to do so; and

   (b) the period of 28 days beginning with the date of service of that notice has ended.

(2) In this section—

   'universal postal service letter box' has the meaning given in section 86(4) of the Postal Services Act 2000;

   'universal postal service pouch-box' has the meaning given in paragraph 1(10) of Schedule 6 to that Act.

225H Section 225F powers as respects bus shelters and other street furniture

(1) The local planning authority may exercise the power conferred by section 225F(6)(a) to remove or obliterate a sign from any surface on a bus shelter, or other street furniture, of a statutory undertaker that is not situated on operational land of the statutory undertaker only if—

   (a) the authority has served on the statutory undertaker notice of the authority's intention to do so;

   (b) the notice specified the bus shelter, or other street furniture, concerned; and

   (c) the period of 28 days beginning with the date of service of the notice has ended.

(2) In this section 'statutory undertaker' does not include an airport operator (within the meaning of Part 5 of the Airports Act 1986).

225I Right to appeal against notice under section 225F

(1) A person on whom notice has been served under section 225F(2) may appeal to a magistrates' court on any of the following grounds—

   (a) that the sign concerned is neither detrimental to the amenity of the area nor offensive;

   (b) that there has been some informality, defect or error in, or in connection with, the notice;

   (c) that the time within which the sign concerned is to be removed or obliterated is not reasonably sufficient for the purpose;

   (d) that the notice should have been served on another person.

(2) The occupier or owner of premises which include a surface to which a notice has been fixed under section 225F(3) may appeal to a magistrates' court on any of the following grounds—

    (a) that the sign concerned is neither detrimental to the amenity of the area nor offensive;

    (b) that there has been some informality, defect or error in, or in connection with, the notice;

    (c) that the time within which the sign concerned is to be removed or obliterated is not reasonably sufficient for the purpose.

(3) So far as an appeal under this section is based on the ground mentioned in subsection (1)(b) or (2)(b), the court must dismiss the appeal if it is satisfied that the informality, defect or error was not a material one.

(4) If an appeal under subsection (1) is based on the ground mentioned in subsection (1)(d), the appellant must serve a copy of the notice of appeal on each person who the appellant considers is a person on whom the notice under section 225F(2) should have been served.

(5) If—

    (a) notice under section 225F(2) is served on a person, and

    (b) the local planning authority bring proceedings against the person for the recovery under section 225F(6)(b) of any expenses,

it is not open to the person to raise in the proceedings any question which the person could have raised in an appeal under subsection (1).

225J Remedying defacement at owner or occupier's request

(1) Subsection (2) applies if—

    (a) premises in England include a surface that is readily visible from a place to which the public have access;

    (b) there is a sign on the surface; and

    (c) the owner or occupier of the premises asks the local planning authority to remove or obliterate the sign.

(2) The local planning authority may—

    (a) remove or obliterate the sign; and

    (b) recover expenses reasonably incurred by the local planning authority in doing that from the person who asked the local planning authority to do it.

(3) In this section 'premises' means building, wall, fence or other structure or erection, or apparatus or plant.

(4) In this section 'sign'—

    (a) includes—

        (i) any writing, letter, picture, device or representation, and

        (ii) any advertisement, but

    (b) does not include an advertisement for the display of which deemed or express consent has been granted under Chapter 3.

CHAPTER V APPLICATION OF PROVISIONS OF CHAPTERS 3 AND 4 TO STATUTORY UNDERTAKERS

225K Action under sections 225A, 225C and 225F: operational land

(1)   This section applies in relation to the exercise by the local planning authority of—

  (a)   power conferred by section 225A(1), or section 324(3) so far as applying for the purposes of section 225A(1), to—

    (i)   enter on any operational land of a statutory undertaker, or

    (ii)   remove a display structure situated on operational land of a statutory undertaker;

  (b)   power conferred by section 225C(10)(a), or section 324(3) so far as applying for the purposes of section 225C(10)(a), to—

    (i)   enter on any operational land of a statutory undertaker, or

    (ii)   carry out any measures to prevent or reduce the frequency of the display of unauthorised advertisements on a surface on operational land of a statutory undertaker; or

  (c)   power conferred by section 225F(6)(a), or section 324(3) so far as applying for the purposes of section 225F(6)(a), to—

    (i)   enter on any operational land of a statutory undertaker, or

    (ii)   remove or obliterate a sign on a surface of premises that are, or are on, operational land of a statutory undertaker.

(2)   The authority may exercise the power only if—

  (a)   the authority has served on the statutory undertaker notice of the authority's intention to do so;

  (b)   the notice specified the display structure, surface or sign concerned and its location; and

  (c)   the period of 28 days beginning with the date of service of the notice has ended.

(3)   If—

  (a)   a notice under subsection (2) is served on a statutory undertaker, and

  (b)   within 28 days beginning with the date the notice is served, the statutory undertaker serves a counter-notice on the local planning authority specifying conditions subject to which the power is to be exercised,

the power may only be exercised subject to, and in accordance with, the conditions specified in the counter-notice.

(4)   The conditions which may be specified in a counter-notice under subsection (3) are conditions which are—

  (a)   necessary or expedient in the interests of safety or the efficient and economic operation of the undertaking concerned; or

  (b)   for the protection of any works, apparatus or other property not vested in the statutory undertaker which are lawfully present on, in, under or over the land upon which entry is proposed to be made.

(5) If—

(a) a notice under subsection (2) is served on a statutory undertaker, and

(b) within 28 days beginning with the date the notice is served, the statutory undertaker serves a counter-notice on the local planning authority requiring the local planning authority to refrain from exercising the power,

the power may not be exercised.

(6) A counter-notice under subsection (5) may be served only if the statutory undertaker has reasonable grounds to believe, for reasons connected with the operation of its undertaking, that the power cannot be exercised under the circumstances in question—

(a) without risk to the safety of any person; or

(b) without unreasonable risk to the efficient and economic operation of the statutory undertaker's undertaking.

(7) In this section 'statutory undertaker'does not include an airport operator (within the meaning of Part 5 of the Airports Act 1986).

PART XII VALIDITY

284 Validity of development plans and certain orders, decisions and directions [England]

(1) Except in so far as may be provided by this Part, the validity of—

(a) [...]

(b) a simplified planning zone scheme or an alteration of such a scheme, whether before or after the adoption or approval of the scheme or alteration; or

(c) an order under any provision of Part X except section 251(1), whether before or after the order has been made; or

(d) an order under section 277, whether before or after the order has been made; or

(e) any such order as is mentioned in subsection (2), whether before or after it has been confirmed; or

(f) any such action on the part of the Secretary of State as is mentioned in subsection (3),

shall not be questioned in any legal proceedings whatsoever.

(2) The orders referred to in subsection (1)(e) are—

(a) any order under section 97 or under the provisions of that section as applied by or under any other provision of this Act;

(b) any order under section 102;

(c) any tree preservation order;

(d) any order made in pursuance of section 221(5);

(e) any order under paragraph 1, 3, 5 or 6 of Schedule 9.

(3) The action referred to in subsection (1)(f) is action on the part of the Secretary of State of any of the following descriptions—

(ya) any decision on an application made to the Secretary of State under section 62A;

(za) any decision on an application referred to the Secretary of State under section 76A;

(a) any decision on an application for planning permission referred to him under section 77;

(b) any decision on an appeal under section 78;

(c) [...]

(d) any decision to confirm a completion notice under section 95;

(e) any decision to grant planning permission under paragraph (a) of section 177(1) or to discharge a condition or limitation under paragraph (b) of that section;

(f) any decision to confirm or not to confirm a purchase notice including—

(i) any decision not to confirm such a notice in respect of part of the land to which it relates, or

(ii) any decision to grant any permission, or give any direction, instead of confirming such a notice, either wholly or in part;

(g) any decision on an appeal under section 195(1);

(h) any decision relating—

(i) to an application for consent under tree preservation regulations,

(ii) to an application for consent under any regulations made in accordance with section 220 or 221, or

(iii) to any certificate or direction under any such order or regulations,

whether it is a decision on appeal or a decision on an application referred to the Secretary of State for determination in the first instance.

(i) any decision on an application for planning permission under section 293A.

(4) Nothing in this section shall affect the exercise of any jurisdiction of any court in respect of any refusal or failure on the part of the Secretary of State to take any such action as is mentioned in subsection (3).

284 Validity of development plans and certain orders, decisions and directions [Wales]

(1) Except in so far as may be provided by this Part, the validity of—

(a) [...]

(b) a simplified planning zone scheme or an alteration of such a scheme, whether before or after the adoption or approval of the scheme or alteration; or

(c) an order under any provision of Part X except section 251(1), whether before or after the order has been made; or

(d) an order under section 277, whether before or after the order has been made; or

(e) any such order as is mentioned in subsection (2), whether before or after it has been confirmed; or

(f) any such action on the part of the Secretary of State as is mentioned in subsection (3),

shall not be questioned in any legal proceedings whatsoever.

(2) The orders referred to in subsection (1)(e) are—

(a) any order under section 97 or under the provisions of that section as applied by or under any other provision of this Act;

(b) any order under section 102;

(c) any tree preservation order;

(d) any order made in pursuance of section 221(5);

(e) any order under paragraph 1, 3, 5 or 6 of Schedule 9.

(3) The action referred to in subsection (1)(f) is action on the part of the Secretary of State of any of the following descriptions—

(za) any decision on an application referred to the Secretary of State under section 76A;

(a) any decision on an application for planning permission referred to him under section 77;

(b) any decision on an appeal under section 78;

(c) [...]

(d) any decision to confirm a completion notice under section 95;

(e) any decision to grant planning permission under paragraph (a) of section 177(1) or to discharge a condition or limitation under paragraph (b) of that section;

(f) any decision to confirm or not to confirm a purchase notice including—

(i) any decision not to confirm such a notice in respect of part of the land to which it relates, or

(ii) any decision to grant any permission, or give any direction, instead of confirming such a notice, either wholly or in part;

(g) any decision on an appeal under section 195(1);

(h) any decision relating—

(i) to an application for consent under tree preservation regulations,

(ii) to an application for consent under any regulations made in accordance with section 220 or 221, or

(iii) to any certificate or direction under any such order or regulations,

whether it is a decision on appeal or a decision on an application referred to the Secretary of State for determination in the first instance.

(i) any decision on an application for planning permission under section 293A.

(4)   Nothing in this section shall affect the exercise of any jurisdiction of any court in respect of any refusal or failure on the part of the Secretary of State to take any such action as is mentioned in subsection (3).

285 Validity of enforcement notices and similar notices

(1)   The validity of an enforcement notice shall not, except by way of an appeal under Part VII, be questioned in any proceedings whatsoever on any of the grounds on which such an appeal may be brought.

(2)   Subsection (1) shall not apply to proceedings brought under section 179 against a person who—

    (a)   has held an interest in the land since before the enforcement notice was issued under that Part;

    (b)   did not have a copy of the enforcement notice served on him under that Part; and

    (c)   satisfies the court—

        (i)   that he did not know and could not reasonably have been expected to know that the enforcement notice had been issued; and

        (ii)   that his interests have been substantially prejudiced by the failure to serve him with a copy of it.

(3)   Subject to subsection (4), the validity of a notice which has been served under section 215 on the owner and occupier of the land shall not, except by way of an appeal under Chapter II of Part VIII, be questioned in any proceedings whatsoever on either of the grounds specified in section 217(1)(a) or (b).

(4)   Subsection (3) shall not prevent the validity of such a notice being questioned on either of those grounds in proceedings brought under section 216 against a person on whom the notice was not served, but who has held an interest in the land since before the notice was served on the owner and occupier of the land, if he did not appeal against the notice under that Chapter.

(5)   [...]

(6)   [...]

286 Challenges to validity on ground of authority's powers

(1)   The validity of any permission, determination or certificate granted, made or issued or purporting to have been granted, made or issued by a local planning authority in respect of—

    (a)   an application for planning permission;

    (aa)   an application for non-material changes to planning permission under section 96A;

    (b)   [...]

    (c)   an application for a certificate under section 191 or 192;

    (d)   an application for consent to the display of advertisements under section 220; or

    (e)   a determination under section 302 or Schedule 15,

shall not be called in question in any legal proceedings, or in any proceedings under this Act which are not legal proceedings, on the ground that the permission, determination or certificate should have been granted, made or given by some other local planning authority.

(2) The validity of any order under section 97 revoking or modifying planning permission, any order under section 102 or paragraph 1 of Schedule 9 requiring discontinuance of use, or imposing conditions on continuance of use, or requiring the alteration or removal of buildings or works, or any enforcement notice under section 172 or stop notice under section 183 or a breach of condition notice under section 187A, being an order or notice purporting to have been made, issued or served by a local planning authority, shall not be called in question in any such proceedings on the ground—

(a) in the case of an order or notice purporting to have been made, issued or served by a district planning authority, that they failed to comply with paragraph 11(2) of Schedule 1;

(b) in the case of an order or notice purporting to have been made, issued or served by a county planning authority, that they had no power to make, issue or serve it because it did not relate to a county matter within the meaning of that Schedule.

288 Proceedings for questioning the validity of other orders, decisions and directions

(1) If any person—

(a) is aggrieved by any order to which this section applies and wishes to question the validity of that order on the grounds—

(i) that the order is not within the powers of this Act, or

(ii) that any of the relevant requirements have not been complied with in relation to that order; or

(b) is aggrieved by any action on the part of the Secretary of State to which this section applies and wishes to question the validity of that action on the grounds—

(i) that the action is not within the powers of this Act, or

(ii) that any of the relevant requirements have not been complied with in relation to that action,

he may make an application to the High Court under this section.

(2) Without prejudice to subsection (1), if the authority directly concerned with any order to which this section applies, or with any action on the part of the Secretary of State to which this section applies, wish to question the validity of that order or action on any of the grounds mentioned in subsection (1), the authority may make an application to the High Court under this section.

(3) An application under this section must be made within six weeks from the date on which the order is confirmed (or, in the case of an order under section 97 which takes effect under section 99 without confirmation, the date on which it takes effect) or, as the case may be, the date on which the action is taken.

(4)   This section applies to any such order as is mentioned in subsection (2) of section 284 and to any such action on the part of the Secretary of State as is mentioned in subsection (3) of that section.

(5)   On any application under this section the High Court—

(a)   may, subject to subsection (6), by interim order suspend the operation of the order or action, the validity of which is questioned by the application, until the final determination of the proceedings;

(b)   if satisfied that the order or action in question is not within the powers of this Act, or that the interests of the applicant have been substantially prejudiced by a failure to comply with any of the relevant requirements in relation to it, may quash that order or action.

(6)   Paragraph (a) of subsection (5) shall not apply to applications questioning the validity of tree preservation orders.

(7)   In relation to a tree preservation order, or to an order made in pursuance of section 221(5), the powers conferred on the High Court by subsection (5) shall be exercisable by way of quashing or (where applicable) suspending the operation of the order either in whole or in part, as the court may determine.

(8)   References in this section to the confirmation of an order include the confirmation of an order subject to modifications as well as the confirmation of an order in the form in which it was made.

(9)   In this section 'the relevant requirements', in relation to any order or action to which this section applies, means any requirements of this Act or of the Tribunals and Inquiries Act 1992, or of any order, regulations or rules made under this Act or under that Act which are applicable to that order or action.

(10)   Any reference in this section to the authority directly concerned with any order or action to which this section applies—

(a)   in relation to any such decision as is mentioned in section 284(3)(f), is a reference to the council on whom the notice in question was served and, in a case where the Secretary of State has modified such a notice, wholly or in part, by substituting another local authority or statutory undertakers for that council, includes a reference to that local authority or those statutory undertakers;

(b)   in any other case, is a reference to the authority who made the order in question or made the decision or served the notice to which the proceedings in question relate, or who referred the matter to the Secretary of State, or, where the order or notice in question was made or served by him, the authority named in the order or notice.

289 Appeals to High Court relating to enforcement notices and notices under s 207

(1)   Where the Secretary of State gives a decision in proceedings on an appeal under Part VII against an enforcement notice the appellant or the local planning authority or any other person having an interest in the land to which the notice relates may, according as rules of court may provide, either appeal to the High Court against the decision on a point of law or require the Secretary of State to state and sign a case for the opinion of the High Court.

(2)   Where the Secretary of State gives a decision in proceedings on an appeal under Part VIII against a notice under section 207, the appellant or the local planning authority or any person (other than the appellant) on whom the notice was served may, according as rules of court may provide, either appeal to the High Court against the decision on a point of law or require the Secretary of State to state and sign a case for the opinion of the High Court.

(3)   At any stage of the proceedings on any such appeal as is mentioned in subsection (1), the Secretary of State may state any question of law arising in the course of the proceedings in the form of a special case for the decision of the High Court.

(4)   A decision of the High Court on a case stated by virtue of subsection (3) shall be deemed to be a judgment of the court within the meaning of section 16 of the Supreme Court Act 1981 (jurisdiction of the Court of Appeal to hear and determine appeals from any judgment of the High Court).

(4A) In proceedings brought by virtue of this section in respect of an enforcement notice, the High Court or, as the case may be, the Court of Appeal may, on such terms if any as the Court thinks fit (which may include terms requiring the local planning authority to give an undertaking as to damages or any other matter), order that the notice shall have effect, or have effect to such extent as may be specified in the order, pending the final determination of those proceedings and any re-hearing and determination by the Secretary of State.

(4B) Where proceedings are brought by virtue of this section in respect of any notice under section 207, the notice shall be of no effect pending the final determination of those proceedings and any re-hearing and determination by the Secretary of State.

(5)   In relation to any proceedings in the High Court or the Court of Appeal brought by virtue of this section the power to make rules of court shall include power to make rules—

(a)   prescribing the powers of the High Court or the Court of Appeal with respect to the remitting of the matter with the opinion or direction of the court for re-hearing and determination by the Secretary of State; and

(b)   providing for the Secretary of State, either generally or in such circumstances as may be prescribed by the rules, to be treated as a party to any such proceedings and to be entitled to appear and to be heard accordingly.

(5A) Rules of court may also provide for the High Court or, as the case may be, the Court of Appeal to give directions as to the exercise, until such proceedings in respect of an enforcement notice are finally concluded and any re-hearing and determination by the Secretary of State has taken place, of any other powers in respect of the matters to which such a notice relates.

(6)   No proceedings in the High Court shall be brought by virtue of this section except with the leave of that Court and no appeal to the Court of Appeal shall be so brought except with the leave of the Court of Appeal or of the High Court.

(7)   In this section 'decision' includes a direction or order, and references to the giving of a decision shall be construed accordingly.

The Town and Country Planning (Enforcement Notices and Appeals) (England) Regulations 2002 (SI 2002/2682)

PART 1 CITATION, COMMENCEMENT, INTERPRETATION AND EXTENT

Citation, commencement and extent

1. These Regulations may be cited as the Town and Country Planning (Enforcement Notices and Appeals) (England) Regulations 2002, and shall come into force on 23rd December 2002.

2. These Regulations shall extend to England only.

Interpretation

3. In these Regulations—

'enforcement notice' means a notice issued under section 172(1) of the Planning Act or section 38(1) of the Listed Buildings Act;

'electronic communication' has the meaning given in section 15(1) of the Electronic Communications Act 2000;

'the Hearings Rules' means the Town and Country Planning (Enforcement) (Hearings Procedure) (England) Rules 2002;

'the Inquiries Rules' means the Town and Country Planning (Enforcement) (Inquiries Procedure) (England) Rules 2002;

'the Inspectors Inquiries Rules' means the Town and Country Planning (Enforcement) (Determination by Inspectors) (Inquiries Procedure) (England) Rules;

'the Listed Buildings Act' means the Planning (Listed Buildings and Conservation Areas) Act 1990;

'local planning authority' means the body who issue the relevant enforcement notice;

'the Planning Act' means the Town and Country Planning Act 1990.

Appendix 2

PART 2 ENFORCEMENT NOTICES UNDER SECTION 172

Additional matters to be specified in enforcement notice

4. An enforcement notice issued under section 172 of the Planning Act shall specify—

(a) the reasons why the local planning authority consider it expedient to issue the notice;

(b) all policies and proposals in the development plan which are relevant to the decision to issue an enforcement notice; and

(c) the precise boundaries of the land to which the notice relates, whether by reference to a plan or otherwise.

Explanatory note to accompany copy of enforcement notice

5. Every copy of an enforcement notice served by a local planning authority under section 172(2) of the Planning Act shall be accompanied by an explanatory note which shall include the following—

(a) a copy of sections 171A, 171B and 172 to 177 of the Planning Act, or a summary of those sections including the following information—

(i) that there is a right of appeal to the Secretary of State against the enforcement notice;

(ii) that an appeal must be made by giving written notice of the appeal to the Secretary of State before the date specified in the enforcement notice as the date on which it is to take effect or by sending such notice to him in a properly addressed, pre-paid letter posted to him at such time that, in the ordinary course of post, it would be delivered to him before that date, or (where electronic communications are used to send such notice to the Secretary of State) by sending the notice to him at such time that, in the ordinary course of transmission, it would be delivered to him before that date;

(iii) the grounds on which an appeal may be brought under section 174 of the Planning Act;

(iv) the fee payable under regulation 10 of the Town and Country Planning (Fees for Applications and Deemed Applications) Regulations 1989 for the deemed application for planning permission for the development alleged to be in breach of planning control in the enforcement notice;

(b) notification that an appellant must submit to the Secretary of State, either when giving notice of appeal or within 14 days from the date on which the Secretary of State sends him a notice so requiring him, a statement in writing specifying the grounds on which he is appealing against the enforcement notice and stating briefly the facts on which he proposes to rely in support of each of those grounds.

(c) a list of the names and addresses of the persons on whom a copy of the enforcement notice has been served.

PART 3 APPEALS

Statement of appeal

6. A person who makes an appeal to the Secretary of State under section 174(3) of the Planning Act or section 39(2) of the Listed Buildings Act against an enforcement notice shall submit to the Secretary of State, a statement in writing—

(i)   specifying the grounds on which he is appealing against the notice; and

(ii)   setting out briefly the facts on which he proposes to rely in support of each of those grounds,

and if such a statement is not included with the appeal he shall deliver it to the Secretary of State not later than 14 days from the date on which the Secretary of State sends him a notice requiring him to do so.

Notification of appeal to the local planning authority

7.—(1) On receipt of the statement under regulation 6 the Secretary of State shall notify the local planning authority in writing that an appeal has been made and copy to them the appeal and, subject to paragraph (2), the statement made under regulation 6.

(2) Nothing in paragraph (1) shall require the Secretary of State to disclose information as to national security or the measures taken or to be taken to ensure the security of any premises or property where, in the Secretary of State's opinion, public disclosure of that information would be contrary to the national interest.

Local planning authority to send a copy of notice to Secretary of State

8. Where the local planning authority receives notification under regulation 7 that an appeal has been made to the Secretary of State, the local planning authority shall send to the Secretary of State, not later than 14 days from the date of that notification, a certified copy of the enforcement notice and a list of names and addresses of the persons on whom a copy of the notice has been served under section 172(2) of the Planning Act or section 38(4) of the Listed Buildings Act, as the case may be.

Statement by local planning authority

9.—(1) Where an appeal has been made to the Secretary of State against an enforcement notice issued by a local planning authority, the authority shall submit to the Secretary of State and any person on whom a copy of the enforcement notice has been served, a statement indicating the submissions which they propose to put forward on the appeal, including—

(a)   a summary of the authority's response to each of the grounds on which the appeal is brought by the appellant;

(b)   a statement whether the authority would be prepared to grant planning permission for the matters alleged in the enforcement notice to constitute the breach of planning control, or grant listed building consent or conservation area consent for the works to which the listed building enforcement notice or conservation area enforcement notice relates, as the case may be, and, if so, particulars of the conditions, if any, which they would wish to impose on the permission or consent.

(2) Any statement which is required to be submitted under paragraph (1) shall be submitted within 6 weeks of the starting date.

(3) In paragraph (2) 'starting date' means the date of—

(a) the Secretary of State's written notice under regulation 10; or

(b) the Secretary of State's written notice under rule 4 of the Hearings Rules, rule 4 of the Inspectors Inquiries Rules or rule 4 of the Inquiries Rules, informing the appellant and the local planning authority that an inquiry or hearing, as the case may be, is to be held,

whichever is the later.

Notice of receipt of all required documents

10. When the Secretary of State considers that he has received all the documents required to enable him to entertain the appeal he shall send a notice to this effect to the appellant and the local planning authority.

Use of electronic communications

10A.—(1) Paragraphs (2) to (7) of this regulation apply where an electronic communication is used by a person for te purpose of fulfilling any requirement in Part 3 of these Regulations to give or send any statement, notice or other document to any other person ('the recipient').

(2) The requirement shall be taken to be fulfilled where the document transmitted by means of the electronic communication is—

(a) capable of being accessed by the recipient,

(b) legible in all material respects, and

(c) sufficiently permanent to be used for subsequent reference.

(3) In paragraph (2), 'legible in all material respects' means that the information contained in the notice or document is available to the recipient to no lesser extent than it would be if sent or given by means of a document in printed form.

(4) Where the electronic communication is received by the recipient outside the recipient's business hours, it shall be taken to have been received on the next working day; and for this purpose 'working day' means a day which is not a Saturday, Sunday, Bank Holiday or other public holiday.

(5) A requirement that any notice or other document should be in writing is fulfilled where that document meets the criteria in paragraph (2), and 'written' and cognate expressions are to be construed accordingly.

(6) Where a person makes an appeal to the Secretary of State under regulation 6 using electronic communications, the person shall be taken to have agreed—

(7) Where a person is no longer willing to accept the use of electronic communications for the purposes of an appeal under these Regulations, he shall give notice in writing—

    (a) withdrawing any address notified to the Secretary of State or to a local planning authority for that purpose, or

    (b) revoking any agreement entered into with the Secretary of State or with a local planning authority for that purpose,

and such withdrawal or revocation shall be final and shall take effect on a date specified by the person in the notice but not less than seven days after the date on which the notice is given.

PART 4 NOTICES ISSUED BY THE SECRETARY OF STATE

Application of Regulations

11. These Regulations, except regulations 7 and 8, apply to enforcement notices issued by the Secretary of State under section 182 of the Planning Act, to appeals made to the Secretary of State against such notices and to appeals against notices issued by him under section 46 of the Listed Buildings Act as they apply to such notices issued by local planning authorities and to appeals made against them as if—

(a)   for references to a local planning authority there were substituted references to the Secretary of State;

(b)   in regulation 4, for 'section 172' there were substituted 'section 182';

(c)   in regulation 5—

    (i)   for 'section 172(2)' there was substituted 'section 182(1)'; and

    (ii) in paragraph (a), after 'sections 171A, 171B and 172 to 177' there were inserted 'and section 182'; and

(d)   for regulation 9 the following were substituted—

    '9.—(1) Where an appeal has been made to the Secretary of State against an enforcement notice which he has issued, the Secretary of State shall serve on the appellant a statement indicating the submissions which he proposes to put forward on the appeal including a summary of his response to each ground of appeal pleaded by the appellant within 6 weeks of the starting date'.

(2) In paragraph (1) 'starting date' means the date of—

(a)   the Secretary of State's written notice under regulation 10; or

(b)   the Secretary of State's written notice under rule 4 of the Hearings Rules, rule 4 of the Inspectors Inquiries Rules or rule 4 of the Inquiries Rules, informing the appellant and the local planning authority that a hearing or inquiry, as the case may be, is to be held,

whichever is the later.

Appendix 2

PART 5 REVOCATION

Revocation and transitional provisions

12.—(1) Subject to paragraph (3), the Town and Country Planning (Enforcement Notices and Appeals) Regulations 1991 ('the 1991 Regulations') are hereby revoked in so far as they extend to England, except regulation 10(2) of those Regulations so far as it amends regulation 11 of the Planning (Listed Buildings and Conservation Areas) Regulations 1990.

(2) Subject to paragraph (3), the Town and Country Planning (Enforcement Notices and Appeals)(Amendment) Regulations 1992 are hereby revoked in so far as they extend to England.

(3) Subject to paragraph (4), any appeal to which the 1991 Regulations applied which has not been determined on the date when these Regulations come into force, shall be continued under the 1991 Regulations.

(4) Where an appeal to which the 1991 Regulations applied is subsequently remitted to the Secretary of State for redetermination in proceedings before any court, the decision shall be redetermined in accordance with these Regulations.

The Town and Country Planning (Enforcement) (Written Representations Procedure) (England) Regulations 2002 (2002/2683)

The First Secretary of State, in exercise of the powers conferred on him by sections 175 and 323 of the Town and Country Planning Act 1990, and of all other powers enabling him in that behalf, hereby makes the following Regulations:

Citation, commencement, and extent

1.—(1) These Regulations may be cited as the Town and Country Planning (Enforcement) (Written Representations Procedure) (England) Regulations 2002 and shall come into force on 23rd December 2002.

(2) These Regulations extend to England only.

Interpretation

2.—(1) In these Regulations—

'the appellant' means a person giving notice of appeal to the Secretary of State;

'document' includes a photograph, map or plan;

'enforcement notice' means a notice issued under section 172(1) of the Planning Act or section 38(1) of the Listed Buildings Act;

'the Enforcement Notices and Appeals Regulations' means the Town and Country Planning (Enforcement Notices and Appeals) (England) Regulations 2002;

'the Listed Buildings Act' means the Planning (Listed Buildings and Conservation Areas) Act 1990;

'local planning authority' means the body who issued the relevant enforcement notice;

'notice of appeal' means a notice of appeal under section 174(3) of the Planning Act or section 39(2) of the Listed Buildings Act;

'the Planning Act' means the Town and Country Planning Act 1990;

'questionnaire' means a document in the form supplied by the Secretary of State to local planning authorities for the purpose of proceedings under these Regulations and for this purpose a form is taken to be supplied where the Secretary of State has published it on a website and has notified a local planning authority of—

(i) publication of the form on the website,

(ii) the address of the website, and

the place on the website where the form may be accessed, and how it may be accessed;

'starting date' means the date of the Secretary of State's written notice to the appellant and the local planning authority under regulation 4;

'written representations' includes supporting documents.

(2) In these Regulations, and in relation to the use of electronic communications for any purpose of these Regulations which is capable of being carried out electronically—

(a) the expression 'address' includes any number or address used for the purposes of such communications, except that where these Regulations impose an obligation on any person to provide a name and address to any other person, the obligation shall not be fulfilled unless the person on whom it is imposed provides a postal address;

(b) references to notices, representations, or other documents, or to copies of such documents, include references to such documents or copies of them in electronic form.

(3) Paragraphs (4) to (7) apply where an electronic communication is used by a person for the purpose of fulfilling any requirement in regulations 4 to 8 of these Regulations that representations or other documents should be sent or submitted to any other person ('the recipient').

(4) The requirement shall be taken to be fulfilled where the document transmitted by means of the electronic communication is—

(a) capable of being accessed by the recipient,

(b) legible in all material respects, and

(c) sufficiently permanent to be used for subsequent reference.

(5) In paragraph (5), 'legible in all material respects' means that the information contained in the document is available to the recipient to no lesser extent than it would be if sent or given by means of a document in printed form.

(6) Where the electronic communication is received by the recipient outside the recipient's business hours, it shall be taken to have been received on the next working day; and for this purpose 'working day' means a day which is not a Saturday, Sunday, Bank Holiday or other public holiday.

(7) A requirement in these Regulations that any notice or document should be in writing is fulfilled where that document meets the criteria in paragraph (4), and (except in regulation 5) 'written' and cognate expressions are to be construed accordingly.

Application

3.—(1) These Regulations apply where, after they come into force, an appellant informs the Secretary of State in the notice of appeal that he wishes the appeal to be disposed of on the basis of written representations.

(2) Where an appeal under section 174 of the Planning Act or section 39 of the Listed Buildings Act is not being disposed of on the basis of written representations and the appellant and the local planning authority inform the Secretary of State that they wish it to be disposed of on that basis, these Regulations apply to the proceedings to such extent as the Secretary of State may specify having regard to any steps already taken in relation to those proceedings.

(2A) Where an appellant (or, as the case may be, the appellant and the local planning authority) so informs the Secretary of State using electronic communications, the appellant shall be taken to have agreed—

(a) to the use of such communications for all purposes of these Regulations relating to his appeal which are capable of being carried out electronically;

(b) that his address for the purpose of such communications is the address incorporated into, or otherwise logically associated with, his communication so informing the Secretary of State; and

(c) that his deemed agreement under this paragraph shall subsist until he gives notice in accordance with regulation 10A that he wishes to revoke the agreement;

and the references in paragraphs (1) and (2) of this regulation to an appeal being disposed of on the basis of written representations shall not be taken to preclude the use of electronic communications in accordance with this paragraph and regulation 2.

(3) These Regulations cease to apply to proceedings if the Secretary of State informs the appellant and the local planning authority that he will give them an opportunity of appearing before and being heard by a person appointed by him for the purpose.

Notification of receipt of appeal

4. The Secretary of State shall, as soon as practicable after receipt of the written notice of appeal, advise the appellant and the local planning authority in writing of—

(a) the starting date;

(b) the reference number allocated to the appeal;

(c) the address to which written communications to the Secretary of State about the appeal are to be sent; and

(d) the ground, or grounds, under section 174(2) of the Planning Act or section 39(1) of the Listed Buildings Act, as the case may be, on which the appeal has been brought.

Notice to interested parties

5.—(1) The local planning authority shall, within 2 weeks of the starting date, give written notice of the appeal to any—

(a)   person on whom a copy of the enforcement notice has been served;

(b)   occupier of property in the locality in which the land to which the enforcement notice relates is situated; and

(c)   other person who in the opinion of the local planning authority is affected by the breach of planning control or contravention of listed building or conservation area control which is alleged in the enforcement notice.

(2) The notice given under paragraph (1) shall include—

(a)   the name of the appellant and the address of the land to which the appeal relates;

(b)   the starting date;

(c)   the reference number allocated to the appeal;

(d)   a description of the alleged breach of control;

(e)   in the case of an appeal against an enforcement notice under section 172 of the Planning Act, a statement setting out the additional matters specified in regulation 4 of the Enforcement Notices and Appeals Regulations;

(f)   the ground, or grounds, under section 174(2) of the Planning Act or section 39(1) of the Listed Buildings Act, as the case may be, on which the appeal is made;

(g)   a statement that representations may be submitted to the Secretary of State within 6 weeks of the starting date and the address to which such representations should be sent;

(h)   a statement that any representations made by any person mentioned in paragraph (1) will be sent to the appellant and the local planning authority; and

(i)   a statement that any such representations will be considered by the Secretary of State when determining the appeal unless any person mentioned in paragraph (1) withdraws them within 6 weeks of the starting date.

Questionnaire

6.—(1) The local planning authority shall within 2 weeks of the starting date submit to the Secretary of State, and copy to the appellant—

(a)   a completed questionnaire; and

(b)   a copy of each of the documents referred to in it.

(2) The questionnaire shall state the date on which it is submitted to the Secretary of State.

Representations

7.—(1) The notice of appeal, the documents accompanying it and any statement submitted under regulation 6 of the Enforcement Notices and Appeals Regulations shall comprise the appellant's representations in relation to the appeal.

(2) The local planning authority may elect to treat the questionnaire, the documents submitted with it and the statement submitted under regulation 9 of the Enforcement Notices and Appeals Regulations as their representations in relation to the appeal; and, where they do so, they shall notify the Secretary of State and the appellant accordingly when submitting the questionnaire or sending the copy in accordance with regulation 6.

(3) If the appellant wishes to make any further representations to those in paragraph (1), he shall submit 2 copies of those further representations to the Secretary of State within 6 weeks of the starting date.

(4) Where the local planning authority does not elect as described in paragraph (2), they shall submit 2 copies of their written representations to the Secretary of State within 6 weeks of the starting date and these shall include—

(a) a summary of the local planning authority's response to each of the grounds on which the appeal is brought; and

(b) a statement as to whether they would be prepared to grant planning permission for the matters alleged in the enforcement notice to constitute a breach of planning control, or to grant listed building consent or conservation area consent for the works to which the listed building enforcement notice or conservation area enforcement notice relates, as the case may be, and, if so, particulars of the conditions, if any, which they would wish to impose on the permission or consent.

(5) Any representations made to the Secretary of State under paragraphs (3) or (4) should be dated and submitted to the Secretary of State on the date they bear.

(6) The Secretary of State shall, as soon as practicable after receipt, send a copy of any representations made to him by the local planning authority to the appellant and shall, subject to paragraph (7A), send a copy of any representations made to him by the appellant to the local planning authority.

(7) The appellant and the local planning authority shall submit 2 copies of any comments they have on each other's representations to the Secretary of State within 9 weeks of the starting date; and the Secretary of State shall, as soon as practicable after receipt and subject to paragraph (7A), send a copy of these further comments to the other party.

(7A) Nothing in paragraph (6) or (7) shall require the Secretary of State to disclose information as to national security or the measures taken or to be taken to ensure the security of any premises or property where, in the Secretary of State's opinion, public disclosure of that information would be contrary to the national interest.

(8) The Secretary of State may disregard further information from the appellant and the local planning authority which was not submitted within 9 weeks of the starting date unless that further information has been requested by him.

(9) Where a party to which this regulation applies elects to use electronic communications for submitting, sending, copying, or sending a copy of any representations, questionnaire or other document, this regulation shall have effect subject to the following modifications—

(a)   where the party so electing is the appellant, in paragraphs (3) and (7) omit the words '2 copies of';

(b)   where the party so electing is the local planning authority, in paragraphs (4) and (7) omit the words '2 copies of'.

Third party representations

8.—(1) If an interested person notified under regulation 5(1) wishes to submit representations to the Secretary of State, he shall do so within 6 weeks of the starting date.

(2) The Secretary of State shall—

(a)   subject to paragraph (2A) send to the appellant and the local planning authority, as soon as practicable after receipt, a copy each of all of the representations received from interested persons; and

(b)   specify a period of not less than 2 weeks within which any comments on the representations must be submitted.

(2A) Nothing in paragraph (2)(a) shall require the Secretary of State to disclose information as to national security or the measures taken or to be taken to ensure the security of any premises or property where, in the Secretary of State's opinion, public disclosure of that information would be contrary to the national interest.

(3) The Secretary of State may disregard comments made by the local planning authority under paragraph 2(b), where they failed to notify interested persons in accordance with regulation 5.

Allowing further time

9. The Secretary of State may in a particular case give directions setting later time limits than those prescribed by the Regulations.

Decision on Appeal

10.—(1) The Secretary of State may proceed to a decision on an appeal taking into account only such written representations as have been submitted within the relevant time limits.

(2) The Secretary of State may, after giving the appellant and the local planning authority written notice of his intention to do so, proceed to a decision on appeal notwithstanding that no written representations have been made within the relevant time limits if it appears to him that he has sufficient material before him to enable him to reach a decision on the merits of the case.

(3) In this regulation 'relevant time limits' means the time limits prescribed by these Regulations or, where the Secretary of State has exercised his power under regulation 9, any later time limits.

Withdrawal of consent to use of electronic communications

10A. Where a person is no longer willing to accept the use of electronic communications for any purpose under these Regulations which is capable of being carried out electronically, the person shall give notice in writing—

(a)   withdrawing any address notified to the Secretary of State or to a local planning authority for that purpose, or

(b)   revoking any agreement entered into with the Secretary of State or with a local planning authority for that purpose,

and such withdrawal or revocation shall be final and shall take effect on a date specified by the person in the notice but not less than seven days after the date on which the notice is given.

Transitional provisions

11.—(1) Subject to paragraph (2), any appeal to which the Town and Country Planning (Enforcement Notices and Appeals) Regulations 1991 ('the 1991 Regulations') applied which has not been determined on the date when these Regulations come into force, shall be continued under the 1991 Regulations.

(2) Where an appeal to which the 1991 Regulations applied is subsequently remitted to the Secretary of State for redetermination in proceedings before any court, and is to be disposed of on the basis of written representations, the decision shall be redetermined in accordance with these Regulations.

The Town and Country Planning (Enforcement) (Hearings Procedure) (England) Rules 2002 (2002/2684)

The Lord Chancellor, in exercise of the powers conferred on him by section 9 of the Tribunals and Inquiries Act 1992 and of all other powers enabling him in that behalf, and after consultation with the Council on Tribunals, hereby makes the following Rules:

Citation, commencement, and extent

1.—(1) These Rules may be cited as the Town and Country Planning (Enforcement) (Hearings Procedure) (England) Rules 2002.

(2) These Rules shall come into force on 23rd December 2002.

(3) These Rules extend to England only.

Interpretation

2. —(1) In these Rules—

'certificate of lawful use or development' means a certificate under section 191 or 192 of the Planning Act;

'document' includes a photograph, map or plan;

'electronic communication' has the meaning given in section 15(1) of the Electronic Communications Act 2000;

'enforcement appeal' means an appeal against an enforcement notice;

'enforcement notice' means a notice under section 172 of the Planning Act or under section 38 of the Listed Buildings Act;

'hearing' means a hearing to which these Rules apply;

'hearing statement' means, and consists of, a written statement which contains full particulars of the case which a person proposes to put forward at a hearing and copies of any documents which that person intends to refer to or put in evidence;

'inquiry' means a local inquiry to which the Town and Country Planning (Enforcement) (Inquiries Procedure) (England) Rules 2002 or the Town and Country Planning (Enforcement) (Determination by Inspectors) (Inquiries Procedure) (England) Rules 2002 apply;

'inspector' means—

(a) in relation to a transferred appeal, a person appointed by the Secretary of State to determine an appeal;

(b) in relation to a non-transferred appeal, a person appointed by the Secretary of State to hold a hearing or a re-opened hearing;

'land' means the land or building to which the hearing relates;

'the Listed Buildings Act' means the Planning (Listed Buildings and Conservation Areas) Act 1990;

'local planning authority' means in relation to—

(a) an enforcement appeal, the body who issued the relevant enforcement notice;

(b) an appeal against the refusal or non-determination of an application for a certificate of lawful use or development, the body to whom that application was made;

'non-transferred appeal' means an appeal which falls to be determined by the Secretary of State, including an appeal which falls to be so determined by virtue of a direction under paragraph 3(1) of Schedule 6 to the Planning Act or paragraph 3(1) of Schedule 3 to the Listed Buildings Act;

'Planning Act' means the Town and Country Planning Act 1990;

'questionnaire' means a document in the form supplied by the Secretary of State to local planning authorities for the purpose of proceedings under these Rules, and for this purpose a form is taken to be supplied where the Secretary of State has published it on a website and has notified the local planning authority, in a manner for the time being agreed between the Secretary of State and the authority for that purpose, of—

(i) publication of the form on the website,

(ii) the address of the website, and

(iii) the place on the website where the form may be accessed, and how it may be accessed;

'the relevant notice' means the Secretary of State's written notice under rule 4(1) informing the appellant and the local planning authority that a hearing is to be held;

'starting date' means the date of the—

(a) Secretary of State's written notice to the appellant and the local planning authority that he has received all the documents required to enable him to entertain the appeal pursuant to regulation 10 of the Town and Country Planning (Enforcement Notices and Appeals) (England) Regulations 2002; or

(b) relevant notice,

whichever is later;

'transferred appeal' means an appeal which falls to be determined by a person appointed by the Secretary of State under Schedule 6 to the Planning Act or Schedule 3 to the Listed Buildings Act.

(2) In these Rules, and in relation to the use of electronic communications for any purpose of these Rules which is capable of being carried out electronically—

(a)   the expression 'address' includes any number or address used for the purposes of such communications, except that where these Rules impose an obligation on any person to provide a name and address to any other person, the obligation shall not be fulfilled unless the person on whom it is imposed provides a postal address;

(b)   references to statements, notices, applications, or other documents or to copies of such documents, include references to such documents or copies of them in electronic form.

(3) Paragraphs (4) to (8) apply where an electronic communication is used by a person for the purpose of fulfilling any requirement in these Rules that a statement or other document should be sent or given to any other person ('the recipient').

(4) The requirement shall be taken to be fulfilled where the document transmitted by means of the electronic communication is—

(a)   capable of being accessed by the recipient,

(b)   legible in all material respects, and

(c)   sufficiently permanent to be used for subsequent reference.

(5) In paragraph (4), 'legible in all material respects' means that the information contained in the notice or document is available to the recipient to no lesser extent than it would be if sent or given by means of a document in printed form.

(6) Where the electronic communication is received by the recipient outside the recipient's business hours, it shall be taken to have been received on the next working day; and for this purpose 'working day' means a day which is not a Saturday, Sunday, Bank Holiday or other public holiday.

(7) A requirement in these Rules that any notice or document should be in writing is fulfilled where that document meets the criteria in paragraph (4), and 'written' and cognate expressions are to be construed accordingly.

(8) A requirement in these Rules to send more than one copy of a statement or other document may be complied with by sending one copy only of the statement or document in question.

Application of the Rules

3.—(1) These Rules apply in relation to any hearing held in England for the purposes of a non-transferred or a transferred appeal made on or after 23rd December 2002 under—

(a)   section 174 of the Planning Act (appeal against enforcement notice);

(b)   section 195 of the Planning Act (appeal against refusal or non-determination of an application for a certificate of lawful use or development);

(c)   section 39 of the Listed Buildings Act (appeal against listed building enforcement notice) or under that section as applied by section 74(3) of that Act (appeal against conservation area enforcement notice);

but do not apply to any hearing by reason of the application of any provision mentioned in this paragraph by or under any other enactment.

(2) Where these Rules apply in relation to an appeal which at some time fell to be disposed of in accordance with the Town and Country Planning (Enforcement) (Inquiries Procedure) (England) Rules 2002 or the Town and Country Planning (Enforcement) (Determination by Inspectors) (Inquiries Procedure) (England) Rules 2002, any step taken or thing done under those Rules which could have been done under any corresponding provision of these Rules shall have effect as if it had been taken or done under that corresponding provision.

Preliminary information to be supplied by local planning authority

4.—(1) The Secretary of State shall, as soon as practicable after it is determined to hold a hearing under these rules, inform the appellant and the local planning authority in writing that a hearing is to be held.

(2) The local planning authority shall within 2 weeks of the starting date—

(a)   send to the Secretary of State and the appellant a completed questionnaire and a copy of each of the documents referred to in it;

(b)   in the case of an enforcement appeal, notify any—

(i)   person on whom a copy of the enforcement notice has been served;

(ii) occupier of property in the locality in which the land to which the enforcement notice relates is situated; and

(iii) other person who in the opinion of the local planning authority is affected by the breach of planning control or contravention of listed building or conservation area control which is alleged in the enforcement notice,

that an appeal has been made and of the address to which and of the period within which they may make representations to the Secretary of State.

Hearing statements

5.—(1) The appellant and the local planning authority shall send 2 copies of their hearing statement to the Secretary of State within 6 weeks of the starting date.

(2) The Secretary of State may in writing require the appellant and the local planning authority to provide such further information about the matters contained in their hearing statement as he may specify; such information shall be provided in writing and the appellant or the local planning authority, as the case may be, shall send 2 copies to the Secretary of State within such period as the Secretary of State may reasonably require.

(3) Any person who was notified about the appeal under rule 4(2)(b), shall send to the Secretary of State 3 copies of any written comments they wish to make concerning the appeal within 6 weeks of the starting date.

(4) The appellant and the local planning authority shall send to the Secretary of State 2 copies of any comments the local planning authority and the appellant wish to make on—

(a)   each other's hearing statement;

(b)   comments made pursuant to paragraph (3); and

(c)   comments made to them by any other person,

within 9 weeks of the starting date.

(5) Subject to paragraph 5(A), the Secretary of State shall send, as soon as practicable after receipt, a copy of any—

(a)   hearing statement received by him pursuant to paragraph (1), further information provided pursuant to paragraph (2) and any comments received pursuant to paragraph (4) from, in each case, the appellant or the local planning authority to the other of those two parties; and

(b)   written comments made by persons pursuant to paragraph (3), to the local planning authority and the appellant.

(5A) Nothing in paragraph (5) shall require the Secretary of State to disclose information as to national security or the measures taken or to be taken to ensure the security of any premises or property where, in the Secretary of State's view, public disclosure of that information would be contrary to the national interest.

(6) The local planning authority shall give any person who so requests a reasonable opportunity to inspect, and where practicable, take copies of—

(a)   the local planning authority's completed questionnaire, hearing statement and any document copied to the authority under paragraph (5); and

(b)   further information provided by the authority under paragraph (2) and comments made by the authority under paragraph (4),

and shall specify in their hearing statement the time and place where such documents may be inspected.

(6A) For the purposes of the previous paragraph an opportunity shall be taken to have been given to a person where the person is notified of—

(a)   publication on a website of any document mentioned in sub-paragraph (a) or (b) of the previous paragraph;

(b)   the address of the website;

(c)   the place on the website where the document may be accessed, and how it may be accessed.

(7) The Secretary of State shall send to the inspector, as soon as practicable after receipt, any hearing statement, document, part of any document or written comments sent to the Secretary of State within the relevant period specified for sending such documents pursuant to paragraphs (1) to (4).

(8) In the case of a non-transferred appeal, the Secretary of State, and in the case of a transferred appeal, the inspector, may in determining the appeal disregard any comments made pursuant to paragraphs (3) and (4) which are sent after the relevant specified period.

Date and notification of hearing

6.—(1) The date fixed by the Secretary of State for the holding of a hearing shall be—

(a)   not later than 12 weeks after the starting date, unless he considers such a date impracticable; or

(b)   the earliest date after that period which he considers to be practicable.

(2) Unless the Secretary of State agrees a lesser period of notice with the appellant and the local planning authority, he shall give not less than 4 weeks written notice of the date, time and place fixed by him for the holding of a hearing to every person entitled to appear at the hearing.

(2A) A written notice shall be taken to have been given by the Secretary of State for the purposes of paragraph (2) where he and any person entitled to appear at the hearing have agreed that notice of the matters mentioned in that paragraph may instead be accessed by that person on a website and—

(a)   the notice is a notice to which that agreement applies;

(b)   the Secretary of State has published the notice on a website;

(c)   not less than 4 weeks before the date fixed by the Secretary of State for the holding of the inquiry, the person is notified of—

   (i)   the publication of the notice on a website,

   (ii) the address of the website, and

   (iii) the place on the website where the notice may be accessed, and how it may be accessed

(3) The Secretary of State may vary the date fixed for the holding of a hearing, whether or not the date as varied is within the period of 12 weeks mentioned in paragraph (1); and paragraph (2) shall apply to a variation of a date as it applied to the date originally fixed.

(4) The Secretary of State may vary the time or place for the holding of a hearing and shall give notice of any such variation as appears to him to be reasonable.

(5) The Secretary of State may in writing require the local planning authority to take one or both of the following steps—

(a)   not less than 2 weeks before the date fixed for the holding of a hearing, to publish a notice of the hearing in one or more newspapers circulating in the locality in which the land is situated;

(b)   to send a notice of the hearing to such persons or classes of persons as he may specify, within such period as he may specify.

(6) Every notice of hearing published or sent pursuant to paragraph (5) shall contain—

(a)   a clear statement of the date, time and place of the hearing and of the powers enabling the Secretary of State or inspector to determine the appeal in question;

(b)   a written description of the land sufficient to identify approximately its location;

(c)   a brief description of the subject matter of the appeal; and

(d)   details of where and when copies of the local planning authority's completed questionnaire and documents sent by and copied to the authority pursuant to rule 5 may be inspected.

Notification of name of inspector

7.—(1) Subject to paragraph (2), the Secretary of State shall notify the name of the inspector to every person entitled to appear at the hearing.

(2) Where the Secretary of State appoints another inspector instead of the person previously appointed and it is not practicable to notify the new appointment before the hearing is held, the inspector holding the hearing shall, at its commencement, announce his name and the fact of his appointment.

Method of procedure

8.—(1) If either the appellant or the local planning authority at any time before or during the hearing is of the opinion that the hearings procedure is inappropriate in determining the appeal and that the appeal should not proceed in this way then they may inform the Secretary of State, before the hearing, or the inspector, during the hearing, of their opinion and the reasons for it and—

(a)   the Secretary of State, before the hearing, shall, after consulting the other party who may inform the Secretary of State of his opinion pursuant to this paragraph, decide whether an inquiry should be arranged instead; or

(b)   the inspector, during the hearing, shall, after consulting the other party who may inform the inspector of his opinion pursuant to this paragraph, decide whether the hearing should be closed and an inquiry held instead.

(2) If at any time during a hearing it appears to the inspector that the hearings procedure is inappropriate, he may, after consulting the appellant and the local planning authority, decide to close the proceedings and arrange for an inquiry to be held instead.

Appearances at hearing

9.—(1) The persons entitled to appear at the hearing are—

(a)   the appellant;

(b)   the local planning authority;

(c)   in the case of an enforcement appeal, any person on whom a copy of the enforcement notice has been served; and

(d)   in the case of an enforcement appeal or an appeal under section 195 of the Planning Act, any person having an interest in the land.

(2) Nothing in paragraph (1) shall prevent the inspector from permitting any other person to appear at a hearing, and such permission shall not be unreasonably withheld.

(3) Any person entitled or permitted to appear may do so on his own behalf or be represented by any other person.

Inspector may act in place of Secretary of State in respect of transferred appeals

10.—(1) This rule applies where a hearing is to be held or has been held for the purposes of a transferred appeal.

(2) An inspector may take such steps as the Secretary of State is required or enabled to take under or by virtue of rules 5(2), 5(5), 6 and 18, in place of the Secretary of State.

(3) Where an inspector requires further information or copies pursuant to rules 5(2) or 18(2) that information or copies shall be sent to him.

Procedure at hearing

11.—(1) Except as otherwise provided in these Rules, the inspector shall determine the procedure at a hearing.

(2) A hearing shall take the form of a discussion led by the inspector and cross-examination shall not be permitted unless the inspector considers that cross-examination is required to ensure a thorough examination of the main issues.

(3) Where the inspector considers that cross-examination is required under paragraph (2) he shall consider, after consulting the appellant and the local planning authority, whether the hearing should be closed and an inquiry held instead.

(4) At the start of the hearing the inspector shall identify what are, in his opinion, the main issues to be considered at the hearing and any matters on which he requires further explanation from any person entitled or permitted to appear.

(5) Nothing in paragraph (4) shall preclude any person entitled or permitted to appear from referring to issues which they consider relevant to the consideration of the appeal but which were not issues identified by the inspector pursuant to that paragraph.

(6) A person entitled to appear at a hearing shall be entitled to call evidence but, subject to the foregoing and paragraphs (7) and (8), the calling of evidence shall otherwise be at the inspector's discretion.

(7) The inspector may refuse to permit the—

(a)   giving or production of evidence; or

(b)   presentation of any other matter,

which he considers to be irrelevant or repetitious; but where he refuses to permit the giving of oral evidence, the person wishing to give the evidence may submit to him any evidence or other matter in writing before the close of the hearing.

(8) The inspector may—

(a) require any person appearing or present at a hearing who, in his opinion, is behaving in a disruptive matter to leave; and

(b) refuse to permit that person to return; or

(c) permit him to return only on such conditions as he may specify,

but any such person may submit to him any evidence or other matter in writing before the close of the hearing.

(9) The inspector may allow any person to alter or add to a hearing statement received under rule 5 so far as may be necessary for the purposes of the hearing; but he shall (if necessary by adjourning the hearing) give every other person entitled to appear who is appearing at the hearing an adequate opportunity of considering any fresh matter or document.

(10) The inspector may proceed with a hearing in the absence of any person entitled to appear at it.

(11) The inspector may take into account any written representation or evidence or any other document received by him from any person before a hearing opens or during the hearing provided that he discloses it at the hearing.

(12) The inspector may from time to time adjourn a hearing and, if the date, time and place of the adjourned hearing are announced at the hearing before the adjournment, no further notice shall be required.

Site inspections

12.—(1) Where it appears to the inspector that one or more matters would be more satisfactorily resolved by adjourning the hearing to the appeal site he may adjourn the hearing to that site and conclude the hearing there provided he is satisfied that—

(a) the hearing would proceed satisfactorily and that no party would be placed at a disadvantage;

(b) all parties present at the hearing would have the opportunity to attend the adjourned hearing;

(c) the local planning authority and the appellant have not raised reasonable objections to it being continued at the appeal site.

(2) Unless the hearing is to be adjourned to the appeal site pursuant to paragraph (1), the inspector—

(a) may inspect the land during the hearing or after its close; and

(b) shall inspect the land if requested to do so by the appellant or the local planning authority before or during the hearing.

(3) Where the inspector intends to make an inspection under paragraph (2), he shall ask the appellant and the local planning authority whether they wish to be present.

(4) Where the appellant or the local planning authority have indicated that they wish to be present the inspector shall announce the date and time at which he proposes to make the inspection during the hearing and shall make the inspection in the company of—

(a)   the appellant, the local planning authority and any other person who has an interest in the land; and

(b)   at the inspector's discretion, any other person entitled or permitted to appear at the hearing who is appearing or did appear at it.

(5) The inspector shall not be bound to defer an inspection of the kind referred to in paragraph (2) where any person mentioned in paragraph (4) is not present at the time appointed.

Procedure after hearing—non-transferred appeals

13.—(1) This rule applies where a hearing has been held for the purposes of a non-transferred appeal.

(2) After the close of the hearing, the inspector shall make a report in writing to the Secretary of State which shall include his conclusions and his recommendations or his reasons for not making any recommendations.

(3) When making his determination the Secretary of State may disregard any written representations, evidence or other document received after the hearing has closed.

(4) If, after the close of the hearing, the Secretary of State—

(a)   differs from the inspector on any matter of fact mentioned in, or appearing to him to be material to, a conclusion reached by the inspector, or

(b)   takes into consideration any new evidence or new matter of fact (not being a matter of government policy),

and is for that reason disposed to disagree with a recommendation made by the inspector, he shall not come to a decision which is at variance with that recommendation without first notifying the persons entitled to appear at the hearing who appeared at it of his disagreement and the reasons for it.

(5) Where persons entitled to appear at the hearing who appeared are notified pursuant to paragraph (4), the Secretary of State shall give them an opportunity to make written representations to him or (if the Secretary of State has taken into consideration any new evidence or new matter of fact, not being a matter of government policy) to ask for the re-opening of the hearing.

(6) Those making written representations or requesting the hearing to be re-opened pursuant to paragraph (5), shall send such representations or requests to the Secretary of State within 3 weeks of the date of the Secretary of State's notification under that paragraph.

(7) The Secretary of State may, as he thinks fit, cause a hearing to be re-opened, and he shall do so if asked by the appellant or the local planning authority in the

circumstances mentioned in paragraph (5) and within the period mentioned in paragraph (6).

(8) Where a hearing is re-opened pursuant to rule (7) (whether by the same or a different inspector)—

(a)   the Secretary of State shall send to the persons entitled to appear at the hearing who appeared at it a written statement of the matters on which further evidence is invited; and

(b)   paragraphs (2) to (6) of rule 6 shall apply as if the reference to a hearing were references to a re-opened hearing.

Procedure after hearing—transferred appeals

14.—(1) This rule applies where a hearing has been held for the purposes of a transferred appeal.

(2) When making his decision the inspector may disregard any written representations, or evidence or any other document received after the hearing has closed.

(3) If, after the close of the hearing, an inspector proposes to take into consideration any new evidence or any new matter of fact (not being a matter of government policy) which was not raised at the hearing and which he considers to be material to his decision, he shall not come to a decision without first—

(a)   notifying persons entitled to appear at the hearing who appeared at it of the matter in question; and

(b)   giving them an opportunity to make written representations to him or to ask for the re-opening of the hearing,

and they shall send such written representations or requests to re-open the hearing to the Secretary of State within 3 weeks of the date of the notification.

(4) An inspector may, as he thinks fit, cause a hearing to be re-opened and he shall do so if asked by the appellant or the local planning authority in the circumstances and within the period mentioned in paragraph (3).

(5) Where a hearing is re-opened pursuant to paragraph (4)—

(a)   the inspector shall send to the persons entitled to appear at the hearing who appeared at it a written statement of the matters on which further evidence is invited; and

(b)   paragraphs (2) to (6) of rule 6 shall apply as if the references to a hearing were references to a re-opened hearing.

Notification of decision—non-transferred appeals

15.—(1) This rule applies where a hearing has been held for the purposes of a non-transferred appeal.

(2) The Secretary of State shall notify his decision on an appeal, and his reasons for it, in writing to—

(a)   the appellant and the local planning authority;

(b)   all persons entitled to appear at the hearing who did appear; and

(c)   any other person who, having appeared at the hearing, has asked to be notified of the decision.

(2A) Notification in writing of a decision and reasons shall be taken to have been given to a person for the purposes of this rule where—

(a)   the Secretary of State and the person have agreed that decisions, reasons, and copies of reports required under this rule to be given in writing may instead be accessed by that person on a website;

(b)   the decision and reasons are a decision and reasons to which that agreement applies;

(c)   the Secretary of State has published the decision and reasons on a website;

(d)   the person is notified of—

   (i)   the publication of the decision and reasons on a website;

   (ii) the address of the website;

   (iii) the place on the website where the decision and reasons may be accessed, and how they may be accessed.

(3) Where a copy of the inspector's report is not sent with the notification of the decision or published on a website in accordance with paragraph (2A), the notification shall be accompanied by a statement of his conclusions and of any recommendations made by him; and if a person entitled to be notified of the decision has not received a copy of that report, he shall be supplied with a copy of it on written application to the Secretary of State.

(4) In this rule 'report' does not include any documents appended to the inspector's report; but any person who has received a copy of the report may apply to the Secretary of State in writing for an opportunity to inspect any such documents and the Secretary of State shall give him that opportunity.

(4A) For the purposes of the previous paragraph an opportunity shall be taken to have been given to a person where that person is notified of—

(a)   publication of the relevant documents on a website;

(b)   the address of the website;

(c)   the place on the website where the documents may be accessed, and how they may be accessed.

(5) A person applying to the Secretary of State under—

(a)   paragraph (3) shall send his application to the Secretary of State within 4 weeks;

(b)   paragraph (4) shall send his application to the Secretary of State within 6 weeks,

of the date of the Secretary of State's decision.

Appendix 4

Notification of decision—transferred appeals

16.—(1) This rule applies where a hearing has been held for the purposes of a transferred appeal.

(2) An inspector shall notify his decision on an appeal, and his reasons for it, in writing to—

(a) the appellant and the local planning authority;

(b) all persons entitled to appear at the hearing who did appear; and

(c) any other person who, having appeared at the hearing, has asked to be notified of the decision.

(3) Any person entitled to be notified of the inspector's decision under paragraph (2) may apply to the Secretary of State in writing, for an opportunity to inspect any documents listed in the notification and the Secretary of State shall give him that opportunity.

(3A) For the purposes of the previous paragraph an opportunity shall be taken to have been given to a person where that person is notified of—

(a) publication of the relevant documents on a website;

(b) the address of the website;

(c) the place on the website where the documents may be accessed, and how they may be accessed.

(4) A person applying to the Secretary of State under paragraph (3) shall send his application to the Secretary of State within 6 weeks of the date of the inspector's decision.

Procedure following remitting of appeal

17.—(1) Where an appeal, for which a hearing has been held, is remitted by any court to the Secretary of State for rehearing and redetermination, the Secretary of State—

(a) shall send to the persons entitled to appear at the hearing who appeared at it a written statement of the matters on which further representations are invited in order for him to consider the appeal further;

(b) shall give those persons the opportunity to make written representations to him on those matters or to ask for the re-opening of the hearing; and

(c) may, as he thinks fit, cause the hearing to be re-opened or an inquiry held instead (whether by the same or a different inspector) and if he re-opens the hearing paragraphs (2) to (6) of rule 6 shall apply as if the reference to a hearing were to a re-opened hearing.

(2) Those persons making representations or asking for the hearing to be re-opened under paragraph (1)(b) shall send such representations or requests to the Secretary of State within 3 weeks of the date of the written statement sent under paragraph (1)(a).

Further time and additional copies

18.—(1) The Secretary of State may at any time in any particular case allow further time for the taking of any step which is required or enabled to be taken pursuant to these Rules, and references in these Rules to a day by which, or a period within which, any step is required or enabled to be taken shall be construed accordingly.

(2) The Secretary of State may at any time before the close of a hearing request from any person entitled to appear additional copies of the following—

(a)   a hearing statement or comments sent in accordance with rule 5; or

(b)   any other document or information sent to the Secretary of State before or during a hearing,

and may specify the time within which such copies should be sent to him and any person so requested shall ensure that the copies are sent within the specified period.

Notices sent

19.   Notices or documents required or authorised to be sent or supplied under these Rules may be sent or supplied—

(a)   by post; or

(b)   by using electronic communications to send or supply the notice or document (as the case may be) to a person at such address as may for the time being be specified by the person for that purpose.

Withdrawal of consent to use of electronic communications

20.   Where a person is no longer willing to accept the use of electronic communications for any purpose which under these Rules is capable of being carried out electronically, the person shall give notice in writing—

(a)   withdrawing any address notified to the Secretary of State or to a local planning authority for that purpose, or

(b)   revoking any agreement entered into with the Secretary of State or with a local planning authority for that purpose,

and such withdrawal or revocation shall be final and shall take effect on a date specified by the person in the notice but not less than seven days after the date on which the notice is given.

The Town and Country Planning (Enforcement) (Determination by Inspectors) (Inquiries Procedure) (England) Rules 2002 (2002/2685)

The Lord Chancellor, in exercise of the powers conferred upon him by section 9 of the Tribunals and Inquiries Act 1992 and of all other powers enabling him in that behalf, and after consultation with the Council on Tribunals, hereby makes the following Rules:

Citation, commencement and extent

1.—(1) These Rules may be cited as the Town and Country Planning (Enforcement) (Determination by Inspectors) (Inquiries Procedure) (England) Rules 2002 and shall come into force on 23rd December 2002.

(2) These Rules extend to England only.

Interpretation

2. In these Rules—

'assessor' means a person appointed by the Secretary of State to sit with an inspector at an inquiry or re-opened inquiry to advise the inspector on such matters arising as the Secretary of State may specify;

'certificate of lawful use or development' means a certificate under section 191 or 192 of the Planning Act;

'document' includes a photograph, map or plan;

'enforcement appeal' means an appeal against an enforcement notice;

'enforcement notice' means a notice under section 172 of the Planning Act or under section 38 of the Listed Buildings Act;

'inquiry' means a local inquiry to which these Rules apply;

'inspector' means a person appointed by the Secretary of State under Schedule 6 to the Planning Act or, as the case may be, Schedule 3 to the Listed Buildings Act to determine an appeal;

'land' means the land or building to which an inquiry relates;

'Listed Buildings Act' means the Planning (Listed Buildings and Conservation Areas) Act 1990;

'local planning authority' means in relation to—

(a) an enforcement appeal, the body who issued the relevant enforcement notice;

(b) an appeal against the refusal or non-determination of an application for a certificate of lawful use or development, the body to whom the application was made;

'outline statement' means a written statement of the principal submissions which a person proposes to put forward at an inquiry;

'Planning Act' means the Town and Country Planning Act 1990;

'pre-inquiry meeting' means a meeting held before an inquiry to consider what may be done with a view to securing that the inquiry is conducted efficiently and expeditiously, and where two or more such meetings are held references to the conclusion of a pre-inquiry meeting are references to the conclusion of the final meeting;

'questionnaire' means a document in the form supplied by the Secretary of State to local planning authorities for the purpose of proceedings under these Rules, and for this purpose a form is taken to be supplied where the Secretary of State has published it on a website and has notified the local planning authority, in a manner for the time being agreed between the Secretary of State and the authority for that purpose, of—

(i) publication of the form on the website,

(ii) the address of the website, and

(iii) the place on the website where the form may be accessed, and how it may be accessed

'relevant notice' means the Secretary of State's written notice under rule 4(1), informing the appellant and the local planning authority that an inquiry is to be held;

'starting date' means the date of the—

(a) Secretary of State's written notice to the appellant and the local planning authority that he has received all the documents required to enable him to entertain the appeal pursuant to regulation 10 of the Town and Country Planning (Enforcement Notices and Appeals) (England) Regulations 2002; or

(b) relevant notice,

whichever is the later;

'statement of case' means, and is comprised of, a written statement which contains full particulars of the case which a person proposes to put forward at an inquiry, and a list of any documents which that person intends to refer to or put in evidence;

'statement of common ground' means a written statement prepared jointly by the local planning authority and the appellant, which contains agreed factual information about the development, breach of condition or works which are the subject of the appeal.

(2) In these Rules, and in relation to the use of electronic communications for any purpose of these Rules which is capable of being carried out electronically—

(a)　the expression 'address' includes any number or address used for the purposes of such communications, except that where these Rules impose an obligation on any person to provide a name and address to any other person, the obligation shall not be fulfilled unless the person on whom it is imposed provides a postal address;

(b)　references to statements, notices, applications, or other documents, or to copies of such documents include references to such documents or copies of them in electronic form.

(3) Paragraphs (4) to (8) apply where an electronic communication is used by a person for the purpose of fulfilling any requirement in these Rules that a statement or other document should be sent or given to any other person ('the recipient').

(4) The requirement shall be taken to be fulfilled where the statement or other document which is transmitted by means of the electronic communication is—

(a)　capable of being accessed by the recipient,

(b)　legible in all material respects, and

(c)　sufficiently permanent to be used for subsequent reference.

(5) In paragraph (4), 'legible in all material respects' means that the information contained in the notice or document is available to the recipient to no lesser extent than it would be if sent or given by means of a notice or document in printed form.

(6) Where the electronic communication is received by the recipient outside the recipient's business hours, it shall be taken to have been received on the next working day; and for this purpose 'working day' means a day which is not a Saturday, Sunday, Bank Holiday or other public holiday.

(7) A requirement in these Rules that any notice or document should be in writing is fulfilled where that document meets the criteria in paragraph (4), and 'written' and cognate expressions are to be construed accordingly.

(8) A requirement in these Rules to send more than one copy of a statement or other document may be complied with by sending one copy only of the statement or document in question.

Application of the Rules

3.—(1) These Rules apply in relation to any local inquiry held in England by an inspector before he determines an appeal made on or after 23rd December 2002 under—

(a)　section 174 of the Planning Act (appeal against enforcement notice);

(b)　section 195 of the Planning Act (appeal against refusal or non-determination of an application for a certificate of lawful use or development);

(c)　section 39 of the Listed Buildings Act (appeal against listed building enforcement notice) or under that section as applied by section 74(3) of that Act (appeal against conservation area enforcement notice), but do not apply to any local inquiry by reason of the application of any provision mentioned in this rule by or under any other enactment.

(2) Where these Rules apply in relation to an appeal which at some time fell to be disposed of in accordance with—

(a) the Town and Country Planning (Enforcement) (Inquiries Procedure) (England) Rules 2002; or

(b) the Town and Country Planning (Enforcement)(Inquiries Procedure) Rules 1992,

any step taken or thing done under those Rules which could have been done under any corresponding provision of these Rules shall have effect as if it had been taken or done under that corresponding provision.

Preliminary information to be supplied by local planning authority

4.—(1) The Secretary of State shall, as soon as practicable after it is determined to hold an inquiry under these Rules, inform the appellant and the local planning authority in writing that an inquiry is to be held.

(2) The local planning authority shall within 2 weeks of the starting date—

(a) send to the Secretary of State and the appellant a completed questionnaire and a copy of each of the documents referred to in it;

(b) in the case of an enforcement appeal, notify any—

  (i) person on whom a copy of the enforcement notice has been served;

  (ii) occupier of property in the locality in which the land to which the enforcement notice relates is situated; and

  (iii) other person who in the opinion of the local planning authority is affected by the breach of planning control or contravention of listed building or conservation area control which is alleged in the enforcement notice,

  that an appeal has been made and of the address to which and of the period within which they may make representations to the Secretary of State.

Notification of name of inspector

5.—(1) The Secretary of State shall, subject to paragraph (2), notify the name of the inspector to every person entitled to appear at the inquiry.

(2) Where the Secretary of State appoints another inspector instead of the person previously appointed and it is not practicable to notify the new appointment before the inquiry is held, the inspector holding the inquiry shall, at its commencement, announce his name and the fact of his appointment.

Service of statements of case, etc

6.—(1) The local planning authority shall, within 6 weeks of the starting date, serve 2 copies of their statement of case on the Secretary of State and, in the case of an enforcement appeal, a copy on any person on whom a copy of the enforcement notice has been served.

(2) The local planning authority shall include in their statement of case details of the time and place where the opportunity will be given to inspect and take copies described in paragraph (13) (and including, in any case in which the local planning authority rely on paragraph (13A), the details mentioned in that paragraph).

(3) The appellant shall, within 6 weeks of the starting date, serve 2 copies of his statement of case on the Secretary of State and, in the case of an enforcement appeal, a copy on any person on whom a copy of the enforcement notice has been served.

(4) The Secretary of State shall, as soon as practicable after receipt, send a copy of the local planning authority's statement of case to the appellant and a copy of the appellant's statement of case to the local planning authority.

(5) The appellant and the local planning authority may in writing each require the other to send them a copy of any document, or the relevant part of any document, referred to in the list of documents comprised in that party's statement of case; and any such document, or relevant part, shall be sent, as soon as practicable, to the party who required it.

(6) The Secretary of State may in writing require any other person who has notified him of an intention or a wish to appear at the inquiry, to serve—

(a)   3 copies of their statement of case on him within 4 weeks of being so required; and

(b)   in the case of an enforcement appeal, simultaneously, a copy of their statement of case on any person specified by the Secretary of State,

and the Secretary of State shall, as soon as practicable after receipt, send a copy of each such statement of case to the local planning authority and to the appellant.

(7) The Secretary of State shall, as soon as practicable—

(a)   send to any person from whom he requires a statement of case in accordance with paragraph (6) a copy of the statements of case of the appellant and the local planning authority; and

(b)   inform that person of the name and address of every person to whom his statement of case is required to be sent.

(8) The Secretary of State may in writing require any person, who has served on him a statement of case in accordance with this rule, to provide such further information about the matters contained in the statement of case as he may specify and may specify the time within which the information shall be sent to him.

(9) A local planning authority or appellant required to provide further information, shall send within the time specified—

(a)   2 copies of that information in writing to the Secretary of State; and

(b)   in the case of an enforcement appeal, a copy to any person on whom a copy of the enforcement notice has been served, and the Secretary of State shall, as soon as practicable after receipt, send a copy of the further information received from the local planning authority to the appellant and a copy of the further information received from the appellant to the local planning authority.

(10) Any other person required to provide further information shall send within the time specified—

(a)   3 copies of that information in writing to the Secretary of State; and

(b)   in the case of an enforcement appeal, a copy to any person on whom a copy of the enforcement notice has been served,

and the Secretary of State shall, as soon as practicable after receipt, send a copy of the further information to the local planning authority and the appellant.

(11) Any person other than the appellant who serves a statement of case on the Secretary of State shall send with it a copy of—

(a)   any document; or

(b)   the relevant part of any document,

referred to in the list comprised in that statement, unless a copy of the document or part of the document in question is already available for inspection pursuant to paragraph (13).

(12) The Secretary of State shall, as soon as practicable after receipt, send to the inspector any statement of case, document, further information and written comments sent to him in accordance with this rule and received by him within the relevant period, if any, specified in this rule.

(13) The local planning authority shall give any person who so requests a reasonable opportunity to inspect and, where practicable, take copies of—

(a)   any statement of case, written comments, further information or other document a copy of which has been sent to the local planning authority in accordance with this rule; and

(b)   the local planning authority's completed questionnaire and statement of case together with a copy of any document, or of the relevant part of any document, referred to in the list comprised in that statement, and any written comments, information or other document sent by the local planning authority pursuant to this rule.

(13A) For the purposes of the previous paragraph an opportunity is to be taken to have been given to a person where the person is notified of—

(a)   publication on a website of the documents mentioned in that paragraph;

(b)   the address of the website;

(c)   the place on the website where the documents may be accessed, and how they may be accessed.

(14) If the local planning authority or the appellant wish to comment on another person's statement of case, they shall send within 9 weeks of the starting date—

(a)   2 copies of their written comments to the Secretary of State; and

(b)   in the case of an enforcement appeal, a copy of their written comments to any person on whom a copy of the enforcement notice has been served,

and the Secretary of State shall, as soon as practicable after receipt, send a copy of the written comments received from the appellant to the local planning authority and a copy of the written comments received from the local planning authority to the appellant.

(15) Any person, other than the local planning authority or the appellant, who serves a statement of case on the Secretary of State under this rule and who wishes to comment on another person's statement of case, shall send, not less than 4 weeks before the date fixed for the holding of the inquiry—

(a)   3 copies of their written comments to the Secretary of State; and

(b)   in the case of an enforcement appeal, a copy of their written comments to any person on whom a copy of the enforcement notice has been served,

and the Secretary of State shall, as soon as practicable after receipt, send a copy of the written comments to the local planning authority and to the appellant.

Statement of matters and pre-inquiry meetings

7.—(1) An inspector may, within 12 weeks of the starting date, send to the appellant, the local planning authority and, in the case of an enforcement appeal, any person on whom a copy of the enforcement notice has been served, a written statement of the matters about which he particularly wishes to be informed for the purposes of his consideration of the appeal.

(2) An inspector shall hold a pre-inquiry meeting—

(a)   if he expects an inquiry to last for 4 days or more, unless he considers it is unnecessary; or

(b)   for shorter inquiries, if it appears to him necessary.

(3) An inspector shall give not less than 2 weeks' written notice of a pre-inquiry meeting to—

(a)   the appellant;

(b)   the local planning authority;

(c)   any other person known to be entitled to appear at the inquiry; and

(d)   any other person whose presence at the pre-inquiry meeting appears to him to be desirable.

(4) The inspector—

(a)   shall preside at the pre-inquiry meeting;

(b)   shall determine the matters to be discussed and the procedure to be followed;

(c)   may require any person present at the pre-inquiry meeting who, in his opinion, is behaving in a disruptive manner to leave; and

(d)   may refuse to permit that person to return or to attend any further pre-inquiry meeting, or may permit him to return or attend only on such conditions as he may specify.

(5) An inspector may request any further information from the appellant or the local planning authority at the pre-inquiry meeting.

(6) The appellant and the local planning authority shall—

(a)   send 2 copies of any further information requested under paragraph (5) to the inspector; and

(b)   in the case of an enforcement notice appeal, send a copy to any person on whom a copy of the enforcement notice has been served,

within 4 weeks of the conclusion of the pre-inquiry meeting.

(7) The inspector shall, as soon as practicable after receipt, send a copy of the further information received from the local planning authority to the appellant and a copy of any further information received from the appellant to the local planning authority.

Inquiry timetable

8.—(1) In respect of inquiries that appear to the Secretary of State likely to last for 4 days or more, the inspector shall prepare a timetable for the proceedings.

(2) In respect of shorter inquiries, the inspector may at any time prepare a timetable for the proceedings at, or at part of, an inquiry.

(3) The inspector may, at any time, vary the timetable prepared under the preceding paragraphs.

(4) The inspector may specify in a timetable prepared pursuant to this rule a date by which any proof of evidence and summary sent in accordance with rule 15(1) shall be sent to him.

Date and notification of inquiry

9.—(1) The date fixed by the Secretary of State for the holding of an inquiry shall be—

(a)   not later than 20 weeks after the starting date unless he considers such a date impracticable; or

(b)   the earliest date after that period which he considers to be practicable.

(2) Unless the Secretary of State agrees a lesser period of notice with the appellant and the local planning authority, he shall give not less than 4 weeks written notice of the date, time and place fixed by him for the holding of an inquiry to every person entitled to appear at the inquiry.

(3) The Secretary of State may vary the date fixed for the holding of an inquiry, whether or not the date as varied is within the period of 20 weeks mentioned in

paragraph (1); and paragraph (2) shall apply to a variation of a date as it applied to the date originally fixed.

(3A) A written notice shall be taken to have been given by the Secretary of State for the purposes of paragraph (3) where he and any person entitled to appear at the inquiry have agreed that notice of the matters mentioned in that paragraph may instead be accessed by that person via a website, and—

(a)   the notice is a notice to which that agreement applies;

(b)   the Secretary of State has published that notice on the website;

(c)   not less than 4 weeks before the date fixed by the Secretary of State for the holding of the inquiry, the person is notified of—

   (i)   the publication of the notice on a website,

   (ii) the address of the website, and

   (iii) the place on the website where the notice may be accessed, and how it may be accessed.

(4) The Secretary of State may vary the time or place for the holding of an inquiry and shall give such notice as appears to him to be reasonable.

(5) The Secretary of State may in writing require the local planning authority to take one or more of the following steps—

(a)   not less than 2 weeks before the date fixed for the holding of an inquiry, to publish a notice of the inquiry in one or more newspapers circulating in the locality in which the land is situated;

(b)   to send a notice of the inquiry to such persons or classes of persons as he may specify, within such period as he may specify; or

(c)   to post a notice of the inquiry in a conspicuous place near to the land, within such period as he may specify.

(6) Where the land is under the control of the appellant, he shall—

(a)   if so required in writing by the Secretary of State, affix a notice of the inquiry firmly to the land or to some object on or near the land, in such manner as to be readily visible to and legible by members of the public; and

(b)   not remove the notice, or cause or permit it to be removed, for such period before the inquiry as the Secretary of State may specify.

(7) Every notice of inquiry published, sent or posted pursuant to paragraph (5), or affixed pursuant to paragraph (6), shall contain—

(a)   a clear statement of the date, time and place of the inquiry and of the powers enabling the inspector to determine the appeal in question;

(b)   a written description of the land sufficient to identify approximately its location;

(c)   a brief description of the subject matter of the appeal; and

(d)   details of where and when copies of the local planning authority's completed questionnaire and any document sent by and copied to the authority pursuant to rule 6 may be inspected.

Notification of appointment of assessor

10. Where the Secretary of State appoints an assessor he shall notify every person entitled to appear at the inquiry of the name of the assessor and of the matters on which he is to advise the inspector.

Appearances at inquiry

11.—(1) The persons entitled to appear at the inquiry are—

(a) the appellant;

(b) the local planning authority;

(c) any of the following bodies if the land is situated in their area and they are not the local planning authority—

  (i) a county or a district council;

  (ii) an enterprise zone authority designated under Schedule 32 to the Local Government, Planning and Land Act 1980;

  (iii) the Broads Authority, within the meaning of the Norfolk and Suffolk Broads Act 1988;

  (iv) a housing action trust specified in an order made under section 67(1) of the Housing Act 1988;

(d) where the land is in an area previously designated as a new town, the Homes and Communities Agency;

(e) in the case of an enforcement appeal, any person on whom a copy of the enforcement notice has been served;

(f) in the case of an appeal under section 195 of the Planning Act, any person having an interest in the land;

(g) the Historic Buildings and Monuments Commission for England where—

  (i) the inquiry relates to an enforcement notice under section 38 of the Listed Buildings Act;

  (ii) the listed building is in Greater London; and

  (iii) if an application for listed building consent had been made for the works set out in the enforcement notice, the Commission would have been notified of the application under a direction given under section 15(5) of the Listed Buildings Act;

(h) any other person who has served a statement of case in accordance with rule 6(6).

(2) Nothing in paragraph (1) shall prevent the inspector from permitting any other person to appear at an inquiry and such permission shall not be unreasonably withheld.

(3) Any person entitled or permitted to appear may do so on his own behalf or be represented by any other person.

413

Appendix 5

Information to be provided by all parties

12. Any person entitled or permitted to appear at the inquiry, who proposes to give, or call another person to give evidence at the inquiry, shall send in writing to the Secretary of State no later than 4 weeks before the inquiry—

(a)   an estimate of the time required to present all their evidence; and

(b)   the number of witnesses that they intend to call to give evidence.

Representatives of government departments at inquiry

13.—(1) Where the Secretary of State or any other Minister of the Crown or any government department has expressed in writing to the local planning authority a view on an appeal and the authority refer to that view in a statement prepared pursuant to rule 6(1), the appellant may, not later than 4 weeks before the date of an inquiry, apply in writing to the Secretary of State for a representative of the Secretary of State or of the other Minister or department concerned to be made available at the inquiry.

(2) Where an application is made in accordance with paragraph (1), the Secretary of State shall make a representative available to attend the inquiry or, as the case may be, send the application to the other Minister or department concerned, who shall make a representative available to attend the inquiry.

(3) A person attending an inquiry as a representative pursuant to this rule shall state the reasons for the expressed view and shall give evidence and be subject to cross-examination to the same extent as any other witness.

(4) Nothing in paragraph (3) shall require a representative of a Minister or government department to answer any question, which in the opinion of the inspector, is directed to the merits of government policy.

Inspector may act in place of Secretary of State

14. An inspector may in place of the Secretary of State take such steps as the Secretary of State is required or enabled to take under or by virtue of rule 6(6) to (10), (14) and (15), rules 9, 22 and 23; and where an inspector requires further information or copies pursuant to rules 6(8) or 23, that information or copies shall be sent to him.

Proofs of evidence

15.—(1) Any person entitled to appear at an inquiry who proposes to give, or to call another person to give, evidence at the inquiry by reading a proof of evidence shall—

(a)   subject to paragraph (2), send 2 copies, in the case of the local planning authority and the appellant, or 3 copies in the case of any other person, of the proof of evidence together with a written summary to the Secretary of State; and

(b)   in the case of an enforcement appeal, simultaneously send copies of these to any person on whom a copy of the enforcement notice has been served,

414

and the Secretary of State shall, as soon as practicable after receipt, send a copy of each proof of evidence together with any summary to the local planning authority and the appellant.

(2) No written summary shall be required where the proof of evidence proposed to be read contains no more than 1500 words.

(3) The proof of evidence and any summary shall be sent to the Secretary of State no later than—

(a)   4 weeks before the date fixed for the holding of the inquiry, or

(b)   where a timetable has been prepared pursuant to rule 8 which specifies a date by which the proof of evidence and any summary shall be sent to the Secretary of State, that date.

(4) The Secretary of State shall send to the inspector, as soon as practicable after receipt, any proof of evidence together with any summary sent to him in accordance with this rule within the relevant period, specified in this rule.

(5) Where a written summary is provided in accordance with paragraph (1), only that summary shall be read at the inquiry, unless the inspector permits or requires otherwise.

(6) Any person, required by this rule to send copies of a proof of evidence to the Secretary of State, or any other person, shall send with them the same number of copies of the whole, or the relevant part, of any document referred to in the proof of evidence, unless a copy of the document or part of the document in question is already available for inspection pursuant to rule 6(13).

(7) The local planning authority shall give any person who so requests a reasonable opportunity to inspect and, where practicable, take copies of any document sent to or by them in accordance with this rule.

(8) For the purposes of the previous paragraph an opportunity shall be taken to have been given to a person where the person is notified of—

(a)   publication of the relevant document on a website,

(b)   the address of the website,

(c)   the place on the website where the document may be accessed, and how it may be accessed.

Statement of common ground

16.—(1) The local planning authority and the appellant shall together prepare an agreed statement of common ground and shall send it to—

(a)   the Secretary of State; and

(b)   in the case of an enforcement appeal, any person on whom a copy of the enforcement notice has been served,

not less than 4 weeks before the date fixed for the holding of the inquiry.

(2) The local planning authority shall give any person who asks, a reasonable opportunity to inspect, and where practicable, take copies of the statement of common ground sent to the Secretary of State.

(3) For the purposes of the previous paragraph an opportunity shall be taken to have been given to a person where the person is notified of—

(a)   publication of the statement of common ground on a website,

(b)   the address of the website,

(c)   the place on the website where the document may be accessed, and how it may be accessed.

Procedure at inquiry

17.—(1) Except as otherwise provided in these Rules, the inspector shall determine the procedure at an inquiry.

(2) At the start of the inquiry the inspector shall identify what are, in his opinion, the main issues to be considered at the inquiry and any matters on which he requires further explanation from the persons entitled or permitted to appear.

(3) Nothing in paragraph (2) shall preclude any person entitled or permitted to appear from referring to issues which they consider relevant to the consideration of the appeal but which were not issues identified by the inspector pursuant to that paragraph.

(4) Unless the inspector otherwise determines, the appellant shall begin and shall have the right of final reply; and the other persons entitled or permitted to appear shall be heard in such order as the inspector may determine.

(5) A person entitled to appear at an inquiry shall be entitled to call evidence and the appellant, the local planning authority and, in the case of an enforcement appeal, any person on whom a copy of the enforcement notice has been served shall be entitled to cross-examine persons giving evidence, but, subject to the foregoing and paragraphs (6) and (7), the calling of evidence and the cross-examination of persons giving evidence shall otherwise be at the discretion of the inspector.

(6) The inspector may refuse to permit the—

(a)   giving or production of evidence;

(b)   cross-examination of persons giving evidence; or

(c)   presentation of any matter,

which he considers to be irrelevant or repetitious; but where he refuses to permit the giving of oral evidence, the person wishing to give the evidence may submit to him any evidence or other matter in writing before the close of the inquiry.

(7) Where a person gives evidence at an inquiry by reading a summary of his proof of evidence in accordance with rule 15(5)—

(a)   the proof of evidence referred to in rule 15(1) shall be treated as tendered in evidence, unless the person required to provide the summary notifies the inspector that he now wishes to rely on the contents of that summary alone; and

(b)   the person whose evidence the proof contains shall then be subject to cross-examination on it to the same extent as if it were evidence he had given orally.

(8) The inspector may direct that facilities shall be made available to any person appearing at an inquiry to take or obtain copies of documentary evidence open to public inspection.

(9) The inspector may—

(a)   require any person appearing or present at an inquiry who, in his opinion, is behaving in a disruptive manner to leave; and

(b)   refuse to permit that person to return; or

(c)   permit him to return only on such conditions as he may specify,

but any such person may submit to him any evidence or other matter in writing before the close of the inquiry.

(10) The inspector may allow any person to alter or add to a statement of case served under rule 6 so far as may be necessary for the purposes of the inquiry; but he shall (if necessary by adjourning the inquiry) give every other person entitled to appear who is appearing at the inquiry an adequate opportunity of considering any fresh matter or document.

(11) The inspector may proceed with an inquiry in the absence of any person entitled to appear at it.

(12) The inspector may take into account any written representation or evidence or other document received by him from any person before an inquiry opens or during the inquiry provided that he discloses it at the inquiry.

(13) The inspector may from time to time adjourn an inquiry and, if the date, time and place of the adjourned inquiry are announced at the inquiry before the adjournment, no further notice shall be required.

(14) Where the Secretary of State expects an inquiry to last for 4 days or more, any person who appears at the inquiry and makes closing submissions, shall before the close of the inquiry, provide the inspector with a copy of their closing submissions in writing.

Site inspections

18.—(1) The inspector may make an unaccompanied inspection of the land before or during an inquiry without giving notice of his intention to the persons entitled to appear at the inquiry.

(2) During an inquiry or after its close, the inspector—

(a)   may inspect the land in the company of the appellant, the local planning authority, any person with an interest in the land and, in the case of an enforcement appeal, any other person on whom a copy of the enforcement notice has been served; and

(b) shall make such an inspection if so requested by the appellant or the local planning authority before or during an inquiry.

(3) In all cases where the inspector intends to make an accompanied site inspection he shall announce during the inquiry the date and time at which he proposes to make it.

(4) The inspector shall not be bound to defer an inspection of the kind referred to in paragraph (2) where any person mentioned in that paragraph is not present at the time appointed.

Procedure after inquiry

19.—(1) Where an assessor has been appointed, he may, after the close of the inquiry make a report in writing to the inspector in respect of the matters on which he was appointed to advise, and where he does so the inspector shall state in his notification of his decision pursuant to rule 20 that such a report was made.

(2) When making his decision the inspector may disregard any written representations or evidence or any other document received after the close of the inquiry.

(3) If, after the close of the inquiry, an inspector proposes to take into consideration any new evidence or any new matter of fact (not being a matter of government policy) which was not raised at the inquiry and which he considers to be material to his decision, he shall not come to a decision without first—

(a) notifying the persons entitled to appear at the inquiry who appeared at it of the matter in question; and

(b) giving them an opportunity of making written representations to him or of asking for the re-opening of the inquiry,

and they shall send such written representations or request to re-open the inquiry to the Secretary of State within 3 weeks of the date of the notification.

(4) An inspector may, as he thinks fit, cause an inquiry to be re-opened, and he shall do so if asked by the appellant or the local planning authority in the circumstances and within the period mentioned in paragraph (3); and where an inquiry is re-opened—

(a) the inspector shall send to the persons entitled to appear at the inquiry who appeared at it a written statement of the matters with respect to which further evidence is invited; and

(b) paragraphs (2) to (7) of rule 9 shall apply as if references to an inquiry were references to a re-opened inquiry.

Notification of decision

20.—(1) The inspector shall, as soon as practicable after reaching his decision, notify his decision on an appeal, and his reasons for it in writing to—

(a)   the appellant and the local planning authority;

(b)   all other persons entitled to appear at the inquiry who did appear; and

(c)   any other person who, having appeared at the inquiry, has asked to be notified of the decision.

(1A) Notification in writing of a decision and reasons shall be taken to have been given to a person for the purposes of this rule where—

(a)   the Secretary of State and the person have agreed that decisions, reasons, and copies of reports required under this rule to be given in writing may instead be accessed by that person on a website;

(b)   the decision and reasons are a decision and reasons to which that agreement applies;

(c)   the Secretary of State has published the decision and reasons on a website;

(d)   the person is notified, in a manner for the time being agreed between him and the Secretary of State, of—

    (i)   the publication of the decision and reasons on a website;

    (ii) the address of the website;

    (iii) the place on the website where the decision and reasons may be accessed, and how they may be accessed.

(2) Any person entitled to be notified of the inspector's decision under paragraph (1) may apply to the Secretary of State in writing for an opportunity to inspect any documents listed in the notification and any report made by an assessor and the Secretary of State shall give him that opportunity.

(2A) For the purposes of the previous paragraph an opportunity shall be taken to have been given to a person where that person is notified of—

(a)   publication of the relevant documents on a website;

(b)   the address of the website;

(c)   the place on the website where the documents may be accessed, and how they may be accessed.

(3) Any application made pursuant to paragraph (2) shall be sent to the Secretary of State within 6 weeks of the date of the decision.

Procedure following remitting of appeal

21.—(1) Where a decision of an inspector on an appeal for which an inquiry has been held is remitted by any court to the Secretary of State for rehearing and redetermination, the Secretary of State—

(a)   shall send to the persons entitled to appear at the inquiry who appeared at it a written statement of the matters on which further representations are invited in order for him to consider the appeal further;

(b)   shall give those persons the opportunity of making written representations to him about those matters or asking for the re-opening of the inquiry; and

(c)   may, as he thinks fit, cause the inquiry to be re-opened (whether by the same or a different inspector) and if he does so paragraphs (2) to (8) of rule 9 shall apply as if the references to an inquiry were references to a re-opened inquiry.

(2) Those persons making representations or asking for the inquiry to be re-opened under paragraph (1)(b) shall send such representations or requests to the Secretary of State within 3 weeks of the date of the written statement sent under paragraph (1)(a).

Allowing further time

22. The Secretary of State may at any time in any particular case allow further time for the taking of any step which is required or enabled to be taken by virtue of these Rules, and references in these Rules to a day by which, or period within which, any step is required or enabled to be taken shall be construed accordingly.

Additional copies

23.—(1) The Secretary of State may at any time before the close of the inquiry request from any person entitled to appear additional copies of the following—

(a)   a statement of case sent in accordance with rule 6;

(b)   a proof of evidence sent in accordance with rule 15;

(c)   any other document or information sent to the Secretary of State before or during an inquiry,

and may specify the time within which such copies should be sent to him.

(2) Any person so requested shall send the copies to the Secretary of State within the period specified.

Service of notices, etc

24. Notices or documents required or authorised to be served, sent or supplied under these Rules may be served, sent or supplied—

(a)   by post; or

(b)   by using electronic communications to serve, send or supply the notice or document (as the case may be) to a person at such address as may for the time being be specified by the person for that purpose.'

Withdrawal of consent to use of electronic communications

24A. Where a person is no longer willing to accept the use of electronic communications for any purpose of these Rules which is capable of being carried out electronically, he shall give notice in writing—

(a)   withdrawing any address notified to the Secretary of State or to a local planning authority for that purpose, or

(b)   revoking any agreement entered into with the Secretary of State or with a local planning authority for that purpose,

and such withdrawal or revocation shall be final and shall take effect on a date specified by the person in the notice but not less than seven days after the date on which the notice is given.

Revocation and savings

25.—(1) Subject to paragraph (2), the Town and Country Planning (Enforcement) (Inquiries Procedure) Rules 1992 ('the 1992 Rules') shall continue to apply to any local inquiry in England held for the purposes of—

(a)   an enforcement appeal; or

(b)   an appeal under section 195 of the Planning Act,

which was made before 23rd December 2002.

(2) Where a decision of an inspector on an appeal to which the 1992 Rules applied is subsequently remitted by any court to the Secretary of State for rehearing and redetermination, the matter shall be redetermined in accordance with these Rules or the Town and Country Planning (Enforcement) (Inquiries Procedure) (England) Rules 2002.

The Town and Country Planning (Enforcement) (Inquiries Procedure) (England) Rules 2002 (2002/2686)

The Lord Chancellor, in exercise of the powers conferred upon him by section 9 of the Tribunals and Inquiries Act 1992 and of all other powers enabling him in that behalf, and after consultation with the Council on Tribunals, hereby makes the following Rules:

Citation, commencement and extent

1.—(1) These Rules may be cited as the Town and Country Planning (Enforcement) (Inquiries Procedure) (England) Rules 2002 and shall come into force on 23rd December 2002.

(2) These Rules extend to England only.

Interpretation

2. —(1) In these Rules—

'assessor' means a person appointed by the Secretary of State to sit with an inspector at an inquiry or re-opened inquiry to advise the inspector on such matters arising as the Secretary of State may specify;

'certificate of lawful use or development' means a certificate under section 191 or 192 of the Planning Act;

'document' includes a photograph, map or plan;

'enforcement appeal' means an appeal against an enforcement notice;

'enforcement notice' means a notice under section 172 of the Planning Act or under section 38 of the Listed Buildings Act;

'inquiry' means a local inquiry to which these Rules apply;

'inspector' means a person appointed by the Secretary of State to hold the relevant inquiry or re-opened inquiry;

'land' means the land or building to which an inquiry relates;

'Listed Buildings Act' means the Planning (Listed Buildings and Conservation Areas) Act 1990;

'local planning authority' means in relation to—

(a) an enforcement appeal, the body who issued the relevant enforcement notice;

(b) an appeal against the refusal or non-determination of an application for a certificate of lawful use or development, the body to whom the application was made;

'outline statement' means a written statement of the principal submissions which a person proposes to put forward at an inquiry;

'Planning Act' means the Town and Country Planning Act 1990;

'pre-inquiry meeting' means a meeting held before an inquiry to consider what may be done with a view to securing that the inquiry is conducted efficiently and expeditiously, and where two or more such meetings are held references to the conclusion of a pre-inquiry meeting are references to the conclusion of the final meeting;

'questionnaire' means a document in the form supplied by the Secretary of State to local planning authorities for the purpose of proceedings under these Rules ', and for this purpose a form is taken to be supplied where the Secretary of State has published it on a website and has notified the local planning authority of—

(i) publication of the form on the website,

(ii) the address of the website, and

(iii) the place on the website where the form may be accessed, and how it may be accessed;

'relevant notice' means the Secretary of State's written notice under rule 4(1) informing the appellant and the local planning authority that an inquiry is to be held;

'starting date' means the date of the—

(a) Secretary of State's written notice to the appellant and the local planning authority that he has received all the documents required to enable him to entertain the appeal pursuant to regulation 10 of the Town and Country Planning (Enforcement Notices and Appeals) (England) Regulations 2002; or

(b) relevant notice,

whichever is the later;

'statement of case' means, and is comprised of, a written statement which contains full particulars of the case which a person proposes to put forward at an inquiry, and a list of any documents which that person intends to refer to or put in evidence;

'statement of common ground' means a written statement prepared jointly by the local planning authority and the appellant, which contains agreed factual information about the development, breach of conditions or works which are the subject of the appeal.

(2) In these Rules, and in relation to the use of electronic communications for any purpose of these Rules which is capable of being carried out electronically—

(a) the expression 'address' includes any number or address used for the purposes of such communications, except that where these Rules impose an obligation on any person to provide a name and address to any other person, the obligation shall not be fulfilled unless the person on whom it is imposed provides a postal address;

(b) references to statements, notices, summaries, applications, or other documents, or to copies of such documents, include references to such documents or copies of them in electronic form.

(3) Paragraphs (4) to (8) apply where an electronic communication is used by a person for the purpose of fulfilling any requirement in these Rules that an application, notice, or other document should be made, sent or given to any other person ('the recipient').

(4) The requirement shall be taken to be fulfilled where the application, notice, or other document or (in the case of an agreement) the text concluding the agreement which is transmitted by means of the electronic communication is—

(a) capable of being accessed by the recipient,

(b) legible in all material respects, and

(c) sufficiently permanent to be used for subsequent reference.

(5) In paragraph (4), 'legible in all material respects' means that the information contained in the notice or document is available to the recipient to no lesser extent than it would be if sent or given by means of a notice or document in printed form.

(6) Where the electronic communication is received by the recipient outside the recipient's business hours, it shall be taken to have been received on the next working day; and for this purpose 'working day' means a day which is not a Saturday, Sunday, Bank Holiday or other public holiday.

(7) A requirement in these Rules that any notice or other document should be in writing is fulfilled where the document transmitted meets the criteria in paragraph (4), and 'written' and cognate expressions are to be construed accordingly.

(8) A requirement in these Rules to send more than one copy of a statement or other document may be complied with by sending one copy only of the statement or document in question.

Application of the Rules

3.—(1) These Rules apply in relation to any local inquiry caused by the Secretary of State to be held in England before he determines an appeal made on or after 23rd December 2002 under—

(a) section 174 of the Planning Act (appeal against enforcement notice);

(b) section 195 of the Planning Act (appeal against refusal or non-determination of an application for a certificate of lawful use or development);

(c) section 39 of the Listed Buildings Act (appeal against listed building enforcement notice) or under that section as applied by section 74(3) of that Act (appeal against conservation area enforcement notice), but do not apply to any local inquiry by reason of the application of any provision mentioned in this rule by or under any other enactment.

(2) Where these Rules apply in relation to an appeal which at some time fell to be disposed of in accordance with—

(a)   the Town and Country Planning (Enforcement) (Determination by Inspectors) (Inquiries Procedure) (England) Rules 2002; or

(b)   the Town and Country Planning (Enforcement) (Inquiries Procedure) Rules 1992,

any step taken or thing done under those Rules which could have been done under any corresponding provision of these Rules shall have effect as if it had been taken or done under that corresponding provision.

Preliminary information to be supplied by local planning authority

4.—(1) The Secretary of State shall, as soon as practicable after it is determined to hold an inquiry under these Rules, inform the appellant and the local planning authority in writing that an inquiry is to be held.

(2) The local planning authority shall within 2 weeks of the starting date—

(a)   send to the Secretary of State and the appellant a completed questionnaire and a copy of each of the documents referred to in it;

(b)   in the case of an enforcement appeal, notify any—

(i)   person on whom a copy of the enforcement notice has been served;

(ii) occupier of property in the locality in which the land to which the enforcement notice relates is situated; and

(iii) other person who in the opinion of the local planning authority is affected by the breach of planning control or contravention of listed building or conservation area control which is alleged in the enforcement notice,

that an appeal has been made and of the address to which and of the period within which they may make representations to the Secretary of State.

Notification of name of inspector

5.—(1) The Secretary of State shall, subject to paragraph (2), notify the name of the inspector to every person entitled to appear at the inquiry.

(2) Where the Secretary of State appoints another inspector instead of the person previously appointed and it is not practicable to notify the new appointment before the inquiry is held, the inspector holding the inquiry shall, at its commencement, announce his name and the fact of his appointment.

Procedure where pre-inquiry meeting is to be held

6.—(1) The Secretary of State shall hold a pre-inquiry meeting—

(a) if he expects an inquiry to last for 4 days or more, unless he considers it unnecessary;

(b) for shorter inquiries, if it appears to him necessary.

(2) Where the Secretary of State decides to hold a pre-inquiry meeting the following provisions shall apply—

(a) the Secretary of State shall send to the appellant and the local planning authority—

    (i) notice of his intention to hold a pre-inquiry meeting; and

    (ii) a statement of the matters about which he particularly wishes to be informed for the purposes of his consideration of the appeal in question;

(b) the local planning authority shall publish in a newspaper circulating in the locality in which the land is situated a notice of the Secretary of State's intention to hold a pre-inquiry meeting and of the statement sent in accordance with paragraph (2)(a)(ii) above; and

(c) the appellant and the local planning authority shall send 2 copies of their outline statement to the Secretary of State within 8 weeks of the starting date.

(3) The Secretary of State shall, as soon as practicable after receipt, send a copy of the local planning authority's outline statement to the appellant and a copy of the appellant's outline statement to the local planning authority.

(4) The Secretary of State may in writing require any other person who has notified him of an intention or a wish to appear at the inquiry to send an outline statement to him, the appellant and the local planning authority.

(5) A person required to send an outline statement under paragraph (4) shall send it to the Secretary of State, the appellant and the local planning authority within 4 weeks of the date on which the Secretary of State so requires.

(6) The pre-inquiry meeting (or where there is more than one, the first pre-inquiry meeting) shall be held within 16 weeks of the starting date.

(7) The Secretary of State shall give not less than 3 weeks written notice of the pre-inquiry meeting to—

(a) the appellant;

(b) the local planning authority;

(c) any person known at the date of the notice to be entitled to appear at the inquiry; and

(d) any other person whose presence at the pre-inquiry meeting appears to him to be desirable.

(8) Rule 11(6) shall apply to a pre-inquiry meeting as it does to the holding of an inquiry.

(9) The inspector—

(a)   shall preside at the pre-inquiry meeting;

(b)   shall determine the matters to be discussed and the procedure to be followed;

(c)   may require any person present at the pre-inquiry meeting who, in his opinion, is behaving in a disruptive manner to leave; and

(d)   may refuse to permit that person to return to or attend any further pre-inquiry meeting, or may permit him to return or attend only on such conditions as he may specify.

(10) Where a pre-inquiry meeting has been held pursuant to paragraph (1), the inspector may hold a further pre-inquiry meeting and he shall arrange for such notice to be given of a further pre-inquiry meeting as appears to him necessary; and paragraph (9) shall apply to such a pre-inquiry meeting.

(11) If the Secretary of State requests any further information from the appellant or the local planning authority at the pre-inquiry meeting, they shall send—

(a)   2 copies of it to him; and

(b)   in the case of an enforcement appeal, a copy to any person on whom a copy of the enforcement notice has been served,

within 4 weeks of the conclusion of the pre-inquiry meeting.

(12) Where the Secretary of State receives further information pursuant to paragraph (11) he shall, as soon as practicable after receipt—

(a)   send a copy of such further information received from the appellant to the local planning authority; and

(b)   send a copy of such further information received from the local planning authority to the appellant.

Statement of matters

7. The Secretary of State may, before an inquiry is held, serve on the local planning authority, the appellant, any person required to serve a statement of case pursuant to rule 8(6) and, in the case of an enforcement appeal, any person on whom a copy of the enforcement notice has been served, a written statement of the matters about which he particularly wishes to be informed for the purposes of his consideration of the appeal.

Service of statements of case, etc

8.—(1) The local planning authority shall—

(a)   within 6 weeks of the starting date, or

(b)   where a pre-inquiry meeting is held pursuant to rule 6, within 4 weeks of the conclusion of that pre-inquiry meeting,

serve 2 copies of their statement of case on the Secretary of State and, in the case of an enforcement appeal, a copy on any person on whom a copy of the enforcement notice has been served.

(2) The local planning authority shall include in their statement of case details of the time and place where the opportunity will be given to inspect and take copies described in paragraph (13) (and including, in any case in which the local planning authority rely on paragraph (13A), the details mentioned in that paragraph).

(3) The appellant shall—

(a)　in the case of an appeal where no pre-inquiry meeting is held, within 6 weeks of the starting date, or

(b)　in any case where a pre-inquiry meeting is held, within 4 weeks of the conclusion of that pre-inquiry meeting,

serve 2 copies of his statement of case on the Secretary of State and, in the case of an enforcement appeal, a copy on any person on whom a copy of the enforcement notice has been served.

(4) The Secretary of State shall, as soon as practicable after receipt, send a copy of the local planning authority's statement of case to the appellant and a copy of the appellant's statement of case to the local planning authority.

(5) The appellant and the local planning authority may in writing each require the other to send them a copy of any document, or the relevant part of any document, referred to in the list of documents comprised in that party's statement of case; and any such document, or relevant part, shall be sent, as soon as practicable, to the party who required it.

(6) The Secretary of State may in writing require any other person, who has notified him of an intention or a wish to appear at the inquiry, to serve—

(a)　3 copies of their statement of case on him within 4 weeks of being so required; and

(b)　in the case of an enforcement appeal, simultaneously, a copy of their statement of case on any person specified by the Secretary of State,

and the Secretary of State shall, as soon as practicable after receipt, send a copy of each such statement of case to the local planning authority and to the appellant.

(7) The Secretary of State shall, as soon as practicable—

(a)　send to any person from whom he requires a statement of case in accordance with paragraph (6) a copy of the statements of case of the appellant and the local planning authority; and

(b)　inform that person of the name and address of every person to whom his statement of case is required to be sent.

(8) The Secretary of State or the inspector may in writing require any person, who has served on him a statement of case in accordance with this rule, to provide such further information about the matters contained in the statement of case as he may specify and may specify the time within which the information shall be sent to him.

(9) A local planning authority or appellant required to provide further information, shall send within the time specified—

(a)   2 copies of that information in writing to the Secretary of State or, as the case may be, the inspector; and

(b)   in the case of an enforcement appeal, a copy to any person on whom a copy of the enforcement notice has been served,

and the Secretary of State or, as the case may be, the inspector, shall, as soon as practicable after receipt, send a copy of the further information received from the local planning authority to the appellant and a copy of the further information received from the appellant to the local planning authority.

(10) Any other person required to provide further information shall send within the time specified—

(a)   3 copies of that information in writing to the Secretary of State or, as the case may be, the inspector; and

(b)   in the case of an enforcement appeal, a copy to any person on whom a copy of the enforcement notice has been served,

and the Secretary of State or, as the case may be, the inspector, shall, as soon as practicable after receipt, send a copy of the further information to the local planning authority and the appellant.

(11) Any person other than the appellant who serves a statement of case on the Secretary of State shall send with it a copy of—

(a)   any document; or

(b)   the relevant part of any document,

referred to in the list comprised in that statement, unless a copy of the document or part of the document in question is already available for inspection pursuant to paragraph (13).

(12) Unless he has already done so, the Secretary of State shall, within 12 weeks of the starting date, send a written statement of the matters referred to in rule 6(2)(a) (ii) to—

(a)   the appellant;

(b)   the local planning authority;

(c)   in the case of an enforcement appeal, any person on whom a copy of the enforcement notice has been served; and

(d)   any person from whom he has required a statement of case.

(13) The local planning authority shall give any person who so requests a reasonable opportunity to inspect and, where practicable, take copies of—

(a)   any statement of case, written comments, further information or other document a copy of which has been sent to the local planning authority in accordance with this rule; and

(b)   the local planning authority's completed questionnaire and statement of case together with a copy of any document, or of the relevant part of any document, referred to in the list comprised in that statement, and any written comments, information or other documents sent by the local planning authority pursuant to this rule.

(13A) For the purposes of the previous paragraph an opportunity shall be taken to have been given to a person where the person is notified of—

(a)   publication on a website of the documents mentioned in that paragraph;

(b)   the address of the website;

(c)   the place on the website where the documents may be accessed, and how they may be accessed.

(14) If the local planning authority or the appellant wish to comment on another person's statement of case, they shall send within 9 weeks of the starting date—

(a)   2 copies of their written comments to the Secretary of State; and

(b)   in the case of an enforcement appeal, a copy of their written comments to any person on whom a copy of the enforcement notice has been served,

and the Secretary of State shall, as soon as practicable after receipt, send a copy of the written comments received from the appellant to the local planning authority and a copy of the written comments received from the local planning authority to the appellant.

(15) Any person, other than the local planning authority or the appellant, who serves a statement of case on the Secretary of State under this rule and who wishes to comment on another person's statement of case, shall send, not less than 4 weeks before the date fixed for the holding of the inquiry—

(a)   3 copies of their written comments to the Secretary of State; and

(b)   in the case of an enforcement appeal, a copy of their written comments to any person on whom a copy of the enforcement notice has been served,

and the Secretary of State shall, as soon as practicable after receipt, send a copy of the written comments to the local planning authority and to the appellant.

(16) The Secretary of State shall, as soon as practicable after receipt, send to the inspector any statement of case, document or further information or written comments sent to him in accordance with this rule and sent to him within the relevant period, if any, specified in this rule.

Further power of inspector to hold pre-inquiry meetings

9.—(1) Where no pre-inquiry meeting is held pursuant to rule 6, an inspector may hold one if he thinks it necessary.

(2) An inspector shall give not less than 2 weeks written notice of a pre-inquiry meeting he proposes to hold under paragraph (1) to—

(a)   the appellant;

(b)   the local planning authority;

(c)　any person known at the date of the notice to be entitled to appear at the inquiry; and

(d)　any other person whose presence at the pre-inquiry meeting appears to him to be desirable.

(3) Rule 11(6) shall apply to a pre-inquiry meeting held under this rule.

Inquiry timetable

10.—(1) The inspector shall prepare a timetable for the proceedings at, or at part of, an inquiry where—

(a)　a pre-inquiry meeting is held; or

(b)　it appears to the Secretary of State likely that an inquiry will last for 4 days or more.

(2) In respect of shorter inquiries or those where no pre-inquiry meeting is held the inspector may at any time prepare a timetable for the proceedings at, or at part of, an inquiry.

(3) The inspector may, at any time, vary the timetable prepared under the preceding paragraphs.

(4) The inspector may specify in a timetable prepared under this rule a date by which any proof of evidence and summary sent in accordance with rule 16(1) shall be sent to the Secretary of State.

Date and notification of inquiry

11.—(1) The date fixed by the Secretary of State for the holding of an inquiry shall be, unless he considers such a date impracticable, not later than—

(a)　subject to paragraph (b), 22 weeks after the starting date; or

(b)　in a case where a pre-inquiry meeting is held, 8 weeks after the conclusion of that meeting.

(2) Where the Secretary of State considers it impracticable to fix a date in accordance with paragraph (1), the date fixed shall be the earliest date after the end of the relevant period mentioned in that paragraph which he considers to be practicable.

(3) Unless the Secretary of State agrees a lesser period of notice with the appellant and the local planning authority, he shall give not less than 4 weeks written notice of the date, time and place fixed by him for the holding of an inquiry to every person entitled to appear at the inquiry.

(3A) A written notice shall be taken to have been given by the Secretary of State for the purposes of paragraph (3) where he and any person entitled to appear at the inquiry have agreed that notice of the matters mentioned in that paragraph may instead be accessed by that person via a website, and—

(a)　the notice is a notice to which that agreement applies;

(b)   the Secretary of State has published that notice on the website;

(c)   not less than 4 weeks before the date fixed by the Secretary of State for the holding of the inquiry, the person is notified of—

(i)   the publication of the notice on a website,

(ii) the address of the website, and

(iii) the place on the website where the notice may be accessed, and how it may be accessed.

(4) The Secretary of State may vary the date fixed for the holding of an inquiry, whether or not the date as varied is within the relevant period mentioned in paragraph (1); and paragraph (3) shall apply to a variation of the date as it applied to the date originally fixed.

(5) The Secretary of State may vary the time or place for the holding of an inquiry and shall give such notice as appears to him to be reasonable.

(6) The Secretary of State may in writing require the local planning authority to take one or more of the following steps—

(a)   not less than 2 weeks before the date fixed for the holding of an inquiry, to publish a notice of the inquiry in one or more newspapers circulating in the locality in which the land is situated;

(b)   to send a notice of the inquiry to such persons or classes of persons as he may specify, within such period as he may specify; or

(c)   to post a notice of the inquiry in a conspicuous place near to the land, within such period as he may specify.

(7) Where the land is under the control of the appellant, he shall—

(a)   if so required in writing by the Secretary of State, affix a notice of the inquiry firmly to the land or to some object on or near the land, in such manner as to be readily visible to and legible by members of the public; and

(b)   not remove the notice, or cause or permit it to be removed, for such period before the inquiry as the Secretary of State may specify.

(8) Every notice of inquiry published, sent or posted pursuant to paragraph (6), or affixed pursuant to paragraph (7), shall contain—

(a)   a clear statement of the date, time and place of the inquiry and of the powers enabling the Secretary of State to determine the appeal in question;

(b)   a written description of the land sufficient to identify approximately its location;

(c)   a brief description of the subject matter of the appeal; and

(d)   details of where and when copies of the local planning authority's completed questionnaire and any document sent by and copied to the authority pursuant to rule 8 may be inspected.

Notification of appointment of assessor

12. Where the Secretary of State appoints an assessor he shall notify every person entitled to appear at the inquiry of the name of the assessor and of the matters on which he is to advise the inspector.

Appearances at inquiry

13.—(1) The persons entitled to appear at the inquiry are—

(a)   the appellant;

(b)   the local planning authority;

(c)   any of the following bodies if the land is situated in their area and they are not the local planning authority—

   (i)   a county or a district council;

   (ii)   an enterprise zone authority designated under Schedule 32 to the Local Government, Planning and Land Act 1980;

   (iii) the Broads Authority, within the meaning of the Norfolk and Suffolk Broads Act 1988;

   (iv)   a housing action trust specified in an order made under section 67(1) of the Housing Act 1988;

(d)   where the land is in an area previously designated as a new town, the Homes and Communities Agency;

(e)   in the case of an enforcement appeal, any person on whom a copy of the enforcement notice has been served;

(f)   in the case of an appeal under section 195 of the Planning Act, any person having an interest in the land;

(g)   the Historic Buildings and Monuments Commission for England where—

   (i)   the inquiry relates to an enforcement notice under section 38 of the Listed Buildings Act;

   (ii)   the listed building is in Greater London; and

   (iii) if an application for listed building consent had been made for the works set out in the enforcement notice, the Commission would have been notified of the application under a direction given under section 15(5) of the Listed Buildings Act;

(h)   any other person who has served a statement of case in accordance with rule 8(6) or who has sent an outline statement in accordance with rule 6(4).

(2) Nothing in paragraph (1) shall prevent the inspector from permitting any other person to appear at an inquiry and such permission shall not be unreasonably withheld.

(3) Any person entitled or permitted to appear may do so on his own behalf or be represented by any other person.

Appendix 6

Information to be provided by all parties

14. Any person entitled or permitted to appear at the inquiry, who proposes to give, or call another person to give evidence at the inquiry, shall send in writing to the Secretary of State no later than 4 weeks before the inquiry—

(a) an estimate of the time required to present all their evidence; and

(b) the number of witnesses that they intend to call to give evidence.

Representatives of government departments at inquiry

15.—(1) Where the Secretary of State or any other Minister of the Crown or any government department has expressed in writing to the local planning authority a view on an appeal and the authority refer to that view in a statement prepared pursuant to rule 8(1), the appellant may, not later than 4 weeks before the date of an inquiry, apply in writing to the Secretary of State for a representative of the Secretary of State or of the other Minister or department concerned to be made available at the inquiry.

(2) Where an application is made in accordance with paragraph (1), the Secretary of State shall make a representative available to attend the inquiry or, as the case may be, send the application to the other Minister or department concerned, who shall make a representative available to attend the inquiry.

(3) A person attending an inquiry as a representative pursuant to this rule shall state the reasons for the expressed view and shall give evidence and be subject to cross-examination to the same extent as any other witness.

(4) Nothing in paragraph (3) shall require a representative of a Minister or government department to answer any question which, in the opinion of the inspector, is directed to the merits of government policy.

Proofs of evidence

16.—(1) Any person entitled to appear at an inquiry who proposes to give, or to call another person to give, evidence at the inquiry by reading a proof of evidence, shall—

(a) subject to paragraph (2), send 2 copies, in the case of the local planning authority and the appellant, or 3 copies in the case of any other person, of the proof of evidence together with a written summary, to the Secretary of State; and

(b) in the case of an enforcement appeal, simultaneously send copies of these to any person on whom a copy of the enforcement notice has been served,

and the Secretary of State shall, as soon as practicable after receipt, send a copy of each proof of evidence together with any summary to the local planning authority and the appellant.

(2) No written summary shall be required where the proof of evidence proposed to be read contains no more than 1500 words.

(3) The proof of evidence and any summary shall be sent to the Secretary of State no later than—

(a)   4 weeks before the date fixed for the holding of the inquiry, or

(b)   where a timetable has been prepared pursuant to rule 10 which specifies a date by which the proof of evidence and any summary shall be sent to the Secretary of State, that date.

(4) The Secretary of State shall send to the inspector, as soon as practicable after receipt, any proof of evidence together with any summary sent to him pursuant to this rule within the relevant period, specified in this rule.

(5) Where a written summary is provided in accordance with paragraph (1), only that summary shall be read at the inquiry, unless the inspector permits or requires otherwise.

(6) Any person, required by this rule to send copies of a proof of evidence to the Secretary of State, or any other person, shall send with them the same number of copies of the whole, or the relevant part, of any document referred to in the proof of evidence, unless a copy of the document or part of the document in question is already available for inspection pursuant to rule 8(13).

(7) The local planning authority shall give any person who so requests a reasonable opportunity to inspect and, where practicable, take copies of any document sent to or by them in accordance with this rule.

(8) For the purposes of the previous paragraph an opportunity is to be taken to have been given to a person where the person is notified of—

(a)   publication of the relevant document on a website,

(b)   the address of the website,

(c)   the place on the website where the document may be accessed, and how it may be accessed.

Statement of common ground

17.—(1) The local planning authority and the appellant shall together prepare an agreed statement of common ground and shall send it to—

(a)   the Secretary of State; and

(b)   in the case of an enforcement appeal, any person on whom a copy of the enforcement notice has been served,

not less than 4 weeks before the date fixed for the holding of the inquiry.

(2) The local planning authority shall give any person who asks, a reasonable opportunity to inspect, and where practicable, take copies of the statement of common ground sent to the Secretary of State.

(3) For the purposes of the previous paragraph an opportunity is to be taken to have been given to a person where the person is notified of—

(a)   publication of the statement of common ground on a website,

(b)   the address of the website,

(c)   the place on the website where the document may be accessed, and how it may be accessed.

Procedure at inquiry

18.—(1) Except as otherwise provided in these Rules, the inspector shall determine the procedure at an inquiry.

(2) At the start of the inquiry the inspector shall identify what are, in his opinion, the main issues to be considered at the inquiry and any matters on which he requires further explanation from the persons entitled or permitted to appear.

(3) Nothing in paragraph (2) shall preclude any person entitled or permitted to appear from referring to issues which they consider relevant to the consideration of the appeal but which were not issues identified by the inspector pursuant to that paragraph.

(4) Unless the inspector otherwise determines, the appellant shall begin and shall have the right of final reply; and the other persons entitled or permitted to appear shall be heard in such order as the inspector may determine.

(5) A person entitled to appear at an inquiry shall be entitled to call evidence and the appellant, the local planning authority and, in the case of an enforcement appeal, any person on whom a copy of the enforcement notice has been served shall be entitled to cross-examine persons giving evidence, but, subject to the foregoing and paragraphs (6) and (7), the calling of evidence and the cross-examination of persons giving evidence shall otherwise be at the discretion of the inspector.

(6) The inspector may refuse to permit the—

(a)   giving or production of evidence;

(b)   cross-examination of persons giving evidence; or

(c)   presentation of any matter,

which he considers to be irrelevant or repetitious; but where he refuses to permit the giving of oral evidence, the person wishing to give the evidence may submit to him any evidence or other matter in writing before the close of the inquiry.

(7) Where a person gives evidence at an inquiry by reading a summary of his proof of evidence in accordance with rule 16(5)—

(a)   the proof of evidence referred to in rule 16(1) shall then be treated as tendered in evidence, unless the person required to provide the summary notifies the inspector that he now wishes to rely on the contents of that summary alone; and

(b)   the person whose evidence the proof contains shall be subject to cross-examination on it to the same extent as if it were evidence he had given orally.

(8) The inspector may direct that facilities shall be made available to any person appearing at an inquiry to take or obtain copies of documentary evidence open to public inspection.

(9) The inspector may—

(a)   require any person appearing or present at an inquiry who, in his opinion, is behaving in a disruptive manner to leave; and

(b)   refuse to permit that person to return; or

(c)   permit him to return only on such conditions as he may specify,

but any such person may submit to him any evidence or other matter in writing before the close of the inquiry.

(10) The inspector may allow any person to alter or add to a statement of case served under rule 8 so far as may be necessary for the purposes of the inquiry; but he shall (if necessary by adjourning the inquiry) give every other person entitled to appear who is appearing at the inquiry an adequate opportunity of considering any fresh matter or document.

(11) The inspector may proceed with an inquiry in the absence of any person entitled to appear at it.

(12) The inspector may take into account any written representation or evidence or other document received by him from any person before an inquiry opens or during the inquiry provided that he discloses it at the inquiry.

(13) The inspector may from time to time adjourn an inquiry and, if the date, time and place of the adjourned inquiry are announced at the inquiry before the adjournment, no further notice shall be required.

(14) Where the Secretary of State expects the inquiry to last for 4 days or more, any person who appears at the inquiry and makes closing submissions, shall before the close of the inquiry, provide the inspector with a copy of their closing submissions in writing.

Site inspections

19.—(1) The inspector may make an unaccompanied inspection of the land before or during an inquiry without giving notice of his intention to the persons entitled to appear at the inquiry.

(2) During an inquiry or after its close, the inspector—

(a)   may inspect the land in the company of the appellant, the local planning authority, any person with an interest in the land and, in the case of an enforcement appeal, any person on whom a copy of the enforcement notice has been served; and

(b)   shall make such an inspection if so requested by the appellant or the local planning authority before or during an inquiry.

(3) In all cases where the inspector intends to make an accompanied site inspection he shall announce during the inquiry the date and time at which he proposes to make it.

(4) The inspector shall not be bound to defer an inspection of the kind referred to in paragraph (2) where any person mentioned in that paragraph is not present at the time appointed.

Procedure after inquiry

20.—(1) After the close of an inquiry, the inspector shall make a report in writing to the Secretary of State which shall include his conclusions and his recommendations or his reasons for not making any recommendations.

(2) Where an assessor has been appointed, he may, after the close of the inquiry, make a report in writing to the inspector in respect of the matters on which he was appointed to advise.

(3) Where an assessor makes a report in accordance with paragraph (2), the inspector shall append it to his own report and shall state in his own report how far he agrees or disagrees with the assessor's report and, where he disagrees with the assessor, his reasons for that disagreement.

(4) When making his decision the Secretary of State may disregard any written representations, evidence or any other document received after the close of the inquiry.

(5) If, after the close of an inquiry, the Secretary of State—

(a)   differs from the inspector on any matter of fact mentioned in, or appearing to him to be material to, a conclusion reached by the inspector; or

(b)   takes into consideration any new evidence or new matter of fact (not being a matter of government policy),

and is for that reason disposed to disagree with a recommendation made by the inspector, he shall not come to a decision which is at variance with that recommendation without first notifying the persons entitled to appear at the inquiry who appeared at it of his disagreement and the reasons for it.

(6) Any person notified under paragraph (5) shall be given the opportunity to make written representations to the Secretary of State or (if he has taken into consideration any new evidence or new matter of fact, not being a matter of government policy) to ask for the re-opening of the inquiry.

(7) Those persons making written representations or requesting the inquiry to be re-opened under paragraph (6) shall send such representations or requests to the Secretary of State within 3 weeks of the date of the Secretary of State's notification under that paragraph.

(8) The Secretary of State may, as he thinks fit, cause an inquiry to be re-opened, and he shall do so if asked by the appellant or the local planning authority in the

circumstances mentioned in paragraph (6) and within the period mentioned in paragraph (7).

(9) Where an inquiry is re-opened under this rule (whether by the same or a different inspector)—

(a) the Secretary of State shall send to the persons entitled to appear at the inquiry who appeared at it a written statement of the matters on which further evidence is invited; and

(b) paragraph (3) to (8) of rule 11 shall apply as if references to an inquiry were references to a re-opened inquiry.

Notification of decision

21.—(1) The Secretary of State shall, as soon as practicable after reaching his decision, notify his decision on an appeal, and his reasons for it in writing to—

(a) the appellant and the local planning authority;

(b) all other persons entitled to appear at the inquiry who did appear; and

(c) any other person who, having appeared at the inquiry, has asked to be notified of the decision.

(1A) Notification of a decision and reasons is to be taken to have been given to a person for the purposes of this rule where—

(a) the Secretary of State and the person have agreed that decisions and reasons required under this rule to be given in writing may instead be accessed by that person on a website;

(b) the decision and reasons are a decision and reasons to which that agreement applies;

(c) the Secretary of State has published the decision and reasons on a website;

(d) the person is notified, in a manner for the time being agreed between him and the Secretary of State, of—

(i) the publication of the decision and reasons on a website;

(ii) the address of the website;

(iii) the place on the website where the decision and reasons may be accessed, and how they may be accessed.

(2) Where a copy of the inspector's report is not sent with the notification of the decision or published on a website in accordance with paragraph (1A), the notification shall be accompanied by a statement of his conclusions and of any recommendations made by him, and if a person entitled to be notified of the decision has not received a copy of that report, he shall be supplied with a copy of it on written application to the Secretary of State.

(3) In this rule 'report' includes any assessor's report appended to the inspector's report but does not include any other documents so appended; but any person who has received a copy of the report may apply to the Secretary of State in writing,

within 6 weeks of the date of the Secretary of State's decision, for an opportunity of inspecting any such documents and the Secretary of State shall give him that opportunity.

(3A) For the purposes of the previous paragraph an opportunity is to be taken to have been afforded to a person where that person is notified of—

(a)   publication of the relevant documents on a website;

(b)   the address of the website;

(c)   the place on the website where the documents may be accessed, and how they may be accessed.

(4) Any person applying to the Secretary of State under paragraph (2) shall send his application to the Secretary of State within 4 weeks of the Secretary of State's determination.

Procedure following remitting of appeal

22.—(1) Where an appeal in respect of which an inquiry has been held is remitted by any court to the Secretary of State for rehearing and redetermination, the Secretary of State—

(a)   shall send to the persons entitled to appear at the inquiry who appeared at it a written statement of the matters on which further representations are invited in order for him to consider the appeal further;

(b)   shall give those persons the opportunity of making written representations to him about those matters or asking for the re-opening of the inquiry; and

(c)   may, as he thinks fit, cause the inquiry to be re-opened (whether by the same or a different inspector) and if he does so paragraphs (3) to (8) of rule 11 shall apply as if the references to an inquiry were references to a re-opened inquiry.

(2) Those persons making representations or asking for the inquiry to be re-opened under paragraph (1)(b) shall send such representations or requests to the Secretary of State within 3 weeks of the date of the written statement sent under paragraph (1)(a).

Allowing further time

23. The Secretary of State may at any time in any particular case allow further time for the taking of any step which is required or enabled to be taken by virtue of these Rules, and references in these Rules to a day by which, or period within which, any step is required or enabled to be taken shall be construed accordingly.

Additional copies

24.—(1) The Secretary of State may at any time before the close of the inquiry request from any person entitled to appear additional copies of the following—

(a)   an outline statement sent in accordance with rule 6;

(b)   a statement of case or comments sent in accordance with rule 8;

(c)   a proof of evidence sent in accordance with rule 16;

(d)   any other document or information sent to the Secretary of State before or during an inquiry,

and may specify the time within which such copies should be sent to him.

(2) Any person so requested shall send the copies to the Secretary of State within the period specified.

Service of notices, etc

25. Notices or documents required or authorised to be served, sent or supplied under these Rules may be served, sent or supplied—

(a)   by post; or

(b)   by using electronic communications to serve, send or supply the notice or document (as the case may be) to a person at such address as may for the time being be specified by the person for that purpose.

Withdrawal of consent to use of electronic communications

25A. Where a person is no longer willing to accept the use of electronic communications for any purpose of these Rules which is capable of being effected electronically, he shall give notice in writing—

(a)   withdrawing any address notified to the Secretary of State or to a local planning authority for that purpose, or

(b)   revoking any agreement entered into with the Secretary of State or with a local planning authority for that purpose,

and such withdrawal or revocation shall be final and shall take effect on a date specified by the person in the notice but not less than seven days after the date on which the notice is given.

Modifications where national security direction given

25B. The modifications set out in the Schedule shall have effect where a direction is given by the Secretary of State under—

(a)   section 321(3) of the Planning Act (planning inquiries to be held in public subject to certain exceptions); or

(b)   paragraph 6(6) of Schedule 3 to the Listed Buildings Act (determination of certain appeals by person appointed by the Secretary of State).

Revocation, saving and transitional provisions

26.—(1) Subject to paragraphs (2), (3) and rule 25 of the Town and Country Planning (Enforcement) (Determination by Inspectors) (Inquiries Procedure) (England) Rules 2002, the Town and Country Planning (Enforcement) (Inquiries Procedure) Rules 1992 ('the 1992 Rules') are hereby revoked in relation to England.

(2) The 1992 Rules shall continue to apply to any local inquiry held for the purposes of—

(a)   an enforcement appeal; or

(b)   an appeal under section 195 of the Planning Act,

made before 23rd December 2002.

(3) Where an appeal to which the 1992 Rules applied is subsequently remitted by any court to the Secretary of State for rehearing and redetermination, the matter shall be redetermined in accordance with these Rules.

SCHEDULE

MODIFICATIONS WHERE NATIONAL SECURITY DIRECTION GIVEN

Interpretation

1. In rule 2(1)—

(a)   before the definition of "assessor" insert—

   "'appointed representative" means a person appointed under—

   (a) section 321(5) or (6) of the Planning Act; or

   (b) paragraph 6(6) of Schedule 3 to the Listed Buildings Act;';

(b)   after the definition of "certificate of lawful use or development" insert—

   "'closed evidence" means evidence which is subject to a security direction;';

(c)   after the definition of 'relevant notice' insert—

   "'security direction" means a direction given by the Secretary of State under—

   (a) section 321(3) of the Planning Act (matters related to national security); or

   (b) paragraph 6(6) of Schedule 3 to the Listed Buildings Act (matters related to national security);'; and

(d)   in the definition of "statement of common ground" after "local planning authority" insert ", or appointed representative, as the case may be,".

Procedure where pre-inquiry meeting is to be held

2. In rule 6—

(a)   for paragraph (3) substitute—

   '(3)   The Secretary of State shall, as soon as practicable after receipt, send a copy of the local planning authority's outline statement to the appellant, a copy of the appellant's outline statement to the appointed representative and a copy of the appellant's open outline statement to the local planning authority.

(3A) In this rule "open outline statement" means such part (if any) of an outline statement as does not include or refer to closed evidence.';

(b)   in paragraph (4) after 'statement to him' insert 'and the open outline statement to';

(c)   in paragraph (5) after 'outline' insert ', or outline open,'; and

(d)   after paragraph (5) insert—

'(5A) The Secretary of State shall, as soon as practicable after receipt, send a copy of any outline statement received in accordance with paragraph (4) to the appointed representative.'.

Service of statements of case etc

3. In rule 8—

(a)   in paragraph (3) for 'copy on any person' substitute 'copy of their open statement on any person';

(b)   in paragraph (4) for 'statement of case to the local planning authority' substitute 'open statement to the local planning authority';

(c)   in paragraph (6)—

    (i)   in sub-paragraph (b) for 'statement of case' substitute 'open statement';

    (ii) for 'send a copy of each such statement of case' substitute 'send a copy of any open statement received by him in accordance with sub-paragraph (a)';

(d)   in paragraph (7)—

    (i)   in sub-paragraph (a) for 'statements of case of the appellant and the local planning authority' substitute 'open statement of the appellant and the statement of case of the local planning authority';

    (ii) in sub-paragraph (b) for 'statement of case' substitute 'open statement';

(e)   in paragraph (16) after 'inspector' insert 'and appointed representative'; and

(f)   after paragraph (16) insert—

'(17) For the purposes of this rule "open statement" means such part (if any) of a statement of case as does not include or refer to closed evidence.'.

Appearances at inquiry

4. In rule 13(1) after sub-paragraph (a) insert—

'(aa) the appointed representative;'.

Proofs of evidence

5. In rule 16—

(a)   in paragraph (1) for "Any person" substitute "Subject to rule (1A), any person";

(b)   after paragraph (1) insert—

'(1A) Paragraph (1B) applies where the proof of evidence includes or refers to closed evidence.

(1B) Where this paragraph applies, any person entitled to appear at an inquiry, who proposes to give, or to call another person to give evidence at the inquiry by reading a proof of evidence, shall—

(a)   send to the Secretary of State 2 copies, in the case of the local planning authority and the appellant, or 3 copies in the case of any other person, of—

(i)   the proof of evidence including closed evidence together with any written summary of it;

(ii)   the proof of evidence excluding closed evidence ("the open proof") together with any written summary of it; and

(b)   simultaneously send copies of the open proof and any written summary of it to any statutory party,

and the Secretary of State shall, as soon as practicable after receipt, send a copy of each open proof together with any written summary of it to the local planning authority and the appellant.';

(c)   in paragraph after 'inspector' insert 'and appointed representative'; and

(d)   in paragraph (5) after 'paragraph (1)' insert 'or (1B)'.

Statement of common ground

6. In rule 17—

(a)   in paragraph (1) after 'ground' insert 'insofar as it does not relate to closed evidence'; and

(b)   after paragraph (3) insert—

'(4) Where the appeal is made by or on behalf of the Crown, the appointed representative and the appellant shall—

(a)   together prepare an agreed statement of common ground insofar as it relates to closed evidence; and

(b)   ensure that the Secretary of State receives it not less than 4 weeks before the date fixed for the holding of the inquiry.'.

Site inspections

7. In rule 19—

(a)   in paragraph (1) for 'The inspector' substitute "Subject to paragraph (1A), the inspector";

(b)   after paragraph (1) insert—

'(1A) Paragraph (1) does not apply where a site inspection will involve the inspection of closed evidence.';

(c)   in paragraph (2) for 'During' substitute 'Subject to paragraph (2A), during';

(d)   after paragraph (2) insert—

'(2A) Where an accompanied site inspection will involve the inspection of closed evidence, paragraph (2) does not apply and the inspector—

   (a) may inspect the land in the company of the appellant and the appointed representative, where one has been appointed; and

   (b) shall make such an inspection if so requested by the appellant or the appointed representative before or during an inquiry.'; and

(e)   in paragraph (4) after 'paragraph (2)' insert 'or (2A)'.

Procedure after inquiry

8. In rule 20—

(a)   after paragraph (3) insert—

'(3A) Where closed evidence was considered at the inquiry—

   (a) the inspector and assessor, where one has been appointed, shall set out in a separate part ("the closed part") of their reports any description of that evidence together with any conclusions or recommendations in relation to that evidence; and

   (b) where an assessor has been appointed, the inspector shall append the closed part of the assessor's report to the closed part of his own report and shall state in the closed part of his own report how far he agrees or disagrees with the closed part of the assessor's report and, where he disagrees with the assessor, his reasons for that disagreement.";

(b)   at the beginning of paragraph (5) insert "Subject to paragraph (5A)"; and

(c)   after paragraph (5) insert—

'(5A) Where the Secretary of State differs from the inspector on any matter of fact mentioned in, or appearing to him to be material to, a conclusion reached by the inspector in relation to closed evidence, the notification referred to in paragraph (5) shall include the reasons for the Secretary of State's disagreement unless—

   (a) the notification is addressed to a person who is neither the appointed representative nor any person specified, or of a description specified, in the security direction; and

   (b) inclusion of the reasons would disclose any part of the closed evidence.'.

Notification of decision

9. In rule 21—

(a)   in paragraph (1) for 'The Secretary of State' substitute 'Subject to paragraph (1B), the Secretary of State';

(b)   after paragraph (1A) insert—

'(1B) Where the Secretary of State's reasons for a decision relate to matters in respect of which closed evidence has been given, nothing in paragraph (1) requires the Secretary of State to notify those reasons to any person other than—

(a) the appointed representative; or

(b) a person specified, or of any description specified, in the security direction.';

(c) in paragraph (2) for 'Where a copy" substitute "Subject to paragraph (2A), where a copy"; and

(d) after paragraph (2) insert—

'(2A) Nothing in paragraph (2) requires the disclosure of any closed evidence to a person other than—

(a) the appointed representative; or

(b) a person specified, or of any description specified, in the security direction.'.

Procedure following remitting of appeal

10. In rule 22—

(a) at the beginning of sub-paragraph (a) of paragraph (1) insert "subject to paragraph (1A)"; and

(b) after paragraph (1) insert—

'1A) Where the matters referred to in paragraph (1)(a) will involve consideration of closed evidence, the Secretary of State shall only send the written statement to—

(a) the appointed representative; and

(b) a person specified, or of any description specified, in the security direction.".

Closed evidence not to be disclosed

11. After rule 25A insert—

'Closed evidence not to be disclosed

25B. Nothing in these Rules shall be taken to require or permit closed evidence to be disclosed to a person other than—

(a)   the Secretary of State;

(b)   the appointed representative; or

(c)   a person specified, or of any description specified, in the security direction.'

Model Forms from Circular 10/97

MODEL PLANNING CONTRAVENTION NOTICE

Important – This Communication Affects Your Property

Town and Country Planning Act 1990 (as amended by the Planning and Compensation Act 1991)

Planning Contravention Notice

Served by: [name of Council]

To: [Name[s] of those thought to be owner[s] or occupier[s] of land or person[s] having any other interest in it] [Name[s] of person[s] thought to be responsible for a possible breach of planning control]

1. This Notice is served by the Council because it appears to them that there may have been a breach of planning control, within section 171 A(1) of the above Act, at the land described below. It is served on you as a person who appears to be the owner or occupier of the land or has another interest in it, or who is carrying out operations in, on, over or under the land or is using it for any purpose. The Council require you, in exercise of their powers under section 171C(2) and (3), so far as you are able, to provide certain information about interest in, and activities on, the land.

2. The Land to Which the Notice Relates

Land at [address or description of land], shown edged red on the attached plan].

3. The Matters Which Appear to Constitute the Breach of Planning Control

[Without planning permission]

[Specify the suspected breach of planning control]

[The failure to comply with a condition or limitation]

4. What You Are Required to Do

Provide in writing, the following information:

(1)

[Specify the information required, having regard to the terms of section 171C(2) and (3)]

(2)

(3)

Time within which the information must be provided: *within twenty-one days,* beginning with the day on which this notice is served on you:

5. *Opportunity to Make Representations in Response to Notice*

If you wish to make an offer to apply for planning permission, or to refrain from carrying out any operations or activities, or to undertake remedial works; or to make any representations about this notice, the Council, or representatives of the Council, will consider them on [date and time] at [address where the person served with the notice may be heard] where you will be able to make any such offer or representations in person at that time and place.

6. *Warning*

It is an offence to fail, without reasonable excuse, to comply with any requirements of this notice within twenty-one days beginning with the day on which it was served on you. The maximum penalty on conviction of this offence is a fine of £1,000. Continuing failure to comply following a conviction will constitute a further offence. It is also an offence knowingly or recklessly to give information, in response to this notice, which is false or misleading in a material particular. The maximum penalty on conviction of this offence is a fine of £5,000.

7. *Additional Information*

If you fail to respond to this notice, the Council may take further action in respect of the suspected breach of planning control. In particular, they may issue an enforcement notice, under section 172 of the 1990 Act, requiring the breach, or any injury to amenity caused by it, to be remedied. [Add any other "likely consequences", in accordance with section 17 I C(5)(a), if appropriate.]

If the Council serve a stop notice, under section 183 of the 1990 Act, section 186(5) (b) of the 1990 Act provides that should you otherwise become entitled (under section 186) to compensation for loss or damage attributable to that notice, no such compensation will be payable in respect of any loss or damage which could have been avoided had you given the Council the information required by this notice, or had you otherwise co-operated with the Council when responding to it.

Dated: *[date of notice]* Signed: *[Council's authorised officer]*

On behalf of:

[Council's name and address]

MODEL ENFORCEMENT NOTICE – OPERATIONAL DEVELOPMENT

Important - This Communication Affects Your Property

Town And Country Planning Act 1990 (as amended by the Planning and Compensation Act 1991)

Enforcement Notice Issued By: [name of Council]

1. This Notice is issued by the Council because it appears to them that there has been a breach of planning control, within paragraph (a) of section 171A(1) of the above Act, at the land described below. They consider that it is expedient to issue this notice, having regard to the provisions of the development plan and to other material planning considerations. The Annex at the end of the notice and the enclosures to which it refers contain important additional information.

2. The Land To Which The Notice Relates

Land at [*address of land*], shown edged red on the attached plan.

3. The Matters Which Appear To Constitute The Breach Of Planning Control

Without planning permission, the erection of a brick-built, single-storey building, and the construction of a driveway leading to it, in the approximate position marked with a cross on the attached plan.

4. Reasons For Issuing This Notice

It appears to the Council that the above breach of planning control has occurred within the last four years. The building in question was substantially completed less than four years ago. The building looks like, and appears to have been designed as, a dwellinghouse. The site is within the approved Green Belt where, with certain exceptions which do not apply in this case, there is a strong presumption against any development. The building appears as an intrusion in this otherwise mainly open, rural landscape. It is contrary to development plan policies and harmful to the visual amenities of the area. The Council do not consider that planning permission should be given, because planning conditions could not overcome these objections to the development.

5. What You Are Required To Do

(i) Remove the building and the driveway.

(ii) Remove from the land all building materials and rubble arising from compliance with requirement (i) above, and restore the land to its condition before the breach took place by levelling the ground and re-seeding it with grass.

6. Time For Compliance

(i) 12 weeks after this notice takes effect.

(ii) 24 weeks after this notice takes effect.

7. When This Notice Takes Effect

This notice takes effect on [*specific date, not less than 28 clear days after date of issue*], unless an appeal is made against it beforehand.

Dated: [*date of issue*] Signed: [*Council's authorised officer*]

on behalf of

[*Council's name and address*]

ANNEX

Your Right Of Appeal

You can appeal against this notice, but any appeal must be received, or posted in time to be received, by the Secretary of State before the date specified in paragraph 7 of the notice. The enclosed booklet 'Enforcement Notice Appeals - A Guide to Procedure' sets out your rights. You may use the enclosed appeal forms.

(a)   One is for you to send to the Secretary of State if you decide to appeal, together with a copy of this enforcement notice.

(b)   The second copy of the appeal form and the notice should be sent to the Council.

(c)   The third copy is for your own records.

What Happens If You Do Not Appeal

If you do not appeal against this enforcement notice, it will take effect on the date specified in paragraph 7 of the notice and you must then ensure that the required steps for complying with it, for which you may be held responsible, are taken within the period[s] specified in paragraph 6 of the notice. Failure to comply with an enforcement notice which has taken effect can result in prosecution and/or remedial action by the Council.

EXAMPLE ENFORCEMENT NOTICE – MATERIAL CHANGE OF USE

Important - This Communication Affects Your Property

Town And Country Planning Act 1990 (as amended by the Planning and Compensation Act 1991)

Enforcement Notice

Issued By: [name of Council]

1. This Notice is issued by the Council because it appears to them that there has been a breach of planning control, within paragraph (a) of section 171A(1) of the above Act, at the land described below. They consider that it is expedient to issue this notice, having regard to the provisions of the development plan and to other material planning considerations. The Annex at the end of the notice and the enclosures to which it refers contain important additional information.

2. The Land To Which The Notice Relates

Land at [*address of land*], shown edged red on the attached plan.

3. The Matters Which Appear To Constitute The Breach Of Planning Control

Without planning permission, change of use of the land from use for agriculture to a mixed use for agriculture and as a road haulage depot.

4. Reasons For Issuing This Notice

It appears to the Council that the above breach of planning control has occurred within the last ten years. The unauthorised use as a road haulage depot is not an appropriate use of the land, which is within a rural area and forms part of the approved Green Belt in the development plan. The site is approached by narrow country lanes which are unsuitable for use by the type and quantity of traffic which the use attracts. The Council do not consider that planning permission should be given, because planning conditions could not overcome these objections.

5. What You Are Required To Do

Stop using any part of the land as a road haulage depot and remove from the land all vehicles and equipment brought on to the land for the purpose of that use. (You may keep on the land any equipment which you use solely for the maintenance of farm vehicles and machinery used for the purposes of agriculture on that land).

6. Time For Compliance

8 weeks after this notice takes effect.

7. When This Notice Takes Effect

This notice takes effect on [*specific date, not less than 28 clear days after date of issue*], unless an appeal is made against it beforehand.

Dated: [date of issue] Signed: [Council's authorised officer]

on behalf of

[Council's name and address]

ANNEX

Your Right Of Appeal

You can appeal against this notice, but any appeal must be **received**, or posted in time to be received, by the Secretary of State **before** the date specified in paragraph 7 of the notice. The enclosed booklet "Enforcement Notice Appeals - A Guide to Procedure" sets out your rights. You may use the enclosed appeal forms.

(a)   One is for you to send to the Secretary of State if you decide to appeal, together with a copy of this enforcement notice.

(b)   The second copy of the appeal form and the notice should be sent to the Council.

(c)   The third copy is for your own records.

What Happens If You Do Not Appeal

If you do not appeal against this enforcement notice, it will take effect on the date specified in paragraph 7 of the notice and you must then ensure that the required steps for complying with it, for which you may be held responsible, are taken within the period[s] specified in paragraph 6 of the notice. Failure to comply with an enforcement notice which has taken effect can result in prosecution and/or remedial action by the Council.

EXAMPLE ENFORCEMENT NOTICE – FAILURE TO COMPLY WITH A CONDITION

Important - This Communication Affects Your Property

Town And Country Planning Act 1990 (as amended by the Planning and Compensation Act 1991)

Enforcement Notice Issued By: [name of Council]

1. This Notice is issued by the Council because it appears to them that there has been a breach of planning control, within paragraph (b) of section 171A(1) of the above Act, at the land described below. They consider that it is expedient to issue this notice, having regard to the provisions of the development plan and to other material planning considerations. The Annex at the end of the notice and the enclosures to which it refers contain important additional information.

2. The Land To Which The Notice Relates

Land at [*address of land*], shown edged red on the attached plan.

3. The Breach Of Planning Control Alleged

On [date of planning permission] planning permission was granted for the erection of a building for use as a retail shop, subject to conditions. One of those conditions was that the premises should not be open for the sale of goods on Sundays or after 1900 hours on any other day. It appears to the Council that the condition has not been complied with, because the premises have been open for the sale of goods on Sundays and after 1900 hours on some other days.

4. Reasons For Issuing This Notice

It appears to the Council that the above breach of planning control has occurred within the last ten years. The building adjoins a residential area. Its immediate surroundings also contain a number of residential flats above shops and other business premises. The sale of goods from the premises on Sundays and late in the evenings attracts large numbers of people to the area both on foot and in vehicles and is causing significant disturbance to nearby residents, at times when they might reasonably expect the area to be relatively peaceful. The Council do not consider that there should be any relaxation of the condition in question, which already permits reasonably long opening hours for the shop.

5. What You Are Required To Do

Stop opening the shop for the sale of goods on Sundays and on other days after 1900 hours.

6. Time For Compliance

7 days after this notice takes effect.

7. When This Notice Takes Effect

This notice takes effect on [*specific date, not less than 28 clear days after date of issue*], unless an appeal is made against it beforehand.

Dated: [*date of issue*] Signed: [*Council's authorised officer*]

on behalf of

[*Council's name and address*]

ANNEX

Your Right Of Appeal

You can appeal against this notice, but any appeal must be **received**, or posted in time to be received, by the Secretary of State **before** the date specified in paragraph 7 of the notice. The enclosed booklet "Enforcement Notice Appeals - A Guide to Procedure" sets out your rights. You may use the enclosed appeal forms.

(a)   One is for you to send to the Secretary of State if you decide to appeal, together with a copy of this enforcement notice.

(b)   The second copy of the appeal form and the notice should be sent to the Council.

(c)   The third copy is for your own records.

What Happens If You Do Not Appeal

If you do not appeal against this enforcement notice, it will take effect on the date specified in paragraph 7 of the notice and you must then ensure that the required steps for complying with it, for which you may be held responsible, are taken within the period[s] specified in paragraph 6 of the notice. Failure to comply with an enforcement notice which has taken effect can result in prosecution and/or remedial action by the Council.

MODEL TREE REPLACEMENT NOTICE

Important - This Communication Affects Your Property

Town And Country Planning Act 1990 (as amended by the Planning and Compensation Act 1991)

Tree Replacement Notice

Tree preservation order: [title] [name of Council]

1. This Notice is served by the Council under section 207 of the Town and Country Planning Act 1990 ("the Act") because it appears to them that

[you have not complied with a duty to plant [a tree/trees] under section 206 of the Act].

[you have not complied with a condition of consent granted under the above tree preservation order to plant [a replacement tree/replacement trees]].

[you have not complied with a duty to plant [a tree/trees] in a conservation area under section 213 of the Act].

2. The Land Affected

Land at [address of land], shown edged red on the attached plan.

3. Reasons For Serving Notice

[On or around [date], a beech tree protected by the above tree preservation order was cut down on the grounds that it had become dangerous. Under section 206 of the Act the owner of the land is under a duty to plant another tree. It appears to the Council that this duty has not been complied with.]

[On [date], the Council granted consent to fell an oak tree protected by the above tree preservation order subject to a condition to plant [a replacement tree or trees] [*give details of condition*]. It appears to the Council that this condition has not been complied with.]

[On or around [date], an ash tree situated in the [title of conservation area] was removed in contravention of section 211 of the Act. Under section 213 of the Act the owner of the land is under a duty to plant another tree. It appears to the Council that this duty has not been complied with.]

[*Then set out any relevant background leading up to the Council's decision to serve the notice (eg references to correspondence with the landowner).*]

4. What You Are Required To Do

You are required to plant [*number, species and size of tree or trees to be planted*] at the place(s) shown on the attached plan.

Time for compliance: [X months from the date stated in paragraph 5 below.]

5. When This Notice Takes Effect

This notice takes effect on [specific date (which must be not less than 28 clear days after date of service)], unless an appeal is made against it beforehand.

Dated: *[date of notice]* Signed: *[Council's authorised officer]*

on behalf of

[Council's name and address]

ANNEX

Your Right Of Appeal

You can appeal to the Secretary of State for [Communities and Local Government][1] against this notice by writing to the Planning Inspectorate, Environment Appeals Team, Room 3/25 Hawk Wing, Temple Quay House, 2 The Square, Temple Quay, Bristol BS1 6PN, Telephone: 0303 444 5584, e-mail environment.appeals@pins.gsi. gov.uk.[2] **Your appeal must be received, or posted in time for it to be received, before [date specified in the notice (at 5 above)].** You can appeal on anyone or more of the following grounds

- that the provisions of the duty to replace trees or, as the case may be, the conditions of consent requiring the replacement of trees, are not applicable or have been complied with;

- that in all the circumstances of the case the duty to replace trees should be dispensed with in relation to any tree;

- that the requirements of the notice are unreasonable in respect of the period or the size or species of trees specified in it;

- that the planting of a tree or trees in accordance with the notice is not required in the interests of amenity or would be contrary to the practice of good forestry;

- that the place on which the tree is or trees are required to be planted is unsuitable for that purpose.

You must also state the facts on which your appeal is based.

Failure To Comply

If you do not comply with this notice, the Council may enter the land, plant the tree(s) and recover from you any reasonable expenses incurred.

---

[1] Author's update.
[2] Author's update.

Advice

If you have any questions about this notice or would like some advice on how to comply with it, please contact [*name, address and telephone number of appropriate Council officer*].

MODEL STOP NOTICE

Important - This Communication Affects Your Property

Town And Country Planning Act 1990 (as amended by the Planning and Compensation Act 1991)

Stop Notice

Served By: [name of Council] To: [name of intended recipient of the notice]

1. On [*date*], the Council issued an enforcement notice (of which a copy is attached to this notice) alleging that there has been a breach of planning control on [*description of the land to which the notice relates*].

2. This Notice is issued by the Council, in exercise of their power in section 183 of the 1990 Act, because they consider that it is expedient that the activity specified in this notice should cease before the expiry of the period allowed for compliance with the requirements of the enforcement notice on the land described in paragraph 3 below. The Council now prohibit the carrying out of the activity specified in this notice. Important additional information is given in the Annex to this notice.

3. The Land To Which This Notice Relates

Land at [*address of land, or description of relevant part of the land to which the enforcement notice relates*], shown edged red on the attached plan.

4. Activity To Which This Notice Relates

[*Specify the activity required by the enforcement notice to cease, and any activity carried out as part of that activity, or associated with it*]

5. What You Are Required To Do

Cease all the activity specified in this notice.

6. When This Notice Takes Effect

This notice takes effect on [*date*] when all the activity specified in this notice shall cease.

Dated: [*date of notice*]

Signed: [*Council's authorised officer*]

On behalf of

[*Council's name and address*]

ANNEX

Warning

This Notice Takes Effect On The Date Specified In Paragraph 6.

There Is No Right Of Appeal To The Secretary Of State For [Communities and Local Government][3] Against This Notice.

It is an offence to contravene a stop notice after a site notice has been displayed or the stop notice has been served on you. (Section 187(1) of the 1990 Act). If you then fail to comply with the stop notice you will be at risk of **immediate prosecution** in the Magistrates' Court, for which the maximum penalty is £20,000 on summary conviction for a first offence and for any subsequent offence. The fine on conviction on indictment is unlimited. If you are in any doubt about what this notice requires you to do, you should get in touch **immediately** with [*Council's nominated officer to deal with enquiries, address and telephone number*]. If you need independent advice about this notice, you are advised to contact urgently a lawyer, planning consultant or other professional adviser specialising in planning matters. If you wish to contest the validity of the notice, you may only do so by an application to the High Court for judicial review.

---

[3]   Author's update.

Appendix 7

MODEL BREACH OF CONDITION NOTICE

Important - This Communication Affects Your Property

Town And Country Planning Act 1990 (as amended by the Planning and Compensation Act 1991)

Breach Of Condition Notice

Served By:. [name of Council]

To: [name[s] of person[s] responsible for the alleged breach of condition]

1. This Notice is served by the Council, under section 187A of the above Act, because they consider that [*a condition*] [*conditions*] imposed on a grant of planning permission, relating to the land described in paragraph 2 below, [*has*] [*have*] not been complied with. The Council consider that you should be required to [*comply*] [*secure compliance*] with the condition[s] specified in this notice. The Annex at the end of this notice contains important additional information.

2. The Land To Which The Notice Relates

Land at [*address of land*], shown edged red on the attached plan.

3. The Relevant Planning Permission

The relevant planning permission to which this notice relates is the permission granted by the Council on [*date of issue of permission*] for [*description of development*] Ref [*Council's reference number*].

4. The Breach Of Condition

The following condition[s] [*has*][*have*] not been complied with:

(1)

(2) [*State the terms of each condition which has not been complied with.*]

(3)

5. What You Are Required To Do

As the person responsible for the breach[es] of condition[s] specified in paragraph 4 of this notice, you are required to [*comply*][*secure compliance*] with the stated condition[s] by taking the following steps:

(1) [*State clearly the steps to he taken in order to*

(2) *to secure compliance with the condition[s] in*

(3) *paragraph 4 above.*]

[and] [ceasing the following activities:-]

(1) [*State clearly the activities which must cease*

(2) *in order to secure compliance with the*

(3) *condition[s] in paragraph 4 above.*]

Period for compliance: 30 days beginning with the day on which this notice is served on you. [*Different periods may be specified for each requirement*].

Dated: [*Date of notice*]

Signed: [*Council's authorised officer*]

On behalf of: [*Council's name and address*]

ANNEX

Warning

This Notice Takes Effect Immediately It Is Served On You In Person Or On The Day You Received It By Post.

There Is No Right Of Appeal To The Secretary Of State For [Communities and Local Government][4] Against This Notice.

It is an offence to contravene the requirements stated in paragraph 5 of this notice after the end of the compliance period. You will then be at risk of immediate prosecution in the Magistrates' Court, for which the maximum penalty is £2,500[5] for a first offence and for any subsequent offence. If you are in any doubt about what this notice requires you to do, you should get in touch immediately with [*Council's nominated officer to deal with enquiries, address and telephone number*].

If you do need independent advice about this notice, you are advised to contact urgently a lawyer, planning consultant or other professional adviser specialising in planning matters. If you wish to contest the validity of the notice, you may only do so by an application to the High Court for judicial review.

---

[4]   Author's update.
[5]   Author's update, the maximum fine in Wales remains £1,000.

Appendix 8

Certificate of Lawful Use or Development

THE TOWN AND COUNTRY PLANNING (DEVELOPMENT MANAGEMENT PROCEDURE) (ENGLAND) ORDER 2010 (2010/2184)

Schedule 8 Certificate of lawful use or development

Town and Country Planning Act 1990: sections 191 and 192
The Town and Country Planning (Development Management Procedure)
(England) Order 2010: article 35

CERTIFICATE OF LAWFUL USE OR DEVELOPMENT

The (a) .... Council hereby that on (b) .... The use/ operations/matter* described in the first Schedule to this certificate in respect of the land specified in the Second Schedule to this certificate and edged/hatched/coloured* (c) .... on the plan attached to this certificate, was/were/would* have been lawful within the meaning of section 191 of the Town and Country Planning Act 1990 for the following reason(s):

....
....

Signed ....(Council's authorised officer)
On behalf of (a) .... Council
Date ....

First Schedule
(d)
Second Schedule
(e)

Notes
1 This certificate issued solely for the purpose of section 191/192* of the Town and Country Planning Act 1990.
2 It certifies that the use/operations/matter* specified in the First Schedule taking place on the land described in the Second Schedule was/were/would have been* lawful, on the specified date and, therefore, was not/were not/would not have been* liable to enforcement action under section 172 of the 1990 Act on that date.
3 This certificate applies only to the extent of the use/operations/matter* described in the First Schedule and to the land specified in the Second Schedule and identified on the attached plan. Any use/operations/ matter* which is/are* materially different from that/those* described or which relate/s* to other land may render the owner or occupier liable to enforcement action.
*4 The effect of the certificate is also qualified by the proviso in section 192(4) of the 1990 Act, which states that the lawfulness of a described use or operation is only conclusively presumed where there has been no material change, before the use is instituted or the operations are begun, in any of the matters relevant to determining such lawfulness.

* delete where inappropriate
Insert:
(a) name of Council
(b) date of application to the Council
(c) colour used on the plan
(d) full description of use, operations or other matter, if necessary, by reference to details in the application or submitted plans, including a reference to the use class, if any, specified in an order under section 55(2)
(f) of the 1990 Act, within which the certificated use falls
(e) Address or location of the site

Appendix 9

Temporary Stop Notice

ODPM CIRCULAR 02/2005

ANNEX: MODEL TEMPORARY STOP NOTICE

IMPORTANT – THIS COMMUNICATION AFFECTS YOUR PROPERTY

TOWN AND COUNTRY PLANNING ACT 1990

(As amended by the Planning and Compensation Act 1991 and the Planning and Compulsory Purchase Act 2004)

TEMPORARY STOP NOTICE

SERVED BY: [name of Council] herein after referred to as 'the Council'.

To: [name of intended recipient of the notice]

1. On [date], the Council has issued this temporary stop notice alleging that there has been a breach of planning control on the land described in paragraph 4 below.

2. This temporary stop notice is issued by the Council, in exercise of their power in section 171E of the 1990 Act, because they think that it is expedient that the activity specified in this notice should cease on the land described in paragraph 4 below. The Council now prohibits the carrying out of the activity specified in this notice. Important additional information is given in the Annex to this notice.

3. The reasons for issuing this notice

[Briefly specify the reasons why the temporary stop notice has been issued. There is no requirement to outline specific policies from the Local Plan.]

4. The land to which this notice relates

Land at [address of land, or description of relevant part of the land to which the temporary stop notice relates], shown edged red on the attached plan.

5. The activity to which this notice relates

[Specify the activity required by the temporary stop notice to cease, and any activity carried out as part of that activity, or associated with it.]

6. What you are required to do

Cease all the activity specified in this notice.

7. When this notice takes effect

This notice takes effect on [date] when all the activity specified in this notice shall cease. This notice will cease to have effect on [date 28 days after it takes effect].

Dated: [date of notice]

Signed: [Council's authorised officer]

On behalf of [Council's name and address]

Nominated Officer [Name of contact officer]

Telephone Number [of Nominated Officer]

ANNEX

WARNING

THIS NOTICE TAKES EFFECT ON THE DATE SPECIFIED IN PARAGRAPH 7.

THERE IS NO RIGHT OF APPEAL TO THE FIRST SECRETARY OF STATE AGAINST THIS NOTICE.

It is an offence to contravene a temporary stop notice after a site notice has been displayed or the temporary stop notice has been served on you. (Section 171G of the 1990 Act). If you then fail to comply with the temporary stop notice you will be at risk of immediate prosecution in the Magistrates' Court, for which the maximum penalty is £20,000 on summary conviction for a first offence and for any subsequent offence. The fine on conviction on indictment is unlimited. If you are in any doubt about what this notice requires you to do, you should get in touch immediately with [Council's nominated officer to deal with enquiries, address and telephone number]. If you need independent advice about this notice, you are advised to contact urgently a lawyer, planning consultant or other professional adviser specialising in planning matters. If you wish to contest the validity of the notice, you may only do so by an application to the High Court for judicial review.

Index